# 中国城市发展报告

## （2010）

主　办

中　国　市　长　协　会

承　办

国际欧亚科学院中国科学中心

《中国城市发展报告》编委会　编

中国城市出版社

·北　京·

**图书在版编目（CIP）数据**

中国城市发展报告.2010/《中国城市发展报告》编委会编.—北京：中国城市出版社，2011.5

ISBN 978-7-5074-2445-4

Ⅰ.①中… Ⅱ.①中… Ⅲ.①城市经济—经济发展—研究报告—中国—2010 Ⅳ.①F299.21

中国版本图书馆CIP数据核字（2011）第070049号

---

责任编辑 孙湛波
装帧设计 美信书籍设计工作室
责任技术编辑 张建军
出版发行 中国城市出版社
地址 北京市海淀区太平路甲40号（邮编 100039）
网址 www.citypress.cn
发行部电话 （010）63454857 63289949
发行部传真 （010）63421417 63400635
发行部信箱 zgcsfx@sina.com
编辑部电话 （010）52732085 52732055 63421488（Fax）
投稿信箱 city_editor@sina.com
总编室电话 （010）52732057
总编室信箱 citypress@sina.com
经销 新华书店
印刷 北京蓝海印刷有限公司
字数 699千字 印张 33
开本 889×1194（毫米） 1/16
版次 2011年5月第1版
印次 2011年5月第1次印刷
定价 398.00元

---

# 《中国城市发展报告(2010)》
# 机构组成名单

**《中国城市发展报告(2010)》总顾问**

路甬祥　全国人民代表大会常务委员会副委员长
成思危　全国人民代表大会常务委员会原副委员长
周光召　全国人民代表大会常务委员会原副委员长
徐匡迪　中国人民政治协商会议全国委员会原副主席
罗豪才　中国人民政治协商会议全国委员会原副主席

**《中国城市发展报告(2010)》顾问**

汪光焘　全国人大环境与资源保护委员会主任委员
王梦奎　国务院发展研究中心原主任
曲格平　全国人大环境与资源保护委员会原主任
刘燕华　国家科技部原副部长
刘　江　国家发展改革委员会原副主任
周干峙　原国家建设部副部长，中国科学院院士，中国工程院院士
赵宝江　原国家建设部副部长
李振东　原国家建设部副部长

**《中国城市发展报告(2010)》理事会**

**理 事 长**：蒋正华　全国人民代表大会常务委员会原副委员长
　　　　　　　　国际欧亚科学院中国科学中心主席
**副理事长**：陶斯亮　中国市长协会副会长
**理　　事**：(以下按姓氏拼音顺序排列)
崔衡德　戴　逢　廖幼鸣　马俊如
毛其智　彭公炳　王长远

中国城市经济学会
广州市都市发展研究会
清华大学建筑学院
北京大学数字中国研究院
中山大学城市与区域研究中心
北京师范大学资源学院
北京凯德欧亚咨询中心有限公司
国家遥感应用工程技术研究中心

**《中国城市发展报告(2010)》工作委员会**

**主任委员：**王长远

**委　　员：**林家宁　方兆瑞　马海鹰

# 序　一

蒋正华

（第九届、十届全国人大常委会副委员长，国际欧亚科学院中国科学中心主席）

《中国城市发展报告》的编写，已步入第十个年头。

21世纪开元之年，中共“十五”届五次全会通过了《关于制定国民经济和社会发展第十个五年计划的建议》（以下简称《建议》），第一次从国家发展的角度提出了城镇化的要求。《建议》指出：随着农业生产力水平的提高和工业化进程的加快，我国推进城镇化条件已渐成熟，要不失时机地实施城镇化战略。为响应中央的决策，中国市长协会自2002年起开始组织编写《中国城市发展报告》，出版了报告的2001—2002卷。

回顾过去的十年，我们欣慰地看到，作为一个系列性出版物，《中国城市发展报告》与中国城镇化进程共同成长。从“十五”到“十二五”，从“积极稳妥推进城镇化”，到“促进城镇化健康发展”，从“把城市群作为推进城镇化的主体形态”，到“构建城市化战略格局”，从“把符合落户条件的农业转移人口逐步转为城镇居民作为推进城镇化的重要任务”，到“坚持以人为本、节地节能、生态环保、安全实用、突出特色、保护文化和自然遗产的原则，科学编制城市规划，健全城镇建设标准，增强城镇综合承载能力”，我国的城镇化道路越走越宽广。

2010年，国内的大事、喜事和难事不断：成功应对国际金融危机冲击，加快转变经济发展方式；上海世博会、广州亚运会胜利举行；全民团结奋斗战胜玉树地震、舟曲泥石流和部分地区严重的旱涝灾害。在党中央和国务院领导下，全国的改革开放不断深化，改善民生成效显著，经济保持平稳较快发展，社会主义政治建设、文化建设、社会建设以及生态文明建设和党的建设取得新的重大进展，经济实力和综合国力进一步增强。

刚刚闭幕的第十一届全国人民代表大会第四次会议，通过了《国民经济和社会发展第十二个五年规划纲要》，标志着中国发展已经站在了一个新的起点上。未来五年，我们将围绕转变经济发展方式的关键领域和薄弱环节，着力解决发展中不平衡、不协调、不可持续的问题，为全面建成小康社会打下坚实基础。同时，《纲要》提出了城镇化率提高4个百分点的预期性指标，要求优化城市化布局和形态，加强城镇化管理，不断提升城镇化的质量和水平。

《中国城市发展报告（2010）》的主题，与2010年成功举办的上海世博会一致：“城市，让生活更美好”(Better City, Better Life)。正是因为这届世博会给世界带来的新希望，让我们有信心应对城市化时代日益涌现的挑战。在构思这一年度主题时，我曾提出：希望《报告》能更多注重“生老病死安稳，衣食住行舒适，家庭亲情融洽，社会沟通顺畅，精神生活充实，环境安全满意”等方面内容；更多关注城市发展中的难点、热点、焦点问题；不断扩大社会影响，将《报告》办成国内、国际认可的文献。我很高兴地看到，本年度报告在民生方面加大了篇幅，加重了分量。

希望编辑部的同志们今后更加努力工作，真正使《中国城市发展报告》成为国内具有权威性、前瞻性、文献性的中国城市问题理论和实践的研究报告，为城市决策者、管理者和研究者提供参考。

2011年3月25日

# 序　二

## 积极稳妥推进城镇化

姜伟新

（住房和城乡建设部部长，中国市长协会执行会长）

“十二五”期间，我国城镇化处于转型发展的关键时期，城镇化水平将超过50%。许多国家在城镇化水平发展到这个阶段之后，都曾不同程度地出现了就业不足、贫富差距拉大、住房短缺、交通拥堵、环境污染等问题。而有的国家没能处理好这些问题，从而出现了发展停滞、社会动荡情况，落入了“中等收入国家陷阱”，这些问题值得我们认真研究。

“十一五”期间，我国城镇化水平从2005年的42.99%提高到2009年的46.59%，年均增加0.9个百分点，城镇化保持了平稳有序的发展趋势，成绩很大。但应看到，上述国家在城镇化相应阶段发生的问题也已经陆续在我国程度不同地出现了，同时我国还有特定国情背景下的新问题，如进城农民市民化、城镇发展模式和城市管理等问题。这些问题如果处理不好，将会影响我国的长远持续发展。“十二五”期间，我们既要保持适当的城镇化发展速度，更要注重提升城镇化质量；既要强调积极进取，把握机遇，有序推进，为拉动内需、扩大就业提供新的增长空间，更要强调有序稳妥，针对我国城镇化发展的客观条件和突出问题，调整结构，优化布局，节能减排，改善民生和转型发展。

“十二五”期间，住房和城乡建设部要在积极稳妥推进城镇化方面做些比较实在的工作。第一，要努力实现“住有所居”的目标，切实解决群众的住房问题。一方面更大规模地推进保障性安居工程建设，同时继续坚定不移地加强房地产市场调控，遏制房价过快上涨。第二，要转变城镇发展模式，积极推进节能减排，推广绿色建筑和绿色交通，着力建设低碳生态城市，实践“两型社会”的目标。第三，着力解决“大城市病”，加强城市建设与管理，加强城市水、电、气、路、热等市政公用设施的建设，建立统一、协调、高效、合理的城市管理体制，提升城市发展质量和城市综合管理水平。第四，统筹城乡发展，积极推进农村现代化，推动城市基础设施和服务功能向农村地区延伸，有序推进“城中村”改造和城乡结合部地区的综合环境整治，提升农村发展能力，让农民享受到城镇化的成果。第五，进一步健全城镇化的体制机制，积极发挥城乡规划的综合调控作用，切实提高城乡规划水平，坚持城乡统筹规划管理，完善规划实施手段。第六，进一步加强研究工作，针对城镇化发展中遇到的新问题，积极开展理论、政策等方面的研究，以指导城镇化实践。

由中国市长协会主办、国际欧亚科学院中国科学中心承办的《中国城市发展报告(2010)》即将出版。本期《中国城市发展报告（2010）》以“城市，让生活更美好”为主题，以积极稳妥推进城镇化为主旋律，在客观总结2010年我国城市发展成绩的基础上，进一步回顾了“十一五”辉煌成就，并展望“十二五”宏伟目标，成为大家了解中国城镇化和城镇发展的一个窗口，希望对大家的学习、工作有所帮助。

2011年3月31日

# 前　言

## 中国特色城镇化与城市现代化问题

汪光焘

（全国人大环境与资源保护委员会主任委员，国际欧亚科学院中国科学中心常务副主席）

最近，国际红十字会发表报告称，全球城市人口首次超越农村人口，城市化进程加快正面临巨大风险。21世纪初，诺贝尔经济学奖金获得者、美国经济学家斯蒂格利茨（J. E. Stiglitz）把中国的城镇化与美国的高科技并列为影响21世纪人类发展进程的两大关键因素。改革开放以来，中国的城镇化一直被世人瞩目。

### 一、中国城镇化的现状与特征

城镇化主要是伴随着现代工业发展和分工细化而产生人口向城市集中的过程。它是一个国家经济、社会发展客观形态的综合体现，是整个社会基本形态的转型。

中国古代曾经出现过世界上最大的城市：长安、北京、南京、杭州等，反映了当时中国的综合国力。近代受到帝国主义列强的侵略，我国城市化水平远远落后于世界平均水平。中华人民共和国建国之初，城镇人口占总人口比例不足11%，仅及世界平均水平的1/3。1949—1957年，伴随“一五”计划的大规模工业化建设，城镇化水平由10.64%提高到15.39%。1958—1978年，城镇化前期起落较大，后期多年徘徊在17%左右。改革开放以来，城镇化进入了一个稳步增长的阶段，城镇化水平从1978年的17.92%提高到2009年的46.6%，年均增长0.93个百分点。

中国城镇化发展体现了以下几个显著特征：

一是城镇化发展始终与农业、农村、农民问题紧密相关。中国是农业大国。新中国成立后的几十年里，通过农业支援工业、农村支援城市建立国家工业化和城镇化基础，成为必然的选择。工农业产品的剪刀差、城乡劳动力的剪刀差，在不同时期支撑着国家的城镇化。可以说，没有农业、农村的发展，城镇的繁荣和发展就没有保障。所以，城镇化过程中，必须妥善解决好“三农”问题，注意增强以工补农、以城带乡的能力。这是实现城乡经济共同繁荣的关键，也是城镇化健康发展的核心问题。

二是地区发展不平衡决定地区城镇化水平差异较大。中国地理环境的空间差异以及资源禀赋和历史发展基础的不同，导致了地区经济社会发展和城镇化水平的差异。东部地区骨干工业带动和乡镇工业异军突起，形成了一批人口经济集聚程度较高的城市群，中西部地区工业发展相对滞后，逐渐形成了以县城为基础，服务农业、农村、农民为主，发展中小城市的格局。在城镇化过程中，必须坚持大中小城市和小城镇协调发展，重视发挥大城市辐射带动作用，重视加强中小城市和小城镇的建设，防止盲目大城市化，并以此带动区域协调发展。

三是中国城镇化将是一个较长的渐进的社会转型过程。中国大陆目前正处于经济体制改革和经济结构调整的双重转折时期。这一时期结构性矛盾突出，就业压力较大，给农业人口向非农产业转移带来特殊困难。“候鸟”式的富余劳动力的转移方式，又是中国的特点。按城镇化水平每年提高近1个百分点计算，2035年前后才能达到70%。中国高峰人口预测在14.86亿~15.44亿之间。城镇化水平达到60%后，将进入后期缓慢增长阶段，届时中国农村仍将有6亿多农民。在这样一个较长的渐进的社会转型过程中，推进城镇化，必须坚持统筹城乡发展，注重新农村建设。

## 二、城镇化与城市可持续发展

中国人口众多、资源紧缺、生态环境脆弱的基本国情，决定了城镇化过程中必须集约利用土地、水、能源等资源，切实保护好生态环境，走可持续的城镇化发展道路。

一是节约利用土地资源，建设集约型城市。土地是十分宝贵的资源和资产，关系到粮食安全，关系到谁养活中国人的问题。城市建设和发展必须十分珍惜和合理利用土地。应当坚持以城乡规划为依据，强化规划的调控作用，合理控制城镇用地规模，优化用地结构和布局，鼓励土地的合理利用和供应。要充分发挥市场机制的配置作用，积极运用经济杠杆，减少土地低效利用和闲置浪费。积极推进土地整理，盘活存量建设用地，提高土地集约利用程度。重视城市地下空间资源的利用，统一规划，综合开发，不断探索土地集约利用的新途径。

二是要节约和保护水资源，建设节水型城市。中国是一个水资源短缺的国家，城市缺水问题尤为突出。目前，600多个城市有400多个缺水，其中100多个严重缺水，水资源短缺已经成为制约经济社会发展的重要因素。因此，城市建设和发展必须坚持开源与节流并重，把节约和保护水资源放在突出位置，做好开发利用水资源和保护城市水源安全的规划；依据本地区水资源状况合理确定城市发展规模，合理确定和调整产业结构。要加强水污染防治，加快污水处理设施建设，提高污水处理能力，重视污水资源的再生利用。特别是要大力推广节水措施，稳步推进水价改革，促进全社会节约和合理利用水资源。

三是要提高能源利用效率，建设节能型城市。能源是经济社会发展的基础。中国经济的高速增长和人民生活水平的不断提高，使其对能源需求始终保持强劲增长态势，能源越来越成为可持续发展的瓶颈制约因素，特别是城市节能问题十分突出。要贯彻实施国家节能减排战略，大力调整优化经济结构，转变发展方式，促进生产节能；大力推广节能措施，促进建筑、交通和生活节能；调整优化能源供应结构，促进清洁能源的开发利用；综合运用各种管理手段，促进节能和新能源开发，推动节约发展、清洁发展、安全发展和可持续发展。

四是要保护历史文化遗产，建设文明型城镇。历史文化遗产和自然生态环境，是宝贵的不可再生资源。保护优秀的历史文化遗产，是继承和弘扬中华民族优秀文化传统的一件大事。一个城市历史文化遗产的保护状况是城市文明的重要标志。在城市发展中必须正确处理建设和保护的关系，尊重城市发展的历史，使城市的风貌随着岁月的流逝而更具内涵和底蕴。优良的生态环境，是现代文明社会和生活质量提高的本质要求。要贯彻实施环境保护的法律法规，加强环境管理，建立环境保护的约束机制；要加强城镇生态建设和保护，增强自然系统的生态服务功能，推进生态文明型城镇建设。

## 三、城镇化与城市的现代化

城市是一定区域经济、政治、文化、信息和服务中心，对经济社会发展有着重要作用。城镇化水平是一个国家工业化、现代化的重要标志。城市现代化是城市经济、社会、环境及生活方式由传统社会向现代化社会发展的转变过程，是综合的、多层次的、全方位的，涉及城市方方面面的深刻变化。

一是发展现代化经济。城镇化的核心是经济发展，以经济发展带动社会的全面发展。城市是经济发展的重点，产业发展是促进经济发展的基本因素。我国目前重要的任务，就是走新型工业化道路。要坚持以信息化带动工业化，以工业化促进信息化。要用高新技术和先进适用技术改造传统产业，加快发展服务业，提高第三产业在国民经济中的比重，尽快形成以高新技术产业为先导、基础产业和制造业为支撑、服务业全面发展的产业格局。

二是建设和谐社会。社会发展与人民幸福安康息息相关。社会现代化，目的是要满足社会日益发展和人的全面发展的需要，促进社会公平正义，共享改革开放的成果，符合绝大多数社会成员和民族文化价值的需要。在城镇化快速发展阶段，要特别注意协调城市不同群体之间的关系，保障城乡居民的各项权益，使低收入市民和进城务工就业农民等社会各类群体均享受到城市发展的成果。要着力保障和改善民生，建立和完善广覆盖的社会保障体系，使全体居民在就业、教育、医疗、养老、住房、最低生活保障等方面享有公平、合理的社会权利。

三是保护人居环境。现代化环境离不开现代化基础设施，现代化的基础设施是现代化城市的重要支撑。现代化城市必须拥有具备良好设施的住房、现代化的市政公用设施、现代化的城市交通、现代化的商业服务和休闲娱乐设施等，为广大居民提供舒适、方便、安全的居住、出行、休闲的条件。良好的生态环境是城市居民生存需求和追求现代化的重要目标。现代化城市要着力进行城市环境综合整治，改善城市大气、水环境，扩大绿地，改善和美化人居环境，提高城市居民生活质量。

四是实现科学管理。在工业化、信息化、城镇化、市场化、国际化的社会发展进程中，现代化管理水平是城市和国家发展水平的集中体现。现代化城市由于它的人口和用地规模较大，功能复杂，发展的要素和功能多元化，必须构建一套完整的科学管理体系才能有效地进行管理和运作。运用现代技术的管理体系，应当以城市的基本信息流为基础，依靠法律、行政、经济、技术和社会等各种手段来引导和调控城市的发展，实现决策的科学化和民主化，确保城市基础设施服务功能安全运行，满足城市经济社会发展和人民生活的需要。这样，才能更好地体现国家综合国力、政府管理能力和国际竞争力的要求。

# 目 录

## 综论篇

## 论坛篇

## 观察篇

## 专题篇

## 案例篇

## 附录篇

# 综论篇

# 2010中国城市发展综述

2010年是我国发展进程中很不平凡的一年。面对复杂多变的国内外环境，中国人民团结一心、开拓前进，社会和谐稳定，民生改善成效显著。经过不懈努力，“十一五”规划确定的目标任务胜利完成，经济实力、综合国力、人民生活水平迈上新的台阶。

中共十七届五中全会通过了《中共中央关于制定国民经济和社会发展第十二个五年规划的建议》。全会指出，制定“十二五”规划，必须高举中国特色社会主义伟大旗帜，以邓小平理论和“三个代表”重要思想为指导，深入贯彻落实科学发展观，适应国内外形势新变化，顺应各族人民过上更好生活新期待；以科学发展为主题，以加快转变经济发展方式为主线，深化改革开放，保障和改善民生，巩固和扩大应对国际金融危机冲击成果，促进经济长期平稳较快发展和社会和谐稳定，为全面建成小康社会打下具有决定性意义的基础。

据初步核算，我国2010年国内生产总值达397983亿元，比上年增长10.3%；第一、第二、第三产业分别增长4.3%、12.2%和9.5%；三次产业占国内生产总值的比重分别为10.2%、46.8%和43.0%。第二产业和第三产业的快速增长，展现出我国工业化和城镇化蓬勃推进的明显变化。

## 一、中国的城镇化进程

城镇化是经济社会发展的客观趋势，也是2010年中国发展关注的焦点。李克强在省部级主要领导干部专题研讨班上的讲话中指出：我国最大的内需在城镇化，最雄厚的内需潜力在城镇化。当前和今后相当长一段时间，我国城镇化处于快速发展阶段。在这个历史阶段，应以加快城镇化为依托，调整优化城乡和区域结构，扩大消费需求和投资需求，促进经济长期平稳较快发展。

### 1. 健康城镇化与制度创新

中共中央国务院《关于加大统筹城乡发展力度，进一步夯实农业农村发展基础的若干意见》，提出“推进城镇化发展的制度创新”的要求，把加强中小城市和小城镇发展作为当前的工作重点。

(1) 深化户籍制度改革，加快落实放宽中小城市、小城镇特别是县城和中心镇落户条件的政策，促进符合条件的农业转移人口在城镇落户并享有与当地城镇居民同等的权益。

（2）多渠道多形式改善农民工居住条件，鼓励有条件的城市将有稳定职业并在城市居住一定年限的农民工逐步纳入城镇住房保障体系。采取有针对性的措施，着力解决新生代农民工问题。统筹研究农业转移人口进城落户后城乡出现的新情况新问题。

（3）大力发展县域经济，抓住产业转移有利时机，促进特色产业、优势项目向县城和重点镇集聚，提高城镇综合承载能力，吸纳农村人口加快向小城镇集中。

（4）完善加快小城镇发展的财税、投融资等配套政策，安排年度土地利用计划要支持中小城市和小城镇发展。农村宅基地和村庄整理所节约的土地首先要补充耕地，调剂为建设用地的，在县域内按照土地利用总体规划使用，纳入年度土地利用计划，主要用于产业集聚发展，方便农民就近转移就业。

（5）继续推进扩权强县改革试点，推动经济发展快、人口吸纳能力强的镇行政管理体制改革，根据经济社会发展需要，下放管理权限，合理设置机构和配备人员编制。

### 2. 统筹推进城镇化与新农村建设

温家宝在2010年政府工作报告中提出：着力提高城镇综合承载能力，发挥城市对农村的辐射带动作用，促进城镇化和新农村建设良性互动。壮大县域经济，大力加强县城和中心镇基础设施和环境建设，引导非农产业和农村人口有序向小城镇集聚，鼓励返乡农民工就地创业。城乡建设都要坚持最严格的耕地保护制度和最严格的节约用地制度，切实保护农民合法权益。推进户籍制度改革，放宽中小城市和小城镇落户条件。有计划有步骤地解决好农民工在城镇的就业和生活问题，逐步实现农民工在劳动报酬、子女就学、公共卫生、住房租购以及社会保障方面与城镇居民享有同等待遇。要让符合条件的农业转移人口逐步变为城镇居民，也要让农民有一个幸福生活的美好家园。

同时，城镇化是解决“三农”问题的重要途径。只有减少农民，才能富裕农民。随着农村富余劳动力和农村人口逐步向城镇转移，农村居民人均占有资源量会相应增加，从而提高农业生产效率和商品化率，增加农民收入。减少农村人口，可以提高农业生产的规模化和市场化水平，促进现代农业的发展。城镇化水平的提高、城市经济实力的提升，可以增强以工补农、以城带乡的能力，有利于改善农村面貌，带动农村经济社会发展。

### 3. 积极稳妥推进城镇化与区域协调发展

中共中央在“十二五”规划建议中提出：

（1）实施区域发展总体战略。加强和完善跨区域合作机制，消除市场壁垒，促进要素流动，引导产业有序转移。

（2）实施主体功能区战略。基本形成适应主体功能区要求的法律法规、政策和规划体系，完善绩效考核办法和利益补偿机制，引导各地区严格按照主体功能定位推进发展。

（3）完善城市化布局和形态。科学规划城市群内各城市功能定位和产业布局，缓解特大城市中心城区压力，强化中小城市产业功能，增强小城镇公共服务和居住功能，推进大中小城市交通、通信、供电、供排水等基础设施一体化建设和网络化发展。

(4) 加强城镇化管理。城市规划和建设要注重以人为本、节地节能、生态环保、安全实用、突出特色、保护文化和自然遗产，强化规划约束力，加强城市公用设施建设，预防和治理“城市病”。

#### 4. 中国的流动人口和农民工

中国的城镇化进程正经历着前所未有的人口流动和迁移。1979—2010 年，全国流动人口从原来的 600 万人增加到 2.21 亿人。在未来二三十年，国内的流动迁移人口还将保持 2 亿 ~3 亿人的规模，其分布、结构、素质的复杂变化，对国家战略规划、政府社会管理和公共服务提出了严峻挑战。

根据《中国流动人口发展报告 (2010)》，我国未来的人口流动将呈现四大基本态势：

(1) 流动人口规模不断增加，但增速逐步放缓。如果我国人口流动迁移政策没有大的变化，到 2050 年流动人口规模可达 3.5 亿人左右，但每年新增流动人口由近 600 万人逐步下降到 2050 年的 300 万人左右。

(2) 经济危机为区域产业结构的调整带来了契机，促进了人口的重新分布。受本次金融危机影响，劳动力需求减弱，长距离人口流动减少，短期内沿海地区人口集聚趋势有所弱化，出现以省会城市为中心的流动态势，但流动人口继续向沿海、沿江、沿主要交通线地区聚集的长期趋势不会改变。

(3) 未来我国流动人口的分布将逐步形成以东部沿海连绵城市带为重心，以内陆城市群为中轴，以西部中心城市为集聚点的流动人口分布格局。

(4) 人口流动由生存型向发展型转变。流动人口受教育年限比全国平均水平略高，年龄结构趋于成年化，性别结构逐步均衡，举家迁移比例上升，在流入地长期定居倾向明显，流动人口的民生问题和服务管理体制改革压力增大。

在中国的流动人口中，数量最大的是外出农民工。2010 年，在本乡镇以外从业 6 个月以上的外出农民工和在本乡镇内从事非农产业 6 个月以上的本地农民工合计，全国农民工总量为 2.42 亿人，其中外出农民工数量为 1.53 亿人。

在农民工中，新生代农民工 (16 岁 ~30 岁) 的总数在 1 亿人左右，他们的文化素质整体较高；大多数人不再“亦工亦农”，而是纯粹从事二三产业；就业主要集中在制造业，在我国经济社会发展中日益发挥主力军的作用。新生代农民工在融入城市的过程中，还存在诸多问题。部分新生代农民工有较大的工作压力，对收入的满意度较低，在“市民”和“农民”的身份认同中处于尴尬境地。他们要想实现在务工地城市长期稳定就业和生活的目标，还需多层次的社会保障，以解决病患时的后顾之忧和失业后的暂时生活困难等。

## 二、快速发展的城乡建设

根据第六次全国人口普查主要数据公报，以 2010 年 11 月 1 日零时为标准时点，全国总人口为133972万人，其中居住在城镇的人口66557万人，占总人口的49.68%。在快速发展的城乡建设进程中，中国又新设了三个城市。根据民政部的批复，云南省人民政府决定撤销蒙自县，设立蒙自市（县级市）；撤销文山县，设立文山市（县级市）；江西省人民政府决定设立共青城市（县级），由省直辖，九江市代管。至2010年年末，中国共有设市城市657个。

**1. 城市建设**

2009年年末，全国设市城市654个，城市城区人口3.40亿人，暂住人口0.36亿人，建成区面积3.81万平方公里。城市市政公用设施固定资产完成投资10641.5亿元，占同期城镇固定资产投资总额的5.48%。

2009年全国城市用水人口3.6亿人，用水普及率96.12%，人均日生活用水量176.58升；城市用气人口3.44亿人，燃气普及率91.41%；集中供热面积38.0亿平方米；城市道路长度26.91万公里，人均城市道路面积12.79平方米，城市道路机械清扫率31.8%；有10个城市已建成轨道交通线路条数33条，长度839公里；有28个城市在建轨道交通线路条数81条，长度1991公里；城市共有污水处理厂1214座，污水处理厂集中处理率65.79%，生活垃圾无害化处理率为71.31%；全年清运生活垃圾、粪便1.79亿吨；城市建成区绿化覆盖率38.22%，绿地率34.17%，人均公园绿地面积10.66平方米。全国共有208处国家级风景名胜区，根据其中198处统计，风景名胜区面积8.1万平方公里，可游览面积3.4万平方公里，全年接待游人4.6亿人次。国家投入34亿元用于风景名胜区的维护和建设。

自1992年起，国家建设部门先后命名了180个园林城市和7个园林城区。2010年，银川市、无锡市、黄山市、吴江市、寿光市被授予“中国人居环境奖”，北京市通州大运河公园建设等35个项目被授予“中国人居环境范例奖”。

**2. 县城建设**

2009年年末，全国有县城1636个。据其中1617个县、13个特殊区域及144个新疆生产建设兵团师团部驻地统计汇总，县城人口1.23亿人，暂住人口1120万人，建成区面积1.56万平方公里。全国县城市政公用设施固定资产完成投资1681.4亿元。县城用水人口1.12亿人，用水普及率83.72%，人均日生活用水量118.6升；用气人口8248万人，燃气普及率61.7%；集中供热面积4.8亿平方米；县城道路长度9.5万公里，人均城市道路面积11.95平方米，机械清扫率13.7%；县城共有污水处理厂664座，污水处理厂集中处理率35.11%；县城建成区绿化覆盖率23.48%；建成区绿地率18.37%，人均公园绿地面积6.89平方米。

自2006年起，国家建设部门先后命名了61个园林县城和15个园林城镇。

**3. 村镇建设**

2009年年末，全国共有建制镇19322个、乡14848个。据16881个建制镇、13886个乡、

667 个镇乡级特殊区域和 271.4 万个自然村（其中村民委员会所在地 56.75 万个）统计汇总，村镇户籍总人口 9.44 亿。其中，建制镇建成区 1.38 亿，乡建成区 0.328 亿，镇乡级特殊区域建成区 0.029 亿，村庄 7.70 亿。全国建制镇建成区面积 3.13 万平方公里，人口密度 5214 人/平方公里；乡建成区 0.76 万平方公里，人口密度 4661 人/平方公里；镇乡级特殊区域建成区 854 平方公里，人口密度 3796 人/平方公里。年末全国有总体规划的建制镇 14387 个、乡 8048 个、镇乡级特殊区域 412 个、有规划的行政村 260457 个。全年村镇规划编制投入达 30.66 亿元。

2009 年，全国村镇建设总投入 9615 亿元，村镇房屋竣工建筑面积 9.73 亿平方米。年末全国村镇实有房屋建筑面积 347.8 亿平方米，人均住宅建筑面积 30.88 平方米。据统计，我国建制镇建成区用水普及率 78.3%，人均日生活用水量 98.9 升，燃气普及率 43.4%，人均道路面积 11.2 平方米，排水管道暗渠密度 4.99 公里/平方公里，人均公园绿地面积 1.92 平方米。乡建成区用水普及率 63.5%，人均日生活用水量 79.5 升，燃气普及率 18.3%，人均道路面积 10.9 平方米，排水管道暗渠密度 3.01 公里/平方公里，人均公园绿地面积 0.84 平方米。镇乡级特殊区域建成区用水普及率 82.4%，人均日生活用水量 80.8 升，燃气普及率 36.8%，人均道路面积 14.0 平方米，排水管道暗渠密度 3.80 公里/平方公里，人均公园绿地面积 2.99 平方米。全国 49.9% 的行政村有集中供水，4.9% 的行政村对生活污水进行了处理，35.0% 的行政村有生活垃圾收集点，17.7% 的行政村对生活垃圾进行处理。

### 4. 战胜玉树地震和舟曲泥石流等重大自然灾害

2010 年，我国地震、洪涝、干旱、台风、泥石流等自然灾害异常严重，造成重大人员伤亡和财产损失。在党中央、国务院和中央军委坚强领导下，各族人民团结奋战、顽强拼搏，奋力夺取抗灾救灾的重大胜利，谱写了中国防灾减灾史上新的篇章。

4 月 14 日，青海省玉树地区发生 7.1 级强烈地震，涉及玉树藏族自治州玉树、称多、治多、杂多、囊谦、曲麻莱县和四川甘孜藏族自治州石渠县等 7 个县的 27 个乡镇，受灾面积 35862 平方公里，受灾人口 246842 人。截至 5 月 30 日统计，地震遇难 2698 人，失踪 270 人。居民住房大量倒塌，学校、医院等公共服务设施严重损毁，部分公路沉陷、桥涵坍塌，供电、供水、通信设施遭受破坏。农牧业生产设施受损，牲畜大量死亡，商贸、旅游、金融、加工企业损失严重。山体滑坡崩塌，生态环境受到严重威胁。

为科学、依法、统筹，有力、有序、有效地推进灾后恢复重建工作，国务院先后发布关于做好玉树地震灾后恢复重建工作和支持恢复重建政策措施的指导意见。政府各部门组织完成了《玉树地震灾后恢复重建总体规划》，力争用三年时间基本完成恢复重建主要任务，使灾区基本生产生活条件和经济社会发展全面恢复并超过灾前水平，生态环境切实得到保护和改善，又好又快地重建新校园、新家园，为建设生态美好、特色鲜明、经济发展、安全和谐的社会主义新玉树奠定坚实基础。

8 月 8 日凌晨，甘肃省甘南藏族自治州舟曲县发生新中国成立以来最为严重的特大山洪泥石流灾害。舟曲县城由北向南 5 公里长、500 米宽的区域被夷为平地，三个村庄和沿河房屋被冲毁，泥石流阻断白龙江、形成堰塞湖，回水使县城部分被淹，供水、电力、交通、通讯中断。灾害主要涉及城关镇和江盘乡的15个村、2个社区，受灾面积约2.4平方公里，受灾人口26470人。人员伤亡惨重，截至10月11日统计，遇难1501人，失踪264人。

灾区广大干部群众和社会各界救援人员不畏艰险、万众一心、科学应对，最大限度解救被困人员，及时救治伤员，妥善安置受灾群众，全面开展卫生防疫，迅速抢修受损基础设施，排除堰塞体险情，疏通白龙江河道，确保了灾区人心安定、民族团结和社会稳定。至2010年年末，城乡居民住房加固维修已基本完成。按照建设“让灾区人民满意，让全国人民放心”的新舟曲的目标要求，按照《舟曲灾后恢复重建总体规划》，力争在2012年年底前，全面完成城乡住房、公共服务和基础设施等各项恢复重建任务，使灾区基本生产生活条件和经济社会发展全面恢复并超过灾前水平。

## 三、城市发展中的焦点与问题

在快速的城镇化进程中，我国发展中不平衡、不协调、不可持续的问题依然突出：经济增长的资源环境约束强化，投资与消费关系失衡，收入分配差距较大，科技创新能力不强，产业结构不合理，农业基础薄弱，城乡区域发展不协调，就业压力和结构性矛盾并存，一些群众反映强烈的问题如教育、医疗、物价、拆迁和食品安全等没有根本解决。如何转变发展方式，大力推进服务型政府建设，努力为各类市场主体创造公平的发展环境，为人民群众提供良好的公共服务，维护社会公平正义，是各级政府长期面对的重大课题。

### 1. 城市环境保护任务繁重

“十一五”以来，我国环境保护事业取得积极进展，环境质量也得到了有效的改善，从环境监测结果来看，地表水水质持续好转，环保重点城市空气质量逐年提高，生态环境质量总体保持稳定，重点流域、重点区域和重点城市的环境质量明显改善。但个别地方和区域污染指标超过国家标准，污染依然严重，环境保护的压力依然较大。突出表现为：

(1) 我国传统的污染物排放量仍然很大，超过环境容量，致使一些地区环境质量达不到国家规定的标准。如我国首次成为世界汽车产销第一大国，机动车污染日益严重，全国约五分之一的城市大气污染严重，机动车尾气排放成为我国大中城市空气污染的主要来源。2010年，全国113个环保重点城市环境空气中主要污染物年均浓度值与《环境空气质量标准》的限值相比较，有30个城市超过国家二级标准，其中省会及以上城市有北京、太原、沈阳、哈尔滨、南京、合肥、济南、郑州、武汉、重庆、成都、西安、兰州、西宁、乌鲁木齐等15个。如北京市的可吸入颗粒物（PM10）年日均浓度值连续多年超过二级标准，二氧化氮的年平均浓度值也在逐年上升；兰州市的空气质量为劣三级。

2010年，全国重点流域水环境质量总体为中度污染，I～III类水质比例为51.9%，IV类和V类为27.3%，劣V类为20.8%。太湖、巢湖、滇池和三峡库区的富营养化依然较重，“水华”现象时有发生。在监测的5个城市内湖中，东湖（武汉）和昆明湖（北京）为IV

类水质，玄武湖（南京）为Ⅴ类水质，西湖（杭州）和大明湖（济南）为劣Ⅴ类水质。

（2）随着我国经济的快速发展，一些新的环境问题也在不断地产生，特别是重金属、持久性有机污染物、土壤污染、危险废物和化学品污染、电子垃圾等，这些污染物的产生都带来一些新的问题。特别是在损害人体健康方面，这类污染物的危害更大。

（3）我国工业化、城镇化加速发展，企业为追求利益最大化而忽视安全生产和环境保护导致安全生产事故和违法排污行为频发，长期以来积累的排污效应使环境不堪重负，自然灾害引发次生环境问题时有发生，群众对环境安全诉求和要求不断提高，环境应急管理工作面临严峻形势。

（4）气候变化和生物多样性等全球性环境问题，已经成为各国利益博弈的焦点。随着我国二氧化碳、二氧化硫等排放量居世界前列，中国的环境问题将承受更多国际压力。

**2. 城市交通面临严峻考验和深刻变革**

2010年是我国城市交通面临严峻考验和深刻变革的一年，也是对以往城市交通策略进行深刻反思的重要时刻。随着城镇化进程和社会经济快速发展，机动车发展速度加快、城市交通问题日益成为地方政府和市民关注的热点问题。

（1）大城市交通拥堵问题日益严重。2010年，全国主要城市交通正面临着整体性的交通拥堵问题，除北京、上海、广州、重庆等一线城市外，济南、南京、武汉、成都等二线城市，甚至一些三线城市，都相继出现了严重的交通拥堵情况。据统计，北京市主干道高峰时间道路饱和度接近1.0，上海、南京、成都、广州分别达到了0.95、0.82、0.8和0.72。严重的交通拥堵在我国部分高速公路干线上也时有发生，如京藏高速进京段2010年6月连续拥堵半个月，司机与旅客苦不堪言。

（2）“停车难”问题日渐突出。由于停车设施总量严重不足、配置不合理、利用效率低和停车管理不到位，“停车难”成为困扰城市交通的又一大难题。占道停车、乱停乱放已经成为普遍现象，城市停车供需矛盾日益突出，停车位数量和汽车保有量形成了巨大反差和缺口。“停车难”的影响不仅仅局限于停车本身，还引发了一系列城市管理问题，如加剧道路拥堵、引发公共纠纷、带来安全隐患、导致交通事故等。

（3）小汽车发展进入快速增长阶段。10年来，我国的汽车产销量由2000年的200多万辆发展到了2010年的1800多万辆。2010年年末，全国民用汽车保有量达到9086万辆，比上年末增长19.3%；私人汽车保有量6539万辆，增长25.3%。民用轿车保有量4029万辆，增长28.4%，其中私人轿车3443万辆，增长32.2%。北京市机动车保有量超过480万辆，私人小汽车超过370万辆，全年销售新机动车91.6万辆。目前，全国机动车保有量超过100万辆的城市已经达到20多个，小汽车出行比例逐年增加，大量的城市土地资源和道路被小汽车占用。

（4）交通需求管理开始受到关注。采取以调节需求为目标的交通需求管理，逐渐成为缓解大城市交通拥堵的重要对策。北京奥运会起实施单双号管理，还将城市重点地区的临时占道停车收费标准由原来的每半小时2.5元提高到了5元，并颁布了错时上下班等十几项交通管理措施。2010年12月，北京市政府出台了《关于进一步推进首都交通科学发展，加大力度缓解交通拥堵工作的意见》等一系列严厉的治理交通拥堵政策措施，包括完善交通规划，疏解中心城功能和人口；加快道路交通基础设施建设；加大优先发展公共交通力度；改善自行车步行交通系统和驻车换乘条件；进一步加强机动车管理；对小客车实施数量调控和配额管理制度等。

### 3. 完善住房保障体系

社会保障性住房制度是国家社会保障体系的重要组成部分，也应是城镇住房供应体系的主体，其实质是政府利用国家和社会的力量解决城镇中低收入家庭的住房问题。从城镇健康发展的目标出发，提供社会保障性住房是各级政府义不容辞的责任，其社会效益高于经济效益。“十一五”期间，全国大力实施保障性住房建设和棚户区改造，使1100万户困难家庭住上了新房。尽管我国城乡人均住房条件至2010年均已超过30平方米，但与人民不断增长的改善居住条件的需求还有较大差距，一些中低收入家庭住房困难，群众反映强烈，社会舆论高度关注。

2010年，我国的住房供应强化了培育市场和保障的“两条腿走路”的体制，以形成多层次的住房保障体系为目标，廉租房、经济适用房、公共租赁住房等为主体的保障性住房建设呈现了加速趋势，全年各类保障性住房和棚户区改造住房开工590万套，基本建成370万套。针对一些中等偏下收入住房困难家庭无力通过市场租赁或购买住房的突出问题，住房和城乡建设部等七部门联合制定了《关于加快发展公共租赁住房的指导意见》，旨在解决城市中等偏低收入家庭住房困难。根据《指导意见》，公共租赁住房供应对象主要是城市中等偏下收入住房困难家庭。有条件的地区，可以将新就业职工和有稳定职业并在城市居住一定年限的外来务工人员纳入供应范围。

同时，加快保障性住房建设，为市场性住房需求减压，缓和住房供求矛盾，也被作为遏制房价持续上涨的一种调控手段。2010年年底，中央经济工作会议进一步明确提出，2011年要加快推进住房保障体系建设，强化政府责任，加大保障性安居工程建设力度，加快棚户区和农村危房改造，大力发展公共租赁住房，逐步形成符合国情的保障性住房体系和商品房体系。

### 4. 加强房地产市场调控

通过不断的实践，中国政府对房地产市场的调控已经彰显了明确的思路：增加有效供给，抑制不合理需求。2010年国务院先后发布了《关于促进房地产市场平稳健康发展的通知》和《关于坚决遏制部分城市房价过快上涨的通知》，不断加大调控力度，增添调控手段。尤为突出的是，采取了经济手段和行政措施并举的办法，从抑制需求、增加供给、加强监管等方面对房地产市场进行全方位、大力度的调控。

初步统计，2010年房地产开发投资48267亿元（占全国GDP比重的12.13%），比2009年增长33.2%。其中，商品住宅投资34038亿元，增长32.9%；办公楼投资1807亿元，增长 31.2%；商业营业用房投资 5599 亿元，增长 33.9%。

针对违法征地拆迁等引发日益增多的社会矛盾，国务院法制办两次在全社会征求对《国有土地上房屋征收与补偿条例》的意见，目的是加快建立健全维护群众权益机制、行政决策风险评估和纠错机制，加强信访、人民调解、行政调解工作，拓宽社情民意表达渠道，切实解决乱占耕地、违法拆迁等群众反映强烈的问题。

《中共中央关于制定国民经济和社会发展第十二个五年规划的建议》要求：加强市场监管，规范房地产市场秩序，抑制投机需求，促进房地产业平稳健康发展。根据“十二五”规划，我国政府将坚定不移地搞好房地产市场调控。加快健全房地产市场调控的长效机制，重点解决城镇中低收入家庭住房困难，切实稳定房地产市场价格，满足居民合理住房需求。未来五年，全国计划新建保障性住房 3600 万套。到“十二五”末，全国城镇保障性住房覆盖率将从目前的 7%～8% 提高到 20% 左右，进一步解决城镇低收入家庭住房困难问题。

## 四、“城市，让生活更美好”

### 1. 成功举办上海世界博览会

2010 年上海世博会，是我国首次举办的综合性世界博览会，举国关注，举世瞩目。围绕“城市，让生活更美好”的主题，秉承和弘扬理解、沟通、欢聚、合作的世博理念，创造和演绎了一场精彩纷呈、美轮美奂的世界文明大展示，成功、精彩、难忘的世博会为祖国和人民赢得了荣耀。

上海世博会是一届规模空前的人类盛会。从 4 月 30 日晚隆重开幕起，上海黄浦江两岸 5.28 平方公里的世博园 169 个展馆内，有 246 个国家和国际组织参展，城市最佳实践区集中了全球遴选出的 80 个城市案例，展示了世界先进的城市发展理念和具体实践。在 184 天会期中，有 7308.4 万人次的海内外游客参观，单日最大客流达到 103.28 万人；共有超过 1200 个中外演出团体来园演出，节目总数超过 1100 个，共上演各类文化演出活动 22900 余场，累计吸引观众逾 3400 万人次。世博会期间共举办 1 场高峰论坛、6 场主题论坛、1 场青年高峰论坛，此前还举办了 53 场公众论坛。

上海世博会是新中国成立以来我国举办的规模最大、持续时间最长的国际活动。世博会的成功举办，实现了中华民族百年世博梦想，向世界展示了中华民族五千年灿烂文明，展示了新中国 60 年特别是改革开放 30 多年的辉煌成就，展示了我国各族人民为实现全面建设小康社会目标而团结奋斗的精神风貌，集中反映了世界经济、科技、文化、社会以及生态文明发展的时代潮流，深入探讨了当今世界人类发展面临的共同课题，增进了我国人民同各国各地区人民的相互了解和友谊，提升了我国国际地位和影响力，增强了全国人民的民族自豪感、自信心、凝聚力。上海世博会的成功实践再次证明，中国人民有信心有能力为人类文明进步作出自己的贡献。

本届世博会让更多的人知道，城市是有可能变得更加健康、更加安全的，城市能够更好地把自然和技术融合在一起。城市里的居民可以获得更加清洁的空气和水，享受更加美好的生活。换句话说，这届世博会给世界带来了新的希望，让我们有信心应对城市化时代日益涌现的挑战。

在10月31日的世博会高峰论坛上发表了《上海宣言》，形成了对全球城市创新与可持续发展的共识，表达了城市时代全球公众对和谐美好城市生活的共同愿景。《宣言》倡议：创造面向未来的生态文明，追求包容协调的增长方式，坚持科技创新的发展道路，建设智能便捷的信息社会，培育开放共享的多元文化，构筑亲睦友善的宜居社区，促进均衡协调的城乡关系。

**2. 光彩夺目的世界人居日庆典**

2010年10月4日是第25个“世界人居日”。由联合国人居署、中华人民共和国住房和城乡建设部、上海市人民政府共同主办的人居日庆典活动在上海举行。世界人居日选择了与正在进行中的上海世博会同样的主题：“城市，让生活更美好”。

在庆典上，中国昆山市人民政府荣获“2010年联合国人居奖”。获奖原因是：昆山市采取创新举措向外来人口提供城市基本服务。每年约80万外来人口来昆山市务工，城市每周举办五场招聘会。在过去的两年间，昆山帮助超过20万人找到工作，新建现代住房使人均居住面积从1999年的12平方米增至目前的40平方米；同时，昆山还保障外来人口充分享有养老金、医疗和其他社会保险，及与本地居民平等的教育机会和公共服务权。

庆典活动还包括：在2008年联合国人居奖得主日照市政府的赞助下，联合国人居署正式启动了汉语网站；联合国人居署、国际欧亚科学院中国科学中心、中国市长协会联合发布了《中国城市状况报告2010/2011》（英文版）；联合国人居署区域技术合作司也展示了该机构有史以来的第一部《亚洲城市状况报告》。由住房和城乡建设部推荐申报的梅州市龙丰垃圾填埋场CDM（清洁发展机制）综合治理、晋城市煤层气综合利用工程、哈尔滨市群力新区生态环境建设、常熟市沙家浜生态环境建设、上虞市曹娥江两岸环境综合整治和中卫市开发保护黄河湿地资源等6个项目荣获2010年“迪拜国际改善人居环境最佳范例奖”全球百佳范例称号。

上海世博会联合国馆总代表阿瓦尼·贝楠博士代表联合国秘书长潘基文先生在庆典上说：“随着全球人口日益以城市人口为主，每年一届的世界人居日提供机会让我们反思如何使城市和城镇成为对于所有人来讲更美好的地方。”

联合国人居署执行主任安娜·蒂拜朱卡在致辞中强调，城市是人类的最大遗产，而且是世界文明最大的成就。对于建设更加美好的城市，使所有人过上更美好生活，建议采取以下五个战略步骤：

（1）改善生活质量，特别是估计10亿居住在世界各地贫民窟和其他低标准住房中的居民的质量。为了使所有人都能够过上更好的生活，就必须改进取得安全和有利于健康的住房、安居、基本服务和保健与教育等社会福利设施的机会。

（2）投资于人力资本。这是促进社会经济发展和更公平地分配城市优势的一个条件。

这还将能够使得各城市和各地区更有效地执行政策，并确保它们适当进行调整，以满足当地需要。

(3) 提升持续经济机会。城市可以通过劳力密集型项目刺激有利于贫困者的持续经济增长。这主要包括公共工程和建筑行业。发展中国家的城市正在开始提供社会保障，使那些历来受到排斥者更好地取得经济机会。

(4) 增强政治包容性。当今越来越多的城市和国家主管部门分享同样的基本哲学：通过增强互动使普通百姓能够参与治理。这意味着促使人们及其街邻参与对话和决策，以此作为地方民主的一个基本方面。

(5) 促进文化包容性。文化历来被排除在常规国际发展议程之外。越来越多的地方发展政策考虑到城市生活的文化层面，例如，社会资本、传统、标识、归属感和最高荣誉感。这将有助于融合少数民族、保存区域价值、维护语言和宗教多样性，解决冲突和保护遗产。

### 3. 促进城市平等和包容的成长

第五届世界城市论坛于2010年3月22日至26日在巴西里约热内卢召开，共有来自世界150个国家的13718名代表实际参加了这次盛会。这是联合国人居署首次在拉丁美洲举办的世界城市论坛，主题为“城市权利：促进城市平等”（The Right to the City：Bridging the Urban Divide）。

第五届世界城市论坛共包括6个对话会议：①推进城市权利；②促进城市平等：包容的城市；③平等获得住房和基本城市服务的权利；④城市的文化多样性；⑤治理和参与；⑥可持续城市化：气候变化中的城市。

当前，全球人口中的城市人口刚刚过半，但快速发展的城市经济生活已经消耗了世界总能源消费的三分之二，并产生了相当比例的废弃物和温室气体。此外，在城市化进程中并非所有城市人口和社会团体都享有同等机会，享受同样的城市服务和供应。在世界各国各地区，都存在着明显的城市发展差异。可持续地共同享有城市化带来的福利，是一个城市的共同目标，必须由政府、私营部门、民间社会和公众共同付出努力，通过各方面的共同行动来彰显城市的权利、弥合城市的差异。

联合国秘书长潘基文说：“当前，全球半数以上人口居住在城市，城市对气候变化问题负有超出比例的责任，城市化是当代‘至关重要的议程’之一。”他敦促与会代表商讨如何解决当前紧迫的城市问题，让所有的人能够得到安全的饮水、卫生、住房和基本服务，让所有人的生活有安全感，让所有的人都获得能够更好的工作机会。

联合国人居署执行主任安娜·蒂拜朱卡说，尽管在过去10年间，联合国千年发展计划确立的“到2020年使至少1亿贫民窟居民生活有明显改善”的目标已经实现，但是从2000年到2010年，贫民窟居民的总数增长了5500万人，目前已经达到8.27亿人，需要引起各方的注意。她说：“独木难撑。政府独木难撑。城市、大企业、公民社会也独木难撑。我们需要清晰协调的伙伴关系和努力！我们需要他们支持，现在就需要，这样，新领导（联合国人居署）才能有万全之备展开行动，协助成员国和所有《人居议程》合作伙伴实现为所有人提供适当住房和可持续城市的理想。”

巴西总统卢拉在开幕致辞时指出：作为集体场所，城市空间属于所有城市居民，具有丰富多样的文化，其社会功能在于保障财富、服务和机会的普遍分配。他说：“实现可以改变城市运营方式的城市设计是有可能的。因为巴西城市投资谨慎，创造了许多就业机会，人民总体生活水平有所提高。”他确信，以里约热内卢这座世界闻名的“奇迹之城”作为论坛的主办地，将有助于促进制定先进的全球城市空间布局解决方案。

论坛闭幕式之前，由联合国人居署牵头的世界城市运动（World Urban Campaign）正式启动。该运动旨在全球、国家和地方政策制定过程中提高可持续城市化的意识并使之主流化。从2010年的里约论坛开始，世界城市运动为各合作伙伴和机构提供一个机制，以便累积知识、专业技能和世界城市论坛的经验，从而改善全球、国家和地方各级的城市政策。人居署旨在通过世界城市运动联合大众、私营部门和公民社会，把可持续城市化提升到全球政府议程的首要位置。

**4. 可持续发展的设计**

面对全球气候变化，国际建筑师协会（UIA）于2009年12月和2010年11月，相继发表了“哥本哈根宣言”和“坎昆公报”，号召进行可持续发展的设计，响应全球的可持续发展战略。

UIA提出：建筑必须从最小的尺度开始直到城市和区域规划的尺度，都使用全面、综合的可持续设计；时刻铭记建筑、景观、自然环境和基础设施都是不断创造可持续未来的基本要素。对形式、几何形状和空间策略的仔细而周到的设计，加上合适的材料、设备和功能分配，可以将资源消耗、温室气体排放以及全部的环境影响减少50%~80%。建筑业——建造、改造与拆除构筑物的过程，以及这些建筑设施整个生命周期的运营过程，为我们今天应对气候挑战提供了一半的机会。

可持续设计始于每个项目的最初阶段，并需要全体利益相关者——业主、设计师、工程师、主管当局、承包商、所有者、使用者和公民社会——共同承担义务。

可持续设计建立在“全生命周期分析与管理”的基础上，包括了建造和未来使用过程中的各个方面。

可持续设计通过设计实现效率最大化。可再生能源、高效能的使用以及环境友好技术在项目概念设想下被整合到最佳的应用状态。

可持续设计意识到所有的建筑和规划项目，都与周围广泛的自然环境紧密关联，是复杂的互动系统的一部分；它们反映了公民日常生活的传统、文化以及社会价值。

可持续设计为健康的建筑寻找健康的材料，推崇尊重生态、尊重社会的土地利用方式，激发、确立和提升审美的敏感。

可持续设计旨在显著减少碳痕迹、有害材料与技术的使用，以及其他由建成环境对自然环境造成的不利影响。

可持续设计致力于改善生活质量、促进地区和全球公平、提高经济福祉，为公民参与与社区营造创造机会。

可持续设计承认地区与全球所有人类间相互依赖的关系。它意识到城市人口必须依靠综合、互动、可持续的城乡体系作为他们的生命保障系统（洁净的水和空气、食品、住所、工作、教育、卫生、文化机遇，等等）。

可持续设计赞同联合国教科文组织的陈述：作为交流、创新和创造的源泉，文化多样性对于人类来说就像生物多样性对于自然界一样必要。

UIA 正在与它的 124 个成员国密切合作，为实施可持续设计战略制定因地制宜的国家级计划。在 2011 年 9 月 UIA 东京世界建筑师大会上将启动这一战略，并督促建筑师采取负责任的态度，致力于通过设计使我们未来的世界走上可持续发展之路。

## 五、小结

2010 年国内的大事、喜事和难事不断：上海世博会、广州亚运会，玉树地震、舟曲泥石流和部分地区严重的旱涝灾害。全国人民面对挑战，有效巩固和扩大应对国际金融危机冲击成果，加快转变经济发展方式，人民生活水平和质量不断提高，经济实力和综合国力进一步增强。历史经验证明，唯有坚定不移地推进改革和发展，唯有始终不渝地维护社会公平正义，唯有充分发挥全体人民的积极性和创造精神，国家才能振兴，民族才能进步，事业才能发展，人民才能安居乐业、心情舒畅，生活才能幸福和更有尊严，城市才能更加美好。

（作者：毛其智，清华大学教授，国际欧亚科学院院士）

# An Introduction of Urban Development in China: 2010

The year 2010 is an unusual one in China's development course. Facing the complicate conditions of domestic and overseas both, the Chinese people have attained social harmonious and stability and significant improvement in livelihood by uniting as one and forging ahead. After unremitting efforts, the objectives and tasks set in the Eleventh Five-Year Plan have been fulfilled successfully; and the economic strength, comprehensive national power and the people's living standard have achieved new heights.

The Fifth Plenum of the $17^{th}$ Central Committee of the Communist Party of China passed the *Proposal of the CPC Central Committee for Formulating the Twelfth Five-year Plan for National Economic and Social Development*. The Plenum pointed out that when drawing up the Twelfth Five-year Plan, we must hold high the great banner of socialism with Chinese characteristics, take Deng Xiaoping Theory and the important thought of Three Represents as our guide, thoroughly apply the Scientific Outlook on Development, adapt to the latest changes in the domestic and international situations, and satisfy the new expectations of the people of all ethnic groups for a better life. Taking scientific development as the theme and accelerating transformation of the pattern of economic development as the main thread, we need to deepen reform and opening up; ensure and improve the people's wellbeing; consolidate and expand upon the success of our efforts to respond to the impact of the global financial crisis; promote long-term, steady and rapid economic development and social harmony and stability; and lay a solid foundation for building a moderately prosperous society in all respects.

According to the preliminary accounting, China's GDP in 2010 reached RMB39798. 3 billion yuan, up by 10. 3% as compared with the prior year; the primary industry, secondary industry and tertiary industry grew by 4. 3%, 12. 2% and 9. 5% respectively, accounting for 10. 2%, 46. 8% and 43. 0% of the GDP proportion. Rapid growth of the secondary and tertiary industry reflects the remarkable change in China's vigorous urbanization and industrialization.

## Ⅰ. China's Urbanization Progress

Urbanization is an objective trend in the social-economic development, also the highlight of China's development in 2010. "China's largest domestic demand rests with urbanization and the strongest domestic demand potential also rests with urbanization". Li Keqiang said at the seminar of major provincial and ministerial leaders. That currently and for a relatively long period of time in the future, China's urbanization will be in a rapid developing stage. In this historical stage, China shall promote the long-term steady and rapid development of economy by accelerating the urbanization, adjusting and optimizing the urban, rural and regional structure, and expanding the consumption demand and investment demand.

### 1. Sound urbanization and institutional innovation

*The Several Proposals of the CPC Central Committee and the State Council on Strengthening the Efforts of Coordinative Urban-Rural Development and Further Consolidating the Basis of Agricultural and Rural Development* advanced the requirement of "promoting the institutional innovation for urbanization development" and took the development of small and medium-sized cities and small towns as the current focus.

(1) Deepen the reform of household registration system and accelerate the implementation and deregulation of the policies regarding the household registration conditions of small and medium-sized cities and small towns, especially county seats and central towns, to promote qualified rural migrants to settle and enjoy the same right and interest as local urban residents.

(2) Improve the living conditions of peasant laborers through multiple channels, encourage capable cities to gradually incorporate peasant laborers with stable career and living in cities for certain years into the urban housing security system. Adopt pertinent measures to solve problems of the new generation of peasant laborers, and study the new situation and new issues occurred after the settlement of rural migrants in urban areas.

(3) Spare no effort to develop county economies and grasp the favorable opportunity of industrial transfer to boost characteristic industries and advantageous projects to gather in counties and key towns, improve the comprehensive carrying capacity of towns and promote rural population to gather in small cities and towns.

(4) Perfect the supporting fiscal, investment and financing policies accelerating the development of small and medium-sized cities and towns, and arrange annual land use plan to support their development. Rural housing land and land saved in village consolidation shall first replenish the arable land; those adjusted for construction shall be used in accordance with the general plan for land use within county's scopes; and those incorporated into the annual land use

plan shall mainly be used for the development of industrial cluster and facilitate the proximate migration and employment of peasants.

(5) Boost the trial of reinforcing the rights of strong counties continuously, promote the administrative system reform of towns featured by rapid economic development and strong population absorption capacity, delegate management powers and set up institutions and staffing in light of the needs of social and economic development.

**2. Balanced promoting urbanization and building a new countryside**

Premier Wen Jiabao proposed in the report on work of the government in 2010 to increase the overall carrying capacity of cities and towns; ensure that cities stimulate the development of surrounding rural areas; and promote positive interaction between urbanization and the building of a new countryside. We will strengthen county economies, improve infrastructure and environmental protection in county towns and hub towns, guide an orderly flow of nonagricultural industries and rural people to small towns, and encourage returned rural migrant workers to start businesses in their hometowns. When developing urban and rural areas, we must adhere to the strictest possible systems for protecting arable land and economizing land use to genuinely safeguard the legitimate rights and interests of farmers. We will carry out reform of the household registration system and relax requirements for household registration in towns and small and medium-sized cities. We will solve employment and living problems rural migrant workers face in cities and towns in a planned and step-by-step manner, and gradually ensure that they receive the same treatment as urban residents in areas such as pay, children's education, healthcare, housing, and social security, and allow eligible workers who have left agricultural work to gradually become urban residents, and develop a beautiful rural environment where farmers can live a happy life.

Meanwhile, urbanization is an important way to solve the issues of agriculture, rural areas and farmers. Peasants cannot get rich unless the number of peasants is reduced. With the migration of rural redundant laborers and rural population to urban areas, the resource per capita of rural residents will go up accordingly, which will improve the production efficiency and commercialization rate of agriculture and increase the income of peasants. The reduction of rural population can enhance the scale and marketization of agricultural production and boost the development of modern agriculture. Urbanization improvement and the enhancement of urban economic strength can strengthen the capability of industry subsidizing agriculture and the city helping power rural growth, to improve the appearance of rural areas and promote rural social and economic development.

**3. Boost the urbanization and regional coordinated development actively and steadily**

In the *Proposal for Formulating the Twelfth Five-year Plan*, the CPC Central Committee put forward:

(1) To implement the general strategy for regional development. Strengthen and perfect the cross-region cooperation mechanism, eliminate the market barriers, promote factor flow and guide the orderly transfer of industries.

(2) To implement the development priority zone strategy. Basically form the laws, regulations, policies and planning system in harmony with the requirements on development priority zones, perfect the performance appraisal methods and interest compensation mechanism, and guide various regions to boost development in light of the positioning of development priority zones.

(3) To perfect the pattern and form of urbanization. Plan city's functional positioning and industrial distribution in the city-groups scientifically, alleviate the pressure of central areas in metropolitans, strengthen the functions of industries in small and medium-sized cities, enhance the public service and residential function of small cities and towns, and boost the integrated construction and network development of infrastructures of large, small and medium-sized cities, such as urban transport, communication, power supply, water supply and drainage, etc.

(4) To strengthen the urbanization management. Urban planning and construction shall highlight people orientation, land and energy saving, environmental protection, safety and practicality, characteristics, protection of cultural and natural heritage, strengthen the restriction of planning, enhance the construction of urban public facilities, also prevent and control the "city disease".

### 4. China's floating population and migrant workers

China's urbanization course is undergoing an unprecedented population movement and migration. From 1979 to 2010, China's floating population increased from the original 6.00 million to 221 million. In the next 20 to 30 years, China's floating and migrant population will be maintained at 200 million to 300 million, whose complicated changes in distribution, composition and quality will file down stern challenge to the national strategic planning, social management and public service of government.

According to 2010 Report on China's Migrant Population Development prepared by the State Population and Family Planning Commission (SPFPC), the floating population of China will show four fundamental trends as stated below in the coming two or three decades:

(1) The floating population will continue to grow but at slower speed. According to the report, by 2050 China will have a floating population of around 350 million while its annual increase will drop from the current level of nearly 6 million to about 3 million on the condition that no dramatic change will be made to China's policies on migration of the population.

(2) This period of global financial crisis has become the right time for adjusting industrial

structure and for redistribution of the population. Due to the influence of the crisis, demands for laborers have declined, and long-distance migration of population and convergence of population in coastal areas abated. The population starts to flow towards provincial capitals. Yet the trend of convergence in areas around seas, rivers and main traffic lines will remain unchanged for a long time to come.

(3) In the future the distribution of floating population of China will feature the extended urban regions in the eastern coastal areas as core zones, inland cities as middle axle and central cities in the west as convergence points.

(4) The subsistence-driven floating population will transform into development-driven floating population. The education level of the floating population is slightly longer than the average level of the country. In the floating population, adults account for increasingly large portion. The gender of males and females tends to be in a rough balance. The migration of whole families will increase but most of them are inclined to settle down in the places they have moved in. Consequently, there will be great pressures associated with the livelihood of the floating population and the reform of the service administrative systems.

A majority of China's floating population are migrant workers. In 2010, the number of migrants was working out of their own villages or towns for 6 months above and local peasant laborers engaging in non-agricultural industry in their own villages or towns for 6 months above reached 242 million, among whom, 153 million worked out of their own villages or towns.

About 100 million migrant workers are peasant laborers of new generation (16 ~ 30 years old), who generally had relatively higher educational level; besides, a majority of them no longer served as workers and peasants concurrently, but solely engaged in the secondary or tertiary industry, mainly in manufacturing, and played an increasingly dominant role in the country's social and economic development. Many problems appeared while migrant workers of new generation got themselves integrated into cities. For example, some new generation migrants sustained heavy work pressure, had low satisfaction on income, were caught in the dilemma of identity recognition between "citizen" and "peasant". Diversified social securities are needed to realize their goals of long-term stable employment and living in cities where they work and solve their fears of trouble in the rear when sick, temporary living difficulties after unemployment, etc.

## Ⅱ. Rapidly Developing Urban-Rural Construction

According to the Communique of the Sixth National Population Census, China's population had grown to 1.3397 billion dated on 1st November 2010, and urban population had risen to 665.57 million, accounting for 49.68 percent of the country's total population. In the process of urban and rural construction enjoying rapid development, China has set up three more new cities. Approved by the Ministry of Civil Affairs, the People's Government of Yunnan Province decided to revoke Mengzi County and establish the City of Mengzi (county-level city); to revoke Wenshan County and establish the City of Wenshan (county-level city); the People's Government of Jiangxi Province decided to establish the City of Gongqingcheng (county-level city) directly under the jurisdiction of the province and actually under the control of the City of Jiujiang by entrusting. By the end of 2010, China had 657 cities officially designated.

### 1. Construction of cities

Based on statistics of Ministry of Housing and Urban-Rural Development, there were 654 cities officially designated across the country at the end of 2009 with a total population of 340 million urban residents, the temporary population was 36 million, and the urban built-up areas amounted to 38100 square kilometers. The total fixed assets investment in the urban municipal service facilities reached RMB1064.15 billion yuan, and accounting for 5.48% of total urban fixed assets investment in the same period.

In 2009, the water supply served a population of 360 million with coverage rate of 96.12%, and daily per capita consumption of domestic water being 176.58 liters; the urban gas serving a population of 344 million with coverage rate of 91.41%; the central heating area extended to reach 3.8 billion square meters; the total length of urban road was 269100 kilometers with per capita area of 12.79 square meters, the mechanical cleaning rate of the urban road was 31.8%; 10 cities had 33 rail transit lines completed with the length up to 839 km; 28 cities had 81 rail transit lines under construction with the length being 1991 km; there were a total of 1214 wastewater treatment plants in cities, and central treatment rate of 65.79%; the domestic garbage harmless treatment rate was 71.31% and total 179 million tons garbage was cleared and transported; the greenery coverage of urban built-up areas was 38.22%, the green space coverage rate was 34.17% with per capita public green space 10.66 square meters. There were 208 state-level scenic spots and historic sites in China, wherein the statistics according to 198 places showed that they covered an area of 81000 square kilometers with 34000 square kilometers open to visitation which added up to 460 million people times for the whole year. The state invested 3.4 billion yuan for maintenance and development of national parks.

Since 1992, the state construction authority had named 180 garden cities and 7 garden urban districts. In 2010, Yinchuan, Wuxi, Huangshan, Wujiang and Shouguang were conferred the China Habitat Award, and 34 projects including Tongzhou Grand Canal Park Construction awarded for Best Practices to Improve the Living Environment in China.

### 2. Construction of county seats

There were 1636 county seats across the country at the end of 2009. Based statistics on 1617 counties, 13 special regions and 144 Xinjiang Production and Construction Corps stations, there are total population of 123 million and temporary residents of 11. 2 million, and built-up area in accounted for 15600 square kilometers. The fixed assets investment in the county seats reached 168. 14 billion yuan. The county seats supplied water to 112 million residents and the water coverage rate was 83. 72% ; daily per capita water consumption was 118. 6 liters; the population supplies with gas was 82. 48 million with coverage rate registering 61. 7% ; the centrally heated area extended to reach 480 million square meters; the length of road in county seats was 95000 kilometer, the average road area per capita was 11. 95 square meters, the mechanical cleaning rate was 13. 7% ; there were total 664 wastewater treatment plants with central treatment rate of 35. 11% ; the greenery coverage rate in county seats built-up area was 23. 48% , and green space coverage rate reached 18. 37% , per capita public green space reached 6. 89 square meters.

Since 2006, the state construction authority had named 61 garden county seats and 15 garden towns.

### 3. Construction of villages and small towns

By the end of 2009, there were 19322 designated towns and 14848 townships in China. Based on the data collected from 16881 designated towns, 13886 townships, 667 township level special regions and 2. 714 million villages (567500 villages accommodate villagers' committees), the total household registered population was 944 million. Among them, there was 138 million people lived in the built area of towns, 32. 8 million in the built area of townships, 2. 9 million in the township level special regions and 770 million villagers. The total built-up area of the designated towns was 31300 square kilometers, the population density was 5214 persons per square kilometer; the township built-up area was 7600 square kilometers, and the population density was 4661 persons per square kilometer; the special township level built-up regions was 854 square kilometers, the population density was 3796 persons per square kilometers. By the end of the year, there 14387 designated towns, 8048 townships, 412 township level special regions, and 260457 administrative villages have made master plans. The master plan making investment in the towns and townships throughout the year reached 3. 066 billion yuan.

The total investment of towns and townships was RMB961. 5 billion yuan in 2009, and the new building completion in towns and villages was 973 million square meters of floor space. At the end of the year, the total floor space of the building stock in towns and villages covered 34. 78 billion square meters, the average residential floor space per capita was 30. 88 square meters. According to the statistics, the designated town water popularity rate was 78. 3% , the average daily water consumption per capita was 98. 9 liters, the gas popularity rate was 43. 4% , the average road area per capita was 11. 2 square meters, the drainage & channel density was 4. 99 kilometers per square kilometer, the average per capita public green space was 1. 92 square meters. Water popularity into rural areas was 63.5%, the average daily water consumption was 79.5 liters, gas popularity rate was 18.3%, the average road area per capita was 10.9 square meters, drainage & channel density was 3.01 kilometers per square kilometer, the average per capita public green space was 0.84 square meters. The water popularity of township level special region was 82.4%, the average daily water consumption per capita was 80.8 liters, the gas popularity rate was 36.8%, the average road area per capita was 14.0 square meters, the drainage & channel density was 3.80 kilometers per square kilometer, the average per capita public green space was 2.99 square meters. Among the administrative villages, 49.9% had central water supply system, 4.9% had domestic wastewater treatment, 35.0% had garbage collection stations and 17.7% had domestic waste treatment.

**4. Conquering the serious natural disasters such as Yushu Earthquake and Zhouqu Mudslide**

In 2010, there were many serious natural disasters in China, such as earthquakes, floods, droughts, typhoons, landslides, causing heavy casualties and property losses. Under the leadership of the CPC Central Committee and the State Council as well as the Central Military Commission, people of all nationalities worked hard together, and struggled to win a significant victory for disaster relief, writing a new chapter in the Chinese history of the prevention and reduction of disasters.

On April 14, Yushu County in Qinghai Province had an earthquake of magnitude 7.1, involved in Yushu, Chengduo, Zhiduo, Zaiduo, Nangqian, QuMalai County in Yushu Tibetan Autonomous Prefecture, and seven counties including Shiqu County in Ganzi Tibetan Autonomous Prefecture in Sichuan, a total of 27 townships. The affected area was 35862 square kilometers, and the population was 246842. Statistics as of May 30 showed that 2698 people died in the earthquake, 270 missing. A large number of housing collapsed, and schools, hospitals and other public facilities were severely damaged. Some roads, bridge collapsed, and power supply, water supply and telecommunication facilities were damaged. The agricultural, livestock production facilities were severely damaged, causing a lot of livestock death. Trade, tourism, finance and processing enterprises suffered serious losses. The ecological environment was threatened seriously because of the landslides and collapsing.

To promote the post-disaster recovery and reconstruction work in a scientific, lawful, coordinated, effective, orderly and effective way, the State Council has issued the guidance to the Yushu Earthquake recovery and reconstruction work as well as the support recovery and reconstruction policies and measures. With the completion of the Yushu Earthquake Recovery and Reconstruction Master Plan, the governmental departments at all levels strive to complete the basic restoration and reconstruction of the main tasks in three years, fully restore the production and living conditions and economic and social development of the affected areas and even exceed the level before, practically perform ecological environment protection and improvement, and rapidly recreate new schools and homes with high quality, thus laying a solid foundation for new Yushu with ecological beauty, distinctive characteristics, economic development, security and harmony.

In the early hours of August 8, Zhouqu County in Gannan Tibetan Autonomous Prefecture of Gansu Province, suffered the most serious torrent & mudslide since the founding of New China. Zhouqu County, an area about 5 kilometers long from north to south and 500 meters wide was razed to the ground, three villages and the houses along the river were washed away. The mudslide blocked Bailong River, formed barrier lake. The back-flowed water flooded part of the county seat. Water supply, electricity, transportation and communications were interrupted. The disasters mainly involved in 15 villages, 2 communities of Chengguan town and Jiangpan township, the affected area was about 2.4 square kilometers, and the affected population was 26470, causing heavy casualties. The statistics as of October 11 showed that 1501 people died and 264 were missing.

The masses and cadres in disaster together with the relief workers from all parts of the country, fearless of danger, worked whole-heartedly and scientifically to cope with the disaster, make the greatest effort rescue the trapped, treat the wounded in time, properly arrange the affected people, carry out a comprehensive health and disease prevention, quickly repair the damaged infrastructure, rule out the danger of the lake, dredge the Bailong River, and ensure the stability of the people in the disaster area, and make sure the national unity and social stability. By the end of 2010, the reinforcement and repair of the houses in the urban and rural areas had been completed. In accordance with the construction objective of new Zhouqu: "Let the people of disaster areas satisfied, make the people throughout the country relieved", and according to the Post-disaster Rehabilitation and Reconstruction Master Plan of Zhouqu, we strive to fully complete the urban and rural housing, public services and infrastructure and other reconstruction tasks by the end of 2012, restore the basic production and living conditions of the affected areas and economic and social development and even exceed the level before.

## Ⅲ. Focused Points and Issues in Urban Development

In China's rapid urbanization course, however, the development is not yet well balanced, coordinated or sustainable. This manifests itself mainly in the following: growing resource and environmental constraints hindering economic growth, imbalance between investment and consumption, large income gap, insufficient scientific and technological innovation capabilities, an irrational industrial structure, continued weakness in the agricultural foundation, uneven development between urban and rural areas and between regions, the coexistence of overall pressure to expand employment and structural shortage of qualified personnel in some industries, defects in systems and mechanisms that hinder scientific development. Moreover, the governments have not yet fundamentally solved a number of issues that the masses feel strongly about, namely the lack of high-quality educational and medical resources, and their uneven distribution; increasing upward pressure on prices, and exorbitant housing price increases in some cities; increasing social problems resulting from illegal land expropriations and housing demolitions; significant problems concerning food safety; and rampant corruption in some areas. How to change the development mode, boost the service-oriented government construction vigorously, make every effort to create equal development environment for various market players, offer desirable public service to the people and safeguard the social equality and justice is the critical long-term topic facing governments at various levels.

### 1. Heavy urban environment protection task

In the Eleventh Five-Year Plan period, China has made significant progress in environmental protection and improved the environmental quality effectively. According to the environment monitoring results, the quality of surface water has turned better; the air quality of key environmental protection cities has been improved year after year; the environmental quality has remained stable as a whole; the environmental quality of key river basins, key regions and key cities has gained remarkable improvement, but the pollution indicators of specific areas and regions are still above the national standards. The pollution is still serious and the environmental protection pressure is still heavy, which is mainly reflected in the following aspects:

(1) The emission of traditional pollutants was still huge in China, and beyond the environmental capacity, which made the environmental quality of some areas fail to come up to the national standards. When China has for the first time become the world's No. 1 in auto output and sale, for example, it confronts the increasingly serious pollution brought by motor vehicles. About one-fifth of cities in the country suffer heavy air pollution. Vehicle exhaust emitted has become the major source of air pollution of large and medium-sized cities. In 2010, among the 113 key environmental protection cities, 30 of them had annual average concentration of major pollutants in urban ambient air excess the national secondary grade as compared with the limits specified in the *Ambient Air Quality Standard*, among which, including 15 provincial capitals and provincial capital-above cities, such as Beijing, Taiyuan, Shenyang, Harbin, Nanjing, Hefei, Ji'nan, Zhengzhou, Wuhan, Chongqing, Chengdu, Xi'an, Lanzhou, Xi'ning and Urumqi. For example, the average daily concentration of inhalable particles (PM10) of Beijing has been above the secondary grade for years. The average annual concentration of nitrogen dioxide has also gone up year after year; the air quality of Lanzhou was inferior grade III.

In 2010, the water environmental quality of key river basins in China was moderate pollution as a whole. The proportion of Grade I ~ III water, Grade IV and V, and Grade inferior V was

51.9%, 27.3% and 20.8% respectively. The Taihu Lake, Chaohu Lake, Dianchi Lake and Three Gorges reservoir area still suffered serious eutrophication. "Algae bloom" had occurred occasionally. Among the five urban lakes monitored, water quality of Donghu Lake (Wuhan) and Kunminghu Lake (Beijing) belonged to Grade IV; water quality of Xuanwuhu Lake (Nanjing) belonged to Grade V; water quality of Xihu Lake (Hangzhou) and Daminghu Lake (Ji'nan) belonged to inferior Grade V.

(2) With the rapid development of China's economy, some new environmental issues also occur continuously, especially heavy metals, persistent organic pollutants, soil pollution, hazardous waste and chemical pollution, electronic waste, etc. The occurrence of these pollutants has brought some new problems, especially their hazards to human health.

(3) With the rapid development of China's industrialization and urbanization, production safety accidents and illegal pollutant discharge due to ignorance of safety production and environmental protection by enterprises pursuing maximum benefit have occurred frequently. The pollutant discharge effect accumulated for a long period of time has overwhelmed the environment. Secondary environmental problems triggered by natural disasters have taken place occasionally. The public has posed higher environmental safety demands and requirements. Environmental emergency management has confronted stern situation.

(4) Global environment problems like climate changes and biodiversity have become the focus of the interest game among countries in the world. Since China leaps into the front ranks of the world in the emission of carbon dioxide and sulfur dioxide, China will sustain more pressure from the world for its environmental issues.

**2. Urban transport confronts stern test and fundamental change**

Year 2010 saw the stern test and fundamental change confronted China's urban transport, and profound review of previous urban transport strategies. With the rapid development of urbanization and social economy, such problems as rapid motor vehicle development and urban transport have become the hot issues concerned by local governments and citizens.

(1) Increasingly serious traffic congestion in large cities

In 2010, traffic congestion was a common problem confronted major cities in China, besides top level cities like Beijing, Shanghai, Guangzhou, Chongqing, etc., secondary large cities like Ji'nan, Nanjing, Wuhan, Chengdu, etc., even some third level cities encountered serious traffic congestion successively. According to statistics, the saturation of trunk roads in Beijing at peak hours was nearly 1.0, and Shanghai, Nanjing, Chengdu, Guangzhou reached 0.95, 0.82, 0.8 and 0.72 respectively. Serious traffic congestion occurred occasionally in trunk roads of some Chinese highways. For example, the section to Beijing in Beijing-Tibet highway suffered a half-month jam in June 2010. Both drivers and passengers suffered untold misery.

(2) Increasingly prominent "parking difficulty"

Given the serious insufficiency, unreasonable allocation and low utilization efficiency of parking facilities and undesirable parking management, "parking difficulty" has become another difficulty puzzling urban transport. On-road parking and irregular parking has become a common phenomenon. The conflict between parking supply and demand has gotten prominent in cities; and parking quantity and the number of motor vehicles held has formed huge contrast and gap. The impact of "parking difficulty" is not limited to the parking itself, but also triggers a series of urban management problems, such as the enhanced traffic congestion, disagreement that leads to discord, hidden safety trouble, traffic accidents caused, etc.

(3) Car development has entered the rapidly growing stage

Over the past decade, China's autos manufactured and sold have increased from more than 2 million in 2000 to more than 18 million in 2010. Till the end of 2010, the number of civil automobiles owned across the nation amounted to 90. 86 million, up by 19. 3% as compared with the end of prior year; the number of private automobiles owned was up to 65. 39 million, up by 25. 3%. The number of civil cars owned reached 40. 29 million, up by 28. 4%, including 34. 43 million private cars, representing an increase of 32. 2%. Beijing had over 4. 80 million motor vehicles and more than 3. 70 million private cars. 916000 new motor vehicles were sold throughout the year. Currently, more than 20 cities have over one million motor vehicles owned. With the year-after-year increase in car proportion, tremendous urban land resources and roads were occupied by cars.

(4) Transportation demand management begins to arouse the attention

The adoption of demand adjustment-oriented transportation demand management has gradually become a significant measure to moderate the traffic congestion in large cities. Beijing implemented the even and odd-number licensed plate management, increased the temporary on-road parking charge in key areas from the original RMB2. 5 yuan per half hour to RMB5 yuan per half hour, also promulgated 10 odd transportation management measures like staggered rush hour plan since Beijing Olympic Games. In December 2010, Beijing Municipal Government promulgated a series of severe policies like the *Opinions on Further Boosting the Scientific Development of Capital Transport and Making Every Effort to Moderate the Traffic Congestion* and measures to solve the traffic congestion, including perfecting the transportation planning, alleviating the function and population of down town, accelerating the construction of road transport infrastructures, giving priority to the development of public transport, improving the bicycle and pedestrian system and park-and-ride condition, further strengthening motor vehicle management, implementing quantity control and quota management to minibus, etc.

### 3. Improve social security housing system

Social security housing system is an integral part of the national social security system, also the main part of the urban housing supply system, whose nature is that the government makes use of the national and social force to solve the housing supply issues of middle and low-income households in cities and towns. Offering social security housing from the objective of urban sound development is the bounden duty of governments at various levels, whose social benefit is higher than the economic benefit. During the Eleventh Five-Year Plan period, China has made every effort to carry out the social security housing construction and slum redevelopment, and enabled 11 million poor families to live in new houses. Though China's urban-rural per capita housing floor space exceeded 30 square meters in 2010, there was still large gap with people's continuously increasing need for improvement of living conditions. The housing difficulty of some middle and low-income households responded strongly by the people has drawn the close attention of the public opinion.

Year 2010 saw the enhancement of "walking on two legs" mechanism in China's housing supply, namely, market and social security approach. Aiming at the establishment of a hierarchical housing security system, the construction of social security housing dominated by low-rent house, affordable house and public rental house assumed the accelerating trend. Construction of 5.90 million units of social security houses and houses for slum redevelopment was launched, among which, 3.70 million had been completed basically. Aiming at the prominent problem that some lower middle income households with housing difficulty cannot rent or purchase house through the market, seven authorities including the Ministry of Housing and Urban-Rural Development drafted the *Guiding Opinions on Accelerating the Development of Public Rental Housing* for the purpose of solving the housing difficulty of middle and low-income households in cities. Capable areas might incorporate newly employed workers and migrant workers with stable career and having lived in the city for certain years into the scope of supply.

Meanwhile, accelerating the construction of social security housing is also taken as a regulatory measure to reduce the housing demand pressure in market, alleviate the housing supply and demand conflict, and contain the continuous housing price hike. Up to the end of 2010, the CPC Central Economic Working Conference further proposed explicitly to accelerate the construction of social housing security system in 2011, strengthen government responsibility, enhance the construction of security comfortable housing project, accelerate slum and rural dangerous housing redevelopment, and spare no effort to develop public rental housing to gradually form the social security housing system and commodity housing system in harmony with national conditions.

#### 4. Strengthen the control over real estate markets

After continuous practice, the Chinese government has reflected the clear idea for real estate market control: increasing effective supply and containing unreasonable demand. In 2010, the

State Council promulgated the *Circular on Promoting the Steady and Sound Development of the Real Estate Markets* and *Circular on Firmly Containing the Overly Rapid Housing Price Hike in Some Cities* successively, strengthened the control continuously and added control measures, in particular, took economic measures and administrative measures concurrently to control the real estate markets vigorously and in an all-round way from such perspectives as demand restriction, supply increase, supervision enhancement, etc.

According to preliminary statistics, in 2010, the real estate development investment reached RMB4826. 7 billion yuan (up to 12. 13% of China's GDP), up by 33. 2% as compared with 2009. Among others, the investment in commodity housing, office building and building for business operation reached RMB3403. 8 billion, RMB180. 7 billion and RMB559. 9 billion yuan, up by 32. 9%, 31. 2% and 33. 9% respectively.

Aiming at the increasing social conflicts aroused by illegal land expropriation and removal, Legislative Affairs Office of the State Council solicited social opinions on the *Regulations on the Expropriation and Compensation of Houses on State-owned Land* twice for the purpose of accelerating the establishment and perfection of civilians' right and interest security mechanism, the risk assessment and error correction mechanism of administrative decisions, strengthening complaint letter and visit, civilian mediation and administrative mediation, expand the social condition and public opinion reflection channel, and solve problems responded strongly by the people, such as illegal arable land occupation, illegal removal, etc.

The *Proposal of the CPC Central Committee for Formulating the Twelfth Five-year Plan for National Economic and Social Development* required to strengthen market monitoring, regulate the real estate market order, contain speculation demand and promote the steady and sound development of the real estate industry. According to the Twelfth Five-year Plan, the Chinese government will control the real estate markets firmly, accelerate the perfection of the long-term mechanism for real estate market control, primarily solve the housing difficulties of middle and low-income households in cities and towns and stabilize the price in real estate markets feasibly to meet the reasonable housing demand of residents. In the next five years, 36 million security houses are to be established. Till the end of the Twelfth Five-year period, the national urban security housing coverage will go up to about 20% from the current 7%~8%; and the housing difficulty of low-income households in cities and towns will be solved further.

## Ⅳ. Better City, Better Life

### 1. Host Shanghai World Expo Successfully

The World Expo 2010 Shanghai is the first time for China to host a comprehensive World

Expo, which drew the attention of both China and the world. Focusing on the theme of Better City, Better Life, adhering to and promoting the World Expo philosophies of understanding, communication, togetherness and cooperation, the World Expo has created and performed a brilliant, magnificent large display of world civilization. Moreover, the successful, brilliant and unforgettable World Expo has won glory for both the country and the people.

World Expo Shanghai is an unprecedented human gathering in terms of scale. Since the grand opening on the evening of April 30, total 169 pavilions in the 5. 28 square kilometer Expo Park along side banks of Huangpujiang River in Shanghai, 246 countries and international organizations participated in the exposition. The urban best practice zone gathered 80 urban cases selected across the world, which exhibited the world's leading urban development concept and practices; during the 184 - day period, the Expo has met 73. 084 million person-time visits of domestic and overseas tourists, with maximum single day traffic of 1032800; over 1200 Chinese and foreign performance groups came to the Expo Park to perform, which gave more than 1100 programs in total; about 22900 cultural performances were presented, which attracted audiences of accumulated 34 million person-time. During the World Expo, 1 summit, 6 theme forums and 1 youth summit were held; besides, 53 public forums were convened before the Expo.

World Expo Shanghai is the largest and longest international activity hosted by China since the establishment of the New China, whose successful convention has realized the centurial World Expo dream of the Chinese, and exhibited the 5000 - year brilliant Chinese culture, the 60 - year great achievements of New China, especially more than 30 years of reform and opening-up, as well as the united spirit of Chinese people, regardless of the ethnic groups, for achieving the objective of building a moderately prosperous society comprehensively, collectively reflected the development trend of world economy, science and technology, culture, society and ecological civilization, discussed the common topics confronted in human development in depth, enhanced the mutual understanding and friendship between the Chinese people and people of other countries and regions, also boosted China's status and influence in the world, and enhanced the national pride, confidence and cohesion of the Chinese people. The successful practice of World Expo Shanghai has again proved that the Chinese people are confident and capable enough to make their own contribution to the progress of human civilization.

This World Expo has made millions of people recognize that cities can become healthier and safer, and cities and integrate nature and technology together better. Urban residents can have access to cleaner air and water, and better life. In other words, this World Expo has brought new hope to the world and made us full of confidence to cope with increasing challenges in the urbanization.

Shanghai Declaration of the World Expo was issued at the World Expo summit on October 31, which was the consensus reached on global urban innovation and sustainable development and an expression of the shared aspiration of people around the world for a Better City, Better Life in the urban time. The Declaration proposed to establish an ecological civilization oriented toward the future, pursue inclusive and balanced growth, insist on scientific and innovative development, build a smart and accessible information society, foster an open and sharing multicultural society, build friendly and livable communities, and pursue balanced urban-rural development.

**2. Brilliant World Habitat Day ceremony**

Day 4 October 2010 is the $25^{th}$ World Habitat Day. The World Habitat Day ceremony hosted by UN-Habitat, Ministry of Housing and Urban-Rural Development of the People's Republic of China and Shanghai Municipal People's Government was held in Shanghai and adopted the same theme as Shanghai World Expo: Better City, Better Life.

At the ceremony, the Kunshan Municipal People's Government, China won the 2010 UN-Habitat Scroll of Honor for an innovative approach to granting migrants the right to essential services in the city. Drawing some 800000 job seekers every year, Kunshan holds five employment fairs every week. In the last two years it has helped more than 200000 people get work, in a city where modern, new accommodation has increased per capita living space from 12 square meters in 1999 to 40 square meters today. The city also ensures that migrants have full access to pension, health and other social security schemes, as well as equal education opportunities, and the same rights to public services as local people.

The ceremony also consisted of the following parts: under the sponsorship of 2008 UN-Habitat Scroll of Honor winner Rizhao government, UN-Habitat launched the official Chinese-language website; UN-Habitat, the China Science Center of International Eurasian Academy of Sciences and China Association of Mayors released *The State of China's Cities* 2010/2011 (English) jointly; UN-Habitat Regional and Technical Cooperation Division also exhibited its first *The State of Asian Cities.* The CDM (Clean Development Mechanism) comprehensive governance of Longfeng Garbage Landfill in Meizhou, coal-bed gas comprehensive utilization project of Jincheng, ecological environment construction of Qunli New Community in Harbin, Shajiabang ecological environment construction in Changshu, Cao'ejiang River side bank environment comprehensive improvement in Shangyu and the Yellow River wetland resource development and protection in Zhongwei, total 6 projects recommended and applied by the Ministry of Housing and Urban-Rural Development won the title of Global Top 100 best practice in the 2010 Dubai International Best Practices to Improve the Living Environment Award.

"As our world grows predominantly urban, World Habitat Day provides an annual opportunity to reflect on how we can make our towns and cities better places for all," said UN Secretary-General Ban Ki-moon in a statement read on his behalf by Dr. Awni Behnam, Commissioner General of the United Nations Pavilion at the Shanghai 2010 Expo.

The Executive Director of UN-Habitat emphasized in her address that cities were the greatest legacy of humanity and the greatest achievement of our civilization. To build better cities and make all people live better life, the following five strategic steps were suggested to be taken:

(1) Improve the quality of life, especially for the estimated 1 billion people living in slums and other sub-standard housing around the world. Improved access to safe and healthy shelter, secure tenure, basic services and social amenities such as health and education are essential to a better life for every individual.

(2) Invest in human capital. This is a condition for socio-economic development and a more equitable distribution of the urban advantage. This will also enable cities and regions to implement policies more effectively and to ensure that they are properly adjusted to local needs.

(3) Foster sustained economic opportunities. Cities can stimulate sustained economic growth for the poor through labour-intensive projects. These include primarily public works and the construction industry. Cities in the developing world are starting to provide social security to give better access to economic opportunities for those traditionally excluded.

(4) Enhance political inclusion. Today, more and more municipal and national authorities share the same basic philosophy: bringing government within the reach of ordinary people through enhanced mutual engagement. This means engaging people and their neighbourhoods in dialogue and participation in decision-making as a fundamental aspect of local democracy.

(5) Promote cultural inclusion. Culture has historically been left out of the conventional international development agenda. More and more local development policies take into account the cultural dimensions of urban life, such as social capital, tradition, symbols, a sense of belonging and pride of place. This helps integrate ethnic minorities, preserve regional values, safeguard linguistic and religious diversity, resolve conflicts and protect the heritage.

**3. Promote the equal and inclusive growth of cities**

World Urban Forum 5 was held in Rio de Janeiro, Brazil from 22 to 26 March 2010. 13718 representatives from 150 counties in the world actually attended this grand gathering. This is for the first time that UN-Habitat held the World Urban Forum in Latin America under the theme of The Right to the City: Bridging the Urban Divide.

World Urban Forum 5 consists of 6 dialogues: Taking Forward the Right to the City; Bridging the Urban Divide: Inclusive Cities; Equal Access to Shelter and Basic Urban Services; Cultural Diversity in Cities; Governance and Participation; Sustainable Urbanization: Cities in a Changing Climate.

Currently, urban population accounts for just over half of the world population, but the rapidly developing urban economic life has consumed two-thirds of the world's total resource consumption, and produced remarkable proportion of the wastes and greenhouse gas. Besides, in the course of urbanization, not all urban population and social groups enjoy the same opportunity or have access to the same urban service and supply. Obvious urban development differentiation is common in countries and regions across the world. It is the common objective of a city to share the benefits brought by urbanization continuously, which is subject to the joint effort of government, private departments, civil society and the public, and common action of all parties to reflect urban rights and make up urban difference.

UN Secretary-General Ban Ki-moon said that: "currently, over half of all people live in cities. Cites bear responsibilities to the climate change beyond its proportion. Urbanization is one of the 'vital agendas' in modern society. He urged participants to discuss how to solve current pressing urban problems and enable all people to have access to safe water, health, housing and basic services, safe life and better job opportunity."

Executive Director of UN-Habitat Mrs. Anna Tibaijuka said that though over the past decade, the goal of "by 2020, to have achieved a significant improvement in the lives of at least 100 million slum-dwellers" set in UN Millennium Development Goals had been realized, but from 2000 to 2010, the number of slum residents increased by 55 million, and reached 827 million now, which deserved the attentions of all parties. She said that it was difficult for any party to make it by itself. A government could not make it. Cities, large firms or the civil society could not make it independently either. We needed clear coordinated partnership and efforts! We needed their support, and we needed it now, only thus, could the new leader (UN-Habitat) take measures with full preparation, assist member countries and all partners of the UN-Habitat Agenda to realize the dream of offer affordable housing and sustainable cities to all people.

Brazilian President Luiz Inacio Lula da Silva pointed out in his opening speech that urban space, as a collective site, belongs to all urban residents and has abundant culture, whose social function lies in guaranteeing the general distribution of wealth, service and opportunity. He said that it was possible to access urban design capable of changing the urban operation mode as Brazil's prudent urban investment has created many employment opportunities and improved the general living standards of Brazilians. He believed that taking Rio, the world's well-known "Marvelous City" as the host of the Forum would be helpful to the drafting of advanced solutions of global urban spatial arrangement.

Prior to the closing of the forum, the World Urban Campaign led by UN-Habitat was launched officially. The Campaign seeks to enhance the consciousness of sustainable urbanization in the drafting of global, national and local policies and make it dominant. Since the 2010 Rio Forum, the World Urban Campaign has offered a mechanism to its partners and institutions for accumulation of knowledge, professional skills and experience of the World Urban Campaign, so that improve the global, national and local urban policies. The UN-Habitat intends to upgrade sustainable urbanization to the first place of global government agendas by uniting the public, private departments and communities though the World Urban Campaign.

**4. Design of sustainable development**

Facing the global climate changes, the International Union of Architects (UIA) issued the "Copenhagen Declaration" and "Cancun Communication" successively in December 2009 and November 2010, proposing to carry out the design on sustainable development and respond to the global sustainable development strategy.

UIA proposes that architecture must utilize holistic, integrative methods from the smallest scale up through that of city and regional planning, never forgetting that buildings, landscapes, the natural environment and infrastructures are all essential elements in the continuous creation of a sustainable future. A careful and considerate design of forms, geometry and spatial strategies, married with the appropriate materials, equipment and functional distribution can reduce the use of resources, greenhouse gas emission and overall environmental impact by 50% to 80%. The building and construction industries, and the processes that create, modify and remove built structures, and, the whole-of-life operation of those facilities represent half of our opportunity to resolve today's climate challenge.

Sustainable by Design begins with the earliest stages of a project and requires commitments between all stakeholders: clients, designers, engineers, authorities, contractors, owners, users and the community.

Sustainable by Design incorporates all aspects of construction and future use based on full Life Cycle Analysis and Management.

Sustainable by Design optimizes efficiency through design. Renewable energies, high performance and environmentally benign technologies are integrated to the greatest practical extent in the project conception.

Sustainable by Design recognizes that all architecture and planning projects are part of a complex interactive system, linked to their wider natural surroundings, and reflect the heritage, culture and social values of the daily life of the community.

Sustainable by Design seeks healthy materials for healthy buildings, ecologically and socially respectful land-use, and an aesthetic sensitivity that inspires, affirms and ennobles.

Sustainable by Design aims to significantly reduce carbon imprints, hazardous materials and technologies and all other adverse human effects of the built environment on the natural environment.

Sustainable by Design endeavors to improve the quality of life, promote equity both locally and globally, advance economic well-being and provide opportunities for community engagement and empowerment.

Sustainable by Design recognizes the local and planetary interdependence of all people. It acknowledges that urban populations depend on an integrated, interdependent, and sustainable rural-urban system for their life support systems (clean water and air, food, shelter, work, education, health, cultural opportunity, and the like).

Sustainable by Design endorses UNESCO's statement that the cultural diversity, as a source of exchange, innovation and creativity, is as necessary for humankind as biodiversity is for nature.

The UIA is working directly with all of its 124 member countries to develop specific, national plans for implementing the Sustainable By Design Strategy. The UIA World Congress in Tokyo in September 2011 will launch the Sustainable By Design Mission, urge architects to adopt due attitude and dedicate to sustainable development of the world through design.

## V. Conclusion

Year 2010 saw continuous great events, happy events and difficulties: Shanghai World Expo, Guangzhou Asian Games, Yushu earthquake, Quanzhou debris flow and serious drought and flood disaster in some areas. All of the Chinese people, in the face of challenges, have consolidated and expanded the achievements made in tackling the global financial crisis effectively, accelerated the conversion of economic development model, improved the people's living standard and quality continuously, also further enhanced the economic strength and comprehensive national strength. The historical experience has proved that only by boosting reform and development firmly, safeguarding the social equality and justice persistently and bringing the enthusiasm and creativity of all people into full play, can the country gain vitality, the nation advance, career develop, people live and work in peace and contentment, the life become happy and dignity, and cities get better.

(Author: Mao Qizhi, Professor of Tsinghua University, Academician, International Eurasian Academy of Sciences)

# 2010中国城市发展十大事件

2010年，我国成功举办了若干大型活动，对城市经济社会的健康发展产生了重大影响。上海成功举办了第41届世界博览会，创造和演绎了一场精彩纷呈、美轮美奂的世界文明大展示；广州成功举办了第16届亚运会，铸造了一届精彩、成功、和谐的体育盛会；深圳隆重纪念经济特区走过30年历程，庆祝取得的辉煌成就。

2010年，我国努力推进和谐社会建设，对促进区域协调、城乡统筹发展具有重要的战略意义。国务院部署全国对口支援新疆工作，推动新疆经济快速发展和社会和谐稳定；国家积极推进创新型城市试点工作，把自主创新作为城市发展的主导战略；中央要求加大城乡统筹力度，努力形成城乡经济社会发展一体化新格局。

2010年，我国发生的重大自然灾害和突发性事故，给人民生命财产和经济社会造成了巨大损失。青海玉树发生7.1级强烈地震，甘肃舟曲发生特大泥石流地质灾害，全国人民众志成城的救灾壮举感天动地；南方多地遭受暴雨袭击，造成部分城市严重内涝；城市突发事故频繁发生，公共安全面临诸多挑战。

## 一、上海世博会取得圆满成功

第41届世界博览会（以下简称“上海世博会”）于2010年5月1日至10月31日在上海市举办，这是在我国举办的首届世界博览会。本届世博会的主题是“城市，让生活更美好”，体现了人类对于未来城市环境中美好生活的共同向往，反映了国际社会对于城市化浪潮、未来城市战略和可持续发展的高度重视。上海世博会会场位于上海市中心黄浦江两岸，南浦大桥和卢浦大桥之间的滨江地区，面积5.28平方公里。

4月30日晚8点，上海世博会开幕式在上海世博文化中心拉开帷幕，国家主席胡锦涛出席并宣布上海世博会开幕。党和国家领导人习近平、李克强、李长春、周永康，国家展览局主席蓝峰，以及来自世界各地的领导人和贵宾出席了开幕式。中外艺术家联袂登台，奉献了一台精彩的大型文艺演出。整台演出分4个章节，气势恢弘、热情洋溢的表演，引起现场观众强烈共鸣。第一章节《相约上海》用明快的歌舞、款款的深情，营造出“海内存知己，天涯若比邻”的浓厚氛围；第二章节《江河情缘》通过多瑙河与长江跨越时空的深情对话，表现了新时代中国海纳百川的胸襟和朝气蓬勃的活力；第三章节《世界共襄》充满浓郁异国情调，传递出世界各地人民对上海世博会的真诚祝愿，赢得现场观众一次次热烈的掌声；最后一个章节《致世博》感人肺腑，表达了繁衍生息在地球上的人们心手相连、共同开创美好生活的深刻主题。

5 月 1 日上午，2010 年中国上海世界博览会开园仪式在上海世博中心举行。中共中央政治局常委、全国政协主席贾庆林出席开园仪式，并同国际展览局主席蓝峰一道为上海世博会开园。

自 5 月 1 日开幕以来，来自全球 246 个国家、国际组织的参展方，通过展示、论坛、表演等形式，一起探讨城市未来发展前景，共同谱写了一曲人类文明和谐共生的激情乐章，生动诠释了“理解、沟通、欢聚、合作”的世博理念，共同成就了一届“成功、精彩、难忘”的世博盛会。上海世博会参观人数达到 7308. 4 万人次，单日最大客流达到 103. 28 万人，创造了世博会历史上的新纪录。通过世博园区异彩纷呈的 184 个日日夜夜，中国圆满兑现“世界给中国一次机会，中国将还世界一片异彩”的申办承诺。

上海世博会是世界文化交流的盛会。184 天会期中，上海世博会园区 33 块场地总共举办了 22925 场精彩纷呈的活动，活动规模空前，创造了世博舞台盛况。246 个参展方中，来自 176 个国家、13 个国际组织、36 个城市和 4 个企业的 1200 余支团队上演了 1172 个精心准备的文艺活动，以及一大批具有民族、民间、民俗特色和浓郁地域文化特色的文艺节目，展示了世界文化的多样性和中华艺术的独特魅力。

世博论坛直接演绎世博会主题，集中体现世博会精神遗产，也是展望未来的重要平台。上海世博会期间共举办了 1 场高峰论坛、6 场主题论坛、1 场青年高峰论坛，此前还举办了 53 场公众论坛。10 月 31 日举行的世博会“城市创新与可持续发展”高峰论坛深入探讨了一系列与城市发展有关的问题，并发表了《上海宣言》，形成了对全球城市创新与可持续发展的共识。

10 月 31 日晚，上海世博会闭幕式在上海世博文化中心隆重举行。国务院总理温家宝出席闭幕式，并宣布上海世博会闭幕。国际展览局主席蓝峰，来自世界各地的领导人和贵宾出席闭幕式，共同庆祝上海世博会取得圆满成功。上海世博会以一届成功、精彩、难忘的世博会载入史册，为祖国和人民赢得了荣耀。

12 月 27 日，上海世博会总结表彰大会在北京人民大会堂隆重举行。中共中央总书记、国家主席、中央军委主席胡锦涛在会上发表重要讲话。胡锦涛强调，上海世博会的成功举办，实现了中华民族百年世博梦想，向世界展示了中华民族五千年灿烂文明，展示了新中国 60 年特别是改革开放 30 多年的辉煌成就，展示了我国各族人民为实现全面建设小康社会目标而团结奋斗的精神风貌，增强了全国各族人民的民族自豪感、自信心和凝聚力。

作为首届以“城市”为主题的世界博览会，上海世博会以“和谐城市”的理念来回应对“城市，让生活更美好”的诉求，积极塑造“和谐城市”的范例。这个理念包括“人与自然的和谐”、“历史与未来的和谐”以及“人与人的和谐”。在上海世博会 184 天的展期里，世界各参展国家和国际组织、城市、企业等，围绕“城市”主题，充分展示城市文明成果、交流城市发展经验，传播先进城市理念，从而为人类的居住、生活和工作探索崭新的模式，为生态和谐社会的缔造和人类可持续发展提供了生动的例证。

上海市借助举办世博会的契机，对城市基础设施进行了升级改造和生态环境改善。从2007—2010年，实施了一批以交通基础设施为重点的世博配套工程项目建设。共有8大类60个项目：包括世博园区内场馆（组织方承建部分）和主要基础设施、浦东世博配套道路、浦西世博配套道路和中心城重点区域城市道路改扩建项目、越江隧道、世博配套能源供应、对外交通及配套工程、轨道交通建设和水门及公交枢纽建设，打造了一个立体化、多元化的综合交通枢纽体系，提升了城市综合交通能力。完成了竹园第一污水处理厂的升级改造，对864项污染企业进行结构调整，清理了黄浦江畔最大的污染源，有效改善了上海的水和空气环境质量。通过道路、交通、绿化、环保等一系列城市公共基础设施的扩建和改造，把上海打造成为一个世界级的生态城市。

**表1 历届世博会一览表**

| 年份 | 举办国城市 | 名称 | 类型 | 展期（天数） | 参观人数（万人） | 主题 |
|---|---|---|---|---|---|---|
| 1851 | 英国伦敦 | 伦敦万国工业产品大博览会 | 综合 | 190 | 604 | 万国工业 |
| 1855 | 法国巴黎 | 巴黎世界工农业和艺术博览会 | 综合 | 180 | 516 | 农业 |
| 1862 | 英国伦敦 | 伦敦国际工业和艺术博览会 | 综合 | 180 | 609 | 农业 |
| 1867 | 法国巴黎 | 第2届巴黎世界博览会 | 综合 | 210 | 923 | 农业 |
| 1873 | 奥地利维也纳 | 维也纳万国博览会 | 综合 | 180 | 725 | 文化和教育 |
| 1876 | 美国费城 | 美国独立百年博览会 | 综合 | 180 | 800 | 庆祝美国百年独立 |
| 1878 | 法国巴黎 | 第3届巴黎世界博览会 | 综合 | 170 | 1616 | 农业 |
| 1880 | 澳大利亚墨尔本 | 万国工农业、制造与艺术博览会 | 综合 | 210 | 1200 | 万国工农业 |
| 1883 | 荷兰阿姆斯特丹 | 阿姆斯特丹国际博览会 | 专业 | 100 | 880 | 园艺 |
| 1889 | 法国巴黎 | 世界博览会 | 综合 | 182 | 2512 | 法国大革命百年，埃菲尔铁塔落成 |
| 1893 | 美国芝加哥 | 芝加哥哥伦布纪念博览会 | 综合 | 183 | 2700 | 哥伦布发现新大陆四百年 |
| 1900 | 法国巴黎 | 第5届巴黎世界博览会 | 综合 | 210 | 5000 | 世纪回顾 |
| 1904 | 美国圣路易斯 | 圣路易斯百周年纪念博览会 | 综合 | 185 | 1969 | 该市成立百年 |
| 1908 | 英国伦敦 | 伦敦世界博览会 | 综合 | 220 | 1200 | 同年举行奥运 |
| 1915 | 美国旧金山 | 旧金山巴拿马太平洋博览会 | 综合 | 288 | 1883 | 庆祝巴拿马运河通航 |
| 1925 | 法国巴黎 | 国际装饰艺术及现代工艺博览会 | 专业 | 195 | 1500 | 宣扬 |
| 1926 | 美国费城 | 美国建国150周年世界博览会 | 综合 | 183 | 3600 | 纪念美国建国150周年 |
| 1933 | 美国芝加哥 | 芝加哥万国博览会 | 综合 | 170 | 2257 | 进步的世纪 |
| 1935 | 比利时布鲁塞尔 | 布鲁塞尔世界博览会 | 综合 | 150 | 2000 | 通过竞争获取和平 |
| 1937 | 法国巴黎 | 巴黎艺术世界博览会 | 专业 | 93 | 870 | 现代世界艺术和技术 |
| 1939 | 美国纽约 | 纽约世界博览会 | 综合 | 340 | 4500 | 建设明天的世界 |
| 1958 | 比利时布鲁塞尔 | 布鲁塞尔世界博览会 | 综合 | 186 | 4150 | 科学 |
| 1962 | 美国西雅图 | 西雅图世界博览会 | 专业 | 184 | 964 | 太空时代的人类 |
| 1964 | 美国纽约 | 纽约世界博览会 | 综合 | 360 | 5167 | 通过理解走向和平 |

续表 1

| 年份 | 举办国城市 | 名称 | 类型 | 展期（天数） | 参观人数（万人） | 主题 |
|---|---|---|---|---|---|---|
| 1967 | 加拿大蒙特利尔 | 加拿大世界博览会 | 综合 | 185 | 5031 | 人类与世界 |
| 1968 | 美国圣安东尼奥 | 美国圣安东尼奥世界博览会 | 专业 | 约 180 | 640 | 美洲大陆的文化交流 |
| 1970 | 日本大阪 | 日本万国博览会 | 综合 | 183 | 6422 | 人类的进步与和谐 |
| 1971 | 匈牙利布达佩斯 | 世界狩猎博览会 | 专业 | 4 | 190 | 狩猎对人与艺术的影响 |
| 1974 | 美国斯波坎 | 世界博览会 1974 | 专业 | 184 | 480 | 庆祝明日的清新环境 |
| 1975 | 日本冲绳 | 冲绳世界海洋博览会 | 专业 | 183 | 349 | 海——充满希望的未来 |
| 1982 | 美国诺克斯维尔 | 诺克斯维尔世界能源博览会 | 专业 | 152 | 1113 | 能源推动世界 |
| 1984 | 美国新奥尔良 | 路易西安纳世界博览 | 专业 | 184 | 734 | 河流的世界 |
| 1985 | 日本筑波 | 筑波世界博览会 | 专业 | 184 | 2033 | 居住与环境 |
| 1986 | 加拿大温哥华 | 温哥华世界运输博览会 | 专业 | 165 | 2211 | 世界通联 |
| 1988 | 澳洲布里斯本 | 布里斯本世界博览会 | 专业 | 184 | 1857 | 科技时代的休闲生活 |
| 1992 | 意大利热那亚 | 热那亚世界博览会 | 专业 | 92 | 800 | 哥伦布 |
| 1992 | 西班牙塞维利亚 | 塞维利亚世界博览会 | 综合 | 176 | 4100 | 发现的时代 |
| 1993 | 韩国大田 | 大田世界博览会 | 专业 | 93 | 1400 | 挑战新的发展之路 |
| 1998 | 葡萄牙里斯本 | 里斯本博览会 | 专业 | 132 | 1000 | 海洋 |
| 1999 | 中国昆明 | 1999 年昆明园艺博览会 | 专业 | 184 | 1000 | 人与自然——迈向 21 世纪 |
| 2000 | 德国汉诺威 | 汉诺威世界博览会 | 综合 | 153 | 1800 | 人类 |
| 2005 | 日本爱知 | 爱知地球博览会 | 综合 | 185 | 2200 | 自然的睿智 |
| 2008 | 西班牙萨拉戈萨 | 萨拉戈萨世博会 | 专业 | 93 | 800 | 水和持续发展 |
| 2010 | 中国上海 | 上海世博会 | 综合 | 184 | 7309 | 城市，让生活更美好 |

资料来源：http://www.expo2010.cn

## 上海宣言

2010 年 10 月 31 日

我们，来自全球各地的参展方和所有参与者，在“城市，让生活更美好”主题的引导下，共同参与第一次在发展中国家举办的注册类世博会。在 184 天的会期里，各具创意的展览展示、精彩纷呈的文化活动、智慧迭出的论坛研讨让我们认识到，人类对美好生活的理解与追求引领城市发展。我们高度认同，必须重新审视城市化过程中人、城市与地球家园的关系。我们一致认为，通过创新来建设和谐城市，是城市可持续发展的解决之道。

今天，50% 以上的人已经居住在城市，我们的星球进入了城市时代。城市化和工业化在带给人类丰富现代文明成果的同时，也伴随着前所未有的挑战。人口膨胀、交通拥挤、环境污染、资源紧缺、城市贫困、文化冲突，正在成为全球性的问题。由于历史和现实的原因，这些现象在发展中国家尤为突出。中国2010年上海世博会在挑战中应运而生，在世博会历史上首次以城市为主题，通过城市最佳实践区和网上世博会等创举，总结实践经验，勾勒未来图景，对解决人类共同面临的难题，进行了开创性的探索。

今天，上海世博盛会即将闭幕，我们高度肯定，世博会作为文明展示与交流平台的重要价值。作为对本届世博会思想成果的总结，我们一致同意发表《上海宣言》，以表达城市时代全球公众对和谐美好城市生活的共同愿景。

我们一致认为，和谐城市，应该是建立在可持续发展基础之上的合理有序、自我更新、充满活力的城市生命体；和谐城市，应该是生态环境友好、经济集约高效、社会公平和睦的城市综合体。我们相信，这样的和谐城市是实现“城市，让生活更美好”的有效途径。

为此，我们共同倡议：

**创造面向未来的生态文明**

城市应尊重自然，优化生态环境，加强综合治理，促进发展方式转变；推广可再生能源利用，建设低碳的生态城市；大力倡导资源节约、环境友好的生产和生活方式，共同创造人与环境和谐相处的生态文明。

**追求包容协调的增长方式**

城市应统筹经济和社会的均衡发展，注重公平与效率的良性互动，创造权利共享、机会均等和公平竞争的制度环境，努力缩小收入差距，使每个居民都能分享城市经济发展成果，充分实现个体成长。

**坚持科技创新的发展道路**

城市应加强科学研究和技术创新，建立和完善科技创新和应用体系；加快科技成果转化，提高民众生活质量，创造新的产业和就业岗位；通过科学研究和技术创新，增强城市的防灾减灾能力；加强科技交流与合作，实行开放与互利共赢的原则，促进全球城市的共同发展。

**建设智能便捷的信息社会**

城市应进一步加大对信息基础设施的投入，通过信息化来加强诸多领域的服务，促进信息与知识的有效传播；构建以信息网络为基础的城市神经系统，自我完善和调整城市的运行效能；加强信息化教育，缩小数字鸿沟，让居民接触与获取更多的信息。

**培育开放共享的多元文化**

城市应积极保护物质和非物质文化遗产，鼓励多元文化繁荣发展；倡导海纳百川的开放精神，积极开展文化间交流与互动，在尊重文化传统和保护文化多样性的基础上进行文化创新，为城市和人类发展提供持久动力。

**构筑亲睦友善的宜居社区**

城市应构建和谐友好的社会环境，通过合理规划，营造文明、安全、宜居的城市社区，在就业、医疗、教育、住房、社会保障等方面提供平等和高质量的公共服务；鼓励公众参与城市规划与管理，关注城市移民的物质需求与精神需求，消除社会隔阂与冲突。

**促进均衡协调的城乡关系**

城市应兼顾与乡村的协调发展，推动区域结构的调整和优化；特别注重推动欠发达地区的发展，加强城市功能向农村的辐射，努力缩小城乡差距，关注弱势群体利益；积极引导城乡对话，实现城乡和谐互动。

我们呼吁，认真总结上海世博会展览展示、论坛和城市最佳实践区的思想成果，汇集各国城市发展的宝贵经验和人类探索城市发展的共同智慧，在全球范围内进行推广，与广大民众共同交流，为城市管理者提供城市建设和管理经验。

我们倡议，将10月31日上海世博会闭幕之日定为世界城市日，让上海世博会的理念与实践得以永续，激励人类为城市创新与和谐发展而不懈追求与奋斗！

## 二、广州举办亚运会和亚残运会

第16届亚洲运动会（以下简称“广州亚运会”）于2010年11月12日至27日在中国广州举行，为期16天。广州是中国第二个取得亚运会主办权的城市，北京曾于1990年举办了第11届亚运会。

广州亚运会共设42个竞赛项目，是亚运会历史上比赛项目最多的一届，包括28个奥运项目和14个非奥运项目，28个奥运项目为：游泳、射箭、田径、羽毛球、拳击、篮球、皮划艇、自行车、马术、击剑、足球、体操、手球、曲棍球、柔道、现代五项、赛艇、帆船、射击、乒乓球、跆拳道、网球、铁人三项、排球、举重、摔跤、棒球、垒球。14个非奥运项目为：保龄球、台球、板球、体育舞蹈、壁球、武术、棋类、藤球、橄榄球、轮滑、空手道、卡巴迪、高尔夫球、龙舟，体育舞蹈、龙舟、轮滑、围棋、象棋、板球等6个项目首度现身亚运赛场。

广州亚运会设三个协办城市，分别是：佛山、汕尾和东莞。三个协办城市四个项目共产生43块金牌。其中，东莞市承办举重项目比赛，产生15块金牌；佛山市承办拳击和花样游泳两个项目比赛，产生14块金牌；汕尾市承办帆船帆板项目比赛，产生14块金牌。

11月12日，广州亚运会在广州市隆重开幕，国务院总理温家宝出席开幕式并宣布本届亚运会开幕。开幕式分为珠江巡游、开幕仪式和文艺表演三大部分。珠江巡游以城市为背景、以珠江为舞台，通过“海上丝路”、“西关风情”、“广府华彩”、“羊城画卷”、“花城锦绣”、“共庆亚运”共6个极具岭南特色的文艺表演、情景展示和群众互动，描绘了一幅千年羊城的画卷，开启了一扇城市风情的窗口，营造了一江欢歌的氛围。文艺表演《启航》以“水”为主题，节目分为序曲、上篇《大地之水》和《海洋之舟》、中篇《白云之帆》、下篇《花城之邀》三个篇章，表达着广州对亚运会的祝福。

在16天的时间里，共有亚洲45个国家和地区的9704名运动员参加比赛，向476枚金牌发起冲击，规模创亚运历史的新纪录。参赛运动员挑战极限，超越自我，刷新了3项世界纪录、15项亚洲纪录和27项亚运会纪录。29个国家和地区获得亚运会金牌，36个国家和地区获得亚运会奖牌，奏响了更快、更高、更强的激情乐章，描绘了团结、友谊、和平的壮丽画卷。

中国体育代表团本届亚运会派出1454人组成的队伍，其中运动员977人，共夺得了199

枚金牌、119 枚银牌、98 枚铜牌，连续八届位居亚运会金牌榜第一，金牌数和奖牌总数都创下了单届亚运历史最高纪录。

11 月 27 日晚，广州亚运会闭幕式在广州海心沙广场隆重举行。国务委员刘延东出席闭幕式，亚奥理事会主席艾哈迈德·法赫德·萨巴赫亲王宣布第 16 届亚洲运动会闭幕。在闭幕式上，亚奥理事会主席艾哈迈德·法赫德·萨巴赫亲王充满激情地说："这是一届精彩绝伦的亚运会，它将永远成为亚运会历史上的宝贵财富，共同珍藏于你我心中。"闭幕式文艺表演凸显亚洲元素，歌颂了亚洲各国和地区运动员的交流和友谊，展示了亚洲多元文化的魅力与融合。大屏幕上各种视觉元素变幻无穷，亚洲各地不同文化以歌舞形式跨越时空和地域，汇聚在岭南。

来自亚洲各国各地区的运动员、教练员和来宾团结交流，顽强拼搏，激情飞扬，共同铸造了一届精彩、成功、和谐的亚运盛会。

第 10 届亚洲残疾人运动会（以下简称"广州亚残运会"）开幕式于 12 月 12 日在广东奥林匹克体育中心隆重举行。国务院副总理李克强出席开幕式并宣布广州亚洲残疾人运动会开幕。开幕式以"大爱、动人、自强不息"为主题，由倒计时与入场仪式，文艺表演的《心声》、《追梦》、《飞翔》三个篇章及点燃圣火等几个部分组成。精彩纷呈、充满人间大爱的运动员入场式和演出令人心潮澎湃，凸显人间真情，启迪人生，使人深切感受到人类一家、互相裨益、互相积聚宝贵的精神财富。

广州亚残运会共设 19 个竞赛大项，包括 17 个残奥会项目和 2 个非残奥会亚洲特色项目（羽毛球、保龄球）：坐式排球、自行车、游泳、硬地滚球、田径、射箭、射击、赛艇、盲人柔道、乒乓球、七人制足球、五人制足球、盲人门球、轮椅网球、轮椅篮球、轮椅击剑、举重、羽毛球、保龄球。参赛运动员约 3000 人，随队官员约 2000 人，另有约 2000 名左右记者和媒体人员、360 多名亚洲残奥委员会大家庭贵宾参加。

在广州亚残运会上，各国运动员健儿表现出了高超的竞技水平和顽强的精神风貌。在 41 个参赛代表团中，有 31 个代表团的运动员分享了 1020 枚奖牌。位列奖牌榜首位的是中国代表团，431 名运动健儿共夺得 391 枚奖牌，其中 185 枚金牌、118 枚银牌和 88 枚铜牌；日本和韩国则分列奖牌榜的二、三位，同样取得了不俗的战绩。

在难忘的 8 天里，亚洲残疾人运动员向亚洲和世界展现了残疾人体育的独特魅力和超越自我、永不言弃的精神，共同创造了亚洲残疾人体育事业的辉煌。

12 月 19 日，广州亚残运会闭幕式在广东奥体中心顺利举行。国务委员刘延东出席闭幕式，亚洲残奥委会主席拿督扎纳尔·阿布扎林宣布广州亚残运会闭幕。闭幕式上，圣火缓缓熄灭，但火种被装入火种灯，永远留在广州。

闭幕式继续开幕式"爱"的主题，以"你让世界从此不同"为主题，体现亚洲大团圆与惜别的情怀。文艺演出包括《天与海》、《叶与脉》、《光与梦》三个篇章，分别用大自然的开阔寓意残疾人心理的开阔，以大自然的胸怀表达残疾人胸怀的宽广，以及大自然给人带来田园式的幸福，共同表达出残疾人带着梦和希望，自强不息的精神。文艺表演利用情境行为、歌曲节目、舞蹈场景来点缀内涵、营造气氛，实现点与面的结合。

广州市借助举办亚运会和亚残运会的机会，全面实施“亚运城市行动计划”和“十年大变”工程，推进城市建设、交通升级和环境整治，促使广州的城市建设速度加快了 5 ~ 10 年。从 2005 年开始，广州投入 1000 多亿元城市重点基础建设资金，实施了 835 项大小工程，完成了整饰城市建筑、绿道网建设及城市道路绿化及设施升级改造，新建了 BRT 快速公交车道、轨道交通，开通了 5 条地铁线路，城市的空气质量与水质量得到明显改善。这些工程建设有效地改善了民生，提升了广州的城市品质和形象。

表 2　广州亚运会奖牌榜

| 排名 | 代表团 | 金牌 | 银牌 | 铜牌 | 合计 |
| --- | --- | --- | --- | --- | --- |
| 1 | 中国 | 199 | 119 | 98 | 416 |
| 2 | 韩国 | 76 | 65 | 91 | 232 |
| 3 | 日本 | 48 | 74 | 94 | 216 |
| 4 | 哈萨克斯坦 | 18 | 23 | 38 | 79 |
| 5 | 中华台北 | 13 | 16 | 38 | 67 |
| 6 | 印度 | 14 | 17 | 33 | 64 |
| 7 | 伊朗 | 20 | 14 | 25 | 59 |
| 8 | 乌兹别克斯坦 | 11 | 22 | 23 | 56 |
| 9 | 泰国 | 11 | 9 | 32 | 52 |
| 10 | 马来西亚 | 9 | 18 | 14 | 41 |
| 11 | 中国香港 | 8 | 15 | 17 | 40 |
| 12 | 朝鲜 | 6 | 10 | 20 | 36 |
| 13 | 越南 | 1 | 17 | 15 | 33 |
| 14 | 印度尼西亚 | 4 | 9 | 13 | 26 |
| 15 | 新加坡 | 4 | 7 | 6 | 17 |
| 16 | 菲律宾 | 3 | 4 | 9 | 16 |
| 17 | 卡塔尔 | 4 | 5 | 7 | 16 |
| 18 | 蒙古 | 2 | 5 | 9 | 16 |
| 19 | 沙特 | 5 | 3 | 5 | 13 |
| 20 | 科威特运动员 | 4 | 6 | 1 | 11 |
| 21 | 缅甸 | 2 | 5 | 3 | 10 |
| 22 | 巴林 | 5 | 0 | 4 | 9 |
| 23 | 巴基斯坦 | 3 | 2 | 3 | 8 |
| 24 | 中国澳门 | 1 | 1 | 4 | 6 |
| 25 | 约旦 | 2 | 2 | 2 | 6 |
| 26 | 阿联酋 | 0 | 4 | 1 | 5 |
| 27 | 吉尔吉斯斯坦 | 1 | 2 | 2 | 5 |
| 28 | 塔吉克斯坦 | 1 | 0 | 3 | 4 |

续表 2

| 排名 | 代表团 | 金牌 | 银牌 | 铜牌 | 合计 |
|---|---|---|---|---|---|
| 29 | 阿富汗 | 0 | 2 | 1 | 3 |
| 30 | 黎巴嫩 | 0 | 1 | 2 | 3 |
| 31 | 孟加拉国 | 1 | 1 | 1 | 3 |
| 32 | 伊拉克 | 0 | 1 | 2 | 3 |
| 33 | 老挝 | 0 | 0 | 2 | 2 |
| 34 | 叙利亚 | 1 | 0 | 1 | 2 |
| 35 | 阿曼 | 0 | 0 | 1 | 1 |
| 36 | 尼泊尔 | 0 | 0 | 1 | 1 |

资料来源：http://www.gz2010.cn

## 三、纪念深圳经济特区建立30周年

30年前，深圳与珠海、汕头、厦门一起被批准建立经济特区；30年后，深圳由原来的一个“小渔村”奇迹般地变成了一座现代化的国际大都市。2010年，深圳市举办了一系列重大活动，纪念深圳经济特区建立30周年，庆祝30年来取得的伟大成就。

8月10日，深圳经济特区建立30周年纪念园竣工。纪念园位于莲花山公园东南角，园内将《春天的故事》、《走进新时代》、《走向复兴》三首经典歌曲的歌词和五线乐谱，用喷砂的方式凸显在纪念园一面浮雕墙的背面，让这座特区纪念园既充满了厚重的历史感，又弥漫着一种浓郁的文化艺术气息。

8月17日，首届深圳合唱节在深圳音乐厅拉开帷幕，深圳儿女以洪亮的合唱，歌颂改革开放的伟大成就，表达对时代的感恩以及对城市的赞美，向特区建立30周年献礼。“庆祝深圳经济特区建立30周年——深圳30年30首合唱歌曲作品评选”同时揭晓，30首合唱歌曲成为深圳合唱的骄傲。

8月20日至21日，国务院总理温家宝深入深圳的企业、科研院所、口岸和社区，就发展战略性新型产业，加快转变经济发展方式进行调研，并于21日专程来到深圳博物馆参观“改革开放总设计师邓小平”大型展览。

8月21日，在深圳经济特区建立30周年之际，中央电视台“心连心”艺术团来深圳慰问演出。两个多小时的精彩演出，从大合唱、大歌舞《春天的故事》、《走进新时代》、《江山》开始，到以大合唱、大歌舞《走向复兴》圆满结束，既回放了深圳过去的创业历程，又展示了深圳今天的改革成就，畅想深圳未来的灿烂前景，共祝深圳明天更美好。

8月22日，为期两天的“经济特区与中国特色社会主义理论研讨会”在深圳开幕，150多位国内知名专家学者聚首中国改革开放的“试验田”和“示范区”，就深圳经济特区发展历程、特区与中国特色社会主义理论体系发展等一系列重大问题进行研讨，为深圳经济特区的科学发展提供有力的智力支持。同日，大型展览“改革开放总设计师邓小平”在深圳博物馆隆重开幕。展览共包括“走出广安”、“戎马生涯”、“艰辛探索”、“非常岁月”、“开创伟业”、“小平您好”、“小平与深圳”七个部分，采用多媒体展示系统以及数字电影放映技术，生动展现了邓小平同志波澜壮阔的人生历程和丰功伟绩。

8 月 26 日，“庆祝深圳经济特区建立 30 周年美术作品展”在关山月美术馆隆重开幕，从深圳市 30 年来具有代表性美术作品中精心遴选出的 94 件精品，用艺术形式精彩表现了特区 30 年发展的光辉历程和建设成就。在深圳博物馆新馆，《深圳改革开放史》展览重新修订布展后，8 月 26 日正式向公众开放，主要反映 1978 年以来深圳改革开放历程以及所取得的经验和成就。

9 月 2 日，“深圳经济特区 30 年 30 位杰出人物”评选结果揭晓。杰出人物评选分创业、创新、模范三个子类，其中袁庚、任正非等 10 人当选杰出创业人物，马化腾、侯为贵等 10 人当选杰出创新人物，吴立民、丛飞等 10 人当选杰出模范人物。本次评选活动吸引了深圳乃至全国各地民众网友的热情参与，总投票数高达 1130 万张。

9 月 3 日，“深圳经济特区 30 年 100 件大事”评选活动揭晓。“全国人大常委会批准在深圳设立经济特区”、“深圳出台最低工资标准”、“百万劳工下深圳”等 100 件影响深圳、触动全国的事件入选。评选产生的 100 件大事中，属经济建设领域的有 29 件，政治建设领域的有 25 件，文化建设领域的有 18 件，社会建设领域的有 28 件。时间分布上，20 世纪 80 年代发生的事件有 42 件，90 年代发生的事件有 24 件，21 世纪以来发生的事件有 34 件。

9 月 6 日，深圳经济特区建立 30 周年庆祝大会在深圳隆重举行，中共中央总书记、国家主席、中央军委主席胡锦涛出席大会并发表重要讲话。胡锦涛指出，兴办经济特区是党和国家为推进我国改革开放和社会主义现代化作出的一项重大决策，是中国共产党人和中国人民在探索中国特色社会主义道路上进行的一个伟大创举。党中央、国务院决定兴办深圳、珠海、汕头、厦门经济特区，随后又兴办海南经济特区，实行特殊政策和灵活措施，发挥它们对全国改革开放和社会主义现代化建设的重要窗口和示范带动作用。

晚上，深圳举行庆祝特区成立 30 周年焰火晚会。焰火晚会以“继往开来、再创辉煌”为主题，共分为“春雷激荡”、“开拓奋进”、“科学发展”、“再创辉煌”四个乐章。19 个品种、145107 发烟花与跃动激光、激昂的音乐一起，交织出一个梦幻美妙的世界。

10 月 11 日，“深圳文化周”在北京中国美术馆开幕，为首都及全国人民献上一道充满特区特色的“文化大餐”。活动期间举办了“庆祝深圳经济特区建立 30 周年美术作品展”、“大型交响音乐会”和“深圳平面设计回顾邀请展”三项重要活动。11 日上午“庆祝深圳经济特区建立 30 周年美术作品展”同时在中国美术馆开幕，50 余件精选出的国画、油画、版画、雕刻、水彩、装置等美术作品，用艺术的形式记录深圳经济特区建立 30 年来的光辉历程和辉煌成就，京城各界千余名观众观看了展览。

12 月 23 日，“深圳经济特区建立 30 周年系列庆祝活动图片展”开幕式在深圳音乐厅举行。与当晚的大型交响合唱诗歌音乐会一道，成为今年深圳市系列庆祝活动的收官之作。

30 年来，深圳等经济特区在党中央、国务院的领导下，不辱使命、敢为人先，在建设中国特色社会主义的伟大历史进程中谱写了勇立潮头、开拓进取的壮丽篇章，创造了世界工业化、城市化和现代化发展史上的奇迹，为全国的改革开放和现代化建设作出了历史性的贡献。

在新的历史征程上，深圳人将秉承“敢为天下先”的精神，转变经济发展方式，加快产业结构升级转型；加强能源资源节约和生态环境保护，建设低碳城市、生态城市，继续充当我国经济发展和城市建设的排头兵，发挥示范和推动作用。

### 深圳经济特区建立30周年历程回顾

1980年8月26日，第五届全国人大常委会第15次会议决定，批准国务院提出的在广东省深圳、珠海、汕头和福建省厦门建立经济特区。

1981年3月，深圳市升格为副省级市。

1982年，蛇口工业区创始人袁庚率先提出“时间就是金钱，效率就是生命”的口号。

1983年，新中国第一张股票“深宝安”发行，深圳第一家股份制企业诞生。

1984年1月25日，改革开放的总设计师邓小平第一次南巡视察深圳，并题词：“深圳的发展和经验证明，我们建立经济特区的政策是正确的。”

1985年，华侨城开始筹建，拉开了中国内地“主题公园”建设序幕。

1986年，深圳市制定了《深圳经济特区国营企业股份制试点的暂行规定》，探索国企股份制改造新路，一些企业进行了股份制改造，其中个别企业还发行了股票。

1987年，深圳市委召开思想政治工作会议，将特区精神归纳为“开拓、创新、献身”。

1988年11月，国务院批准深圳市在国家计划中实行单列，并赋予其相当于省一级的经济管理权限。

1989年，百万劳工下深圳，形成了特殊的移民潮，深圳成为最早聚集打工者的城市之一。

1990年，深圳证券交易所成立，成为中国内地两大证券交易所之一。

1991年，深圳南星玻璃制品有限公司成为首家获得ISO 9000质量体系认证的单位，这是中国内地企业获取的第一张ISO 9000证书。

1992年，邓小平再次视察深圳并发表南方谈话，为建设中国特色社会主义指明正确方向，带来了一个思想解放的春天。

1993年，深圳设立金融中心，对活跃、组织和监督货币市场起到了积极作用。

1994年，江泽民视察深圳，勉励特区“增创新优势，更上一层楼”。

1995年，深圳掀起“二次创业”，以适应特区优惠政策逐渐变成普惠制的新形势。

1996年，深圳地王大厦竣工，成为当时亚洲第一高楼、世界第四高楼。

1997年，深圳初步建立社会主义市场经济十大体系，基本完成了从计划经济到社会主义市场经济的过渡。

1998年，《深圳市政府审批制度改革实施方案》出台，开创中国内地审批制度改革先例。

1999年，首届中国国际高新科技成果交易会在深圳举行，其后发展成为“中国科技第一展”。

2000年，首座邓小平塑像在莲花山揭幕，表达了深圳人民对改革开放总设计师的崇高敬意。

2001 年,《深圳市土地交易市场管理规定》颁布实施，这是中国内地第一部土地交易的地方性法规。

2002 年，深圳市实行国有大型企业国际招标改革，在探索国有企业产权主体多元化方面实现了突破。

2003 年，胡锦涛视察深圳，要求深圳“加快发展，率先发展，协调发展”。

2004 年，深圳地铁正式通车，城市轨道交通体系建设拉开序幕。

2005 年，深圳被评为首批全国文明城市，标志着深圳城市文明建设提高到了新的水平。

2006 年,《深圳市实施“走出去”战略规划纲要》出台，深圳首次把“走出去”列入城市重点发展战略。

2007 年，深圳成功申办 2011 年第 26 届世界大学生夏季运动会，成为大运会历史上最年轻的主办城市。

2008 年，国家发改委《珠三角地区改革发展规划纲要》确定深圳“一区四市”的定位，即综合配套改革试验区、全国经济中心城市、国家创新型城市、国际化城市和中国特色社会主义示范市。

2009 年，深圳证券交易所创业板开市交易，中国多层次资本市场进一步完善。

2010 年，国务院批准深圳经济特区范围扩大到深圳全市，深圳经济特区面积从 327.5 平方公里扩大至 1952.8 平方公里。

（资料来源：http://www.sina.com.cn）

## 四、国务院部署对口支援新疆工作

2010 年 3 月 29 日至 30 日，全国对口支援新疆工作会议在北京召开。国务院副总理李克强出席会议并发表重要讲话。会议指出，进一步加强和推进对口支援新疆工作，是中央新时期新疆工作总体部署的重要组成部分，是贯彻两个大局思想、促进区域协调发展的战略举措，是发挥社会主义制度优越性、巩固和发展各民族大团结的重要体现，是增强自我发展能力、促进新疆跨越式发展的有效途径，是促进社会和谐稳定、实现新疆长治久安的必要保证。

会议强调，要按照中央的决策部署，建立起人才、技术、管理、资金等全方位对口支援新疆的有效机制，把保障和改善民生放在支援的优先位置，着力帮助各族群众解决就业、教育、住房等基本民生问题，着力支持新疆特色优势产业发展。今年要深入调查研究，编制专项规划，加强人员培训，抓紧做好对口援疆的前期准备。明年起全面实施对口援疆工作。

会议要求，有关省（市）全方位加大对口支援新疆工作力度，力争 5 年内使新疆特别是南疆地区经济发展明显加快，各族群众生活明显改善，城乡面貌明显改观，公共服务水平明显提高，基层组织建设明显加强；经过 10 年的不懈努力，最大限度地缩小新疆与内地差距，确保 2020 年实现全面建设小康社会目标。新疆工作在党和国家事业发展全局中具有特殊重要的战略地位，进一步推进新疆加快发展和长治久安，需要全国各方面的大力支持。开展对口支援新疆工作，是贯彻落实中央关于新疆工作决策部署、发挥中国特色社会主义制度优越性、巩固和发展各民族大团结的重大举措。

4月23日，中共中央政治局召开会议，研究推进新疆维吾尔自治区跨越式发展和长治久安工作，中共中央总书记胡锦涛主持会议。会议指出，新疆工作在党和国家事业发展全局中具有特殊重要的战略地位，要认真总结新疆工作宝贵经验，深入分析新疆发展和稳定面临的新情况新问题，把新疆经济社会发展搞上去，把新疆长治久安工作搞扎实，是具有全局和战略意义的重大而紧迫的任务。会议强调，要坚持走具有中国特色、符合新疆实际的发展路子，全面推进经济建设、政治建设、文化建设、社会建设以及生态文明建设和党的建设，促进新疆区域协调发展，人民富裕，生态良好，民族团结，社会稳定，边疆巩固，文明进步，确保实现全面建设小康社会奋斗目标。会议要求，要集中力量优先保障和改善民生，使新疆各族群众生活更加富裕幸福，要坚持党的民族政策和宗教政策，促进新疆不同民族、不同宗教信仰群众和谐相处，巩固和发展新疆社会和谐稳定的局面，要坚持中央关心支持，东中部地区支援和新疆各族干部群众自力更生、艰苦奋斗相结合的方针，认真做好对口支援新疆工作。

5月17—19日，中共中央、国务院在北京召开新疆工作座谈会，国家主席胡锦涛、国务院总理温家宝出席会议并发表重要讲话。这次会议是在我国全面建设小康社会进入关键时期、新疆发展和稳定面临重大机遇和挑战的新形势下召开的。会议全面总结了新中国成立以来特别是改革开放以来新疆发展和稳定工作取得的成绩和经验，深刻分析了新疆工作面临的形势和任务，进一步明确了当前和今后一个时期做好新疆工作的指导思想、主要任务、工作要求，对推进新疆跨越式发展和长治久安作出了战略部署。

胡锦涛指出，新形势下新疆工作的目标任务是，坚持走具有中国特色、符合新疆实际的发展路子，全面推进经济建设、政治建设、文化建设、社会建设以及生态文明建设和党的建设，到2015年，新疆人均地区生产总值达到全国平均水平，城乡居民收入和人均基本公共服务能力达到西部地区平均水平，基础设施条件明显改善，自我发展能力明显提高，民族团结明显加强，社会稳定明显巩固；到2020年，促进新疆区域协调发展，人民富裕，生态良好，民族团结，社会稳定，边疆巩固，文明进步，确保实现全面建设小康社会的奋斗目标。

温家宝对今后一个时期新疆经济社会发展工作作出了具体部署。要求加快推进以改善民生为重点的社会建设，着力扶持贫困地区发展；加强基础设施和生态环境建设；大力发展特色优势产业；从战略层面扩大新疆内外开放，努力打造我国向西开放的桥头堡；努力提高新疆生产建设兵团综合实力，发挥在稳疆兴疆中的特殊作用；举全国之力，把新疆这块伟大祖国的宝地建设得更加美好。

6月3日，全国对口支援新疆工作骨干培训班在中央党校举行。中央政法委书记周永康出席开班式并讲话。他强调，援疆工作队伍要认真学习贯彻中央新疆工作座谈会和全国对口支援新疆工作会议精神，充分发挥建设队、工作队、宣传队的作用，为推进新疆跨越式发展和长治久安贡献智慧和力量。

表 3　各地对口支援新疆情况一览表

| 省(市) | 对口支援地区 | 援疆计划和思路 |
|---|---|---|
| 北京市 | 和田地区的和田市、和田县、墨玉县、洛浦县及新疆生产建设兵团农十四师团场 | 建设五大示范项目:和田市棚户区改造一期工程、和田县抗震安居房暨新农村建设工程、墨玉县设施农业建设工程、洛浦县人民医院病房楼建设工程、兵团农十四师红枣加工基地建设工程 |
| 广东省 | 喀什地区疏附县、伽师县、兵团农三师图木舒克市 | 未来五年,广东省安排资金 96 亿元对口援建喀什地区"两市三县";在 2010 年年底前完成对口支援总体规划及公共服务、基础设施、产业发展、城乡建设等各专项规划的编制工作 |
| 广东省深圳市 | 喀什市、塔什库尔干县 | 着力帮助改善人民生活,把人、财、物重点投向民生领域,切实解决对口支援地区群众最直接、最现实、最紧迫的民生问题 |
| 江苏省 | 克州的阿图什市、阿合奇县、乌恰县,伊犁州 10 个县(市),以及兵团农四师、农七师 | 把保障和改善民生作为对口支援工作的重中之重 |
| 上海市 | 喀什区巴楚县、莎车县、泽普县、叶城县 | 把支援重点放在群众最为关注的民生问题与可持续发展问题上 |
| 山东省 | 喀什地区疏勒县、英吉沙县、麦盖提县、岳普湖县 | 着力支持民生保障项目建设;着力培育特色优势产业;以智力帮扶为重点,着力强化人才援疆工作;着力推进农村基层政权和基层组织建设 |
| 浙江省 | 阿克苏地区的 1 市 8 县和新疆生产建设兵团农一师的阿拉尔市 | 突出改善民生;突出干部、人才支援;突出项目支援;突出产业培育和资源开发利用 |
| 辽宁省 | 塔城地区 | 把受援地区各族群众最为关注的住房等民生问题作为对口支援的工作重点 |
| 河南省 | 哈密地区、兵团农十三师 | 做好六个方面的工作,加强工作的对接,实现优势互补,实现豫新两地共同发展 |
| 河北省 | 巴音郭楞蒙古自治州、兵团农二师 | 把保障和改善民生放在对口支援工作的优先位置,把资金、人才、技术、智力等更多投向民生项目,让广大群众切身感受到对口支援的成果 |
| 山西省 | 农六师五家渠市、昌吉回族自治州阜康市 | 以企业为骨干,与新疆各族人民友好相处,实现互利共赢 |
| 福建省 | 昌吉回族自治州的昌吉市、玛纳斯县、呼图壁县、奇台县、吉木萨尔县、木垒县六个县市 | 把重点更多地放在与群众切身利益相关的生产生活条件上,着力解决受援地区群众最直接、最现实的困难和问题,大力帮助各族群众解决就业、教育、住房等基本民生问题 |
| 湖南省 | 吐鲁番地区 | 科学编制对口支援各项规划;把促进科学发展作为对口支援的突出任务;把改善民生放在对口支援的优先位置;充分利用好湖南的优势;精心组织好重大项目建设 |
| 湖北省 | 博尔塔拉蒙古自治州博乐市、精河县、温泉县与兵团农五师 | 选择切合实际的援助项目,切实满足当地需要,着力解决博州和农五师经济社会发展的瓶颈和难点问题,切实加强受援方的造血机能 |
| 安徽省 | 和田地区皮山县 | 突出重点,坚持当前与长远相结合、输血与造血相结合、硬件与软件相结合、政府与市场相结合 |
| 天津市 | 和田地区的民丰、策勒和于田三个县 | 采取 10 项措施,做好新一轮对口支援工作 |
| 黑龙江省 | 阿勒泰地区福海县、富蕴县、青河县和新疆生产建设兵团十师 | 围绕农业产业化、矿产资源开发、地质勘探等领域,加强协调沟通,不断拓宽合作渠道,通过技术支援、资本输出、人才共享、合作开发,促进两地民族团结和经济共同发展 |
| 江西省 | 克孜勒苏柯尔克孜自治州阿克陶县 | 通过五年的对口援建,力争使阿克陶县经济总量、财政收入、县城规模实现三个翻番,经济发展综合水平达到江西省县(市)的平均水平 |
| 吉林省 | 阿勒泰地区阿勒泰市、哈巴河县、布尔津县和吉木乃县 | 把对口支援的重点放在着力改善生存性民生问题、保障性民生问题和解决安全性民生问题上,让群众得到实惠 |

资料来源: http://www.xjjs.gov.cn

## 五、大力推进国家创新型城市试点

中共十六届五中全会作出建设创新型国家的战略决策后，全国各地、各部门积极响应，努力探索中国特色的创新发展道路，促进经济社会发展向创新驱动转变。国家发展改革委在2008年启动深圳市创建国家创新型城市试点工作的基础上，2010年再次部署开展创建国家创新型城市试点工作。

2010年1月6日，国家发展改革委下发了《关于推进国家创新型城市试点工作的通知》(发改高技［2010］30号)，原则同意大连、青岛、厦门、沈阳、西安、广州、成都、南京、杭州、济南、合肥、郑州、长沙、苏州、无锡、烟台等城市申报的创建国家创新型城市总体方案，支持这16个城市开展创建国家创新型城市试点。

创建国家创新型城市目的是把自主创新作为城市发展的主导战略，作为经济社会发展的主要驱动力，作为产业结构优化升级的中心环节，显著提高发展质量和效益，从根本上转变发展方式。开展国家创新型城市试点，是深入落实科学发展观的客观要求，是增强国家自主创新能力的有效手段，是推进创新型国家建设的重要战略选择，对实施区域发展总体战略、促进城乡统筹发展具有极为重要的意义。

为深入推进国家创新型城市的建设，国家发展改革委会同有关部门，加大对试点城市自主创新基础能力的投入，促进科技、教育、人才等计划向试点城市倾斜，大力推进试点城市产业结构优化升级，鼓励试点城市“先行先试”，突破各种瓶颈制约，为全面探索中国特色创新型国家建设道路提供借鉴。

1月10日，科技部同意北京市海淀区等20个城市（区）为国家创新型试点城市（区），并在召开的全国科技工作会议上为试点城市（区）授牌。这20个试点城市（区）分别为：北京市海淀区、天津市滨海新区、河北省唐山市、内蒙古自治区包头市、黑龙江省哈尔滨市、上海市杨浦区、江苏省南京市、浙江省宁波市、浙江省嘉兴市、安徽省合肥市、福建省厦门市、山东省济南市、河南省洛阳市、湖北省武汉市、湖南省长沙市、广东省广州市、重庆市沙坪坝区、四川省成都市、陕西省西安市、甘肃省兰州市。

开展创新型城市（区）试点工作，是贯彻落实党中央国务院关于增强自主创新能力、建设创新型国家战略部署的重要举措，是加强国家创新体系和区域创新体系建设、推动城市创新发展的积极探索。科技部将把推动试点作为部省会商优先议题，集成项目、基地、人才、政策等资源加强引导和支持。通过深入开展试点工作，充分发挥示范带动作用，大力推进自主创新，促进科学发展，加快创新型城市（区）建设进程，努力为建设创新型国家做出更大的贡献。

4月，科技部批复石河子市、海口、郑州、西宁、南昌、昆明、太原、景德镇、昌吉、常州等18个城市为第二批国家创新型试点城市。根据科技部制定的《创新型城市建设监测评价指标（试行）》，创新型试点城市需要完成创新投入、企业创新、成果转化、高新技术产业、科技惠民、创新环境共6个一级指标和25个具体监测指标。创新型城市试点工作需坚持“突出自主创新，坚持改革开放，强调各具特色，体现总体布局，加强协同支持”等基本原则，还将结合自身特点与发展需求，围绕确立城市创新发展战略、加快经济发展方式转变、促进经济社会协调可持续发展、大力增强企业自主创新能力、加强创新人才培养和创新基地建设、加强创新服务体系建设、营造激励创新的良好环境、推进体制改革和管理创新等八个方面的任务展开，还要突出重点，力求突破，作出示范。

表4　科技部制定的创新型城市建设监测评价指标（试行）

| 一级指标 | 二级指标 |
|---|---|
| 创新投入 | 每万人劳动力从事 R&D 人员数量(人/万人) |
| | 万名就业人口中受过高等教育人数所占比重(%) |
| | 全社会 R&D 投入占 GDP 比重(%) |
| | 地方财政科技拨款占地方财政支出的比重(%) |
| 企业创新 | 企业 R&D 投入占企业销售收入的比重(%) |
| | 消化吸收费用占技术引进经费的比重(%) |
| | 规模以上企业中拥有研发机构的企业所占比重(%) |
| | 高新技术企业占企业总数的比例(%) |
| 成果转化 | 百万人口发明专利授权数(件/百万人) |
| | 百万人口技术市场成交合同额(万元/百万人) |
| | 百万人口拥有的有效商标注册量(个/百万人) |
| | 本市拥有自主创新产品和国家级新产品数量(个) |
| 高新产业 | 高技术产业增加值占工业增加值的比重(%) |
| | 生产性服务业产值占服务业产值的比重(%) |
| | 主要污染物排放量减少幅度(%) |
| | 万元 GDP 综合能耗(吨标煤) |
| | 全员劳动生产率(万元/人) |
| 科技惠民 | 百人口国际互联网用户数(户/百人) |
| | 城市空气质量指数(%) |
| | 城市污水处理率(%) |
| | 公众基本科学素养 |
| 创新环境 | 科技进步法落实情况 |
| | 激励自主创新政策落实情况 |
| | 对外开放和国际科技合作情况 |
| | 其他本地有特色、有创造性的创新政策措施情况 |

资料来源：http://www.gov.cn

## 六、中央要求加大城乡统筹力度

2010年发布的中央一号文件要求加大统筹城乡发展的力度，这标志着我国的城乡统筹事业将从局部的探索试点逐步转入全面推进阶段。

2010年1月1日，一项打破户籍壁垒，旨在推进沈阳经济区建设的超常举措开始实行：沈阳、鞍山、抚顺、本溪、营口、阜新、辽阳和铁岭等8个城市之间统一了户口管理标准，取消了农业和非农业户口划分，将每一个自然人统称为“居民”，以具有合法固定住所、稳定职业和生活来源为基本落户准入条件，放宽城市户口迁移限制，对消除因城乡身份不同而产生的户籍歧视及各种差别待遇、实现公民身份平等具有重要意义。

1月31日，新华社授权发布2010年中央一号文件《中共中央、国务院关于加大统筹城乡发展力度，进一步夯实农业农村发展基础的若干意见》，提出要建立健全农业社会化服务的基层体系，转变农业发展方式，协调推进工业化、城镇化和农业现代化，破除城乡二元结构，构建以工促农、以城带乡的长效机制，努力形成城乡经济社会发展一体化新格局。

2月，《求是》杂志刊载中央政法委书记周永康的文章，提出要加快推进户籍管理制度改革，着力解决流动人口就业、居住、就医、子女就学等问题，探索“以证管人、以房管人、以业管人”的流动人口服务管理新模式，提升流动人口服务管理水平。

4月28日，国务院总理温家宝主持召开国务院常务会议，审议并原则通过《关于2010年深化经济体制改革重点工作的意见》。会议强调推进城乡改革，深化土地管理和户籍制度改革。

6月，上海出台了公共租赁房政策，公共租赁房的供应对象除户籍人口外，还包括持有《上海市居住证》和连续缴纳社会保险金达到规定年限的外来人口。这是上海首次明确把非户籍人口纳入政府主导的住房保障工作的范围。

8月1日，《重庆市统筹城乡户籍制度改革农村居民转户实施办法（试行）》开始实施。作为中国统筹城乡综合配套改革试验区的重庆市以解决农民工城镇户口为突破口，开始全面启动户籍制度改革。重庆全市40个区县807个派出所开始全面受理符合条件的农村居民转户变市民的申请，这标志着重庆以适度放宽主城区、进一步放开区县城、全面放开乡镇落户条件，推动千万农民进城的户籍制度改革正式进入到实施阶段。该项改革迎来一个标志性时刻：在重庆市渝中区购房的农民工陈刚从重庆市公安局治安总队政委郭金严手中接过了重庆市主城区的户口簿——该户口簿被称为重庆户籍新政“第一本”。按照计划，重庆338.8万农村人口将在2011年年底前转为城镇居民。到2020年，重庆市户籍改革将实现1000万农村人群转户为城镇人口，全市户籍人口城镇化率达到60%以上。

8月2日，北京市向社会发布《首都中长期人才发展规划纲要（2010—2020年）》，首次明确提出，北京将逐步推行京津冀地区互认的高层次人才户籍自由流动制度。

9月，继浙江温州市试点5个镇级市后，山东省也宣布将启动镇级市试点，计划用3~5年时间将省内20多个中心镇培育成小城市。按照温州“镇级市”试点方案，这些试点镇将扩大土地使用权、财政支配权、行政审批权和事务管理权。而广东省则仿照温州市启动了“简政扩权”改革。

10月，广州市委、市政府审议通过了《广州市农民工及非本市十城区居民户口的城镇户籍人员积分制入户办法》，规定原则上农民工积满85分可提出入户申请，符合积分制条件的农民工从此可以入户广州，成为“新广州人”。

10月18日，《中共中央关于制定国民经济和社会发展第十二个五年规划的建议》指出，要统筹城乡发展，积极稳妥推进城镇化，加快推进社会主义新农村建设，促进区域良性互动、协调发展。在统筹城市和新农村建设方面，应遵循社会发展的规律，认真考虑农民的利益诉求，避免出现“挑着扁担上电梯”的现象。

11月，甘肃省制定了从生产一线工人、农民中考试录用公务员工作的总体方案，确定12月底前展开试点工作。在此前，包括山东、安徽在内的一些省份，已经陆续开展过各种形式的针对农民群体或农村干部群体招录公务员的工作，但明确以工人、农民两个群体为对象正式开展这一试点工作，甘肃省起步较早。

11月16日，四川成都市正式出台《关于全域成都城乡统一户籍实现居民自由迁徙的意见》，提出将在2012年实现城乡统一户籍，民众可自由迁徙，并享有平等的基本公共服务和社会福利。各方对此评价颇高，认为这是对中国实施了数十年户籍制度的一次根本性的突破。成都新政的魄力，除了落实公民的自由迁徙权、实施“统一的住房保障制度”、“城乡统一公共服务”，由此消除城乡二元结构之外，最大的亮点是农民进城落户将保留其在农村的宅基地使用权、土地承包经营权。从当年的“裸身出村”到如今的“穿衣进城”，成都市在制度上化解了缺乏城市生存能力的农民在“被市民”后面临的生存危机，将进城落户的主导权交到了农民手里，进而把城市化的政府主导型转变为市场主导型。

12月8日，河北省公安厅出台深化户籍制度改革的实施办法，进一步放宽了城市落户条件，凡在县城以上城市稳定居住6个月以上或购置住房的，均可登记为城镇户口。这一政策也被称为“落户条件全国最宽、配套政策全国最全”的户口迁移政策。

### 日本避免“城乡二元结构”的政策和措施

日本在20世纪前半叶因追求发展工业，一度出现工农收入和城乡差距拉大等现象。但此后，日本通过根本性制度安排，从源头上避免“城乡二元结构”的形成，实现了较为均衡的统筹发展。

在经济高速发展时期，日本政府的一系列根本性制度安排成为日本避免“城乡二元结构”出现的核心因素。

首先，城乡居民享受同等的政治经济待遇，在房籍、政治权利、社会保障和人员流动等政策上对城乡居民一视同仁，避免人为造成城乡差别。

战后经济高速发展时期，日本大量农民离开土地进城工作，有些大企业甚至采用“集团就职”方式，到农村中学整班招收毕业生进城务工。对此，日本政府一方面为新进城务工的农民提供与城市居民相同的社会保障和市民身份；另一方面严格要求企业保障劳动者就业，采用“终身雇佣制”等方式确保农民在进城后不会因失业而陷入困境。这在很大程度上避免了农民在“失地”后再“失业”所带来的严重后果，避免了城市出现“流民”阶层。

其次，消除阻碍人员、资金等经济要素在城乡间流动的壁垒，促进各种资源向农村和落后地区流动。

在大量农村人口进城的同时，也有很多日本城市居民希望到农村和小城镇居住或投资从事农业经营。为此，日本建立了较为完善的农业耕地和农村住宅流转体制，鼓励城市人口到农村居住或投资。从城市“下乡”从事农业经营的居民，往往会给农村带来一定的资本，这有利于农业生产集约化。此外，还有很多老年城市居民退休后到大城市远郊或地方小城镇购房生活，其中有些人还租用或购买小块土地耕作。这一方面减轻了东京、大阪等超大城市的人口压力，另一方面也给地方带来大量投资并拉动个人消费。

最后，重视城市化过程的总体布局，避免出现“城乡结合部”和“贫民窟”。

在经济高速发展时期，日本也经历过大城市人口迅速增长的阶段。以东京为例，1955—1970年期间，每年净流入人口30万~40万人。但由于东京的城市规划以放射状大容量轨道交通为依托，沿轨道交通站点（多为过去的小城镇）建设生活服务、文化娱乐和治安配套完善的居民区，包括大学教授等较为富裕人士在内的、大量在东京工作的居民选择在距东京市中心数十公里的千叶县和埼玉县等地居住。

由于规划合理、配套齐全，日本很多大城市带动了周边大片区域发展，东京周边的“首都圈”和大阪神户周边的“阪神圈”等发达经济圈应运而生。

日本通过建立统一的社会保障体系、建设高标准的卫星城和小城镇、维持农产品较高价格以保障农民收入等措施，打通了城乡之间存在的各种壁垒。

第一，统一社会保障体系和宽松的户籍制度是城乡居民相互流动的前提。在日本，居民的养老、失业和医疗保险全国统一，不以地区或身份区分，居民转移户籍几乎不受限制。这使得日本全国人员流动较为方便，解除了农民进城或城市居民“下乡”的后顾之忧。

第二，高标准建设大城市外围卫星城和小城镇是大城市减轻人口压力的前提条件。日本很多大城市的外围卫星城和小城镇的基础设施、生活服务、文化娱乐等条件与大城市中心区相差无几，吸引了很多城市居民前去居住。充分利用好包括退休老人、不必每天通勤的上班族、小企业主及其雇工等群体的资本和消费需求，在很大程度上促进了日本中小城市和小城镇的发展，既避免了大城市人口过快膨胀，又拉动了农村发展，有力促进了城乡平衡和区域平衡。

第三，采取各种措施维持农产品较高价格以保障农民收入。为增加农民收入，日本在对外贸易中多利用高关税、高检疫检验标准等有形或无形“保护壁垒”，在国内则通过农协等行业组织或地区组织维持农产品较高价格。这实际上是以城市消费者出资的形式对农业进行隐形补贴。同时，为保障城市低收入阶层人群的基本生活，日本政府通过补贴等方式使国内市场鸡蛋、牛奶和面包等基本食品的价格处于较低水平。

按照人口和国土比例，日本的人口密度约为中国的3倍，且其国土山地多，平原少。在这种基本国情下，日本不仅实现了城乡共同富裕和高度城市化，还发展了农业，确保了大米完全自给和大部分蔬菜自给。以日本的情况来看，我国无论在大城市郊区、中小城市和小城镇建设方面，还是在农业集约化、精细化方面，都具有巨大潜力。

（资料来源：http://www.sina.com.cn）

## 七、青海玉树发生7.1级强烈地震

2010年4月14日7时49分，青海玉树发生了7.1级强烈地震，造成2698人遇难，270人失踪，12135人受伤，1.5万户民房倒塌，有10万户灾民转移安置，给人民生命财产和经济社会发展造成了巨大损失。在党中央、国务院和中央军委的坚强领导下，全党全军全国各族人民众志成城、团结奋战，开展了艰苦卓绝的抗震救灾工作，夺取了抗震救灾斗争的重大胜利。

4月14日，为做好青海玉树抗震救灾工作，国务院成立抗震救灾总指挥部，国务院副总理回良玉任总指挥，有关部门负责同志任副总指挥。下设抢险救灾、群众生活、卫生防疫、基础设施保障和生产恢复、地震监测、社会治安、宣传、综合八个工作组。

4月15日，国务院总理温家宝飞抵青海玉树地震灾区，考察灾情，慰问各族干部群众，指导抗震救灾工作。

4月17日，中共中央政治局常务委员会召开会议，全面部署当前青海玉树抗震救灾工作。中共中央总书记胡锦涛主持会议。会议强调，要以更加顽强的精神、更加迅速的行动、更加科学的方法，克服一切艰难险阻，坚决做好抗震救灾各项工作。

4月18日，中共中央总书记、国家主席、中央军委主席胡锦涛来到玉树地震灾区，视察灾情，看望、慰问受灾群众和救援人员，实地了解救灾工作面临的突出困难，指导解决影响救灾工作进展的瓶颈问题。

4月21日，全国举行哀悼活动，深切哀悼青海玉树地震中遇难的同胞。北京天安门、新华门和全国人大常委会、国务院、全国政协、中央军事委员会、最高人民法院、最高人民检察院所在地，全国和驻外使领馆，都下半旗志哀。全国停止公共娱乐活动，以表达对青海玉树地震遇难同胞的深切哀悼。

4月30日，国务院发布《青海玉树地震抗震救灾捐赠资金使用管理监督办法》（国务院抗震救灾总指挥部发明电［2010］2号），要求切实做好青海玉树地震抗震救灾捐赠资金的使用管理监督工作，确保捐赠资金合理配置、规范使用。

5月1日，国务院总理温家宝再次来到青海玉树，看望受伤灾民，慰问医疗救治人员，并了解灾后重建情况，指导抗震救灾和恢复重建工作。

5月10日，青海省委、省政府宣布青海玉树灾后重建现场总指挥部正式成立，转入受灾群众进一步过渡安置和科学规划震后重建新阶段。

5月19日，国务院总理温家宝主持召开国务院常务会议，研究部署玉树地震灾后恢复重建工作。提出用3年时间基本完成恢复重建主要任务，使灾区基本生产生活条件和经济社会发展全面恢复并超过灾前水平。

5月24日，国务院发布了《关于做好玉树地震灾后恢复重建工作的指导意见》（国发[2010] 14号），提出力争用三年时间基本完成恢复重建主要任务，使灾区基本生产生活条件和经济社会发展全面恢复并超过灾前水平，生态环境切实得到保护和改善，又好又快地重建新校园、新家园；为建设生态美好、特色鲜明、经济发展、安全和谐的社会主义新玉树奠定坚实基础。

5月31日，国务院发布了《关于支持玉树地震灾后恢复重建政策措施的意见》（国发[2010] 16号），提出支持和帮助玉树地震灾区恢复重建，统筹和引导社会各方面力量，又好又快重建新校园、新家园，建设社会主义新玉树；保证用三年时间基本完成恢复重建主要任务，使灾区基本生产生活条件和经济社会发展全面恢复并超过灾前水平。

6月9日，国务院下发《关于印发玉树地震灾后恢复重建总体规划的通知》（国发[2010] 17号），提出力争用三年时间基本完成恢复重建主要任务，使灾区基本生产生活条件和经济社会发展全面恢复并超过灾前水平，实现居民拥有新家园、生态迈上新台阶、设施得到新改善、城乡呈现新面貌、社会和谐新局面的重建目标。

8月18日，中共中央、国务院、中央军委下发《关于表彰青海玉树全国抗震救灾英雄集体和抗震救灾模范的决定》，决定授予玉树藏族自治州抗震救灾指挥部等225个集体“全国抗震救灾英雄集体”荣誉称号；授予王玉虎等330名个人“全国抗震救灾模范”荣誉称号，追授松尕等4名同志“全国抗震救灾模范”荣誉称号。

8月19日上午，中共中央、国务院和中央军委在青海西宁市隆重举行全国抗震救灾总结表彰大会。表彰抗震救灾英雄集体和抗震救灾模范，弘扬伟大抗震救灾精神，激励全党全军全国各族人民以先进模范人物为榜样，奋力把我国改革开放和社会主义现代化建设伟大事业推向前进。中央和地方等1000多人参加了大会。

### 2010年全球7.0级以上地震一览

2010年以来，全球多个国家和地区发生了较大震级的地震，其中7.0级以上的地震有：

1月12日，海地发生了里氏7.0级大地震，地震的震中位于内陆，距离海地首都太子港仅有16公里，震源深度仅为10公里。

2月27日，智利发生8.8级强震，这场地震发生在康塞普西翁东北115公里处，震源深度35公里。同日，在日本琉球群岛发生7.2级地震，震源深度约为33公里。

4月14日，中国青海玉树发生7.1级地震，震源深度约为33公里。

4月11日，位于太平洋的所罗门群岛发生7.1级强烈地震，震中位于所罗门群岛基拉基拉市西南97公里处，震源深度为52公里。

5月28日，南太平洋岛国瓦努阿图发生里氏7.2级地震，震中位于瓦努阿图圣埃斯皮里图岛西北224公里处，震源深度为36公里。

6月13日，印度尼科巴群岛和印尼苏门答腊岛西北部海域发生里氏7.7级强烈地震，震中位于尼科巴群岛的米沙以西155公里处，震源位于地表以下34公里处。

6月16日，印度尼西亚发生7.1级地震，震源深度为30公里。

6月26日，西太平洋的所罗门群岛附近发生里氏7.1级地震，震中位于所罗门群岛首都霍尼亚拉东南224公里处，震源深度约为30公里。

7月24日，菲律宾棉兰老岛附近海域发生7.2级地震，震源深度约为590公里。

8月10日，南太平洋岛国瓦努阿图发生里氏7.5级地震，震中位于首都维拉港西北46公里处，震源位于地表以下66公里处。

8月12日，厄瓜多尔首都基多东南171公里处发生7.1级地震，震源深度为200公里。

8月14日，关岛西南海域发生里氏7.2级强烈地震，震中位于关岛首府阿加尼亚西南约375公里处，震源深度约为4.7公里。

9月4日，新西兰第二大城市克赖斯特彻奇遭里氏7.0级地震，震源深度为20公里。

9月30日，印度尼西亚发生里氏7.4级强烈地震，震中位于巴布亚省西伊连伊里安地区卡伊马纳市东南141公里处，震源深度为25公里。

10月22日，墨西哥加利福尼亚湾发生里氏7.0级地震，震源深度约为10公里。

10月25日，西苏门答腊省明打威群岛南巴盖岛附近发生了里氏7.2级地震，震中位于西苏门答腊省明打威群岛南巴盖岛西南78公里处，震源深度为10公里。地震还引发了海啸。

12月22日，日本小笠原群岛附近海域发生里氏7.4级地震，此次地震震中位于小笠原群岛海域，震源深度为10公里。

（资料来源：http://www.china.com/）

## 八、甘肃舟曲发生特大泥石流灾害

2010年8月8日凌晨，甘肃省甘南藏族自治州舟曲县发生特大山洪泥石流灾害，共造成1501人遇难，264人失踪，受伤住院人数72人，2万多人受灾，给当地人民生命财产造成重大损失。在党中央、国务院和中央军委的坚强领导下，灾区广大干部群众和社会各界救援人员不畏艰险、万众一心、科学应对，最大限度解救被困人员，及时救治伤员，妥善安置受灾群众，全面开展卫生防疫，迅速抢修受损基础设施，排除堰塞体险情，疏通白龙江河道，确保了灾区人心安定、民族团结和社会稳定，取得了抢险救援阶段的重大胜利。

8月8日中午，国务院总理温家宝率国务院有关部门负责人赶赴受灾地区，指挥抗灾救灾工作。

8月10日，国务院办公厅印发了《关于有序做好支援甘肃舟曲灾区有关工作的通知》（国办发明电［2010］22号），要求国务院各有关部门要加强指导和协调，及时帮助灾区解决抗灾救灾工作中的困难和问题。

8月15日，全国举行哀悼活动，深切哀悼在这次灾害中遇难的同胞。这是继汶川地震和玉树地震后，中国历史上第三次，也是2010年第二次为自然灾害中的遇难同胞举行全国性哀悼活动。

8月21日，国务院总理温家宝再次来到舟曲灾区，看望受灾群众，慰问坚守救灾一线的部队官兵，实地指导抢险救灾和恢复重建工作。

9月9日，经过兰州军区救援部队昼夜奋战，舟曲县城被淹主城区清淤工作全部完成，1.2公里长的淤塞河道、150多万方的淤积量被疏通，群众生产生活秩序逐步恢复正常。

10月18日，国务院下发《关于支持舟曲灾后恢复重建政策措施的意见》（国发［2010］34号），提出根据受灾程度，重点支持舟曲县受灾严重的城关镇居民住房、公共服务、基础设施以及灾害防治等方面恢复重建，同时兼顾舟曲县江盘乡等其他受灾乡镇恢复重建。

11月4日，国务院下发《关于印发舟曲灾后恢复重建总体规划的通知》（国发［2010］38号），提出2010年年底前舟曲灾区将基本完成城乡居民住房维修加固任务，并在2012年年底前，全面完成城乡住房、公共服务和基础设施等各项恢复重建任务，使灾区基本生产生活条件和经济社会发展全面恢复并超过灾前水平。

12月2日，中央组织部印发命名表彰决定，授予甘肃省舟曲县公安局党委等31个基层党组织“防汛抗洪救灾先进基层党组织”称号，授予马德华等22名共产党员“防汛抗洪救灾优秀共产党员”称号，追授袁友等23名共产党员“防汛抗洪救灾优秀共产党员”称号。

## 历史上发生的特大泥石流灾害

目前世界上有50多个国家存在泥石流的潜在威胁。由于生态环境日益遭到破坏，进入20世纪后，全球泥石流暴发频率急剧增加，而且还发生过几次特大泥石流，造成严重人员和财产损失。

1970年，秘鲁的瓦斯卡兰山暴发泥石流，500多万立方米的雪水夹带泥石，以每小时100公里的速度冲向秘鲁的容加依城，造成2.3万人死亡，灾难景象惨不忍睹。

1981年7月9日，我国四川大渡河南岸利子依达沟暴发特大泥石流。泥石流体冲毁了成昆铁路尼日车站北侧跨越利子依达沟口的利子依达大桥，摧毁了行驶中的列车，造成300余人死亡，146人受伤。

1985年，哥伦比亚的鲁伊斯火山泥石流，以每小时50公里的速度冲击了近3万平方公里的土地，其中包括城镇、农村、田地，哥伦比亚的阿美罗城成为废墟，造成2.5万人死亡，15万家畜死亡，13万人无家可归，经济损失高达50亿美元。

1998年5月6日，意大利南部那不勒斯等地突遭罕见的泥石流灾难，造成100多人死亡，2000多人无家可归。

2005年，菲律宾雅加达西南部一个村庄遭遇泥石流袭击，造成至少140人死亡。

2006年2月17日，菲律宾中东部莱特省发生特大泥石流，摧毁了两座村庄中的数百间房屋，造成200人死亡、1500人失踪。

2010年8月7日，我国甘南藏族自治州舟曲县突降大暴雨，县城北面的罗家峪、三眼峪泥石流倾泻而下，由北向南横扫县城，沿河大面积房屋被冲毁，共造成1478人遇难、287人失踪、2万多人受灾。

（资料来源：http://www.china.com.cn）

### 泥石流灾害的应急避险

泥石流是指在山区或者其他沟谷深壑、地形险峻的地区，因为暴雨暴雪或其他自然灾害引发的山体滑坡并携带有大量泥沙以及石块的特殊洪流。泥石流具有突然性以及流速快、流量大、物质容量大和破坏力强等特点。泥石流常常会冲毁公路铁路等交通设施甚至村镇等，造成巨大损失。

我国泥石流的分布明显地受地形、地质和降水条件的控制。特别是在地形条件上表现得更为明显。

1. 泥石流在我国集中分布在两个带上。一个是青藏高原、盆地，另一个是东部的低山丘陵或平原的过渡带。

2. 在上述两个带中，泥石流又集中分布在一些沿大断裂、深大断裂发育的河流沟谷两侧。这是我国泥石流的密度最大、活动最频繁、危害最严重的地带。

3. 在各大型构造带中，具有高频率的泥石流又往往集中在板岩、片岩、片麻岩、混合花岗岩、千枚岩等变质岩系及泥岩、页岩、泥灰岩、煤系等软弱岩系和第四系堆积物分布区。

4. 泥石流的分布还与大气降水、冰雪融化的显著特征密切相关。即高频率的泥石流主要分布在气候干湿季较明显、较暖湿、局部暴雨强度大、冰雪融化快的地区，如云南、四川、甘肃、陕西、西藏等。低频率的稀性泥石流主要分布在东北和南方地区。

专家认为，泥石流、滑坡、崩塌的发生也有迹可循。坡度较陡或坡体呈孤立山嘴或为凹形陡坡、坡体上有明显的裂缝、坡体前部存在临空空间或有崩塌物，这说明曾经发生过滑坡或崩塌，以后还可能再次发生；河流突然断流或水势突然加大，并夹有较多柴草、树木，深谷或沟内传来类似火车的轰鸣或闷雷般的声音，沟谷深处突然变得昏暗，还有轻微震动感，这些迹象都能确认沟谷上游已发生泥石流。

如果不幸遇上泥石流，不要惊慌，必须遵循规律采取以下应急避险措施：

根据各种现象判断泥石流发生之后应立即逃逸，选择最短最安全的路径向沟谷两侧山坡或高地跑，切忌顺着泥石流前进方向奔跑；不要停留在坡度大，土层厚的凹处；不要上树躲避，因泥石流可扫除沿途一切障碍；避开河道弯曲的凹岸或地方狭小高度又低的凸岸；不要躲在陡峻山体下，防止坡面泥石流或崩塌的发生；长时间降雨或暴雨渐小之后或雨刚停，不能马上返回危险区，泥石流常滞后于降雨暴发；白天降雨较多后，晚上或夜间密切注意雨情，最好提前转移、撤离。切忌在危岩附近停留，不能在凹形陡坡危岩突出的地方避雨、休息和穿行，不能攀登危岩。

（资料来源：http://www.bjkp.gov.cn）

## 九、南方部分城市发生严重内涝

2010 年入汛以来，我国先后出现多次大范围的强降雨过程，全国洪涝灾害呈东西并发、南北并发、多灾并发态势，洪灾范围之广、大江大河水位超警之多，都是 1998 年以来所罕见的。汛前降水偏多和入汛后频繁的强降水过程，使得江河湖库水位超警戒线后居高不下，全国七大江河流域均发生洪水。其中，437 条河流发生超警以上洪水，111 条河流发生了超过历史实测记录的特大洪水，长江上游干流出现了 1988 年以来的最大洪水，三峡水库出现建库以来最大洪峰流量。

5 月至 7 月期间，我国共出现 14 次强降雨天气过程。洪涝灾害主要发生在福建、江西、广西、贵州、四川、湖南、重庆、湖北、安徽、广东、云南等省、自治区。各地暴雨、江河洪水、山洪、泥石流、滑坡、城市内涝等多种洪涝灾害频繁发生。受强降雨影响，全国共有 269 座县级以上城市受淹，其中，广州、武汉、重庆、深圳等大城市遭受严重内涝。

5 月 7 日至 8 日，广州各区普降大暴雨，在 12 个小时之内，降雨量超过 213 毫米，全市受浸严重，广州市中心城区严重内涝，内涝点达到 118 个，其中，89 处为新增内涝点，44 处严重水浸。广州的一些主干道如广州大道、广园路等，有的地方水深达 3 米。全市共有 935 人受灾，87 个镇（街）受淹，38 间房屋倒塌。暴雨造成了交通瘫痪，车辆、行人被困途中数小时，部分地铁线路停运，200 多辆快速公交车被困，白云机场 138 个航班被延误。广州市气象台自有预警信号以来首次发布全市性暴雨红色预警信号。

5 月 13 日，株洲市遭受暴雨袭击，城区多个路段出现严重内涝，许多地势低洼的道路、学校、民房、商店等被淹，积水最深处达 1 米，部分路段交通一度中断。沿江路路基湘江河堤发生塌方，影响株洲部分地区的用水和用电。

5 月 23 日起，深圳普降大到暴雨，两天一夜的大雨可谓是“暴雨倾城”。5 月 23 日当天，深圳全市平均降雨约 110 毫米，而两天来深圳市累计降雨量普遍在 100 毫米至 300 毫米之间，其中最大降雨出现在宝安区大浪街道，高达 263 毫米。大雨造成深圳多处街道、民宅、工厂遭到水浸，受灾严重的大浪、龙华、观澜、石岩等街道以及部分交通干线共出现 30 余处不同程度的积水和内涝，最严重处水深约 1 米。

6 月 9 日，广西梧州市区一场强降雨一个小时之内就达到了 120 多毫米，暴雨致使梧州市区多个路段发生严重内涝，共有 8 个路段出现严重积水。其中，内涝最严重的地方为市政府广场和新兴二路两广市场加油站附近路段，市政府广场内涝积水最严重时，水深约为 1.5 米，一些商铺、车库被淹，多条道路交通拥堵。

6 月 19—20 日，中共中央政治局常委、国务院总理温家宝来到广西梧州市，实地察看汛情、灾情，慰问奋战在抗洪救灾一线的干部群众，主持召开会议，部署防汛抗洪救灾工作。

6 月 29 日，合肥市大雨倾泻而下，猛烈的降雨在巢湖路、步行街等多个街区形成内涝，聚集的雨水深及腰部。安徽省气象观测站网资料显示，14 时至 16 时巢湖路降雨量 72.1 毫米，达暴雨级别。

7 月 9 日，一场强降雨袭击重庆主城区，导致渝北、酉阳和沙坪坝等地区多处路段积水严重，城区部分路面积水深达 3 米，多处内涝，造成交通拥堵，92 个航班延误。

7 月 13 日，大雨造成安徽省安庆市区街头严重积水，城区多条主干道被淹。一些地势低洼的居民小区不同程度受淹，大量住户被困家中。其中华庭小区积水最深时一度达 3 米，1.2 万多名居民被困。

7月13日，持续强降雨6天后，武汉中心城区累计最大降雨量达292毫米，全市江湖水库水位持续上涨，渍水路段达41处，中心城区内涝严重，江汉区新华下路沿线人行道上渍水达30厘米，5米高的铁路桥涵洞被淹去近半，最深积水处超过2米，整条道路交通基本瘫痪。

7月23日，中共中央政治局常委、国务院总理温家宝在湖北考察防汛抗洪工作。他要求坚持按科学规律防汛抗洪，切实做好防御更大洪水、应对更大灾难的准备，统筹做好经济社会发展和抗洪救灾工作，努力实现全年经济社会发展目标。

7月26日，浙江省温岭市突下大暴雨。在短短3天时间内，温岭全市平均降雨量348.9毫米，使温岭城区严重积水，城区交通基本瘫痪，数百辆轿车当街被淹，5500家工矿企业停产。

专家分析，2010年我国暴雨雨量多、雨强大、范围广，超出了排涝体系标准，造成了部分城市中心城区大面积严重内涝。

## 部分发达国家的城市排水经验

**法国** 法国巴黎城区下水道均建于地面以下50米，管道采用多功能设计理念，中间是宽约3米的排水道，两旁是宽约1米、供检修人员通行的便道。基于对地面雨水流量的充分估计，巴黎城区主干道的井盖孔密且直径大，平均每50米就有一个下水口，住宅区内的下水道进水口较大。城区总数达2.6万个下水道盖、6000多个地下蓄水池，均统一编号，由1300多名专业人员负责维护。

**美国** 美国把全国划分为13个流域，每个流域均建立了洪水预警系统，每天进行洪水预报，最长的洪水预报是3个月。此外，美国还利用先进技术，对洪水可能造成的灾害进行及时预测，发布警示信息。美国早已有强制性防城市内涝的法律，多个州都立法规定，城市新开发区域必须实行强制的“就地滞洪蓄水”，对城市内涝防范、治理措施以及问责手段也规定得相当详尽。近几十年来，美国政府还致力于以雨水回收利用为重点的工程措施，在许多城市建造了由屋顶蓄水池、井、草地、透水地面等组成的地表回灌系统，收集的雨水可直接或经适当处理后用于冲厕所、洗车、浇绿地、消防和回灌地下等。

**日本** 日本政府规定：在城市中新开发土地，每公顷土地应附设500立方米的雨洪调蓄池。在城市中广泛利用公共场所，甚至住宅院落、地下室、地下隧洞等一切可利用的空间调蓄雨洪，防止城市内涝灾害。比如，降低操场、绿地、公园、花坛、楼间空地的地面高度，在遭遇较大降雨时可蓄滞雨洪；在停车场、广场铺设透水路面或碎石路面，并建设渗水井，加速雨水渗流等。此外，在东京、大阪等特大城市建设地下河，直径十几米，长度数十公里，将低洼地区雨水导入地下河，排入海中。东京下水道系统以污水和雨水采用同一管道排放为主，用于管道清扫和维护管理的检查井超过47万个，平均每33米就有一个检查井。

**荷兰** 荷兰鹿特丹市位于海平面以下，经常面临海水倒灌的威胁，同时城区洼地众多，排涝压力颇大。为有效应对这种情况，鹿特丹开创了其独有的“水广场”防涝及雨水利用系统。水广场顺地势而建，由形状、大小和高度各不相同的水池组成，水池间有渠相连。平时是市民娱乐休闲的广场，暴雨来临，就变成一个防涝系统。由于雨水流向地势低洼的水广场，街道上就不会有积水。所有水池布成一张循环网络，雨量大时，从大水池中分流到沟渠，雨量小时，水又回流到大水池。雨水还能被抽取储存为淡水资源。

**德国** 为提高城市排涝能力，德国城市居民区一般采用人工湖或构造水景观，或者通过绿地、花园或人工湿地增加雨水入渗。如采用透水砖铺装人行道，增加透水层，减少硬质铺装等。德国汉堡建有容量很大的地下调蓄库，洪水期可以发挥很强的调度水量作用。在柏林，由于广泛推行城市集雨措施，不仅提高了城市的防涝能力，而且实现了对雨水的最大收集利用。此外，德国还通过不断提高城市绿化率来减少雨水径流。在立法保障方面，德国立法规定在新建小区之前，无论是工业、商用还是居民区，均要设计雨洪利用设施，否则，政府将征收雨洪排放设施费和雨洪排放费。

**捷克** 2002年，一场百年一遇的洪水袭击捷克首都布拉格市，大片城区被淹没。洪水中，一个叫约瑟夫的城区却未被水淹，原因是其配备了一种新型的防洪系统，许多可移动的铝合金防汛板构成这一系统的主体。在平时，这些防汛板被放置在某些区域，在洪水来临时，只需要一天时间，这些防汛板就能建立一道坚固的防线。布拉格政府在之后多年的时间里努力构建足以保护全城的防汛城墙，在下次洪水来临时，布拉格只需一天就能够完成部署全长17116米的防汛系统。

（资料来源：http://www.163.com/）

## 十、城市公共安全面临诸多挑战

随着城市化进程的加快和城市人口的不断增加，城市资源相对短缺、基础设施投入不足和管理薄弱等问题日益突出，进而衍生了许多突发事件，城市公共安全面临诸多挑战。

辽宁阜新重大交通事故。2010年5月23日，辽宁省阜新市境内长深高速公路彰武段发生一起逆行货车与客车相撞的特别重大道路交通事故，造成33人死亡、24人受伤，直接经济损失2403万元。这是一起由货车严重超载且逆行、大客车严重超员且超速行驶而引发的特别重大生产安全责任事故。29名事故责任人受到党纪、行政处分。

郑州输水管道爆裂。6月24日，郑州市东周水厂输水管道爆裂，影响了东区30万人72小时的生活用水；11月17日，郑州市柿园水厂供水主干管爆裂，造成80万居民停水；11月22日，中法原水有限公司（原白庙水厂）南侧的外运公司家属院内一条出厂水干管再次发生爆裂，造成郑州120平方公里范围内的居民停水，这是影响区域最大的一次爆管事故。

大连输油管道爆炸。7月16日，位于辽宁省大连市大连保税区的大连中石油国际储运有限公司原油罐区输油管道发生爆炸，造成原油大量泄漏并引起火灾，事故造成1500吨的原油泄漏，海面污染面积达50平方公里；10月24日，大连中石油国际储运有限公司油库再次发生火灾；12月15日，中石油大连新港储油灌区附近区域发生今年以来的第三次火灾，3人在火灾中遇难。

南京燃气泄漏引发爆炸。7 月 28 日，位于南京市栖霞区迈皋桥街道的南京塑料四厂地块拆除工地发生地下丙烯管道泄漏爆燃事故，共造成 22 人死亡、120 人住院治疗，直接经济损失 4784 万元。原因是由于个体拆除施工队擅自组织开挖地下管道，现场盲目指挥并野蛮操作挖掘机挖穿地下管道，导致丙烯大量泄漏，迅速扩散后遇点火源引发爆燃，造成重大安全生产事故。按照有关规定，对 18 名事故责任人依法依纪进行了严肃处理。

上海公寓楼发生火灾。11 月 15 日，上海市中心胶州路靠近余姚路附近的一座 28 层的公寓楼发生火灾，事故造成 58 人死亡、70 多人受伤。受党中央、国务院委托，国务委员、公安部部长孟建柱 15 日深夜率国务院工作组紧急赶赴上海，指导火灾事故救援及善后工作，并宣布成立国务院上海火灾事故调查组。调查组认为，导致这起火灾事故的一个重要原因是大楼装修工程被违法违规层层分包。

北京城市交通陷入“瘫痪”。2010 年 9 月 17 日，一场小雨使北京市的城市交通陷入“瘫痪”，晚高峰提前约一个小时出现，高峰峰值时段全市拥堵道路超过 140 条，拥堵主要集中在二环、三环、四环等环路的连接路口。根据北京交管部门的信息，在平日早高峰，早 6 时 30 分到 8 时 30 分，北京的拥堵路段多达 100 条左右；到上午 9 时，仍有近 90 条城市主干线和城市快速路上的汽车时速低于 20 公里。

北京只是全国城市“豪堵”的一个缩影。综观国内城市，无论北京、广州、上海等大城市，还是郑州、兰州、西安、长沙等二三线城市都出现了“堵局”，交通拥堵已经成为老百姓极为憎恨但却见怪不怪的“城市病”。在我国一些大城市市区，机动车平均时速已经下降到 12 公里，而在市中心，机动车时速更是只有 8 公里到 10 公里。普通自行车时速为 15 公里左右，开车不如骑车快，已不是笑话，而是生活中真实的一幕。

据公安部交管局发布的数据显示，截至 2010 年年底，我国机动车保有量已达 1.99 亿辆，其中汽车 8500 多万辆。全国 667 个城市中，约有三分之二的城市交通在高峰时段出现拥堵。拥堵的城市由大城市向中小城市扩散，拥堵日期由上下班高峰期向全天拥堵转变，各地“堵城”现象频发，道路拥堵已成为一些城市的常态。

## 部分发达国家应对城市交通拥堵的主要措施

**新加坡**　新加坡政府主要通过高税费和推行拥车证制度这两种手段来实现对岛内汽车总量的控制。推行拥车证制度的目的是把车辆增加数目控制在一个可以承受的水平上。拥车证有效期 10 年，其发放数量由政府控制，购车者以竞标方式获得，拥车证价格依市场供求关系上下浮动。在新加坡，不仅购买汽车的代价很高，使用汽车的成本也不低。除汽油费、停车费、维修保养费用、每年的保险费、路税、车检费等必不可少的费用外，在狮城驾车还要负担新加坡特有的电子公路收费。新加坡的电子公路收费系统在不同时段，对进入市中心的车辆收取 0.5～2.5 新元不等的费用，以便达到限制市中心车辆总数，平衡车流，进而使整体交通环境更为顺畅的目的。新加坡政府一方面严格限制车辆的增加和使用，另一方面也花费很大力气不断改造和完善交通网络。目前，新加坡已经建成八条贯穿全岛的快速路，交通网用地占国土总面积的

12%。新加坡各主要道路的交通设施也比较完善，交通标志、标线一应俱全，清晰醒目。驾车者也大多比较遵守交通规则，交通秩序井然。

**德国** 德国有发达的交通网，保证道路基本畅通。德国国土面积不大，但却拥有世界最长的高速公路网，而且高速公路网还在扩大，路面还在加宽。所有的交通参与者遵守交通规则是保持道路通畅的另一个根本原因。在德国城市的街道上，几乎见不到交通警察，所有的交通几乎全由信号灯以及路牌来指示。德国交通管理法规成熟，《道路交通法规》、《道路交通许可法规》和《刑法法典》这3部法规各有明确的适用范围，既规定了执法者和违章者的权利和义务，也规范了交通管理部门的执法尺度和透明度。在市内，行人遵守交通规则也为道路畅通作出了贡献。

**法国** 首先，严把驾照关。法国驾照考试通过率一直不高，一次性通过者更是凤毛麟角；其次，严把车检关。检测人员认可车况后必须在有关单据上签字，如在一定期限内因车况问题导致事故，检测人员将被追究法律责任。这一制度使作为执法者的交管部门与车检服务商角色严格分离，私营车检中心会因法律责任重大而对车辆进行严格检测，保证上路行驶的车辆都是安全车；再次，法国公路网四通八达，路面状况良好，而且交通标识设置堪称一流；最后，在路管方面，法国大量使用“电子警察”，即车辆监视器。

**日本** 尊重弱者、步行者优先、道路使用者依法各行其道、道路交通管理者依法执法，是日本实现交通文明的最关键因素。交通管理部门想方设法扩大道路容量、科学合理调整交通需求量，是日本解决交通拥堵、减少事故、保持交通畅通的又一个关键因素。主要办法包括修建环形路、迂回路、立交桥、拓宽道路增加车道、发展公共交通等。日本大都市的轨道交通都很发达，最为人称道的则是规划设计合理和配套设施齐全。东京都中心区的交通枢纽站，不管是市内地铁换乘市内电车，还是由市内电车、地铁换乘城郊电车或新干线，大都在站内就可实现，不少车站的出站口直通大型商场、大型娱乐场和公司大楼，避免了人流二次拥堵，对缓解路面交通压力非常有效。此外，许多城市在远离市中心的地方都建有大型停车场，目的就是鼓励那些住在城郊的人进市内上班和办事时换乘电车或地铁等公共交通设施，缓解市内交通压力。严格执法并不断加大对违规违章车辆的处罚和打击力度，也是日本缓解交通拥堵、减少伤亡事故和保持交通畅通的关键因素之一。

（资料来源：http://www.chinanews.com.cn/）

（作者：邵益生，中国城市规划设计研究院副院长、研究员，国际欧亚科学院院士；周长青，中国城市规划设计研究院高级工程师）

# 2010中国城市经济发展述评

2010年，面对复杂多变的国内外经济环境、严峻挑战和各种压力，党中央、国务院牢牢把握经济发展的正确方向，采取有力措施，消释国际金融危机的冲击及影响，加快转变经济发展方式，加强和改善宏观调控，发挥市场机制作用，农业基础得到加强，经济结构调整步伐加快，改革开放不断深化，改善民生成效显著，不仅使2010年国民经济仍然保持稳定和较快增长，而且全面完成了“十一五”规划确定的目标任务。城市作为国家的空间主体，城市经济作为国民经济的支柱，在2010年同样取得了辉煌的成就，并对整个国民经济的发展发挥了中坚和支柱的作用。

## 一、2010年中国城市经济运行基本情况

### 1. 我国宏观经济的总体态势及城市的贡献

2010年，我国全年国内生产总值（CDP）达397983亿元，按可比价格计算，比上午增长10.3%，增速比上年提高了1.1个百分点。分季度看，第一季度同比增长11.9%，第二季度增长10.3%，第三季度增长9.6%，第四季度增长9.8%。分产业看，第一产业增加值40497亿元，增长4.3%；第二产业增加值186481亿元，增长12.2%；第三产业增加值171005亿元，增长9.5%。三次产业的比例为：10.1:46.9:43.0。

在全国经济发展中，城市经济的地位更加显现和突出。众所周知，第二、第三产业主要依托于城镇。在2010年国内生产总值的增长中，第二产业和第三产业的增长比例远高于第一产业，从而使第二、第三产业的比重在2010年有明显的提高，从2009年的89.4%提高到89.9%，提高了0.5个百分点。这充分说明了2010年我国工业化和城市化的明显推进和变化。（详见表1）

从各省、自治区、直辖市的情况看，凡是经济实力较强、发展较快的省市，其城市化水平、城市的数量，尤其是大中城市的数量，城市的经济实力都比较强，处于全国发展的前列。

表 1　第十一个五年规划期间国内产业结构的变化

| | | 2006 年 | 2007 年 | 2008 年 | 2009 年 | 2010 年 |
|---|---|---|---|---|---|---|
| 绝对值（亿元） | 国内生产总值 | 211923.0 | 257305.6 | 300670.0 | 335353 | 397983 |
| | 第一产业 | 24040.0 | 28627.0 | 34000.0 | 35477 | 40497 |
| | 第二产业 | 103162.0 | 124799.0 | 146183.4 | 156958 | 186481 |
| | 第三产业 | 84721.4 | 103879.6 | 120486.6 | 142918 | 171005 |
| 比例（%） | 国内生产总值 | 100.0 | 100.0 | 100.0 | 100.0 | 100.0 |
| | 第一产业 | 11.3 | 11.1 | 11.3 | 10.6 | 10.1 |
| | 第二产业 | 48.7 | 48.5 | 48.6 | 46.8 | 46.9 |
| | 第三产业 | 40.0 | 40.4 | 40.1 | 42.6 | 43.0 |

例如，广东省2010年经济总量迈上新台阶，全年国民生产总值达45472.83亿元，比上年增长12.2%，高出预期目标3.2个百分点，居全国各省、自治区、直辖市的第一位。这与珠江三角洲城市的发展，特别是广州、深圳、佛山等城市的经济实力及发展有着密切的联系。

又如，浙江省虽然国民生产总值居全国第四位，但是人均GDP、城市化水平、产业结构在省区中居于全国前列。2010年，全省国民生产总值为27227亿元，比上年增长11.8%。人均GDP为52059元（按年平均汇率折算为7690美元），增长10.1%。三次产业增加值结构由2005年的6.7:53.4:39.9调整为2010年的5.0:51.9:43.1。浙江城市化率已经达到59%，居各省、自治区、直辖市的前列，同时积极推进新型城市建设。

**2. 2010年全国城市经济的发展**

城市是国家及各省、自治区、直辖市的经济中心和支柱，代表着先进的生产力和生产方式，在国家经济发展方式转变和经济结构调整优化中，在改善民生，提高居民生活质量中，城市发挥了积极和明显的作用。

（1）直辖市的经济发展

在直辖市中，上海居于榜首，初步核算，全年实现生产总值16872.42亿元，按可比价格计算，比上年增长9.9%。分产业看，第一产业增加值114.15亿元，下降6.6%；第二产业增加值7139.96亿元，增长16.8%；第三产业增加值9618.31亿元，增长5%。分季度看，一季度生产总值增长15%，二季度增长10.7%，三季度增长9.2%，四季度增长5.9%。第二产业占42%，第三产业已经占57%，而第一产业已下降到不足1%。

北京紧随其后，2010年北京市地区生产总值（GDP）为13777.9亿元，比上年增长10.2%，完成了GDP“保十”的目标，增幅与上年持平。

天津市，2010年全市生产总值突破9000亿元，达到9108.83亿元，比上年净增1586.98亿元，增长17.4%。分三次产业看，第一产业增加值149.48亿元，第二产业增加值4837.57亿元，第三产业增加值4121.78亿元。三次产业的比例为：1.6:53.1:45.3。

重庆市2010年全市国内生产总值为7800亿元。

人均GDP涉及城市人口的统计口径和统计方法，北京、上海、天津的人均生产总值居于全国的前列，远远超过其他省、自治区、直辖市的水平。2010年，上海、北京、天津的人均GDP均已超过1万美元，重庆也达到4000多美元。

2010年，四个直辖市的国内生产总值达47559.15亿元，占全国国内生产总值的11.95%。

（2）计划单列市和部分省会城市的经济情况

计划单列市或副省级城市在我国城市经济乃至整个国民经济中具有举足轻重的地位，在一定程度上决定我国经济发展的总态势。2010年，我国副省级城市的GDP总量达到83277.53亿元，增长速度都在12%以上，高于全国10.6%的水平，最高的长沙达20%，其次如成都（16%）、深圳（16%）、长春（15.6%）、大连（15.2%）、厦门（15.1%）和武汉（15%）等城市，其增长速度都超过15%，在一定程度上起到了引领省区经济运行和发展的作用。副省级城市的人均GDP平均达到72034元，大大超过1万美元。

在副省级城市中，按GDP比较，有10个城市的GDP已经超过5000亿元，进入所谓城市5000亿元的俱乐部。（具体见表2）

表2　2010年国内生产总值过5000亿元的计划单列市经济情况

| 顺序号 | 城市 | 2010年GDP（亿元） | 增速（%） | 人口数（万人） | 人均GDP（元） |
|---|---|---|---|---|---|
| 1 | 广州 | 10604.48 | 13.0 | 795 | 133390 |
| 2 | 深圳 | 9500.00 | 16.0 | 891 | 106622 |
| 3 | 杭州 | 5945.82 | 12.0 | 683 | 87054 |
| 4 | 成都 | 5500.00 | 16.0 | 1140 | 48246 |
| 5 | 青岛 | 5500.00 | 13.0 | 763 | 72084 |
| 6 | 武汉 | 5200.00 | 15.0 | 836 | 62201 |
| 7 | 大连 | 5150.00 | 15.2 | 585 | 88034 |
| 8 | 宁波 | 5125.80 | 12.4 | 571 | 89769 |
| 9 | 南京 | 5075.00 | 13.3 | 630 | 80556 |
| 10 | 沈阳 | 5015.00 | 14.0 | 717 | 69944 |

资料来源：根据各城市人代会的政府工作报告或政府网站公布的统计公报整理

四个直辖市和15个计划单列市的GDP总量130836.68亿元，占2010年全国GDP总量的32.87%。

（3）其他城市的经济发展

中央直辖市和计划单列市只占我国城市数量的绝小部分，其他630多个大中小城市以及城镇是我国城市的基础，也是城市经济的基础。它们的经济运行和发展，同样决定着我国经济命运和城乡经济关系，以及城镇居民的民生。2010年，无论是东中西部城市，还是中小各类城市，以及城镇，其经济的各领域、各系统、各部门都在正常、健康地运行，得到稳步的发展。

无锡市，预计全市地区生产总值达到5750亿元，同比增长13%左右，高于年度预期目标1个百分点，五年来，全市地区生产总值实现翻番，超额完成“十一五”规划目标。按常住人口计算人均地区生产总值13780美元。完成地方财政一般预算收入511.9亿元，同比增长23.1%，高于年度预期目标11.1个百分点，超额完成“十一五”规划目标。

数据显示，2010年，厦门四个季度的GDP累计增速分别为17.7%、17.0%、16.2%和15.1%，增速由年初的高位运行向趋于稳定发展。其中，第一、二、三次产业增加值分别为23.00亿元、1026.86亿元和1003.88亿元，分别增长3.2%、20.4%和9.7%。

东北老工业基地和西部地区的一些城市迅速崛起，经济得到快速增长。如2010年，鸡西市预计地区生产总值实现413亿元，增长15%；全口径财政收入实现59.3亿元，增长39.4%，财政一般预算收入26亿元，增长41.3%；全社会固定资产投资165亿元，增长45%；规模以上工业增加值95亿元，增长（现价）42.4%；外贸进出口总额7.1亿美元，增长41.7%；社会消费品零售总额118.8亿元，增长18.9%；城镇居民人均可支配收入13007元，增长12%，农民人均纯收入7636元，增长33.1%。

广西玉林市初步统计，全年地区生产总值834亿元，增长15.3%；财政收入68.96亿元，增长26%；全社会固定资产投资615亿元，增长38.3%，高于全区平均水平。

### 3. 城市经济发展的主要动力

2008年，我国城市经济受到世界金融危机的冲击和影响，2009年在国家采取一系列应对措施，实现了恢复性的增长，而2010年在转变经济发展方式和优化经济结构的指导下，城市经济重新步入稳定、全面、协调、较快发展的轨道。城市经济发展从主要依靠投资和出口刺激，逐步转变为主要依靠扩大消费拉动，表现为城市市场较为活跃，消费品市场更为繁荣。2010年，全年社会消费品零售总额达154554亿元，比上年增长18.4%；扣除价格因素，实际增长14.8%。其中，城镇消费品零售额133689亿元，增长18.8%。

但是，总体来说，城市经济主要仍然是通过第二产业的发展，特别是工业的发展来促进城市经济的发展。一般说来，工业的增长快于第三产业的增长。

天津市，2010年工业增加值4410.70亿元，增长20.8%，对全市经济增长的贡献率达到63.5%。

厦门市，从经济增长速度看，工业对GDP增长的贡献最大，贡献率每季度均超60%，全年拉动GDP增长9.9个百分点。其中，规模以上工业依然是推动全市经济发展的重要力量，2255家规模以上工业企业完成工业总产值3670.82亿元，比上年增长33.9%，第三产业对GDP增长的贡献率为34.2%，拉动GDP增长4.7个百分点。

### 4. 积极安排就业，切实保障民生

就业是城市经济的重要内容，是提高城市居民生活水平、保持社会安全稳定的基础，就业结构是城市产业结构的体现。所以，积极切实地安排就业，解决失业居民的安置和救济，

以及解决进城市农民工的工作，成为2010年经济发展的重要内容和经济工作重点。许多城市由于后金融危机时期的经济迅速发展，就业岗位大幅度增长，劳动力供不应求，甚至一时出现“民工荒”，更多城市实现了充分就业。据国家有关部门公布的数据，2010年全国城镇新增就业1168万人，为全年目标900万人的130%；下岗失业人员再就业547万人，为全年目标500万人的109%；就业困难人员就业165万人，为全年目标100万人的165%。截至2010年年末，全国实有城镇登记失业人员908万人，城镇登记失业率为4.1%，比上年年底降低0.2个百分点。当然，失业的状态是不完全相同的，失业的原因存在许多复杂的情况。

城市发展“以人为本”，民生是城市经济发展的目的和根本。民生包含广泛的范围和丰富的内容，2010年保障民生方面取得明显的发展。

由于各省、自治区、直辖市、各城市的经济发展水平、经济结构、社会结构、居民构成、财政实力等方面的不同和差异，民生工程的内容、标准、方式、程序等千差万别，但重点是切实解决中低收入阶层和困难群体的生活问题，创造了一个和谐、安定和有保障的生活环境。

## 二、2010年城市经济发展中的热点和突出特点

2010年，城市经济发展经历了复杂的局面和多变的过程，反映出异乎寻常的变化和特点。主要是：

### 1. 转变经济发展方式和优化城市经济结构

2009年年底召开的中央经济工作会议明确指出，2010年我国经济发展的任务之一是“加快发展方式转变，推进经济结构战略性调整”，不断提高经济发展的质量。各城市以中央经济工作会议精神为指导，充分利用金融危机冲击所带来的世界市场结构变化而形成的产业结构调整的有利时机，加快产业结构的优化、转型和升级。

（1）经济发达城市产业结构日趋合理

产业结构的调整是发展方式转变的核心和重要手段，所以，东部沿海地区的经济发达城市，特别是大中城市，努力实现产业结构的调整、优化和转型。北京、上海、广州等一些经济发展水平较高的大城市和特大城市，已经跨入城市发展产业结构的先进水平，进入三次产业的“三二一”的发展阶段，即第三产业占主导地位，第二产业保持发展的优势，而第一产业从绝对值或比重来说，已经降为附属的地位。如北京，2010年，第三次产业的比例已经超过75%，在全国城市中居于领先地位，可与经济发达国家的城市，如纽约、东京、巴黎等世界城市相提并论。2010年，上海三次产业的比例为：0.7:42.3:57.0。在第三产业中，现代服务业和高端服务业的发展和完善，为上海建设成为“三个中心”奠定了坚实的产业基础。广州、深圳、杭州等城市，第三产业也进入了一个新的发展时期。

（2）大批工业城市加快产业结构的转型

许多工业城市，在继续发挥第二产业优势的前提下，加速了第三产业的发展，特别是现代

服务业的发展，改变了传统的产业结构模式。改革开放30多年来，苏州三次产业比例不断调整，从1978年的28.1:55.7:16.2，到2004年的2.2:65.7:32.1，再到2009年的1.8:58.8:39.4，2010年三次产业比例为1.7:57.8:40.5。三次产业的逐年变化，反映了苏州市在工业化、城市化进程中，由“工业型经济”向“服务型经济”转型和发展的努力和进展。

(3) 高科技产业、新兴产业发展迅速

高新技术产业、战略性新兴产业得到迅速发展，甚至成为城市经济新的增长极。工业设计、软件信息服务、现代物流和电子商务等生产性服务业加快发展；现代装备业、汽车工业、船舶制造等先进制造业快速发展，其产量和产值都有大幅度的增长，从而改变了工业内部的行业结构和产品结构；高端新型电子信息、新能源汽车、半导体照明等战略性新兴产业得到长足的发展，在广州和深圳等城市开始形成国家高技术服务业基地。一些城市正成为国家新能源汽车推广应用示范城市。生物医药、新材料、航空产业、节能环保等新兴产业逐步成为一些城市的主导产业或支柱产业，其增加值达到相当规模，远远超过一些传统工业。

(4) 文化产业在城市经济发展崛起

在第十一个五年规划期间，发展文化产业上升为我国推动经济发展和产业转型的引擎地位。2009年，国务院发布了《文化产业振兴规划》，提出“使文化产业成为国民经济新的增长点”。作为推动整个国民经济发展的一个重要的、关键的领域。党的十七届五中会会再次提出，“推动文化产业成为国民经济的支柱产业”。从世界经济发展看，文化与经济密切结合并融为一体的“创意经济”或“文化创意产业”是一种正在全球兴起的新的“发展范式”，对发展中国家更是一种“发展选择”。它表现出创意、文化、经济和技术之间复杂的交互作用，拥有创造收入、扩大就业和增加出口收益的潜力，同时也促进社会包容、文化多元性和人类社会的发展。文化产业创意经济是以文化、技巧、信息为核心，将经济、文化、技巧和艺术有机结合、配合、渗透和覆盖于产业之中，其核心是知识密集和技巧密集的新兴产业，并通过知识产权的应用，实现财产和就业双增长的创新型经济形态。我国城市的历史古迹、文化艺术、社会民族等文化资源极其丰富，有着众多历史文化名城市，蕴藏着非常丰富的非物质文化遗产。所以，具有加速城市文化产业发展的基础和条件。

2009年，我国全国文化产业国内外市场规模达到8000亿元，文化产业增加值占同期GDP的2.5%，2010年得到了进一步的重视和发展。2010年4月，央行等九部委联合出台了《关于金融支持文化产业振兴和发展繁荣的指导意见》后，金融业对文化产业发展的推动作用进一步加强，双方互利共赢的效果也逐步显现。广东省预计2010年文化产业增加值占生产总值比重达5.6%。北京、长沙等城市文化产业已经成为城市经济独树一帜的重要方面军。

(5) 城市经济发展的转型，建设创新型城市

城市经济发展方式的转变经常体现为城市经济发展的转型。不同类型的城市，其转型方式、途径和表现是不同的。一是资源型城市的转型。资源型城市（包括资源型地区）是以本地区矿产、森林等自然资源开采、加工为主导产业的城市类型，如煤炭城市、矿业城市、石油城市、林业城市等；二是一般城市的转型，如单一工业城市的转型等。2010年我国资

源型城市的转型取得积极的进展，一些资源型城市摆脱了对单一资源的依赖，调整产业结构，走上综合的、多元的、高端的城市经济发展新路子，促进新型工业城市的建立。浙江城市发展依靠产业结构优化，重点发展高附加值制造业，加快发展现代服务业，逐步形成以服务经济为主的产业结构新格局，经济增长从主要依靠工业带动向工业服务业协同带动的根本转变。

当今社会是一个信息社会，信息化正全方位地改变着经济社会的发展模式，促使信息化和城市化互相推动，城镇体系与信息网络空间融为一体，共同构成城市经济发展的空间网络节点，并通过这种节点不同程度地参与国内外的经济联系，从而形成新的城市经济网络体系。城市作为专业化分工的空间载体，是人才、信息等高端要素的集聚地，各种新经济业态不断衍生，成为城市经济的新增长点。所以，“数字城市”作为城市经济的技术支撑，其兴起和发展成为必然趋势。目前，浙江等省市正以“数字城管”为突破口，加快“数字城市”建设，提高城市信息化水平。

在城市转型发展中，建设创新型城市正成为一股重要的潮流。在国家发改委和科技部的推动下，一批城市被列为建设创新型城市的试点，为城市经济的升级转型注入新的活力和动力。

### 2. 城市群经济发展和产业转移

随着科学技术的进步，社会生产力的发展，特别是交通通信事业日新月异，城市已经不再是孤立地、单独地发展经济，而是相互参与、渗透、包容和支撑，从而形成新的大小不等、各具特色的区域经济，出现了城市群、城市带、城市圈等新的城市形态。

“十一五”规划期间，国务院和相关部门制定和出台了一系列促进地区经济、城市群、经济圈发展的战略、规划和政策。如，《国务院关于进一步推进长江三角洲地区改革开放和经济社会发展的指导意见》和《规划》，国家发展与改革委员会公布《珠江三角洲地区改革发展规划纲要（2008—2020 年）》。继上海浦东新区、天津滨海新区被国务院批准成为国家综合改革试点之后，2007 年，国务院批复成都—重庆作为统筹城乡综改试验区，武汉城市圈和长株潭城市群作为两型社会的综改试验区，以及其他众多的城市群发展规划等。

这些战略、规划、政策和措施加速形成城市间的合理分工和有效合作，有力地促进了城市经济的增长和发展，形成新的经济结构和布局，而且在 2010 年都收到了明显的成效。

在广东，实施了珠三角基础设施、产业布局、公共服务、城乡规划、环境保护等五个一体化规划和“四年大发展”工作方案，使珠三角区域经济一体化进程加快，加速推进珠三角城际轨道交通建设。广佛地铁正式通车运营，佛肇城际轨道开工建设，城市间实现年票互认。深莞惠跨界河流污染联防联治积极推进，其结果，2010 年全年珠三角地区规模以上工业增加值、全社会固定资产投资、地方财政一般预算收入分别增长 16.5%、18.2% 和 24.4%。

在环杭州湾、温台、浙中等人口和城市密集地区，加快发展形成若干用地少、就业多、要素集聚能力强、人口合理分布的城市群；在人口比较分散的西南地区，重点发展现有城市、县城和建制镇，从而在全省形成特大城市、大城市、中小城市和小城镇协调发展的格局。

随着城市群、经济圈的建立和发展，产业转移成为新的发展趋势和国家战略措施，2010年年初，国务院正式批准《皖江城市带承接产业转移示范区规划》，从而有力地促进合肥、芜湖等众多中小城市的崛起和发展。广东省34个省产业转移园预计实现产值1850亿元、税收约100亿元，分别比上年增长104%和88%。加快促进农村劳动力转移就业，全年免费培训农村劳动力84.7万人，实现转移就业147.1万人。

**3. 居民住房与房地产业的发展**

房地产业和居民住房是2010年城市乃至全社会最为关注的热点，更是社会争论的焦点，同时是国家宏观调控的重点。房地产业是国家加速城市化时期，城市经济的支柱产业，它不仅是解决城镇居民住宅的有效手段之一，更是城市经济发展的增长极，对带动城市其他领域的经济增长具有不可替代的作用。当然，房地产业与居民住房既有联系又有区别，不能混为一谈。居民住房不能完全依靠房地产业来解决，房地产业作为一类经济产业具有自己的功能、特点和属性。2010年，全年全社会固定资产投资278140亿元，其中城镇固定资产投资241415亿元，占86.80%，而房地产开发投资为48267亿元，比上年增长33.2%，其中12月份为5570亿元，增长12.0%。全年增长幅度远远高于全社会和城镇固定资产投资的增长速度，房地产开发投资占总投资的17.35%，占城镇固定资产投资的比重高达20%。据统计，全年住宅地产项目的投资占国内生产总值（GDP）的6.1%。个别城市更为突出，如上海全年完成全社会固定资产投资总额5317.67亿元，比上年增长0.8%。其中，房地产开发投资1980.68亿元，增长35.3%，占37.25%；宁波市2010年全市完成全社会固定资产投资2206.5亿元。其中，完成房地产开发投资557.3亿元，同比增长48.8%，增速同比提高27.1个百分点，占总投资的比例为25.26%。由此可见一斑。

2010年，全国地产市场十分活跃。为了保证和支持城市工业及各项产业的发展、满足城市房地产业发展和各项城市基础设施建设的需要，2010年全年，建设用地供应总量达428212.04公顷，同比增长34.2%，达到近年最高水平，在建设用地供应总量中，工矿仓储用地占35.7%，房地产开发用地占35.8%。房地产用地的比重提高了3.5个百分点。

资料显示，全国30个省区市（不含西藏和新疆建设兵团）住房用地实际供应12.54万公顷，比2009年住房供地增加4.9万公顷，同比增长64.1%。其中，保障性住房用地2.47万公顷，同比增加124.5%。与前几年的供地情况同口径相比，保障性住房、中小套型普通商品房和其他住房实际用地10.89万公顷，同比增长42.5%。

全国商品房销售面积10.43亿平方米，比上年增长10.1%；商品房销售额为5.25万亿元，增长18.3%。尽管如此，无论是一线城市，还是二、三线城市，商品住宅的售价不断上升，而且个别城市房价涨幅惊人，明显脱离一般居民对普通商品房的购买能力和消费水平。据统计，6月份70个大中城市房价环比出现0.1%的降幅，7、8月份环比持平，但9月份以来环比连续上涨。12月份，70个大中城市新建住宅销售价格环比上涨了0.3%；二手住宅销售价格环比上涨 0.5%，涨幅比上月扩大 0.2 个百分点。几年来，商品住房价格连续、累计上涨幅度较大，特别是一线城市已经出现房价过快上涨的势头，引起部分城市居民的不满，也引起中央及决策层的高度关注。为抑制部分城市房价过快上涨，促进房地产业的健康发展，2010 年国家出台多轮房地产调控措施。虽然房价继续上涨，但房地产景气指数有所回落。2010 年 12 月份，全国房地产开发景气指数为 101.79 点，比 11 月份回落 1.41 点，比上年同期回落 1.87 点。

受国家楼市调控政策等因素影响，房地产业增加值增幅由上年增长 47.4% 回落到下降 18.2%，对 GDP 的影响达 1.3 个百分点。

### 4. 城市财政与土地出让金收入

财政是城市经济发展的重要内容，是各项城市建设和社会事业发展的基础。随着城市经济的发展，城市财政收入不断增长，财政实力愈来愈雄厚，这为城市实施各项建设，营造各项民生工程，举办各种公共事业，应对自然灾害和处理应急事件，提供了可靠的稳定的财力保障。从目前显示的数字分析，2010 年，城市财政收入都得到了大幅度的上升。如，天津市全年地方财政收入完成 1068.81 亿元，增长 30.1%。其中，税收收入 776.65 亿元，增长 26.6%，增幅比上年提高 14.2 个百分点。

与此同时，城市为支持产业和各项事业的发展，通过出让土地获得一定的出让金收入。据不完全统计，2010 年，全国土地出让金（土地出让合同价款）收入为 2.71 万亿元，同比增长 70.4%，其中招拍挂出让总价款 2.6 万亿元，达到近几年来的最高水平。出让合同价款中，房地产用地和工矿仓储用地出让合同价款同比分别增长 76.3% 和 36.1%，占出让合同价款比例分别为 87% 和 11%。同年，土地出让合同价款总收入约相当于国家财政收入的三分之一。有的城市土地出让合同价款收入异乎寻常。中国指数研究院的监测数据显示，同年，全国 120 个城市土地出让金总额为 18814.4 亿元，同比增加 50%。其中北京、上海和大连三个城市土地出让金收入突破 1000 亿元。作为预算外财政收入的土地出让合同价款，相当于城市地方财政收入的比重已超过 50%，甚至占 80% 以上或更高，形成城市财政对土地出让的依赖，即所谓的“土地财政”。

不过，需要指出的是，土地出让合同价款中的一部分与城市财政具有同样的意义或作用，但是两者存在一定的区别。一是土地出让金是土地交易收入，不是税收收入；二是土地出让金视土地出让情况或土地市场景气状况而定，是不稳定的收入；三是土地出让金价款是总收入，需要扣除城市政府获得土地的成本和土地获得过程中和出让过程中的许多费用；四是国家已经对土地出让金的支出做了明确的规定，即专款专用，不能挪作他用，不列入城市财政预算，而作为预算外收入。尽管如此，目前的这种状况并不是完全正常的，仍然需要进一步地研究和解决。

## 三、2011 年及“十二五”规划时期城市经济展望

2011 年是 21 世纪第二个十年的开始，是我国第十二个五年规划开局之年。无论从空间

上，还是时间上，2011 年城市经济的健康、稳步和较快发展，对整个国家经济社会的发展和建设有着重要的意义。

2011 年城市经济的发展仍然面临着经济格局深刻变化和经济竞争不断加剧的严峻的国际环境，国内经济发展的深层次矛盾更加尖锐和凸显，对城市经济形成一定的压力。但是，城市经济发展同样存在许多新的优越条件和有利因素，蕴藏着巨大的潜力，特别是经过几十年的发展，奠定了一个坚实的发展基础，积累了丰富的建设经验，掌握了更成熟的领导艺术。所以，2011 年我国城市经济仍然会保持着较快的增长势头，将更有力地全面推进经济结构的调整和优化，居民经济收入和生活水平进一步提高，民生事业更趋于完善，使城市经济、社会和文化更和谐、协调的发展。主要体现在以下方面。

**1. 积极稳妥推进城镇化，提高城市经济发展质量**

城市化率的高低与城市经济发展相互促进。城市化水平的提高，直接带来城市经济的发展，城市经济的发展有力地促进城市化的加速。不仅如此，城市化的正确道路与城市经济总量增长之间，城市化的形态与城市经济结构，包括产业结构、空间结构、分配结构之间，城市化的布局与城市经济发展质量之间有着密切的联系。各省、自治区、直辖市在中央正确的方针、战略和政策的指导下，2011 年全国城市化率仍将继续以较快的速度提高，即以接近 1% 的增长速度提高，城市经济仍然会快于全国整体速度发展，也就是说，城市的 GDP 增长率会高于全国的增长率。但是，不同地区、不同类型、不同规模城市的经济增长率会存在一定的差异。中部地区、中等城市可能会成经济增长最快的城市，而经济发达地区的城市，特别是特大城市和大城市，重点可能会转移到城市经济的发展质量，提高城市自身品位。从全国来说，将更注重城市化的道路、结构、形态和方式，使大中小城市、各类型城市、众多城镇，更好地发挥功能和优势，促进经济的协调发展，促进城乡一体化发展，从而提高城市经济的发展质量。可以预见，中小城市和中小企业在 2011 年和在“十二五”期间将会发挥更重要的作用。

**2. 转变经济发展方式，努力推进城市现代化建设**

全面分析我国城市经济发展过程和水平，可以发现城市之间的差异非常明显，而且差距还在不断拉大。目前，我国不少城市的硬件建设，特别是基础设施和商业设施建设已经称得上现代化，可以与经济发达国家的城市相媲美，相当一部分城市居民的实际经济收入和现实生活达到较高水平。近几年国务院关于长三角、珠三角发展战略、规划和政策的文件中，明确要求这些地区，特别是大中城市“再用更长一段时间，率先基本实现现代化”，“为我国全面建设小康社会和实现现代化做出更大贡献”。对经济发达地区的先进城市来说，发展的不仅是总量，而且是结构。需要改变粗放型的经济发展方式，解决经济发展中、城市现代化建设中的薄弱环节，克服城市间产业结构的同构现象，使城市发展进入一个新的时期。同时，以城市现代化为目标来进一步推动城市经济的和谐、较快和可持续发展，实现经济先进城市带动和支持相对落后城市以及城镇和农村的加速发展。

### 3. 全面改善民生，积极扩大居民消费

城市作为经济中心，不仅仅是生产基地、商业中心和服务中心，而且必然是消费中心。消费是经济发展的目的，也是经济发展的动力，是民生的重要内容。整个城市居民的消费实质就是民生。提高城市的消费力，扩大居民消费是继 2010 年后继续刺激 2011 年城市经济发展强大的内在动力。

维护社会的稳定，保持经济发展的持久动力，发挥消费对经济的拉动作用。根据国外的经验，扩大和稳定中产阶层是最重要的因素。通过经济的增长，分配制度的完善，经济结构（特别是分配结构）的调整，财政政策的完善，等等，逐步形成以城市为依托，达到一定数量和比例的中产阶层，从而促进消费力的较快发展，实现消费的多元化、理性化和持久化，并成为未来五年城市经济发展的重心。

### 4. 深化经济体制改革，加强城市经济管理

与城市经济发展相比，经济管理是城市发展中的薄弱环节。由于经济管理的落后，不仅经济效率低下，经济效益受损，而且造成严重浪费，灾害不断，蒙受重大生命和经济损失。所以，落实科学发展观，强化法制建设，掌握先进的管理理念，采用科学的管理技术和方法，发扬学习和创新精神，加强城市经济宏观、中观和微观管理，是 2011 年及“十二五”规划期间的任务。

目前，城市经济发展中出现和存在的大量问题，都有着深层次的制度、体制和机制方面的原因，必须通过改革来解决。许多不相适应的经济制度、机制和体制，仍然阻碍城市经济更健康、更有效和更快的发展。特别是在经济分配、资源管理、土地利用、市场运行、环境保护、生态建设、公共服务等领域，存在诸多不完善之处，需要继续深化改革，进一步解放生产力，使 2011 年的城市经济更加繁荣。

（作者：杨重光，中国社会科学院研究员，中国城市经济学会副会长）

# 2010中国房地产市场综述

2010年被业界称为"中国房地产宏观调控频次最密集的一年"、"中国房地产史上调控最严厉的一年"，"保民生，稳房价"是2010年房地产市场调控的主旋律。

2010年年初，高速开局；二季度，调整回落；8、9月份，房屋销售价格出现反弹，政府再次密集出台了第二轮调控政策；四季度房屋销售价格出现缓慢回落。通过调控，房地产供给增加较快，尤其是保障性住房的供给取得了突破性进展；需求增幅减小；房价继续上涨，但涨幅回落，其中房屋租赁价格上涨较快。

从全国房地产开发景气状况来看，以3月份为分水岭，前扬后抑。

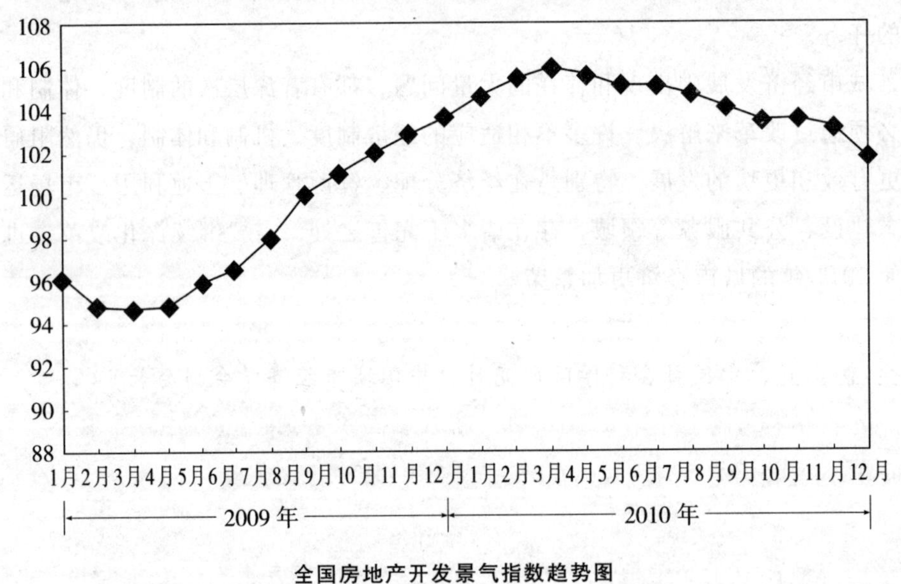


**全国房地产开发景气指数趋势图**

资料来源：国家统计局

## 一、保障性住房建设规模创历史之最

为解决城市中低收入家庭住房困难，中国住房供应正在加紧培育市场和保障的"两条腿走路"的体制。2010年以形成多层次的住房保障体系为目标，廉租房、经济适用房、公共租赁住房等为主体的保障性住房建设呈现了加速趋势。截至目前，已有超过 1000 万个中国住房困难家庭通过保障性住房解决了住房困难。

中国政府在 2007 年开始大规模启动保障性住房建设，各地基本实现了对住房困难的低保家庭应保尽保。2008 年和 2009 年，政府加大了保障房建设的力度和速度，使保障性住房建设进入新的发展阶段。2010 年，中国保障性住房规模建设创下历史之最，计划建设 580 万套。

而据有关政府部门公布的数据显示，2010 年全国各类保障性住房和棚户区改造住房开工 590 万套，基本建成 370 万套；农村危房改造开工 136 万户，基本竣工 108 万户，均超额完成年初国务院部署的任务。

同时，加快保障性住房建设，为市场性住房需求减压，缓和住房供求矛盾，也被作为遏制房价持续上涨的一种调控手段。2010 年年底，中央经济工作会议进一步明确提出，2011 年要加快推进住房保障体系建设，强化政府责任，加大保障性安居工程建设力度，加快棚户区和农村危房改造，大力发展公共租赁住房，逐步形成符合国情的保障性住房体系和商品房体系。

## 二、房地产开发投资、新开工面积房、土地购置面积均出现大幅增长

2010 年全国房地产市场运行情况如下：

### 1. 房地产开发投资完成情况

（1）全国房地产开发投资大幅增长，达到 48267 亿元，比上年增长 33.2%，增幅高于上年同期 17 个百分点，固定资产投资增幅高于上年同期约 9 个百分点，为 1998 年以来最高水平。其中，商品住宅投资 34038 亿元，增长 32.9%，占房地产开发投资的比重为 70.5%。

（2）全国房地产开发企业房屋施工面积，尤其是房屋新开工面积大幅增长。施工面积达到 40.55 亿平方米，比上年增长 26.6%；新开工面积达到 16.38 亿平方米，增长 40.7%。房屋竣工面积小幅增长 4.5%，为 7.60 亿平方米，其中，住宅竣工面积 6.12 亿平方米，增长 2.7%。

（3）全国房地产开发企业完成土地购置面积 4.10 亿平方米，比上年增长 28.4%，是近年购置土地增长最快的一年。

土地购置费 9992 亿元，增长 65.9%。据世联监测数据统计，2010 年北京、上海、大连三个城市的土地出让金收入均超过了千亿元。其中，北京为 1629 亿元；上海为 1513 亿元；大连为 1158 亿元。

全国 70 个大中城市土地交易价格同比涨幅保持高位，全年同比上涨 19.85%，环比上涨 14.74%。居住用地价格涨幅最高，全年环比累计上涨 18.6%。其中，高档住宅用地环比累计上涨 25.3%。

### 2. 商品房销售情况

全国商品房销售面积为10.43亿平方米，比上年增长10.1%，增幅减小32个百分点。其中，商品住宅销售面积为92118万平方米，同比增长8.0%，增幅低于上年同期46个百分点。由于在紧锣密鼓的楼市调控下，投资者对商品住宅的预期发生变化，投资对象转向办公楼和商业营业用房。办公楼销售面积为1844.7万平方米，同比大幅增长21.9%，但增幅低于上年同期9个百分点；商业营业用房销售面积为6783.8万平方米，大幅增长了29.9%。但增幅低于上年同期5.7个百分点。

这种预期的变化，也反映到商品房销售额方面。2010年，商品房销售额5.25万亿元，比上年增长18.3%。其中，商品住宅销售额增长14.4%，而办公楼大幅增长了31.2%，商业营业用房更大幅增长了46.3%。

### 3. 房地产开发企业资金来源情况

在国内贷款因调控政策而增幅较小的同时，企业自筹资金和利用外资大幅增加。房地产开发企业本年资金来源72494亿元，比上年增长25.4%。其中，国内贷款12540亿元，增长10.3%；利用外资796亿元，增长66.0%；自筹资金26705亿元，增长48.8%；其他资金32454亿元，增长15.9%。在其他资金中，定金及预收款19020亿元，增长17.3%；个人按揭贷款9211亿元，增长7.6%。

据商务部统计资料显示，2010年新设或增资的外资房企数量突破了1000家。另据多家顾问公司发布的分析报告显示，2010年外资在全国重点城市大宗物业投资的活跃程度也远远超过2009年。

### 4. 70个大中城市房屋销售价格情况

12月份，全国70个大中城市房屋销售价格同比上涨6.4%，涨幅比11月份缩小1.3个百分点；环比上涨0.3%。

新建住宅销售价格同比上涨7.6%，涨幅比11月份缩小1.7个百分点。其中：商品住宅销售价格上涨8.5%（其中普通住宅销售价格上涨7.2%，高档住宅销售价格上涨12.8%）；经济适用房销售价格上涨1.0%。与11月相比，新建住宅销售价格上涨0.3%。其中，商品住宅销售价格上涨0.3%（其中普通住宅销售价格上涨0.4%，高档住宅销售价格上涨0.2%）；经济适用房销售价格上涨0.1%。

二手住宅销售价格同比上涨5.0%，涨幅比11月份缩小0.6个百分点；环比上涨0.5%，比11月份扩大0.2个百分点。

房屋租赁价格方面，多数城市上涨较快。全年同比上涨6.0%，环比累计上涨8.1%。其中，普通住宅租赁价格上涨最快，全年累计上涨17.9%。

必须认识到，12月份全国70个大中城市房屋销售价格同比上涨能控制到6.4%，二手住宅销售价格同比上涨能控制到5.0%，这完全是采取了一系列调控政策的积极成果。如果不是进行这样严厉的调控，完全有可能出现更剧烈的房价上涨。

### 5. 房地产市场发展的动因分析

（1）国民经济回升向好，是房地产经济持续快速发展的根本动力。2010 年，面对极为复杂的国内外经济环境和极为严峻的各类自然灾害和各种重大挑战，党中央、国务院审时度势，科学决策，带领全国各族人民，深入贯彻落实科学发展观，加快转变经济发展方式，加强和改善宏观调控，发挥市场机制作用，有效巩固和扩大了应对国际金融危机冲击成果，国民经济运行态势总体良好。

据国家统计部门初步测算，全年国内生产总值 397983 亿元，按可比价格计算，比上年增长 10.3%，增速比上年加快 1.1 个百分点。全年全社会固定资产投资 278140 亿元，比上年增长 23.8%，增速比上年回落 6.2 个百分点，扣除价格因素，实际增长 19.5%。货币供应量稳定增长，金融机构人民币各项贷款余额 47.9 万亿元，比年初增加 7.9 万亿元；各项存款余额 71.8 万亿元，比年初增加 12.0 万亿元。城乡居民收入稳定增长。全年城镇居民家庭人均总收入 21033 元，比上年增长 11.5%。其中，城镇居民人均可支配收入 19109 元，增长 11.3%，扣除价格因素，实际增长 7.8%。宏观经济的回升，必然带动房地产部门经济的发展。

（2）城市化速度加快，是房地产经济持续快速发展的客观要求。有专家认为："由于部分人口的流动，乡村常住人口加城镇常住人口肯定少于全国总人口。统计中国城市人口数量的有效办法是调查农村常住人口。以此估算，中国当前的城市化率为 50%～55%，而非各界认定的约 47%。"

城市化进程的加快，又是与近几年来区域规划的大举编制和实施密切相关的。2009 年，国家先后批复了珠三角、福建海西、江苏沿海等 9 个区域规划。2010 年，又批准了海南国际旅游岛、皖江城市带、青海省柴达木循环经济试验区、沈阳经济区、长三角、重庆两江、大小兴安岭、深圳前海、山西综合改革配套改革实验区等。这些区域发展规划项目，在有力促进区域经济发展的同时，也给房地产市场带来了固定资产投资增加、人口聚集加速、居民收入水平提升、区域地产升值、市场需求旺盛等诸多市场利好。

（3）流动性充沛，是房地产经济持续快速发展的必要条件。过去两年，中国实行的是适度宽松的货币政策。由此注入的大量流动性，使 2010 年下半年物价压力剧增，引致下半年中央政府在"保增长、防通胀、稳房价"之间进行艰难的平衡。

流动性过度充沛，既带来了需求旺盛、供求失衡、房价高企的负面现象，但也给 2010 年房地产开发投资、新开工面积房、土地购置面积均出现大幅增长提供了资金条件。因此，2010 年楼市调控的重点之一，就是根据市场态势，寻求两者的平衡点，及时地调节流动性。

## 三、2010 年房地产大事回顾

通过不断的实践，中国政府对房地产市场的调控已经彰显了明确的思路：增加有效供给，抑制不合理需求。在此一以贯之的思路下，2010年加大了调控力度，增多了调控手段。尤其突出的是，采取了经济手段和行政措施并举的办法，从抑制需求、增加供给、加强监管等方面对房地产市场进行全方位、大力度的调控。

在抑制投资、投机等不当需求方面，采取了差别化信贷、限购、上调住房公积金贷款利率，对使用公积金贷款购买多套住房进行限制等多项政策措施。

在增加有效供给方面，采取了大幅增加土地供给并提高保障房用地的比重、减免税费以鼓励保障房建设、金融支持保障房建设等政策措施。

在加强市场管理，促进房地产市场健康发展方面，出台了系列政策，加强对企业融资、土地开发、商品房交易等环节的管理，规范房地产企业及相关人员行为，促进房地产市场健康发展。

2010年房地产调控的轨迹记述如下：

1月7日，为进一步加强和改善房地产市场调控，稳定市场预期，促进房地产市场平稳健康发展，国务院办公厅发布了《关于促进房地产市场平稳健康发展的通知》，要求各地增加保障性住房和普通商品住房有效供给；合理引导住房消费抑制投资投机性购房需求；加强风险防范和市场监管；加快推进保障性安居工程建设；落实地方各级人民政府责任。

1月13日，国务院新闻办召开新闻发布会，就《国务院办公厅关于促进房地产市场平稳健康发展的通知》、《关于推进城市和国有工矿棚户区改造工作的指导意见》的相关情况进行了通报。住房和城乡建设部、国家发改委、财政部、国土部、人民银行和银监会六部门负责人分别就保障房建设、土地供应、房贷政策等问题提出具体措施，以更好地落实《关于促进房地产市场平稳健康发展的通知》，遏制部分城市房价过快上涨、维护房地产市场平稳健康发展。

2月1日，备受社会各界关注的《国有土地上房屋征收与补偿条例（征求意见稿)》正式向公众公开征求意见。征求意见稿共五章四十一条，分别对适用范围、征收程序、征收补偿、关于非因公共利益的需要实施的拆迁等问题予以了明确规定。

3月5日，国务院总理温家宝在十一届全国人大三次会议上指出，要促进房地产市场平稳健康发展。坚决遏制部分城市房价过快上涨势头，满足人民群众的基本住房需求。一是继续大规模实施保障性安居工程。二是继续支持居民自住性住房消费。三是抑制投机性购房。四是大力整顿和规范房地产市场秩序，完善土地收入管理使用办法，抑制土地价格过快上涨。

3月18日，国资委召开新闻发布会，公布了央企地产业务的具体情况。国资委表示，除16家以房地产为主业的中央企业外，还有78家不以房地产为主业正在加快进行调整重组，在完成企业自有土地开发和已实施项目等阶段性工作后要退出房地产业务。

4月17日，国务院发出《关于坚决遏制部分城市房价过快上涨的通知》，要求进一步落实各地区、各有关部门的责任，坚决遏制部分城市房价过快上涨，切实解决城镇居民住房问题。通知说，近期部分城市房价、地价又出现过快上涨势头，投机性购房再度活跃，需要引起高度重视。各地区、各有关部门必须充分认识房价过快上涨的危害性，认真落实中央确定的房地产市场调控政策，采取坚决的措施，遏制房价过快上涨，促进民生改善和经济发展。建立考核问责机制，对稳定房价、推进保障性住房建设工作不力、影响社会发展和稳定的，要追究责任。

4 月 19 日，住房和城乡建设部发出《关于进一步加强房地产市场监管完善商品住房预售制度有关问题的通知》，要求各地切实负起责任，加大查处力度，强化房地产市场监管。通知说，房地产市场监管是政府加强房地产市场宏观调控的重要手段，对维护我国房地产市场平稳健康发展具有重要意义。

5 月 5 日，住房和城乡建设部、民政部、财政部联合印发了《关于加强廉租住房管理有关问题的通知》。《通知》针对部分地方廉租住房管理中出现的房源闲置、出借，日常管理和维修养护资金不落实，准入退出管理机制不完善、日常监管和服务不到位等问题，作出了有关规定。

5 月 24 日，国土资源部、监察部通报了清查出来的逾 61 万亩的“未报即用”违法用地，16 个地级市被点名。所谓“未报即用”违法用地，是指未办理用地申报手续就违法占用土地。根据国土资源部清查的结果，有 31 个省区市不同程度存在“未报即用”违法用地现象，其中国家和省级重点项目超过三成。截至 2010 年 3 月 25 日，全国范围内共清理出 2007 年 10 月—2009 年 10 月期间的“未报即用”违法用地案件 36872 宗，涉及土地总面积 61.3 万亩，其中耕地面积 27.2 万亩。各地清查出的“未报即用”违法用地案件中，立案率 96%，结案率 86%。共收缴罚款 15.67 亿元，拆除建筑物面积 1470 万平方米，没收建筑物面积 3124 万平方米，复耕土地面积 3.42 万亩。

6 月 4 日，住房和城乡建设部、中国人民银行、中国银行业监督管理委员会发出通知，对商业性个人住房贷款中第二套住房认定标准进行了规范。通知规定，商业性个人住房贷款中居民家庭住房套数，应依据拟购房家庭（包括借款人、配偶及未成年子女）成员名下实际拥有的成套住房数量进行认定。对不能提供 1 年以上当地纳税证明或社会保险缴纳证明的非本地居民申请住房贷款的，贷款人按第二套（及以上）的差别化住房信贷政策执行；商品住房价格过高、上涨过快、供应紧张的地区，商业银行可根据风险状况和地方政府有关政策规定，对其暂停发放住房贷款。为坚决遏制部分城市房价过快上涨，国务院近期决定，对贷款购买第二套住房的家庭，首付款比例不得低于 50%，贷款利率不得低于基准利率的 1.1 倍；对贷款购买第三套及以上住房的，大幅度提高首付款比例和利率水平。

6 月 12 日，住房和城乡建设部等七部门联合制定的《关于加快发展公共租赁住房的指导意见》正式对外发布，旨在解决城市中等偏低收入家庭住房困难。根据《指导意见》，公共租赁住房供应对象主要是城市中等偏下收入住房困难家庭。有条件的地区，可以将新就业职工和有稳定职业并在城市居住一定年限的外来务工人员纳入供应范围。公共租赁住房的供应范围和供应对象的收入线标准、住房困难条件和租金水平，由市、县人民政府确定。已享受廉租住房实物配租和经济适用住房政策的家庭，不得承租公共租赁住房。符合廉租住房保障条件的家庭承租公共租赁住房的，可以申请廉租住房租赁补贴。《指导意见》明确，发展公共租赁住房实行省级人民政府负总责、市县人民政府抓落实的责任制。

7月12日，住房和城乡建设部有关负责人表示：《国务院关于坚决遏制部分城市房价过快上涨的通知》（国发［2010］10号）下发后，各地区、各部门认真贯彻落实，部分城市房价过快上涨的势头得到了遏制。下一阶段，住房和城乡建设部将督促各地继续坚定不移地贯彻《通知》内容，严格执行差别化的住房信贷政策，加快推进保障性住房建设和各类棚户区改造；继续加强房地产市场监管，促进房地产市场平稳健康发展。

8月5日，住房和城乡建设部、财政部、发改委、人民银行、审计署和银监会联合发出《关于做好利用住房公积金贷款支持保障性住房建设试点工作的通知》，要求项目贷款必须定向用于试点项目，严禁挪作他用。经济适用住房和列入保障性住房规划的城市棚户区改造项目安置用房建设贷款，贷款期限最长不超过3年；政府投资的公共租赁住房建设贷款，贷款期限最长不超过5年。

8月19日，国土资源部发布，截至5月底，全国共上报房地产违法违规用地宗数3070宗，面积约18.84万亩。在各类房地产违法违规用地中，闲置土地成为房地产用地违法违规的主要问题。国土部表示，随着闲置土地成为房地产用地违法违规的主要问题，土地闲置"政府原因"比例大、查处难、结案率低等问题日益突出。从清理数据来看，因政府和客观原因造成闲置的约占六成以上。"政府原因"包括规划调整，土地出让时未做完拆迁，后期拆迁不力，土地出让后办理手续出现拖延等。下一步，国土部将督促各地加快查处进度，务必于10月底前基本完成查处任务，并研究探索建立解决房地产用地违法违规问题的长效机制。

8月21日，中共中央政治局常委、国务院副总理李克强在江苏省常州市主持召开加快保障性安居工程建设工作座谈会并讲话。李克强强调，实施保障性安居工程，要从各地实际出发，突出重点，分类指导。2010年全国要建设廉租住房、公共租赁住房、棚户区改造安置住房等580万套。

9月21日，国土部、住房和城乡建设部联合发出通知，力推保障房建设落实、严格土地出让管理，成为通知的亮点。通知明确，企业违约开发土地、因自身原因土地闲置一年的，都将禁止竞买资格。另外，通知要求，市、县国土和建设部门，要共同建立保障性住房、棚户区改造住房、公共租房、中小套型商品住房行政审批快速通道。

9月29日，为进一步贯彻落实《国务院关于坚决遏制部分城市房价过快上涨的通知》、巩固房地产调控成果、促进房地产市场健康发展，住房和城乡建设部、国土资源部、监察部发出通知，要求各地立即研究制定贯彻落实该文件的实施细则。房价过高、上涨过快、供应紧张的城市，要在一定时间内限定居民家庭购房套数。住房和城乡建设部、监察部等部门将对省级人民政府稳定房价和住房保障工作进行考核与问责。要依法查处经纪机构炒买炒卖、哄抬房价、怂恿客户签订"阴阳合同"等行为；对房地产开发企业土地闲置、改变土地用途和性质、拖延开竣工时间、捂盘惜售等违法违规行为，要继续加大曝光和处罚力度；对有上述违法违规记录的房地产开发企业，要暂停其新购置土地。

10月15日，温家宝总理在十七届五中全会发表《关于制定国民经济和社会发展第十二个五年规划建议的说明》。《说明》中提出，要完善符合国情的住房体制机制和政策体系。

住房问题涉及群众切身利益，必须形成合理的社会预期和有效的调控体系。要强化各级政府职责，加大保障性安居工程建设力度。合理引导住房需求，抑制投机需求。

10 月 21 日，住房和城乡建设部发布《关于印发〈物业承接查验办法〉的通知》。《办法》中要求，开发商与物业买受人签订的物业买卖合同，应当约定其所交付物业的共用部位、共用设施设备的配置和建设标准。建设单位应当在物业交付使用 15 日前，与选聘的物业服务企业完成物业共用部位、共用设施设备的承接查验工作。该《办法》自 2011 年 1 月 1 日起施行。

10 月 28 日，财政部、国家税务总局联合发布《关于支持公共租赁住房建设和运营有关税收优惠政策的通知》。《通知》指出，对公租房建设用地及公租房建成后占地免征城镇土地使用税；对公租房经营管理单位建造公租房涉及的印花税予以免征；对公租房经营管理单位购买住房作为公租房的，免征契税、印花税等数项税收优惠政策，力促公租房建设。

11 月 3 日，住房和城乡建设部、财政部、人民银行、银监会发布《关于规范住房公积金个人住房贷款政策有关问题的通知》。《通知》指出，一些缴存职工使用住房公积金个人贷款购买第二套及以上住房，并非完全用于自住，全部不符合《住房公积金管理条例》规定。同时，《通知》规定，使用住房公积金个人住房贷款购买首套普通自住房，套型建筑面积在 90 平方米及以下的，贷款首付款比例不得低于 20%；套型建筑面积在 90 平方米以上的，贷款首付款比例不得低于 30%。

11 月 12 日，中国银监会要求各信托公司应立即对房地产信托业务进行合规性风险自查，督促信托公司在开展房地产信托业务时审慎选择交易对手，加强信托资金运用监控，严控对大型房企集团多头授信、集团成员内部关联风险，积极防范房地产市场调整风险。

11 月 15 日，最高法院公布《〈中华人民共和国婚姻法〉若干问题解释（三）》征求意见稿。其中规定，夫妻一方婚前签订不动产买卖合同，以个人财产支付首付款并在银行贷款，婚后不动产登记于首付款支付方名下的，离婚时可将该不动产认定为个人财产，尚未归还的部分贷款为不动产权利人的个人债务。婚后由一方父母出资购买的不动产，产权登记在出资人子女名下的，可视为对自己子女一方的赠与，应认定该不动产为夫妻一方的个人财产。有配偶者与他人同居，为解除同居关系约定了财产性补偿，一方要求支付该补偿或支付补偿后反悔主张返还的，法院不予支持；但合法婚姻当事人以侵犯夫妻共同财产权为由起诉主张返还的，法院应受理并根据具体情况作出处理。

11 月 17 日，国家审计署公布 19 个省市 2007—2009 年政府投资保障性住房审计调查结果，显示 1.5 亿元廉租房保障金被挪用，2132 户不符合条件的家庭获得补贴或住房，6 个城市套取中央投资补助资金 6129 万元。

12 月 1 日，住房和城乡建设部出台《商品房屋租赁管理办法》，旨在加强商品房屋租赁管理，规范商品房屋租赁行为，维护租赁双方当事人合法权益。《商品房屋租赁管理办法》于 2011 年 2 月 1 日起施行，1995 年发布的《城市房屋租赁管理办法》同时废止。

12 月 3 日，住房和城乡建设部向各地发出《关于报送城镇保障性安居工程任务的通知》，明确提出，2011 年计划建设保障性安居工程任务是 1000 万套，并要求各地方政府调整之前上报的“2009—2012年保障性住房建设规划”和地方“十二五”保障性住房建设规划。新增的建设任务以公共租赁房为主。到2011年年底基本完成747万户城镇低收入家庭住房困难问题。

12月15日，国务院法制办公布《国有土地上房屋征收与补偿条例（第二次公开征求意见稿)》，再度就“新拆迁条例”立法征求公共意见。根据意见稿，行政强制拆迁将取消，需由政府申请法院强制执行。

12月16日，国土资源部以国家土地督察机构的名义约谈土地违法情况严重的12名地方政府行政“一把手”，就土地违法问题进行通报，同时要求被约谈地方政府积极整改。

12月23日，国家统计局表示，房地产价格统计改革取得阶段性进展，通过网络公开征求意见的《住宅销售价格统计调查方案》从2011年起实施。

12月27日，住房和城乡建设部发布通知，宣布调整住房公积金存贷款利率，从2010年12月26日起，开展住房公积金支持保障性住房建设项目贷款试点的城市，贷款利率按照五年期以上个人住房公积金贷款利率上浮10%执行。五年期以下（含五年）及五年期以上个人住房公积金贷款利率均上调0.25个百分点。

12月28日，国家土地督察机构在线土地督察系统全面开通，督察核心业务全部实现网上运行。在线督察借助实时动态监控平台，可逐步实现对土地全程监控监督；同时，优化了督察业务流程，压缩了自由裁量权，减少了督察过程人为因素的干扰，实现了“土地在网络上监管，权力在阳光下运行”。在线土地督察系统建立了对土地流向、流量和流速的监督。

（作者：张元端，中国房地产研究会名誉副会长）

# 2010中国城市土地利用

2010年是我国经济社会发展最为复杂的一年，经济增长速度在高增长态势下逐步走稳，投资保持较高增速，货币投放趋于平衡，工业生产呈较快增长势头，房地产市场运行高位反弹。在土地利用与管理方面，土地政策参与宏观调控的手段进一步多元化，通过科学安排用地计划，加大土地供应力度，改进用地审批制度，严格土地批后监管等各项措施，增强了国家重点项目和民生工程用地的保障能力。土地宏观调控在促进经济平稳较快发展，特别是促进经济结构调整和发展方式转变中发挥了积极作用，也促进了城市的健康发展。

## 一、2010年城市土地利用的基本情况

### 1. 科学安排用地计划，城市建设用地总量稳步增长，结构更为合理

为应对金融危机和自然灾害，在用地计划和安排上，扩增量、放流量、挤存量，加快用地审批，保障扩内需、保增长与灾后重建项目及时落地。2010年新增建设用地计划总量42.67万公顷。其中，农用地32.67万公顷，耕地22.67万公顷，均较2009年有所提升。

土地供应优先保障重点建设项目和保障性住房等民生项目。2010年全国土地供应总量42.8万公顷，同比增长34.2%，为近年来最高水平。36个重点城市土地供应总量同比增长22.4%，其中，供应同比增长的城市达27个。从供应结构看，工矿仓储用地、房地产用地分别占土地供应总量的35.7%、35.8%，房地产用地供应比例同比提高3.5个百分点，工矿仓储用地所占比重下降1.7个百分点。土地供应结构进一步优化。

同时，适应加快经济发展方式转变的要求，制定相关政策严禁向“两高一资”、产能过剩和重复建设项目供地，严格控制新上建设项目供地，优先保障战略性新兴产业和低碳经济产业的用地需求。

### 2. 全面落实调控政策，城市住宅用地供应量大幅上升，保障房用地应保尽保

为遏制房价过快上涨，2010年中央出台了一系列房地产调控政策，经济手段和行政手段并用，从抑制需求、增加供给、加强监管等多方面对房地产市场进行调控。国土资源部采取了加大土地供应、公开供地计划、调节土地供应结构、加大保障房用地供应等多项措施。

2010年全国房地产开发用地安排15.3万公顷，30个省、自治区、直辖市（不含西藏）住房实际供地12.5万公顷，比2009年间增加4.9万公顷，同比增长64.1%。其中，保障性住房用地2.47万公顷，同比增加124.5%。与前几年供地情况同口径相比，保障性住房、中小套型普通商品房和其他住房实际用地10.89万公顷，同比增长42.5%。

保障性住房用地优先供应，中央确定的580万套保障性住房用地应保尽保。2010年全国保障性住房用地2.47万公顷中，用于直接安排经济适用房和廉租房用地1.59万公顷，棚户区改造用地0.87万公顷，两类保障性住房用地供应量占住房用地总量的19.7%，创历史新高。中央确定的580万套保障性安居工程建设目标用地得到足额保障。

**3. 强化土地市场建设，土地资源资产特性进一步显化，城市地价稳步上升**

深入推进国有土地有偿使用制度改革，及时出台新修订的划拨用地目录；坚持和完善土地招牌挂制度，推动工业用地弹性出让和租赁制；推动土地供应由“价高者得”的单一目标向完善市场、保障民生等多目标管理转变。

2010年全国各地共出让土地29.2万公顷，比上年同期增长32%；出让总价款2.71万亿元，同比增长57.8%。其中，招拍挂出让土地面积25.7万公顷，同比增长37.4%，招拍挂出让土地面积占出让总面积的比例达88.3%；招拍挂出让价款2.6万亿元，同比增长59.7%，招拍挂出让价款占出让总价款的比例达到96.0%。土地资源市场化配置程度持续稳步提高，土地资产特性进一步显化。

房地产市场快速升温引致土地价格稳步攀升。在经历了力度最大、手段最多、持续时间最长的调控政策后，2010年年末房地产市场重新火暴。中国城市地价动态监测系统数据显示，综合地价第一季度涨幅较2009年第四季度有所趋缓，但仍保持较高的涨幅；二季度调整回落，涨幅较一季度趋缓；三季度出现反弹，环比增速较上一季度有所回升；政府再次密集出台了第二轮调控政策，但四季度综合地价环比增幅加速回升。全国地价总体水平呈上升态势，综合、商业、居住和工业地价环比增幅均为本年度最高。

到2010年年底，全国主要城市综合地价平均值为2882元/平方米，比上年增长了229元/平方米，同比增幅8.62%。其中，商业用地地价最高，为5185元/平方米，比上年增长了473元/平方米，同比增幅10.03%；其次为居住用地，4245元/平方米，比上年提高了421元/平方米，同比增幅11.02%；工业用地地价最低，为629元/平方米，比上年提高了32元/平方米，同比增幅5.29%。

**4. 加强融资平台监管，适度控制土地抵押贷款增幅，抵押贷款率趋于稳定**

落实国家房地产市场调控政策，加强地方融资平台管理，适当控制土地抵押的杠杆率，强化房企土地开发利用对上市融资的影响，进一步弱化了土地资本化的风险。一是土地抵押面积和贷款总量持续增长。2010年，全国84个重点城市抵押面积净增374平方公里，抵押贷款净增9206亿元，比年初的土地抵押面积（2208平方公里）、土地抵押贷款金额（2.6万亿元），分别增加了16.9%和35.3%。二是储备用地抵押贷款增长较快。2010年储备用地抵押贷款占比由年初的14%上升到年末的16%。截至2010年年底，储备用地抵押贷款量较大的城市是：北京2469亿元、重庆916亿元，上海680亿元。三是土地抵押贷款率稳定在50%左右。2010年新增抵押贷款率为50.9%，略高于2009年的50.3%。

## 二、面临的形势和问题

当前，城市土地利用与管理存在的主要问题有：

**1. 城市经济发展过度依赖土地出让收入，土地利用潜在风险进一步加大**

近十年来，各地通过土地出让筹集资金，极大地加快了城市化建设的进程，但由此引发的资源、社会问题和矛盾也日益显化，并有进一步加剧的趋势。1993年分税制改革之后，土地出让收入全部纳入地方预算，近年来，各地土地出让收入占地方一般预算收入的比重逐年提升，部分地方甚至超过了60%。

基于土地出让带来的巨大收益，多数地方都热衷于利用土地创造财政收入、进行融资以推动城市发展，再通过城市发展不断扩大土地经营，形成了“土地—财政—金融”发展模式。征地卖地冲动不断增强，对土地管理秩序产生巨大冲击。2010年，84个重点城市土地抵押贷款总额达3.52万亿元，同比增长35.3%，超过了同期固定资产投资规模的增速。这些融资在相当程度上建立在对未来土地收益增长的预期上，一旦土地市场出现波动，可能引发严重金融风险。这种吃饭靠财政、建设靠“卖地”的局面，在我国现实人多地少的基本国情下很难持续。

政府在土地配置中的多重身份助长了城市建设对土地财政的过度依赖。经济发展方式转变背景下的市场经济要求政府制定合理规则，通过法律、经济手段建立和维护公平统一、兼顾效益的市场秩序。而当前政府兼有管理主体、产权主体和受益主体的多重身份，其经营职能与管理职能目标相悖，效益与公平很难兼顾。国有土地一级市场政府垄断，农转用中征收范围大、补偿标准低，计划经济拿地，市场经济卖地，巨大利差引致了地方政府扩张用地的内在冲动，土地资源节约集约利用受到极大冲击，也进一步触发了中央保护耕地与地方谋求发展用地、政府以地生财与农民权益受损等诸多资源、社会矛盾问题。

**2. 城市土地闲置、低效利用问题仍较突出，节约集约用地机制还有待健全**

党的十七届五中全会提出了节约优先的战略，明确要把建设资源节约型、环境友好型社会作为加快转变经济发展方式的重要着力点，国务院和部已密集出台了资源保护和节约集约利用政策文件。但当前，资源保护和节约集约利用的激励机制仍未健全，土地资源粗放浪费现象依然较多，城市土地闲置、低效利用等问题仍较普遍，其中以房地产项目和违规新设、扩大的开发（园）区内工业项目用地闲置现象最为集中。

闲置土地的原因复杂，处置的任务艰巨。原因主要有：一是由政府及其部门因素造成闲置。如未能及时拆迁腾地、城市规划调整、政府未“净地”出让、土地前期开发未达到出让合同约定条件等政府原因造成的闲置。二是国土部门与规划、建设、财政、金融等部门在土地用途、规划前置和供后监管几个方面缺乏工作衔接。如国土的土地用途分类与规划部门的用途分类标准不一致，与建设部门在项目竣工核验方面衔接不够，没有充分利用财税政策和金融政策遏制土地闲置浪费等。三是因企业存在债务纠纷，导致法院暂时无法处置；同时，农村集体建设用地粗放利用。部分地区农村居民点布局分散，住房建新不拆旧，存在空心村、宅基地利用效率不高及资源浪费等现象，违法占地、少批多占和“一户多宅”的现象尚未得到完全控制。

节约集约用地的相关政策机制还不完善。一是各地有关节约集约用地的地方性规章相对滞后。目前已出台节约集约用地政策（包括责任机制和考核机制），大多数是市县级政府或国土资源部门制发的文件，法律效力有限。二是对闲置土地的认定、处置、土地使用权的收回均无具体的可操作办法，实施起来阻力大，导致闲置土地真正完全按法律法规规定依法处理到位的不多。

**3. 房地产市场土地供应调控形势复杂，压力增大，计划完成情况差异较大**

2010年，国家对房地产市场调控政策密集出台，市场对调控政策反复博弈，多因素作用下房地产市场健康运行面临复杂局面，各地加大了土地市场供应量，优化供地结构，确保保障性住房、棚户改造和自住性中小套型商品房建房用地不低于住房建设用地供应总量的70%。但是在一些城市，第四季度地住宅地价增长幅度较第三季度有所提高，土地市场再次活跃，土地价格仍居高不下，甚至再现“地王”，地价隐现上涨苗头。

究其原因，一方面是开发商对宏观经济形势尚未有充分的认识，对楼市还有看涨的预期。虽然部分开发商受到调控影响，资金开始趋紧，但仍有相当数量的房企现金充裕，有较为强烈的购地需求，仍在大规模进行抢地；同时，通胀预期愈演愈烈，资本在土地上避险、资金保值增值的心态也促使开发商有拿地的冲动。另一方面，不少地方政府没有完成2010年的土地出让任务，为冲刺年度土地出让目标而开闸放地，使得供需两旺。目前，房地产市场的复杂形势考验了地方政府的调控能力，需增强对房地产市场的敏锐性，把握好供地节奏和时序。

从全国住房用地供应计划执行情况来看，2010年全国30个省、自治区、直辖市（不含西藏）住房供地计划完成率为67.9%，房地产市场实际土地供应与计划相比有较大差距，总体存在落实不平衡的问题。原因主要有：一是2010年是住房用地供应计划编制的第一年，各地前期调研和论证不够充分，预测不够准确。二是住房供地计划、住房建设计划之间的衔接不够。从全年情况看，住房供地计划编制公布在前，保障性住房建设计划和棚户区改造计划编制在后，虽然有一定的衔接，但由于保障房目标尚未确定，计划下达较晚，使得供地计划规模偏大。三是一些地区出于争取补助资金和年度新增建设用地计划指标的考虑，住房建设规模和用地规模偏大。四是部分地区地方财政困难，融资渠道有限，资金落实不了，建设项目难以推进。五是少数项目用地仍实行毛地出让，在房价上涨带动拆迁成本上升的背景下，阵地拆迁进展缓慢，造成已批准的土地不能及时转变成有效供给，影响了计划的实施。

## 三、对策和建议

随着刺激性政策的逐步退出、房地产新政的出台、地方投融资平台的清理、结构性调整力度的加强等政策的实施，下一阶段宏观经济发展的不确定性在增加。而宏观调控政策预期趋紧、流动性释放的渐进性和通胀压力，增大了城市土地市场运行的复杂性。为此，从保障城市土地利用角度出发，建议：

### 1. 科学编制土地供应计划，全力服务经济结构调整和发展方式转变

科学编制土地供应计划，保障经济发展对建设用地的合理需求。一是继续实行有保有控的土地政策，做到保、促、控有机结合。确保国家重大基础建设用地、保障性住房用地、城镇化发展就业和民生用地、战略性新兴产业和低碳经济产业用地。提出土地政策促进产业结构优化升级的措施，制定支持中小企业发展的用地政策。对用地集约的国家鼓励类外商投资项目优先供应土地。落实好限制、禁止供地项目用地政策。严格执行《限制用地项目目录(2010 年本)》和《禁止用地项目目录（2010 年本)》。二是加强房地产市场土地供应调控，加强与财政、金融、证监等部门联动，防范系统性风险。加大房地产建设用地指标安排量，特别是增加保障性住房和普通商品房用地计划指标，加大中小户型、中低价位普通商品房用地供应。完善国有土地招拍挂出让制度，大力推进房地产用地出让预申请制度。三是建立健全预警在先、关口在前、协同应对，以经济手段为核心的土地宏观调控体系，逐步形成信息整合全、分析判断准、政策引导稳、相机决策快、调整力度慎的调控机制。

加强国土资源节约集约利用，促进国土资源利用方式根本转变。一是继续发挥规划的管控和引导作用，优化资源利用结构和布局，制定促进产业转型升级项目供地目录，以资源利用结构调整推动需求结构、产业结构、要素投入结构的全方位调整。二是大力推广和实施资源节约集约模式，突出节约优先，运用土地政策积极推动经济结构调整。三是适当提高工业用地供应门槛，加强用地强度、投资强度审核，建立新增建设用地计划动态管理考核机制。四是严格差别供地政策，有效引导投资方向，推进产业结构调整和区域合理布局，对战略性和高新技术产业用地提供优惠政策保证优先用地，不向“两高一资”、产能过剩和重复建设项目供地。同时，加大存量挖潜，提高建设用地节约集约利用水平。

### 2. 加大房地产土地供应动态监测力度，确保房地产用地调控政策落实到位

进一步加强土地市场动态监测监管，增强审核功能，及时制止地方违规出让行为，以及全程监管高价地，防违约、防欠款、防闲置。一是加大建设用地批后监管力度。在土地“招拍挂”之后，更应通过防止囤地、明确开工竣工时间、禁止捂盘惜售等市场整顿方法，来调控高价地最终转嫁给消费者的行为。二是加强地价动态监管，加大信息披露力度。适应不动产税制改革需要，借鉴日本、韩国等国家公示地价的经验，进一步加强城市地价动态监测，健全中央和地方分级维护、同质可比的地价监测样点网络，适时发布全国和区域性分用

途的地价指数等权威信息，正确引导公众。三是密切关注形势变化，加大研究分析和政策储备力度。重点对土地供应、项目用地开发利用等情况进行动态监测。特别要加强对房地产企业土地取得、开发、使用的监管，及时向社会发布相关信息，引导居民消费。

进一步明确房地产调控目标，落实调控政策。一是研究制定出台保障性住房供地扶持和规范制度，加强保障性住房用地供后监管，确保保障性住房用地供应计划落实到位。二是确保保障性住房建设用地供应，加大公租房和中小套型普通商品住房用地，制订合理的用地计划，使保障性住房享有用地的“优先权”。三是针对近期出现的高地价情况，要采取有力的土地政策，在合理的土地转让价格基础上，增加土地供应，并在土地供应环节加强监管。

**3. 稳步推进国土资源有偿使用制度改革，推动完善收益分配制度**

全面深化有偿使用制度改革，构建促进和保障科学发展的新机制，促进经济又好又快发展。

一是推动完善土地收益分配制度。规范国有土地使用权出让收支管理，确保土地增值收益主要用于农业、农村和农民；建立国有土地收益基金，遏制片面追求土地收益的短期行为；改革土地出让批租制，探索年租制；建立耕地保护补偿机制，从根本上调动耕地保护的积极性。

二是进一步显化土地市场主体。处理好政府与市场的关系，强化政府的土地管理的公共服务职能，弱化政府的土地经营职能，增强市场主体在土地资源配置中的动力和活力。逐步实现从政府主导的土地资源配置方式向以产权为基础的市场配置方式转变，规范集体土地入市，加快建立城乡统一的土地市场，完善市场规则、丰富资源配置手段，坚持和完善招拍挂制度，提高土地市场运行的规范性。

三是深化土地有偿使用制度改革。更好地发挥市场在土地资源配置中的基础性作用，建立完善反映市场供求状况、资源稀缺程度和环境损害成本的资源价格形成机制，推进国家机关办公和交通、能源、水利等基础设施（产业）、城市基础设施以及各类社会事业用地的有偿使用。加快土地税费制度改革，提高土地保有成本，探索将土地闲置费改为土地闲置税，促进土地节约集约利用。

（作者：田彦军，中国土地勘测规划院地价所主任工程师，研究员；郑伟元，国土资源部耕地保护司研究员）

# 2010中国城市交通进展

2010年是我国城市交通面临严峻考验和深刻变革的一年。随着我国城镇化进程和社会经济快速发展，机动车发展速度加快、城市交通问题日益凸显，已经成为城市政府和市民关注的热点社会问题。科学配置交通资源、落实优先发展公共交通的战略、构建支撑城市可持续发展的综合交通体系、推进新技术在城市交通领域中的应用等成为城市交通发展面临的十分紧迫的问题，也是缓解交通拥堵的重要对策。

## 一、城市交通问题成为社会焦点和国家领导关注的民生问题

### 1. 大城市交通拥堵问题日益严重

随着经济的发展，汽车逐步走入了寻常百姓家。然而，当人们在享受汽车文明的同时，饱受交通拥堵的困扰也与日俱增。尤其是2010年9月17日，一场小雨即引发了北京交通大堵车，全市143条路段拥堵，整个市区的交通近乎瘫痪。9月20日，温总理作出重要批示："17日的交通大拥堵是多方面原因造成的，但也反映了汽车增长过快、城市交通承载过大等问题。必须进一步完善城市规划，采取综合措施应对和解决可能越演越烈的堵车问题。"

有很多像北京这样的城市，整个路网已经脆弱到了有一点外因就可能导致较大范围的拥堵。从9月底到10月初，北京、上海、广州、重庆等一线城市，还有济南、南京、武汉、成都等二线城市，甚至一些三线城市，都相继出现了严重的交通拥堵以及停车难的情况。此外，严重的交通拥堵在我国部分高速公路干线上也时有发生，如京藏高速进京段2010年6月连续堵半个月，8月份堵了9天，司机与旅客苦不堪言。据统计，在大城市中，北京市主干道高峰时间道路饱和度接近1.0，上海、南京、成都、广州分别达到了0.95、0.82、0.8和0.72。北京、广州、上海、深圳、天津、南京、成都和济南的居民上班单程平均耗时分别为52分钟、48分钟、47分钟、46分钟、40分钟、37分钟、31分钟和29分钟。全国主要城市交通正面临着整体性的交通拥堵问题。

当前，我国的城市正处于快速城市化发展期，机动化水平快速提高，城市交通供需矛盾也处于最严重时期，以北京为代表的我国大城市交通拥堵正在呈现拥堵程度加剧化、拥堵范围扩大化、拥堵时间延长化等特征。交通拥堵已经由交通问题上升为从普通老百姓至国家领

导人普遍关心的社会民生问题，各城市政府也将治理交通拥堵问题作为“十二五”期间最核心的工作之一。

**2. 城市“停车难”问题日益突出**

“停车难”是困扰城市交通的又一大难题。由于停车设施总量严重不足、配置不合理、利用效率低和停车管理不到位，导致了城市停车供需矛盾日益突出，如今城市街头、商业区、医院、中小学校、住宅小区等，占道停车、乱停乱放已经成为普遍现象，停车位数量和汽车保有量形成了巨大反差和缺口。“停车难”的影响不仅仅局限于停车本身，还引发了一系列城市管理问题，如加剧道路拥堵、引发公共纠纷、带来安全隐患、导致交通事故等。

停车难，也是世界上许多国家共同面临的问题，各国采取了各种办法。但中国由于人口在城市快速积聚与城市土地资源越来越匮乏的国情，必须从实情出发，必须把停车设施建设与加强管理，作为交通需求调节的有效手段来统筹解决。

**3. 小汽车发展进入快速增长阶段**

近十年，我国的汽车产量由原来的200万辆发展到了2010年的1400多万辆，城镇居民的可支配收入由原来的平均6000元增长到现在的1.6万元。在汽车供应能力大大增强、居民购买力提高和相关鼓励政策的作用下，全国民用汽车拥有量年均增长16.34%，其中私人汽车拥有量年均增长24.7%。根据公安部交管局10月份发布的数据，我国机动车保有量达到了1.99亿辆，其中汽车保有量超过了8500万辆，成为继美国之后的全球汽车保有量第二大国。北京民用汽车拥有量年均增长15%左右，其中私家车拥有量年均增长22%。截至2010年12月底，北京机动车保有量超过480万辆，私人小汽车超过370万辆，机动车全年增加91万辆。目前，全国机动车保有量超过100万辆的城市已经达到20多个，且增长速度还在加快。小汽车出行比例逐年增加，大量的城市土地资源和道路被小汽车占用。2009年，北京市小汽车出行占34%。

**4. 公交优先战略进入攻坚阶段**

早在2004年，国家就已经明确了公共交通在城市交通中的优先地位，国家政策的确立为城市公交的发展提供了良好的条件。为了更好地满足大众市民出行需要，一些城市加快实施轨道交通建设及加密轨道线网，也越来越注重发挥常规公交的衔接优势。

城市轨道交通进入大建设期。2010年12月30日，北京市同时开通长达108公里的5条地铁线路（房山线、昌平线一期、15号线一期、亦庄线和大兴线），运营及在建线路达到14条，运营里程达到336公里，这5条线都是中心城区的外围线，为调整北京城市结构、降低城区人口密度打下重要基础。到2015年，北京再新增10条线路，地铁规划里程将达580公里。到2020年，北京轨道交通线路预计将达到1000公里。未来五年，广州也将规划新建地铁线路9条，武汉计划每年将开通一条轨道交通，天津地铁2、3、9号线也正在加紧建设中，投入运营后将与已开通的1号线形成贯通南北、勾连东西的骨干网基础结构，与即将建设的地铁5、6号线一道，基本形成城市轨道交通体系。

完善快速公交和常规公交建设。广州市将在现有128.5公里公交专用道的基础上，加大对中心城区早晚高峰公交专用道的施划力度，到2013年施划公交专用道214公里，总里程超过300公里，实现公交车辆早晚高峰较快通行，对已设置公交专用道、公交线路密集、客流量较大且交叉口有条件的主干道进行公交优先信号配置。济南市到2015年，城市公共交通客运量占总出行比重将达到28%以上，万人拥有公交车达到18标台以上，公交专用道总长度达到180公里，快速公交网络力争达到100公里。

从中央到地方对公共交通的发展十分重视，各地也加快了包括城市轨道、快速公交以及常规地面公交的建设，出现了令人可喜的变化。但是，也应清醒地看到，公共交通的整体服务水平依然不高，尚没有成为居民机动化出行的首选或者主体。目前，我国36个大城市的公交出行分担率刚刚达到20%，由于公共交通在速度、灵活性和舒适度等方面与小汽车的差距，所以建立与小汽车具有较强竞争力的公共交通服务体系的任务十分艰巨，需要付出持久和全方位的努力。如何在城镇化快速发展过程中实现两个结构性转变，即以公共交通引导的城市布局结构和以公共交通为主体的机动化交通出行结构的转变，都是城市规划和交通规划面临的重大课题。

**5. 交通需求管理开始受到关注**

传统的改善交通拥堵手段，如拓宽道路、修建快速路、立交桥等增加设施的方式过于简单，而以牺牲步行、自行车空间为代价来提高小汽车通行能力的做法也受到了越来越多的质疑。从短期看，我国城市结构性交通拥堵仍将持续较长时间，甚至还会有进一步加剧的可能，严重的城市交通形势呼唤着缓解拥堵措施尽早出台。

交通拥堵既是发达国家大城市普遍遇到过的难题，也是发展中国家大城市发展中面对的问题。纽约、伦敦、巴黎、东京、首尔等发达城市分别在20世纪40、60、70和90年代发生了较为严重的交通拥堵。目前，这些城市已经处于城市化的成熟期，机动车保有量基本实现零增长，城市交通总体趋于稳定，交通拥堵状况有所缓解。

我国大城市采取以调节需求为目标的交通需求管理措施成为缓解交通拥堵的重要对策。北京市在2008年奥运会期间实施单双号管理的措施，2009年实施每周少开一天车的措施，同时还将北京站、北京西站、王府井、前门、西单商业街、中关村、CBD、金融街等13个重点地区的临时占道停车收费标准由原来的每半小时2.5元提高到了5元。2010年年初又出台了错时上下班等十余项交通管理措施。2010年12月北京市人民政府先后出台了《关于进一步推进首都交通科学发展，加大力度缓解交通拥堵工作的意见》、《北京市小客车数量调控暂行规定》、《北京市小客车数量调控暂行规定实施细则》、《北京市非居住区停车价格调整方案》、《关于对非本市进京载客汽车采取交通管理措施的通告》等一系列严厉的治理交通拥堵政策措施，引起了全社会的广泛关注。措施主要包括完善交通规划，疏解中心城功能和人口；加快道路交通基础设施建设；加大优先发展公共交通力度；改善自行车步行交通系统和驻车换乘条件；进一步加强机动车管理；提高交通管理和运输服务水平等六个方面28

项政策。

2010年上海世博会通过差别化停车收费、封存公车、扩大摩托车限行等措施保障城市交通畅通。广州亚运会期间也实施了单双号限行、公车定额停驶等交通需求管理措施，并取得了一定成效。天津、深圳、哈尔滨、沈阳、南昌、济南、郑州等众多城市也在积极研究实施交通需求管理的应对政策。

## 二、高铁建设向城际铁路倾斜，城市交通在区域统筹中地位提高

### 1. 区域性交通建设快速推进

随着京津、武广以及2010年郑西、沪宁、沪杭等高速铁路的相继开通运行，启动了一个高速化发展的铁路新时代。高速铁路营业里程已经达到7531公里，从而令城市与城市之间，开始进入了“分分钟”的时代。2010年12月7至9日，第七届世界高速铁路大会在北京召开，这是自1992年国际铁路联盟（UIC）发起该会议以来，首次在欧洲以外的国家举行。中国已成为世界上高速铁路发展最快、系统技术最全、集成能力最强、运营里程最长、运营速度最高、在建规模最大的国家。

高速铁路的建成改变了人们的时空观念，带动沿线城市及区域间的经济联系，促进产业结构的优化，加快了工商、旅游、物流和交通的发展。城镇之间的联系已经进入区域同城化的时代。2009年年底开通的武广高铁，即催生了沿线的投资热潮。根据《人民日报》相关报道，2010年第一季度，武汉、咸宁两市GDP同比增长均为15.9%，其中旅游业收入分别增长36.5%、166.7%，房地产开发投资分别增长72.7%、44.9%，城镇以上固定资产投资分别增长36.5%、58.8%，实际外商直接投资分别增长21.4%、25.7%，社会消费零售总额分别增长17.8%、21.8%。

### 2. 高铁建设向城际铁路倾斜

2010年9月20日，我国中部地区第一条城际高铁——昌九城际铁路正式开通运营，首次开通南昌至九江、南昌至武汉间250公里动车组，实现江西南昌与湖北武汉两个中部省份省会城市的高速通达。10月26日，沪杭城际高铁正式通车营运，运行最高时速达到416.6公里，刷新世界铁路运营试验的最高时速，沪杭高铁的运营严格按照列车时刻表执行，从早上6:12到晚上9:00，每天开行50对高铁动车，沪杭高铁上海虹桥站也同步正式启用，与沪宁高铁、虹桥机场第二航站楼等实现零换乘。12月30日，我国东北地区第一条高速城际铁路长吉城际铁路正式开通，铁路西起长春站，东至吉林站，全长111公里，设计时速250公里。12月31日，广珠城际铁路开始试运行，列车最高时速达到250公里，从广州市到珠海市仅需40分钟左右。

2011年年初，沪宁高铁、沪杭高铁、福厦高铁、海南东环高铁、昌九城际、广珠城际、长吉城际、成灌铁路和太中银、包西、宜万铁路也将首次投入春运，让广大旅客享受到铁路

现代化建设的成果。此外，宁安（南京—安庆）、长株潭（长沙—株洲—湘潭）、渝万（渝北—万州）、武咸（武汉—咸宁）、武黄（武汉—黄石）城际、青烟荣威（青岛—烟台—荣成—威海）等城际铁路建设正处于建设施工高潮。2011 年，京沪、哈大（哈尔滨—大连）、京石（北京—石家庄）等高铁有望建成通车。

江苏计划到“十二五”期末，所有地级市间都要贯通时速 200 公里以上的高速铁路。广西计划“十二五”期将形成以南宁为中心的“一二三小时”城际高速铁路网，基本建成布局合理、结构清晰、功能完善、衔接顺畅的现代化快速铁路运输网络，全面进入高铁时代。

#### 3. 城市交通在区域统筹中地位提高

随着城市发展空间的拓展和交通时距的延长，城市交通区域化、区域交通城镇化的趋势越来越明显，城市交通的范围不再局限于城市内部，城市交通的目标也不再仅仅是关注城区内交通资源的最优配置，需要扩展至区域范围。区域交通在构成与总量上以城市节点为主的交通模式也越来越显现，城市交通与区域交通开始打破部门藩篱，逐步走向一体化规划。

区域性的交通设施，如国家铁路、城际铁路、航空、高速公路等在城镇的集聚是其发挥作用与效益的重大保障。城市综合交通必须协调、统筹与服务于区域交通设施的合理布局。城市综合交通规划的研究范围、内容、方法等方面也都将发生新的改变。当前，有关高铁车站选址与城市布局的关系、高铁与支线航空竞争关系的争论以及各种交通方式在通道和站点的选择上，都需要站在城镇化总体发展的基础上进行综合协调和统筹优化。因此，伴随城镇化发展以及国家高速铁路等区域性交通设施建设的快速推进，城市交通的区域统筹作用越来越明显。

### 三、探索实践以节能减排为目标的绿色交通受到重视

节能减排是我国对国际社会的庄严承诺，也是国内转变发展模式的客观需要，城市交通应在节能减排方面作出重要贡献。

#### 1. 实践绿色交通活动

以提倡公交、步行、自行车等交通方式为核心的绿色交通实践活动在社会上引起了很大反响。由住房和城乡建设部倡导的无车日活动已经进入了第四年，活动主题分别是——绿色交通与健康、人性化街道、健康环保的自行车与步行交通、绿色交通与低碳生活，参加城市已经扩大到了 129 个。2010 年 7 月，重庆、杭州、济南、昆明、昆山、常熟 6 个城市经住房和城乡建设部审查，成为全国第一批自行车与步行交通系统示范项目建设城市，以构建“安全、公平、便捷、连续、舒适、低碳”的慢行出行环境为目标，建设特色地区慢行交通系统。2009 年，科技部和财政部共同启动了十城千辆的电动汽车示范工程，计划每年发展十个城市，在公交、出租车等领域推出 1000 辆新能源汽车。城市绿色交通的实践反映了人

们对健康机动化的向往，但要得到全社会总体的认同与实践，仍然任重而道远。

### 2. 探索绿色出行的交通规划方法

2010年2月，住房和城乡建设部颁发了《城市综合交通体系规划编制办法》、《城市综合交通体系规划编制导则》，规范了城市综合交通体系规划的编制和实施，统筹考虑与优化配置各种交通资源，提高道路网整体通行能力；强调将步行与自行车系统列为城市综合交通的组成部分，在道路断面、通行空间的配置上，必须考虑给行人、自行车留下空间，必须改变一切都给机动车让路的做法，建立以公共交通为主的绿色交通系统。在规划中，应确立步行与自行车系统网络布局框架及规划指标，同时需合理设置自行车、步行等与公共交通的衔接换乘，发挥绿色交通的整体效益。2010年11月，北京市发布了《北京城区行人和非机动车交通系统设计导则》，其主要内容包括：行人和非机动车交通系统中的人行设施设计通行能力与服务水平、过街设施、无障碍环境设施的设计、照明的设计等。这为指导本市行人和非机动车交通系统的规划设计及管理提供了依据，为创造良好的交通环境，构建和谐交通，鼓励绿色出行，提供了技术保障。

在城市交通规划中积极探索绿色出行的规划方法，在中新生态城、曹妃甸生态城的规划之后，2010年又启动了广州知识城，对绿色交通模式作了进一步探索，规划“绿线”、“黄线”、“红线”三级自行车网络，即慢行专用道路、休闲健身道路与沿路自行车道三类，为建设宁静、和谐的城市新区作出了贡献。

## 四、城市交通与土地利用、城市功能的互为关系成为关注重点

由于大城市土地利用和房价推高的影响，一些城市形成了工作单位集中在中心区域，而居住地主要集中在外围区域的格局，从而出现了明显的潮汐式交通特点。以北京市为例，受西郊、北郊、南郊等大型居住区的影响，双向交通流之比达1:3，甚至在局部地段达1:6。据北京市统计，早高峰期间，进城机动车是出城机动车的1.4倍，晚高峰期间，出城机动车是进城机动车的1.85倍。

### 1. 城市土地利用影响交通流分布

城市规划和空间布局不合理，交通流分布不均衡，是引发城市交通问题的重要原因之一。以北京市为例，《北京城市总体规划（2004—2020年）》提出在北京市域范围内，构建“两轴—两带—多中心”的城市空间结构，试图对单中心格局进行调整。但六年来的现实情况是：望京、亦庄、天通苑、回龙观等边缘组团迅速膨胀，而宜建的独立“新城”迟迟见效甚慢，使中心城区的“大饼”越摊越大。这些拥有数十万人口的超大型居住区功能单一，缺乏企业和商业中心落户，缺乏就业机会。这种同心圆式的土地利用模式，只会使城市中心区的交通流量越来越大，而交通资源的调整已很困难，交通拥堵状况越来越严重。2010年，北京市区交通拥堵指数从奥运会后的5.1升至6.7，已属于中度拥堵等级。英国伦敦在二战

结束后通过实施大伦敦规划，将市区的就业功能向外围新城疏散，成功地带动了人口疏散，推动了区域的平衡发展，从根本上缓解了市区的交通拥堵和环境污染。所以，城市的土地利用必须与交通条件与承载力相匹配，必须与交通规划相衔接，而现在土地利用与交通规划两张皮的做法，土地利用无视交通规划、无视交通设施能力的做法，只能使交通问题更为严峻。

### 2. 城市功能不平衡影响交通出行

城市发展不平衡也是带来城市交通问题突出的客观问题之一。以北京为例，南城北城除了经济发展、教育资源、居民收入存在较大差距之外，南城的交通基础设施发展也严重滞后于北城。而随着南城一些大型居住区的增加、大型交通枢纽（北京南站、六里桥交通枢纽）的运营使用，道路交通压力剧增，但是路网系统等基础设施建设远远跟不上交通量增加的步伐，道路密度、道路等级、轨道交通网络密度等均明显低于北城，导致原本交通运行情况较好的南城也出现严重恶化。

城市功能与规模的发展，直接影响交通需求的形态与供给的方式。调整完善城市规划，进一步协调交通结构、交通方式与产业布局、居住配置的关系，建立科学的交通影响分析机制，是城市规划与交通规划的关键切入点。交通系统与城市空间、土地利用的协调发展，交通系统引导土地利用的模式应是城市规划的首要任务。

## 五、新技术应用逐步加快，大型活动交通组织经验已经成熟

### 1. 新技术在交通领域的应用逐步加快

我国以智能交通系统为代表的新技术在城市交通中的应用已有十多年的历史，从“十五”期间的智能交通科技攻关计划的实施，到“十一五”期间863计划等，科技为智能交通系统发展起到了良好的引领和支撑作用。如驾驶员安全辅助、安全预防、安全管理等防护技术；交通信息采集、处理和发布技术；定位技术、车辆自动识别技术和移动通信技术。基于信息共享实现多种运输方式的共享机制与平台成为智能交通技术发展的热点，同时也为解决城市综合交通问题提供了智力保障。

为大型国际活动提供服务的智能化交通管理系统达到了国际水平，在中国举办的奥运会、世博会和亚运会，为中国开发和应用智能交通提供了极好的机会。北京、上海、广州均围绕大型国际活动的交通管理和服务开发和集成应用各种为交通管理和出行服务的智能化技术，建成了大规模的智能交通管理系统和交通信息服务系统。

2009年温家宝总理参观无锡物联网产业基地，提出“感知中国理念”后，物联网这一名词迅速广为人知，形成了一种热潮。物联网、云计算、智慧地球等新理念、新技术在交通领域逐渐得到了应用。2010年年底，由交通信息采集、交通信号控制、非现场执法、数字视频监控、指挥分中心、交通诱导发布六大系统组成的无锡市惠山智能交通示范工程就充分

体现了物联网核心技术的应用。

随着城市交通需求的不断提高和技术的进步，交通新技术的核心理念、关键技术和主要内容也在不断完善和丰富。目前，我国已有568个城市建成了集接处警、信息采集、交通控制于一体的交通指挥中心，390个城市主干道实现了交通信号智能控制。适应城市发展需求，结合城市交通管理要求和交通的具体特点，充分运用新技术手段，构建具有中国特色的新一代智能交通系统已具备基础条件并成为可能。

### 2. 大型活动交通组织的经验已经成熟

继2008年北京奥运会交通组织的探索之后，2010年上海世博会、广州亚运会等重大国际活动相继拉开帷幕，为大型活动的交通组织积累了丰富的经验。北京、广州举办的奥运会和亚运会，主要特征是短期性的大型体育赛事，交通需求较明确（可通过运动员、官员、裁判、售票观众等推算），交通出行保障的时效性要求高，主要场馆安排在城市中心区外围，对城市日常交通的影响相对有限。因此，北京采取了单双号限行等一系列机动车禁限令，广州在亚运会期间全市范围内禁行黄标车，所有持有绿色环保标志的机动车也将按单双号限行等强制性的交通管理措施。为期半年的上海世博会累计吸引超过7000万游客，展览时间长，交通需求不明确（每日的游客规模无法预测，且不均衡性很大），会场选址在市中心区域，博览会交通与日常交通的叠加影响较大。因此，上海主要采取多元化集约交通方式，引导性的交通需求管理政策，兼顾大型活动和社会日常交通需要。虽然各个城市在具体的交通组织与管理模式上不完全相同，但是城市对于大型活动的组织思路基本是一致的，均是通过鼓励公交优先消化大型活动产生的交通需求，尽量控制个体机动交通方式的使用。这一经验也可以指导未来中国城市的日常交通管理与发展。

2010年8月北京奥运会开幕两周年之际，《北京奥运交通丛书》正式出版，丛书共分8册，从需求、规划、建设、运行、政策、科技、应急管理等各个方面，贯穿申办、筹办、举办全过程，对北京奥运交通进行了较为全面的论述。该丛书也是奥运史上第一部对奥运交通进行全面系统呈现、总结的书籍。

## 六、交通安全问题依然严峻，文明交通理念渐入人心

### 1. 交通安全问题依然严峻

2010年5月3日，公安部挂牌成立了道路交通安全研究中心，标志着道路交通安全越来越多地受到了政府的重视。2010年7月，山东省政府下发通知，专门就进一步加强全省道路交通安全工作作出安排部署，并对道路设施建设健全做了详细的规定：要求新建、改建、扩建道路时，交通信号灯、交通标志、交通标线及其他交通安全设施必须一应俱全；对于双向六车道以上城市道路，全面设置中间物理隔离设施。2010年11月5日，中国关心下一代工作委员会在北京人民大会堂正式启动了“全国中小学生交通安全教育”活动。据不

完全统计：交通事故和溺水造成的学生死亡人数超过了全年事故死亡总人数的60%，而且交通事故伤亡的数量呈逐年上升趋势，全国每年约有2万多名中小学生因交通事故伤残、死亡。全国中小学生交通安全教育活动以最大限度减少交通意外对中小学生健康成长造成的伤害，减轻家庭和社会的经济负担为原则，将保险、急救、医疗机构三方共同引入到中小学生交通事故救治方案中，建立了“绿色救助通道”。

### 2. 文明交通理念渐入人心

文明交通是体现社会文明程度的一个“晴雨表”。近年来，机动车发展迅速，一些大城市正在步入汽车时代。但是，人们的交通文明素质与现代交通文明的要求还不相适应，传统的不文明交通陋习相当普遍，驾驶人酒后驾驶、争道抢行、乱鸣喇叭、车辆乱停乱放以及行人过马路不走过街天桥和人行横道、逆向骑车、跨越道路隔离设施等不文明交通行为时常发生。2009年，在全国范围内展开的酒后驾驶违法行为专项整治行动，得到了社会各界的广泛关注和支持，这从一定程度上反映出全社会对文明交通的呼唤，凸显了人民群众在逐步满足物质文明需求后对精神文明的强烈需求。

文明交通理念的深入，特别是公民文明交通素质的提高，是一个渐进的潜移默化的过程。2010年1月26日，中央文明办、公安部联合启动为期三年的“文明交通行动计划”。全国各地通过精心组织活动、广泛开展媒体宣传、大力开展秩序整治、推动示范创建工作等形式，提高居民积极参与文明交通的主动性，对改善交通秩序、提高通行效率、减少交通事故，为全社会创造和谐的交通环境氛围打下了良好的基础。

## 七、小结

2010年是我国城市交通面临严峻挑战和深刻变革的一年，也是对以往交通发展策略进行深刻反思的重要时刻。2010年11月26日，中国工程院土木、水利与建筑学部和中国城市规划学会城市交通学术委员会联合在苏州市举办了为期两天的“中国大城市交通规划研讨会”。会议围绕大城市交通发展模式与方向为主题开展了深入的交流与探讨，就如何按大交通理念做好综合系统规划、缓解城市交通拥堵对策、绿色交通规划与实践、交通规划变革与创新、交通政策思考等内容建言献策，并呼吁树立科学的城市交通发展理念，即节约资源的发展理念、服务民生的发展理念、和谐有序的发展理念、科学决策的发展理念。

2011年是实施“十二五”规划的开局之年，也是城市交通的规划、建设、管理等全面进入攻坚阶段的一年。如何破解目前城市交通所遇到的困难和挑战，是一项任重而道远的课题，需要各部门、各方面、各系统的积极参与、协调和配合，更需要全方位的考量和探索。

（作者：王静霞，国务院参事，住房和城乡建设部城市交通工程技术中心教授级高级规划师）

# 2010中国城市市政公用设施建设

市政公用设施是城镇经济和社会发展的重要基础设施，是城市经济社会发展的重要载体，直接为城镇居民生产生活提供必需的普遍服务，具有显著的基础性、先导性和公用性。市政公用设施发展直接关系到社会公众利益，关系到人民群众生活质量，关系到城市经济和社会的可持续发展。2010年，各地以改善城市人居环境为目标，抓住节能减排和市政公用行业服务质量及运行安全两条主线，采取积极有效措施切实加快市政公用设施建设，转变城市建设发展方式，推动城市建设事业健康发展，较好地实现了“十一五”规划目标，为“十二五”规划实施奠定了良好的基础。

## 一、基本概况

市政公用设施继续保持较快增长，特别是城镇污水、垃圾处理设施建设快速发展，设施水平又有较大提高。2009年年末，全国城镇总人口6.22亿，城镇化率46.60%。全国共有设市城市654个，城市城区人口3.40亿人，暂住人口0.36亿人，建成区面积3.81万平方公里。城市市政公用设施固定资产完成投资额首次突破万亿元大关，达10641.5亿元，占同期全社会固定资产投资总额的4.73%，占同期城镇固定资产投资总额的5.48%，道路桥梁、轨道交通、园林绿化分别占城市市政公用设施固定资产投资的46.5%、16.3%和8.6%。

全国城市市政公用设施水平现状为：用水普及率为96.12%，燃气普及率为91.41%，污水处理率为75.25%，生活垃圾无害化处理率为71.31%，建成区绿化覆盖率38.22%，人均公园绿地面积10.66平方米，人均道路面积12.79平方米，全国城市轨道交通线路建成运营总长度839公里。

——城市供水和节水。城市供水总量496.7亿立方米。其中，生产运营用水166.8亿立方米，公共服务用水63.1亿立方米，居民家庭用水169.6亿立方米，用水人口3.6亿人。城市节约用水62.9亿立方米，节水措施总投资19.8亿元。

——城市燃气和集中供热。人工煤气供应总量361.6亿立方米，天然气供气总量405.1亿立方米，液化石油气供气总量1340.0万吨。用气人口3.44亿人。蒸汽供热能力9.3万吨/小时，热水供热能力28.6万兆瓦，集中供热面积38.0亿平方米。

——城市道路桥梁和轨道交通。城市道路长度26.91万公里，道路面积48.19亿平方米，其中人行道面积10.59亿平方米；全国有10个城市已建成轨道交通线路条数33条，长度839公里，车站数558个，其中换乘站116个，配置车辆数4801辆。

——城市园林绿化。城市建成区绿化覆盖面积149.4万公顷，建成区绿化覆盖率38.22%；建成区园林绿地面积133.8万公顷，建成区绿地率34.17%；公园绿地面积40.2万公顷。

——城市市容环境卫生。全国城市道路清扫保洁面积44.7亿平方米，其中机械清扫面积14.2亿平方米，机械清扫率31.8%。生活垃圾清运量1.57亿吨，无害化处理量1.1亿吨，无害化处理能力35.6万吨/日。

——城市排水和污水处理。全国城市污水处理规模9052万立方米/日，年处理污水总量279.3亿立方米，削减化学需氧量（COD）超过700万吨。

## 二、城市市政公用设施建设进展

### 1. 城市市政公用设施供给能力稳步提升

2009年，全国城市市政公用设施新增供水日综合生产能力968万立方米，天然气储气能力623万立方米，集中供热蒸汽能力3045吨/小时，热水能力14349兆瓦，道路长度9188公里，轨道交通运营线路长度264公里，排水管道长度2.87万公里，城市污水处理厂日处理能力946万立方米，城市生活垃圾无害化日处理能力2.4万吨。市政公用设施供给能力快速增长，增强了城市综合承载能力，基本适应城镇化快速发展阶段人民群众日益增长的需要。

### 2. 市政公用事业领域节能减排工作任务顺利完成

一是超额完成“十一五”规划和政府工作报告确定的城镇污水处理目标。截至2010年12月，全国共建成城镇污水处理厂2800座，有15个省（市）实现了县县建有污水处理厂，超额完成了新增城镇污水日处理能力1500万吨的任务。二是城镇供热计量改革工作有效推进，累计完成北方采暖地区既有居住建筑供热计量及节能改造面积1.67亿平方米，超出“十一五”期间任务的11.3%。三是城市道路照明淘汰低效照明产品、严格控制公用设施和大型建筑物装饰性景观照明能耗工作进展良好，加强了对城市景观照明的能耗监管，会同有关部门共同组织开展半导体路灯应用示范工程项目，推广使用节能、环保的照明新技术、新产品，城市绿色照明理念得到进一步落实。

### 3. 城市建设管理相关法规制度进一步完善

结合新形势下市政公用设施发展需要，及时组织制定和修订完善相关法规制度。一是《城镇燃气管理条例》的颁布，对进一步加强城镇燃气管理，保障燃气供应，防止和减少燃气安全事故，保障公民生命、财产安全和公共安全，促进燃气事业健康发展发挥重要作用。

二是修订出台《城市照明管理规定》，将管理范围从原来的道路照明管理拓展到道路照明与景观照明并重，将管理内容从道路照明设施管理拓展到城市照明规划、建设、维护和监督全过程的管理，重点突出城市照明节能管理。三是《城市综合交通体系规划编制办法》、《关于城市停车设施规划建设及管理的指导意见》、《关于进一步推进供热计量改革的意见》、《关于进一步加强动物园管理工作的意见》、《中国人居环境奖评价指标体系（试行）》、《城市园林绿化评价标准》（GB/J50563－2010）、《城镇污水处理工作考核暂行办法》等一系列文件相继印发，对进一步指导和规范城市综合交通、供热计量改革、园林绿化、城镇污水处理和人居环境建设等发挥积极的作用。

#### 4. 市政公用事业服务质量和安全运行水平进一步提高

一是青海玉树、甘肃舟曲等灾区市政公用事业抢险救灾工作取得实效。2010年，全力以赴地完成了青海玉树、甘肃舟曲、吉林洪涝灾区的应急供水、市容环卫设备保障及灾后恢复重建指导工作。向灾区提供支援物资，及时组织有关专家赶赴灾区一线，帮助做好应急供水、建筑垃圾处理、道路桥梁评估工作。针对今年极端恶劣天气频发的情况，积极指导各地采取有效防范措施，降低灾害对城建行业造成的损失。二是城市供水、供气、供热和轨道交通建设等市政基础设施安全管理工作进一步加强。开展了对全国所有设市城市和县城4500多个公共供水厂的普查工作，督导各地做好城镇供水、供气、供热、道路桥梁安全和反恐工作，指导大连、贵阳等地妥善处理好燃气事故。印发了《关于加强城市轨道交通安防设施建设工作的指导意见》，指导各地科学规划、优化设计、加强轨道交通安防设施建设。三是加强了动物园安全管理制度建设，坚决纠正对动物园进行租赁、承包等违规经营行为，保障动物园安全运营。

#### 5. 城市人居环境建设不断加强

一是数字化城市管理工作全面推进。组织召开了“全国数字化城市管理工作总结交流会暨节约型数字化城市管理论坛”，数字化城市管理在各地城市精细化管理实践中发挥了重要作用。截至目前，全国共有128个城市（区）建成数字化城市管理系统。二是人居环境评价体系进一步完善，着重解决目前城市人居环境工作中的住房改善、社区服务、公共安全、生态环境、资源节约等难点和焦点问题，同时，引入第三方社会调查机构组织开展居民对城市人居环境的感受调查，并将调查结果作为重要的考核内容，人居环境改善工作更贴近百姓生活、更符合百姓的需要。三是加强了对城市综合交通体系建设的指导。指导各地统筹近远期发展，形成支撑城市可持续发展的综合交通体系。积极引导各地缓解城市停车难和交通拥堵，组织开展“2010年中国城市无车日”活动，开展了“城市步行和自行车交通系统示范项目”工作，促进城市绿色交通出行方式的普及。四是加强对城镇园林绿化建设的监督、指导和服务。以国家园林城市创建和监督考核为抓手，督促各地做好园林绿化工作，对国家园林城市进行了全面复查。组织专家组对国家城市湿地公园保护管理情况进行了普查，加强城市湿地资源保护和城市生物多样性保护工作。

### 6. 城市建设领域基础研究工作扎实推进

针对近年来工作中遇到的城市建设领域的热点难点问题，如城市供水水质、生活垃圾处理、极端天气条件下的内涝灾害、城市地下管线安全管理等，组织专家加强基础调查研究，有针对性提出对策建议。完成了全国范围内的城市生活垃圾处理调研，完成了《关于我国城市生活垃圾处理情况的调研报告》，会同有关部门印发了《生活垃圾处理技术指南》，指导各地选择适宜的生活垃圾处理技术路线；同时，提出了进一步加强城市生活垃圾处理工作的意见。

## 三、城市市政公用设施建设的形势分析

多年来，尽管我国的城镇化和城市市政公用设施建设取得显著成绩，但我们清醒地认识到我国是在经济全球化深入发展和国际竞争日益加剧的背景下进入城镇化快速发展阶段的，面临着错综复杂的矛盾和问题。

### 1. 城市人居环境改善任务艰巨

城镇化水平是一个国家工业化、现代化的重要标志。目前发达国家城市化率一般接近80%，一些人均收入与我国接近的周边国家也已达到60%以上，相比之下我国的城镇化发展还有很大潜力。“十二五”是我国城镇化发展的关键时期，城镇化水平将达到并超过50%。我国城镇化水平每提高1个百分点，就要有1000万农村人口进入城镇，城镇的就业吸纳能力和基础设施承载能力压力巨大，城市居民对人居环境的要求不断提高。城市人居环境的改善跟不上城镇化人口转移的速度和广大城市居民日益增长的物质文化要求。要努力加强城市基础设施和公共服务设施建设，提高市政公用设施服务的覆盖面和保证率。根据城市拓展的需要，有序推进工业危险源搬迁和“城中村”改造，消除城市安全隐患，增加中心城区公共活动空间。

### 2. 城市发展模式需要转变

我国人多地少，宜居空间、能源资源、环境容量是城镇化发展的主要制约因素，随着城镇化的推进，人地矛盾和资源环境压力还将进一步加剧，粗放的城镇发展模式难以为继。“十二五”期间，我国城市发展要更加注重完善城市功能，提高宜居生活水平。不仅要完善城市布局和形态，促进大中小城市和小城镇协调发展，也要科学规划城市群内部各城市功能和产业定位，提升城市的综合承载能力。引导特大城市功能疏解和产业结构优化，缓解中心城区压力，避免“城市病”。积极建设低碳生态城市。制定低碳生态城市发展目标和评价指标体系，推行IID理念，推广技术的集成应用。着力提高绿色建筑比重，加快对既有老旧建筑的供热计量及节能改造，推广供热供气的计量化。加强城市资源循环利用设施建设，提高可再生能源利用率。大力发展绿色交通，减少城市交通能耗和空气污染。努力增加城乡绿色

空间，保护和建设湿地，提高碳汇能力。

**3. 城市管理手段有待创新**

当前，部分城市交通拥堵、环境污染、抵御自然灾害和应对突发事件的能力不足等问题凸显，“城中村”、城乡结合部等成为管理盲区，管理手段简单粗放，方法陈旧落后，与现代城市的要求差距很大。提高城市综合管理和服务水平。建立统一、协调、高效、合理的城市管理体制，调动各方面积极性。要创造管理手段，利用现代信息技术，推进数字化城市管理，提高城市动态管理、精细管理水平。要建立高效的城市公共安全保障体系，提高大城市、特大城市应对突发事件的应急反应能力。

## 四、城市市政公用设施建设的任务

“十二五”期间，城市建设要合理把握城镇化发展的规模、速度、节奏，全面深入贯彻落实科学发展观，以落实节能减排任务、保障和改善民生、提高市政公用事业服务质量和安全运行水平为主线，求真务实，真抓实干，着力解决与人民群众密切相关的热点、难点问题，推动城市建设事业健康发展。要加强对不同地区城镇市政公用设施发展的分类指导，东部经济发达地区要着力提高城镇发展质量，促进城乡市政公用设施一体化；中部地区要提高各级城镇综合承载能力；西部地区要重点发展条件好的城镇，促进边关城镇的发展。

**1. 提高城镇供水、排水设施建设和运行水平**

一是抓紧做好《城镇排水与污水处理条例》、《节约用水条例》、《生活饮用水卫生监督管理办法》的研究和制定工作。抓紧编制并实施《全国城镇供水设施改造与建设规划(2011—2020年)》，加快城镇供水设施改造与建设，加强供水水质检测监测能力和应急能力建设。研究应对突发事件的应急供水工作机制和措施。实施全国城市供水水质督察，完善并启用“全国城镇供水管理信息系统”。

二是加快编制《全国城镇污水处理和再生利用设施建设“十二五”规划》，指导各地着力加强污水处理厂配套管网和雨污分流管网建设，推进污泥无害化、资源化处理处置，因地制宜加快中小城市和镇、西部地区的污水处理设施建设。加强城镇污水处理设施建设和运行指导和监管，进一步完善“全国城镇污水处理管理信息系统”和《城镇污水处理工作考核暂行办法》。研究制定《城镇污水处理厂污泥处理处置技术指南》，指导城镇污水处理厂污泥处理处置设施建设与示范，开展全国城市排水系统排涝能力的普查和评估。

三是在城市节水方面，要继续抓好城市节约用水工作，总结交流节水型城市创建工作经验，组织开展节水型城市的复查和“全国城市节约用水宣传周”活动。

**2. 加强城市生活垃圾处理能力建设**

一是编制“十二五”生活垃圾处理设施建设规划。注重区域统筹和集中处理，解决生活垃圾处理设施区域共享问题，各城市要编制生活垃圾处理设施规划，严格实施《城乡规划法》和《城市黄线管理办法》，保障设施建设用地，禁止擅自改变用途，严格控制周边建设活动。

二是推进生活垃圾分类。36个大城市等有条件的地区，要重点研究实施垃圾分类的政策措施，重点开展有害垃圾单独收运，家庭干湿垃圾分类收集和餐饮业、单位餐厨垃圾分类收集工作；抓好餐厨垃圾资源化利用和无害化处理试点，启动建筑垃圾调查研究，出台加强建筑垃圾管理、推动建筑垃圾资源化利用的政策措施。

三是通过继续开展生活垃圾处理设施等级评定，完善生活垃圾处理管理信息系统，实现设施建设和运行有效监管，确保设施高标准建设、规范运行、达标排放。

### 3. 推进供热计量和城市照明节能

一是继续以供热计量改革为工作主线，全面推行按用热量计价收费制度。会同有关部门研究制定“十二五”支持北方采暖地区既有建筑供热计量改造政策，完成供热企业税费减免工作，制定减免实施政策，将减免政策和推行按用热量计价收费制度相挂钩。加强供热能耗监测，开展建立供热企业能耗监测统计平台的试点工作。加快城镇供热管网改造。逐步建立冬季供热采暖应急保障省级联络员制度，动态掌握煤炭储备、煤价变化和重点城市企业的运行状态。适时召开推进供热计量改革工作会议，开展供热计量改革技术培训工作。

二是继续推进城市绿色照明工作，促进城市照明系统节能。大力推广高效节能照明灯具，促进可再生能源在城市照明方面的应用。修改完善城市照明管理与节能考核标准，建立城市照明能效考核制度，严格控制景观过度照明。继续抓好半导体照明试点示范工程，指导试点示范实施单位做好设计方案论证、运行维护管理、检测评估以及节能投资效果对比分析。争取国家有关部门扩大财政奖励补贴政策，支持城市照明节能工作。

### 4. 加强城市综合交通规划建设

一是科学规划，发挥规划的调控作用。贯彻落实《城市综合交通体系规划编制办法》，加快城市综合交通体系规划的编制与实施，处理好城市综合交通体系与其他交通子系统的关系，统筹考虑、优化配置各种交通资源。研究制定《城市轨道交通线网规划编制办法》，进一步规范城市轨道交通线网规划的编制，加强城市轨道交通线网规划指导和监督管理，加强城市轨道交通近期建设规划的审查工作，推进城市轨道交通健康、可持续发展。

二是加强设施建设，提高城市综合交通承载能力。研究制定缓解城市交通拥堵的政策文件，指导各地科学推进城市交通基础设施建设。加快推进公交专用道、公交场站等公共交通设施的建设，推动优先发展城市公共交通战略的实施。继续开展“城市步行和自行车交通系统示范项目”工作，发挥示范作用，研究制定加强城市步行、自行车交通系统规划建设的指导意见，促进各地加快城市和自行车交通系统建设。贯彻落实《关于城市停车设施规划建设及管理的指导意见》，加强技术指导，加快城市停车设施建设，进一步缓解城市停车难的问题。

三是加大宣传力度，倡导绿色出行。继续开展“中国城市无车日活动”，加强对城市绿色交通的宣传，倡导更多的人选择绿色交通出行方式。

**5. 改进城市管理模式**

一是要破解城市地下管线综合管理难题。有关部门针对当前城市地下管线综合管理出现的问题，完善政策和相关制度，创新管理手段和运行机制，促进城市安全运行。推进城市地下管线管理立法工作，促进《城市地下管线管理条例》出台，建立城市地下管线综合协调监管机制，编制城市地下管线综合规划，推进市政综合管廊的建设、减少“马路重复开挖”，结合数字城管加强地下管线的信息化建设。

二是全面推广数字化城市管理模式。在全国地级以上城市全面推进数字化城市管理工作，指导地方不断完善管理体制和机制，拓展覆盖面积和管理内容，向深度和广度延伸发展（如地下管线、城市安全等领域），提高管理效率，加强城市综合管理。确保城市环境改善，城市安全运行，人民群众满意。

三是要贯彻实施《城镇燃气管理条例》。组织开展《条例》的宣贯培训工作，清理废止和修订燃气有关规章和文件。组织编制全国燃气发展规划。制定燃气经营许可制度等管理办法以及供应质量和服务标准规范，明确相关政策问题。抓好燃气安全运行工作，研究建立燃气供应保障机制，促进城镇燃气老旧管网改造。适时会同有关部门开展液化气市场的整顿工作。

四是要进一步加强市政道路桥梁设施管理工作。针对市政设施养护工作体制的现状，推进改革，抓好市政道路桥梁的养护维修工作、检测评估工作、档案信息管理工作和应急处理处置工作。适时启动《城市道路管理条例》修订工作，编制《市政工程设施养护维修估算指标》。

**6. 改善城镇人居环境**

以创建国家园林城市和中国人居环境奖为载体，全面贯彻新颁布的《中国人居环境奖评价指标体系》（试行），推动人居环境改善。

一是进一步健全城市园林绿化法规、标准体系，修订《城市绿化条例》、《城市动物园管理规定》、《国家重点公园管理办法》和《国家城市湿地公园管理办法》，抓紧制定《公园绿地管理办法》；组织编制国家标准《动物园设计规范》、《公园设计规范》、《城市绿线划定技术规程》等。

二是跟踪行业发展动态，加强对地方园林绿化工作的指导和服务。要积极引导、推动各地因地制宜开展“绿道”建设，以园博会、园林城市创建等为平台积极推广半导体照明工程建设、配合实施城市步行、自行车交通系统建设以及地下管网建设管理，将城市公园绿地作为城建司各处业务展示宣传的一个窗口。

三是进一步督促各级城市加快编制（修编）和实施城镇绿地系统规划，严格实施城市绿线管制制度，重点解决老旧城区的绿地总量不足和分布不均衡等难点问题。指导各地按照建设节约型、生态型和功能完善型园林的要求加强城市园林绿化建设，不断完善城镇绿地系统在节能减排、防灾避险等方面的综合功能，全面提升城市园林绿化行业建设管理水平。

四是做好国家园林城市（县城、城镇）、国家生态园林城市创建指导服务工作。积极配合各地住房城乡建设主管部门，组织专家对创建城市给予全过程的指导服务，帮助申报城市、县、镇做好工作；充分发挥有关单位的专家力量，加强对国家重点公园、城市湿地公园、动物园等建设管理情况的监督检查；加强国家城市湿地资源保护，加大城市规划区内生物多样性保护力度，建立城市园林绿化动态监管系统，利用遥感技术等科技手段，对各级城市园林绿化规划、建设和管理情况实施动态监管。

（作者：李如生，住房和城乡建设部城市建设司副司长；严盛虎，住房和城乡建设部城市建设司主任科员）

# 2010 中国城市信息化进展

城市信息化是国家信息化在城市的集中体现。其任务是综合运用信息技术和相关技术手段，通过实现城市规划、建设、管理、服务和安全保障，以及城市经济、社会和生态等不同层面的数字化、网络化、智能化，提升城市的整体信息化水平，为政府、企业和公众提供高效率、高质量、低成本的信息服务和决策支持，从而提高城市规划、建设、管理、服务及安全保障的能力和效率，提高民众的生活质量。

2010 年，我国城市信息化建设和应用取得了一系列新的进展，为城市的社会经济发展提供了有力的支撑，主要成就包括：城市网络发展迅速，三网融合进入试点；城市地理空间信息共享与服务取得重要进展；城市网络地图服务开始步入规模化、规范化；城市有关领域的信息化应用继续向深度和广度推进；城市信息化在上海世博会、广州亚运会中发挥重大作用；云计算、物联网等信息化技术发展迅速等。从总体上看，2010 年我国城市信息化发展呈现三大特征：一是信息化发展更理性化，应用需求成为城市信息化建设的主要导向；二是信息化亮点频现，如公众版国家地理信息公共服务平台、信息技术应用于世博会和亚运会、基于位置服务的社交网络等；三是随着新技术的不断成熟和许多基础工作的逐步积累，城市信息化蓄势待发，对未来城市的发展将提供更有力的支撑和保障。

## 一、城市网络发展迅速，三网融合进入试点

### 1. 互联网发展呈现新特点

2011 年 1 月，中国互联网络信息中心（CNNIC）在京发布了《第 27 次中国互联网络发展状况统计报告》。该报告显示，截至 2010 年 12 月底，我国网民规模达到 4.57 亿，较 2009 年底的 3.84 亿增加了 7330 万人；2010 年互联网普及率攀升至 34.3%，较 2009 年的 28.9% 提高了 5.4 个百分点。从纵向对比来看，“十一五”末的 2010 年较“十五”末的 2005 年（网民规模 1.11 亿，互联网普及率 8.5%）取得了飞速的发展，变化十分显著。

在 2010 年全国 4.57 亿网民中，城市网民规模为 3.52 亿，占整体网民的 72.7%，同比增长 26.9%。这表明城市网络发展是我国网络发展的主体，而且城市网络发展速度较快、势头强劲。其中，北京、上海、天津、重庆 4 个直辖市的网络普及率分别达到 69.4%、

64.5%、52.7%、34.6%，高出全国平均水平。同时，城市化率较高的沿海省份，诸如广东（55.3%）、浙江（53.8%）、福建（50.9%）、辽宁（44.4%）、江苏（42.8%）等，网络普及率也高于全国平均水平。

2010年我国网络发展呈现以下5个特点：（1）宽带网普及率较高，宽带网民规模达4.5亿，有线（固网）用户中的宽带普及率高达98.3%；（2）手机网民规模较大，手机网民达到3.03亿，依然是拉动我国总体网民规模攀升的主要动力；（3）网络购物增长较快，网络购物用户年增长48.6%，预示着更多的经济活动步入互联网时代；（4）企业网络应用普及，92.7%的中小企业接入互联网，42.1%的中小企业利用互联网进行过营销；（5）基础网络安全明显改善，2010年遭受过病毒或木马攻击的网民降至45.8%（2009年为56.6%），有过账号或密码被盗经历的网民也降至21.8%（2009年为31.5%）。

**2. 光纤网络发展迅速**

2010年，在国内大力拉动内需以及推广3G建设、FTTH（光纤到户）建设、三网融合和电力光纤推广等多重因素的影响下，中国的光纤光缆行业迎来了“爆炸性”增长的一年。

2010年3月，工业和信息化部等七部委联合发布了《关于推进光纤宽带网络建设的意见》，提出3年内光纤宽带网络建设投资将超过1500亿元，新增宽带用户超过5000万。

数据显示，截至2010年9月底，中国联通宽带用户数累计达到4598万户，中国电信宽带用户累计达到6107万户。中国电信计划2010年下半年和2011年追加投资150亿元，主要用于宽带建设。“十二五”期间，我国将加快光纤宽带网络建设，预计未来三年，国内三网融合及宽带光纤接入的投资将达6000亿~7000亿元。

**3. 3G持续发展，准4G初显身手**

2010年4月，工业和信息化部等八部门联合发布《关于推进第三代移动通信网络建设的意见》，提出2010—2011年3G网络建设的总投资将达到2400亿元。

2010年，全国3G用户净增3683.4万户，累计达到4705.2万户。其中，中国联通全年净增1132万户，达到1406万户；中国移动全年净增1729.4万户，达到2070.2万户；中国电信全年净增822万户，达到1229万户。

2010年4月15日，全球首个TD-LTE“准4G”演示网络在上海世博园开通。2010年5月1日，上海世博会开幕，中国移动TD-LTE接受了检验，世博场馆TD-LTE“准4G”现场实测数据传输速率达70Mbps，是现有3G技术的十几倍。2010年11月，更大规模的TD-LTE演示网在广州亮相，服务于亚运会。TD-LTE技术是“准4G”体系中我国唯一拥有核心知识产权的技术标准，具有高带宽和高频谱利用率等特点，特别适合承载高速数据业务。据报道，工业和信息化部2010年12月批复了准4G标准TD-LTE规模试验总体方案。中国移动2011年将在北京、上海、广州等7个城市建成超过1000个基站的TD-LTE“准4G”规模技术试验网络。

#### 4. 三网融合进入试点

2010 年 1 月初，国务院常务会议决定加快推进电信网、广播电视网和互联网三网融合，并明确提出阶段性目标和重点工作。按照部署，我国三网融合将分“两步走”，2010—2012 年重点开展广播电视和电信业务双向进入试点；2013—2015 年，总结推广试点经验，全面实现三网融合发展，普及应用融合业务。此项部署标志着三网融合正式进入实质性推进阶段，而三网融合将刺激广播电视及电信运营商对光纤网络建设的投入，给光纤光缆产业的发展带来新的机遇。

2010 年 7 月 1 日，第一批三网融合试点地区（城市）名单出炉，包括：北京市、上海市、哈尔滨市、南京市、杭州市、武汉市、深圳市、大连市、厦门市、青岛市、绵阳市以及长株潭地区等。目前，这些城市基本上都已经开始试点的实质性工作。

城市网络的进一步发展，无疑将为未来城市信息化建设和成果应用提供更强大的支持。

## 二、城市地理空间信息共享与服务取得重要进展

#### 1. 数字城市地理空间框架建设广受关注

国家测绘局组织实施的我国数字城市地理空间框架建设试点和推广的城市目前已达 130 个，其中近 60 个城市基本建成，成果已在 30 多个领域、众多专业部门以及人民群众生活中得到广泛应用。数字城市不仅成为宣传城市的靓丽名片、扩大城市影响的重要窗口，也成为测绘部门推动应用、展示实力、提升形象的重要载体。

2010 年 3 月，《中国新闻》两会特刊数字城市专辑集中展示了数字西安等一批我国数字城市地理空间框架建设的成果，吸引了广泛关注。

2010 年 9—11 月，国家测绘局组织人民日报、新华社、光明日报、经济日报、中央人民广播电台、中央电视台、科技日报、新华网、人民网、中国测绘报等 10 家中央主要新闻媒体，前往临沂、徐州、嘉兴、太原、郑州、惠州、潜江以及北京市西城区等数字城市试点城市（或城区）进行实地采访，开展了“数字城市中国行”宣传报道活动。通过众多大众新闻媒体对数字城市的宣传，展示了数字城市建设的成效与作用。

2010 年 11 月，针对数字城市地理空间框架建设中存在的主要问题，国家测绘局发布《关于进一步加快推进数字城市建设的通知》，要求加大推广力度，进一步做好数字城市地理空间框架建设和应用工作。

#### 2. 公众版国家地理信息公共服务平台开通

2010 年 10 月，国家测绘局宣布，我国公众版国家地理信息公共服务平台“天地图”网站开通。作为中国区域内数据资源最全的地理信息服务网站，将从根本上改变我国传统地理信息服务方式，全面提升信息化条件下国家地理信息公共服务能力。

“天地图”是国家地理信息公共服务平台的重要组成部分，其目的是通过互联网为公众、企业提供权威、可信、统一的地理信息服务，使基础地理信息更好地服务大众，打造互联网地理信息服务的中国品牌。

“天地图”采用了权威、标准、高清晰度的地理信息数据，主要包括：全球范围的1:100万矢量地形数据、500 米分辨率卫星遥感影像，全国范围的 1:25 万公众版地图数据、导航电子地图数据、15 米分辨率卫星遥感影像、2.5 米分辨率卫星遥感影像，全国 300 多个地级以上城市的 0.6 米分辨率卫星遥感影像，总数据量约 30TB。所有数据都根据互联网地图使用需求进行处理，包括电子地图制图、地理实体构建、地名地址统一、影像拼接匀色、地图缓存切片、脱密处理等。处理后的电子地图总瓦片数近 30 亿，在线服务数据量近 10TB。

随着“天地图”开发应用的不断深入，地理信息数据资源将继续丰富，特别是省、市测绘部门建设的“数字省区”及“数字城市”成果，将以网络互联、服务聚合的形式纳入到“天地图”中。

### 3. 城市地理信息标准化、共享与服务技术取得新进展

2010 年 5 月，住房和城乡建设部颁布了行业标准《城市地理空间信息共享与服务元数据标准》（CJJ/T144 – 2010）。该标准规定了元数据的内容、扩展方式及元数据获取、管理与发布等，适用于城市地理空间信息共享与服务元数据的建立、管理和发布。

2010 年，全国地理信息标准化技术委员会（SAC/TC230）基本完成了我国地理信息标准化“十二五”规划的制定工作。在未来五年，将着力实施与优化国家地理信息标准体系，全面完成地理信息资源建设、地理信息开发利用和地理信息公共服务等重点领域标准的制、修订任务，积极开展标准前期基础研究和实验验证，努力推进标准的宣传培训、贯彻和服务。

为满足数字中国及数字城市地理空间框架与地理信息公共服务平台建设的急需，规范地理信息数据产品及应用服务，促进地理信息资源的互联互通和高效开发应用，全国地理信息标准化技术委员会组织全国有关部门和专家，于 2010 年完成了《地理信息分类与编码规则》、《地理信息数据产品规范》、《地理信息服务》、《地理信息万维网地图服务接口》、《地理信息目录服务规范》和《地理信息注册服务规范》等 6 项国家标准的编制工作，这些标准有望于 2011 年年初颁布实施。

2010 年年初，国家测绘局主持开展了“数字城市地理信息公共平台国产软件测评”工作，共有 42 套软件申报参评，经测评，8 套为“优秀软件”、6 套为“合格软件”。

2010 年 11 月，上海市科委组织召开专家组论证会，对《上海市地理信息公共服务平台关键技术研究》进行开题评审。项目旨在通过对基础地理信息服务模式与关键技术的研究，逐步实现成果转化，推动全市信息化进程。“上海市地理信息公共服务平台”的建设有利于提高上海的政府行政管理效能，有利于推动长三角区域联动发展，适应国家信息化发展的方向，对提高上海的基础地理信息服务和城市信息化发展具有长远的意义。

### 4. 地理信息产业发展明显增速

2010年，我国地理信息产业取得了长足的发展。企业数量增加，规模不断扩大，一些IT企业也涉足地理信息产业。目前，已有6家企业进入创业板、中小板，还有3家企业在美国NASDQ上市。2010年产业总产值有望突破1000亿元。武汉、哈尔滨、西安等地的地理信息产业园已经发挥良好效益，山东、江苏、浙江等多个省市也正在积极筹划或建设地理信息产业基地，积极推动地理信息产业规模化、集约化发展。

国家测绘局与北京市政府合作，建设国家地理信息科技产业园。园区位于北京国门商务区，总占地面积1000亩左右，产业园于2010年11月28日奠基，项目总投资约150亿元人民币，预计在2013年建成投入使用。园区将以国家地理空间信息公共服务平台建设为龙头，通过标准化体系建设，带动基础测绘、数据加工、系统集成、服务外包、设备制造等相关业务的发展，形成相对完整的地理空间信息服务产业链。投入使用后，园区拟吸引国内外地理空间信息企业100家以上，预计年产值达到200亿元。

## 三、城市信息化应用继续向深度和广度推进

### 1. 数字化城市管理试点工作取得实效

2010年6月，住房和城乡建设部在河北省秦皇岛市召开了全国数字化城市管理工作总结交流会暨节约型数字化城市管理论坛，对数字化城市管理试点工作情况进行了总结，并对下一步相关工作进行了部署。

自2005年全国开展数字化城市管理试点工作以来，截至2010年5月，全国已经建成和正在建设数字化城市管理的城市达到128个，全国36个大城市中有30个已经完成或正在开展数字化城市管理工作。数字化城市管理试点工作的开展，搭建了政府与群众沟通的平台，提高了城市综合管理效率和水平。突出表现在三方面：一是城市管理队伍处理现场问题的速度大大加快，原来需要几天解决的问题，现在几个小时，甚至几分钟就能得到反馈和解决；二是网络整合能力越来越强，不少城市数字化城管平台越来越被管理部门所倚重，越来越为老百姓所喜爱，已经成为现代化城市管理不可缺少的手段；三是通过数字化城市管理带动了城市的各行各业信息化管理，促进了城市数字化产业的发展。

2010年，数字化城市管理一方面向广度推进，住房和城乡建设部决定在全国地级以上城市全面推广数字化城市管理新模式；另一方面也在向深度拓展，许多城市积极整合资源，挖掘潜力，扩大应用覆盖的地域和业务领域，实现与应急预案、综合执法等业务的协同。

### 2. 普查图电子化服务第六次全国人口普查

在国家863计划“国家统计遥感业务系统关键技术研究与应用”重点项目的支持下，国家统计局在2010年全国第六次人口普查中利用GIS和遥感技术进行普查区划分和普查图

电子化。全国32个直辖市、省和自治区开展了这项工作，基本实现了居委会和村委会（社区）的普查区及普查小区数据的电子化，条件较好的地区实现了建筑物数据的电子化。在此基础上，建立全国人口普查图数据库，将普查获得的人口数据定位到普查区和普查小区，甚至到建筑物，以实现人口数据的空间化，为城市空间布局和空间结构优化提供数据支持。北京市建立了由6563个普查区、71451个普查小区和200多万个建筑物构成的人口普查地理空间数据库。普查图电子化工作为人口普查数据的开发利用以及统计地理信息系统的建设奠定了基础。

**3. 城市警用地理信息系统建设进展显著**

警用地理信息系统是公安部确定的“金盾工程”二期建设的核心平台之一，也是国家“十一五”科技支撑计划的重点项目。公安部于2009年9月启动了警用地理信息系统试点和首批示范城市建设工作，2010年在全国启动了第二、三批示范建设。目前，全国共启动4个省级示范和120个示范城市，其中第一批芜湖和武汉示范于2010年通过公安部示范验收；上海、常州、苏州已通过公安部组织的验收测试。

警用地理信息系统面向各级业务公安机关、各业务警种，依据“人”、“案（事）件”、“物品”、“机构”、“地点”公安五要素，从“地点”的维度整合各种公安业务信息资源，服务于日常警务工作需要和突发事件的应急指挥调度。警用地理信息系统将公安机关现有地图资源统一整合起来，提供统一的地理信息服务，使底图数据在各业务单位之间交换、共享和整合，实现警务信息的地图可视化，为各级领导提供更形象、更直观的展示方式，并利用系统提供的空间数据和警务模型分析数据，提高警务综合分析、辅助决策和指挥调度能力，促进了公安行业信息化。

目前，警用地理信息标准建设已形成了一个标准体系，其中的大部分标准已经完成。

**4. 城市个人住房信息系统建设迅速推进**

为加强房地产市场的宏观调控，根据国务院有关文件要求，住房和城乡建设部启动了全国住房信息系统的建设。2010年6月，住房和城乡建设部在山东省青岛市召开了加快住房信息系统建设工作现场会，总结了近年来各地在推进房屋登记信息系统建设工作中取得的进展和经验，提出要在房屋登记信息系统建设的基础上，加快推进个人住房信息系统建设。建设的总体思路是，以城市住房信息系统建设为重点、以房屋登记数据为基础，建立部、省、市三级住房信息系统网络和基础数据库，全面掌握个人住房的基础信息及动态变化，为科学制定相关政策提供技术支持，为实施房地产市场宏观调控政策、提高行业管理和社会服务水平创造条件。

个人住房信息系统建设，实行部、省、市一起抓落实，重心在城市的工作机制。各城市要加快完成市、区、县系统的整合，尽快建立市一级统一的数据库，实现数据的集中统一和互联互通，加快实现全市住房信息的全覆盖；各省（区）、市负责组织建立省级住房信息系统和省级基础数据库，配合住房和城乡建设部建立全国住房信息系统和基础数据库的相关工作；住房和城乡建设部将制定全国住房信息系统建设的总体规划和系统建设框架、制定相关技术标准，搭建部与省级住房信息系统联网平台。

按计划，2013年年前，个人住房信息系统基本实现全国联网。为此，住房和城乡建设部确定40个城市作为全国个人住房信息系统重点建设城市。在2010年11月召开的“个人住房信息系统建设座谈会”上要求2011年10月底前完成部与40个重点城市的个人住房信息系统联网工作。

## 四、城市信息化支撑世博会、亚运会的成功举办

### 1. 世博会——从信息技术层面阐述“城市，让生活更美好”主题

2010年5月1日至10月31日，以“城市，让生活更美好”为主题的世博会在上海成功举办。信息技术在世博会园区管理与服务方面得到了充分的展现，发挥了巨大作用。

信息技术支撑了世博会的运行。世博会建立了75个机房和40多个应用系统，部署了130个通信服务设施、1万多个摄像头和10万台电子终端设备。其中的亮点包括：一是40多个应用系统基于统一的信息平台构建，涉及物流、安保、票务、交通、售检票、设施运营等各种应用。二是搭建了网上世博会——“世博网”，营造了一个访问者和实体世博会进行互动的网络平台；首次对世博会进行网上直播，利用网络打造“永不落幕的世博会”。三是新一代通信网、无线宽带、RFID和传感网、互联网、多媒体、智能视频处理、定位导航等先进的技术在世博会上都得到了广泛的应用，如构建了中国自主研发的TD-LTE准4G网络规模演示网，理论峰值速率在上、下行分别达到了50Mbps和100Mbps。该示范网对中国无线网络的发展起到重要的推进作用。四是世博会门票全部采用了无线射频技术（RFID），借助电子标签无线电波传递唯一的序列号来识别门票。

除支撑世博会运行外，信息技术还为人们展现了未来的城市生活。在太空家园馆，可以看到如何利用物联网技术来管理冰箱中的食物，利用智能技术来管理城市的交通。在IT企业馆中，展示了2020年上海城市生活的一天，当卢浦大桥发生事故，如何智能化地协调城市交通、城市医疗救护、城市监管等各个层面的问题。世博会气象馆展出了我国自主研发的触摸式三维天气信息展示系统，通过大屏幕触摸系统，可在数字三维地球上快速精确显示全球三维背景下的卫星云图、天气实况和预报、雷达拼图等气象信息数据，展现高温、暴雨、大风沙尘、雾霾等天气实况，演示台风移动轨迹，从而帮助人们迅速追踪天气最新变化趋势。

应该说，各种信息技术的应用使世博会成为数字城市和智慧城市的样板，从信息技术层面上深刻阐述了“城市，让生活更美好”的主题。

### 2. 亚运会——信息技术为体育盛会成功举办提供重要保障

2010年11月，广州成功地举办了第十六届亚运会。信息技术为这一重要体育盛会的成

功举办提供了十分重要的支撑和保障。为了确保亚运会的召开，亚运会组委会以“数字广州”为基础，打造了“数字亚运”系统工程。

“数字亚运”系统工程以运动会信息系统和计时记分成绩处理系统为赛事技术核心，以场馆信息技术基础建设、网络通信与信息安全、场馆技术支持等其他项目为基础，以组委会办公信息系统及其相关业务系统为支撑，共同组成规模庞大、技术复杂、领域广阔、协作接口最多的信息服务体系。亚运会新建光缆网络 8 万多纤芯公里，覆盖亚运会所有 69 个场馆，开通信息点 7000 个，配置计算机、电视机等设备 1.7 万多台，为 4.5 万名工作人员提供了高效的数字集群指挥系统，为媒体和参会人员提供 40 多种综合信息服务。总指挥部信息平台（MOC）成为汇聚 20 多项赛事运行信息的信息汇集发布中心、资源调度中心和可视化监控指挥中心。亚运管理专网承载了办公应用、视频会议、公众综合信息服务、视频安全监控、应急处理和综合指挥调度、车辆调度、统一新闻发布、统一信息门户等赛会运行服务功能。语音通信和宽带互联网两大通信网络通过整合调配社会资源，广泛应用 TD-LTE、无线城市、WLAN、手机电视等高新技术，确保了亚运场馆、相关场所、重点公共区域实现高容量通信和 100% 无缝覆盖。

信息技术在广州亚运会上应用的亮点包括：（1）高速网络：中国移动推出了继上海世博会后更大规模的 TD-LTE 准 4G 演示网服务亚运会；中国电信在广州市内提供了 4000 多个免费 WiFi 热点，在广东省范围内有 20000 多个 WiFi 热点对公众免费开放。（2）高清转播：广州亚运会首次采用高清技术向全球转播精彩比赛，高清转播占到整个电视转播任务的三分之一左右。（3）智能调度：建立了智能化的交通指挥调度系统，为参与亚运会运输服务的 3500 多辆车提供了智能化、电子化和可视化的指挥调度功能，使得为 3.1 万多名注册人员提供的抵达、离开、训练、比赛、开闭幕式等 23 项交通服务高效平稳。（4）地图服务：应用 GIS 技术进行场馆管理、提供亚运会地图服务等。

## 五、城市网络地图服务步入规模化和规范化阶段

### 1. 主要网络运营服务商和智能手机商进入网络地图服务与导航领域

在城市公众地理信息服务方面，互联网地图服务和卫星导航服务一直走在前列。目前，互联网地图服务和卫星导航服务已经成为支持公众生活的重要工具。人们利用互联网地图，可以查询地址、搜索地名、安排出行路线、标注地物等；利用车载或智能手机的位置服务，可以选择安全、快捷的出行路线，享受由此带来的工作、生活、休闲便利。

目前，我国从事互联网地图服务的网站已达到数万个。2010 年 9 月，腾讯 QQ 地图正式上线。至此，我国几大主要网络运营服务商新浪、搜狐、网易、百度、腾讯等均加入了网络地图服务行列，主要门户网站均提供在线地图服务。主要网络运营服务商开展网络地图服务，一方面显示出网络地图服务业务的巨大商业价值，另一方面也为网络地图的规模化、持续化发展打下了基础。

与此同时，随着智能手机的日益普及，智能手机厂商开始加速进军网络地图服务和卫星导航领域。目前主要品牌的智能手机都能提供地图和导航服务。智能手机厂商提供免费的地图和卫星导航应用服务，对卫星导航市场带来了巨大冲击，但同时也将带动位置服务市场的进一步发展。目前，位置服务与社交网络的集成应用受到青睐，有可能引爆位置服务市场迅速扩大。

**2. 国家开始加强互联网地图服务的监管**

为促进我国互联网地图服务的健康有序发展，引导地图服务网站正确刊登、发布和使用地图，我国2010年对互联网地图服务开始建立准入制度。4月，国家测绘局、工业和信息化部、国家安全部、工商总局、新闻出版总署、国家保密局、总参测绘局等7部门发布了《关于加强地理信息市场监管工作的意见》。5月，国家测绘局出台了《互联网地图服务专业标准》。按照该标准，取得互联网地图服务甲级测绘资质的单位，可以从事地图搜索、位置服务，地理信息标注服务，地图下载、复制服务，地图发送、引用服务等四类服务；取得互联网地图服务乙级测绘资质，可以从事前两类服务，但不得从事后两类服务。

截至2010年年底，已有100多家互联网地图服务网站获得了资质，还有近100家向测绘行政主管部门提出了资质申请。获得资质或正在申请资质的地图服务网站占应申请单位总数的50%以上。获得和正在申请互联网地图服务甲级测绘资质的单位中包括多家中外合资公司。

## 六、云计算和物联网等城市信息化新技术快速发展

**1. 城市信息化进入云计算时代**

城市信息化离不开新技术的支持。2010年，在各种新技术中，云计算和物联网等技术受到进一步关注。

云计算被认为是继大型机、个人计算机和互联网后的第四次IT革命。IT进入云计算时代，将改变城市信息化状况和我们的工作及生活方式。云计算的核心思想是将大量用网络连接的计算资源统一管理和调度，构成一个计算资源池向用户提供按需服务。它在系统的可扩展性和规模性、资源的动态分配管理、服务模式等方面都具有突出的优点，对于实现资源的广泛共享和增值应用具有重要意义。据统计，2010年，云计算在百度和谷歌上的搜索量快速增长，已经受到行业内外的普遍关注。

我国已把云计算作为新一代IT产业研发与应用的重要领域之一。2010年8月，上海市颁布了推进云计算产业发展行动方案，即“云海计划”，按照这个计划，上海将被打造成亚太地区的云计算中心，并为全国提供优质的云计算基础设施服务。2010年10月，国家发改委、工业和信息化部确定北京、上海、深圳、杭州、无锡五个城市开展云计算服务创新发展试点。重庆、东营、佛山等地也先后制定了云计划发展规划。许多企业更是把云计算作为未

来投资的重点，如华为、用友、阿里巴巴、伟库、浪潮、云天科技等都发布了云服务策略。

云计算无疑将为我国城市信息化建设和应用提供有力的技术支撑，值得密切关注。据预测，云计算市场将以28%的复合年增长率迅速扩张，云计算在我国的市场规模有望在3年内突破1万亿，到2012年，云计算技术将相当普及。

**2. 物联网与智慧城市开始走出概念**

2010年，物联网和智慧城市开始走出概念，进入实施阶段。2010年10月，国务院发布《关于加快培育和发展战略性新兴产业的决定》。其中提出发展新一代信息技术产业，包括：加快建设宽带、泛在、融合、安全的信息网络基础设施；推动新一代移动通信、下一代互联网核心设备和智能终端的研发及产业化；加快推进三网融合，促进物联网、云计算的研发和示范应用等。2010年10月，国家发改委、工业和信息化部、科技部、中科院和江苏省人民政府在无锡共同举办2010中国国际物联网（传感网）博览会，这是近年来中国物联网产业规模最大、层次最高、影响力最深远的行业盛会。与此同时，《中国物联网产业发展年度蓝皮书（2010）》在无锡发布。蓝皮书包括环境篇、概述篇、产业篇、应用篇、技术篇、战略篇、展望篇、附录篇等内容，对物联网产业进行了全面系统的阐述。

2010年，智慧城市受到进一步关注。智慧城市是以信息、知识和脑力资源为支撑，通过透明、充分的信息获取，广泛、安全的信息传递，有效、科学的信息处理，均衡而有效地提高城市运行和管理效率，从而提高城市发展的创新性、有序性和持续性，更好地服务于市民。2010年6月世博会期间，IBM在上海举办了“2010智慧城市全球峰会”，来自全球38个国家、22个行业、180座城市的800多位城市与地区领导、行业与企业领袖及专家与学者出席峰会。峰会研讨围绕“挑战、现实、机遇”三大方向展开，探讨全球在建设智慧城市方面的实践与经验。

2010年11月，科技部和湖北省政府主办的“2010中国智慧城市论坛大会”在武汉召开，近300余人出席了论坛大会。与会代表共同交流和探讨我国智慧城市的发展思路，分享研究成果。9月，宁波市委召开工作会议，对当前及今后一段时期宁波市智慧城市建设工作进行了全面部署，出台了《中共宁波市委宁波市人民政府关于建设智慧城市的决定》，确定了智慧宁波建设的发展目标。11月，厦门市人民政府与中国电信福建公司签订“智慧厦门”信息化战略合作协议。未来5年，中国电信福建公司将投入不少于50亿元资金，在厦门建设具有世界先进水平的“智慧网络”，重点实施无线宽带城市、电子商务综合服务平台等项目，加快下一代互联网、物联网等建设，推进电信网、计算机网、广播电视网“三网融合”试点工作等。

## 七、扎实推进城市信息化可持续发展

2010年，我国城市信息化领域各种信息、技术与学术交流活动十分频繁。除上述“数字城市中国行”、全国数字化城市管理工作总结交流会暨节约型数字化城市管理论坛、中国国际物联网（传感网）博览会等外，还有：7月，在沈阳召开的由亚太地区城市信息化合作办公室与中国计算机用户协会主办的“2010中国城市信息化峰会暨AMD杯第二届中国城市信息化50强发布会”。会上发布了“第二届中国城市信息化50强”、“中国城市信息化杰出供应（服务）商”和“中国城市信息化领军人物”，北京、上海、宁波、沈阳等50个城市入选城市信息化50强，同时以“交流、协作、促进”为宗旨的“中国城市信息化推进论坛”也宣告成立。10月，以“信息化促进城市科学发展”为主题的2010全球城市信息化论坛在上海召开，来自全球五大洲40个国家54个城市、49个国际组织和机构的350多名代表参加论坛，论坛讨论了信息技术创新发展、引领未来城市生活等议题，并通过了《全球城市信息化论坛宣言》，确定在上海设立全球城市信息化论坛秘书处。11月，住房和城乡建设部在北京召开“第五届中国数字城市建设技术研讨会暨设备博览会”，多位信息化研究领域的院士、著名学者在论坛上发表主题演讲；设立的六个分论坛分别就国内外数字城市建设及产业化发展、“十一五”期间我国数字城市发展的政策导向、城乡信息资源建设管理与服务、数字城市管理与发展、城市三维地理信息技术、无线城市及3G、物联网在城市信息化建设中的应用、建筑业信息化、数字房产及房屋权属生命周期管理等城市信息化热点问题进行了研讨。11月，神州数码在成都召开2010合作伙伴大会，并联合众多厂商倡议建立中国数字城市产业联盟。住房和城乡建设部信息中心主办《数字城市》杂志已经五周年，经过五年的发展，共出版了51期，累计发行达40余万册，覆盖全国各省、市（地区），得到业界人士的广泛好评和行业企业的大力支持。此外，中国地理信息系统协会除继续评选地理信息系统优秀工程外，还首次开展了地理信息科技进步奖的评选。所有这些活动，为我国城市信息化的发展起了重要的促进作用。

回顾2010年我国城市信息化进展，我们认为，尽管城市信息化发展迅速，但也存在许多不足。主要是：从中央到地方城市信息化的管理体系不够清晰，城市信息化涉及的领域众多，许多政府部门都在开展信息化建设工作，但缺乏强有力的部门来统一运筹城市信息化的总体发展；城市信息化总的服务层次还较低，基本上还是在为城市的发展提供辅助和支持，真正能起到提升作用的还很少；城市信息化的应用服务模式以及信息化的效果等尚需要进一步创新和发展。

当前，我国城市现代化建设和经济社会发展仍十分迅速，对信息化应用的需求将不断提升；随着城市经济实力的增强将使城市信息化有可能获得更多的资金支持；城市信息化核心技术的发展和突破也将使应用成本进一步降低。城市信息化无疑将面临新的更大的机遇。城市群和区域的统筹发展、住房保障的实施、社会管理与社区服务的创新、智能交通的升级、公共安全管理和服务的推进，以及基于位置服务的公众生活服务支持（如社交网络和网络购物）等，将成为未来一段时间我国城市信息化服务的重点。

根据我国的国情，当前在城市信息化建设实践中，应在积极发挥市场机制的基础上，继续强化城市政府的主导作用；让城市政府而不是政府的某个部门成为城市信息化建设的主导者，让城市信息化建设成为城市基础设施建设的重要组成部分。此外，还应进一步更新城市信息化建设的理念，加强城市信息化规划的制定与落实，提高对规划实施的监控力度，积极使用信息化适用的新技术、新方法，切实做好城市信息化建设和运行的资金与人才保障，扎扎实实地推动城市信息化的进一步可持续发展。

（作者：王丹，建设综合勘察研究设计院有限公司研究员；党安荣，清华大学建筑学院教授；梁军，北京超图软件股份有限公司副总裁；何建邦，中国科学院资源与环境信息系统国家重点实验室研究员，国际欧亚科学院院士）

## 参考文献

[1] http://www. ccw. com. cn
[2] http://www. cnnic. net. cn
[3] http://www. expo2010. cn
[4] http://www. gz2010. cn
[5] http://www. miit. gov. cn
[6] http://www. mlr. gov. cn
[7] http://www. mohurd. gov. cn
[8] http://www. sbsm. gov. cn
[9] http://www. 3snews. net
[10] 住房和城乡建设部信息中心，《数字城市》杂志，2010（1～12）

# 论坛篇

# 建设生态城市，促进绿色发展

城市是人口的主要集聚地，也是人类经济、政治、科技和文化活动的中心。工业革命二百多年来，城市化快速发展，为人类创造了巨大的物质和精神财富。与此同时，城市的发展也付出过沉重的环境代价。20 世纪 70 年代，联合国教科文组织发起的“人与生物圈”计划研究中提出了生态城市的概念，并将其付诸实践。今天，寻求自然化、人文化、生态化已经成为城市建设的大趋势，促进人与自然和谐相处，代表着城市发展的新潮流。建设生态城市对于促进绿色复苏，实践以人为本的科学发展观具有重要意义，也是促进我国实现可持续发展的重要途径。

## 一、建设生态城市是实现绿色复苏的重要途径

2008 年开始的席卷全球的金融危机，表面上看是对经济增长的冲击，本质上是对传统发展模式的冲击。值得欣慰的是，各国在采取金融救援和刺激措施时，并没有忽视生态环境保护，在世界范围内开启了一轮发展绿色经济、推动绿色复苏的浪潮。

据统计，在危机应对中，全球范围与绿色经济相关的投资总额达到 4360 亿美元，占世界应对危机的经济刺激政策总投资的 15.6%。美国实施了“绿色新政”，宣布未来十年内在绿色能源领域投资 1500 亿美元，创造 500 万个就业机会，并且制定了绿色能源法案。欧洲在其 2020 年计划中提出，将把可再生能源比重提高到 20%，在 2013 年前投资 1050 亿欧元支持发展绿色经济。日本也制定了相应的绿色经济发展计划，宣布扩大绿色经济规模，建立一个总额为 45 亿日元的基金，为企业减排融资提供“贴息”。

发展绿色经济，促进绿色复苏，不仅可以节能减排，而且能够更加有效地利用资源、扩大市场需求、提供新的就业岗位，是发展经济与保护环境的重要结合点。从未来趋势看，随着全球绿色经济的发展和绿色技术的进步，经济“绿色化”不仅不会成为增长的负担，而且将成为经济增长的重要引擎。

建设生态城市有利于推动绿色经济发展，培育新的经济增长点。生态城市建设本身需要一定的投入，比如对民用住宅、办公大楼、工厂、学校、公共基础设施等实施节能改造，利用新能源发电，推广绿色家电，采用节能环保的公共交通工具，建设智能电网等，都可以带动基础设施、基础产业的发展，推动低碳、节能、循环经济产业的投入，有利于增加绿色投

资，扩大绿色消费。由于生态城市均拥有良好的自然和人文环境，这种价值巨大的无形资产对吸引人才集聚、带动各方投资、促进经济发展有不可估量的影响，因此，建设生态城市在实现绿色复苏中的重要作用正得到国际社会的广泛重视，并成为世界环境与发展领域的一个新趋势。

## 二、建设生态城市实践了以人为本的科学发展理念

传统城市建设中往往出现各种各样的“城市病”，比如贫民窟广布、交通拥堵、空气污染、水资源短缺、传染病肆虐等，很难与美好的宜居生活相联系。与传统城市相比，生态城市更加适合人类居住。生态城市应以人类宜居为重心，创造优美舒适的工作环境和生活环境，形成低碳的生产生活方式，保持一定面积湿地用于调节城市气候，提高淡水的循环利用率，搞好垃圾的无害化处理等。换句话说，它将用更多的绿色空间、绿色社区打造人们的绿色生活，用低排放的产业模式、先进的科学技术、优美的自然景观、良好的人文环境、便利的交通设施，满足人们的工作需求、发展需求、精神需求和健康需求。

与传统城市相比，生态城市更加注重建立民众利益共享的体制机制。生态城市建设要以城市民众利益为先，建立涉及利益相关者共同参与的政策制定和决策机制，树立“人人参与，人人爱护”城市生态文明的理念，实现公共服务的均等共享，让所有人享有平等的就业机会，享受住房、基础设施和公共服务设施的权益，享有充分的食物、清洁的水和空气，享有平等的教育医疗机会，以及享有平等的获取资源的机会。生态城市将提供更多的包容性，尊重人的全面发展，增加对外来人口和不同阶层的亲和力、凝聚力，提升城市居民个体和集体的幸福感。

与传统城市相比，生态城市遵循“人与自然和谐共生”的价值观念。城市管理者要师法自然，将自然融入城市，处理好产业发展与自然生态的关系，营造清洁高效的生产环境，减少对生态环境的破坏和对自然系统的索取，处理好经济社会与自然系统的关系，建立安全、卫生、友善、景观的服务环境。同时，生态城市还需要处理好社会生态与自然生态的关系，提高城市的人口承载能力、对外开放程度，提倡适度消费、就近上班等健康的生活方式，提供人性化、自然化和公平化城市管理服务；处理好人类发展与资源禀赋的关系，因地制宜创造不同特色，较少对自然环境做大的改动，将历史原貌与现代建筑创造性融合在一起。

当然，发展生态城市在实践以人为本的科学发展理念时，不是将人凌驾于自然之上，也不是把利己、功利和享乐作为生活态度，而是将“人与自然和谐共生”作为发展前提，同时追求物质与精神财富的创造和积累。良好生态环境的创造，首先通过城市的布局来解决。可以说，发展生态城市，就要通过合理规划城市的生态格局、产业发展、建筑布局、人口规模，创造最佳的人与自然和谐的生态城市系统，走生产发展、生活富裕、生态良好的文明发展道路。

## 三、建设生态城市是对可持续发展道路的有益探索

我国高度重视城市发展的可持续问题。党的十七大报告指出，要建设生态文明，基本形成节约能源资源和保护生态环境的产业结构、增长方式、消费模式。积极主动应对气候变化，把节能减排作为“十一五”国民经济和社会发展规划的约束性指标，公布了《节能减排综合性工作方案》和《应对气候变化国家方案》，在节能减排方面作出了巨大努力。在这些战略和方案指引下，城市在产业、建筑、交通和环境的规划和建设方面都形成了一套可持续发展的思路。在加快转变经济发展方式中，我们坚持走中国特色城镇化道路，促进大中小城市和小城镇协调发展，着力提高城镇综合承载能力，发挥城市对农村的辐射带动作用。

城镇化发展充满机遇，也面临许多挑战。我国从1995年开始加快城镇化，平均每年有1540万农村人口迁移到城镇。2009年，城镇化率已达到46.6%。未来20年还将延续这一趋势。今后几十年，我国经济还会保持较快的发展速度，不论是大城市还是中小城市，大都面临着人口增加、面积扩大和旧城改造的任务。到2015年，我国将从一个以农业人口为主的国家，转型为一个以城市人口为主的国家。从现在到2030年，将有3亿多人口从农村转移到城镇。中国城镇化将成为中国经济增长的新引擎，也会为拉动全球经济稳定增长做出贡献。但是，应当看到，在如此大规模的城镇化过程中，需要同时解决好人口老龄化、社会保障体系不健全、城市基础设施不完善、生态环境恶化、能源消耗超常增长等方面的问题。

城镇化进程的稳步推进需要破解转变城市发展模式，不能继续采取传统的经济发展和城市发展模式。以往城市建设的经验已经证明，一个城市只有走可持续发展的道路，才能为公众提供高质量的生活，才能有持久发展的活力。生态城市建设为我国城市实现可持续发展提供了重要的方案和思路。国际上一些城市按照生态城市的理念来规划和建设，取得了巨大成功。国内近年也涌现了一批循环经济城市、绿色城市、低碳城市和生态城市。

在未来的城市建设中，我国应借鉴发达国家城市发展经验，探索适合我国国情的生态城市发展模式，紧紧围绕“加快转变经济发展方式”，实现可持续发展。在城市规划设计、基础设施建设、产业体系构建和生态环境保护等城市建设环节，以是否符合生态文明内涵为标尺，衡量城市发展的质量，确定城市发展的方向。生态城市的建设应当充分发挥科学技术的支撑作用。世界各国建设生态城市的探索和实践经验表明，规划技术、管理技术和产业技术对于实现城市的可持续发展至关重要。生态城市建设要坚定不移地走科技含量高、经济效益好、人力资源优势得到充分发挥的可持续发展模式。

（作者：曾培炎，中国国际经济交流中心理事长）

# 完整社区与和谐社会

## 一、世博会点燃智慧的火炬

从1851年英国伦敦召开万国工业博览会至今，世博会已经走过了159年的历史，它既展示了从工业革命至今每一时代人类文明的成果，浓缩了历史的经验和教训，又是人类实现“理想国”梦想的场所，创造了新的历史，为后世发展奠定了基础，引领着时代前进的方向。

在1900年巴黎博览会期间，英国生物学家、规划理论家帕特里克·盖迪斯（Patrick Geddes）共举行了134次特别会议，举办了800个班（每班都有40~50人参加），宣传城市发展与区域主义理念——曾经引领了城市发展的方向。上海世博会期间，有关方面也在杭州、苏州、南京等地举办了各种论坛，汇聚了多方的智慧与思想。今天，世博会已闭幕，大量的展览馆将拆除，但我们有理由相信，它所点燃的凝聚着智慧的火炬，必将照亮21世纪人居事业的发展之路，让生活更美好。

## 二、“城市即人民”

从20世纪初，特别是第二次世界大战以后，城市规划领域出现了不同的方向。一种是“自上而下”的，从宏观上关注城市、地区、城市连绵区等的发展。另一种是“自下而上”的，以社区为基础规划城市，采用小规模的形式，致力于提升普通民众的生活质量和社会凝聚力，如邻里单位（Neighborhood Unit）理论等。

远在第二次世界大战期间，许多有识之士在战火烽烟中即开始思考和讨论战后住宅与城市重建的问题。亨利·丘吉尔（Henry Stern Churchill）1945年出版的《城市即人民》（*The City is the People*）一书，强调人是城市的核心，没有人，城市就无从存在，应关注基本的邻里规划。其思想深刻，影响深远。

这些学术思想和研究成果都激荡着那个年代年轻而又充满热情的规划学人。以我自己为例，20世纪40年代在滇西参加抗战，眼见战争破坏下的中国城乡满目疮痍，由此下定了投身建筑与城市规划事业的决心。1945年受到梁思成先生的鼓励与赞许，并于1946年年初应其邀请到清华任教。其间有机会了解到邻里单位的理论，很受启发，当读到《城市即人民》一书时，更是顿然领悟。又在学校旁听费孝通先生的《城市社会学》、《乡村社会学》课程，经过多方阅读与思考，写出了我关于城市规划的第一篇习作论文，形成“完整社会单位的理论”的概念。

改革开放以来，中国城市快速发展，城市规划与区域理论结合起来指导大城市发展、城市化推进等问题，取得了很大进展，也进行了大量的社区建设。但社会发展日新月异，很多实际问题既有的社区无法解决，这不得不说是中国学术界的遗憾。

社区本身是一个社会学概念，人是城市的核心，社区是人最基本的生活场所，社区规划与建设的出发点是基层居民的切身利益。不仅包括住房问题，还包括服务、治安、卫生、教育、对内对外交通、娱乐、文化公园等多方面因素，既包括硬件又包括软件，内涵非常丰富，应是一个“完整社区”（Integrated Community）的概念。在社会整体转型的今天，建设“完整社区”正是从微观角度出发，进行社会重组，通过对人的基本关怀，维护社会公平与团结，最终实现和谐社会的理想。

例如，社区养老问题：中国已逐渐步入老龄化社会，家庭养老问题日趋普遍，这对单个家庭来讲是难题，但若依靠社区进行合理有效的组织就能有所缓解。又如，残疾人康复问题：如今人们致残的因素很多，病人自医院就医后回到家中仍需进行康复治疗，这就需要社区为他们提供必要的场所、设施和专业服务人员。再如，青年工作者的居住问题：学校毕业的青年人，海外归来的游子逐步融入大千城市，正当奋发有为，却每每“蜗居”一隅，难于“安居乐业”，施展抱负。

今天的中国已进入所谓“后单位”时代，由各事业单位的“大院”分头负责渐转向由社会负责，因此必须丰富社区的内涵，建设“完整社区”，承担综合功能，解决社会问题。

“完整社区”的建设首先是对物质空间匠心独运的创造性设计，以满足现实生活的需求。很多既有的小区设计僵化教条、考虑不周，留下了至今难以解决的后遗症，所谓的“物业”一般只能管理安全、维修。例如，北京海淀区蓝旗营小区，是清华和北大老师共同居住的社区，在国务院副总理的直接关怀下，才得以在2000年年底建设完成，但如今，公共空间匮乏，步行环境恶劣，甚至小区内都发生车辆相撞的事故，芳邻偶遇，竟无处交流，遑论居民的生活质量。

“完整社区”的建设更是一项系统的社会工程，社区精神与凝聚力的塑造至关重要。联合国及诸多学者所倡导的社区发展，其核心正在于组织和教育民众，要从社区的共同意识、友邻关系、公共利益和需要出发。因此，社区建设中还应加强民主评议及对公共利益的关心，使城市建设的科学原理从“普通常识”和“平凡真理”进一步成为社会共识，形成良好的社会风气，引导群众的广泛参与，形成完整社区，进行社会重组，共建和谐社会。

## 三、“安得广厦千万间，大庇天下寒士俱欢颜”

从中国当前的社区发展来看，主要是以房地产开发为主的建设经营模式，市场经济起主导作用。虽推进了住房建设，实则存在很大缺陷，导致房价暴涨不下，广大中低收入社会群体住房短缺。美国学者凯瑟琳·鲍尔（Catherine Bauer）1934 年出版的《近代住宅》（*Modern Housing*）一书中，即指责当时住宅经营为奢侈的投机（the Luxury of Speculative），指出："不好的制度不能产生好的住房，但只有良好的制度也不一定能产生好的住房。"从 20 世纪初到现在，社会发生了巨大的变化，但仍可认识到市场经济并不是万能的，不能盲目遵循美国房地产的发展途径，而荷兰、新加坡、我国香港等地建设"社会住宅"的经验值得我们借鉴。"住者有其房"是 1947 年梁思成随孙中山提出的"耕者有其田"而最早提出的，是人民群众普遍的渴望，在社会转型的大背景下，我们更要思考如何利用自身的智慧来解决时代的问题，在住房建设中加强社会主义的内涵。

中国历史上有良好的社会传统，至今仍是我们在社区建设中可以借鉴的宝贵财富。从孔子的"里仁为美"到杜甫的"安得广厦千万间，大庇天下寒士俱欢颜"，传统知识分子始终秉持着实现社会整体安居乐业的宏愿，并以实际行动努力践行。例如，北宋著名政治家、文学家范仲淹，兴置"义庄"周济宗族穷人，并在家乡创办"义学"培养乡里子弟，其济世情怀令今人感佩。

对比本文前述"自上而下"的规划来说，"自下而上"的社区规划虽然不足，但也不是没有新生的萌芽，社区规划还需要积极的倡导与规划。社区问题、住房问题的解决要依靠社会建设与重组，需要凝结着人类智慧的创造，以及多个地方、各规划单位、多学科、多领域的共同努力，以解决实际的生活问题，建立良好的居住环境秩序，建设完整社区，迈向和谐社会，真正实现"城市，让生活更美好"!

（作者：吴良镛，中国科学院院士，中国工程院院士，清华大学人居环境研究中心主任，清华大学建筑与城市研究所所长）

# 岭南近现代优秀建筑·1949—1990卷

1949—1990年，或许可以称为岭南建筑的“黄金时代”。在这50多年里，北园酒家、山庄旅舍、友谊剧院、矿泉旅舍、白云宾馆……一座座将“建筑”与“园林”有机结合的岭南建筑，曾经独领风骚，与“京派”、“海派”鼎足而立，三分天下，何其风流。2010年8月20日，一部还原现代岭南建筑历史的专著——《岭南近现代优秀建筑·1949—1990卷》在广州首发，再现岭南建筑辉煌。

## 岭南建筑科学文化的价值（序）

石安海同志托人带《岭南近现代优秀建筑·1949—1990卷》初稿给我，邀我写序。病后初愈，拜读华章，20世纪70年代参观岭南建筑所留下的印象重新展现在眼前，对曾经活跃的岭南建筑大师的崇敬之情又生。

先说“地区建筑”。在20世纪30年代，西方所谓“国际式”建筑思潮兴起时，就有人针锋相对地提出了“地域建筑形式”的主张。此后两种论争此起彼伏，直到今天。“地域建筑论”就世界看，意大利、法国以及北欧、中东、中南美等国家和地区都有自己的建筑特征。中国对整个世界来说，也是地区（东方或远东）。但中国有56个民族，分布在各个地区，不能简单地用“民族形式”来概括。例如：江南、皖南、巴蜀、云贵等，都有自己的文化传统，各个地区的地理气候特点、经济生活、社会情况和人文特色各不相同。岭南地区就属于这种情况。

说岭南建筑，不能不涉及泛岭南文化，包括绘画、雕塑、音乐、戏剧、建筑、园林、文学以及工艺美术、烹饪等等。即以近现代而论，不同艺术门类也多有其独到之处，代表人物、代表作品等会集为整体，互相影响，相得益彰，丰富多彩。即以绘画而论，我因幼时就热爱此道，20世纪30年代就知道有画家高剑父、陈树人，到后来，又有关山月、黎雄才以及我的老师邓白等。

岭南建筑的创造首先从功能出发。该地区独特的亚热带季风气候使得遮阳与通风的要求成为创作的前提。在20世纪50年代后，岭南建筑师就敢为天下先，在建筑创作中抵制“学苏”时期一度风靡的复古主义和形式主义，在建筑功能满足的前提下再进行建筑风格的探索，使得“岭南风格”逐渐形成并走向成熟。其中有对外来建筑思潮的吸收与扬弃，有与岭南庭园建筑的结合与创造，有依据岭南文化内涵创造的南越王博物馆等优秀建筑作品。

这本书并不是“建筑人物志”，但是重要作品与关键人物直到精辟的建筑思想多有列入：除前辈人物林克明先生外，陈伯齐、夏昌世、龙庆忠先生抗战时期都曾执教于重庆大学，我奉之为师辈。夏之鼎湖山庆云寺东侧教工休养所，依山就势，与寺院平台之结合，无愧为“岭南建筑的先驱”。后来的大师有佘畯南、莫伯治先生等，他们创造性的实践对岭南建筑特色的形成、发展居功甚伟。

谈到这里，又必须涉及地方领导的关注对岭南建筑风格的形成的作用。广州的朱光市长我未见过，知之不多，但从书中可以读到对他领导作风的赞扬。林西我曾晤面，他对建筑的热爱以及独特的见解在同行中口碑甚佳。另一方面是建筑师们兢兢业业的创造。以我所见证的佘畯南的几件“小事”为例：一次是我来广州，去白天鹅宾馆的建筑工地参观，见到类似本书插图所载的情形。佘畯南虽然在发高烧，但丝毫没有停止工作，披着一件棉军大衣在现场指挥。另一件是他们的“星期六建筑师”活动，利用公休时间下乡参加咨询工作，服务于郊区建设，我曾随着他们走访番禺、顺德等地。这些事情都给我留下了很深的印象。

处在中国对外交往南大门的当代岭南建筑师的创作是成功的。他们创造了一系列建筑精品，为新中国成立后的现代建筑史增添了光辉的篇章。但对于理论的全面整理和分析尚有滞后，尚不能说已经形成学派。而本书前言与绪论中，对于岭南建筑的概念与特征作了中肯而扼要的分析：在文化多元、宽容共存、多样杂陈的现象中，岭南建筑师不仅面对自然气候条件，如“夏氏遮阳”对建筑物理学之提倡，还有人文历史的兼容并蓄、建筑与环境的结合、地方风格的创新，以及对“平衡于经济实用与美观得体的简秀风格”的分析等等，正是本书对岭南建筑理论和信念所作的较完整的总结，对当代人居环境科学历史与理论的建构深有启发。

还有一点虽然在本书中已经提起注意，但仍值得更加重视。在城市化的高潮中，一些历史建筑包括近现代建筑的精品由于房地产的开发频遭拆毁。类似的情况在日本也曾经出现过，赖特的东京帝国饭店就不幸被拆除，事后不少人为之惋惜。建筑精品确实难得，城市也不能“失去记忆”。岭南建筑本身的发展过程是历史也是文化，特别是代表时代的一些标志性建筑更应得到重视和保护。

读完本书，有一个感想，过去建筑史研究往往偏向古代，自开展对近现代的研究以来，已经取得了丰硕的成果。但近现代的地域建筑，特别是新中国成立以后的当代建筑也应该梳理。一个时期的地域建筑的形成有一定的必然性和偶然性，一个地域的成功，对于其他地域来说不一定必须奉为经典，这方面值得探索的题目还很多。寂寞的建筑理论应该活跃起来。这本《岭南近现代优秀建筑·1949—1990卷》的出版可喜可贺，希望对其他地区也有可借鉴之处。

（作者：吴良镛，中国科学院院士，中国工程院院士，清华大学人居环境研究中心主任，清华大学建筑与城市研究所所长）

# 有益的总结，深刻的启示（在首发式上的发言）

《岭南近现代优秀建筑·1949—1990卷》出版发行，可喜可贺。这是一部关于区域文化和本土建筑的力作，是一部引人入胜的成功作品：阅读言简意赅的文字，欣赏精彩珍贵的图片，品味技艺精湛的画稿，获得的不仅是一种阅读的享受，更会有多方面的收益和启示。特别是对于建筑工作者来说，本书会引导你去思索某种类型的建筑与其区域位置、自然禀赋、人文资源和场所环境有着必然而直接的关系，而这些要素又通过建筑语言作出强烈的表达而加以固化，从而形成典型化的特色与个性。书中介绍了大量的案例，通过作者的分析评述，你会感受到岭南建筑在风格上的特质和气质上的惯性，而这些正是当代建筑设计最缺少的东西。当今，不同地域的城市之间同质化现象越来越明显，这一印象的最直观的感受是建筑的趋同，这是城市化快速推进的中国建筑界必须认真对待的现实。我们在放眼全球大量吸收国外先进建筑文化的同时，还必须回望自己的历史和家园，从丰富而独特的建筑遗产和文化传统中，去汲取营养，滋补创意思维，提高创新能力。《岭南近现代优秀建筑·1949—1990卷》的编纂在这方面做了有益的工作。本书立足于岭南，提示我们：不要忘记传统和本土，创新不是克隆舶来品，必须在承续传统的基础上去创新。因此，很有必要不断增强我们的典籍意识、理论意识、精品意识和遗产意识。

一是典籍意识。本书对1949—1990年间一系列优秀岭南建筑作品、关键人物和重要事件，进行了全面回顾与评述，是对当代岭南建筑发展历程的一次总结。作者从考察建筑实例入手，从1951年的华南土特产品展览建筑群，到1989年的西汉南越王墓博物馆，文图并茂，历数家珍，尽展新中国成立之后岭南建筑之精华，内容丰富、资料翔实，堪称近现代优秀岭南建筑的典籍。长期以来，由于我们缺乏典籍意识，不少珍贵的资料多有散失，每每因之造成不可挽回的损失，令人痛心疾首。本书的出版，首先在岭南建筑方面做了弥补，为我们留下了可以保留的记忆。随着时间的推移，这些资料将越发显示出它的珍贵和价值。

二是理论意识。本书在整理大量建筑实例的基础上，从学术的角度，研究总结出岭南建筑的五个方面的主要特征，这是本书的核心价值所在。在国际化、全球化浪潮猛烈冲击下，在城市快速生长、更新周期加快的背景下，在南北西东城市之间性格模糊、风貌趋同、特质式微的现实面前，本书的研究成果和学术观点，让建筑学人眼前为之一亮：业界的有识之士还是在坚持理论的探索，这是难能可贵的。中国建筑设计的软肋在于缺乏学术理论支撑、少有建筑评论引导和风格流派的探讨，基本上是跟在国外建筑师和建筑潮流的后面亦步亦趋。尽管跟得很紧，但跟在后面就意味着被边缘化，因此，难以走出国门参与世界市场的竞争。我国幅员辽阔，自然条件差异大，造就了具有不同区域特色的建筑文化，只要我们多关注自己，多研究一些本土的东西，多探索一些地域的特色，我们就会多一份文化自觉和民族自信，建筑就会少一些克隆，多一些创新，城市就会少一些浅薄低俗，多一些文化内涵。据悉，广东提出要建设文化强省，加强岭南建筑研究，弘扬岭南建筑文化传统，创新岭南建筑流派，当属题中之意。本书的编辑出版，可以说是个好的开头。

三是精品意识。本书在介绍建筑作品的同时，推出了主创建筑师，可谓让读者见物又识人。以广州为中心的岭南建筑界，有一大批素质很高的建筑大师。他们根植厚重的岭南文化沃土，并处在对外交流和改革开放的前沿，在吸收传统文化技能的基础上兼收并蓄、不断创新，屡屡推出许多建筑精品，造就了独树一帜的岭南建筑。纵观全书实例，我们可以鲜明感受到，岭南建筑：一是有文脉，是从珠三角这片热土中长出来的，而不是从外地搬来的；二是尊重自然和环境，它们是适应亚热带气候条件的；三是建筑意象具有自由、疏朗、明快、秀丽的南国气质，既有眷恋乡土的情愫，又有开放包容的心态，是很有"人缘"的建筑。应该看到，潜藏在这些精品后面的，是建筑师的社会责任和职业操守、建筑师的敬业热忱和团队精神、建筑师的不断追求和精品意识。这些都是我们应该认真学习和传承的，尤其是处在高速度开发建设时期的执业建筑师，应以他们为榜样，都应该具有这种品格。城市管理者、高层决策者也都应该具有这种素质。这样，我们的城市就会少一些失误和遗憾。

四是遗产意识。本书中某些精品佳作，可望经受住时间的检验而成为建筑设计的经典之作，这是一批宝贵的文化遗产。本书主编石安海先生无不痛心地披露：不少优秀的岭南建筑已经惨遭损毁。他提出"保护当代优秀建筑不受破坏刻不容缓"。其实，这种情况不仅在珠三角地区，在全国（特别是经济发达、开发建设速度较快的地区）都是屡见不鲜的事实。吴良镛先生在本书序言中也强调，对这些现象"值得更加重视"。本书的这些观点和意见，相信会得到多数人的赞同和支持。我们都要增强遗产意识。谈到遗产，我们可能对古建筑遗存，特别是文物，比较注重保护（尽管也有的遭到"灭顶之灾"），但对近现代建筑的保护则还没有真正提到日程上。这里有个遗产意识问题。文物是文化遗产，但遗产不一定都是文物。巴西利亚是个新兴城市，20 世纪 50 年代末作为新首都开始建设，1960 年开埠，27 年后，于 1987 年被列为世界文化遗产。可见，只要有独特的文化艺术价值，近现代的东西也能成为文化遗产。希望本书出版后，广东省能对近现代岭南建筑在本书基础上列出优秀项目保护名录，通过地方立法挂牌保护，或许是亡羊补牢，尤为未晚。

最后，要感谢本书的编著者，他们之中不少人是广东建筑界的宿将，是这批优秀建筑的亲历者、见证者，也是某些项目的设计者、建造者。他们熟知这段历史。可以看得出，他们是带着一份责任，带着一种特殊感情来编著这本书的。我想，这也是为什么先选择 1949—1990 年作为首卷出版的原因之一吧。岭南建筑文脉源远，1949 年前仍有一大批优秀建筑遗存；1990 年后的新岭南建筑，又在创新发展。另外，广东岭南建筑师在外地和境外也有不少优秀设计作品。所以，优秀的岭南建筑，还应该有姊妹篇出版，我们期待着新书的问世。这样，必将对岭南建筑的新发展，也为推动全国建筑理论研究和学术探索，做出积极的贡献。

（作者：宋春华，中国建筑学会理事长，中国房地产协会会长，中国房地产经纪人协会会长）

# 以迎办亚运为契机，全面提升城市规划建设管理科学化水平

2010 年是广州的“亚运之年”、“大变之年”和“跨越之年”。这一年，广州圆满、成功、精彩地举办了亚运史上规模最大的第 16 届亚洲运动会和首届亚洲残疾人运动会。同时，我们紧紧抓住筹办“两个亚运”的有利契机，以“迎接亚运会，创造新生活”为主题，在全力筹办好赛会活动的同时，坚持亚运为城市发展服务的工作导向，把筹办工作与加快转变经济发展方式、建设优美舒适的宜居城乡、展示提升市民文明素养和城市文明形象、提高市民群众幸福指数、强化国家中心城市功能紧密结合起来，加快国家中心城市和全省宜居城乡“首善之区”的建设步伐。特别是坚持“办赛事，办城市”的理念，按照中央政治局常委李长春同志关于广州城市环境面貌“到 2010 年一大变”的要求和中央政治局委员、广东省委书记汪洋同志提出的建设成为广东宜居城乡“首善之区”、实现“天更蓝、水更清、路更畅、房更靓、城更美”的目标，加快推进实施 2010 年城市环境“大变”工程计划、亚运城市行动计划和“花园城市”建设行动纲要，全力以赴推进以空气环境、水环境、人居环境及交通环境为重点的迎亚运城市环境综合整治，把筹备亚运的过程变成为推动城市环境建设科学化、上水平的过程，使广州城市建设和发展的步伐大大提速，城市环境面貌发生了巨大变化。

一是城市发展空间明显提升，功能布局明显优化。“山、水、城、田、海”的城市格局趋于定型，“南拓、北优、东进、西联、中调”的城市空间发展战略有序实施，多中心、组团式、网络型的城市结构基本形成，城市空间布局更加合理，区域功能定位更加明晰，城市发展内涵更加优化。2009 年年底城市建成区面积达到 927.1 平方公里，市区范围从 1998 年的 1443.9 平方公里增加到 3718.8 平方公里。

二是基础设施支撑功能显著提升，城市综合承载力明显增强。以新白云机场、南沙深水港、广州南站为龙头，以城市轨道交通和高快速路网为骨干，形成了立体式、现代化综合交通网络体系，城市综合承载能力、辐射带动能力显著提高。至亚运前已开通运营 8 条线路、236 公里地铁网络，比 1998 年增加 217.5 公里，比 2004 年增加 199.4 公里；城市道路总长度 5686 公里，比 1998 年新增 3778 公里。

三是城市面貌焕然一新，生活环境更加宜居。2010 年全市空气质量优良天数达到 97.8%，比 2004 年提高 13 个百分点，空气质量连续 5 年优于国家二级标准。2009 年以来新

建污水处理能力相当于历史形成的污水处理能力的总和，全市生活污水集中处理率达到85%，中心城区接近90%，是1998年污水处理率21.68%的4倍多；珠江广州段水质从劣V类提高到IV类标准，总长388.5公里的121条河涌整治后水质明显改善，再现岭南水乡特色；亚运前西江引水工程竣工通水，600万市民喝上了放心的优质水。全市公园数达到232个，比1998年增加了170个；建成区绿地率达35.5%，人均公园绿地面积达15.01平方米，分别比1998年增长9.62个百分点和8.64平方米。打造了一批人文历史景观和“一河三岸”旅游观光城市名片，陈家祠广场、荔枝湾涌、沙面等12个区域升级为岭南文化体验片区，广州塔、海心沙亚运公园、花城广场成为新的旅游和文化热点。

## 一、坚持科学统筹，系统有序整体推进城市“大变”工程

城市环境面貌关系亚运成功举办，关系国家中心城市建设，关系市民群众生活品质和水平。能否实现城市环境面貌“大变”目标，是对广州城市建设管理能力的一次大考。我们坚持一手抓经济发展，一手抓环境建设，统筹兼顾、整体部署，突出重点、扎实有序，以超常规的思维、超常规的手段、超常规的举措、超常规的大干掀起“大变”热潮，推动城市建设全面转型升级。

一是把“大变”与建设国家中心城市紧密结合起来。统筹考虑“大变”与城市总体发展战略规划实施，在深入推进“大变”中同步拓展城市空间结构、优化城市功能布局，增强交通基础设施支撑力，为加快国家中心城市建设打下了坚实基础。

二是把“大变”与加快转变经济发展方式紧密结合起来。坚持在“大变”中加快推进产业结构调整优化，实施中心城区产业“退二进三”、“腾笼换鸟”，积极推进产业和劳动力“双转移”，大力开展“三旧”改造，推动了产业高端化发展。

三是把“大变”与“创造新生活”紧密结合起来。坚持以“迎接亚运会，创造新生活”为主题，牢固确立“办赛事、办城市”理念，全力推进城乡环境综合整治，为市民群众营造整洁、舒适、优美的人居环境，提升了城市品位和市民生活品质。

四是把“大变”与提升城市文明程度紧密结合起来。坚持在“大变”中努力营造优良的城市软环境和昂扬向上的城市精神，使经济实力与城市活力、文明魅力相映生辉，国家中心城市形象得到更好展现。

## 二、坚持规划引领，明确城市定位和发展目标

注重规划引导，2000年，广州率先编制《广州城市建设总体战略概念规划纲要》，以拓展城市发展空间为核心，提出了将广州建设成为适宜创业发展、适宜生活居住的国际性区域中心城市和山水型生态城市的目标，以及“南拓、北优、东进、西联”的空间发展战略，及时解决了当时条件下城市发展方向、发展思路等战略性问题。

2000年6月、2005年5月，经国务院批准，先后两次调整市域行政区划，城市格局从

传统的“云山珠水”向“山、水、城、田、海”的立体式山水型转变，使广州从沿江城市成为真正的滨海城市，为实现“大变”拓展了广阔的发展空间。

2006年，回顾检查战略规划纲要实施情况，进一步修改完善规划纲要，并编制实施新一轮城市总体规划，增加了“中调”战略。城市空间发展布局进一步优化，形成了五大片区一主多副的空间格局，重点区域发展提速，各组团功能互补性和基础设施配套水平明显提升。

2009年9月，重新修编城市总体发展战略规划，提出了城市发展从外延式扩张向内涵优化提升转型的战略思路，明确提出以建设国家中心城市为总目标，加快建设国际商贸中心和世界文化名城，开始了城市建设发展的新跨越。在规划的有序引导和有效调控下，高标准规划建设新区，精细化改造提升老城区，搭起了城市面貌脱胎换骨的结构框架。

## 三、坚持夯实基础综合整治，加快建设优美舒适的宜居城乡

始终坚持以人为本，以建设全省宜居城乡的“首善之区”为目标，大力推进基础设施建设，着力优化提升城市功能布局，全力开展城市环境综合整治，着力为市民群众创造更加宜居的生活环境。

一是大力加强交通基础设施建设。坚持优先发展城市交通，高起点规划、高标准建设新机场、新港口、新火车站等大型交通枢纽设施，大力推进快速轨道和高快速路网建设。武广客运专线已经开通，广珠城际铁路、广深港客运专线等城际轨道交通线网以及贵广、南广、广珠的大型轨道交通工程加快推进，构建了市域高等级道路系统“四环十九射”基本骨架和中心城区“三环八联十八射”环形放射格网加“十八横十八纵”交通主干道。完成全市177条、共483.63公里道路人中修升级改造，全年新增市政道路长度约40.3公里。全力推进地铁网和BRT建设，实现7条地铁线网同时运行，中山大道22.9公里BRT公交项目投入营运。目前，地铁日均客流量达到410万人次，占公交客流总量的31.8%；BRT公交日均客运量80万人次，是亚洲客运量最大的BRT线路。注重交通管理政策的科学规划和实操演练，分三阶段实施15项整治措施，着力改善城市交通拥堵现状。高标准建设城市无障碍设施，共新建和改造盲道1129.34公里、坡道11827个，设置了1000套盲人过街音响信号装置，健全了覆盖全市道路、公共交通设施、公共活动和服务场所的无障碍设施，城市无障碍环境得到了明显改善。

二是高标准建设城市新中轴线等城市功能区。把筹办亚运作为城市战略规划实施的助推器，高标准规划建设广州城市新中轴线，在珠江新城开通了国内首条全地下、无人驾驶的旅客自动输送系统，在花城广场建设了国内一次性开发规模最大的综合性地下空间项目，珠江新城各项配套设施更加完善，CBD功能日渐凸显；建设了海心沙亚运公园、广州塔、国际金融中心（西塔）、广州歌剧院、省博物馆新馆、广州图书馆新馆等一系列具有国际水准、现代风格、岭南特色的城市新地标，打响了“城市客厅”新名片，成为广州新的商贸文化旅游休闲中心。

三是加快推进空气污染治理。实施“空气整治50条”和新31条，2008年以来淘汰1139家企业的燃煤小锅炉和91家落后水泥企业，关停23个小火电项目，整改或关停11个重点行业4413家挥发性有机物排放企业；提前实施机动车国Ⅲ、国Ⅳ标准，全面实施机动车环保标志管理，在城区260平方公里的区域限行黄标车。2007年1月起，在市中心区全面实施摩托车禁行，淘汰摩托车39万辆，每年减少2.44万吨污染排放量。

四是集中开展水环境综合治理。2008年年底，广州把水环境治理作为政府民生“一号工程”来抓，按照“截污清淤、雨污分流、调水补水、堤岸建设”的标准系统治水、综合治水，在不到两年时间里完成388公里、121条河涌整治工程，完成中心城区160个社区的雨污分流改造，新建成38座污水处理厂、1094公里污水管道，每天减少直排珠江污水80万吨。目前，全市市政污水管网达到2907公里，污水处理厂56座，生活污水处理能力提升到465.18万吨/日，全市生活污水集中处理率达到85%，中心城区接近90%，饮用水提前两年在全国大城市中率先全面达到新国标要求。

五是扎实推进人居环境综合整治。推动老城区1512个社区环境综合整治，成片改造后每个社区配套建设了社区服务中心、社区卫生服务中心、小公园、文化活动中心、视频监控系统。同步实施道路升级改造、建筑立面整治、园林绿化和光亮工程，共整治城市道路483公里，对31190栋旧建筑进行翻新，完成架空线落地埋设456公里，新建完善1215.91公里排水管（其中雨水管782.54公里，污水管433.37公里）。加大力度查控违法建设、整治违法广告招牌和城市“六乱”。城市管理年活动期间在全市范围集中开展查处违法建设、整治“六乱”、打击无证照生产经营食品违法行为、出租屋整治和流动人员管理等专项重点行动。目前，流动人员和出租屋基本实现了100%登记管理，2010年共清拆违法建设133万平方米，拆除违法户外广告15317块、招牌34120块，整治清理占道经营、乱张贴乱拉挂33.5万多宗。

六是精细做好城市绿化美化亮化工作。持续推进“青山绿地”工程建设和迎亚运绿化升级改造，重点实施18条主干道绿化升级改造，对主干道沿线198座、230公里人行天桥、高架桥、立交桥进行绿化美化，对城市出入口道路绿化景观进行升级，打造了一批精品绿化工程，形成了富有广州“四季花城”特色的绿化景观，建成贯通全市城区和98个街镇总长1060公里的绿道。完成中心城区主干道两侧和亚运会场馆周边32宗“烂尾楼”的整治任务。实施以12座跨江大桥、21公里珠江两岸、4.6公里城市新中轴线为主体的光亮工程。截至2010年，全市累计新增绿地面积24625公顷，森林覆盖率达到41.4%，林木绿化率达到44.8%。

七是积极开展“三旧”改造。从2008年起，对旧城区、旧厂房、旧城镇实施全面改造，进一步优化城市空间布局，改善城市环境面貌。138个城中村目前已有19个完成或正在实施改造，中心城区纳入第一批“退二进三”的企业全部完成关闭或搬迁，涉及用地面积71.5公顷的16个旧厂房改造项目已获得审批，正加快推进实施。

八是精心保护传承优秀传统文化。按照“有序控制，先保护、后开发”和“修旧如旧、建新如故”的原则，加强历史文化古迹的整治修复，传承旧城历史文脉，确保旧城空间肌理和整体格局得到最大维护。坚持历史文脉保护与环境改善相结合，维系非物质文化遗产。注重提升品质，注入文化内涵，打造文化亮点工程。10 多年来，先后完成了广州大剧院、广州新图书馆、南越王博物馆整治工程、南越王宫博物馆、辛亥革命纪念馆、大元帅府、陈家祠、南海神庙、黄埔古港等大型公共文化设施建设改造。

## 四、坚持改革创新，建立有利于城市建设管理科学发展的体制机制

着力推进体制、机制和管理创新，以创造性实践解决了城市建设整治超常规发展面临的突出问题。

一是深化行政管理体制改革。整合部门资源，建立以业务归口管理为主的大部门管理制，推行建管分离，2008 年以来规划、建设、水务、林业园林等实现了部门统管、城乡统筹，如改革水务治理体制，把治水工作集中到市水务局，解决以往上下游分治、多头管理的问题。2009 年成立城市管理委员会，实现了从综合执法到管理与执法的有机统一。

二是改革运行机制。按照“重心下移、立足基层”的思路，推动城市建设管理事权下移，建立了“两级政府，三级管理，四级网络”的城市管理体制。在为时一年多的大规模集中治理水环境中，将原来由市职能部门负责的工作加以分解落实，将治水工作事权下移到区（县级市），进一步明确工作目标和责任，充分发挥区（县级市）一级的主体作用；同时，深化考核奖惩机制改革，建立了一套严格的考核机制，并立下“军令状”，大大调动各责任主体的积极性、主动性和创造性，为打赢治水攻坚战创造了条件。

三是推进融资平台改革。2008 年年底，抓住国际金融危机中蕴藏的机遇，利用国家实行鼓励地方加大基础设施等投入拉动内需的政策，成立城市建设投资集团、水务投资集团等七大融资平台，加大市场融资力度，高强度推进城市规划建设整治项目的实施运作，探索出一套切实可行的城市建设资本化运作模式。如通过市场运作，政府只借资 4000 万元给项目公司作为启动资金，其余资金由企业融资解决建起广州塔。

四是深化审批制度改革。创新政府管理方式，优化审批职能配置。1999 年以来，先后进行三轮行政审批制度改革，共清理行政审批事项 2700 多项。同时完善行政审批配套制度和监管体系，营造了良好的政务环境。

五是改革考核奖励机制。建立严格的考核机制，重大事项签订责任状。对工作成效明显、在规定时限内完成的，予以表彰奖励，对工作不到位、推进不力、拖延完成的，实行严格问责，从而大大调动了各责任主体的积极性、主动性和创造性。

六是严格规范管理。从教育引导、制度建设、监督检查等方面加强工程建设质量，确保“大变”工程成为“阳光工程”、“放心工程”。制定完善建筑企业诚信综合评价体系及工程项目监管制度、工程项目采购（招标）工作配套制度、大额专项支出项目监督检查办法、资金集中支付制度等。实行工程管理、审核管理、资金管理“三权分离”，保证“大变”工程建设、资金使用、人员廉洁“三个安全”。强化工程建设质量管理，定期组织开展质量监督执法检查，以严明纪律和严格问责确保交出明白账、放心账。

十年“大变”翻开了广州城市规划建设的崭新一页。但提升城市建设管理水平永无止境，必须与时俱进、优化提高、不断推进。进入后亚运时期，广州将认真总结“大变”工作中的好做法、好经验，坚定战略目标不动摇，弘扬亚运精神不懈怠，深化“创造新生活”内涵不停步，加快推进城市发展转型升级，不断提升城市规划建设管理科学化水平，努力建设全市人民幸福生活的美好家园。一是进一步完善城市发展战略规划，引领城市新一轮发展，加快建设国家中心城市，建成面向世界、服务全国的现代化国际大都市。二是完善交通基础设施体系，增强城市综合承载能力，加快建设珠江三角洲“一小时城市圈”的核心。三是加快建设“花园城市”，继续扎实推进城市交通优化、绿化升级、城中村改造、水环境和空气污染治理等工作，大力提高生态文明水平，真正把广州打造成宜居宜业的国际“花园城市”。四是建立健全城市环境整治、建设和管理长效机制，提高城市管理科学化、精细化、人性化水平，坚决杜绝“大变”后可能出现的反弹现象，巩固、提升和优化城市环境。五是精心培育城市之魂、活力之源，不断丰富升华新时期广州人精神，大力建设传统与现代完美融合、厚重与时尚交相辉映、岭南文化风情与时代文明风采并茂的世界文化名城。

（作者：张广宁，广东省委常委，广州市委书记）

# 创新型城市建设在中国

伴随着知识经济的萌发与经济全球化的进程，创新型城市的发展迅速崛起，逐步成为国内外经济、社会和区域发展的一个具有战略性意义的亮点，也成为学者们研究的热点。在我国，创建创新型城市的活动也已呈现出一道亮丽的风景线，赢得了社会各界的热切关注。

本文首先介绍创新型城市在国内外的发展态势，接着分析创新型城市建设在我国迅速发展的动因，最后对我国建设创新型城市的战略意义提出若干看法。

## 一、创新型城市的发展态势

创新型城市的崛起虽然迅速，令世人眼花缭乱，但对它的内涵、发展理论、发展模式等问题依然处于探索阶段。目前，远未达到确切地认识与严格地统计分析的时候。好在已有大量的学者就此展开了深入研究，为创新型城市的发展趋势分析提供了参考性思路。关于创新型城市的定义，国内外学者看法各异，各种各样定义很多。本文的定义是：以创新引领发展的现代化城市。

### 1. 创新型城市在世界各国发展的宏观态势

与创新型城市有关的论文和介绍很多，由于篇幅有限，取其中一个受到国内外学者广泛关注的机构所做的研究，作一概括的介绍。

英国罗伯特·哈金斯协会运用世界知识竞争力指数 WKCI（World Knowledge Competitiveness Index）模型对全球最佳表现地区或城市的知识容量、能力、可持续性以及将知识转换成经济价值和该地区居民的富裕程度进行整体综合测评。2002 年首次发表知识竞争力排行榜。2003 年起至 2005 年，扩大到 125 个地区或城市，覆盖了北美、欧洲、亚洲、大洋洲（北京、上海、天津和珠三角地区增列），包括了经济增长活跃的中国、印度和东欧的中心城市和地区；2008 年报告进一步扩大到 145 个地区或城市（除北京、上海、天津外，江苏、浙江、山东增列，珠三角地区被广东替代）。其中北美占 63 个（57 个在美国）；欧洲 54 个；亚太 28 个。我国最关注的世界高技术产业的基地城市和新兴的创意产业中心城市皆被涵盖。部分典型地区的 WKCI 综合指数 2003—2005 年的排序如表 1、表 2 所示：

表1　典型区域，城市的 WKCI 指数排序

| 地名 | 2003 年/指数 | 2004 年/指数 | 2005 年/指数 |
|---|---|---|---|
| 圣何塞 | — | — | 1/295.3 |
| 旧金山 | 1/228.7 | 1/259.0 | 3/239.1 |
| 华盛顿 | 20/144.2 | 23/149.7 | 23/142.4 |
| 柏林 | 93/70.0 | 87/67.8 | 87/71.1 |
| 斯德哥尔摩 | 18/147.0 | 15/170.7 | 8/190.8 |
| 伦敦 | 66/93.9 | 46/111.4 | 56/105.8 |
| 大巴黎 | 54/105.4 | 34/133.5 | 29/136.3 |
| 东京 | 15/149.8 | 38/123.8 | 22/143.4 |

表2　国外典型地区知识密集率及排序

| 地名 | 2003 年/指数 | 2004 年/指数 | 2005 年/指数 |
|---|---|---|---|
| 圣何塞 | — | — | 1/1.84 |
| 旧金山 | 2/1.48 | 1/1.89 | 8/1.54 |
| 华盛顿 | 43/1.09 | 48/1.10 | 56/1.02 |
| 柏林 | 72/0.93 | 67/0.93 | 58/1.01 |
| 斯德哥尔摩 | 18/147.00 | 7/1.49 | 2/1.69 |
| 伦敦 | 86/0.83 | 56/0.97 | 90/0.82 |
| 大巴黎 | 84/0.85 | 47/1.11 | 51/1.06 |
| 东京 | 57/1.02 | 71/0.91 | 46/1.07 |

世界知识经济领先城市和地区的表现，前 20 名（以美国和个别西欧国家的中心城市为主）与后 20 名（以中国、印度和东欧国家的中心城市为代表）位序较稳定。处于中间的近百个城市或地区则变化较大，反映了各自发展驱动力的差异。这一差异从一个侧面反映了创新型城市发展的多样性与曲曲折折的探索过程。

**2. 我国创新型城市的兴起**

（1）我国创新型城市建设起步迅速

中国是当前世界上倡导和创建创新型城市最活跃的国家之一。2006 年 1 月 4 日，中共深圳市委、深圳市人民政府作出了《关于实施自主创新战略建设国家创新型城市的决定》，在全国率先举起了建设创新型城市的旗帜。此后一年时间里，据调查，先后有 106 个城市提出了建设创新型城市的奋斗目标，数量占到全国 661 个建制市的 16%。这些城市分布于全国 27 个省、市、自治区，包括北京、上海、天津和重庆 4 个直辖市，21 个省会城市，一批非省会的副省级市、地级市和县级市。当然，近几年步入创新型城市建设行列的城市急速增加，估计有 200 多个。

(2) 我国城市的创新发展任重道远

如果运用WKCI综合指数分析我国参评的六个地区WKCI综合指数(2003—2005年的排序如表3),其知识创新能力与城市的知识经济发展程度,相对而言存在着一定差距,大多处于起步发展阶段。但是,处于不同发展阶段的城市都会从实际出发,探索适合自身的创新发展的道路。目前,我国的深圳、上海、大连等已经形成加速创新发展的城市建设模式。这是值得总结与借鉴的。

表3 我国参评城市的WKCI指数排序

| 地名 | 2003年/指数 | 2004年/指数 | 2005年/指数 |
|---|---|---|---|
| 北京 | 120/38.0 | 117/27.4 | 119/27.7 |
| 上海 | 121/36.4 | 119/17.5 | 112/40.2 |
| 天津 | 122/25.8 | 121/10.3 | 122/15.7 |
| 珠三角 | 85/74.8 | 118/23.8 | 115/32.9 |
| 香港 | 102/61.4 | 106/53.5 | 118/27.7 |
| 台湾 | 103/60.6 | 102/57.4 | 99/61.3 |

表4 我国参评地区知识密集率及排序

| 地名 | 2003年/指数 | 2004年/指数 | 2005年/指数 |
|---|---|---|---|
| 北京 | 86/0.85 | 111/0.57 | 114/0.51 |
| 上海 | 119/0.59 | 122/0.27 | 101/0.63 |
| 天津 | 91/0.81 | 123/0.27 | 118/0.42 |
| 珠三角 | 22/1.23 | 121/0.33 | 115/0.46 |
| 香港 | 104/0.74 | 99/0.66 | 121/0.56 |
| 台湾 | 81/0.86 | 83/0.82 | 77/0.89 |

中国社会科学院从市场规模、经济增长、生产效率、资源节约、经济结构和生活水平六个方面,利用标准的客观数据对我国200个城市的国际竞争力进行评估。虽然没有直接从创新发展的角度分析,但其评估内容的六大方面已经包含了创新发展的引导意图,还是具有参考价值的。他们的评估显示,我国城市的国际竞争力虽然整体水平低,但是增长速度快,提升潜力巨大。根据《全球城市竞争力报告(2005—2006)》(社科文献出版社)发布的全球110个城市综合竞争力的排名,进入榜单的中国城市共有22个(包括中国香港、中国澳门以及中国台湾地区)。其中排名最高的是香港,位居全球第19名,其次是台北,占据第48位。中国大陆排名最高的是上海,居于全球第69位,接下来依次是北京、深圳、广州等。值得注意的是:排行榜上的中国城市主要位于70~100名之间,且以东南沿海经济较为发达,开放程度较高的城市为主,如深圳、广州、杭州、苏州、大连、青岛、南京、珠海、温州等。在综合2004年、2005年、2006年连续三年的中国城市竞争力排名中,中国内地、港

澳和台湾地区表现出了不同的特点和趋势。香港保持了领头羊地位，竞争力优势尽显；澳门排名稳定，预示较大潜力；台湾地区的几个城市出现疲态，2006年较之2005年竞争力排名显著下滑；浙江省城市竞争力有所下降，环渤海城市竞争力上升。

(3) 创新型城市的发展趋势

在科学发展观的引领和国家实施“十一五”国民经济与社会发展规划及中长期科学和技术发展规划纲要的大背景下，考察各地建设创新型城市的决策、部署和实践，我国创新型城市的发展正呈现以下重要趋势：

① 创新型城市的内涵、战略和评价指标体系的研究进一步深入，对创新型城市建设起到指导作用。

② 创新型城市的经济与产业结构正按照发展绿色经济、低碳技术和循环经济的方针，自觉向绿色化、特色化和高端化发展，对我国产业结构的调整发挥引领作用。

③ 自主创新战略已成创新型城市建设的主导战略，对知识产权的创造、应用和保护起到有力的推动作用。

④ 以企业为主体、产学研有效结合的技术创新活动蓬勃发展，对科技体制改革的深化起到促进作用。

⑤ 科技创新创业的投入大幅增加，支持创新与产业化的金融工具创新更趋活跃。

⑥ 科学创新方法学和现代项目管理的推广应用日益受到高度重视，并在提升自主创新能力和投入效率与效益上发挥重大作用。

⑦ 支持创新创业的服务体系和基础设施更加完善，信息基础设施——特别是宽带服务设施的升级与普及和三网融合的试点，将起重要支撑作用。

⑧ 学习型城市与创新型城市建设紧密结合，将为创新创业的可持续发展营造良好的社会氛围。

⑨ 政府更加重视职能的转变和行政服务效率的提高，并成为城市竞争力的重要因素。

⑩ 创新型城市将更具开放意识，并通过“引进来”、“走出去”、“接得通”、“联得上”，积极促进国内外创新资源的集聚、整合、交流与合作。在创新型城市密集的区域，尤其是长三角、珠三角和环渤海地区，创新型城市间的合作交流与错位发展将有力地促进创新集群的形成，并成为跨行政区的区域创新体系的枢纽。

## 二、建设创新型城市是时代发展的必然

与创新型国家、国家创新体系等一样，创新型城市也是经济社会发展实践的产物，是学者对于一些具有典型意义的国家或地区发展经验的总结与概括。创新型城市的出现应以1996年为具有里程碑意义的一年。这一年，经济合作与发展组织（OECD）在其科学技术和产业发展展望报告中，系统地提出了以知识为基础的经济概念，并称OECD主要国家的经济已是以知识为基础的经济。此后，美国总统的国情咨文和世界银行1998年的年度报告都正式使用了“知识经济”这一概念，“知识经济”得以确认。随之，以西欧、北欧发达国家主

导，积极开展了关于知识经济的深入系统研究，并将研究的重点聚焦到经济表现最佳的中心城市地区，揭示了创新型城市崛起的状态，反映了创新型城市对世界经济的主导引领作用。

创新型城市崛起的速度如此之快，范围如此之广，影响如此之大，被关注的程度如此之高，在战略层面中地位如此之重，充分向人们证明：这绝非偶然。创新型城市的崛起是有其深刻的历史背景与鲜明的时代烙印的。

**1. 科技进步是创新型城市发展的本因**

城市发展是社会进步的集中体现，创新型城市的崛起是社会现代发展的一种表现。显然，创新型城市崛起的根源在于社会发展的内在动力，而不仅仅局限于城市自身。推动社会发展的多种因素相互关联，构成了具有多层次和复杂性的社会发展动力系统。在这一动力系统中，依照因素作用的性质、范围和形式，可以区分为根本的、基本的、直接的或次要的动力。无需证明的是，推动社会发展的根本动力是生产力和生产关系的关联，而最终发挥决定作用的力量是生产力的发展水平。生产力是生产要素与生产方式的综合。与生产力发展水平相适应，社会经历了原始文明、农业文明、工业文明。在工业文明时期，开创了以依赖于资本、资源、劳力的工业经济发展模式。科技进步始终是决定生产要素水平与生产要素关联形式的核心力量，因而也是社会发展的主要推动力量。从一定意义上讲，社会发展过程就是科技进步的过程，人类社会的文明史就是一部科技演化史。

自 20 世纪 70 年代以来，科技进步快速发展，知识产出迅猛增加，科学、技术与经济、社会的关系越来越紧密，科技成果转化越来越迅速，科技第一生产力的地位越来越明显。由此引发了生产力形态的一系列演变：一是知识对经济贡献率越来越大，而资本贡献率逐步下降，以知识为基础的无形资产对经济发展贡献成为主导因素。这就是早年熊比特、弗里曼、伦德瓦尔等提炼、形成创新理论的生产力基础。二是知识经济逐步发育。在科技进步推动的知识生产与社会创新活动基础上，以非物质性产品生产的第三产业（特别是现代服务业）取代工业经济时代的第二产业的主导地位，成为知识经济时代发挥拉动作用，支撑一、二产业技术改造升级的主导产业。三是生产方式与发展模式发生转变。知识的主导地位引发生产要素的组合关系发生巨变。知识取代资本的地位，人才取代劳力的地位，无形资产取代资源的地位。在工业经济时代展现的是依托资本、资源、劳力的传统工业经济模式；而在知识经济时代，取代传统工业经济模式的是依托知识、人才、信息的知识经济模式，通常简称为创新发展模式。这里的创新发展模式，就是以知识生产为基础、创新为驱动、知识经济为特征的新型发展模式。四是知识社会逐步形成。作为经济基础的知识经济以及知识经济所依赖的引导创新的社会网络，决定了社会理念、社会管理、社会组织、社会生活都发生相应的转变。为了简便，这里统称为适应知识经济的知识社会的形成。基于这一发展，在 20 世纪 70—80 年代，高技术产业兴起，以美、日、欧为代表进行了一轮产业结构的重大调整，带动了 20 世纪 90 年代以美国为首的新经济的发展。

城市作为一定区域范围内政治、经济、文化、宗教、人口等的集中之地和中心所在，伴随着知识经济的出现，自然成为创新发展方式取代传统发展方式的开拓者，成为知识创造基地与依赖创新能力竞争发展的前卫。这就是创新型城市崛起的根本的内在原因。

**2. 国际竞争是创新型城市发展的诱因**

(1) 经济全球化的新趋势

科技进步在推动知识经济发育的同时，也借助知识经济的扩张促进了经济的全球化发展和科技国际化趋势。一个源自掌握知识制高点的发达国家夺取国际竞争优势的技术壁垒工具，直接导致了世界以创新能力为核心、以知识产权为手段的国际竞争新格局的形成。而具有创新能力的跨国公司，力图实现在世界范围生产要素的有效配置并获取最大效益的经营理念，引导企业国际化经营的新发展。由此导引出国际经济发展的新特征，包括：生产的全球化，跨国公司越来越成为世界经济的主导力量；市场的全球化，国际贸易迅速发展，国际贸易成为世界经济的火车头；资金的全球化，国际金融迅速发展，巨额资金在各国之间自由流动，国际直接投资迅速增长；科技开发和应用的全球化；信息传播的全球化。对世界各国经济在生产、分配、交换和消费环节的全球趋同化的趋势，称为经济全球化。实质是由于生产力的发展所引起的生产要素在全球范围流动，以寻找更有利的投资场所的过程。面对经济全球化发展，整合国际创新资源、形成有国际优势的创新能力，参与全球化国际布局的竞争，成为新时代创新发展的一个重要特征。

(2) 全球化伴随区域经济的崛起

经济全球化发展并不是世界经济的平均化，不是经济利益的平摊化，而是超竞争能力者获取利益的国际化。全球化并非各民族完全地同质化，而是在全球经济文化整合的进程中显现其区域或民族的异质性与特色。全球化必然伴随区域化和民族化的过程。由此，竞争主体的特色化、优势化是获取经济全球化利益的法宝。特色化、优势化的核心内容在于集聚、整合国际创新资源的能力，形成有国际优势的创新能力，参与全球化国际布局竞争的能力。在某种条件下，全球化与区域化是同一个问题的两个方面，区域化是全球化实现的一种形式。区域经济的空间尺度可以小到中心城市为核心的经济区，可以大到跨行政区、跨国、跨洲。随着知识经济的兴起与经济全球化发展，跨行政区划、跨国界的区域经济一体化也在广度、深度和影响力以及对全球经济发展的贡献方面，形成了浩浩荡荡的历史潮流。例如，欧盟一体化的进程并逐步东扩、美洲自由贸易区的形成、非洲联盟的出现、亚洲一体化趋势。我国海峡"大三角"以及东部产业带也是经济基础最好、区位优势最显著的区域，显示为东亚经济走廊增长潜力最大的区域。

其实，区域经济发展已有长久的历史，区域经济理念也逐步创新。自19世纪初以来，先后出现过杜能的"农业区位论"、韦伯的"工业区位论"、克里斯塔勒的"中心地理论"和廖什的"市场区位论"等。第二次世界大战以后，从科技进步与经济发展的影响，进一步出现威尔逊的"动态区位论"，皮鲁的"增长极理论"以及弗利曼、纳尔逊、伦德瓦尔等区域"创新体系"理论。区域创新理论为知识经济时代区域经济发展提供了社会发展创新的思路，对于微观尺度的城市经济、中观尺度以大都市圈组团为核心的区域经济，以及宏观尺度上经济一体化进程都起到了引导作用。

(3) 区域经济提升城市功能

在社会发展进入21世纪之后，知识经济萌发、经济全球化发展、区域经济崛起，都大大提升了城市的竞争地位与创新功能，由此引发出全球加速城市化的进程。高技术化、全球化和城市化成为21世纪发展的三大特征。那些世界顶尖的战略家们已经看得很清楚，世界的未来是属于那些能够接触和采用新技术的国家，而其核心是国家中具有创新活力的城市，创新型城市是城市化的一个新的高级阶段。从某种意义上来说，创新型城市就是城市的现代化和高技术产业化。

**3. 创新战略是我国创新型城市兴起的直接动因**

(1) 我国创新发展战略方针的引导

2006年新年伊始，党中央国务院即在北京隆重召开了全国科学技术大会。中共中央总书记、国家主席胡锦涛发表了重要讲话，中共中央国务院作出了《关于实施科技规划纲要，增强自主创新能力的决定》，正式提出了建设创新型国家的战略目标和“自主创新，重点跨越，支撑发展，引领未来”的新时期科技工作的指导方针。国务院随即公布了国家中长期科学和技术发展规划纲要，国家发改委和科技部等部门也公布了“十一五”科技发展专项规划，在全国引起巨大反响。各地在贯彻落实大会精神和中央《决定》过程中，纷纷以党委和政府的名义作出决定，提出建设创新型地区（省区）和创新型城市的目标，把增强自主创新能力、建设创新型城市作为提升城市（地区）综合竞争力的主导战略，响应和落实中央建设创新型国家的伟大号召。

(2) 转变经济发展模式紧迫性的鞭策

“十五”计划期间，中央一再强调要树立和落实科学发展观，加强宏观调控，大力转变经济发展模式，调整产业结构，转变增长方式，发展循环经济，建设资源节约型、环境友好型社会。“十一五”规划期间，这一战略方针的落实更为紧迫。城市——尤其是中心城市，是国民经济的基石和枢纽，无论是资源开发型城市、制造业中心城市，或外商投资主导的外向型产业城市，在贯彻落实科学发展观和中央经济方针中，负有重任。依靠科技进步和创新，实现由“中国制造”向“中国创造”的转变，由“投资驱动”主导向“创新驱动”主导转变，由依赖资源和能源消耗向发展循环经济转变，走可持续发展的道路，已在许多城市形成战略共识。在建设创新型城市的名单上，我们可以清晰地看到这一动向。

(3) 多年实施“科教兴国”战略的深化

在20世纪90年代，我国即确定实施“科教兴国”战略。许多城市相应确定了实施“科教（技）兴市”的战略，包括：深化科技和教育体制改革，大力发展科技教育事业；促进企业技术创新，提升传统产业劳动生产率；积极发展高新技术及其产业化，培育知识经济基础；加强信息基础设施建设，建设数字城市和学习型城市；依靠科技和教育，促进经济和社会的可持续发展。这些都为新时期实施建设创新型城市战略奠定了良好的基础。

(4) 我国区域经济战略部署的推动

当前，我国把握历史发展战略机遇期，进入转变经济发展方式，调整经济结构，建设创新型国家，推动全面建设小康社会战略目标的实现、加快现代化快速发展的历史新阶段。为实现现代化建设新阶段的宏伟目标，需要大力促进区域经济协调发展，形成若干各具特色的经济区和经济带，构建优势互补、共同发展的区域经济新格局。对此，国家已经从四个层次上作出了重大战略部署。

一是构建以中心城市为核心的行政区域技术创新体系，推动区划经济特色化发展。二是适应我国幅员广大、差异突出的特点，提出西部大开发战略、中部崛起战略、振兴东北工业基地战略以及鼓励和支持条件较好的东部率先发展等。三是推动具有大城市组团发展潜力、可以显示重要增长极带动作用的经济核心区创新发展。现在已经取得快速发展成效的有泛珠江三角洲，正在形成实力的有长江三角洲，已经启动酝酿的有京津唐或环渤海地区三个，具有潜在能力有待挖掘的是台海经济区，需要扶持整合实力的是武汉、成都、西安三角带所代表的经济区。四是推动跨国界的大经济区域发展。已经启动“10+3”为基础的东亚经济合作区，开始考虑的有亚洲经济一体化，正在以经贸为核心进行探索的有东北亚合作区、西北亚合作区、西南亚合作区等。

(5) 构建国家创新体系是城市创新发展的基本要求

建设创新型国家需要国家创新体系的支撑。《国家中长期科技发展规划纲要》提出了我国国家创新体系建设的基本框架，其中包括宏观调控体系、区域技术创新体系、企业为主体的产学研结合的微观创新体系、军民结合的技术创新体系、科学创新体系以及科技创新资源与支撑体系等。而居于承上启下地位的区域创新体系具有重要的战略意义。区域创新体系的核心在于中心城市的城市创新体系的建设。

从国际创新大趋势来看，抓好创新型城市建设，中国将独领21世纪风骚。中国是一个大国，一些发达地区或大城市可以与一个中小国家比拟，如果能通过国家计划来促进一批城市率先进入创新型城市行列，则将加快具有国际影响力的创新区域的建成，大大加快创新型国家的建成。从国家宏观角度，实施“抓中间，带两头”的战略措施，抓好创新型城市建设，是适应中国国情、有中国特色自主创新道路的新路径。从地区经济发展角度，加速城市向创新型城市转变是其发展的战略捷径。科技部在2008年的工作部署中也指出：加大科技计划对区域发展的引导和支持，提出对区域科技发展的指导性意见；进一步完善和加强部省会商制度，着力抓好“一把手”工程，在资源、智力、政策服务等方面加大支持；要形成长期机制，带动地方的科技创新投资，落实好国家项目和地方重大项目的实施。

自从中央提出建设创新型国家的目标以来，各地纷纷积极响应。据2008年统计，全国已有106个城市在市委市政府主持下，提出建设创新型城市的目标，其中有38个建有国家高新区。天津、深圳、合肥等市还向科技部提出了“部市共建”的要求。这不仅涉及地方发展的全局，也是国家科技工作不可忽视的宏观态势。创新型城市是创新型国家的基础和支柱，是国家创新要素资源最密集的地区，是企业为主体、产学研结合方针的落脚点，也是科技行政管理部门统揽全局、推进区域创新体系和国家创新体系建设、深化科技体制改革、落实十七大精神极好的抓手。当前，完善国家创新体系和区域创新体系，深化科技体制改革，建设创新型城市已经成为一项事关我国能否建成创新型国家的战略措施，这将成为推动城市创新发展的强劲动力，逐步展现出我国创新型城市探索、发展的崭新局面。

## 三、创新型城市建设的战略意义

### 1. 从创新发展和人类社会发展的视角来审视

从系统维度来审视，创新型城市建设是国家创新体系建设的突破口，它属于中观层次，国家是宏观层次，企业是微观层次。国家创新体系建设从中观层次突破比从微观层次突破影响作用更大。中观层次突破必然带动微观层次的突破，微观层次突破是中观层次突破的基础，但不会自动实现中观层次的突破。

国内外都认为创新发展是人类社会发展的新阶段，依靠创新推动和引导社会的科技、教育、经济、文化、政治的发展以及与环境的协调发展。但创新并不是今天才有的，创新是人类固有的本能，有了人类也就有了创新。人类社会由原始社会、农业社会、工业社会到现在的知识社会，从根本上来说，都是靠创新推动的。创新造就了人类的生存和发展，也促进了人类文明的进步。那么，为什么到现在才提出创新发展呢？这就要从创新发展的内涵与外延来探索。创新概念最简洁明了的表述是英国沿用了十几年的定义：创新是新思想的成功应用[1]。创新发展实际上应包含两部分内容：一个是创新自身的发展；另一个是创新外延的发展。创新自身的发展推动着创新外延的发展，创新外延的发展又推动着创新自身的发展，这是一个正反馈关系。到了知识经济、知识社会时代，这个正反馈关系的巨大威力才开始涌现出来。

现代社会无论是创新主体还是创新方式、创新方法、创新过程和创新结果，都有了很大的实质性发展。已有的创新是分散的，以个体为主的特征，思维方式上是还原论的线性思维方式。即使这样，这些特点也使创新取得了很大成就。历史上出现过很多科学家、技术发明家，他们的创新性成果推动了科技进步，促进了生产力的发展，使人类社会先后步入到农业社会、工业社会以至今天的知识社会。另一方面，已有的创新基本上是在物质、能量领域中，科学革命、技术革命以及由此引发的产业革命都是在这两个领域中出现的。而真正在信息领域中出现的革命性发展，是在20世纪末才出现的，由此引发的产业革命正方兴未艾。这场以计算机、网络、通信为核心的信息技术革命，不仅推动着物质、能量领域中的科学革命、技术革命和产业革命，同时也推动着人类自身的发展，出现了人—机结合、以人为主的思维方式，人类更加聪明了，创造性更强了。在信息、知识、智慧三个层次上，以及三个层次的结合上，都比过去有了巨大发展。这场信息技术革命改变了人们的思维方式、研究方式、工作方式、生产方式、生活方式、教育方式以至娱乐方式，特别是创新方式。这就是知识经济、知识社会出现的背景。目前仅仅是这场信息革命的先声，更大的发展还在后头。

在这种趋势下，创新发展呈现出系统性特点，更注重的是整体，是整体涌现。如果说，以往的创新主要在微观层次，如研究所、大学、企业等，那么，现在已进入到中观和宏观层次，出现了创新体系，特别是国家的创新体系，已成为国家行为。

创新自身的发展除了客观因素外，还有来自人类的主观因素，这就是方法论的转变，由过去以还原论方法为主开始向以系统论方法为主的转变。近 20 年来国内外出现的复杂性和复杂系统研究就是这个转变的标志。这个转变的后效作用将会更大。

国家创新体系是有层次结构的复杂系统，这就是国家的宏观层次，区域或地方的中观层次，以及企业、科研院所、大学等构成的微观层次。每个层次都有自己的特点和功能，但又相互作用，相互关联，相互影响。只有层次之间相互协调了，系统的整体优势才能发挥出来。从这个角度来看，国家创新体系建设应该在三个层次上以及三个层次的相互关联、相互作用、相互影响上下功夫，不能顾此失彼。

但我们又不能面面俱到，点点都抓。必须要有重点，抓重点带动全面。那么，重点又是什么呢？从我国实际情况来看，宏观层次上的重点，应是建立科学的决策与管理体系，加强创新型政府的建设；中观层次上应是创新型城市建设；微观层次上是创新型企业和企业集群。应该指出，中观层次有承上启下的作用，所以它又是重中之重。这样一来，三个重点抓住了，也就抓住了国家创新体系建设的“纲”，纲举目张，可以带动整个国家创新体系的建设。

综上所述，我们可以看出，创新型城市建设是国家创新体系建设的突破口，从中观层次突破比从微观层次突破影响作用更大，而中观层次突破必然带动微观层次的突破，微观层次突破是中观层次突破的基础，但不会自动实现中观层次的突破。

一个创新型国家必须有一些创新型城市和一批创新型企业来支撑，否则，创新型国家只是个概念口号和空架子。

### 2. 从国际竞争和全球化视角来看

抓创新型城市建设，对于中国最大限度地分享全球化带来的利益具有重要意义。

2007 年，由美国国家情报委员会主持撰写，上千位资深专家参与的《大趋势——2020 年的世界》指出：“在我们看来，全球化是一个占主导地位的‘主导潮流’，其力量无处不在，以至于将显著地影响 2020 年世界的其他主要潮流的形成。”“全球化所带来的利益不可能是均等的，全球化的最大受益者将逐渐集中到那些能够接触和采用新技术的国家和集团、采用新技术政策的国家。”那些世界顶尖的战略家们已经看得很清楚，世界的未来是属于那些能够接触和采用新技术的国家，而其核心是国家中具有创新活力的城市。美国诺贝尔经济学奖得主斯蒂格里茨曾说：“美国的高技术产业化和中国的城市化是 21 世纪最重要的大事。”创新型城市是城市化的一个新的高级阶段，从某种意义上来说，创新型城市就是城市的现代化和高技术产业化。

### 3. 从区域经济发展来看

区域的概念比较宽泛，小到一个城市的区，大到几个国家聚集的区。本文指的是一个城市的范围。根据 2008 年统计，全国 661 个建制市中已有 106 个城市提出要建创新型城市。创新型城市能否建成的关键要看能不能有效聚集创新资源，以及这些资源在当地能否发挥更高的效率。关于创新型城市建设评价指标体系的构思中采用三个一级指标，创新投入、创新产出和创新环境，正是用来说明这一关键的。

前面已经提到，从建设创新型国家和国家创新体系来看，创新型城市建设是突破口，是抓中间、带两头战略的核心。因此，可以这么说，创新型城市能否建成将决定我国能否建成创新型国家。像中国这么一个大的国家，而且发展极不平衡，国家制定政策需要统筹方方面面。而对一个城市来说，就具有较多的灵活性。因为人才、技术和资本等创新资源具有很强的流动性，每个城市可以招引全国甚至全球的资源，但本地的资源也可能外流。而创新资源的流向则决定于哪里有更加适宜创新的环境。为什么许多原本在上海、北京创新创业的公司都跑到深圳去创业，获得了成功？为什么大量创新产品出在深圳？就因为深圳的创新环境好，创业成本低。只有一所大学的深圳却吸引了大量优秀人才和资金，形成了一个漩涡。如果我们能在东、中、西各地搞一些漩涡，必将大大加速我国的均衡发展。这就是建设创新型城市战略意义所在。

陈清泰对这种创新创业环境有一个很好的描述[2]。他说："适宜的环境包括'软环境'和'硬环境'。概括地讲，就是基础设施，公司创立和退出的方便性，大学的水平和教育发展程度，人员的素质和人才流动的灵活性，诚信环境和融资成本，风险投资、管理咨询、注册会计师等专业服务水平，技术和产权交易市场发育程度，当地经济活动与国际市场对接的程度，司法公正和司法效率，政府监管的规制性、稳定性和透明度，政府的服务能力和行政效率等。一个地区如果能建立起自由创业、创新和分散决策的体制机制，严格的实物产权、知识产权保护的法律环境，鼓励竞争、崇尚创新、宽容失败的社会文化，就能充分调动企业家精神，使那些有创新欲望的人有充分施展才能的条件，使那些成功的创新能得到应有的回报，使创新失败的人有机会东山再起，从而使本地成为创新人才聚集的洼地、技术创新的乐园、企业家创业的天堂、高科技创业公司的栖息地。"

陈清泰又说："创新活动还具有明显的聚集效应。创新资源聚集之势一旦形成，创业者和企业都将从技术外溢和反馈，不同专业、不同思维方式人员的交流和思想碰撞，技术信息共享，技术能力互补，成功与失败的示范效应，甚至你追我赶的创业创新氛围中受益。众多创新企业共同的'中间需求'会刺激针对创新活动的风险投资、管理咨询、猎头公司、注册会计师、律师等专业服务的发展，会使技术交易市场更加活跃，从而使有意创新的企业在这里可以方便地获得创新资源和良好的服务，使这里的创新有更高的成功率和效率。""企业无力改变外部环境，但他们可以在不同地区之间选择。因此，地方政府关注本地产业升级的重点不是直接指挥企业做什么和不做什么，而是实施有利于调动企业家创新精神的政策，下大功夫创造有利于创新资源聚集的区域经济环境。"

由若干大城市聚集起来构成的大经济圈的创新体系建设也引起了广泛关注，例如：以上海、苏州、杭州、宁波和南京为核心的长三角经济圈；以广州、深圳、香港和澳门为核心的珠三角经济圈；以北京、天津、青岛和大连为核心的环渤海经济圈。仅这三个经济圈就占了全国 GDP 的 64%，人口 4 亿，占全国总人口的 37%。这么强大的经济圈，其创新体系的设计将对我国以及世界经济的发展产生重大战略影响。

总之，无论从重要性来看，还是从可操作性来看，抓创新型城市建设是最佳选择。中央各部委为了鼓励自主创新，出台了许多激励政策。把这些政策很好地统筹起来，选择若干示范城市贯彻实施，定会取得很好的结果。现在有些部委已经这么做了，但是，如能很好地统筹起来，齐心协力建设创新型国家，一朵朵创新型城市之花将会迅速开遍祖国大地。

（作者：孔德涌，国际欧亚科学院院士，中国软科学研究会常务副理事长；邹祖烨，国际欧亚科学院院士，北京凯德欧亚咨询中心有限公司总裁）

**参考文献**

[1] Department for Innovation, Universities and skill, UK, Innovation Nation, March, 2008, PP. 12

[2] 陈清泰. 在培育新兴产业中的政府作用 [N]. 科技日报，2010年6月系列报道

# 中国数字城市群建设与管理

2010年11月，中国“数字城市群建设和管理学术研讨会”在香港举行，研讨会由国际欧亚科学院（中国）、香港中文大学太空与地球信息科学研究所、中国科学院区域可持续发展分析与模拟重点实验室联合主办。近年来，随着区域城市化进程的快速推进，城市群逐渐成为中国经济发展的主要力量。面对区域一体化和信息化的时代要求，以及资源短缺、环境保护等诸多问题，城市信息化协作的重要性日益凸显，有必要在“数字城市”的基础上进一步开展“数字城市群”建设。然而，目前中国在“数字城市群”的研究和建设仍处于起步阶段。本文着重探讨了“数字城市群”的内涵与定位，分析了中国“数字城市群”的建设需求与发展策略，为中国数字城市群的统筹发展提出了中肯的见解。

## 一、数字城市与数字城市群

### 1. 数字城市起源与发展

“数字城市”的概念源于美国副总统戈尔1998年1月21日提出的“数字地球”，是指综合运用卫星遥感、互联网、虚拟现实等信息获取、通信、存储、表现等技术对城市的基础设施、地理、经济、社会和人文等信息等进行动态监测、组织管理和应用服务的多功能、智能化的技术系统，具有智能化、数字化和网络化特征[1]。

随着城市发展和信息化水平提升，“数字城市”已成为现代城市发展的重要特征之一[2]。“数字城市”发展过程大致可分三个阶段：（1）信息基础设施建设阶段，数据库建设与信息资源共享是这一阶段的主要任务；（2）以应用服务为中心的全面发展阶段，大力发展城市规划、灾害防治、环境保护等应用系统，面向市民的公共信息服务也越来越受到重视；（3）以知识管理和智能决策为中心的成熟阶段，“数字城市”与经济社会的运转紧密结合，实现信息采集、目标分析和决策方案产生、评价、执行和反馈的自动化、智能化，从而提高整个社会的管理水平和运行效率。

作为城市的信息化映像，数字城市在发展过程中随着新技术的应用和城市内涵的扩充不断丰富和充实。目前的主流趋势是技术上向无线和智能方向发展，即发展无线城市、智慧城市；内涵上随着城市协作和区域一体化向“数字城市群”方向发展[3]。

### 2. 数字城市群内涵与定位

随着区域城市化进程的推进，城市之间的信息、资源、人员、资金等要素互动、流通越来越密切，逐步形成“城市群”的发展格局。城市群内的分工协作是提升城市群竞争力的突破口，是城市群建设的重要内容。面对信息化发展的特征与要求，一个可持续的城市群发展建构，必然需要以数字技术、信息技术、网络技术的广泛运用作为支撑[2]，这种需求为“数字城市群”发展提供了有利契机。

“数字城市群”建设是从单一城市的数字化、信息化建设，逐步走向城市之间的协同发展，进而形成“数字城市群”的发展网络。“数字城市群”是区域协同发展与信息化建设的必然趋势，通过跨政府部门、跨行政区域的政府、企业、学术团体和公民之间的协作，以城市群 GIS 为公共基础平台，共建和共享地理、人口、经济、资源等信息基础设施，发展多种多样的信息化应用系统，服务于区域规划管理和居民生活改善[4]。“数字城市群”应具备以下特点：(1) 以数字城市为基础的网络化区域信息系统工程；(2) 跨行政区域统筹协调，跨政府部门共建共享；(3) 需要政府、企业、学术团体等多方参与、协作和投资；(4) 需要互联网、无线网、城市空间数据等信息基础设施的支撑；(5) 服务于政府管理、企业决策与公众信息；(6) 为各种用户提供多样化的表现、分析、决策支持等服务。

“数字城市群”不是若干数字城市简单组合，而是数字城市在更大区域范围内以网络形式有序延伸和扩充。“数字城市群”建设强调城市的统筹协调，注重信息基础设施的共建与共享，服务于城市群协同发展。“数字城市群”与数字城市有以下区别：(1) 数字城市主要服务于某些部门对城市的管理，数字城市群更偏重于为区域一体化提供服务；(2) 数字城市由一个政府组织建设，数字城市群建设与管理需要在多个政府、多个行政部门之间统筹协调；(3) 数字城市是单一城市的信息化建设与应用，数字城市群是多个城市信息化的整合与共享；(4) 数字城市强调企业级数据库，数字城市群则为跨组织的信息化平台，需要网络化的信息基础设施。

## 二、中国城市群发展与数字城市群建设

面对国内外日趋激烈的竞争环境，城市群发展成为中国城市化发展的重要趋势。城市群的本质就是众多城市的一体化发展[5]，而信息化建设是推进一体化的重要手段。通过城市群的信息化建设，将提升区域综合管理能力，有利于城市群内城市之间的统筹协调，从而推进城市群发展。

### 1. 中国城市化与城市群发展

城市化快速发展正是中国当前城市发展的重要特征之一。2009 年，中国的城市化率已达到 46.6%，某些相对发达地区的城市的城市化水平已接近或超过世界发达国家平均水平。在快速城市化发展的进程中，市场经济的发展、人口的流动、信息技术的进步等，都极大地

推动着城市之间的交流与合作。同时，面对能源资源瓶颈、生态环境日趋严峻等问题，城市发展亟需更宽广的合作领域和更融洽的协同发展，这些都成为城市群发展的重要推动力。

近几年，面对城乡互动、区域一体的时代要求，城市群发展成为中国城市化发展的重要趋势。中国现已发展形成近30个城市群，几乎遍及各个省区，其中较为成形的城市群有15个，包括长三角、珠三角、京津冀、辽中南、山东半岛、海峡西岸、环鄱阳湖、皖江、中原、武汉、长株潭、北部湾、成渝、关中和太原城市群。统计资料表明，这15个城市群以14.2%的国土面积，承载了47%的全国人口，创造了70%以上的工业总产值和地区生产总值，利用外资额更是在80%以上。这些城市群已成为中国最有发展潜力的地区，并将成为中国国民经济发展的重要支撑点[6][7]。

然而，中国目前尚处于城市群发展的初级阶段，产业同构、基础设施重复建设等现象显得较为严重。以长三角城市群为例，在宁波北仑港货源不足、江苏沿海建有多处上万吨级泊位的情况下，上海又投资建设了洋山港口，造成很大的资源浪费。此外，长三角16个城市，以电子信息业为重点发展产业的有12个，选择汽车业的有11个，选择石化的有9个[8]，导致严重的产业同构。这些现象说明，城市之间的统筹协调仍然是中国城市群当前发展面临的首要问题。

**2. 中国数字城市群建设需求**

区域一体化是促进中国城市群发展的关键，城市群GIS则为城市群协调管理提供了有力支持[9][10]，但是统筹城市群整体规划，改善资源要素流通环境，建设可持续发展的合作平台，实现网络化公共信息服务等更需要通过“数字城市群”建设，发展综合、交互的数字化平台。

（1）为城市群规划与管治提供新平台。城市群规划与管治是城市群发展的核心问题也是首要问题，城市之间统筹协调是城市群规划与管治的重点，也是难点[11]。一方面，合理的城市定位、地域结构和用地功能是城市群健康发展的基础；另一方面，城市群通信网络、交通网络、生态网络等共建共享是促进城市联动、推进城市群一体化发展的必要条件。为此，国内各大城市群相继成立了区域协调组织，如“长三角城市经济协调会”，并制定了一些合作协议。这些协调机构与合作机制必须要有信息共享平台和综合分析工具作为支撑，才能进行科学合理的规划与管理。“数字城市群”将跨区域的行政部门、企业、机构集聚在一起，不仅形成了网络化的信息共享平台，并且集成了各种分析应用系统，从而支持城市群统筹规划和跨区域管理，促进城市协同发展。

（2）为城市间要素流通营造新环境。城市群各城市间资金、能源、人员、信息等要素流通是城市群形成与发展的重要机制。为推进资源优化配置，促进城市群经济协调发展，需要为城市群要素流通营造新环境。一是传统产业转型的需求，面对经济全球化，有必要转变组织模式和管理方法，提高生产要素流通效率。二是城市群产业优化重组的需求，产业同构、同质竞争是长期以来一直困扰中国城市群发展的主要问题之一，需要政府予以适当合理的引导，调整生产要素流通，优化产业结构与布局。“数字城市群”建设将通过信息化加强市场经济的活动性和政府宏观调控的科学性，从而改善城市间要素流通，有利于传统特色经济的发展壮大和区域经济的协调发展。

（3）为区域可持续发展提供有力支持。近年来，伴随着生态文明、绿色低碳等理念逐渐在中国城市发展中落实和深化，中国城市群的可持续发展已经是大势所趋。城市群的可持续发展需要综合考虑城市群的区域特点，妥善处理城市群经济社会发展与生态环境保护的矛盾。虽然数字城市可以为城市可持续发展提供决策支持，但是可持续发展问题往往是区域性的。例如，长三角城市群面临的太湖污染问题，长株潭城市群推动“两型社会”建设等，仅仅依靠单个城市的数字化建设已经难以应对。因此，有必要建设“数字城市群”，一方面可以为经济、社会、环境综合评估提供数据共享平台和强有力的分析工具，支持资源环境要素的合理配置；另一方面可以对城市群发展进行动态监测与模拟，为可持续发展战略制定提供科学依据。

（4）为提升城市公共信息服务开辟新途径。数字城市建设带动了信息共享和智能化服务，大大提高了居民生活质量。然而，随着城市群的发展，城市之间的联系将日益紧密，交通、旅游、就业、经济等公共信息服务需求将由城市内部扩展为城市群一体化。因此，需要开展“数字城市群”建设，为公众提供更为丰富的信息资源和网络化的智能服务。同时，社会发展对公众参与提出了更高的要求。我们注意到完善的公众参与机制是国外城市群得以形成良好区域管治的前提之一，但中国城市群发展中公众参与的渠道仍然十分有限。因此，有必要积极建设“数字城市群”，通过Web-GIS、三维仿真等技术，畅通公众参与城市群事务的渠道。

## 三、中国数字城市群发展策略与技术方法

自1999年11月首届“数字地球”国际研讨会在北京召开以来，中国“数字城市”建设已卓有成效，在城市交通、教育、城市管理、城市安全、智能交通等方面已逐步建立起政府、企业、社区与民众的信息共享与良性互动的平台，为“数字城市群”建设与管理奠定了坚实的基础。然而，“数字城市群”涉及众多参与方，除了技术上的问题，数据、资金、人员等统筹协调也势必遇到各种困难，必须提前制定统筹协调的一体化策略，保障“数字城市群”建设的顺利展开。

### 1. 城市群信息一体化

截至2010年，中国已在70个城市先后开展了“数字城市”试点建设工作，部分已完成了政府信息系统、社会保障信息系统、交通管理信息系统、电子商务交易系统等开发及试用，为构建“数字城市群”奠定了良好的基础。但同时我们也看到，各地的信息化建设仍存在严重的“诸侯割据”现象，各地各系统之间缺乏交互性，产生了“信息孤岛”。这不仅造成社会资源的极大浪费，也将阻碍“数字城市群”的发展进程。

“数字城市群”是“数字城市”在更大区域范围内的有序延伸和扩充，强调以“数字城

市”为基础的信息整合与系统集成。城市群信息一体化是实现“数字城市群”的重要条件，是保障“数字城市群”建设与管理的基本战略。城市群信息一体化要求竖立“一盘棋”的大局观，积极推动部门、企业之间的良性互动，为“数字城市群”发展营造良好环境。

“数字城市群”建设与管理需要从三个层次把握城市群信息一体化。一是政府层面，通过成立数字城市群建设管理委员会，在整体规划、推进应用、建章立制、协调共谋等方面发挥主导作用，大力推进政府公共信息资源的公开、开发、利用；二是企业层面，着力发挥企业的主体作用，建立行业信息资源开发利用的公共平台，推进行业基础信息和信用信息的共享；三是公众层面，以满足公众对社会公益性和公共信息资源的需求为目标，重点推进涉及公众利益的农产品、食品、药品信息和社会保障、医疗卫生、治安以及人员流动等方面的信息共享[12]。

建立区域数字城市联盟是推进城市群信息一体化的重要手段。“区域数字城市联盟”将促进城市的交流互动，有利于跨区域、跨组织的统筹与协调。例如，苏州、无锡、常州于2003年成立了“区域数字城市联盟”，通过多次交流讨论，逐步就加强城市信息资源的共享度、共建共享城市公共信息服务体系等合作达成一致，极大地推动了区域信息一体化。

**2. 数据技术标准化**

标准化是信息共享和系统兼容的前提条件，是“数字城市群”建设的重要基础。随着“数字城市”的推进，中国在标准化方面已经做了大量卓有成效的工作。但由于涉及面太广，标准化工作相当复杂，国内还没有形成统一的数字城市标准体系，不同标准之间的不协调现象较为突出，导致了数据质量参差不齐、系统框架各异的情况，给数据共享、交换带来极大不便[13]。因此，加快完善数据标准和技术标准，是中国“数字城市群”建设管理的当务之急。

“数字城市群”的信息服务是跨区域、多层面的，但数据资源必须按照标准统一建设[14]。这当中，一是数据库建设标准化。为减少重复建设和资源浪费，相关部门有必要按照统一标准建设同类数据库。如，逐步建设以规划、房管、土管等部门为基础的统一的“空间地理基础信息库”；以统计部门为基础的统一的“政府宏观经济数据库”；以劳动、公安、民政、教育、地税、国税等部门为基础的统一的“人口基础信息库”等。二是城市群地理坐标系统标准化。经济、社会、地理、文化等多源数据必须集成到统一的空间框架下，才能实现多源信息的叠加分析，服务于决策支持。譬如，以空间定位来说，由于历史原因，中国各城市有的使用国家坐标系，有的使用城市独立直角坐标（地方坐标系），造成数据混乱，影响分析决策，必须尽快统一城市群坐标系统，制定统一的空间定位管理体系。

在技术标准化方面，需要通过规范系统框架和数据接口，实现信息交换、管理、应用高度协同。地理信息基础框架是“数字城市群”建设的根本平台，2000年，中国国家测绘局正式提出了构建“数字中国”地理空间基础框架的思路，规范并逐步展开数字化地理空间基础框架的研究与实践[15]，通过建立统一的城市地理信息公共平台，为各类专业信息的交换整合及应用系统的搭建提供支撑。但是，中国目前仍缺乏科学、实用的“数字城市”建设总体框架，有必要进一步完善相关的技术标准，通过构建统一的数据层、应用层、服务层框架体系和规范的数据接口，实现“数字城市”的互联互通，保障“数字城市群”建设与管理。

### 3. 基础应用融合化

“数字城市群”城市群范围内的信息化建设，可以说是若干“数字城市”的集成与整合。在“数字城市”建设已取得了显著成效的情况下，中国的“数字城市群”建设应充分利用各城市在“数字城市”方面的建设成果，统筹协调，重点推进跨区域、跨行业、跨部门的基础应用融合化，构建网络化的信息服务体系。

目前的工作可以包括：一是城市群行政业务应用系统的融合化，规范协调面向行政办公自动化、政府决策支持、公众服务等不同层面的数据接口和业务平台，实现跨区域同一层面应用服务的交互共享。二是城市群企业商务应用系统的融合化，将电子商务与企业内部管理集成，保证产、供、销、售后服务的业务流程连贯、畅通，并及时响应外部供应链以及市场供求的变化，加快生产要素流通与资源优化配置。三是城市群公共服务应用系统的融合化，提供“同城化”信息服务，如，城市交通、社会保障等“一卡通”服务，实时交通、气象等数据共享与联合发布，提高市民生活质量，加强城市交流。

为确保信息资源共享，真正实现基础应用融合化，就要融合各种城市智能网络，实现城市群各系统间互联互通[16]，并以互联、集群的方式构建立体的、多层面的应用服务体系。同时，还要建立相应的制度体系和协调机构，加强区域合作力度，确保跨区域信息化工程的顺利实施。

### 4. 空间三维可视化

2D－GIS 技术已经在“数字城市”中得到了较深入的应用，多维空间信息的展示与分析更加需要三维空间可视化的支持[17]。目前，3D－GIS 技术、VR 技术、4D 数据融合集成技术正日趋成熟，中国“数字城市群”建设应开拓创新，积极发展以“43VR”（地理数据 4 维化，地图数据三维化，规划设计 VR（Virtual Reality，虚拟现实）化）为亮点的三维可视化“数字城市群”[18]。

具有 4D 数据的城市基础地理信息公共平台是实现三维可视化“数字城市群”的基础。一方面，做好 4D 数据的采集工作，为三维场景建模提供高质量的数据基础；另一方面，三维数据虽然能够提供更加直观、准确的基础资料，但是，三维数据的组织与重建比二维数据复杂得多，有必要探讨合理有效的三维数据结构和管理技术。同时，还需要进一步探索快速、准确的三维建模技术，尤其是实时三维重建技术，为城市群应急管理提供服务。

3D－GIS 技术和 VR 技术是建设三维可视化“数字城市群”的核心技术。3D－GIS 将为城市信息查询和分析提供新视野，更为直观的空间查询与分析将有助于对城市群物流、人流、信息流进行集中而有效的控制和管理，从而更好地促进城市的协同发展。同时，VR 技术通过视觉、听觉、触觉、形体、手势或口令等进行多重感知，提供身临其境的感知环境，不仅为城市群的发展规划提供良好的实验和模拟条件，实现城市超越现实的虚拟化运行、分析和评价，并且大大降低专业门槛，为公众参与提供有益的帮助。

## 四、小结

随着中国城市群观念日益深化，城市之间信息共享与交换更加频繁和迫切，“数字城市群”成为中国城市群发展的必然趋势。虽然国内关于“数字城市群”的研究目前还比较少，但是2006年以来的“数字城市”试点工程建设已经为“数字城市群”的发展奠定了良好的基础。实际上，正是由于区域城市信息化协作的需要，一些地区“数字城市群”的实际行动略早于相关研究。总体上看，中国“数字城市群”研究上目前处于理论探讨和框架设计阶段，建设上则处于经验交流和信息共享的水平。

跨区域、跨部门、跨行业的统筹协调是“数字城市群”建设与管理的核心，但是由于观念、意识、国情等方面因素，中国的“数字城市群”在数据共享、系统集成上遇到了一定的瓶颈。对此，不仅要加强技术创新，促进信息资源的互联互通，还要从政策、制度、管理等方面入手，消除信息交换壁垒，畅通数据共享渠道，才能真正实现区域信息一体化。

城市群统筹协调是“数字城市群”建设的重要条件，反过来，通过建设城市群信息共享平台，提供网络化的信息服务，也会促进城市群内城市的协同发展。在经济全球化与社会信息化的时代背景下，“数字城市群”建设必将为中国城市群发展带来新的机遇，为城市经济发展和改善人民生活质量做出突出的贡献。

（作者：林珲，国际欧亚科学院院士，香港中文大学教授）

### 参考文献

[1] 承继成，李琦，林珲．数字城市——理论、方法与应用［M］．北京：科学出版社，2003

[2] 简逢敏，王剑．区域协同，建构和谐数字城市群——以长三角城市群发展为例［A］．第一届数字城市群建设和管理学术研讨会论文集［C］，2010

[3] 赵小锋，孙艳伟．数字城市群与无线城市群的对比研究［A］．第一届数字城市群建设和管理学术研讨会论文集［C］，2010

[4] 林珲，孔云峰．关于发展中国城市群GIS的探讨［J］．地理与地理信息科学，2004，20（2）：8－12

[5] 徐康宁，赵波，王绮．长三角城市群：形成、竞争与合作［J］．南京社会科学，2005，（5）：1－9

[6] 黄顺江．我国城市群发展现状与趋势［A］//中国城市发展报告，2010

[7] 姚士谋，李青，武清华，等．我国城市群总体发展趋势与方向初探［J］．地理研究，2010，29（8）：1345－1354

[8] 曹宏苓．长三角经济一体化的现状、困惑与制度机制的创新——对国际区域经济一体化经验的借鉴［J］．南京社会科学，2008，（5）：25－30

[9] 李红敏，袁敏，姚国章．长三角一体化进程中城市群GIS建设研究［J］．南京邮电大学学报（社会科

学版)，2009，11 (4)，19 - 26

[10] 向红梅．长株潭城市群区域地理信息系统的建设方法探讨 [J]．测绘与空间地理信息，2010，33 (1)：87 - 89

[11] 姚士谋，陈振光，吴松，等．我国城市群区战略规划的关键问题 [J]．经济地理，2008，28 (4)：529 - 534

[12] 董晓华，金毅．推进长三角区域信息一体化研究 [J]．浙江统计，2009，(6)：5 - 7

[13] 王丹．我国数字城市建设成就、问题与发展建议 [A]．全国地理信息产业峰会，2009

[14] 陈述彭．"数字城市"与时俱进 [J]．地球信息科学，2002，(3)：35 - 37

[15] 陈军．论数字化地理空间基础框架的建设与应用 [J]．测绘工程，2002，11 (3)：1 - 6

[16] 林拓，申立．中国城市群发展模式的基本面向与信息化、智能化战略取向 [A] //第一届数字城市群建设和管理学术研讨会论文集 [C]，2010

[17] 王军，周伟，田鹏，李娜．城市三维基础地理信息系统在城市规划中的应用 [J]．工程勘察，2010，(11)：56 - 61

[18] 郝力．中外数字城市的发展 [J]．国外城市规划，2001，(3)：2 - 4

# 发展低碳经济，促进经济社会发展方式转变

## 一、低碳经济概述

低碳经济最早出现于英国政府文件，2003年能源白皮书《我们能源的未来：创建低碳经济》。作为第一次工业革命的先驱和资源并不丰富的岛国，英国充分意识到了能源安全和气候变化的威胁，它正从自给自足的能源供应走向主要依靠进口的时代。按目前的消费模式，预计2020年英国80%的能源都必须进口，所以，必须通过发展低碳经济来摆脱窘境。2006年，前世界银行首席经济学家尼古拉斯·斯特恩牵头作出的《斯特恩报告》指出，全球以每年GDP 1%的投入可以避免将来每年GDP 5%~20%的损失，呼吁全球向低碳经济转型。随后，低碳理念在生产发展和社会发展的各个层面迅速地推广。

低碳经济是指在可持续发展理念指导下，通过技术创新、制度创新、产业转型以及新能源开发等多种手段，尽可能地减少煤炭、石油等高碳能源消耗，在减缓全球气候变化的同时保持经济和社会发展的高速增长，实现“碳生产率”（单位二氧化碳当量排放所产生的GDP）大幅度增加的经济发展模式，是一种实现经济社会发展与生态环境保护双赢的经济发展形态。低碳经济的内涵包括使用非碳能源、循环利用二氧化碳、固持二氧化碳、开展低碳生活、进行碳交易等。作为人类活动最为集中的地区，城市（特别是处于发展过程中的生产型城市）的发展模式和发展轨迹成为全球低碳发展的关注焦点，“低碳城市”的概念开始受到学术界、国际组织和各级政府的广泛关注。低碳城市是指以低碳经济为发展模式及方向、市民以低碳生活为理念和行为特征、政府公务管理层以低碳社会为建设标本和蓝图，通过转变经济发展模式、消费理念和生活方式，实现减少碳排放的城市发展模式和社会发展方式。低碳城市不仅是一个经济领域的概念，而且涉及城市的制度结构、空间结构、环境特征等各方面内容，城市的低碳转型需要通过低碳技术创新、经济结构优化、转变消费模式等手段来实现。低碳城市是实现低碳社会的重要内容。

## 二、低碳时代的到来是人类社会发展的必然规律

表面上看，低碳经济是因温室效应、气候变化而提出的，而更深层次的原因是以化石能

源为基础、以蒸汽机为标志的工业社会经历了200多年的发展，遇到了诸多瓶颈。一是资源瓶颈，这样的工业除消耗大量化石能源资源外，还消耗大量矿产资源、水资源、土地资源。二是环境瓶颈，化石能源使用带来的排放以及工业过程和消费过程产生的大量废弃物已对经济社会的可持续发展带来挑战，环境容量不断被压迫。三是知识瓶颈，支撑传统工业发展的科学理论和技术已缺少创新动力，全人类、全社会已经遇到了创新的危机。回顾20世纪60年代以来，几乎没有新的科学原理、重大发现、革命性的技术以及大师级科学家诞生，而虚假、泡沫、浪费等现象日趋严重。四是生活方式瓶颈，上述工业社会的发展已难以支撑以美国为代表的高消费生活方式的持续发展。因此，人类社会在经历了农业社会、工业社会之后，向低碳社会进行转型是历史发展的必然规律。而低碳经济的发展模式尚无现成理论可依据，无现成经验可借鉴，无现成模式可仿造，需要人类共同探索、创新。

## 三、低碳时代中国面临的挑战

低碳经济的提出与传统经济社会发展模式有关，而传统的发展模式是靠高碳的化石能源支撑的，所以，实现低碳社会要解决的核心问题就是能源问题。

对于发展低碳经济，中国面临诸多挑战，其中能源问题是最大的挑战。当前，能源面临五个方面的挑战：能源结构、能源需求、能源供给、能源技术、能源政治。

第一是能源结构的挑战。世界能源结构中，化石能源的天然气、石油和煤炭基本上各占30%左右。而中国是以煤炭为主的能源大国，煤炭占了70%左右。而煤的使用，使得能源利用效率低、环境成本高，而且这样一种能源结构在较长一段时间内也是无法改变的。估计到2050年，煤炭在我国能源结构中还将是主力能源，虽然比例会不断下降。

第二是能源需求的挑战。现在中国能源消费的总量已经位居世界第二，进入21世纪以来，基本上年均增长接近10%，而这几年GDP的增长，也是10%左右。一方面，发展惯性要求继续保持较高发展速度，另一方面，为实现社会主义现代化的目标，中国的经济也必须保持较高增长速度，而要发展就必须依靠能源，即便在低碳社会，同样需要大量能源。而目前的化石能源是难以满足这一需求的。

第三是能源供给的挑战。中国的煤炭很多，但开采和运输条件很差，开采技术不发达，因此，供给能力是有限的。我们过去曾经是石油输出国，现在已经是石油进口国了，石油进口超过了总需求量的50%，存在供给安全的问题。天然气可采储量就更少了。

第四是能源技术的挑战。中国能源利用效率低，中国能源利用总效率仅为36.81%，而世界的平均水平是50.32%，即便是印度（40.06%）、巴西（62%）这样的发展中国家都比我们高。这个问题反映出我国能源利用技术水平相对于世界许多国家都还较低。

第五是能源政治的挑战。我国石油进口已超过了50%。我们周边的孟加拉国、印度、印度尼西亚、马来西亚、泰国、科威特、卡塔尔等国，都是处在对能源需求快速增加的过程，也就是说，我们周边的这些国家未来都可能因能源问题与我们产生摩擦。实际上这些摩擦已经产生了，将来的问题可能会更加严重。据预测，截至2020年，亚太地区自给能源与能源总需求的矛盾将变得很突出，自给率最多也只有1/4左右。处理不好能源问题将会给这个地区带来不稳定因素。因此，能源问题已不是简单的经济问题，同时也可转变为政治问题。

## 四、我国低碳经济发展状况

作为发展中国家，中国还没有受到国际上强制减排的要求。但改革开放以来，中国经济增长迅速，并且由于技术水平和发展方式等原因，温室气体排放量已跃居世界前列，降低温室气体排放的国际压力越来越大。作为一个负责任的大国，中国在国际舞台上逐渐展现出积极的姿态，在哥本哈根会议前就对外宣布了控制温室气体排放的行动目标，即到2020年，单位国内生产总值二氧化碳排放比2005年下降40%～45%。

目前，中国正处于工业化的中后期，大规模的城市基础设施、住房建设以及城市人口对交通运输、电力消费等公共设施的更高要求，都将直接导致能源消费和温室气体排放的高增长。如何摒弃发达国家19世纪的高能耗、高污染、低效率的发展模式，实现经济的可持续发展？低碳之路无疑为中国城市的可持续发展提供了一条新的途径。2010年8月，国家确定了将广东等五省八市作为低碳发展的试点省市，积极探索低碳发展新模式。目前，我国的各级政府已将发展低碳经济，促进经济发展方式转变提到议事日程，在许多会议和公开场合都会提及相关话题，并且都在制定相关的规划。

## 五、发展低碳经济的主要抓手

发展低碳经济，促进经济发展方式转变，目前应做好以下几方面的工作。

### 1. 发展碳交易服务市场

在向低碳社会变革过程中，各行各业无论是自觉还是不自觉，是愿意还是不愿意，一些约束性的指标和要求将要相继诞生，人类将会在生产、生活及产品上标明“碳足迹”，以形成新的经济体系（考虑资源禀赋、环境容量、经济效益、社会承载）。比如：据英国专家计算，我们日常的一封电子邮件的碳足迹为：一封垃圾邮件的碳足迹0.3克$CO_2e$；一封正常邮件的碳足迹0.4克$CO_2e$；一封长而乏味邮件的碳足迹50克$CO_2e$。又比如，使用手机的碳足迹为：平均每天使用少于2分钟碳足迹47千克$CO_2e$；平均每天使用少于1小时碳足迹1250千克$CO_2e$；每年全球移动电话产生的碳足迹总量为$1.250\times10^8$吨$CO_2e$。因此，一些量化目标将作为约束性指标纳入中国国民经济和社会发展中长期规划，并制定相应的国内统计、监测、考核体系。建议及早启动碳足迹的计算方法和相关软件的研究开发工作，发展碳交易服务业。

### 2. 科学制定节能减排考核指标

我国节能减排的潜力巨大。在哥本哈根会议上，我国政府郑重承诺：至2050年，单位

GDP能耗比2005年下降40%～45%，节能减排有潜力贡献近一半，也必须达到一半。但是，目前的单位GDP能耗的节能考核指标只考虑总量，而掩盖了重点能耗行业节能效果。因为，通过调整产业结构可以实现单位GDP能耗下降，但重点能耗行业的能耗情况可能依旧没变。另外，在这样的指标体系下，为了追求单位GDP能耗下降，有可能造成一些低能耗的行业重复建设、重复投资、重复生产，产生极大浪费。因此，节能考核指标除考虑总能耗外，还应考虑重点行业、重点领域、重点产品降低能耗的指标，应进行同行业能耗比较。

**3. 大力发展节能建筑**

中国是发展中国家，建筑自然是重要的支柱产业之一。温家宝总理在2003年的政府工作报告中指出：要大力推进建筑节能，大力发展省地节能环保型建筑。建筑是一个大行业，包括材料、技术、设备、设计、施工、使用、管理和服务等方方面面，是一个产业链长、关联产业面宽的行业。建筑行业与能源和环保关系密切。全球建筑行业消耗的能源占总能的50%，消耗的水占总用水的42%，消耗的材料占总材料的50%，占用的土地占所利用土地的48%，而建筑行业产生的污水、大气污染、固体垃圾等也很大。

当前，值得一提的是有一个利用新能源的符合绿色环保概念的新型城市——吐鲁番新城正在创建。这是在国家提出新疆要实现跨越式发展的大好机遇下，新疆各地州都在探索建设“宜居、生态”示范城市的新模式。由于吐鲁番气候独具特色，太阳能、浅层地能、风能等可再生能源极其丰富，具备太阳能大规模利用的有利条件。2009年吐鲁番实施“宜居”战略，提出择址建设“低碳、生态、宜居”新区的理念，城市的规划、建设工作得到国家、自治区的高度支持与关注。2009年7月新疆维吾尔自治区人民政府将其列为“自治区和谐生态城区暨城乡一体化示范区”。2010年国家能源局批准创建“国家新能源示范城市”。吐鲁番示范区规划总面积8.8平方公里，规划总人口6万人。主要建设目标是在规划期内(2010—2020年)，充分利用丰富的清洁能源和生态技术，打造干旱炎热地区人居环境改善的示范区，建设适合西部气候条件的可持续城市新区。在这个大背景下，由国际欧亚科学院中国科学中心联合北京市建筑设计研究院、广州市城市规划勘测设计研究院、中国电子工程设计院和中国气象局风能太阳能资源评估中心，以及相关领域的专家组成中国可持续城市研究中心，以科学求实的工作态度，深入研究吐鲁番新区发展概念规划、新区总体规划和近期发展规划，在规划阶段就充分考虑了建筑与屋顶太阳能光伏发电系统的结合，微电网与光伏发电系统的结合，气象预测与光伏发电功率预测的结合等因素，从而对屋顶光伏发电系统、微电网、气象预测及功率预测系统等建立统一的监测管理平台，以最大限度地平衡示范区内市电、自发电与耗电之间的关系，提高能源使用效率，减少光伏电站对公共电网的冲击。同时探索适合新能源发展的政策和管理措施，为建立能源节约型、环境友好型社会目标的实现做有益的尝试。2010年5月破土建设的示范区以一期起步区2.86平方公里75万平方米居民建筑和配套公共建筑为研究对象，按照“太阳能发电自发自用、余量上网、不足部分从大电网购电”的理念，提出该试点作为示范项目实施。与此同时，配套新城区的绿色交通规划、绿色生态旅游规划等也在按计划进行。

但是，我们也应该注意到，中国的建筑行业发展迅速，而且以每年约20亿平方米的速度增加，而现在符合建筑节能要求的建筑还不足1%，这既是一个具有很大发展潜力的经济增长点，又是在节能减排上需要认真注意努力达标的行业。

**4. 建立以城市生活垃圾的资源化循环利用工业园**

城市生活垃圾是城市人生活过程排出的废弃物，它包括厨余、果叶、废纸、废塑料、废橡胶、废玻璃、废金属、废木料及沙石等。这些物质的85%是可作为资源加以再生利用的，如果将灰渣作为建筑施工的基土的话，则城市垃圾可以全部被利用。比如：每回收1吨废钢铁可炼钢0.9吨，比用矿石冶炼节约成本47%，空气污染减少75%，水污染降低97%；从汽车、摩托车上“退役”的废旧轮胎能被还原成价格不菲的燃油。利用厨余垃圾经过生物技术堆肥制成的有机肥是最天然、最优质的肥料，如果将现有的厨余转化为有机肥，其产量与目前使用的化肥量相当。

建议建立“城市生活垃圾的资源化循环利用工业园”，将垃圾预处理、资源化循环利用、终处理系统以及相关环保产品和装备业、环境监测管理、环保服务业、投融资体系集中于工业园内，以形成城市生活垃圾为对象的循环经济工业园区。

**5. 发展非化石燃料交通工具**

2000年城镇居民家庭平均每百户小汽车拥有量仅为0.5辆，2006年则已增加到了4.32辆。如果中国每5人拥有一辆小汽车（荷兰人均水平），则全国达到2亿辆，每3人拥有一辆小汽车（日本人均水平），则全国达到4亿辆，每2人拥有一辆小汽车（美国人均水平），则全国达到7亿辆。轿车的大幅增长将导致中国能源（石油）消耗的增长，而我国石油储量是难以支撑这样发展的。因此，大力发展非石化燃料交通工具是刻不容缓的，且是未来具有很大发展潜力的产业。

可喜的是，中国政府大力支持、推动和推广的新能源汽车——电力驱动汽车已经上路，如中国自主品牌的比亚迪新能源汽车，其动力电池和启动电池都是自主研发生产的绿色环保电池，不会对环境造成任何危害，它所含有的化学物质均可在自然界中被环境以无害的方式分解吸收。可见，低碳经济将促进生产生活方式转变、产业结构调整和技术进步。我们应抓住这些难得的机遇，加强自主创新，提高国际竞争力。

（作者：陈勇，国际欧亚科学院院士，中国科学院广东分院院长）

**参考文献**

[1] 国家新能源示范城市吐鲁番示范区太阳能屋顶光伏电站暨微电网试点项目（报告）. 北京，2011-2

# 观察篇

# 2010年全国“两会”城乡规划建设热点问题综述

2010年十一届全国人大三次会议和十一届全国政协三次会议（以下简称“两会”）分别于3月5日至14日和3月3日至13日在北京召开。“两会”期间，与会人大代表和政协委员纷纷建言献策。据统计，人大会议期间代表团和代表共提出506件议案，同时收到代表提出的建议、批评和意见7418件；政协会议期间大会提案组共收到提案5430件。这些提案、议案在会后都统一交有关部门进行深入研究和落实。

根据互联网第三方数据服务机构万维数据的统计，网民对其中的370项提案和议案关注度较高，其中教育、住房和法制类最受关注，约占38%（见表1）。

表1　“两会”提案议案受网民关注程度

| 关注度 | 关注领域 | 受关注比重 |
|---|---|---|
| 高关注 | 教育、住房、法制 | 38% |
| 中等关注 | 文化、医疗、收入分配、三农、社会保障、反腐倡廉、经济发展、民主监督 | 35% |
| 低关注 | 食品安全、就业、环保、金融、国防、长假、行政区域划分、拉动内需 | 11% |
| 其他 | | 16% |

注：根据万维数据“2010‘两会’热点提案关注度报告”整理

“两会”期间，有关城乡规划建设方面的提案和议案依然占据一定比重。与往年相比，2010年“两会”城乡规划建设的热点的提案和议案呈现三个主要特征：一是有关民生问题仍然是主要热点，保障房建设和房价仍然是代表委员们关注的内容；二是根据新的发展形势出现了一些新的热点，如低碳城市建设、公共租赁房建设等；三是议题相对集中，区域发展方面的内容明显减少，更多地关注中西部地区和低收入人群。

本文重点从五个大类进行综述，即低碳城市、住房和房价、农村城镇化和城乡统筹、区域发展与振兴、土地制度与规划管理。

## 一、低碳城市

面对全球气候变暖、生态环境破坏加剧的严峻挑战，发展低碳经济已成必然趋势，温总理在政府工作报告中要求："大力开发低碳技术，推广高效节能技术，要努力建设以低碳排放为特征的产业体系和消费模式，积极参与应对气候变化国际合作。"这个问题引起了"两会"代表委员们的热议。据统计，"两会"与"低碳"有关的议案、提案占总量的10%左右，这些议案和提案都与低碳城市建设有一定关系，为低碳城市的建设和城乡规划提供了各种设想、思路和建议。

九三学社在"关于推动我国低碳经济发展的提案"中认为，气候变化已对我国经济社会发展产生了很大影响，以提高能效、发展清洁能源为核心，以转变发展方式、创新发展机制为关键，以经济社会可持续发展为目标的低碳发展，应该是今后我国经济社会发展的必然战略取向。为此，建议"将中国特色低碳发展道路确定为经济社会发展的重大战略"，并实施若干低碳发展的重大行动计划。其中重点实施能源结构调整、绿色能源开发利用、绿色建筑、公共交通、农村沼气化和陆地生态碳循环等重大行动计划。九三学社的提案还建议在东、中、西部经济发展水平不同的地区，建立若干低碳发展试验区，探索低碳发展经验。

九三学社在《关于推广低碳生活、提升社会可持续发展能力的建议》的提案中建议，在探索中国特色低碳发展道路上，应以发展新能源、节能环保、绿色建筑、新能源汽车等低碳产业为抓手，加快推进产业结构调整，加快经济方式转变。

农工党中央《关于合理开发新能源，发展绿色经济的建议》的提案认为，倡导低碳发展方式很重要的方面就是要构建新能源经济政策体系。提案建议采取补贴措施，鼓励电网企业改造设备和技术，把风能和太阳能等输出不稳定的电能纳入电网；调整财政补贴结构，将给予新能源装备生产企业的补贴与其技术创新程度挂钩，对新能源产品的消费补贴与节能效果挂钩；通过制定碳税政策逐步建立和完善全方位的资源与环境政策体系，建立国家可再生能源或低碳经济基金，支持发展绿色经济和低碳经济发展。

致公党中央在《积极应对气候变化，走中国特色低碳发展道路》的提案中提出，要结合节能减排工作和正在制定的"十二五"规划，尽快将低碳发展战略落实到地方，特别是东部、南部沿海发达地区。

全国工商联房地产商会在《关于积极推广绿色低碳技术、推动绿色建筑发展》的提案中认为，应"将推广绿色低碳技术与建筑纳入'十二五'规划之中"。提案建议今后政府应在土地政策、税收政策、产业政策方面对绿色低碳建筑进行改革和倾斜，改变以单纯的"价高者得"的土地出让办法。

台盟在《关于推进我国低碳产业发展》的提案中建议，请相关部门结合"十二五"规划制定出低碳经济的"国家方案"和行动路线图，与国家的"发展规划"、"能源规划"、"循环经济规划"和节能减排规划相衔接，形成一个可操作性强的低碳经济发展蓝图。

## 二、住房与房价

随着房价的持续上涨和住房矛盾的日益凸显，住房与房价问题仍然是本届"两会"的热点话题之一。与往届不同的是，本届两会的话题除了如何稳定房价外，更多地关注保障性住房问题。其中，关于公共租赁房等议案都是首次在“两会”上出现。

全国政协委员郑惠强的提案提出，为解决廉租房和经济适用房之间的“夹心层”住房困难，各地政府应借鉴新加坡、我国香港等地经验，大力建设公共租赁房。他认为，加快公共租赁房体系建设，既可以平抑房价，减轻更多家庭的买房负担，又可以有效解决新就业大学生、外来务工人员等“夹心层”的住房困难。

致公党中央《建立合理的保障性住房管理机制》的提案认为，调整和完善土地供应结构，加大保障性住房在房地产市场中的比例，是解决我国当前房地产市场问题的关键。为此，建议加大住房保障工作的统一协调力度，成立各级社会保障性住房建设与管理办公室，具体负责保障性住房的整体协调工作；调整土地供应结构和二手房交易结构，明确规定保障性住房和商品房土地供应的比例，坚决杜绝保障房在交易环节的盈利空间；建立严格的保障房准入退出机制，确保社会保障性住房实现有效流转；要特别关注外来务工人员的住房问题，在农民工集中区域集中建设符合农民工特点的住房。

中国国民党革命委员会中央委员会提案认为，当前畸高的房价严重脱离经济发展水平和居民购买力，老百姓改善住房的需求和低购买力与高房价之间的矛盾正逐步演化成房地产市场最主要、最尖锐的矛盾。为此，建议改革中央与地方的财政税收关系体制，开征房产税，提高土地供应量，改善招标办法，继续压低出让地价；对存量土地转移过程积极监控，对土地转手增加项目成本形成约束；改变土地出让金收取方式，对居住类用地的土地使用权出让可改为在土地出让期限内分年度收取；开发商不在预定年限内建房出售的，收取高额的土地空置费用。出售后的土地使用费由房主逐年向政府缴纳，或并入物业税缴纳；改革或取消当前的住房预售制度。

全国人大代表宗庆后在《关于改革供地方式，进行二次房改建立三三制住房制度的建议》中提出“三种住房制度，三类供地方式，三支队伍参与”，简称“三三制住房制度”和“三三制房改方案”、“三三制房改路线图”。改革目标是建立“低端有保障，中端买得起，高端有选择”的多层次良性发展的住房供应体系。同时他还提出建议改革供地方式，发展四定两竞公共住房。

九三学社在《关于抑制房价过快上涨》的提案中建议，进一步健全住房保障体系，加大经济适用房土地供应，加快市场投放速度；严格限制经济适用房的转让；落实廉租住房制度建设的目标责任制，落实以财政预算安排为主的多渠道筹措廉租房建设资金的规定；完善管理制度，建立严格的申请、审批和退出制度；健全住房保障对象档案，对廉租住房保障对象实施动态管理；合理确定廉租住房保障标准，逐步扩大廉租住房覆盖面。同时建议：积极推进公共租赁住房建设，建立政府补贴下的、以企业为主体的运行机制。

## 三、农村城镇化与城乡统筹

农村城镇化和城乡统筹建设的问题依然是今年两会的热点话题之一，与会代表和委员对如何在新时期加强城乡统筹工作、如何引导农村城镇化提出了观点和建议。

九三学社在《关于完善“十二五”城镇化规划的建议》的提案中认为，“十二五”规划应该重点关注城镇化进程中的发展策略和资源配置问题，并妥善处理好以下几方面的关系：一是增加城市土地供应与提高农地利用率和产出率，促进农业集约经营的关系；二是合理选择城镇化发展重心与降低流域中上游人口承载系数，鼓励内地人口向沿海地区自然迁移的关系；三是发展中小城镇特别是沿海中小城镇与改革财税收入分配体制，提高地方政府负债与融资能力的关系。

民建中央在《推进农民工市民化，促使城镇化协调发展》的提案中明确提出，当前我国经济社会正处于加速发展的重要战略机遇期，城镇化发展，尤其是加快发展中小城市和县城的城镇化战略是我国最大的内需所在。提案提出六条建议措施：把放开中小城市户籍与农民工市民化作为当前城镇化和扩大内需的战略重点，促进区域城镇化的协调发展与大中小城镇体系合理化；完善创业扶持政策，加强创业服务，加快城镇安居工程建设，实现农民工的“创业梦”和“安居梦”，让进城农民工安居乐业；加大政府对城镇化的财政投入，探讨土地融资的新模式，解决农民工创业和发展中小企业的融资难问题；创新城镇化建设筹资机制，放宽民间投资的准入，构建政府和民间共同在城镇化方面投资的新格局，用好政府发动型和民间发动型的两种城镇化机制；推进农民工市民化进程，实现进城农民工与市民的平权，加快城镇新老居民公共服务均等化，积极应对新生代农民工面临的问题，帮助农民工实现“城市梦”；加强城镇化的科学规划，在继续推动东部城市圈发展的同时，更加注重在中西部地区依托县城发展壮大一批中小城市，实现城镇化的均衡发展。

全国政协委员宗庆后认为，农村劳动大军在城市与乡村以及各个城市之间的无序摆动，不仅导致了劳动力这一重要社会资源在迁徙过程中的巨大浪费，也增加了社会成本。同时，由于大城市生活成本高，农村劳动力亦无法长期在大城市生存，也就实现不了真正的农村剩余劳动力转移，改变不了乡镇依然落后的现状这一国情。而发展县域经济，在中小城镇实现工业化和城市化，就能够就地吸收农村劳动人口，实现城乡统筹协调发展。他建议：控制大城市工业用地指标，迫使企业迁移到地、县；对迁移到中小城市、乡镇就业定居的农民给予适当的补贴；进一步鼓励乡镇民营企业与乡镇企业的发展，积极扶持乡镇兴办农产品深加工企业及为大企业加工配套的乡镇企业的发展，就地消化部分农村劳动力，加快农村发展；发展乡镇医疗、文化、教育事业，改善居住环境。全国人大代表廖国勋也持同样的观点，他认为县域经济是统筹城乡的突破口，国家应支持做大县域经济，农民在县城打工并变成城镇居民，然后逐渐把土地流转出来。

全国政协委员迟福林提出，要让大量农民从土地上转移出去，首先需要解决农民工转为市民的问题。全国人大代表、重庆发展改革委主任杨庆育认为，应给农民工同等待遇，特别是要对进城农民工及其子女进行职业技能培训，让农民工有安居房，有社会保障。全国人大代表陈云贤提出公共服务向农村延伸，是大幅度提高农村生活质量的前提。全国政协委员郑新立指出，要把农村潜在的消费需求变为现实的需求，从而变为拉动经济增长的强大动力。全国政协委员瞿振元认为，农民新建住房愿望很强，可以与新农村建设、土地整理等结合起来，事半功倍。而全国人大代表张育彪则认为，城镇化不是要消灭农村，城镇不能过度扩张，不能侵占农民利益；城镇和农村应当各有分工、互相补充；在大力推动城镇化的同时，还应当积极推动农业产业化，提高农民收入。全国政协委员李冬玉认为，如果农民的宅基地能够有偿退出后，可以用建设用地指标置换的资金到城市里买房，或者能享受城市保障性住房，这对于鼓励农民进城是很好的方式。

## 四、区域发展与振兴

随着我国东部地区逐渐进入工业化后期和后工业化阶段，区域发展与振兴的话题相比往届两会的提案和议案有所减少，但更多的委员和代表对我国中西部地区城市群和区域发展的关注有所增加。

致公党中央针对当前长三角地区仍然面临的产业同构、无序竞争、区域公共基础设施和信息资源难以完全共建共享，环境保护与产业转移的压力不断增大等问题提出四点建议：深化区域产业结构调整，优先发展战略性新兴产业和支持科技创新，培育新的经济增长点；打破行政区划限制，使资本、技术、人才、信息等要素在区域内有序流动，实现企业的跨区域合作；努力实现产业转移与对接，推进安徽融入长三角区域合作与发展；以区域环境政策一体化为目标，建立区域环境保护协调机制。

全国工商联《关于建立“兰西银经济区”，进一步推动西部大开发》的提案认为，西部地区地理位置独特，自然资源和产业优势突出，但目前还缺少真正意义上的经济增长极。应该把甘肃、青海、宁夏三省区联合起来，突出农牧业、矿产和绿色能源等优势，建设“兰州—西宁—银川经济区”（简称为“兰西银经济区”），纳入国家区域发展的大格局之中，促进区域发展和板块的崛起。这对于推进西部大开发战略的实施、促进民族地区的繁荣稳定，具有一定战略意义。为此建议：由国家发改委牵头，组织国家有关部门和专家从国家层面论证建立“兰西银经济区”的必要性和战略意义；加大对西部欠发达地区的支持力度，在甘肃、青海、宁夏三地联合打造“兰西银经济区”，并纳入国家总体区域发展战略；把“兰西银经济区”与已经成立的经济区发展结合起来，优势互补，共同发展，使“兰西银经济区”与成渝经济区、关中经济区成为我国西部真正的“西三角”。

全国政协委员王全书以及多名驻豫全国政协委员联名提交了《关于设立中原城市群农业现代化工业化城镇化协调科学发展示范区的建议》的提案，认为设立示范区就是要通过优化开发空间布局，促进产业向城镇集聚、人口向城镇集中，探索一条以不牺牲农业和生态环境为代价的新型工业化、城镇化道路，同时进一步推进城乡统筹、产业集聚、产城融合、城际开放，增强“三化”协调发展水平，提升区域整体实力和综合竞争力，构筑河南乃至中部地区具有较强集聚效应和辐射带动作用的核心增长极，加快形成东中西互动、优势互补、相互促进、共同发展的区域协调发展新格局。

全国政协委员陈世强认为，加快大别山地区的区域经济合作与发展，具有重要的政治意义、经济意义和社会意义。建议要建立促进大别山区发展的统一协调、规划、合作联动组织。从产业布局、社会事业发展、基础设施建设等方面统筹考虑，整合大别山区资源，制定大别山区发展总体规划，启动大别山区振兴战略。通过建立合作联动机制，指导和引导鄂豫皖三省之间的相互沟通和协商，形成联动机制。

全国政协委员周汉民认为，边境沿边开放不仅关系到对外开放整体水平的提高，更关系到边疆稳定和民族团结，对构建和谐的国内国外环境都具有重大战略意义。他建议从中央和国家层面作出统一部署和周密安排，使边境经济合作区从以边贸带动为主的单一发展模式转变为贸易、投资、加工制造、旅游等协调带动的综合发展模式；出台优势产业发展指导目录，扶持加工贸易和高附加值产业发展；出台惠边政策，边境经济合作区内生产型企业享受所得税优惠；提供基础设施专项贷款；开展人民币结算试点，落实边贸采用人民币结算全额退税政策。

农工党中央提案认为，在唐山湾地区将会出现以绿色发展为主要标志的新型工业化、城市化、生态化和信息化的循环经济和和谐社会建设的新模式，它将成为环渤海崛起的核心发动机之一。因此，应加大滨海新区北翼唐山湾地区的开放改革力度，统筹区域规划、建设和管理，给予该地区一定的政策、体制和机制扶持。提案建议：设立国家级生态文明和绿色发展示范区；在唐山湾曹妃甸开展综合配套改革，创新机制体制；加强唐山湾地区重大交通基础设施建设，推进京津唐一体化；进一步加大对唐山湾曹妃甸生态城建设的支持力度；设立唐山湾曹妃甸综合保税区。

## 五、土地制度与规划管理

针对当前农村集体建设用地使用权流转存在的产权主体不清、隐形市场活跃、违法用地屡禁不止、相关配套政策不完善、收益分配不规范、农村集体建设用地利用规划和村镇规划相对滞后等诸多问题，两会代表和委员提出了他们解决问题的思路和建议。

全国政协委员高金榜认为，应明确农村集体建设用地产权主体，通过土地登记发证，理清乡镇、村、村民小组三类主体的产权界限，避免产权主体虚置与权能重叠。为此，他提出八条建议：进一步规范农民集体经济组织，明确农村集体建设用地产权主体，并通过土地登记发证，理清乡镇、村、村民小组三类主体的产权界限，避免产权主体虚置与权能重叠；建立健全统一的市场和服务体系，完善市场管理规定和交易规则，为农村集体建设用地使用权流转提供相关服务；参照国有土地使用权流转的税费标准，建立和完善农村集体建设用地使用权流转的税费体系，实现“同地、同权、同价”；建立合理的农村集体建设用地使用权流转收益分配机制，确保农村集体和农民成为流转收益的主要获得者，同时确保集体和国家土地收益不流失；积极推进土地承包经营权依法流转，鼓励试点农村宅基地使用权有偿退出政策，推动长期进城并在城镇具有相对固定职业的农民真正转变为城镇居民；完善农村土地利用规划和村镇规划，大量减少人口较少的自然村，使人口逐步向城镇和中心村集中；强化土地用途管制，集体建设用地的安排必须符合土地利用总体规划；加快推进《土地管理法》等相关法律的修改和完善，从根本上解决农村集体建设用地使用权流转的法律问题。

全国政协委员蔡继明认为，城乡集体建设用地应同地同权同价，深入推进土地产权变革，给予农村土地真正完整的产权。建立农民进城与农地退出机制，加快农村土地流转，完善关于自愿放弃、转让土地的相关规定，使土地这种生产要素能够活起来。全国政协委员吴正德认为，要建立农村集体建设用地流转后村民的保障机制，不能简单推行“宅基地换房”和“土地换社保”的做法。

全国政协委员蔡克勤、谢俊奇在提案中建议，做好城乡发展规划，科学合理地安排农村产业发展与城镇建设用地，严格控制用地总量，严格控制非农建设占用耕地，依照土地管理法律法规，做到有保有压；对违法用地必须严格查处，落实耕地保护责任制和科学发展的量化考核长效机制；加快农村集体土地的确权、登记、颁证工作，赋予农民及农村集体合法土地权利，提高他们保护土地资源的自觉性；严格农村集体建设用地流转管理，尊重和保障农民的合法权益，规范流转行为。在试点的基础上，积极稳妥地推进制度创新。

中国民主促进会中央委员会的提案对规范有序开展农村土地整治工作提出建议：坚持增减挂钩，重点开展农田整治；坚持政府领导，建立共同推进工作的机制；注重统筹规划，有效控制整治规模；尊重农民意愿，确保农民受益；坚持量力而行，防止大拆大建；强化考核监管，确保工作实效；出台配套文件，保证实施力度。

除了上述五大类问题外，两会话题还涉及城市发展、生态建设、历史文化遗产保护和具体的城市规划技术规范等问题。这些问题虽然并不集中，但也反映了两会代表和委员对城乡规划建设问题的深入思考和观察。

全国政协委员王顺生关于《加快深圳特区内外一体化进程推动深圳实现科学发展》的提案获16位委员联名签署。闫小培委员认为“将特区扩大至关外，不仅可以解决特区内外软硬环境建设差距巨大的问题，‘一市两法’难题也可以迎刃而解!”王顺生委员认为，目前深圳特区内外发展不平衡，基础设施、投资环境、单位面积土地经济产出量、公共服务水平、法治环境等方面都存在一定的差距，“一市两法”、“一市两制”已成为深圳实现科学发展的制约因素。因此，加快特区内外一体化进程，是深圳实现科学发展的迫切要求。

全国政协委员刘德旺提出要保护和建设好京津冀最美湿地“衡水湖”。他认为，保护衡水湖对于保护京津冀乃至华北地区的生态安全具有重要意义。衡水湖是南水北调东线工程的调蓄枢纽，对保证东线调水工程顺利实施和水质安全具有举足轻重的作用。鉴于此，刘德旺提出建议：加快湿地保护立法步伐；加大工作协调力度，促进各项支持政策与项目的落实；将衡水湖列入国家“十二五”规划和长远发展规划；统筹协调生态建设用地；建立生态用水补偿机制。

2009年“两会”期间，国家文物局长单霁翔就提出了加强大遗址保护的建议。本届“两会”上全国人大代表陈宝根再次提出建议，在西安设立“国家大遗址保护特区”。陈宝根认为西安的大遗址保护存在如下问题：数量多、面积大，涉及多个行政区，协调难度大；经济发展用地之间的矛盾日益突出；文物保护经费缺口很大。对此，建议在西安设立“国家大遗址保护特区”，成立大遗址保护特区管理委员会，享受国家级文物保护等各项优惠政策。同时建议国家有关部门尽快出台针对大遗址保护的专门条例、法规和相关的技术标准规范，出台大遗址保护管理条例和大遗址保护特区条例，将大遗址保护纳入有法可依、有章可循的轨道。

全国政协委员单霁翔针对北京历史城区整体保护提交提案。他建议调整北京历史城区内的现有行政区划，以二环路为界，将现在分属东城、西城、宣武、崇文四个行政区的历史城区内的用地加以整合，形成统一的中央行政区。他认为中央行政区应该具有独特的功能。第一，中央行政区作为我国政治中心的核心地段，要为党中央、国务院领导全国工作和开展国际交往服务；第二，中央行政区是我国文化中心的核心地段，要为来自全国的民众提供享受高雅文化服务；第三，中央行政区是古都的核心地段，要为国内外来宾领略博大精深的中国传统文化提供良好的环境。

全国政协委员吴鸿针对“中国丹霞”申遗提交提案。2009年中国丹霞六处系列提名地顺利完成了IUCN专家的现场考察评估，2010年将面临IUCN的评估推荐和在巴西召开的第三十四届世界遗产大会上接受世界遗产委员会21个委员国的审查表决。为成功申遗，他提出如下建议：一是外交部、文化部及中国联合国教科文组织全委会将中国丹霞申遗工作纳入外事工作议事日程，确定专人负责IUCN专家和世界遗产委员会21个委员国的协调沟通工作。二是发改委、财政部、国土资源部、环境保护部、国家林业局、国家旅游局进一步加大对中国丹霞六个系列提名地的地质遗迹及生态环境的保护、监管、游览设施建设的投入，在项目支持和资金安排上给予倾斜支持。三是住房和城乡建设部进一步加强对中国丹霞申遗工作的组织领导，安排专人负责此项工作的统一指挥和组织协调，带领和指导六地做好最后冲刺的相关工作。

中国民主促进会中央委员会提交提案，针对当前生活垃圾焚烧出现的问题提出建议：第一，坚持垃圾分类，政府必须切实投入，提供垃圾分类所需的配套基础设施。第二，规划选址公开。在充分论证基础上，对焚烧厂进行规划和整体布局；建立和完善听证制度，决策信息过程公开透明；新开发区域的规划方案提前向社会公布，并强制要求开发商向购房者公示；制定相应的补偿机制，从经济利益、公共服务等方面给予利害关系人合理的补偿和平衡。第三，准入门槛从严。必须有资质、有经验的企业才能进入；招标过程公开透明，接受阳光监督；将能否做到垃圾焚烧全程公开，作为是否上马的重要指标。第四，技术严格把关。建议环保总局会同科技部、国家质量监督检验总局共同完善焚烧相关技术标准，宣传普及较成熟技术，对危害较大的不成熟技术进行改造或予以淘汰；将垃圾焚烧处理技术纳入国家“十二五”科技规划，加大技术攻关。

民革中央在提交全国政协的一份大会发言中指出，避免在地震活动带建设危险工程，提高建筑物的抗震能力，是目前对付震灾最有效的手段。因此，要尽快在全国范围进行地震风险评估，高烈度区尤应禁止建学校等人员密集性建筑物。建议迅速在全国范围内开展地震风险评估，尤其需要在我国主要地震带的人口密集区展开此项调查。调查评估内容必须每隔一定时间更新一次，并在一定范围内向社会公布。

（作者：王建军，广东省佛山市南海区国土城建和水务局总规划师，高级规划师）

# 城市保障性住房问题观察

保障性住房是近年来中国城市最具热点的议题之一。从互联网搜索引擎一点便可搜索到关于该题材的上千万网页，足见它受关注的程度。同时，保障性住房也是各界最为纠结的一个城市议题。从政府角度来看，由于建设量有限，使它的惠及面难以铺开，就以该项工作启动较早的广州情况来看，保障性住房年竣工量所占城市住房年竣工总量的比重还很小。而分配和管理环节上产生的问题又使得2006年后重新启动的保障性住房政策，在城市的具体落实显得脆弱而不稳定。从民众角度来看，“僧多粥少”的保障房供求现实使得绝大多数缺房群体望房兴叹。

从社会角度来看，众多专家和学者提出的具有良好社会效应的保障房制度体系和实施措施常常是理想与现实的背离。为避免人为制造贫困聚集而提倡保障房分散建设无疑是一种理想的模式，但能够提供分散建房的用地缺乏往往又成为瓶颈。北京、广州等大城市于2006年后试图构筑的各阶层群体对应收入相互连接的“双特困廉租房——经济适用房——租赁性保障房——限价房”的多层次保障链条，在现实操作上成效也不大。广州市推出的限价房措施有疾而萎缩，北京的租赁性保障房也仅具象征性意义。可以说，保障房体系实质上至今尚未成熟。

## 一、保障性住房制度体系的建设：2006年后全面启动

### 1. 制度体系的建设

城市保障房制度体系并非城市的新议题，它的发展已有相当长的时期。

“保障性住房”首次正式出现在1994年7月《国务院关于深化城镇住房制度改革的决定》① 中，被界定为以中低收入家庭为对象、具有社会保障性质的经济适用住房；其范畴在1998年7月的政策文件《国务院关于进一步深化城镇住房制度改革加快住房建设的通知》② 中被扩充为最低收入租赁廉租房、中低收入家庭购买经济适用房等两类住房。这两类住房也

① 资料来源：http://www.law110.com/law/guowuyuan/2018.htm

② 国发［1998］23号。资料来源：http://china.newssc.org/system/2008/11/05/011255389.shtml

是现行保障房制度体系的核心。我国从1994年提出至2006年，保障性住房已经历了12年的试行期。

## 专栏一：中国城镇保障性住房的类型

保障性住房在不同国家和地区有着不同的概念内涵。第二次世界大战后，特别是20世纪60年代以来，西欧、北美、新加坡，以及我国香港等发达国家和地区的“保障性住房”在政府力量的全力运作下，其概念和运作模式都曾发生变化，但都表现出惊人的共性，主要体现在“保障方式”、“保障力度”、“供应机构”、“保障对象”等关键词上。例如，保障方式包括“租赁和出售”，保障力度体现为“社会可支付水平”，保障对象则是以经济收入衡量的“中低收入群体”，供应机构是“政府及其所属非营利机构或接收租金补贴的私人非营利组织”、“私人合作组织”。而定义保障性住房的核心关键词则是“保障力度”和“保障对象”。

中国的保障性住房虽然目前尚未有缜密严谨的界定和对应的类型划分。但根据上述界定模式，结合国家出台的相关政策及出现的住房类型，通过核心关键词“保障力度”和“保障对象”，应将凡是通过划拨方式获得土地或以政府指导价出售，以住房困难群体或低收入住房困难群体为保障对象的住房类型，均纳入保障性住房的范畴。再结合另外两个关键词“保障方式”和“供应机构”，我国的保障性住房的概念内涵可界定为：“由城市政府及其他辅助机构推出的、面向住房困难或住房和收入双困难的户籍家庭出租或出售的非营利住房。”据此，我国保障性住房所包含的住房类型可以有六类。

表1　保障性住房概念所包含的住房类型

| 住房类型 | 保障方式 | 保障对象① | 保障力度 | 保障机构 |
|---|---|---|---|---|
| 经济适用房 | 出售 | 收入、住房双困 | 不超过成本价3%的微利价 | 地方政府 |
| 解困房 | 出租② | 住房困难 | 准成本租金 | 地方政府 |
| 安居房 | 出售 | 住房、收入困难③ | 成本价 | 地方政府 |
| 廉租房 | 出租 | 住房、收入特困 | 1元/平方米·月 | 政府、单位④ |
| 单位集资建房 | 出售 | 住房困难 | 成本价 | 单位 |
| 个人集资合作建房 | 出售 | 住房困难 | 成本价 | 住房合作社 |

（资料来源：根据马晓亚博士论文《广州市保障性住区的发展特征及其影响机制》）

① 注：保障对象都指户籍人口。

② 根据1995年《广州市解困房租赁管理试行办法》（穗国房字［1995］第135号）（文件来源：http://www.law110.com/law/city/guangzhou/200301072.htm），解困房实行短期出租政策，1999年房改时根据房改政策以成本价进行出售。

③ 根据《广州市安居工程实施方案》（穗府［1997］14号）（文件出处：http://law.baidu.com/pages/chinalawinfo/1679/24/b314dafd71e8454b1d8dd9d375ea299a_0.html）重在解决单位体制内住房困难家庭住房问题；其次是中低收入、住房困难的社会分散群体。

④ 根据《广州市城市廉租住房保障制度实施办法》（穗府［2007］48号）（文件出处：http://www.law110.com/law/city/guangzhou/2006law110200301190.html），廉租房包括公房租金核减和实物配置两种方式，其中公房租金核减是指承租市直管房和各单位自管房的低收入住房困难家庭，按照廉租房租金标准给予减收租金，因此，廉租房房源的供应机构包括单位。

1998年城镇住房双轨供应体制全面运行以来，保障性住房制度体系的建设未被赋予重要使命，在双轨制中仍处于次要地位。事实上，自1996年房地产被确立为拉动经济增长的新增长点后到2006年，城镇住房供应一直采取“市场”一条腿走路，本应由城镇保障性住房制度体系为中低收入者支撑起的住房供给却几乎完全被推向市场。这一时期的缺失体现在两个方面：一是相关政策的缺失，从1999年5月国务院发文《城镇廉租住房管理办法》时，到2004年3月出台《城镇最低收入家庭廉租住房管理办法》，这中间长达5年的期间，相关部门并未出台有关城镇保障性住房的任何政策；二是保障性住房在2003—2005年的两次商品房市场宏观调控政策中从未被提及，直到2006年5月出台的“国六条”中关于住房供给结构的调控，才见到有关部门对住房产业发展思路的反思，使城镇住房从经济消费问题上升到政治民生问题，中低收入阶层成为政府着重关注的对象。2007年8月的《关于解决城市低收入家庭住房困难的若干意见》，正是城镇保障性住房制度体系开始受到重视的体现。

表2　2003—2006年房地产市场的宏观调控政策链条

| 时间 | 政　策 | 调控层面 |
| --- | --- | --- |
| 2003年 | 《关于促进房地产市场持续健康发展的通知①》 | 1998—2003年从开发生产到销售交易到物业管理等各个环节的制度建设过程出现的问题 |
| 2005年 | 《关于切实稳定住房价格的通知②》 | 对市场中的供应结构、居民消费能力、非供求因素导致的房价上升等引起重视 |
| 2006年 | 《关于调控市场的六条意见③》 | 调控住房市场供应结构、房价 |

**2. 制度体系的实施：2006年前，历史遗留问题是解决重点**

与新加坡、日本、欧美和我国香港等不同，中国内地城镇保障性住房制度体系的实施过程更多地携带了历史的痕迹，计划经济时期的福利公房制度遗留的住房问题捆住了保障性住房制度建设前行的脚步。2006年前，许多大城市保障性住房的供给深受计划经济时期的福利公房制度的影响，导致新旧住房制度体系交替阶段，政府机关、国有企事业单位内一部分人出现住房困难的问题。尽管该时期新体系下的收入住房双困难的社会分散群体也被容纳进去，但并不是被保障主体。

① 政策文献来源于 http://www.sdpc.gov.cn/cyfz/fwyfz/t20070516_143901.htm。国发[2003]18号

② 政策文献来源于 http://www.hebjs.gov.cn/govinfo/TCFL/FGGW/SGFXWJ/200803/t20080328_95151.htm。国发[2005]8号

③ 政策文献来源于 http://news.gz.soufun.com/subject/guoliutiao/

## 专栏二：2006年前保障性住房制度在北京、广州等地的实施

北京市在20世纪90年代初便致力于保障性住房的建设。1993年颁布的《北京市康居工程实施方案》是该市启动保障房建设的具有标志意义的行动。虽然市办公厅于1994年下发的《关于开展住房困难户调查的通知》明确将住房困难户的范围界定为“市属委、办、局、总公司系统职工”、“区、县属单位职工”和“来自街道办的无单位依托的居民”，但从1993年的10万平方米康居住宅的最终流向看，至少在早期，历史遗留问题是其解决重点。据1993年9月份的统计，各单位认购面积达9.03万平方米，由无单位依托的困难户买走的却是九牛一毛，少之又少。虽然政府为促进销售于1994年调整了相关分配政策，但有些问题仍未能解决①。

除康居工程对党政机关、国有企事业单位的住房困难职工重点照顾外，1998年更名为经济适用房的保障房仍显得对该类群体有所倾斜。首先，根据北京市于1998年颁布的《关于加快经济适用住房建设的若干规定》，“单位利用自有用地自建经适房以保障本单位内部职工”仍在政策框架内。市政府在1998年确定的首批19个经适房项目中，4个项目是单位自建经适房项目，另一著名特大型项目回龙观，是由市政府面向国家公务员、科技人员、教师组织开发的规划总建筑面积达550万平方米的科教文化居住区。换句话说，该项目仍是主要针对单位体制内家庭的（当然也包含部分来自社会的中低收入家庭）。而且，根据国务院《关于进一步深化城镇住房制度改革加快住房建设的通知》，1998年开工的经济适用房仍可由单位购买，并按照房改政策出售给本单位职工②。

北京保障性住房的建设过程表明，历史遗留问题一定程度上是政府在2006年前的重要解决对象。

从广州的建设实践也可看到，2006年前历史遗留问题在很大程度上是解决重点。《广州市志》、《广州房地产志》等文献所载，广州保障房行动始于1986年。而在1985年的房屋普查中，11642户人均居住面积低于2平方米的家庭全部属于单位体制内住户。据此，《关于解决广州市人均2平方米以下困难户住房问题的方案》被制定和推行。该项工作一直持续到1998年，而保障范围逐步扩大到单位体制内人均居住面积低于5平方米、7平方米的住房困难家庭以及新增无房户。这表明，1998年前，广州的保障房主要用于解决历史遗留问题。

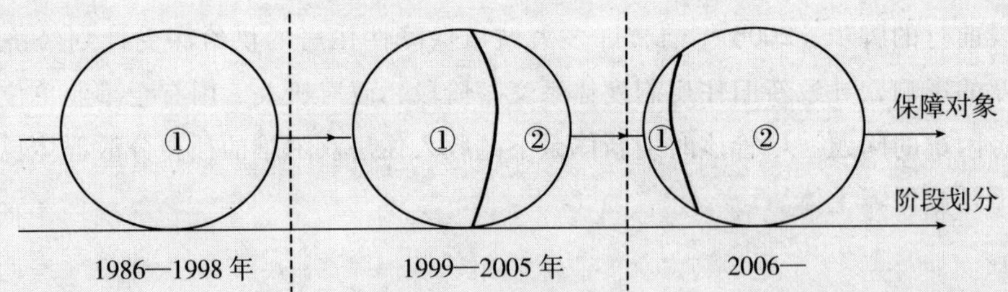


注：①代表公有单位体制内的住房困难家庭；②代表中低收入—住房困难的社会分散群体

（资料来源：马晓亚博士论文《广州市保障性住区的发展特征及其影响机制》）

① 北京市城建系统康居工程调查组．关于康居工程实施情况的调查报告．北京房地产杂志，1995（5）

② 张燕生．北京首批经济适用住房开始认购单位仍可购买．北京房地产，1998（11）

1999—2006 年，尽管该时期保障范围进一步扩大到社会群体和被拆迁户，但从实际的建设成果看，广州市的保障房仍主要面向单位体制内的住房困难家庭。在此期间，市政府共建成数十处保障性住房，都是面向党政机关和教师、医疗系统职工。专门针对社会分散群体的仅有两个小型项目，而且是利用商品房源推出来的。而来自社会的分散群体更多的是被见缝插针地安置在各个时期建成的仍有空置住宅的保障性住区中。

### 3. 制度体系的完善：2006 年后全面启动

2006 年国务院出台《关于调控市场的六条意见》（即“国六条”），针对中低收入阶层的中小户型商品房的调控，预示着保障性住房制度的建设将要重新启动。“国六条”对城市住宅发展思路进行反思，中低收入阶层成为政府的主要关注对象。2007 年 8 月国务院出台的《关于解决城市低收入家庭住房困难的若干意见》是对“国六条”的进一步深化，标志着保障房制度的建设正式启动，并将掀开崭新的一页。主要表现在三个方面：

首先，2006 年后重新启动的保障房制度体系带有较少的旧制度痕迹。尽管新的框架下单位自建房开禁（1998 年后单位自建房被禁止），规定有土地的国有大中型企业可为本单位住房困难职工建设住房，虽被外界视为这是用新瓶装旧酒的方法来继续解决历史遗留问题的措施，但总体上，新框架着重将被保障对象瞄准了社会上的户籍分散群体。各地政府通过制定较为完善的评分系统对申请者的住房情况进行审核，以确保经济最困难者、年龄高者、身残无劳动能力者先行得到保障。另一方面，保障性住房的建设行动也印证了这种转向。2006 年后各城市政府开始专门针对具有城镇户籍的社会中低收入群体，启动新一轮的实物配给，使该类群体成为新建的保障性住区的居住主体，而不是先前被见缝插针地安置在政府专门为单位体制内住房困难家庭所建设的保障性住区中。

其次，2006 年后，保障性住房制度体系系统地得到完善。1999 年“市场提供商品房、政府提供保障性住房”的城镇住房双轨供应制度正式建立之时，“政府为中低收入者提供经济适用房、为最低收入者提供廉租房”的双轨保障机制也同时形成。但长期以来，“只售不租”的经适房制度得以重点实施，廉租房制度的实施却十分缓慢且一度停滞。2006 年后，在经适房制度备受指责之时，廉租房制度得到了各界的重新思考和审视，国务院制定政策敦促各城市政府加强廉租房供应规模，使之成为与经适房制度并行的保障制度。也就是说，2006 年之后，保障性住房制度体系进入了双轨保障制度平行运行的阶段。

最后，2006 年后，保障性住房制度体系得到进一步的扩充。新的保障方式及其相应的保障对象被容纳进来，并得到了初步的实施。这些新的保障方式主要包含面向中低收入群体的限价房和面向外来务工人员或大学毕业生的租赁性保障房。由此，保障性住房制度体系形成了对应收入相互连接的各阶层群体的“双特困廉租房——经济适用房——租赁性保障房——限价房”的多层次保障链条。

## 二、保障性住房的建设行动：涉及城市发展的多个领域

自从着手建立并逐步推行保障性住房制度以来，保障性住房的建设行动就伴生着一些问

题。政府虽下大力气不断对相关政策进行调整和修补进行引导，但在保障性住房的分配环节、保障性住区后续形成的社会生态、后续的管理层面以及它的空间落实和保障性住区的内部设施补给等方面，还是不时出现各种矛盾和纠纷。

**1. 保障性住房的分配环节**

“经济适用房到底‘经济’了谁”，自1998年北京率先面向社会推出保障性住房以来，这种来自分配环节的质疑之声便风生水起。如果说，早期的分配不公是由于那时经济适用房担负着扩大内需、拉动经济增长的重任，而导致其在分配环节没有完善系统的分配政策和防漏措施可依，以及由于允许单位购买经济适用房的宽松政策而导致其注定无法针对性惠贫而引起较大的反响。但是，2006年后，保障性住房制度经过新一轮的修补和完善，新建保障性住房的分配不公却并未消失，在对申请者的身份识别和核查机制尚不健全的情况下，“有空可钻”的现象仍时有发生。

在深圳、北京等地的经适房小区出现了不少“名车房主”，而真正急需的人却没有住进保障房。尽管各地出台的针对申请者资格审查的政策和防漏措施越来越严，但保障房审查存在着的先天不足，从根本上难以遏制申请者的“钻空”行为。下面以深圳为例：

**专栏三：深圳保障房审核越查越细，漏洞不断冒出**①

在保障性住房申请中，“猫鼠戏”持续上演。保障房审核存在漏洞，主管部门的相关人员叹息：“现在就是越查越细，但是不断有新的漏洞冒出。”南方日报于2010年10月26日报道，深圳房产审查有四难：31万栋历史遗留违法建筑没有建立全市统一数据库；没有房产证的非农民数量也不少；原住民宅基地难查；外地房产全国未联网。这四大难题令现行保障房审查制度对房产情况的审查十分被动。此外，资产外移到境外也很难查。深圳市人大代表举例，有人为了申请保障房，三年前就把资产转移到国外，使得资产审查变得很难。另外，还有婚姻作假也不好核实。

审查中的漏洞让审核人员倍感头疼。他们虽竭尽全力，在复审工作中新增工商审查，但还是没权限审查财产。最为关键的市级终审层面，虽动用全国各大城市罕见的联合性终审，即联合民政部门，并在市公安、规划、国土、人力资源和社会保障、地税以及金融办、信息办、人民银行等相关职能部门的协助下，对申请家庭户籍、车辆、住房、保险、个税、存贷款、证券、残疾等级及优抚对象等情况进行审查核实，即“九查九核”，但对上文提到的房产审核四大难题、境外资产、婚姻作假等方面依然作用有限。

在审核机制存在先天缺陷的情况下，部分保障房难免再次流入不符合申请条件的非中低收入者手中，在一定程度上来说，这也是“分配不公”的表现。

---

① 筛选自：http://www.cnstock.com/index/gdbb/201010/951556.htm；作者，周昌和；来源，南方网2010－10－27

### 2. 保障性住房的大规模集中建设

“居住分异”和“贫困集聚”开始成为中国城市社会空间的一种表征，也逐渐受到学界的关注，学者呼吁更多的社会融合。2006 年后，经适房和廉租房的大规模成片建设，在保障房分配制度的作用下所形成的同质性社会生态空间，一定程度上会导致城市居住分异。这种现象受到学界和社会的质疑，认为是政府人为制造贫困集聚。

根据学者们对城市贫困集聚的研究，当前中国城市普遍存在着市场力量自发和历史遗留通过市场过滤作用所产生的老城衰退邻里、退化的工人居住区和外来人口集聚区等三大本地化和异地化集聚类型。2006 年后大规模成片开发的保障房住区作为政府反贫困的重要措施，无疑在客观上又导致贫困集聚的新类型，成为中国城市贫困集聚的第四类①。

而与传统的三类贫困集聚区相比，2006 年后新建保障性住区的贫困特征不尽相同。就老城衰退邻里而言，以南京为例，老龄化人口、下岗失业工人和低收入家庭是构成其社会生态的主要群体②。就退化的工人居住区而言，以安徽芜湖为例，原从事轻工、纺织、机械等国有企业及其衍生性生活服务业的产业工人，因国有企业改制和传统产业提升而被迫失业或另谋职业，他们成为主要生态群体。就外来人口集聚区而言，以雇佣者身份进入城市并从事工业生产和低端服务业的青壮年劳动力，是形成以“城中村”为主要集聚形态的边缘社区的主要生态群体③。而新建保障性住区一定程度上显示出更加综合性的、最贫困的集聚性特征。规模较大的广州金沙洲新社区就是一个例子。

#### 专栏四：广州金沙洲新社区的低收入集聚特征

金沙洲新社区汇集了具有广州城市户籍的按月领取最低生活保障金的群体和劳动性收入低于特定标准的家庭。这是一个通过廉租房和经适房政策而筛选出的广州户籍最贫困的群体集聚的保障性住区。

第一，该住区表现出“高度失业集聚”的特征。在确定为廉租户的 110 位受访者中，有 72.7% 处于失业状态。从对其在此居住的家庭成员就业情况的问卷调查得知，夫妻双方都工作的双职工家庭仅占 2.9%；而没有成员工作的家庭则占 55.2%。而在包含经适房住户、廉租户和拆迁安置户的 176 名受访居民中，住区整体的实有失业率仍达 61.3%，而没有人工作的家庭该指标为 38.3%，远远超过其他低收入集聚区类型。

第二，关于收入来源。居民的收入贫困除体现出广州保障房政策所规定的贫困度外，着重体现了“极度贫困”的经济特征。就廉租户的收入水平看，低于政府低保线（365 元/月·人）的群体所占比重高达 48.6%。如果算上该住区的经适房住户和拆迁户，该住区的“极度贫困程度”也未得到缓解，人均收入低于640元的家庭高达63.7%，而完全依靠政府救济的家庭则

① 陈云．城市贫困区位化与社区重建．中南民族大学学报（人文社会科学版），2009，29（1）：86－89

② 刘玉亭．转型期城市低收入邻里的类型、特征和产生机制：以南京为例．地理研究，2006，25（6）：1073－1082

③ 吴晓．“边缘社区”探察——我国流动人口聚居区的现状特征透析．城市规划，2003，27（7）：40－45

占35.9%。

第三，该住区居住群体的年龄结构特征表现出高度老龄化以及青壮年等生力军群体严重缺失。住区所有群体中，作为家庭核心和生产力中坚的年龄在22～40岁的中青年群体所占比重仅为32.5%，而50岁以上的中老年群体所占比重竟高达25.42%。

第四，在受教育程度上，该住区表现出文化素质普遍偏低的特征。廉租户群体中具有“大专或技术院校”及以上学历的群体仅为9.2%。

第五，该住区有较多的单亲家庭、身残病弱者集聚。

**3. 保障性住区的管理制度缺陷**

我们注意到，一些成功解决了低收入者居住问题的发达国家和地区，它们在公共住区的管理上也有其成功之处，大都建立了较为成功的公共住区管理制度。例如，我国香港公屋区的管理可谓成熟高效，对出售型公共屋邨和廉租公共屋邨分而治之，分别建立不同的管理制度。出售型公共屋邨由于“居者有其屋”计划的推行，使得其居住者有权选择物业服务公司，而被采取了市场化的管理模式。廉租公共屋邨需要政府的直接参与，但为了提高管理效率，也引进社会化的专业私营物业管理公司，实行经营服务社会化的管理模式。健全的制度使得香港公共屋邨的日常运作平稳而有序。

相比之下，中国内地无论是新建的还是早期的保障性住区，都存在一些这样那样的管理问题。发生在新旧保障性住区的物业管理纠纷、物权侵权维权纠纷、管理“只理不管”现状等问题频频见诸报端，说明在该类住区管理制度尚未成熟和完善，有时还会令新老住区陷入管理困境。

观察我国保障性住区管理特征的演变历程和现状，可将该类住区的管理模式划分为三种类型：类商品房住区的“自主社会化”的住区自治模式、政府主导的“半自主社会化”的模式和“政府联合社会力量共同管理”的非自主社会化模式。而从该类住区管理模式的演变趋势看，新建的保障性住区（尤其是廉租住区或经适房和廉租房混合住区）将继续采取并不断优化“政府联合社会力量共同管理”的非自主社会化模式，老旧的及续建的以出售型经适房为主的保障性住区则逐步完成向“自主社会化”的住区自治模式转型。在该类住区管理的实践过程和管理模式的转型、完善过程中，不时还会产生一些管理环节上的问题。

物业管理纠纷是该类住区中最为常见的问题类型。如旧保障性住区在由政府主导的非自主社会化的管理实践中，及在向业主自治的自主社会化管理转型的过程中，出现掌握管理决策权的政府下属物业管理公司有时未经业主投票同意便擅自收取特定管理费的现象。以广州市的聚德花苑为例，该住区在2008年前缺乏业委会，管理决策权在很大程度上由广州市住保办下属棠苑物业管理公司掌握，曾经发生物管公司向每户征收1500元安装防盗网、防盗门，被指出货不抵值后又不及时退款；还曾经发生物业管理公司在业主入住前承诺向每户每月征收20元的小区管理费，但实际却按每平方米1元来收取，甚至以最高每平方米1.7元的价格收取，引起部分业主不满，甚至以不交管理费作为抗议。

物权侵权维权纠纷是该类住区在管理环节上发生的最具影响的问题类型。在旧保障性住区的管理过程中，由于规划与建设行动错位引起的侵权维权事件较多，而且多发生在管理模式由政府主导的非自主社会化向自主社会化过渡和演变的阶段。例如，北京天通苑住区内的公立学校被转成民办，学费高昂。业主向物管公司及建设单位交涉，并向上级政府部门反映，迟迟没有结果，导致到了学龄的业主孩子无法就近上学。在建设单位侵权、不把建设好的教育设施的产权交给政府的情况下，责任单位北京市住保办处理力度不够，使得业主的维权行为变得十分艰辛，维权过程相当漫长。又如，行政部门要对广州市聚德花苑住区中央的原社区卫生设施进行改造，2005 年区卫生局引入民营资金，拟兴建带有太平间的综合性专业肿瘤医院。由于治疗辐射、医疗垃圾等处理的问题，该住区业主先后自发组织与广州市相应行政部门进行沟通和斡旋，最后到法庭上寻理。就是这样，业主的话语权仍不能得到充分表达。

物业管理“只理不管”的管理现状是新建的以廉租房或其与经适房混合布局的保障性住区最为明显的一类问题。这主要是由政府联合社会力量共同管理的管理模式导致的。在此种模式下，“市住保办”、“物业管理公司”和“居民”之间缺乏正常的联系机制。“市住保办”出于社会责任进行管理，“物业管理公司”要讲求利润，在利润空间不足时，会缺乏服务动力，居民缺乏自治组织而又缺少强有力的维权渠道，这些相关主体之间松散的缺乏制衡关系的管理机制，使得该类住区的管理低效在所难免。以广州金沙洲新社区为例，作为以廉租户和经适房住户混居的大型住区，按“市住保办”的相关规定，该住区的物业费用极低，非电梯楼房 0.5 元/月・平方米，高层电梯楼房 1 元/月・平方米。在利润空间微乎其微的情况下，社会化的物管公司只得压缩经营成本，雇佣能接受更低工资的女性应聘者来负责治安管理和卫生清洁，还要尽可能地压缩服务人员规模。从而导致一线工作人员“拿低工资干重活”，使得新社区的管理工作不尽如人意。可见，“只理不管”现象实在是一种管理困境。

#### 4. 保障性住区的空间布局边缘化，设施供应难以为继

保障性住区的空间布局边缘化和设施供给也是关于该类住区的一个老话题。中国各大城市保障性住区的空间布局几乎都呈现出边缘化的分布特征。根据张永波[①]的研究，北京保障性住房的空间布局呈现出远离中低收入人群就业密集区、远离经济型公共交通服务设施、远离公益性服务设施的特征。张祚[②]对武汉 2007 年在建的经适房项目空间布局的分析得出三个边缘化的特征，即逐步向内环以外区域转移、多分布在城中村区域、远离了规划中的快速交通线路。马晓亚[③]通过对广州自 1986 年后各个政策阶段所建成的保障性住区的整体区位特征和空间分布趋势进行分析，得出的结论是：绝大多数保障性住区与就业岗位集中、公共

① 张永波，翟健．北京市保障性住房空间布局探讨——和谐城市规划//2007 年中国城市规划年会论文集

② 张祚，李江风．经济适用房空间分布对居住空间分异的影响——以武汉市为例．城市问题，2007（7）：96－101

③ 马晓亚．广州保障性住区的发展特征及其影响机制研究．中山大学博士论文

服务设施良好、公共交通便利的城市中心均比较远。分布趋势上，保障性住区的用地选址逐步外移，各政策阶段的保障性住区呈圈层向外分布，远离城市中心和发展成熟的局部区域。

保障性住区空间布局的边缘化，一定程度上导致了中低收入群体难以分享城市公共设施福利。

除此之外，由于规划滞后、供应量不足等原因，保障性住区内部的设施供应也难以为继，这在大多数大型保障性住区中普遍存在。例如，广州的形象工程——棠德花园，由于停车空间的规划缺位，造成车辆严重挤占道路等停车难的问题。北京的大型保障性住区——天通苑，其公立中学到2004年才建成开学，足足滞后了6年，而其规划的三甲医院难产，何时建成还未知。广州的大型成熟住区——聚德花苑，规划的社区医院却被异化为肿瘤专科医院。

保障性住区内外设施供应的难以为继，是影响中低收入群体生活的最重要因素。如何改善保障性住区被边缘化的区位，让居住类群体充分享用其高度依赖的城市公共设施，是城市建设和发展中面临的重大课题之一。如何保证该类住区内部设施的充分与及时，也是保障性住区项目规划中需要得到重视的重要环节。

（作者：马晓亚，郑州大学建筑学院讲师；袁奇峰，中山大学地理科学与规划学院教授）

# 四川灾区震后城镇恢复重建状况观察

2008年5月12日14时28分，四川省汶川地区发生8.0级特大地震，数万同胞在灾害中不幸遇难，数百万家庭失去世代生活的家园，数十年辛勤劳动积累的财富毁于一旦。根据民政部发布的灾害范围评估结果，汶川地震波及四川、甘肃、陕西、重庆、云南等10省（区、市）的417个县（市、区），总面积约50万平方公里。其中极重灾区包括四川省汶川县、北川县、绵竹市、什邡市、青川县、茂县、安县、都江堰市、平武县、彭州市等10个县（市），重灾区共41个县（市、区），一般灾区共186个县（市、区）。极重灾区和重灾区总面积共132596平方公里，乡镇1271个，行政村14565个。

2010年10月，根据联合国开发计划署技术援助项目的安排，有关方面组成了震后城镇恢复重建考察组，走访了地震极重灾区——汶川、北川和青川及其部分城镇，现结合有关方面公布的材料，将初步观察结果汇总如下。

## 一、灾区城镇受损情况

汶川特大地震是新中国成立以来破坏性最强、波及范围最广、救灾难度最大的一次地震，震区最大烈度达11度，余震3万多次，受灾群众超过4625万人。

一是人员伤亡严重。据民政部报告，截至2008年9月25日12时，四川汶川地震已确认69227人遇难，374643人受伤，17923人失踪。

二是房屋大面积倒塌损坏。共倒塌房屋778.91万间，损坏房屋2459万间，需要紧急转移安置受灾群众1510万人。四川省有347.6万户农房受损，其中126.3万户需重建，221.3万户需维修加固；城镇住房有31.4万套需重建，141.8万套需维修加固。北川县城、汶川映秀镇等一些城镇几乎夷为平地。

三是产业发展受到严重影响，6443个规模以上工业企业一度停工停产，主要产业、众多企业遭受重创，直接经济损失8451亿多元。

四是基础设施严重损毁，生态环境和大量文化自然遗产遭到严重破坏。震中地区周围的16条国道省道干线公路和宝成线等6条铁路受损中断，电力、通信、供水等系统大面积瘫痪。根据四川省、甘肃省和陕西省建设厅提供的灾损情况，统计得出51个县（市、区）极重灾区和重灾区受损水厂供水能力112.2万立方米/日，受损供水管长2296公里，受损污水处理厂处理能力59.3万立方米/日，受损排水管长799公里，天然气受损设施能力172万立方米/日，受损燃气管线2409公里，受损垃圾处理能力950吨/日，损毁道路3717公里，损毁桥梁752座，绿地受损763公顷。

## 二、灾区城镇重建的主要进展

经历了100多个难忘的抗震救灾日日夜夜，灾区军民在党中央、国务院和中央军委坚强领导下，在国务院抗震救灾总指挥部直接指挥下，有力有序有效地展开了气壮山河的抗震救灾斗争，竭尽全力抢救被困群众，最大限度减低了灾害损失，灾后安置有序推进。截至2008年9月10日，据住房和城乡建设部报告，地震灾区的过渡安置房（活动板房）已全部安装完成，共安装677131套。抗震救灾随即进入灾后恢复重建的阶段。

2008年9月19日，国务院印发了《汶川地震灾后恢复重建总体规划》，提出力争用三年左右时间完成恢复重建的主要任务，基本生活条件和经济发展水平达到或超过灾前水平，努力建设安居乐业、生态文明、安全和谐的新家园，实现家家有房住、户户有就业、人人有保障、设施有提高、经济有发展、生态有改善的目标。

在全国人民的大力支持下，灾区城镇重建取得重大进展。截至2010年9月28日，纳入国家重建规划的29700个重建项目已开工99.3%，完工85.2%；概算总投资8613亿元已完成7365.9亿元，占85.6%，完成9月底前完成投资和项目85%以上的总体目标。18个对口支援省市在四川灾区确定的3860个项目已全部开工，建成3430个，占88.9%；完成投资692.9亿元，占90%。各对口支援省市与灾区携手合作，规划建设了24个特色产业园区和农业示范园区，落实产业合作项目438个，资金178亿元。

——受灾群众住房条件得到极大改善。震后一年半，148.5万户农房重建全部完成；震后两年，25.9万套城镇居民住房基本竣工。

——重建城镇初展新姿。38个重点重建城镇中，汶川、北川、青川县城和映秀、汉旺镇等37个城镇形成主体功能。唯一一个“整体异地重建的县城”——北川羌族自治县新县城灾后重建工程基本完成。

——农村重建有序推进。农村村庄布局、村容村貌得到较大改善。农业重建项目已完工71.5%，完成投资82.2%。

——公共服务设施功能明显提升。学校、医院、体育馆、福利院等公共设施明显改善。其中，规划重建的3002所学校完工91.2%；2010年春季开学时，灾区学生已全部告别板房教室。

——基础设施保障能力显著增强。一批关系长远的交通、水利、电力等基础设施重大项目相继完工或正在建设。其中，交通恢复重建项目完工87%，投资完成90%。

——产业在重建中优化升级。新批准设立5个省级开发区，灾区现代农业聚集区和绿色经济示范区加快建设，受援双方联建的产业园，成为灾区承接产业转移、增加“造血”功能的载体。其中，需要重建的2400户规模以上受损工业企业已全部恢复生产，旅游业在

2009年底已恢复到震前水平。

——防灾减灾能力增强。四川省共排查地质灾害隐患11384处，新发现隐患点5033处，纳入《汶川地震灾后恢复重建地质灾害防治专项规划》的2334处重大地质灾害治理项目全部开工，其中完工47.9%，28674户农户地质灾害搬迁避让任务完成23374户。地震灾区地质灾害防治能力显著增强。

——生态环境进一步改善。坚持自然修复与人工治理相结合，在岷江、嘉陵江、涪江上游地区实施生态修复工程。四川省林业灾后重建项目开工98.6%；完成林草植被恢复350万亩，占规划任务的76.1%。

——文化得到保护和弘扬。民族文化和地震遗址保护工作进一步加强，76个文化项目开工49个，占65%。都江堰两馆、绵竹年画村、安县文化中心、江油李白纪念馆和汶川地震博物馆等项目陆续竣工，北川羌族民俗博物馆主体工程已经完工。

## 三、灾区城镇重建的主要经验

### 1. 充分发挥制度优势

灾后恢复重建的历史奇迹是在社会主义制度下创造的，中国特色社会主义是中华民族伟大复兴之基。在灾后恢复重建中，党中央、国务院总揽全局，科学决策，充分发挥社会主义制度集中力量办大事的优势，为灾后恢复重建提供了经济、技术和人才保障。社会主义市场经济体制的不断完善，国家经济实力和综合实力的极大增强，为灾后恢复重建奠定了坚实的物质基础。

### 2. 建立对口援助机制

灾后恢复重建是一项十分艰巨的任务。为举全国之力，加快地震灾区灾后恢复重建，并使各地的对口支援工作有序开展，国务院办公厅于2008年6月11日下发了《汶川地震灾后恢复重建对口支援方案》，按照“一省帮一重灾县”的原则，依据支援方经济能力和受援方灾情程度，合理配置力量，建立了灾后恢复重建对口支援机制。对口支援期限按3年安排。东部和中部地区共19个省市，对口支援四川省的18个县（市），以及甘肃省、陕西省受灾严重地区。在国家的支持下，集各方之力，基本实现灾后恢复重建规划的目标。

### 3. 建立重建协同机制

为保障灾后重建工作的有序开展，及时建立了重建协同机制。一方面，国务院成立了汶川地震灾后恢复重建工作协调小组，省、市（县）相应成立了由政府主导，企业、社会团队和个人共同参与的重建机构，一定程度上实现了跨地区、跨部门的协调，有效引导了各方重建主体互相配合。同时，重视监督机制的创新，建立重建目标考核体系，优先考核灾区各级领导班子和干部政绩。高效的多方协同机制使政府和民间力量互动，形成了多方合力，而强有力的自上而下的组织领导体制则使上下级政府间互动，保证了重建执行力。

**4. 吸纳社会力量广泛参与重建**

《汶川地震灾后恢复重建条例》明确指出：在灾后重建中应坚持“政府主导与社会参与相结合”的原则。在灾后重建中，社会力量在产业重建、文化重建、生态重建、心理重建等方面发挥了重要的作用。资金短缺是灾后重建中的最大瓶颈，直接制约重建进程。四川灾后重建早期曾面临1.3万亿资金缺口，单纯依靠政府难以解决。对此，我国政府充分调动各方主体的积极性，创新筹资方式，拓展筹资渠道，构建一个公开、透明、监督有力、多渠道的筹资机制，实现财政拨款、社会募集、对口支援、市场运作等多渠道筹资，为完成重建任务提供资金保障。截至2009年9月30日，国内外共筹集社会捐赠款物797.03亿元，1300多万名志愿者参与汶川地震抗震救灾，并得到国际组织和外国政府提供的多项援助。

**5. 将重建工作纳入法制化轨道**

规划是科学援建工作、合理安排项目的重要依据，也是灾区灾后城镇重建、长远发展的需要。汶川地震发生后，党中央、国务院高度重视，尽一切能力抗震救灾和开展灾后重建工作，先后出台了诸多重建规划方案和条例，先后发布了一系列重建规划，指导灾后重建工作。如在震后不到一个月，就公布了《汶川地震灾后恢复重建条例》（国务院令第526号），讨论通过了《国家汶川地震灾后重建规划方案》。此后，陆续发布了《关于地震灾区恢复生产指导意见》（国办发［2008］52号），《关于进一步做好地震灾区医疗卫生防疫工作的意见》（国办发［2008］54号），《国务院关于支持汶川地震灾后重建政策措施的意见》（国发［2008］21号），《国务院关于做好汶川地震灾后恢复重建工作的指导意见》（国发［2008］22号），《汶川地震灾后恢复重建总体规划》（国发［2008］31号）。还有《城镇体系专项规划》、《城乡住房建设专项规划》、《农村建设专项规划》、《市政公用设施重建规划》、《风景名胜区重建规划》等相关规划。各受灾市、县也分别制定了相关的重建规划，指导灾后重建工作，保证了灾后重建的安全性和规范性。2008年6月8日国务院公布实施的《汶川地震灾后恢复重建条例》，是我国首次为一个地方地震灾后恢复重建制定的条例，标志着灾后恢复重建工作纳入了法制轨道。

## 四、灾区城镇重建中存在的一些问题

**1. 部分城镇设施重建的选址存在安全隐患**

由于灾区适宜城镇建设用地较为紧张，因此在城镇重建过程中，部分城镇设施或住房仍建在存在地质风险的地区。特别是城镇周围的部分山体，由于地震，使得山体存在一定程度的破碎，遇到强降雨时，容易引发泥石流，从而可能对山下的城镇设施或住房造成破坏。如2010年8月8日凌晨在甘肃省甘南藏族自治州舟曲县发生的特大山洪泥石流灾害，就是一

2008 年“5·12”地震前的北川老县城

2008 年“5·12”地震后的北川老县城

2008 年“9·24”泥石流后的北川老县城

北川新县城所在地原貌（2009 年 12 月）

北川新县城航拍图（2010 年 9 月）

北川新县城近景（2010 年 10 月）

个深刻的教训。

按照重建过程中相关政策的规定，灾后毁损农房农户先领取补助金，然后以农户自修自建为主的方式进行农房的维修和重建。但在重建过程中，部分农户对受损房屋只是简单维修，或仅以少量补助资金修建房屋，而保留原部分损坏房屋继续使用，结果，一方面，由于重建资金使用不到位，部分农房的维修或加固质量不高，农房的安全隐患依然存在；另一方面，农房重建优先选择原址，使得部分在地质灾害易发地区的农房依然面临地震、泥石流的威胁。

**2. 部分设施的重建与运行管理脱节**

在城镇重建过程中，对口援助单位大多按照高标准援助受灾地区，很多新设施、新工艺、新装备在灾区得到广泛建设。这种做法一方面使得受灾地区的城镇建设进度大幅度加快、城镇化的质量大幅提高，但另一方面也增加了设施的使用成本，并对管理提出了更高的要求。部分设施的操作要求较高的技能水平，当地居民掌握起来难度较大，先进设施并不一定能很好地发挥作用；部分设施的维修维护和使用成本较大，或在灾区较难买到合适的配件，或者配件的价格过高，致使一些设施常处在“待运行”状态。这些问题在对口援建期间可能并不突出，援建单位可以负责设施的运行、维护和管理，但当援建单位撤出后，问题会逐渐凸显出来。如何做好设施的恢复重建与后续运行管理的对接，关系到援建设施能否持续有效利用，需要援建双方共同付出更多努力。

**3. 城镇发展的产业支撑能力有待提高**

产业是维系城镇发展的根本。在重建过程中，对口援建单位均安排了资金援建灾区建设，但大部分的对口援助资金的使用方向为城乡住房、市政基础设施和学校等公用设施建设，对产业方面的投资比例相对偏小。但如果缺乏产业支持，居民将缺少增加收入的机会，城镇缺少持续发展的动力。如在广东援建汶川的82亿资金中，产业恢复项目的援建投资约6.74亿元，仅占援建资金的8.22%；在北川新县城重建首期投入的218个项目95.5亿元中，市场服务体系建设安排的资金仅为2.61亿元。因此，需要进一步加大产业扶植力度，避免出现灾区城镇居民“住别墅、吃红薯”的现象。

此外，新引入工业项目对灾区比较优势资源的整合能力不强，也是产业重建过程中存在的问题之一。灾后重建产业项目一般纳入对口支援规划，园区招商由援建双方共同推进，因而这些项目基本是援建省市的优势产业，具有显著的“嵌入式”特征，与当地的产业基础存在明显的差异，不具备整合当地资源的比较优势。特别是有些项目的主要原料和市场都“双向在外”，在不具备区位优势的条件下，其产业竞争力必然被削弱。同时，在整个地震灾区缺乏产业布局合理协调的情况下，产业同构的矛盾已有所显现，这必将对区域协调和分工合作产生负面影响。

**4. 对口支援中的经济收支不平衡**

由于支援方省市和受援方县区在财政收入、人口等方面差异较大，资金分配和支出存在较严重的不平衡。一方面，受援方接受分配资金的不平衡，国务院的要求是各支援省市每年对口支援按不低于本省市上年地方财政收入的1%考虑。按照2007年各省、自治区、直辖市地方财政收入及其年度增长预计，人均分配对口支援资金三年平均约2万元，最高的是广东省支援的汶川县，三年约7.7万元，最低的是黑龙江省支援的剑阁县，三年约2500元，二者相比，差距在30倍以上。另一方面，支援方的支出也存在不平衡。一些地方财力相对较弱的省份负担较重，如河南、湖南、江西、安徽等支援省，其2007年人均地方财政收入和支出均低于受援的四川省。

由于汶川地震影响空前，对口支援的投入在某些方面很难保持客观和理性的态度。有学者建议应及早研究其中的一些负外部性问题，如对受灾地区的投入是否会影响对其他地区的必要投入，那些受灾程度相似的其他地区能否得到与汶川地震对口支援同样的待遇，等等。

#### 5. 部分公共设施建设规模偏大

在重建过程中，灾区城镇从提高人民群众社会文化水平和生活质量的角度出发，在各自区域内按照较高标准建设了大量的中小学校、卫生院所，以及体育馆、博物馆、文化馆等设施，在部分地区存在土地占用偏多，建设规模偏大、建设标准偏高等问题，造成设施的利用程度不高、运行成本偏大。此外，很多地区提出建设地震遗址保护区和纪念（场）馆。据不完全统计，已初步规划20多处，数量偏多，个别规划建设的单个遗址纪念（场）馆规模偏大，造成保护内容重复，无法突出保护重点。在灾区城镇重建过程中，由于具体项目的建设资金来源不同，部分基础设施项目（以中小学校为多）是由资金捐赠单位或对口援助单位提出的建设要求，也是造成公用设施建设规模偏大、建设标准偏高等问题的原因之一。

### 五、几点认识和建议

#### 1. 建立对口援建的长效合作机制

在援建任务结束后，“省——县”对口援建形式也将结束，由对口支援向对口合作、无偿支援向互惠合作转变，成为当前及今后最现实和可行的选择。应进一步建立援建省市与受援县区合作的长效机制，合作的重点由灾后城镇设施、住房重建向智力帮扶、产业发展等方面转移。在处理援建方与灾区利益方面，逐渐改变灾后重建中对口援建灾区单方面受益的局面，寻求产业有前景、市场有需求和有价值的合作产业项目，建立援建方与灾区在人才、技术、资源、市场、文化、劳动力等方面的市场化合作，促进援建方与灾区长期的、可持续的合作。同时，应尽快制定相关政策，对促进与保障灾后对口合作长期发展所需的土地、税收、工商、信贷、服务等方面给予明细化的政策性优惠和支持。

#### 2. 加大政府对城镇产业的扶植力度

产业重建是解决灾区群众的就业问题和收入问题根本途径，具有长期性、战略性意义，是一个任重道远的重建进程，必须加大政府的扶持力度。对于正处于工业化初中期的川、甘、陕等受灾地区，产业重建不应是简单的产业恢复与再建，而是要将灾后产业重建与产业结构调整升级、工业化进程结合起来，坚持“硬件”与“软件”相结合、“输血”与“造血”相结合、当前和长远相结合。灾后产业重建需要重新考虑灾区的环境承载能力、资源禀赋、生产要素分布等，要根据资源环境承载能力、产业政策和就业需要，以市场为导向，以企业为主体，合理引导受灾企业原地恢复重建、异地新建和关停并转，支持发展特色优势产业，推进结构调整，促进发展方式转变，扩大就业机会。

**3. 加强对震区地质灾害易发区的建设管理**

据统计，灾区在震前已有55.7%的面积存有地质灾害，震后这一比例激增至74.2%。通过两年多的生态修复，目前这一比例正逐渐降低。在汶川、青川等极重灾区，由于地震导致部分山体松动、岩层破碎，因此简单的植树造林等人力作用，并不能有效消除滑坡、泥石流等地质灾害隐患。除北川外，灾区城镇均为原地重建，城镇周围的地质灾害隐患依然存在。因此，要加强对震区地质灾害易发区的管理，加强地质灾害防治知识宣传，依靠群众和专业队伍对地质灾害进行科学防治，建立完善地质灾害群测群防体系，建立健全地质灾害防治部门联动机制是保障。同时，应仔细权衡局部地区地质灾害治理工程成本与地质灾害影响地区城镇设施搬迁或异地重建成本的大小，尽量选择经济成本小、社会影响小的方式治理或规避地质灾害。

（作者：毛其智，清华大学教授，国际欧亚科学院院士；邵益生，中国城市规划设计研究院副院长、研究员，国际欧亚科学院院士；张志果，中国城市规划设计研究院助理研究员）

# 近年来我国区域规划发展概述

## 一、引言

1949—2000年，中国的区域规划实践先后两次兴起、繁荣：一是20世纪50年代以工业布局设计为核心的国家经济复兴规划及80年代以国土开发整治为目标的国家建设布局规划[1]。进入21世纪，随着经济全球化和区域一体化两大进程的深化发展，中国经济发展模式也将由外向型增长导向转变为外需与内需共同发展导向。区域，特别是跨越不同层级行政单元的地域系统，在国民经济社会发展中的地位和作用将变得更加重要，成为全球竞争重要的空间载体[2][3]。而2008年全球金融危机的爆发促成了国家第三次区域规划高潮的来临。国务院以空前的速度先后批复了《珠江三角洲地区改革发展规划纲要》等15个区域规划，将区域发展上升到国家战略层面，尝试通过加快区域发展步伐以缩小地区间经济发展的不平衡，促进区域协调发展，并通过一些重大项目的建设带动更大区域发展，减弱金融危机对我国的不利影响。

本文试图通过全面梳理近年来十余个区域规划编制的背景、规划思路、定位与主要内容，以及在实践上取得的进展情况，对本轮区域规划的总体特点进行简要评价，并展望了进一步研究的方向。

## 二、我国新一轮区域规划实践概述

从2008年开始，国务院先后批复珠江三角洲、海峡西岸、横琴岛等15个区域规划，这在中国区域规划历史上极为罕见。这些区域规划的空间分布很广，涵盖了我国大部分省区，从东部、中部、东北部到西部，从沿海到内陆。从区域规划类型看，有改革发展、经济合作、产业转移、生态循环经济、旅游、区域合作等六大类。

与前两轮区域规划相比，本轮区域规划在定位与内容方面更为丰富，最为显著的表现在改变了以往以落实国民经济社会发展计划空间手段为主的“角色”，形成了以公共政策为“切入点”的规划编制与政策实施思路，赋予了地方政府更多的发展自主权，这在区域规划思路、组织主体、战略定位与内容等多方面都有所体现。

### 1. 规划思路

国家层面主要按照三条线索来推进新一轮区域规划：（1）基于加快重点地区发展；（2）基于落实重大发展战略；（3）围绕地区区域开拓空间[4]。而实际上，通过对已批准的15个区域规划进行剖析，可以发现当前我国区域规划的编制思路是充分贯彻落实国家层次要求的。其中重点地区开发包括了两类区域：一方面，要促使具有较好发展基础的地区率先和加快发展，如长三角、珠三角地区、横琴岛等地区规划的编制渗透了“排头兵”的角色；另一方面，要推动欠发达地区、贫困地区后来居上，实现跨越式发展，包括图们江地区、甘肃省、皖江城市带、北部湾等地区；在落实国家提出的重大改革和发展战略方面，黄河三角洲高效生态区建设规划、鄱阳湖生态经济区建设规划、安徽皖江城市带承接产业转移示范区规划、促进中部地区崛起规划、甘肃省循环经济总体规划等都贯彻落实了资源节约型战略、环境友好型战略、产业转移战略、开发开放战略等国家战略；围绕区域开拓空间方面的主要表现为江苏沿海地区发展规划、关中—天水经济区发展规划、辽宁沿海经济带发展规划、中国图们江区域合作开发规划纲要、广西北部湾经济区发展规划等打破了传统的行政区划的阻隔，通过综合功能的开发促进区域一体化发展，力争实现区域内各城市的协调发展。

### 2. 组织主体

新一轮出台的区域规划虽被上升到国家战略层面，作为国家抵抗金融危机消极影响的主要手段之一，但从组织主体上来看，地方政府仍是最为积极主动的力量。大部分规划为地方政府主动提出，并进一步获得中央政府的批复认可。较之以前的两轮区域规划，本轮规划可以说是中央与地方政府协调的结果，在与国家重大战略方向保持一致的同时，更加符合地方发展的实际需求和利益。这也反映出中央政府在干预区域经济政策的思路发生重大变化：由“自上而下”的中央组织向“自下而上”的地方政府主导区域开发战略转型。这更有利于发挥地方政府的积极性、主动性和创造性。

### 3. 战略定位与内容

新一轮区域规划的战略定位更加强调推进落实国家重大战略实施，强调在更大区域范围内的地位，强调加快重点地区的发展与产业升级，推动区域功能整合等方面。

首先，规划强调在科学发展观的指导下，根据区域自身资源环境的承载力、开发条件和潜力，以及自身所处的发展阶段，提出具有浓厚地域特色的战略目标定位。如珠江三角洲地区要成为“探索科学发展模式试验区，深化改革先行区……世界先进制造业和现代服务业基地，全国重要的经济中心”，继续承担改革先锋的重任，并在更大的区域范围内发挥更大的作用，而长江三角洲地区则要在世界城镇群中谋求一席之位，成为“亚太地区重要的国际门户，全球重要的现代服务业和先进制造业中心，具有较强国际竞争力的世界级城市群”；海峡西岸经济区则要依托自身优越地缘优势，发展成为“两岸人民交流合作先行先试区域，服务周边地区发展新的对外开放综合通道”；横琴岛毗邻澳门，将进一步发展成为

"'一国两制'下探索粤、港、澳合作新模式的示范区，深化改革开放和科技创新的先行区，促进珠江口西岸地区产业升级发展的新平台"。

其次，规划强调经济发展方式的转变。在公布区域规划的同时，国家也高调公布了汽车、钢铁等十大产业振兴规划，意图依托区域规划和产业振兴规划共同促进经济发展方式的转变。其中产业规划直接着眼于产业升级和产业调整，而结合产业转移和产业升级的区域规划政策更具有宏观战略性和针对性，以促进产业结构调整升级。如《珠江三角洲地区改革发展规划纲要》提出建设世界先进制造业和现代服务业基地，全国重要的经济中心。

再次，规划优先考虑特色区域板块的崛起。从区域规划的功能定位与编制内容进行剖析，多数区域规划都有各自期望和战略重点，存在较为显著的定位及功能分工，这样避免了各区域发展的"无的放矢"、"一哄而上"，在一定程度上实现了不同区域板块间的相互协作和良性互动。如海西经济区要发挥独特的对台优势，努力构筑两岸交流合作的前沿平台；辽宁沿海经济带要起到拉动东北地区经济发展作用；江苏沿海地区的发展有利于提升江苏经济社会整体发展水平、缩小苏南苏北发展差距；关中—天水经济区是支撑西安统筹科技资源改革；黄河三角洲强调发展高效生态经济等。

最后，规划内容中涉及了国家对规划区域的政策倾斜，赋予其在某些领域"试点"或"先行先试"的权利。如《珠江三角洲地区改革发展规划纲要》将珠三角定位为"探索科学发展模式试验区、深化改革先行区"，赋予了珠江三角洲地区发展更大的自主权，为全国科学发展提供示范，要求珠三角先行先试，全面推进经济体制、政治体制、文化体制、社会体制改革。在《纲要》的全文中，关于试验区、先行区、示范区、开发新区、重要基地、重大项目、中心、试点等的提法共有150个。其中试验区和先行区有5个、示范区有8个、开发新区有11个、改革试点有6个，并点名授予了珠三角各市一系列试点权。深圳是全国综合改革配套试验区，珠海是社会管理综合改革试点，佛山、中山、惠州是统筹城乡发展综合改革试点等。而《横琴岛总体发展规划》将横琴岛定位为"'一国两制'下探索粤、港、澳合作新模式的示范区"，赋予了其在通关制度、金融创新、产业和信息化政策、土地管理制度等方面进行改革创新方面的权利。(见表1)

**表1　近年来主要区域规划一览表**

| 所处地区 | 规划名称 | 颁布时间 | 战略意义 | 战略定位 | 主要内容 | 创新点 | 地域范围 |
|---|---|---|---|---|---|---|---|
| 东部地区 | 珠江三角洲地区改革发展规划纲要 | 2009年1月7日 | 应对国际金融危机，推进经济结构战略性调整 | 探索科学发展模式试验区，深化改革先行区，扩大开放的重要国际门户，世界先进制造业和现代服务业基地，全国重要的经济中心 | 包括构建现代产业体系、提高自主创新能力、基础设施、统筹城乡发展、区域协调发展、社会事业发展、体制机制新优势、规划实施的保障机制等12部分 | 包括行政管理体制创新、深化经济体制改革、推进社会管理体制改革、推进民主法制建设、充分发挥经济特区的改革开放先行作用等5项内容 | 以广东省的广州、深圳、珠海、佛山、江门、东莞、中山、惠州和肇庆为主体，辐射泛珠江三角洲区域 |

续表 1

| 所处地区 | 规划名称 | 颁布时间 | 战略意义 | 战略定位 | 主要内容 | 创新点 | 地域范围 |
|---|---|---|---|---|---|---|---|
| 东部地区 | 关于支持福建省加快建设海峡西岸经济区的若干意见 | 2009 年 5 月 14 日 | 北承长江三角洲，南接珠江三角洲，开展与台湾地区合作 | 两岸人民交流合作先行先试区域，服务周边地区发展新的对外开放综合通道，东部沿海地区先进制造业的重要基地，我国重要的自然和文化旅游中心 | 包括基础设施建设、自主创新能力培养、区域协调发展、社会事业发展、生态文明建设、保障措施等 9 部分 | 包括建立城乡统一的建设用地市场、金融改革与创新、行政管理体制改革等方面 | 以福建省为主体，涵盖浙江、江西、广东共 4 个省份 |
| | 横琴岛总体发展规划 | 2009 年 6 月 24 日 | 构建粤、港、澳紧密合作的新载体，共建珠澳国际都会区，重塑珠海发展新优势、培育珠江口西岸地区新的增长极 | “一国两制”下探索粤、港、澳合作新模式的示范区，深化改革开放和科技创新的先行区，促进珠江口西岸地区产业升级发展的新平台 | 包括意义、总体要求和发展目标、空间布局、产业发展、基础设施、公共服务设施、生态环境、开发管理模式、保障措施、近期建设行动计划等 10 部分 | 创新通关制度、查验监管模式、鼓励金融创新、产业和信息化政策、土地管理制度改革等方面的创新 | 横琴岛 |
| | 江苏沿海地区发展规划 | 2009 年 7 月 14 日 | 连续中国沿海经济区发展 | 我国重要的综合交通枢纽，我国沿海新型的工业基地，我国重要的土地后备资源开发区，生态环境优美、人民生活富足的宜居区 | 包括发展基础与重大意义、总体要求与发展目标、空间布局、重大基础设施建设、产业发展、城乡发展、海域滩涂资源开发、生态建设与环境保护、保障措施等 9 部分 | 包括深化行政管理体制改革、建立生态建设和环境保护新机制、创建良好的法制环境 | 连云港、盐城、南通 |
| | 黄河三角洲高效生态经济区发展规划 | 2009 年 12 月 1 日 | 对接天津滨海新区、发挥环渤海经济圈重要成员作用 | 依托山东半岛城市群和济南城市圈，对接天津滨海新区，服务环渤海，面向东北亚，以建设高效生态经济区为目标 | 包括发展背景、总体要求、空间布局、生态环境保护、产业体系、基础设施、社会事业、创新体制机制、规划实施和保障等 9 部分 | 推进行政管理体制改革、财税体制改革、金融改革与创新、土地管理体制改革等 | 营和滨州、潍坊北部寒亭区、寿光市、昌邑市、德州乐陵市、庆云县、淄博高青县和烟台莱州市 |
| | 关于推进海南国际旅游岛建设发展的若干意见 | 2009 年 12 月 31 日 | 对全国调整优化经济结构和转变发展方式具有重要示范作用 | 世界一流的海岛休闲度假旅游胜地 | 包括总体要求、生态文明建设、旅游业管理服务、服务业发展、城乡一体化进程、基础设施建设、社会建设、新型工业发展、保障措施等 9 部分 | 将在政策、资金、项目安排等方面给予特殊扶持，并在投融资政策、财税政策、土地政策、开放政策进行创新 | 海南省 |
| | 长江三角洲地区区域规划 | 2010 年 5 月 23 日 | 处于转型升级的关键时期，必须进一步增强综合竞争力和可持续发展能力 | 亚太地区重要的国际门户，全球重要的现代服务业和先进制造业中心，具有较强国际竞争力的世界级城市群 | 包括发展基础、战略定位、区域协调发展、城乡统筹、产业发展与布局、自主创新、基础设施建设、生态环境保护、社会公共服务、体制改革、对外合作、组织实施等 12 部分 | 深化行政管理体制改革、推进非公有制经济发展和国有企业改革、加快市场体系建设（推动市场一体化）、开展重大改革试验、加强法制环境建设等 | 上海市和江苏省的南京、苏州、无锡、常州、镇江、扬州、泰州、南通，浙江省的杭州、宁波、湖州、嘉兴、绍兴、舟山、台州 |

续表 1

| 所处地区 | 规划名称 | 颁布时间 | 战略意义 | 战略定位 | 主要内容 | 创新点 | 地域范围 |
|---|---|---|---|---|---|---|---|
| 东北地区 | 辽宁沿海经济带发展规划 | 2009年7月1日 | 提升辽宁乃至整个东北地区对外开放水平 | 对外开放的重要平台、东北亚重要的国际航运中心、具有国际竞争力的临港产业带、生态环境优美和人民生活富足的宜居区 | 主要背景、战略意义、战略构想、主要任务、空间新格局、主要政策措施等6部分 | 深化政府管理体制改革、加快社会信用体系建设、加强金融生态环境建设,建立激励机制,搭建融资平台,为境外资金和域外资金流入构建融资洼地。拓宽融资渠道等 | 大连、丹东、锦州、营口、盘锦、葫芦岛 |
| 东北地区 | 中国图们江区域合作开发规划纲要 | 2009年8月30日 | 推进中国图们江区域国际合作以及东北地区的对外开放 | 我国沿边开放开发的重要区域,我国面向东北亚开放的重要门户,东北亚经济技术合作的重要平台,东北地区新的重要增长极 | 包括意义、总体要求、开发开放先导区、与国内区域联动、与图们江国际区域合作、规划实施保障等6部分 | 统筹安排区域内新增建设用地计划指标、对区域内建设项目的审批、核准、备案等方面,给予优先支持。设立交通基础设施建设、口岸建设专项资金等 | 吉林省长春市、吉林市部分区域和延边朝鲜族自治州 |
| 中部地区 | 促进中部地区崛起规划 | 2009年9月23日 | 加快中部地区崛起 | 粮食生产基地、能源原材料基地、现代装备制造及高技术产业基地和综合交通运输枢纽 | 包括重大意义、发展目标、粮食生产基地建设、能源原材料基地建设、高技术产业基地建设、交通运输枢纽建设、重点地区发展、规划实施等11部分 | 积极推进武汉城市圈、长株潭城市群"两型社会"综合配套改革试验区建设。加快推进资源节约、生态环境保护、产业结构优化升级、科技和人才管理、土地管理、对内对外开放、财税金融等重点领域和关键环节的机制体制创新。 | 山西、安徽、江西、河南、湖北、湖南 |
| 中部地区 | 鄱阳湖生态经济区规划 | 2009年12月12日 | 探索生态与经济协调发展的新路子,探索大湖流域综合开发的新模式 | 全国大湖流域综合开发示范区,长江中下游水生态安全保障区,加快中部崛起重要带动区,国际生态经济合作重要平台 | 包括发展背景、总体要求、生态建设、环境友好型产业发展、构建生态文明社会、促进区域协调发展、深化改革开放、保障措施等9部分 | 鼓励在生态环保方面先行先试,形成有利于生态与经济协调发展的体制环境 | 南昌、景德镇、鹰潭、九江、新余、抚州、宜春、上饶、吉安 |
| 中部地区 | 皖江城市带承接产业转移示范区规划 | 2010年1月12日 | 有利于推动产业结构调整升级,推进区域协调发展,探索承接产业转移科学途径 | 长三角拓展发展空间优选区,全国重要的先进制造业和现代服务业基地,中部地区崛起的重要增长极 | 包括背景、发展目标、空间布局、产业承接园区建设、产业承接发展重点、基础设施支撑、资源节约和环境保护、保障措施等10部分 | 鼓励大胆探索,先行先试,深化改革,完善政府服务,建立高效运作的行政和社会管理体制,加快构建规范透明的法治环境 | 安徽的合肥、芜湖、马鞍山、铜陵、安庆、池州、巢湖、滁州和宣城 |

续表 1

| 所处地区 | 规划名称 | 颁布时间 | 战略意义 | 战略定位 | 主要内容 | 创新点 | 地域范围 |
|---|---|---|---|---|---|---|---|
| 西部地区 | 关中—天水经济区发展规划 | 2009 年 6 月 10 日 | 承接东中部地区产业转移，促进区域协调发展 | 全国内陆型经济开发开放战略高地，统筹科技资源改革示范基地，全国先进制造业重要基地，全国现代农业高技术产业基地，彰显华夏文明的历史文化基地 | 包括发展基础、总体要求、空间布局、构建创新型区域、产业发展、基础设施、生态环境、公共服务、改革开放等 10 部分 | 包括了体系创新、技术创新、环境创新等内容 | 陕西省西安、铜川、宝鸡、咸阳、渭南、杨凌、商洛（部分区县）和甘肃省天水所辖行政区域 |
| | 甘肃省循环经济总体规划 | 2009 年 12 月 24 日 | 循环经济 | 重要的生态屏障和陆路交通枢纽 | 包括基本状况、工作基础、目标、主要任务、重点项目和支撑技术、资源支撑与环境影响分析、保障措施等 7 部分 | 加大循环经济支撑技术的研发推广力度 | 甘肃省 |
| | 广西北部湾经济区发展规划 | 2008 年 2 月 21 日 | 有利于推动广西经济社会全面进步，从整体上带动和提升民族地区发展水平，保障边疆稳定；有利于深入实施西部大开发战略 | 中国—东盟开放合作的物流基地、商贸基地、加工制造基地和信息交流中心 | 包括发展背景、总体思路、空间布局、产业发展、基础设施、社会建设、生态环境、开放合作、保障措施等部分 | 推进行政管理体制、市场体系、土地管理制度等综合配套改革，大胆试验，开拓创新；加强人口综合管理制度改革等 | 南宁、北海、钦州、防城港四市所辖行政区域 |

资料来源：根据相关规划资料整理，详见参考文献［5］～［19］

## 三、区域规划特点的简要评价

### 1. 全国区域经济战略新版图初定，各个区域板块协调发展

本次区域规划在全国范围内覆盖面非常广，这在一定程度上说明中国正从优先发展东部沿海的非均衡的区域发展战略，转变为均衡发展战略，将促使全国经济战略布局的重组，初步确定了国家区域经济战略的新版图。从新一轮的区域规划的内容可以看出，各地区正不断探索、谋求适合自身发展需求的道路。

若按照东部、中部、西部地区、东北部进行分类，该“四大板块”已被批准的区域规划数量分别为 7 个、2 个、3 个、3 个，东部地区的区域规划数量仍占优势，同时也兼顾了中部、西部和东北地区，区域开发在空间上开始趋向协调。

另外，四大板块在定位上也各有侧重：东部地区要在技术、人才、资本、开放程度以及

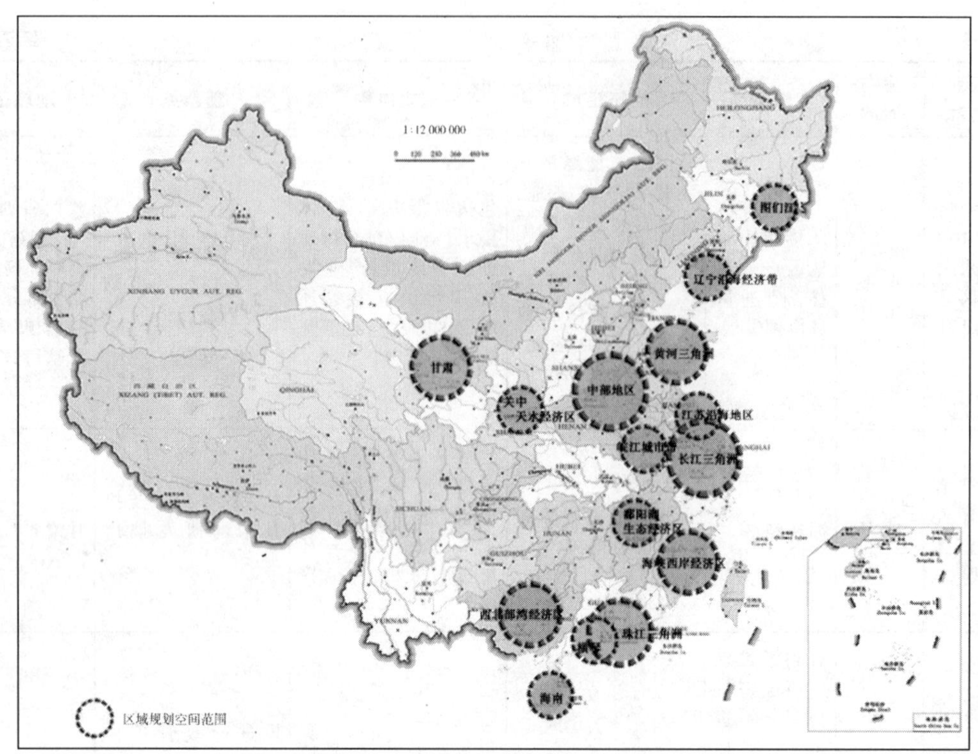


图1 各区域规划空间位置分布图

城市化水平等方面继续保持领先水平；中部地区则要充分发挥地理优势“联东带西”；西部地区把大力推进特色优势产业发展提到战略高度；而东北地区致力于传统产业与技术的升级。

**2. 自下而上推进，“问题导向”的特征较为显著**

如前文所述，本轮区域规划主要是由地方政府自下而上主导的，拥有多方面的“试验”权力，它不仅能体现国家的战略意图，考虑地方的比较竞争优势，而且能够最大限度地激发地方政府的积极性和创造性，有更多的制度创新和实验的自主权力。

各地区的规划虽因地制宜，产业发展侧重点不同，但面对全球范围内产业价值链的转移机遇，都将服务业的发展上升到重要地位。另外，根据地区城市化的实际存在的具体问题，在东部、东北部地区的规划内容中以城乡统筹为主，中部和西部地区则重点分析新农村建设。在协调区域空间时，中西部地区及东北地区多倾向于架构类似于城镇体系规划的空间规划，而东部地区由于城市发展、经济发展相对成熟很多，在空间问题上更多的关注区域协调、统筹布局，即区域间差异化发展，突出各自特色，以进一步强化区域合作，增强竞争优势，力求在全球的城市群中占一席位置。

**3. 特殊政策的倾斜变得更为重要**

除了已经批准的15个区域规划外，国内其余地区也正在积极编制、申报区域规划，出现此种“区域规划热”的重要原因是考虑到争取更多的资金和项目的需要。而更主要的目的还是在“政策”，尤其是金融创新政策和土地创新政策。

因为当前业已出台的诸多区域规划，在实质上还是围绕经济建设与发展这一核心，为区域经济的发展提供特殊的政策环境支持。可以看到，在每个区域规划中，农村土地管理制度的改革创新都是最为重要的内容。无论是农村集体土地所有权、宅基地使用权、集体建设用地使用权的确权登记，城乡增减挂钩，宅基地抵押，还是农村建设用地和承包权的流转，都是这些规划的重要内容[20]。

## 四、小结

国家将本轮区域规划上升为国家战略的初衷是希望地方充分发挥经济建设主动性，结合自身特色、因地制宜，发挥自己的资源优势，真正实现产业模式的转型和经济内生性的增长，另外，也试图通过每个地方突出经济发展亮点，“以点带面”，内部多极发力，形成区域均衡增长的新的发展局面。在这种局势下，当前我国区域发展战略的空间布局形态形成了从南到北、由东向西、从沿海到内地，多极发展、齐头并进的态势。而我国新一轮的区域改革试验也进入到一个深化的阶段。

但短时间内如此大规模规划的出台过于粗放，往往在微观的制度安排上不能落实到位，并且基于不同发展目标出台的区域规划在短期内不能完全体现其效益，需要充分重视规划的贯彻实施，而国家有关部门也要对规划所提出的重点任务的推进情况进行全面跟踪，切实发挥区域规划的指导和约束作用[4]。另外，区域规划的法制建设、协调机制、分工协作等方面亟需改善[21]，这也是下一步需要继续深入研究的方向。

（作者：魏宗财，广州市城市规划勘测设计研究院规划研究中心工程师；廖远涛，广州市城市规划勘测设计研究院规划研究中心副总规划师；翟青，南京大学地理与海洋科学学院）

**参考文献**

[1] 胡序威．中国区域规划的演变与展望［J］．地理学报，2006，61（6）：585－592

[2] 胡云峰，曾澜，李军，等．新时期区域规划的基本任务与工作框架［J］．地理研究，2010，29（4）：6－9

[3] 魏宗财，甄峰．区域一体化影响下的宁杭城市带构建研究［J］．世界地理研究，2006，15（3）：60－67

[4] 戚常庆，李健．新区域主义与我国新一轮区域规划的发展趋势［J］．上海城市管理，2010，19（5）：36－41

[5] 广西北部湾经济区发展规划，http://baike.baidu.com/view/3206702.htm

[6] 珠江三角洲地区改革发展规划纲要，http://politics.people.com.cn/GB/1026/8644751.html

[7] 关于支持福建省加快建设海峡西岸经济区的若干意见，http://baike.baidu.com/view/3293393.htm

[8] 横琴总体发展规划，http://www.customs.gov.cn/tabid/399/ctl/InfoDetail/InfoID/211231/mid/60432/Default.aspx? ContainerSrc = [G] Containers%2f_ default%2fNo + Container

[9] 江苏沿海地区发展规划，http://baike.baidu.com/view/2528675.htm

[10] 黄河三角洲高效生态经济区发展规划，http://biz.zjol.com.cn/05biz/system/2010/06/17/016692274_04.shtml

[11] 关于推进海南国际旅游岛建设发展的若干意见，http://baike.baidu.com/view/3254986.htm

[12] 长江三角洲地区区域规划，http://www.china.com.cn/policy/txt/2010-06/22/content_20320273.htm

[13] 辽宁沿海经济带发展规划，http://baike.baidu.com/view/3337635.htm

[14] 中国图们江区域合作开发规划纲要，http://www.chinanews.com.cn/cj/news/2009/11-17/1968343.shtml

[15] 促进中部地区崛起规划，http://www.china.com.cn/policy/txt/2010-01/12/content_19218531.htm

[16] 鄱阳湖生态经济区规划，http://www.jx.xinhuanet.com/jxzw/2010-02/22/content_19070288.htm

[17] 皖江城市带承接产业转移示范区规划，http://www.gov.cn/gzdt/att/att/site1/20100324/001e3741a2cc0d13bd3c01.pdf

[18] 关中—天水经济区发展规划，http://baike.baidu.com/view/3201996.htm

[19] 甘肃省循环经济总体规划，http://baike.baidu.com/view/3128914.htm

[20] 商汤．从区域规划大潮说创新［J］．中国土地．2010（7）：1

[21] 孙承平，李鲁静，王东升．区域规划、产业转型与区域发展——2010年“十二五”区域规划学术研讨会观点综述［J］．中国工业经济，2010（7）：146-151

# 中国城市热岛问题综述

19 世纪初英国气象学者 Lake Howard 在对伦敦城区和郊区的气温进行同时间的对比观测时，首次发现了城区气温比其四周郊区气温高的现象，并把这种现象称为“Urban Heat Island”或“Hot-island Effect”，即“城市热岛”和“热岛效应”[1]。此后，各国学者对不同位置、不同类型、不同大小的城市做了大量城郊气温对比观测，均发现了类似的现象。“城市热岛”就成为了城市气候中最普遍存在的典型特征之一。

改革开放以来，随着我国经济的迅速发展，城市化也取得巨大进展，城市化水平从1978 年的 17.9% 提高到 2009 年的 46.6%。随着城市数量和规模的不断扩大，人口不断向城市集中，人为热排放迅速增长，城市建筑物猛增，城市热岛现象变得越来越严重，从一般的气象问题逐渐成为最为突出的城市环境问题。北京最大热岛强度达到 9℃[2][3]，广州达到7.2℃[4]，上海达到 6.9℃[3]，如此高强度城市热岛不仅会带来夏季酷热的天气，提高城市空气污染水平，还会造成各种异常的城市气象，如暖冬、暴雨等，对城市居民生活、工业生产和经济发展产生很大的影响。因此，中国的城市热岛问题已经成为学者、管理者以致民众广泛关注的焦点。从 20 世纪 80 年代开始，国内众多学者就开始采用各种研究方法研究中国各城市的热岛效应问题。本文拟对中国城市热岛的研究进行综合论述，来探讨中国当前的城市热岛的特征、影响因素和产生的影响等问题。

## 一、中国城市热岛的主要特征

### 1. 具有显著的周期性：夜晚强，白天弱；工作日强，周末弱；季节变化复杂

国内外研究表明，城市热岛的日变化主要有两种模式：

一是 Oke 根据中纬度地区城市大量实测记录归纳出的理想状态模式[5]（见图 1a），即在地形平坦，天气晴朗、风速小等条件下，城市热岛强度夜晚强，白昼午间弱。二是Nkemdirim 和 Truch 在对加拿大的卡尔加里观测基础上提出的双峰模式[6]（见图 1b），热岛强度一天中有两个峰值，最高峰值出现在上午，次峰值出现在晚上，最低值出现在午后。

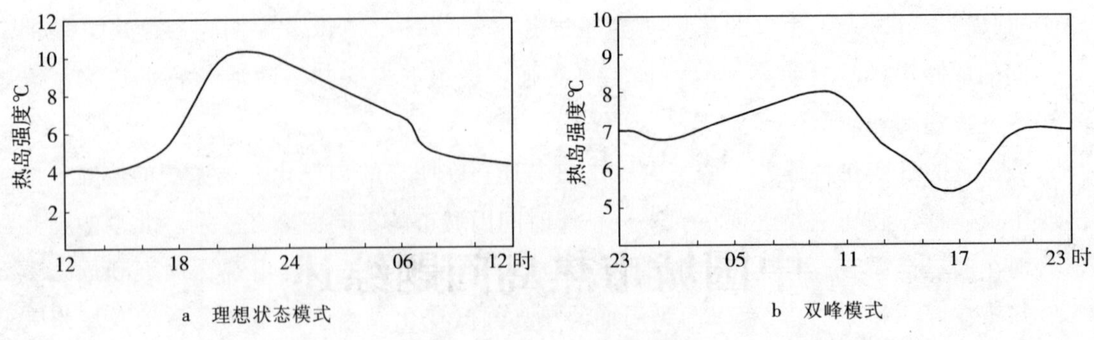


a 理想状态模式

b 双峰模式

**图1 城市热岛强度日变化**

理想状态模式产生的原因主要是由于下垫面性质不同，造成城郊昼夜增温、降温速度的差别，从而引起昼夜的热岛强度差别。午后随着太阳高度角的减小，郊区空旷，天穹可见度小，有效辐射强，大气失热快。特别是日落前后，空气层结稳定降温率更大。城区因下垫面温度高，白天蓄积的热量多，地面长波辐射和湍流显热提供给城区大气的热量较多，因此城区气温下降缓慢，相对于快速降温的郊区大气来说，就形成了夜间城市热岛。热岛强度以日落后3～5小时为最强，子夜以后，城、郊气温冷却率相近，热岛强度逐渐减小。日出以后郊区气温增温率大于城区。到了近中午的时候一般风速比夜间大，湍流增强，城区与郊区间的水平和垂直方向的混合增强，城、郊气温差别更小，热岛消失。在有些地区反而会出现郊区气温高于城区的城市"凉岛 Cool Island"[7]。双峰模式的两个峰值的出现与城市人为热排放和风向、风速及大气稳定度的日变化密切有关。高纬度城市，如：卡尔加里人为热排放一天有两个高峰分别在上午9时与晚上21时，同时城区从日落后至上午10点前均盛行西北向风，由于地形的关系风速偏小，大气层结稳定，因此在9～10时和21～22时出现热岛强度的高峰值[6]。由此可见，双峰模式是在特殊的人为和天气条件下出现的日变化形式。

中国城市热岛的日变化大都与理想状态模式变化一致，夜晚强、白昼午间弱。不过夜间的最大强度和白天的最小强度出现时间各有不同。北京在3～5时日出前热岛强度达到最高值，平均热岛强度接近2.7℃，在12～16时达最低值0.9℃[8]。上海城市热岛在23时左右达到最高峰2.1℃，9时达到谷底为－0.8℃[9]。昆明热岛效应以夜间最为明显，最高值出现时刻为3时[10]。兰州以2时热岛效应最为明显，而14时效应较小，平均热岛强度分别为3.6℃、1.4℃[11]。

在冬季由于人为热排放的影响较为显著，中国一些城市热岛强度的日变化也会出现类似与卡尔加里的双峰模式情况。合肥市夏季热岛强度的基本特征与理想状态模式曲线非常相似，夜晚强，白昼午间弱，大约21～23时最强，9～12时最小[12]。而冬季却与双峰模式的日变化特征接近，热岛强度有两个峰值，分别在8时、18时前后，与城市里早晚上下班高峰车流量增多对应，正午时最弱[13]。这反映了冬、夏两季人类活动、能源消耗量的不同。北京1971年秋季日变化是单峰模式，在清晨5时左右热岛强度达到最大值，其值为6℃左右。中午前后，其值最低，有时甚至出现负值。而冬季热岛强度日变化具有明显的双峰值现象（峰值出现时间是8时和20时，其强度分别是5℃和4.5℃），主要原因是由于冬季是北京地区的取暖季节，人工释放的热量明显超过其他季节（以用煤量为例，冬季是夏季的二倍）人们的取暖活动具有明显的时间性，热岛强度峰值的形成与取暖活动有密切关系[14]。上海初冬也曾观测到类似的现象[15]。

除了显著的日变化特征外，中国的城市热岛还存在明显的周变化，其振荡的波峰一般主要出现在工作日，波峰主要出现在周末，具体时间因城市的不同而略有差别。北京的强热岛主要出现在周三至周五，弱热岛出现在周六至周一[16]；上海的波峰出现在周五和周六，而波谷恰好落在周一和周二[17]。以周为周期的热岛强度变化成因主要与人类活动及城市大气污染物排放的“周末效应”[19]有显著的关系，在工作日，工厂或机动车辆等排放的人为热和大气污染物比周末要多，热岛受人为热和大气污染物的驱动，有些地方在时间上会滞后1~2天[17]。

热岛强度的季节变化十分复杂，它主要视区域气候条件和城市人为因素而异，没有一定的模式。按照最强热岛效应出现的季节，中国的城市热岛的季节变化大致可以分成冬强型、春强型、夏强型和秋强型四种类型（见表1）。冬强型的热岛强度冬季最强，北京[8][16][20][21]、天津[22][23]和昆明[24]等就属于这一类型。北京的热岛强度以冬季最强，春、秋季次之，夏季为最小，冬季市中心的温差在0.8℃以上，夏季只有0.5℃[20]。春强型春季热岛强度最高，代表城市有南京[25]、成都[26]和西安[27]等。南京的热岛强度3—5月份的春季为最高，11月至次年1月份的秋冬季比较低[25]。夏季热岛强度最高的属于夏强型，重庆[28]、唐山[29]和乌鲁木齐[30]等均属于该类型。重庆在一年中，夏季城乡温差较大，热岛最强，冬季仅次于夏季，而春秋两季城乡温差较小[28]。秋季热岛强度最强的为秋强型，广州[31][32]和杭州[33][34]等城市均属于该类型。广州月平均热岛强度具有明显的季节变化特征，总体上呈“U”字形变化，其中11月份热岛强度最高，7月份最低[31]。

**表1　中国主要城市热岛强度的季节变化**

| 类型 | 城市 | 季节变化 |
|---|---|---|
| 冬强型 | 北京 | 冬季最强，春、秋季次之，夏季最小 |
| | 天津 | 冬季最强，春季次之，夏秋季较弱 |
| | 昆明 | 冬季大于夏季 |
| 春强型 | 南京 | 3—5月的春季最高，11月至次年1月的秋冬季比较低 |
| | 成都 | 春季最强，冬季次之，夏季最弱 |
| | 西安 | 春季最强，冬、夏季次之，秋季最弱 |
| 夏强型 | 重庆 | 夏季最强，冬季次之，春秋最弱 |
| | 唐山 | 夏秋季节比冬春季节明显 |
| | 乌鲁木齐 | 夏季6—8月最大 |
| 秋强型 | 广州 | 11月份最高，7月份最低 |
| | 杭州 | 基本上呈秋>夏>春>冬 |

由于不同季节的热岛效应增长速度不同，同一城市在不同时期季节变化也不同。兰州

1990年之前，春季和夏季的热岛效应要强于秋季，秋季热岛效应比冬季更显著。在1990年之后，由于冬季和秋季热岛效应的增强，使得兰州一年四季间热岛效应的变化减小了，季节性差异表现不明显[35]。上海1955年平均气温差秋季10、11月为最大，以夏季6、7月为最小[36]；1998—1999年冬季最大，秋季次之，春、夏季最小[37]；2004—2005年春季4月的城市热岛强度最大，可达3.7℃，11—2月最低[9]。

**2. 热岛效应增强趋势显著，2000年后开始出现缓解迹象**

目前国内对热岛效应的变化趋势的研究表明，中国城市的热岛效应增强趋势显著（见表2），热岛强度和热岛面积随时间保持持续增长趋势，增温主要发生在20世纪80年代以后，但2000年之后，由于城市环境整治工作的开展，北京[38]、上海[39][40][41]、南京[25]和沈阳[42]等大城市热岛效应的增强趋势出现了缓解迹象。1960—2000年北京城市热岛强度具有清楚年际增温，年平均热岛强度的增温率为0.309℃/10a。从1960年开始上升，到1962年达到极大，此后下降，1969年达到最低点，此后强度开始波动式的上升。20世纪80年代后上升速度加快[20]，但2002—2003年北京市超过2℃以上的强热岛现象发生天数有所下降[38]。这说明1999年开始实施的北京市环境综合整治工程对缓解城市热岛有一定的作用。上海近50年来，城郊温差增温率为0.230℃/10a。在20世纪90年代前，城郊温差变化比较平稳，最大值没有超过0.4℃；90年代后，温差呈锯齿状上升，温差最大值出现在2004年，达到1.6℃[39]。另一方面，1960—1970年的热岛面积（温差大于0.8℃的区域）局限在市区的100km$^2$范围内，但从1980年开始突然扩大到400km$^2$以上，增加了3倍；到90年代后期扩展到近郊地区，热岛面积超过800km$^2$，达到60~70年代的8倍[41]。2000—2006年的城郊年均温差为1.27℃，仍保持增加，但增加率有所减缓。这说明上海2000年后的绿地建设和环境规划对热岛效应有减弱作用[39][40]。

表2 中国主要城市热岛强度倾向率（以平均气温为指标）

| 城市 | 倾向率(℃/10年) | 时间段 | 跃变点 |
|---|---|---|---|
| 北京 | 0.309[20] | 1960—2000年 | 1981年 |
| 上海 | 0.230[39] | 1951—2006年 | 20世纪90年代 |
| 广州 | 0.529[31] | 1980—2005年 | |
| 南京 | 0.109[25] | 1961—2005年 | 1977年 |
| 天津 | 0.110[43] | 1964—2003年 | 20世纪80年代中期 |
| 武汉 | 0.235[44] | 1960—2005年 | 20世纪80年代中后期 |
| 沈阳 | 0.270[42] | 1960—2006年 | |
| 西安 | 0.322[27] | 1959—2007年 | 1980年、1993年 |
| 唐山 | 0.170[29] | 1977—2006年 | 1993年 |
| 兰州 | 0.371[18] | 1956—2005年 | 1981年 |
| 宁波 | 0.260[45] | 1961—2005年 | |
| 石家庄 | 0.066[46] | 1961—2000年 | 20世纪80年代 |

热岛强度的增温率存在季节差别。北京冬季的增温率最大，春、秋季次之，夏季为最小，冬季热岛强度的年际变化为0.365℃/10a，夏季热岛强度0.258℃/10a[20]。天津热岛强度增幅在秋季最强、春季最小，分别为0.16℃/10a和0.06℃/10a[43]。沈阳春、夏、秋、冬季热岛强度增幅分别为0.23℃/10a、0.33℃/10a、0.30℃/10a和0.23℃/10a，夏季最强，秋季次之，春冬最小[42]。

平均气温、最高气温和最低气温均可以用来表示城市热岛强度，这三个指标表示的热岛强度的增温率也是不同的。一般来说，最低气温的增温率最高，平均气温次之，最高气温最小。兰州以年平均、最高和最低气温表示的城市热岛强度的增温率分别为每10年0.371℃、0.169℃和0.654℃[18]。南京用年平均气温计算获得的热岛强度增幅为0.109℃/10a。最高气温增幅为0.031℃/10a，最低气温增幅为0.167℃/10a[25]。武汉以年平均、最低和最高气温表示的城市热岛强度增幅率分别为0.235℃/10a、0.425℃/10a和0.034℃/10a[44]。

**3. 具有“陡崖—高原—高峰”的水平分布结构，大城市还出现了多中心的非均匀结构和中心位置的漂移现象**

城市热岛的水平分布与下垫面性质有着密切的关系。热岛一般出现在人口密集、建筑物密度大、工商业最集中的地区；而郊区有较好的植被覆盖，或者农田密布，热岛强度小。Oke根据加拿大多个城市多次观测热岛现象的数据总结了城市热岛水平分布基本的特征：城市周围的乡村气温较低，从乡村到城市近郊过渡时会出现气温陡然上升的“陡崖”（cliff）；到了城区上空气温梯度比较平缓，因城市下垫面性质的差异略有起伏，称为“高原”（plateau）；到了市中心区人口密度和建筑密度及人为热释放量最大的地点，气温最高，称为“高峰”（Peak）[47]。

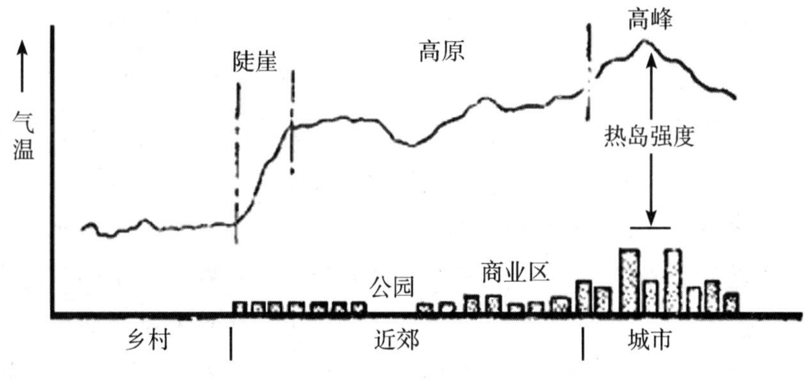


**图2　城市热岛温度坡面示意图**

中国很多城市的热岛结构也具有“陡崖—高原—高峰”的水平分布特征。北京从霞云岭站到房山站气温急剧升高，这是由于郊区农村到城市边缘的近郊区下垫面发生巨大变化，所引起的气温陡然升高，被称作“陡崖”（cliff）。由房山站至北京站气温在高水平上起伏，气温梯度比较平缓，这是因城市下垫面性质基本相同下的地区差异而引起的气温波动，被称作“高原”（plateau）。到了城市中心区，是人口密度和建筑密度及人为热释放量最大的地

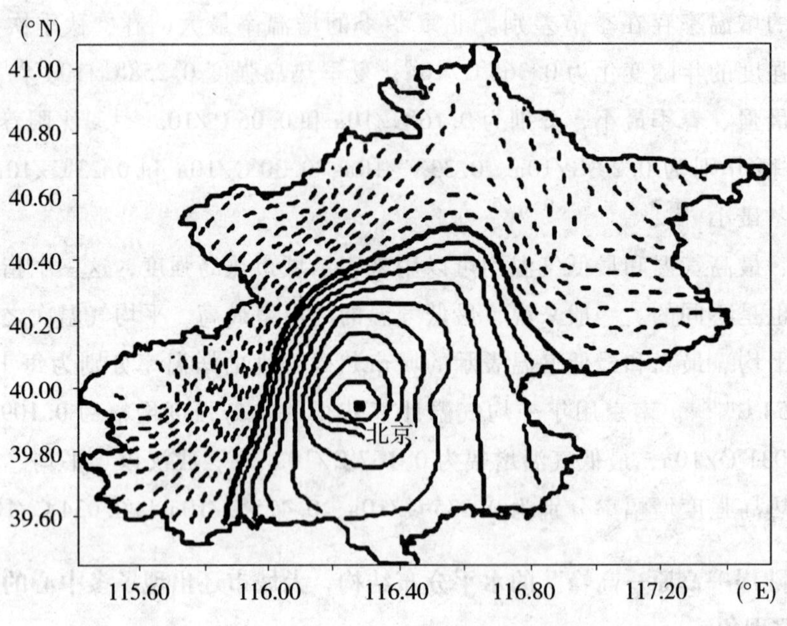


**图3 北京市热岛（1960—2000年各站年平均局地气温）**

每隔0.1℃画一条等值线，粗实线为零线，实线为正值线，虚线为负值线

点，气温也最高（北京站），被称作“高峰”（peak）。“高峰”过后再向东北，其基本特征如“高原”、“陡崖”等都存在，但不对称，气温要比西南低[20]。重庆市热岛有两个中心，一个在人口稠密的市中区，一个是钢铁和电力工业集中的大渡口区。热岛中心等温线呈椭圆形分布，其长轴走向与重庆市冬季盛行风向（NNE）一致；在中梁山和铜锣山、真武山之间的槽谷，即城区范围内，各测点位温差异不大，最大位温差只有0.4℃，但在铜锣山、真武山之外的郊区，位温递减较快，位温梯度与山脉垂直[48]。在西安[49]、天津[23]等地也观测到了类似的水平分布结构特征。

此外，随着城市规模的扩大，北京[16][50][51]、广州[32]、深圳[52]、上海[53]、杭州[33]、兰州[54]等大城市还出现了多中心的非均匀镶嵌式结构，热岛中心位置随时间出现漂移现象。北京在夏季白天14时只有一个强热岛中心，位于四元桥附近，另外在知春里、丽泽桥附近有两个次热岛中心。在20时出现4个热岛中心，分别位于大观园、白家庄、四元桥以及知春里附近。2时在大观园、白家庄、知春里附近还存在3个强热岛中心。到8时则只剩下大观园附近一个强热岛中心[16]。兰州早上8:30城关区有2个热中心，主要出现在能耗大、热源强度高的工业区。下午14:30城关区主要有3个热中心，主要出现在人口和建筑密集的商贸区、高能高耗工业区及大型生活住宅区。晚上20:30城关区有2个热中心，主要出现在高耗能工业区和火车站等人口密集的区域[54]。

**4. 具有随着高度的增加而逐渐减弱的垂直结构**

城市热岛强度不仅在水平方向上是非均匀分布，在垂直方向上还会随高度而变化。一般来说，白天变化复杂，晚上热岛强度在近地面部分最大，随着高度的增加而减小。到了一定高度之后，城市气温反较郊区低，出现“交叉效应”，温差为0的高度被称为“热岛高度”。国内很多城市都观测到了这一现象[15][23][28][55][56]。昆明测得地面附近城市增温效应显著，热岛中心出现在城中心偏东北处，随着高度增加，其强度逐渐减弱，且热岛中心逐渐向西南侧偏移，在50m高度，热岛中心强度仅为地面附近的26.7%，出现在城西南附近[55]。南京热岛强度基本随高度增加而减小，在约400m高度的时候城市和郊区温差较小[57]。

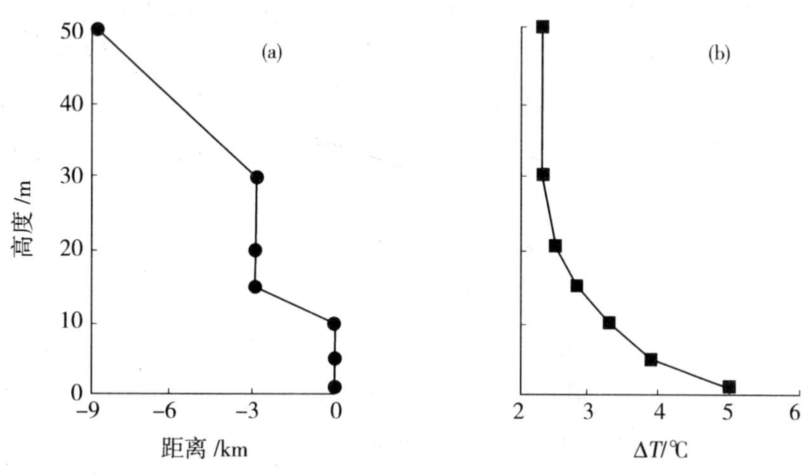


**图4 昆明最大热岛效应出现位置（a）及强度（b）**

热岛高度与城市规模、建筑物高度、下垫面粗糙度、时间、风速等因素有关。据日本河村武的研究[58]，在没有高层建筑物的人口为10万左右的城市，热岛效应影响高度小于30m。昆明夜间的热岛高度超过50m，昼间低于50m[55]。重庆的热岛高度在23:00和5:00最高，日出以后逐渐下降[48]。天津热岛顶高夏季平均为700m，上限可达900m，冬季平均高度为270m，最高为600m[23]。Oke在加拿大蒙特利尔市观测发现，当风速小的时候（0～3m/s），地面城市热岛强度很大。但因热岛强度随高度递减的速度快（中间有小的曲折），热岛伸及到600m高度为止。在风速为3～6m/s时，近地面层城市热岛强度较弱，但其热岛强度随高度递减的速度慢（中间亦有小曲折），热岛伸及的高度却比较大，在900m高度处温差仍为正值[59]。

## 二、影响城市热岛的因素

城市热岛的形成和变化受到城市化的人为因素和自然因素共同作用下影响。人为因素包括下垫面性质的改变、人为热和大气污染物、城市规模、形状和布局等，自然因素包括自然地理位置、天气条件等。

### 1. 下垫面性质

市、郊区下垫面性质的差异是城市热岛形成和强度变化的重要原因。城市中除少量绿地外，绝大部分是人工铺砌的道路、广场、建筑物和构筑物。这些下垫面与郊区农田绿野相比不透水面积要大得多。降雨后，雨水很快从排水管道流失，因此在城市中供蒸发蒸腾消耗的热量远比郊区少，而用于下垫面增温和向空气输送的湍流显热则比郊区多。这就使城区下垫面温度常常会比郊区高，形成“城市热岛”。另一方面，城市中建筑物参差错落，形成很多高宽比不同的“城市街谷”。在白天太阳照射下，由于城市街谷中墙壁和墙壁之间，墙壁和地面之间的多次的反射和吸收，在其他条件相同的情况下，能够比郊区获得较多的太阳辐射能。同时又因为墙壁、屋顶和地面的建筑材料又具有较大的导热率和热容量，城市下垫面在白天吸收和储存的能量远比郊区多。在夜间墙壁和屋檐等都会发射长波辐射，再加上“城市街谷”中风速比较小，热量不容易外散。因此在日落之后，城区下垫面温度和近地面气温下降速度都比郊区慢。城、郊在日落后降温率的不同，是城市热岛夜晚比白天更为显著的重要原因[7]。

城区不同土地利用/覆盖类型的地表温度差异是造成城市热岛多中心的非均匀水平结构的主要原因，土地利用/覆被类型的空间格局总体上决定了热场的分布格局。对上海市区而言，居民用地对热岛强度的贡献最大，其次是道路广场，第三是工厂用地。其中，居民用地占各类土地热贡献总和的1/3，道路广场和工厂用地的热贡献之和占1/3，其他各类土地的热贡献占1/3[60]。西安市土地覆被类型亮温分布由高到低：商业和工业用地、未利用地、居民住宅用地、绿地、水体；亮温与植被指数有良好的反相关关系[61]。福州不同的土地利用/覆被类型存在温度差异：城市建筑用地 > 裸地 > 耕地 > 林草地 > 水体，城市建筑用地和裸地对地表温度的贡献最大，水体和林草地具有较好的降温作用[62]。上海[63]、北京[64][65]、深圳[66]、成都[67]、哈尔滨[68]、武汉[69]等地均发现植被绿地状况与城市热岛呈现明显反相关分布，下垫面类型及其组合主要通过植被覆盖的分布对地表温度产生影响，城市绿化覆盖率越高，城市地表温度越低，夏季尤为显著。

**2. 人为热和大气污染物**

城市人为热排放是造成和影响热岛效应的另一个重要原因。城市人为热也就是人类活动产生的废热，主要来自机动车辆、工厂车间、空调运转、居民烹饪及建筑物向外散发的热量等[70]。人为热排放对城市热岛的影响具有双重作用：一方面，直接增加了城市的热量，特别是在夏季和冬季；另一方面，城市人为热排放的同时，也大量排放煤灰、粉尘及各种污染气体，其中较多的是 $CO_2$、$N_2O$、$H_2O$、$CH_4$、CFC 等温室气体，形成覆盖在城市上空的“尘罩”与“气罩”，加重了城市热岛的强度[71]。广州市城市温度场的分布由高到低依次为：旧型工业区—新型工业区—老城区—新城区—郊区—农村，热岛效应的首要原因是工业、运输业集中地的热量排放[72]。南京市存在三个分布范围较广且连续的热岛中心，主要分布在南京市的工业区，而并非出现在人口密集、经济繁荣的商业区和居住区，工业热源是南京市热岛形成的一个重要因素[73]。人为热的释放是西安热岛效应产生与加重的主要因素。其中城市耗电量是最主要的影响因素，关联度达到 0.9148，工厂、汽车、空调及家庭炉灶和饭店等大量消耗的能源释放出大量的废热进入大气中，使城市热岛效应更加严重；反过来，城市热岛效应的加重又使得城市耗电量进一步增加，形成恶性的循环。城市里的机动车对热岛效应的影响也不容忽视，关联度为 0.7594。城市里昼夜营运的车辆不仅排放出大量的污染尾气，还随之释放出大量废热，加重城市底层的热污染，对城市热岛起到推波助澜的作用[74]。

在影响城市热岛的污染物之中，大气总悬浮颗粒物（TSP）的作用较为显著。长沙市城市热岛效应与 TSP 污染在空间与时间分布上都具有耦合关系。TSP 污染的分布特征和热岛强度分布状况基本一致，都是由市中心往外逐渐减轻。TSP 高值区，城区呈高温区，反之亦然。月平均热岛强度与 TSP 浓度在时间上呈正相关关系[75]。沈阳热岛效应强度与 TSP 浓度有较好的相关关系，其相关系数为 0.58，TSP 浓度越大，城市热岛越明显[76]。另一方面，TSP 污染会影响城市热岛的日变化。白天大气悬浮颗粒粒子可以反射太阳辐射，降低城区的日照时间，使白天的热岛强度减弱。夜间城区由于大气悬浮颗粒的存在不利于热量的散失，使城郊温差加大，进而使热岛强度加强。

**3. 城市规模、形状和布局**

城市规模、形状和布局也会对城市热岛的强度和空间分布产生显著的影响。城市规模的影响表现为：城市人口越多，城市规模越大，热岛效应越明显。据研究，城市的热岛强度 1 万人口达到 0.11℃，10 万人口达到 0.32℃，100 万人口达到 0.91℃[77]。Mitchel 根据美国 77 个城市的资料，论证城市最大热岛强度与城市人口的平方根有很好的正相关关系[78]。Oke 根据北美和欧洲 20 多个城市资料统计出最大热岛强度与城市人口数的对数呈线性关系[79]。北京城市热岛强度和总人口对数呈线性相关关系，其长期变化相关系数为 0.76[21]。上海[39]、兰州[35]、西安[27]各个季节热岛效应与人口数量之间有很强的相关性。北京的热岛强度与基本建设投资总额、基础设施投资总额、房屋竣工面积和住房竣工面积的相关系数，分别为 0.7051，0.5975，0.8766 和 0.8747（超过了 0.1% 信度）。房屋竣工面积每增加 100 万 $m^2$，北京城市的热岛强度增加 0.04℃，或当北京城市基本建设投资总额每增加 100 亿 $m^2$，北京城市温度要比远郊区高出 0.16℃[20]。2001—2008 年，由于城市扩张，无锡市城市建成区面积由 163.7$km^2$ 增加为 203.0$km^2$，而城市热岛效应中较强—极强面积相应由 4.03$km^2$ 增长到 55.02$km^2$[80]。

城市形状和布局主要影响城市热岛的空间分布特征。无锡市城市扩张主要呈现出集中发展和条带状发展，主要集中在沿京杭大运河的苏、锡、常中心线，太湖沿岸以及几个开发区。而城市热岛分布与城市扩张呈现出空间分布的一致性，热岛主要也分布在上述地区[80]。北京城市热岛多尺度非均匀空间分布特征与中高层建筑群空间布局存在显著的相关性。城西、城东北以及城南等中高层建筑群密集区为强热岛区，而城区南北向古建筑群中轴区和海淀区北部园林绿地等地区为相对弱热岛区[81]。长沙城区热岛效应与城市规划呈对应关系，热岛效应最显著的区域为二环线内，并从中心沿三环逐渐向郊区减弱[82]。

**4. 自然环境**

因地理位置、气候条件和地形地貌的差异而引起城市自然环境的差异，也会对城市热岛的强度和空间分布特征产生影响。韩国南部的沿海城市的年平均日最大热岛强度比内陆城市要低[83]。国内也发现类似的情况，沈阳、大连都是综合性特大城市，重工业发达，但热岛最大强度沈阳（5.27℃）比大连（2.61℃）高1倍多。造成此差别的主要原因可能是由于沈阳、大连两城市各自的地理位置和气候特点引起的。虽然两市都属于温带季风气候，但沈阳地处辽河平原，而大连位于辽东半岛南端且濒临黄海和渤海，受海洋影响较大，气候温和湿润，缓解了城市热岛强度[84]。上海盛夏存在一个从西北指向东南的温度梯度，平均梯度约为0.8/24km。这是由于上海地形呈三角形半岛，西连大陆，东北和东南两边临水的海陆地形差异决定的，因为夏季海温低于陆温，上海地区又盛行偏东风，造成气温从邻近海面的东南郊区向内陆的西北郊区逐渐升高[60]。中国位于北纬30°以北的城市比以南的城市热岛效应更为严重，春季和夏季沿海城市的热岛效应比内陆城市要弱，但在秋季和冬季正好相反[85]。广州地势东北高、西南低，北部和东北部是低山丘陵，西北部地势平坦开阔，南部是冲积平原，珠江自西而东穿过市区的南部。荔湾区是市区地势最低的地区。这样的自然地理环境使广州城市热岛的水平分布偏于市区的西南部，热岛中心位于荔湾区人民南路附近，气温自热岛中心向四周递减。北面的等温线分布较东面和南面密些[86]。重庆市温度的分布明显地受到了山脉和河流等地形因素的影响，地形的分布格局与温度分布的基本格局是一致的。在有山脉的地区，由于海拔高，温度明显降低，低温范围与山脉走向一致。在长江和嘉陵江的河谷地带，由于海拔较低，并且河谷地带不太利于夜间降温，因此沿这两条河流形成了带状分布的高温带[87]。

**5. 天气条件**

在同一时期，同一个城市其下垫面、人为热和污染等条件基本相似，但其热岛现象却时强时弱，时有时无。主要的原因是城市热岛的出现除了城市本身的内部原因外，还取决于当时的天气形势和气象条件。大量观测事实证明，大气层结稳定的、气压梯度小、风速小、天气晴朗少云或无云的天气形势才有利于城市热岛的形成。天气晴朗少云或无云，使白天日照充足，太阳直接辐射使城区下垫面储存到足够多的热量；大气层结稳定的、气压梯度小、风速小使得城郊在水平方向和垂直方向动力交换作用小，有利于城市热岛的形成。Park发现热岛强度随风速的增加而减弱，在热岛盛行的时刻，当风速增大时，由此引起的动力交换作用也将增大，这往往使得热岛强度减弱[88]。北京强的“城市热岛”现象都是在静风或软风（蒲氏1级）条件下出现的，此时热岛强度均值达4.6℃；当风速增大到微风（蒲氏3级）或以上时，城市热岛消失[89]。风是影响上海地区高温分布和强度的最主要气象要素。东风和南风带来海上的冷平流，使全市高温强度降低。而城市热岛的加热作用，使下风方的降温幅度为上风方的降温幅度的一半，造成市区内高温中心向西转移，全市的热岛效应范围向下风方的西部郊区扩展。相反，西风带来大陆的暖平流使上风方的高温强度增强，城市热岛的加热作用使下风方的增温幅度大于上风方的增温幅度，导致市区高温中心向东转移，全市的热岛效应范围向下风方的东部郊区扩展。这是所谓的热岛下游效应。风对城市热岛的热扩散作用使城市热岛面积总是比市区面积大[60]。就平均情况来说，广州无论冬夏都是夜间风速较白天小，夜间大气层结稳定并常有逆温出现，有利于热岛的形成，白天风速较大，尤其是市区湍流作用比较强，不利于热岛的形成，所以广州的平均热岛强度日变化是夜间强，白天弱[86]。Ackerman[90]发现热岛强度随着云量的增加而减弱。广州测得年热岛强度变化与云量的相关系数为 -0.76，与晴天日数的相关系数为 0.74[86]。北京晴天时热岛强度大，80%的热岛强度在 2℃以上；阴天时热岛强度小，80%的热岛强度在 2℃以下[89]。

## 三、城市热岛的影响

### 1. 加剧城市高温出现的频率和高温灾害

研究结果表明，城市热岛对中国一些地区的气温序列产生了显著的影响。北京地区 1961—2000 年整个时期由于热岛效应加强因素引起的国家气象观测站平均年温度变化速率为 0.16℃/10a，对全部增温的贡献达到 71%；近 20 年来尤为显著达到每 10 年增暖 0.33℃，对该时期全部增温的贡献达到 49%[91]。深圳 1979 年以来，城市热岛效应导致年平均气温增暖 0.243℃/10a，占深圳总体增暖的 36.3%[92]。长三角城市带增温效应使得区域的年平均气温在 1961—2005 年间增加了 0.072℃，其中 1991—2005 年间增温幅度为 0.047℃；年最高气温升高了 0.162℃，其中 1991—2005 年间增温幅度为 0.083℃，表明 1991—2005 年间长江三角洲城市带的空间扩展正在改变区域温度变化趋势，且这种增温趋势显著[93]。华北地区在国家气象观测站观测的年平均气温和年平均最低气温上升趋势中，城市化造成的增温分别为 0.11℃/10a 和 0.20℃/10a，对全部增温的贡献率分别达 39.3% 和 52.6%[94]。近 40 多年来甘肃省城市热岛效应对国家气象观测站年平均温度的增温贡献率为 18.5%，对城市站年平均温度的增温贡献率为 37.6%[95]。值得一提的是中国东北部城市热岛的贡献程度，无论是 1954 年以来还是 1979 年以来均很小，即使影响最为显著的年份，冬季平均最低气温，对其贡献也均不到 5%[96]。西北地区总体来说城市效应在全区温度增暖中所占比例较小，增暖主要为自然因素导致[97]。

热岛引起的增暖现象还存在季节差异。北京地区热岛效应对暖季的增暖贡献比冷季大，热岛贡献冬季为 56.1%，而夏季为 76.1%[91]。兰州热岛增温贡献率最大的是春、夏季气温，而不是冬季气温[18]。华北地区城市化增温以冬季为最大，夏季最小[94]。甘肃省城市热岛效应对季节增暖的贡献率则为春季最大，夏季次之，秋冬季最小[95]。

城市热岛效应不仅对区域气温有较大的影响，且有可能是夏季酷热的重要原因。1995 年以来，北京由于热岛效应夏季高温天气（≥35℃）日数有增加的趋势[50][98]。而且夏季平均热岛指数随着环境温度的升高呈上升趋势，在环境温度越高时，城市热岛对温度的增幅作用越明显。北京环境场气温达到 35℃的天气过程时，平均热岛指数为 1.65℃。随着环境温度的升高，平均热岛指数也呈上升的趋势，在出现 39℃以上的极端高温天气情况下，平均热岛指数最强，达到了 3.28℃[99]。城市热岛影响上海高温日和热浪过程的空间分布。由于城市热岛的存在，表现出市中心区比近郊区和远郊区具有更多的热日天数、更高的极端最高气温、更长的高温持续时间[100]。1960—1980 年上海城市站（龙华站）与郊区站（崇明站）的高温日数之比平均为 1.9，极端最高气温城市站比郊区站平均高 1.0℃。1981—2000 年城市站与郊区站的高温日数之比平均增加到 5.1，两站的极端最高气温差平均扩大到 1.7℃。可见，近 20 年来热岛效应加剧了上海市区夏季高温灾害的程度[41]。

**2. 增强城郊空气对流，影响降水的分布**

热岛效应影响着云的形成和运动[101]，对局地降雨及降雨机制产生影响。在一定的天气形势背景和热力、动力的适合条件下，城市热岛对降水产生“诱导”或增幅作用[102][103]，增加的区域集中在市中心及其下风向范围。主要是由于在静风的条件下，热岛使得城区气压相对较小，乡村较冷的空气流向城区，形成局部空气对流，产生降雨[104]。陈云浩等对上海研究表明：不同的热力背景对下垫面降雨分布有不同影响，降雨量依次从自然背景、低温背景、高温背景递增。在自然背景下，年降雨为 974.2mm，在低温背景下则为 1027.2mm，增加 53mm，增加幅度为 5.4%，而高温背景下年降雨则为 1075.7mm，增加了 101.5mm，增幅为 10.4%[105]。北京冬季盛行北风气流，在城区及南部近郊区，冬季降水日数和降水量都在明显增加，在北部郊区，热岛效应强迫产生的边界层下沉运动有可能造成局地降水天气过程相对减少，夏季盛行南风气流，随着城市热岛效应的增强，发生在北部近郊区的弱降水天气过程趋于增多。尽管南部平原郊区的相对降水日数变化不大，但降水量在相对减少[106]。广州地区研究发现，2005 年 8 月 4 日夜间和 7 日午后发生在广州城区的两次雷暴的形成均与城市热岛相关。城市热岛引起局地气流发生辐合并引发对流发展，对流降水发生的时间和位置均与城市热岛的演变及其相应的辐合区有良好对应关系，对流易在城市热岛发展较强的时段和位置上发生，而且受城市的影响。两次雷暴在移动经过广州城区时均得到了进一步发展，最强的对流回波出现在中心城区上空，降水也集中落在中心城区。所有这些特征表明两次雷暴的形成和发展均与城市热岛的影响有关[107]。

**3. 影响城市地区大气环境质量，加重大气污染**

一般认为，当天气尺度的风速较小时，边界层大气由于城市热岛的存在，可以在城市形成一个低压中心并产生指向城市的气压梯度力，在低层造成向内的辐合流场和上升气流。在几百米的高度上，空气又以相反的方向从城市向郊外流出并下沉，形成一个闭合的热岛环流（见图 5）。在存在城市热岛效应的情况下，城区排放的污染物会随着环流扩散到郊区，在郊区沉降后随近地风返回到城区，加重了城区的污染物浓度，并且起着循环污染的作用[108]。在城市热岛中心的上升热气流中，含有大量的尘埃和烟雾，一部分尘埃上升后并降落在城市周围，一部分则停留在空中形成“微尘云”。郊区低层污染物在热岛环流的作用下，聚集在城市上空，而空气中大量尘埃的存在，易于雾的形成。在夜晚气温降低使得水汽凝结形成雾，雾下沉并成为烟雾。这种烟雾使得能见度降低，对人类的呼吸产生危害，严重时会造成空气污染事件。城市热岛越强，污染物和烟雾的浓度越大，危害性也就越强[109]。而热岛的垂直分布，使得空气污染物在一定高度不易扩散，加重污染。Jonsson 等人[110]的研究表明

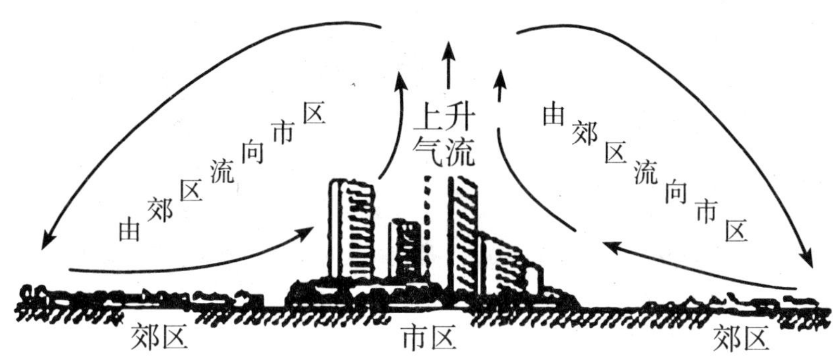


图5 城市热岛环流示意图

达累斯萨达姆（Dares Salaam）城区颗粒物浓度在夜间高于郊区，且浓度与夜间城市热岛强度呈正相关。Kevin 等[111][112]也认为城市热岛可以影响混合层高度，进而影响地面污染物浓度。徐祥德[113]认为城市区域尺度热岛由强弱程度不同的“次生”热岛效应结构“合成”，可引起局地次生尺度环流辐合结构，导致大气污染程度加重。

（作者：王晓云，国家气象局副司长）

## 参考文献


［1］Howard L. Climate of London deduced from meteorological observation［J］. Harvey and Darton，1833，1（3）：1－24

［2］窦建奇．关于城市“热岛效应”的思考［J］．武汉城市建设学院学报，2001，18（3－4）：76－78

［3］申绍杰．城市热岛问题与城市设计［J］．中外建筑，2003，5：20－22

［4］杨士弘．城市生态环境研究［M］．广州：中山大学出版社，1991：64

［5］Oke T R，Maxwell The energetic basis of the urban heat island［J］. Q J R Meteorol Soc，1982，108（45）：1－24

［6］Nkemdirim，L. C.，Truch，P.，Variability of temperature fields in Calgary，Alberta Atmospheric Environment，1977，12：809－822

［7］周淑贞，束炯．城市气象学［M］．北京：气象出版社，1994：263－265

［8］谢庄，崔继良，陈大刚．北京城市热岛效应的昼夜变化特征分析［J］．气候与环境研究，2006，11（1）：69－75

［9］朱家其，汤绪，江灏．上海市城区气温变化及城市热岛［J］．高原气象，2006，25（06）：1154－1160

［10］何云玲，张一平，刘玉洪，等．昆明城市气候水平空间分布特征［J］．地理科学，2002，22（06）：724－729

［11］白虎志，任国玉，方锋．兰州城市热岛效应特征及其影响因子研究［J］．气象科技，2005，33（06）：492－500

［12］石春娥，王兴荣，吴必文，等．合肥市夏季热岛特征研究［J］．南京气象学院学报，2005，28（05）：672－678

［13］严平，杨书运，王相文，等．合肥城市热岛强度及绿化效应［J］．合肥工业大学学报，2000，23

(3): 348 - 352

[14] 周明煌，曲绍厚，李玉英，等. 北京地区热岛和热岛环流特征［J］. 环境科学，1980 (04): 12 - 19

[15] 焦敦基，陈达铭，张锦秀. 上海初冬的城市热岛［J］. 自然杂志，1983，6 (01): 54 - 56

[16] 郑祚芳，刘伟东，王迎春. 北京地区城市热岛的时空分布特征［J］. 南京气象学院学报，2006，29 (05): 694 - 699

[17] 江田汉，束炯，邓莲堂. 上海城市热岛的小波特征［J］. 热带气象学报，2004，20 (05): 515 - 522

[18] 马玉霞，王式功，魏海茹. 兰州市近50年城市热岛强度变化特征［J］. 气象科技，2009，37 (06): 660 - 665

[19] 章志芹，唐健，汤剑平. 无锡空气污染指数、气象要素的周末效应［J］. 南京大学学报（自然科学），2007，43 (6): 643 - 654

[20] 于淑秋，卞林根，林学椿. 北京城市热岛“尺度”变化与城市发展［J］. 中国科学（D 辑），2005，35 (S1): 97 - 106

[21] 季崇萍，刘伟东，轩春怡. 北京城市化进程对城市热岛的影响研究［J］. 地球物理学报，2006，49 (01): 69 - 78

[22] 韩素芹，郭军，黄岁樑，等. 天津城市热岛效应演变特征研究［J］. 生态环境，2007，16 (02): 280 - 284

[23] 孙奕敏，边海. 天津市城市热岛效应的综合性研究［J］. 气象学报，1988，46 (03): 341 - 348

[24] 施晓晖，顾本文. 昆明城市气候特征［J］. 气象，2001，27 (03): 38 - 41

[25] 邱新法，顾丽华，曾燕，等. 南京城市热岛效应研究［J］. 气候与环境研究，2008，13 (06): 807 - 815

[26] 钱妙芬，石风云. 成都市城市热岛特征初探［J］. 成都气象学院学报，1988 (01): 1 - 10

[27] 张宏利，陈豫，张纳伟锐，等. 西安市热岛效应变化特征与城市人口发展研究［J］. 水土保持研究，2009，16 (4): 131 - 136

[28] 任启福. 重庆城市热岛效应［J］. 重庆环境科学，1992，14 (3): 37 - 42

[29] 龚宇，余森，王璞，等. 典型重工业城市热岛效应特征分析——以唐山市为例［J］. 资源科学，2010，32 (6): 1120 - 1126

[30] 王珊珊，艾里西尔·库尔班，郭宇宏，等. 乌鲁木齐地区气温变化和城市热岛效应分析［J］. 干旱区研究，2009，26 (03): 432 - 440

[31] Zhou Kai, Ye Youhua, Peng Shaolin, Variations of urban heat island and its relationships with total suspended particulates in Guangzhou, China［J］. Ecology and Environment. 2008, 17 (5): 1861 - 1867

[32] 江学顶，夏北成，郭泺，等. 广州城市热岛空间分布及时域—频域多尺度变化特征［J］. 应用生态学报，2007，18 (01): 133 - 139

[33] 鲍淳松. 杭州夏季城市热岛特点与绿化覆盖率的关系［J］. 杭州科技，2002 (2): 32 - 33

[34] 骆杨，周锁铨，孙善磊，等. 杭州城市热岛空间分布及时域—频域多尺度变化特征［J］. 生态环境学报，2009，18 (6): 2200 - 2205

[35] 李卓仑，王乃昂，轧靖，等. 近40年兰州城市气候季节性变化与城市发展［J］. 高原气象，2007，26 (03): 586 - 591

[36] 周淑贞，张超. 上海城市热岛效应［J］. 地理学报［J］. 1982，37 (04): 372 - 382

[37] 束炯，江田汉，杨晓明. 上海城市热岛效应的特征分析［J］. 上海环境科学，2000，19 (11): 532 - 534

[38] 刘熙明，胡非，李磊．北京市夏季城市热岛特征及其近地层气象场分析［J］．中国科学院研究生院学报，2006，23（1）：70－76

[39] 曹爱丽，张浩，张艳，等．上海近50年气温变化与城市化发展的关系［J］．地球物理学报，2008，51（6）：1663－1669

[40] 漆梁波．近10年上海盛夏高温及热岛强度变化趋势［J］．气象科技，2004，32（06）：433－437

[41] 丁金才，周红妹，叶其欣．从上海市热岛演变看城市绿化的重要意义［J］．气象，2002，28（02）：22－24

[42] 万志红，万志强．沈阳市热岛动态及其影响因子分析［J］．防灾科技学院学报，2008，10（04）：7－11

[43] 韩素芹，郭军，黄岁樑，等．天津城市热岛效应演变特征研究［J］．生态环境，2007，16（2）：280－284

[44] 陈正洪，王海军，任国玉．武汉市城市热岛强度非对称性变化［J］．气候变化研究进展，2007，3（05）：282－287

[45] 丁烨毅，陈有利，黄鹤楼．宁波市城市热岛效应特征分析［J］．浙江气象，2008，29（4）：28－32

[46] 刘学锋，阮新，谷永利．石家庄地区气温变化和热岛效应分析［J］．环境科学研究，2005，18（05）：11－15

[47] Oke TR，Cleugh HA. Urban heat storage derived as energy balance residuals［J］. Boundary-Layer Meteorology，1987，39：233－245

[48] 李子华，唐斌，任启福．重庆市区冬季热岛和湿岛效应的研究［J］．地理学报，1993，48（04）：358－367

[49] 刘加平，林宪德，刘艳峰，等．西安冬季城市热岛调查研究［J］．太阳能学报，2007，28（08）：245－249

[50] 王郁，胡非．近10年来北京夏季城市热岛的变化及环境效应的分析研究［J］．地球物理学报，2006，49（01）：61－68

[51] 王今殊，李贵才，刘玉洁，等．北京地区陆表温度空间分布特征［J］．测绘科学，2009，34（06）：218－222

[52] 宋艳，余世孝，李楠，等．深圳特区表面温度空间分异特征［J］．生态学报，2007，27（04）：1489－1499

[53] 邓莲堂，束炯，李朝颐．上海城市热岛的变化特征分析［J］．热带气象学报，2001，17（03）：273－280

[54] 李国栋，王乃昂，张俊华．兰州市城区夏季热场分布与热岛效应研究［J］．地理科学，2008，28（05）：709－715

[55] 张一平，何云玲，马友鑫，等．昆明城市热岛效应立体分布特征［J］．高原气象，2002，21（06）：604－610

[56] 陈二平，武永利，张怀德，等．太原市城市热岛效应的分析研究［J］．山西气象，1991（01）：22－24

[57] 刘红年，蒋维楣，孙鉴泞，等．南京城市边界层微气象特征观测与分析［J］．南京大学学报（自然科学），2008，44（1）：99－107

[58] 河村武编．都市大气环境．东京大学出版会，1979

[59] Oke，T. R.，East. C，The urban boundary layer in Montreal［J］. Boundary Layer Meteorol，1971（1）：

411 - 437

[60] 丁金才，张志凯，奚红，等. 上海地区盛夏高温分布和热岛效应的初步研究. 大气科学，2002，26 (03)：412 - 420

[61] 解修平，周杰，张海龙，等. 基于 Landsat TM 的西安市城市热岛效应研究. 河北师范大学学报（自然科学版），2007，31（03）：397 - 417

[62] 季青，贺伶俐，余明，等. 基于 Landsat ETM + 数据的福州市土地利用/覆被与城市热岛的关系研究. 福建师范大学学报（自然科学版），2009，25（06）：106 - 114

[63] 延昊，邓莲堂. 利用遥感地表参数分析上海市的热岛效应及治理对策 [J]. 热带气象学报，2004，20 (05)：579 - 586

[64] 张佳华，侯英雨，李贵才，等. 北京城市及周边热岛日变化及季节特征的卫星遥感研究与影响因子分析 [J]. 中国科学（D 辑），2005，35（S1）：187 - 194

[65] 江樟焰，陈云浩，李京. 基于 Landsat TM 数据的北京城市热岛研究 [J]. 武汉大学学报（信息科学版），2006，31（02）：121 - 125

[66] 张小飞，王仰麟，吴健生，等. 城市地域地表温度—植被覆盖定量关系分析——以深圳市为例 [J]. 地理研究，2006，25（03）：369 - 377

[67] 陈辉，古琳，黎燕琼，等. 成都市城市森林格局与热岛效应的关系 [J]. 生态学报，2009，29（09）：4865 - 4874

[68] 冯欣，应天玉，李明泽，等. 哈尔滨市热岛效应与绿色空间消长的关系 [J]. 东北林业大学学报，2007，35（05）：55 - 60

[69] 张春玲，余华，宫鹏，等. 武汉市地表亮温与植被覆盖关系定量分析 [J]. 地理科学，2009，29 (05)：741 - 744

[70] FAN H L，SAILOR D J. Modeling the impacts of anthropogenic heating on the urban climate of Philadelphia：a comparison of implementations in two PBL schemes [J]. Atmospheric Environment，2005，39（01）：73 - 84

[71] 彭少麟，周凯，叶有华，等. 市热岛效应研究进展 [J]. 生态环境，2005，14（04）：574 - 579

[72] 马跃良，陈彧，蔡睿. 广州市城区热岛效应的遥感应用研究 [J]. 云南地理环境研究，2009，21 (01)：83 - 88

[73] 苏伟忠，杨英宝，杨桂山，等. 南京市热场分布特征及其与土地利用/覆被关系研究. 地理科学，2005，25（06）：697 - 704

[74] 陈志，俞炳丰，胡汪洋. 城市热岛效应的灰色评价与预测 [J]. 西安交通大学学报，2004，38（09）：985 - 988

[75] 曹进，曾光明，石林，等. 基于 RS 和 GIS 的长沙城市热岛效应与 TSP 污染耦合关系 [J]. 生态环境，2007，16（01）：12 - 17

[76] 张云海，李法云，刘闽. 沈阳城市热岛变化趋势及其与 TSP 相关关系的初步分析 [J]. 环境保护科学，2004，30（02）：1 - 3

[77] Karl T R，Diaz H F，Kukla G. Urbanization：its detection and effect in the United States climate record [J]. Journal of Climatology，1988，1：1099 - 1123

[78] Mitchell，J. M. Jr.，The thermal climate of citis. Symp. Air over Cities. Symp. Air over Cities，U. S. Public Health Serv.，Publ. SEC Tech. Kept.，A62 - 5，1961，131 - 145

[79] Oke，T. R.. City size and the urban heat islands. Atmospheric Environment，1973，7：769 - 779

[80] 夏叡，李云梅，王桥，等．无锡市城市扩张与热岛响应的遥感分析［J］．地球信息科学学报，2009，11（05）：677－684

[81] 程兴宏，徐祥德，张胜军，等．北京地区热岛非均匀分布特征的卫星遥感—地面观测综合变分分析［J］．气候与环境研究，2007，12（05）：683－693

[82] 屈右铭，蔡荣辉，霍林，等．MODIS数据以及变分订正技术在长沙城市热岛特征分析中的应用［J］．湖南农业大学学报（自然科学版），2010，36（01）：100－106

[83] Kim Y，Baik J. Daily maximum urban heat island intensity in large cities of Korea［J］. Theor Appl Climatol 2004（79）：151－164

[84] 纪瑞鹏，张喜民，李刚，等．沈阳等6城市热岛效应卫星监测研究［J］．辽宁气象，2000（4）：22－23

[85] L. J. Hua，Z. G. Ma，W. D. Guo. The impact of urbanization on air temperature across China. Theoretical and Applied Climatology. 2008，93：179－194

[86] 杨士弘，张茂光，曾荣青．广州城市热岛分析［J］．华南师范大学学报（自然科学版），1984（02）：113－118

[87] 何泽能，李永华，陈志军．重庆市2006年夏季城市热岛分析［J］．热带气象学报，2005，24（05）：527－533

[88] Park H S. Features of the heat island in Seoul and it s surrounding cities［J］. Atmos. Environ.，1986，20：1859－1866

[89] 王喜全，王自发，郭虎．北京“城市热岛”效应现状及特征［J］．气候与环境研究，2006，11（05）：627－636

[90] Ackerman B. Temporal march of the Chicago heat island［J］. J. Climate Appl. Meteor.，1985，24：547－554

[91] 初子莹，任国玉．北京地区城市热岛强度变化对区域温度序列的影响［J］．气象学报，2005，63（04）：534－541

[92] 司鹏，李庆祥，李伟，等．城市化对深圳气温变化的贡献［J］．大气科学学报，2010，33（01）：110－117

[93] 谢志清，杜银，曾燕，等．长江三角洲城市带扩展对区域温度变化的影响［J］．地理学报，2007，62（07）：717－727

[94] 周雅清，任国玉．城市化对华北地区最高、最低气温和日较差变化趋势的影响［J］．高原气象，2009，28（05）：1158－1166

[95] 白虎志，任国玉，张爱英，等．城市热岛效应对甘肃省温度序列的影响［J］．高原气象，2006，25（01）：90－95

[96] 司鹏，李庆祥，李伟．城市化进程对中国东北部气温增暖的贡献检测［J］．气象，2010，36（02）：13－22

[97] 方锋，白虎志，赵红岩，等．中国西北地区城市化效应及其在增暖中的贡献率［J］．高原气象，2007，26（03）：579－585

[98] 宋艳玲，张尚印．北京市近40年城市热岛效应研究［J］．中国生态农业学报，2003，11（04）：126－129

[99] 郑祚芳，范水勇，王迎春．城市热岛效应对北京夏季高温的影响［J］．应用气象学报，2006，17（S1）：48－54

[100] 谈建国，郑有飞，彭丽．城市热岛对上海夏季高温热浪的影响［J］．高原气象，2008，27（S1）：144－150

[101] Bornstein R，L eRoyM. Urban barrier effects on convective and frontal thunder storms［C］. Extended Abstracts，Fourth Conf. on Mesoscale Processes，Boulder，CO.，25—29 Jan，1990

[102] Shepherd J M，Pierce H，NegriA J. Rainfall modification by major urban areas：Observations from spaceborne rain radar on the TRMM satellite［J］. J. Appl. Meteor.，2002，41：689－701

[103] 束炯．上海城市在热岛和海风锋影响下特大暴雨的初步分析［J］．华东师范大学学报（自然科学版），1987（04）：81－87

[104] Bornstein R，L in Q L. Urban heat islands and summertime convective thunderstorms in Atlanta：three case studies［J］. Atmospheric Environment，2000，34：507－516

[105] 陈云浩，史培军，李晓兵．不同热力背景对城市降雨（暴雨）的影响（Ⅰ）——降雨分布的空间差异．自然灾害学报，2001，10（02）：37－42

[106] 孙继松，舒文军．北京城市热岛效应对冬夏季降水的影响研究［J］．大气科学，2007，31（02）：311－321

[107] 蒙伟光，闫敬华，扈海波．热带气旋背景条件下的城市效应与广州夏季雷暴［J］．中国科学（D辑：地球科学），2007，37（12）：1660－1668

[108] 张凯杨，许春晓，崔桂香，等．城市热岛成因及其对污染物扩散影响的数值模拟．气象与环境学报，2007，23（03）：10－15

[109] 彭希珑，邹寒山，何宗健．城市热岛效应对城市生态系统的影响及其对策研究．江西科学，2003，21（03）：257－259

[110] Jonsson P，Bennet C，Eliasson I，et al. Suspended particulate matter and its relation to the urban climate in Dares Salaam，Tanzania［J］. Atmospheric Environment，2004，38：4175－4181

[111] Kim S W，Yoon S C，Won J. G，et al. Ground-based remote sensing measurements of aerosol and ozone in an urban area：A case study of mixing height evolution and its effects on Ground-level ozone concentrations［J］. Atmospheric Environment，2007，41：7069－7081

[112] Kevin C，Christian H，Barry L. Estimating the effects of increased urbanization on surface meteorology and ozone concentrations in the New York City metropolitan region［J］. Atmospheric Environment，2007，41：1803－1819

[113] 徐祥德，周秀骥，施晓晖．城市群落大气污染源影响的空间结构及尺度特征［J］．中国科学，2005，35（增刊）：1－19

# 现代休闲产业与休闲经济

新中国成立60年来，已产生了翻天覆地的变化。从解放之初在贫困线上挣扎到改革开放后小康生活的到来，人民的生活也发生了巨大改变；从先生产后生活，到休闲经济的出现，从农业社会到工业社会、信息化社会，如今又迎来了休闲产业时代。休闲经济将通过引入休闲规划，引导人们进入更积极、更高质量的生活。

## 一、休闲经济概况

### 1. 休闲经济的产生

休闲产业是工业化社会高度发达的产物，19世纪中叶初露端倪，20世纪80年代进入快速发展的时期。1999年第12期美国《时代》杂志，封面文章描绘的就是新世纪初的社会形态。文章指出，随着知识经济时代的来临，将使未来社会以史无前例的速度变化。2015年前后，发达国家将进入“休闲（经济）时代”，休闲将成为人类生活的重要组成部分。据美国权威人士预测，休闲、娱乐活动、旅游业将成为下一个经济大潮，席卷世界各地。专门提供休闲的产业在2015年将会主导劳务市场，在美国的国民生产总值中将占有一半的份额，各种创新技术可以让人把生命中的50%的时间用于休闲。

休闲经济的出现是社会发展的必然，休闲经济首先是建筑于一个生产力高度发展的社会——普遍的“有闲”和“有钱”构成了它的物质基础。而传统经济学在学科范围内对整个社会普遍“有闲”与“有钱”的消费行为的阐释已显得力不从心，与传统经济学相比，休闲经济更侧重“以人为本”。

### 2. 休闲经济的特征与本质

休闲经济是以人的休闲消费、休闲心理、休闲行为、休闲需求为考察对象，以满足人的个性、多样性、多元性发展为目的，研究人类休闲行为和经济现象之间互动规律的一门人文社会科学。休闲经济依托的四大产业包括了旅游产业、娱乐产业、体育竞赛与健身产业、文化产业，是经济领域非常重要的部分。

休闲经济的表现形态主要侧重人的体验、欣赏、情感表达方式，以及由此传递出的供给与消费需求信息。使各类服务、市场、营销、企业策划、产品生产、社会组织的出发点都能建筑于这些方面的基础之上。

休闲经济考察的对象不仅是物，更重要的是人，包括人的休闲动机、休闲心理、休闲模式以及非物质形态休闲资源的科学合理配置等。

休闲是消费活动的重要条件之一。休闲消费的需求涉及每一个人，它不仅具有经济和营销意义，而且具有重要的文化和社会意义。这个新的消费需求，不仅仅是物质方面的产品，而更多的是满足休闲消费需要的文化精神产品。由此，它将引起新的产业链和新的社会文化关系的变化。

休闲经济在经济学研究范围的拓展中崛起，经济学研究范围的拓展，又是在与其他学科的交叉与融合中进行的。而休闲经济尤其需要借助哲学、社会学、心理学、行为学、市场营销学等多学科的介入，休闲经济与传统经济有很大的差别。

休闲经济是在经济结构和社会结构发生变革的基础上，突出“以人为本”，强调社会和谐、生态、环保、低能耗、高效益，以无形资源替代有形资源，以经济资本、文化资本、社会资本、人力资本共同推进经济繁荣为己任，以物质财富和精神财富相平衡的一种崭新的经济形态。

**3. 休闲经济的社会影响**

（1）参与经济创造

我国现行的休假制度在推动休闲经济的形成、促进休闲产业的发展等方面作用是巨大的，尤其为促进产业结构的调整、拉动内需、解决失业、盘活经济、繁荣市场立下了汗马功劳。“黄金周”的消费热潮充分体现了我国休闲经济的发展潜力。

（2）带动消费、调节再分配

近100年来，随着物质生产的极大丰富，事实上，“消费已成为为数众多的人的主要休闲选择”。如果没有夜生活和周末，娱乐业将会崩溃；如果没有假期，旅游业将会衰落。实际上，是休闲使得工业资本主义走向成熟。在这里，休闲新的合理性被展现出来了。正是由于休闲消费的普遍存在，才使各种休闲产业不断诞生，从而为解决就业创造了条件。

（3）影响未来工作方式

休闲作为一个新的社会经济现象，对人类未来工作方式必将产生深刻的影响：

1）知识经济社会的来临，使得社会生产力以空前的速度向前发展，人为物质生产而付出的社会必要劳动时间越来越少，而人的闲暇时间将越来越多；

2）休闲对于人的“行为状态”发挥着其他形态不能替代的作用；

3）工作与休闲的界限会越来越模糊；

4）整个社会的人文关怀情结会越来越普遍；

5）在休闲产业从事服务的人越来越多，未来的工作更需要爱心和诚信；

6）城市建设发展的现实与未来需要研究休闲经济，宜居城市更需要研究休闲经济，高速城市化的中国城市尤其需要研究休闲经济。

(4) 休闲经济与其他经济活动的相互作用

奥运经济几乎涵盖了休闲经济的全部领域，北京奥运会的成功举办对中国和北京的影响是广泛而深远的，对举办城市也是一次巨大的挑战，其重要的影响有：

1）休闲经济的四大产业（旅游产业、娱乐产业、体育竞赛与健身产业、文化产业）都是奥运会最直接受益的产业。从申奥成功开始，四大产业尤其是北京的四大产业发展，迎来了历史的转折点，无论规模、层次、质量都上了一个新台阶。

2）休闲经济又为解决后奥运时期经济低谷效应问题提供了最好的渠道。国家和北京为奥运会投入资金达数千亿元人民币，奥运会后很多场馆在相当长的时间里只有很少几次的利用，大量场馆的闲置，占用了大批资金，如果经营不好，将给北京造成巨大的财政负担。而正是休闲经济的大发展，很好地解决了这个问题，尤其是奥运项目旅游，迎来了后奥运时期的大发展，并取得了良好的经济效益。

3）奥运经济对区域和城市经济整体发展的影响。最近，北京的道路交通拥堵成了电视、报纸的头条新闻，而10年前一场关于奥运村选址的讨论，在当时引发了不小的轰动。中央电视台还在黄金时段由主持人与规划专家进行了热烈的讨论，其中讨论的热点是奥运村应选址在北京中轴线的北部（即奥运村现址），还是选址在北京与天津之间靠近北京东南部。最后的结果是大家有目共睹的，奥运会已经举办，并已取得巨大的成功，但由于奥运村选址所引发的争论并未结束，北京的道路交通拥堵再次引发了人们对当初奥运村选址的关注。这也从一个侧面反映了休闲经济对城市建设发展的影响，影响奥运村选址的因素有很多，有政治的，经济的（包括休闲经济的）以及奥运本身的。不少专家认为：将奥运村建在北京和天津之间，是北京调整城市结构由单中心转变为多中心城市的最后一次机会了，也是彻底解决北京城市交通拥堵以及其他城市弊端的唯一途径。争论还在继续，带给人们思考的问题是，休闲经济对城市发展的影响是越来越大了，城市发展建设也需要越来越多地关注休闲经济。

## 二、中国休闲经济存在的问题

从目前中国的生产力水平看，休闲显然已成为我们这个时代的特征之一，虽然我国城市大部分劳动人口仍从事第二产业制造业的劳动，总体上仍有相当比例的人群已经从繁重的体力劳动中解放出来；标志着人从满足现实的基本生活需要转向对精神生活的向往；标志着计划经济体制向市场经济体制转变的过程中，已由传统的生产——消费模式逐渐地转向消费——生产的模式；标志着人开始从有限的发展转向全面地发展自己的历史阶段。

### 1. 休闲需求中存在的问题

尽管近几年我国休闲经济有了很大的发展，但实际上人们只是在工作和休闲时间上与世界接轨，而在休闲的意识、形式和内容上仍然在很大程度上沿袭着传统，只是用更多传统意义上的休息（而非休闲）来填充新的闲暇时间。休闲需求指向的相对单一，反映了休闲意识的落后，制约着休闲产业的发展。因此，倡导科学健康丰富的休闲活动，清除各种意识障碍，是走向大众休闲时代的前提。

**2. 休闲供给中存在的问题**

由于长期以来强调重视劳动，轻视休闲，休闲的供给严重不足。不仅公共性供给不足，商业性供给也相对匮乏。

**3. 对休闲经济认识的问题**

各地政府对休闲经济与区域和城市社会经济整体发展的相互作用还缺乏深刻的认识。快速城市化阶段的中国迫切需要对休闲经济有更深刻的了解和运用（包括城市规划中是否需要更多地考虑休闲经济的成分）。

对休闲经济的重要性认识还不够。旅游产业、娱乐产业、体育竞赛与健身产业、文化产业是休闲经济的主要支撑。人们对它们之间的联系和作用机制、休闲经济本身的特点和规律、贡献尚缺乏深入研究，人们还没有认识到休闲经济与生产经济具有相等的社会地位，且休闲经济的地位和比重正在快速提高，普遍的休闲经济社会即将到来（发达国家部分已经进入休闲经济时代），对其深入研究的必要性和迫切性正日益显现（北京后奥运时代的发展，上海后世博时代的发展就是一个最好的例证）。

传播信息上的不平衡。目前我国休闲业发展刚起步，经营性娱乐场所多而公益性的休闲设施少。同时在传播信息方面也表现出明显的不平衡：娱乐信息多而知识信息少；模拟信息（如主题公园等）、虚假信息和冗余信息多（如神怪世界等）而真实信息少（如博物馆等）；人文信息多（如民俗、民间故事和文学名著衍生的主题公园等）而自然信息少（如自然历史博物馆等）。这种不平衡严重制约着人们休闲活动的多样化与进一步提高。

总而言之，休闲经济就是人类社会发展到一定阶段时的产物，是历史的必然。

## 三、休闲产业发展

休闲产业是以旅游业、娱乐业、服务业为龙头形成的经济形态和产业系统，已成为国家经济发展的重要支柱产业。

休闲产业涉及国家公园、博物馆、体育（运动项目、设施、设备、维修等）、影视、交通、旅行社、导游、纪念品、餐饮业、社区服务以及由此形成的产业群（链）。休闲产业不仅包括物质产品的生产，而且也为人的文化精神生活的追求提供保障。

在欧美国家，休闲产业十分发达。有关数据表明，美国的休闲产业已处于国民生产总值第一的位置，其就业人口占全部劳动力的四分之一。

**1. 中国目前的休闲方式及特征**

在我国，休闲方式更多地依靠电视等大众传媒。据抽样调查，城市居民平均每天用于看电视、听广播、阅读报刊杂志的时间占一天休闲时间总量的48.6%。同时城市居民的休闲生活更多依靠的是各种音响电器等工业产品和专业演艺人员，更多地涉足商业休闲娱乐场所，并紧跟时尚。这些都是典型的工业社会休闲文明的特征。

我国国民目前存在着涣散松弛、休闲和工作时间混淆不清的时间结构以及不遵时守时的习惯，是有其经济体制上的原因，在一定程度上也是小农的时间观念在制度层面和懒散的时间利用方式上的反映。

**2. 美国出现的后工业社会休闲文明形态及社会观念**

美国已进入后工业化的知识社会发展阶段，知识社会特点为：

休闲价值升值，从最大限度地进行经济增长转而通过生活方式的变化而最大限度地保证生存幸福，最大限度地提高生活质量。知识社会的主要生产力要素是知识、是创新和创造力。对自由时间的需求上升必然导致休闲地位上升和时间价值的升值。

休闲对以人为本的社会结构来说，反映了人生价值观的变化。人们把时间看得比金钱更重要，可说是美国这个国家的主流“消费心态”。

到2015年，人类将走出信息时代的高峰期而进入休闲时代，首先是在美国，休闲经济产值将占到GNP的50%以上。

**3. 新型休闲形态引发的社会问题**

如果觉得时间成为一种最稀缺资源的话，那么这种短缺不是为了进行经济生产，而是“希望以一种历史上从未有过的高速度来消费产品和体验人生”，“渴望享受一切使人愉快的经历，渴望尽可能多地参与人类体验，这是一种极度的贪婪”。人们花钱买种种感受：体验赌博，环游欧洲，观看他人的隐私，乘橡皮筏漂流，通过种种治疗来改变人际关系，以及诸如此类人们想买的体验。人们对不同生活体验的追求总体上呈上升趋势。

**4. 休闲产业类别**

休闲产业的具体服务项目涉及购物中心、宾馆、田径运动场、高尔夫球场、网球俱乐部、篮球俱乐部、健身俱乐部、剧院、主题公园（如迪斯尼乐园）、游泳池、私人经营的休闲会所（含游泳池）、划船俱乐部和码头、马术场、收费的垂钓园、出租的钓鱼船、天然小径探险、岩洞探险、风景浏览、狩猎向导、射击场、台球厅、网吧、棋牌室、保龄球馆、滑雪场、溜冰场、假日农场、度假牧场、度假宿营地、野营中心、探险旅行和野炊场所等。

还有那些为以上活动提供咨询服务，进行经营管理和那些生产、配送、销售各类休闲活动器材和娱乐装备的行业。

**5. 休闲产业的发展趋势**

休闲产业的“娱乐因素”将成为产品与服务竞争的关键，在这种“娱乐导向消费”的趋势下，会有越来越多的产品、服务提供娱乐功能和娱乐因素，只要能让人感受到轻松有趣，跟休闲娱乐甚至文化艺术有关的人、事、物都是娱乐经济不可或缺的组成部分。“娱乐经济时代”会继“服务经济”之后进入“体验经济时代”。

商品、服务对消费者来说都是外在的，但体验是内在的，是个人在形体、情绪、知识上参与的所得。各人的体验不会完全一样，因为体验来自个人的心境与事件的互动。创造体验是娱乐的核心。

感情、故事、传奇、生活方式将构成休闲商品的主要价值，人们在购买一种休闲商品时很少注意它的使用功能，人们的注意力将主要集中在休闲商品中所包含的伦理方面、社会方面、情感方面的价值。

所谓的“休闲经济时代”、“娱乐经济时代”、“体验经济时代”、“梦幻经济时代”都是以时间商品化为特征的“超资本主义”经济时代。在21世纪前50年内，情感、体验、故事、娱乐、传奇、生活方式，将构成休闲商品的主要价值和“卖点”，而娱乐因素、情感、体验等等将渗透到休闲产品和服务之中，构成休闲产业竞争力的关键因素，信息技术、网络技术将为人们提供无所不能的服务，日常生活中将出现大量购买休闲商品的活动。

## 四、休闲产业发展的成功案例

2004年3月，东莞市获得全国“篮球城市”称号。说到东莞篮球，就不能不提到宏远篮球俱乐部，一个诞生在广东著名的体育之乡东莞的篮球俱乐部。

### 1. 发展历程

1993年12月28日，广东宏远篮球俱乐部在东莞成立。1995年，宏远男篮第一次参加甲级联赛就获得亚军（冠军是著名的八一队）。2003年，宏远成了CBA宣布唯一实现赢利的俱乐部，此后每个赛季，都实现了年均百万余元的赢利。

2003—2004年、2004—2005年、2005—2006年俱乐部又连续三个赛季夺得了CBA联赛总冠军。继CBA联赛三连冠后，宏远（东莞银行冠名）再次站在2007—2008年，2008—2009年CBA联赛的巅峰，并取得第十一届全运会男篮冠军。自2002—2003年赛季起，连续7个赛季进入CBA总决赛。

宏远俱乐部成立以来，为国家队输送了李群、朱芳雨、杜锋、易建联、王仕鹏等国家队员。最近，又向国家队输送了未来之星陈江华。宏远的篮球成就值得骄傲。

### 2. 经验总结

东莞现已拥有三家职业篮球俱乐部——宏远男篮、新世纪男篮和骏达女篮。作为中国成功的（体育）休闲产业，他们的发展历程值得关注，成功有赖于：

*(1) 经济发展环境*

珠三角进入休闲经济初级阶段。东莞是著名的体育之乡，有良好的群众体育基础（除篮球外，足球、游泳、田径、龙舟等体育项目也有出色的成绩）。目前，东莞市有2314个向公众免费开放的篮球场，1044 个学校室外篮球场，工厂、企业和机关事业单位露天篮球场 1 万多个。作为一个地级市，东莞的篮球运动场馆规模令人叹服，这是宏远篮球运动成功的基础。

（2）发展模式

当初，宏远俱乐部创立目的是为宏远集团进行品牌宣传，广东宏远俱乐部是国内第一个完全市场化运作的篮球俱乐部。宏远俱乐部和广东省运动技术学院合作共建，球员的关系、产权、经营权均属于宏远，学院进行业务指导。这一运作模式从俱乐部成立之日起，至今已有 10 余年。

俱乐部的主要收入来自三个方面：门票、冠名和广告（电视转播费等），主要服务对象是赞助商、球迷、媒体。其中，球票占的份额很大，宏远俱乐部是全国经营最好的篮球俱乐部。

俱乐部的发展前景取决于 CBA 以及中国篮球的整体环境，只有 CBA 水平真正提高了，全国篮球球市发展起来了，置身其中的俱乐部才能有更多的发展空间。

## 五、小结

人类对“进步”本身的看法正在发生根本的变化。传统意义上的进步往往意味着物质生活水平的不断提高。时至今日，物质财富的极大满足，促使人们渴望追求充实的精神生活。进步将越来越意味着不断地提高生命质量，讲求生活品位，而且希望以一种更为健康的方式生存下去。千百年来，人类一直在致力于改造世界，而在新的世纪中，人类将更多地致力于改造自身。

（作者：容志军，广州市都市发展研究会）

### 参考文献

[1] 吴承照．现代城市游憩规划设计理论与方法．1998

[2] 王雅林，董鸿扬．构建生活美．2003

[3] 吴承忠．奥运机遇拉动下的北京休闲经济发展．2005

[4] 经济展望．经济展望杂志社，2009（07，11）

# 快速城市化进程中几个土地问题的反思

## 一、引言

历史地看，国家的发展，甚至人类社会的发展，实际上是一个逐步城市化的过程，只不过在现代社会，这个过程加速了。改革开放后，我国社会经济发展重新进入到正轨，在经济体制改革的强力推动之下，迅速进入到了快速城市化时期。城市化水平从改革开放之初的不到20%增长到迄今的将近50%，城市数量从最初的不到200个增长到600多个，建制镇数量达到2万多个，城市人口超过6亿人。快速的城市化已经并将继续成为我国经济增长的主要贡献因素，成为带动我国经济增长的火车头[1]。

随着城市化水平的日渐提高，大都市区、城市群、城市连绵地区不断增多，城市区域化、区域城市化已经成为新时期我国城市化的重要趋势。城市的发展离不开土地，土地是城市发展的空间载体，是与物质资本、人力资本同等重要的资本要素。在城市化的进程中必然伴随着区域土地结构的变化，主要表现为非农业用地不断增多、农用地不断减少以及土地价格的不断上升。在我国，改革开放后，作为经济体制改革重要组成部分的土地制度改革取得了重大突破，在传统计划经济向现代市场经济的重大转型中扮演了极其重要的角色，成为中国城市快速扩张、空间优化及工业高速发展的重要动力。一方面，早期廉价的土地资源成为我国吸引境外投资、激发民间投资的重要优势，推动了我国自下而上的快速工业化，郊区城市化推动了城市规模的大幅度扩张；另一方面，土地的“招拍挂”出让为各城市政府带来了巨额的地租收入，为快速的城市发展提供了雄厚的物质基础。回顾30年来我国的土地制度改革，可以发现，虽然我国的土地制度改革成就卓著，但是仍存在许多复杂问题与矛盾尚待解决。毫无疑问，土地制度作为城市化机制的核心，其影响社会经济的长远走势与城市化的进程，土地制度的改革仍然是我国经济体制改革的一个重点。基于此，本文将在检视当前我国城市化进程中土地财政过度依赖、房地产市场失调、土地低效利用等问题的基础上，重点从土地有偿使用制度、土地产权制度和土地市场制度等角度出发进行剖析和反思，并尝试探索相应的改革路径。

## 二、主要问题

### 1. 土地有偿使用与土地财政依赖

土地财政即地方政府过度依赖土地所带来的相关税费和收入的现象[2]。建国以后至改革开放以前，我国对城市土地实行的是无偿、无限期、无流动性的管理制度，对土地的使用配置通过行政划拨方式进行，土地使用不合理、效率低、土地资产流失、城市财政拮据等问题严重[3]。20 世纪 70 年代末和 80 年代初，我国开始以土地作为股份与外商合资，广东和上海等地开始试点实行土地使用权有偿转让。1987 年深圳经济特区突破了当时《宪法》对出租土地的禁令，敲响了土地拍卖第一槌。1988 年七届全国人民代表大会第一次会议通过了《宪法（修正案）》，明确规定“土地的使用权可以依照法律的规定转让”。同年，七届全国人大常委会议通过了《关于修改〈中华人民共和国土地管理法〉的决定》。修改后的《土地管理法》明确规定，“国有土地和集体所有的土地的使用权可以依法转让”，“国家依法实行国有土地有偿使用制度”。这次适宪性修改，一举扫清了土地使用制度改革面临的法律障碍，为土地作为生产要素进入市场开辟出一条法治之路，也为地方政府提供了一条“生财之道”。当时规定，在进行必要扣除后，土地出让金实行中央与地方分成。从 1994 年至今，土地出让金不再上缴中央财政，全部留归地方。从此之后，土地出让金收入成为地方政府预算外收入的重要来源。

20 世纪 90 年代，我国的土地出让主要采取的是协议出让的形式，即地方政府以协议的形式向土地需求者出让土地，投资者与地方政府就土地价格进行协商谈判，议价空间较大，寻租机会较多，导致土地出让中的国有资产流失和腐败问题。2001 年《国务院关于加强国有土地资产管理的通知》出台，明确规定四类经营性用地一律实行土地使用权招标、拍卖和挂牌出让。由于经营性用地使用权出让大多使用拍卖的形式，而以拍卖方式获取土地的主要标准是价高者得。近年来，我国地方政府的土地出让收入持续大幅度增加。2005 年全国土地出让收入仅为 2000 多亿元；2006 年全国土地出让收入为 7000 亿元人民币；2007 年全国土地出让收入超过 12000 亿元人民币；2008 年土地出让收入 9600 多亿元人民币；2009 年土地出让收入 1.59 万亿元人民币[4]；而 2010 年土地出让收入达到 2.7 万亿元，同比增 70.4%；“十一五”期间，我国土地出让收入超 7 万亿元[5]。一些城市的年土地出让收入超千亿元，个别城市的土地出让收入已占城市财政收入的半壁江山。

### 2. 城市快速扩张与土地低效利用

我国实行的是土地公有制，其中城市土地为国家所有，农村土地为集体所有，政府部门在土地的保护和合理利用上负有非常重要的责任。但由于发展的冲动、区域间的竞争以及制度滞后和监控缺位，导致土地利用还比较低效粗放，浪费现象严重。其中最主要的表现是快速城市化进程中的城市无序蔓延扩张，主要表现在土地非农化的速度明显超过了人口增长的速度，而单位建设用地效益较低。以北京市为例，1996—2004 年间非农建设用地共增加了 965 平方公里，年均增长率为 4.62%，相当于同期总人口增长速度的两倍多，而单位经济增长消耗的土地较多，每增加亿元 GDP 需增加建设用地 36 公顷[6]。再以杭州为例，其主城建成区面积从 1990 年的 69 平方公里增长到 2005 年的 255.09 平方公里，增长了 3.69 倍，而主城非农业人口则从 1990 年的 109.97 万人增长到 2005 年的 190.29 万人，增长了 1.73 倍，城市建成区面积相对城市人口增长来说明显过快[7]。

由于建设用地的粗放利用，我国城市建设用地的利用效益普遍偏低[8]。即便是深圳、上海等经济发达，土地资源非常紧张的地区，建设用地的利用效益，与新加坡、我国香港等地相比，仍然有较大差距（见图 1）。

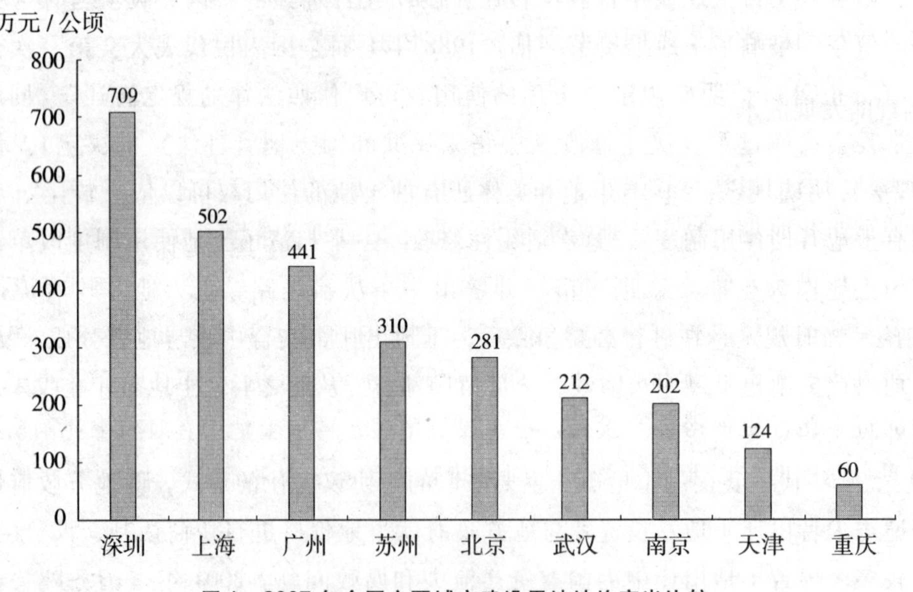


**图 1　2007 年全国主要城市建设用地地均产出比较**

资料来源：广州市土地利用总体规划（2006—2020 年）

### 3. 房产市场发育与市场调控失调

近年来我国房地产市场在快速发育的同时存在明显失调现象，主要表现在三个方面：一是价格失调。房地产价格上涨过快，与市民收入的增长不成比例，房价收入比高位运行，中低收入者的购房压力持续增加。2010 年城镇居民人均可支配收入约为 18900 元，农民工年均工资为 19200 元。按城镇居民每人 30 平方米和农民工家庭人均 20 平方米，以及城镇居民和农民工家庭每户分别有 3、3.5 口人计算，其房价收入比分别为 8.76、10.06。其中，城镇居民房价收入比比 2009 年的 8.3 上升了 0.46。按照房价收入的支付能力及家庭负债风险性考虑，房价收入比保持在 3 ~ 6 较为合适；而按照目前的收入比水平，直接后果就是，85% 的需购买新住宅的城镇居民家庭都无力购买[9]。二是功能失调。随着近年房价的持续高位运行、股市的低迷，住房的保值增值作用日渐突出，成为一种越来越重要的投资品。相当一部分消费者是基于投资套利而不是居住需要购买住房，房地产市场炒风日盛。三是对象失调。住房分配高度不均衡。少数高收入阶层拥有众多住房，而真正需要住房的中低收入阶层购买不起住房。房价过高，已经成为我国最为突出的民生问题。房地产市场失调导致城市生活压力越来越大，“宜居性”不断降低。由于缺乏适宜的住房，外来人口对城市的认同感、归属感降低，房价高昂的城市越来越难以吸引优秀的人才，从而阻碍了城市化进程。

## 三、问题分析

我国是一个发展中国家，一个人口众多、地域辽阔的大国，一个正处于从落后封闭迈向富强开放、从传统农业国家向现代城市国家转型、从计划经济体制向市场经济体制转型的国家。所以，分析当前我国土地问题必须在整个时代的大背景下进行。

### 1. 客观的发展需求

我国土地问题的出现与我国处于快速城市化的发展阶段有着非常密切的关系。近年来我国处于快速城市化时期，城市土地需求量大，而土地管理又非常严厉，建设用地指标有限。因此，城市土地供需失衡，土地价格急剧上升。有关研究显示，近年来我国土地出让收入的增加，主要是由于价格大幅度攀高所导致，并不是因为出让土地数量的增多。一个个“地王”的相继涌现，推高了地价与房价。而房价的暴涨，又反过来使得地价进一步上涨。同时，土地的资本化，更使得地产投机、房产投机增多，再加上消费者对未来我国房地产价格还将上涨的心理预期，以及通货膨胀、国际热钱等因素，从而使得我国房地产价格持续上涨，调控效果不佳。

当前，我国土地问题的出现也与地方政府的发展压力有关。以GDP为风向标的发展水平和政绩考量客观上迫使地方政府比拼经济总量与增长速度、城市规模与现代化设施，一味地强调将城市做大做强，而忽视经济发展的质量、社会的公平正义和谐、资源利用的可持续性，形成典型的“见物不见人”的局面。这一局面的直接结果是，将发展简单地归化为增长，各城市热衷于扩充空间、圈占土地，竞相让利（包括压低产业地价和过量供给土地）以吸引工业投资，促进工业总产值的快速增加，同时通过发展产业获得巨额的土地出让收入以壮大地方财力。一度被崇尚尔后又被广为诟病的“经营城市”的理念是这种“发展”的产物，同时也写照了国人对发展内涵的领悟过程。

### 2. 转型期的制度滞后

我国正处于社会转型期，当前土地问题的出现与我国目前的有关制度设计有着十分密切的关系，其中，中央—地方财权、事权划分又是一个非常重要的因素。客观地说，1994年的分税制改革在不减少地方财政支出的情况下将“财政上收”。随着财权的部分上收和事权的逐渐下放，地方政府承担了较多事务，如地方政府在教育、医疗卫生、社会保障、住房、城镇建设等方面均承担着非常重要的责任，但财力却有限。因此，地方政府只能尽力开拓财源，其中，土地就是一个重要的财源。

土地财政的产生有两个基本原因或曰条件。首先，我国尚是一个发展中国家，正处于快速城市化阶段，政府财力有限，也缺乏人才、技术，唯一能利用的资源就是土地。因而“土地财政”对于缓解地方政府财力不足、公共品供给融资难，创造就业机会和提升城市化水平等都有很大促进作用。赵燕菁[10]就认为土地财政模式适用于城市化的加速阶段，财政税（物业税）模式适用于城市化的稳定阶段。“土地财政”解决了地方政府债务市场缺位、政府信用不足的困难，通过土地收益高额回报，地方政府在城市化最困难的起步阶段筹集了大量资金，而土地收益反过来又支持了产业的发展——正是由于大规模的地方政府补贴，才支持了中国产品超乎寻常的竞争力，才有了大规模的农民工就业，才有了中央财政收入的高速增长，才使得中国城市得以提供远较同等经济水平国家更高水平的公共服务。因此，“土地财政”是中国经济高速成长的主要动力，也是近年来所谓“中国发展模式”的核心。从历史的眼光来看，这一模式堪称我国改革开放以来一个重要的制度创新[10]。此外，现行的土地批租管理制度容许土地出让年期可达70年（工业用地50年）且一次性收取出让金。地方政府任期一般一届五年，如果通过银行贷款融资，五年之内需要归还，如不归还则形成债务。试想，一个市长如果卸任时欠了很多债务，他贡献再大，评价也可能是负面的。但通过土地筹措资金，相当于一借就是70年，且无须偿还，何乐而不为呢。

目前的土地出让制度对于土地财政而言，是一种透支行为，将未来几十年的钱提前借用了，不但可能助长短视行为，还可能孕育巨大的财政和金融风险，危及整个国民经济的可持续发展。国有土地毕竟是一种特殊的公共资源，如果将土地供应目标定位于地方财政的利益最大化，这有悖于其基本属性，也有悖于国有即为全民所有这一基本属性。在这种利益联结机制下，难免产生高价地进而产生高房价，房价不断上涨，就会导致住房不断向富裕家庭集中，大多数居民家庭获得住房的能力减弱、机会减少[11]。有学者认为应从日本长达近20年的经济泡沫、土地泡沫吸取教训：经济增长不能过度依赖土地，否则将会增大土地资源的“尾效”（Growth drag），即土地资源对经济增长形成阻力[12]。

**3. 市场分割**

新中国成立以后，我国基于户籍管理、人口迁移等制度建立了独特的城乡二元制度。城乡二元结构以放缓农村发展为代价换取工业和城市的优先发展。但是，实践证明，落后的农村、农业、农民支撑不了工业的现代化、城市的现代化，更促进不了农村、农业、农民的发展。十一届三中全会后，我国建立了联产承包责任制，推动了农村社会经济的快速发展，而粮食产量的连续增加、农村生产效率快速提高导致了农村剩余劳动力增多，为我国快速城市化提供了前提条件。

虽然随着城市各项综合改革措施的推进，土地市场迅速发展，成为社会主义市场经济体系的重要组成部分。但我国的土地市场仍然沿袭了城乡二元结构的传统：城市土地为国有土地，可以依法流转，因而发育形成了土地一级市场和土地二级市场。而农村土地则为集体土地，有限的流转只能局限在集体经济组织内部，不可直接用作为城市建设用地。因此，我国城乡土地市场是分割的，土地不能在城乡间双向的自由流动。农村集体土地变身为城市国有土地的唯一途径是经过城市政府的“征用”。农村土地只能用作农业生产，又不可流转与转变用途，经济价值很低，而一旦被征用为城市土地，其往往身价倍增。因此，农业用地和城市建设用地之间的巨大价格差，导致了城市政府有着难以抑制的征地冲动。低成本的土地获取难以避免土地的低效利用和浪费。也由于征地的低成本与土地房产市场的高回报导致政府与农民之间的博弈，引发征地管理的矛盾和冲突。

### 4. 区域差异

改革开放后，我国经济高速发展，但是，区域差异也在显著扩大，区域发展不平衡问题突出。其中主要表现在东中西部地区差异、城乡差异、大中小城市间的差异。就东中西部地区差异而言，2000 年东部 GDP 与中西部和东北地区合计 GDP 相差 4833 亿元，2009 年差距扩大到 27109 亿元[13]。就城乡差异而言，2000 年基尼系数达到了 0.437，超过了国际公认的 0.4 的警戒线，进入了收入分配差距较大阶段，到 2008 年，居民收入分配系数已高达 0.458[13]。而大中小城市间的差异，则主要表现在大城市依靠其行政影响力可以获得更多资源、依靠其集聚效益可以获得更好的经济效益、吸引更多的境内外投资、提供更多就业机会而呈现出更快的发展势头，也可以为市民提供更好的基本公共服务。

我国区域差异的持续扩大导致了人口、投资进一步向东部沿海发达地区集中，向大城市尤其是一线城市集中。这一方面导致发达地区的人地矛盾十分剧烈，城市过度膨胀，环境和生态问题越来越突出，影响了这些地区的可持续发展。另一方面人流、物流、资金流和信息流的过度集中加剧了土地和房产市场供需矛盾，房地产市场失调，影响社会和谐。

## 四、路径思考

土地问题是一个极其复杂、相互关联、风险叠加的问题集合，因此，土地问题的解决需要从多方面考虑政策设计与制度安排。以下仅从土地管理的角度提出关于解决上述问题的路径思考。

### 1. 秉承科学发展精神

如前所述，土地问题产生的重要原因是由片面追求经济增长、忽视了资源保护与社会公平正义所致，因此，我们有必要以可持续发展理念来调整和完善我们的土地政策。西方有一个谚语“罗马不是一天建成的”，显然我们的城市化也将是一个持续的过程。急功近利，急于求成，势必欲速则不达。我们可以从三个方面研究可持续的土地管理路径。

首先，要真正树立科学发展观、“包容性增长”的理念，改变 GDP 至上、盲目追求发展速度的政绩观。为此，要形成自上而下科学合理的政绩考核机制，以此来引导地方政府树立正确的政绩观，加快转变经济增长方式、城市发展方式，将民生幸福、和谐发展、可持续发展作为首要的发展目标，也作为最重要的政绩考核指标。要理顺中央—地方政府财权、事权关系，在激励地方积极发展经济的同时，也要引导地方形塑合理的经济发展模式，即“不是为了发展经济而发展经济”，要让经济的发展回归其终极目标——人的发展。

其次，要进一步深化土地制度的改革。30 年前，土地制度的改革，开启了我国改革开放的序幕，推动了我国农业、工业、城市经济的持续快速发展；30 年后，土地制度的改革步入了“深水区”，不但涉及经济发展的速度、质量、竞争力，也涉及社会的公平正义、资源的持续利用，因而任重而道远。要以制度的改革创新来强化耕地的保护、促进经济的健康发展、提升城市化水平、保障社会公平正义。其中，关键是要完善土地产权制度，改革土地有偿使用制度，严格限制土地征用范围，提高土地保有成本，抑制“以地生财”的内在冲动，防范土地金融风险。

最后，要以规划为龙头有序组织土地的保护与开发利用。土地利用规划是市场经济条件下我国政府土地进行管理、经济进行干预的重要手段。土地利用规划对于土地的开发利用、用途管制应有长期安排，不仅应规划规模、发展方向，还应规划发展时序，并区隔刚性与弹性、近期与远期、经济发展与社会公平，应进一步完善土地利用规划的编制方法、编制内容，提升土地利用规划的系统性、科学性、合理性、操作性。

**2. 与发展水平相协调**

因地制宜是任何政策设计的基本原则，土地政策亦不例外。建立差别化的土地管理政策，主要原因是不同地区有着不同的经济发展水平、土地资源赋存，也面临着不同的土地需求、土地问题。就目前情况而言，土地政策更多的是强调普适性而忽略了针对性，这在一定程度上影响了区域发展与宏观调控的预期效果。因此，亟需根据区域社会经济发展水平的差异，加快构建差别化的区域土地政策体系，形成适合不同区域的土地管理政策，从而因地制宜地破解不同区域面临的土地问题，保障不同区域社会经济健康、可持续发展。对发达地区来说，矛盾的主要方面是建设用地紧缺与建设用地低效利用并存、土地出让价格急剧上涨引致的“土地财政”与高房价，因此，对发达地区应着眼于调整土地政策推动产业升级转型、提升产业用地利用效率，同时，改革土地出让方式，提高物业持有成本，抑制房价持续上涨之势。而对于发展中地区来说，存在的主要问题是资本缺乏，投资乏力，为吸引投资可以适当降低土地“门槛”，以通过“土地财政”为地方经济发展进行资本原始积累，优化城市投资环境，加快城市建设。换言之，土地管理政策应与时俱进，具有动态特征，与相应的区域发展水平相适应、相协调。

**3. 一体化的土地市场**

城乡土地市场的分割是导致我国城乡二元发展、地价和房价暴涨、农村资本稀缺、人口流动无序等问题的重要根源。建立城乡一体化的土地市场应是可探讨的我国土地制度深化改革的重要方向，也是一项非常紧迫的任务，其目标是建立主体平等、产权清晰、规则一致、竞争有序的城乡统一土地市场，让农民携土地一起直接参与工业化和城市化，而不是仅仅以农民工的身份进入城市。在政策上尽快研究改革因土地所有制不同就被赋予不同权利的二元结构，尽量避免地方政府既是土地管理者又是土地经营者，既当“裁判员”又当“运动员”，避免由于利益冲突引起土地征用过程中的矛盾，也有利于消减“土地财政”问题，同样可以让全体社会成员成为城市化的利益共同体和城市化的推手。

一体化的土地市场中更需要强化和优化政府的调控和监控职能。一是要加强土地利用规划与土地用途管制，建立健全土地流转制度，完善土地交易管理制度，避免土地投机、土地垄断、地价暴涨等问题的出现，严防市场失控。集体土地自由流转、农用地转用的根本前提是符合土地利用规划与土地用途管制，符合城市化的总部署。二是要平衡城市化带来的利益分配。城市化带来的土地增值应该为全社会共享，农民通过土地直接进入市场得到的价值应该通过合理的调节机制荫及全体社会成员，防止从一个极端走向另一个极端。

## 五、小结

改革开放以后，我国迅速进入了快速工业化、城市化时期，社会经济发展迅速，并实现了从传统封闭的计划经济国家向现代开放的市场经济国家的转变，一跃成为世界第二大经济体，土地制度改革成为推动我国快速城市化的重要动力。但是，快速的城市化进程中也暴露出了许多土地问题。比如，一方面是建设用地紧缺，另一方面是土地粗放利用；一方面是“土地财政”带来滚滚财源，另一方面是房价高昂，普通市民购房日益困难。土地问题成为阻碍我国经济社会健康发展的一大障碍。以上土地问题归结起来，均是发展中的问题，转型中的困惑，是“成长性骨痛”，导致土地问题产生的原因十分复杂。未来土地制度的改革，应以有利于长远发展、公平发展、城乡统筹发展为目标，着力于建立城乡统一土地市场，提高产业用地的利用效率和效益，逐步形成符合可持续科学发展原则的、差别化的区域土地政策，促进城市化进程协调发展。

（作者：郭仁忠，国际欧亚科学院院士，教授）

### 参考文献

[1] 王小鲁．城市化与经济增长［J］．经济社会体制比较，2002，（1）：23－32

[2] 林燕．土地财政的形成、危害及改革措施［J］．中国国土资源经济，2010，（2）：17－20

[3] 许学强，周一星，宁越敏．城市地理学（第二版）［M］．北京：高等教育出版社，2009

[4] 阮煜琳．国土资源部：近十年土地出让收入6.9万亿［EB/OL］．http://news.qq.com/a/20100203/002310.htm，2010－02－03

[5] 吴鹏．去年全国土地转让收入2.7万亿元同比增70.4%［EB/OL］．http://www.chinanews.com/cj/2011/01－08/2774258.shtml，2011－01－08

[6] 蒋芳，刘盛和，袁弘．北京城市蔓延的测度与分析［J］．地理学报，2007，62（6）：649－658

[7] 刘卫东，谭韧骠．杭州城市蔓延评估体系及其治理对策［J］．地理学报，2009，64（4）：417－425

[8] 广州市国土资源和房屋管理局．广州市土地利用总体规划（2006—2020年），广州，2010

[9] 陈佳贵．经济蓝皮书：2011 年中国经济形势分析与预测［M］．北京：社会科学文献出版社，2010

[10] 赵燕菁．财产税与城市化模式之变［J］．瞭望，2010，(39)：42－45

[11] 财经杂志．土地解密［EB/OL］．http://finance.sina.com.cn/g/20060222/18242364373.shtml，2006－02－22

[12] 李磊，张换兆，朱彤．土地“尾效”、泡沫与经济增长［J］．日本研究，2008，(3)：31－35

[13] 杨荫凯，刘利，杨俊涛．我国区域发展不平衡的基本现状与缓解对策［J］．中国经贸导刊，2010，(13)：36－37

# 专题篇

# 2010年“城市，让生活更美好”上海世博会综述

## 一、上海世博会的申办过程

### 1. 百年梦想

1893年，清末广东著名改良主义思想家郑观应在《盛世危言》中提到在上海举办世界赛会。1910年，上海名医陆士谔在其小说《新中国》中预言100年后在上海浦东举办万国博览会，并提到建有高架、立交桥和隧道。

20世纪50年代，中国共产党早期的领导人张闻天曾向毛泽东主席、周恩来总理、陈毅副总理建言，希望在建国10周年内举办一次国际博览会。之后，上海市市长汪道涵1985年4月第一次正式决定对上海举办1989年世博会做可行性研究。1988年7月、1993年2月，上海市政府多次组织专人研究上海举办世博会一事。

### 2. 中央决策

1998年底，上海市领导指示有关部门就上海举办2010年世博会进行可行性调研。1999年2月12日，市委、市政府主要领导对《关于2010年世界综合博览会的情况报告》作出批示，同意申办世博会。5月31日，上海市政府第34次常务会议决定启动2010年世博会申办工作。7月21日，上海市政府向国务院提出申办请示。11月18日，国务院领导批复同意上海的申办请示。12月，经国务院批准，中国驻国际展览局首席代表在国际展览局第126次大会上宣布中国申办2010年世博会。2000年3月17日，国务院办公厅发出“关于成立2010年上海世界博览会申办委员会的通知”，经朱镕基总理批准，国务委员吴仪担任申办委员会主任。

### 3. 制定申办2010年上海世博会工作方案

根据国际展览局的要求，世博会申办国必须提交申办报告，详细说明申办理由、举办地的政治经济文化环境，以及举办条件和措施。从2001年4月起，在国家申博委领导下，中

央有关部门、上海市有关部门的官员、学者200多人，齐心协力历时8个多月完稿，2002年1月30日提交给国际展览局。中国的申办报告共三册、15万字、400多张图片。第一册是报告正文，对国际展览局提出的12大类问题作了系统回答和全面阐述。正文前面是江泽民主席和朱镕基总理的支持信。第二册是场馆规划设计报告，包括选址地区的概况、设计理念、总体规划、主要场馆与标志性建筑的形象设计等内容。第三册是对报告正文的详细阐述和必要补充，包括参展合同、政府承诺书和支持信、附件、介绍上海概况的小册子等。国际展览局对中国申办报告的评价是：计划可行，质量卓越，无愧于一届伟大的世博会。

**4. 陈述与游说**

外交部、外经贸部、贸促会和上海市等申办委成员单位和国务院有关部门通过请国家领导人、驻外使领馆、在外投资企业、在华外资企业、外国驻华机构、华人华侨等方面做工作，开展多层面、多形式的游说拉票工作。期间，我国领导人共向有关国家领导人致电、致函或捎口信31次，在出访、会见、出席国际会议等活动中直接做有关国家领导人的工作；先后派出申博游说团组37批次，其中以中国国家元首特使名义进行申博游说的团组18批次，游说范围基本覆盖了国际展览局所有成员国。国务委员吴仪率代表团参加第131次大会，国务院副总理李岚清、国务委员吴仪率团参加第132次大会，分别作了非常精彩的陈述。整个申办过程，采取了对88个成员国“人盯人”的办法，把游说拉票工作坚持做到投票最后一刻，争取了广泛的支持。

## 二、上海世博会的筹办过程

**1. 概况**

2010年上海世博会是我国第一次举办的注册类世界博览会。自2002年我国成功申办以来，经过8年筹备，上海世博会于2010年5月1日开幕，10月31日闭幕，历时184天。本届世博会以“城市，让生活更美好”为主题，秉承“理解、沟通、欢聚、合作”的理念，充分展示了丰富多彩的人类文明成就，汇集了全球探索城市发展的共同智慧，创造了多项世博会的新纪录，成为人类文明的盛会，把世界博览会推向了新的里程碑。

上海世博会选址在特大城市中心地区，占地面积5.28平方公里，其中，凭票进入的围栏区面积3.28平方公里，配套服务区面积2平方公里，横跨黄浦江两岸，230多个展馆等公共建筑面积达250万平方米。

参展主体包括190个国家、56个国际组织、18个国际企业或企业联合体，以及国内31个省、自治区、直辖市和港澳台地区。

上海世博会的主要内容是展览、论坛和活动。参展方的展馆包括42个自建馆、42个租赁馆、11个联合馆、18个企业馆和80个城市最佳实践案例展示。主办方的展馆包括中国馆，5个主题馆，31个省、自治区、直辖市馆以及港澳台馆。论坛包括1场高峰论坛、6场主题论坛和若干场公众论坛。各类文化演艺活动超过 2 万场次，平均每天多达 100 场。

整个世博会期间，共有 7308 万人次入园参观。其中外国游客 425 万人次，平均每天近 40 万人次，单日客流最高达到 103 万多人次，创下世博会参观总人数和单日客流纪录。中国国家馆接待参观者近 930 万人次。

园区内设有 4 条地面公交线路、5 条观光线、1 条轨道交通专用线、5 条越江轮渡航线、8 条水门航线。共设置了 56 个参观者服务点、1.15 万米排队休息长凳、11 万个坐凳座位、1854 个直饮水龙头、1.1 万个厕位、4.2 万个降温喷头、3 万个餐位，平均每天提供餐饮 25 万多份，发放了 1 亿份世博导览图、1800 万把清凉扇。2 万多参展方人员和 16 万多工作人员服务世博。

园区周边设 24 个停车场 6796 泊位。其中，大车位为 5394 个，小车位为 1402 个。世博旅游巴士专用停车场实际停放车辆共 48.91 万辆，实际进场车辆共 76.59 万辆。

**2. 主题策划——从主题选择到项目落地**

主题是世博会的灵魂。上海世博会的主题演绎经历了选择确定、深化推介、项目落地等阶段。

1999 年 5 月，在上海市政府启动世博会申办工作的同时，就成立了上海世博会主题研究组，由上海市人民政府发展研究中心牵头。要求世博会的主题必须符合 21 世纪世界发展的大趋势，遵循体现时代特征、体现国家特色和城市特点、可参与度大、可展示性强等原则。在研究的准备阶段，提出了 32 个主题，大致可归纳为以城市、文明和文化、探索与创新、环境、信息为主线，以及具有发散性思维六类。后将“城市和生活”作为申办 2010 年上海世博会的主题的核心内容。2001 年 5 月 2 日，在中国政府向国际展览局递交的《2010 年世博会申请函》中，上海世博会主题的英文表述“Better City，Better Life”先行对外公布。不久又发布了经过仔细推敲而确定的祈使句式的中国表述“城市，让生活更美好”。同时，还确定了 5 个副主题，它们分别是：城市多元文化的融合、城市经济的繁荣、城市社区的重塑、城市科技创新、城市和乡村的互动。这 5 个副主题基本涵盖了当前人类城市问题的 5 个方面。

世博会上主题呈现方式主要有三种：展示、论坛和活动。其中，展示最为重要，246 个国家和国际组织的展馆，主办方的中国馆、5 个主题馆、公共参与馆和阳光生命馆，31 个省、自治区、直辖市馆和港澳台馆，18 个企业馆，以及城市最佳实践区，共计 350 多个展馆都需要对主题进行延展。为了便于策展人按照 5 个副主题分别设置主题馆的内容，组织方完成了世博会的“主题内容结构”指导原则，其中提出了与 5 个副主题有联系又有区别的 5 个概念领域——城市人、城市生命、城市星球、城市足迹和城市梦想。

其中，诠释运用中国智慧实现城市化进程的中国馆、体现主办方对世博会主题理解的主题馆展示策划从 2005 年 4 月至 2009 年末历经了 5 个阶段，最后形成了以“城市发展中的中华智慧”为主题的中国馆展示方案，和以“城市人”、“城市生命”、“地球”、“城市未来”和“城市足迹”为主题的主题馆展示方案。

城市最佳实践区集中了全球遴选出的80个城市案例，展示了世界先进的城市发展理念和具体实践。

世博会论坛对难以进行展示的世博会主题相关问题进行全球化的讨论，通过高峰论坛、主题论坛和公众论坛，让各层次的民众有深入了解世博会主题的机会，集中体现世博会精神遗产，也是展望未来的重要平台，最终发表了《上海宣言》，形成对全球城市创新与可持续发展的共识。

上海世博会是世界文化交流的盛会，来自176个国家、13个国际组织、36个城市和4个企业的1200余支团队上演了1172个具有民族、民间、民俗特色和浓郁地域文化特色的文艺节目。中国31个省、自治区、直辖市和港澳地区在上海世博会组织了936场“中国元素”省区市活动周文艺表演，共表演了124个节目。

**3. 硬件建设——从选址调整到场馆建设**

2010年世博会选址在上海城市中心的黄浦江两岸区域，是上海城市发展与改造的重点地区。2004年4月，通过面向全球26家知名设计单位征集世博园区规划设计方案，经过多次评审、综合、优化，最终形成现在实施的上海世博会规划方案。区域内涉及企事业单位272家、1.8万多户居民，为了尽可能少影响现有的住宅建筑，设计单位多次调整红线范围。同时，对园区内30万平方米旧建筑进行了改造利用，节省了办博资金，最大限度地保留了城市文明遗存和历史记忆。

园区以“一主多辅”的规划布局，形成“园、区、片、组、团”5个层次的布局结构：即5.28平方公里的世博园、3.22平方公里的世博会围栏区、5个功能片、12个平均用地10公顷左右的展馆组、26个平均用地2~3公顷的展馆团。工程建设分为场馆建筑和市政设施两大类，其中场馆建筑又分为永久性项目和临时性项目两种类型。永久性场馆建筑主要包括中国馆、主题馆、世博中心、演艺中心和世博轴（合称“一轴四馆”）、世博村、城市最佳实践区，以及白莲泾、世博、后滩三大公园；临时性场馆建筑主要包括浦东园区的11个联合馆、42个租赁馆，42个外国和国际组织自建馆；浦西园区的世博会博物馆、综艺大厅、足迹馆、未来馆、18个企业自建馆等。市政设施包括浦东和浦西园区的永久道路、高架步道、水门码头、水电气等配套项目以及到达园区的越江隧道、轨道交通等大市政项目。园区单体建设项目超过200个，总建筑面积约230万平方米，是世博会有史以来占地面积最大且建设总量最大的园区。

园区建设面临规模和数量空前庞大、复杂，总建筑面积达到230万平方米，而且投资主体多，设计需求不确定，调整工作量大，建设工期非常紧迫，多种系统调试量大、集成度要求高等问题。在组织方的严格管理之下，坚持做到注重以人为本，注重绿色、低碳、环保，集中体现最新科技成果，实现了高质量建设。

**4. 国际招展——从招展邀请到参展服务**

本届世博会吸引了190个国家和56个国际组织参展，国际参展方数量为历届世博会之最，参展的发展中国家数量为历届世博会之最。190个参展国家中，包括尚未与我国建立外交关系的19个国家。

2006年3月22日，温家宝总理亲自签发中国政府参展邀请函后，国际社会积极响应。组织方紧紧依靠外交部、商务部、贸促会、上海市和中国政府总代表，积极依靠我驻外机构，与外国驻华使领馆、外交部驻外使馆、驻联合国使团的保持联系沟通，建立有效工作机制，连续举办了七届世博论坛，先后召开四次参展方大会。编制了上海世博会《注册报告》、《一般规章》和《特殊规章》等法律文件，制定实施了通关、税收、外汇、签证等方面的一系列世博会优惠政策和便利措施。此外，组织方安排了总额1亿美元的援助资金，建造了11个联合馆，免费提供给150多个发展中国家和国际组织使用，把联合馆建设成了上海世博会的亮点之一，履行了申博承诺。

国内参展方面，组织方依靠由组委会联络小组牵头的国内参展联络机制，实现了国内31个省、自治区、直辖市和港、澳地区参展，并与国台办一同促成了台湾参展。

城市最佳实践区是上海世博会的首创。组织方通过面向全球公开征集城市最佳实践区自荐参展案例，并组织了联合国人居署、国际展览局、世界银行以及国内的建设部、科技部专家组成的国际遴选委员会，对来自五大洲的近30个国家、80多个城市的106个案例进行评选，最终选出80多个案例在园区内单独约15公顷面积参展。

企业参展方面。世博园区共规划了18个企业馆，国内企业馆共13个，其中包括3个民营企业馆和1个台资企业馆，展示了我国企业的良好形象。

参展服务方面。组织方组建了由规划、建设管理、消防、税务、工商、海关、环保、出入境等39个部门入驻的参展者服务大厅，为参展者提供70多项"一门式"服务，高效、便捷。建设布展期间，参展者服务联席会议机制定期召开会议，共同协商、解决参展问题达数百个。组织方面向全球征集了16大类、近300家服务供应商为参展者提供服务。除埃及、黑山、拉脱维亚和伊拉克因参展进程启动较晚，未能按期开馆外，其余展馆均于2010年5月1日开馆。展馆规模之大，是历届世博会之最。开幕期间，组织方加强与参展方沟通交流，举办了9次上海世博会总代表指导委员会会议，切实帮助参展方解决各类具体问题，成功应对了高温酷暑、单日百万超大客流、台风雷暴天气等考验。还先后组织了191场国家馆日和国际组织荣誉日活动，以及上海区县结对、长三角城市友谊日活动。

**5. 宣传推介——为提高世博会知晓度的各种努力**

为了提升世博会知晓度，推广上海世博会主题，组织方编写了《2010年上海世博会沟通推介计划》，针对不同目标受众和不同阶段，制定相应的战略和执行计划，配合参展事务、市场开发等工作，在全球范围内提升世博会和上海世博会的认知度和参与度。

组织方在园区内建设了世博会有史以来规模最大、设施最全的媒体服务中心，为中外记者提供专业化服务。总面积约为3500平方米的国际广播电视中心，设有10个电视直播室、4个广播直播室、5个网络直播室、6个园区透明演播室和3个电视单边点，并提供用于高标清电视制作、信号传输的各种技术服务，及时将世博会期间各国各类报道输送出去。

开幕前，为时三年的“上海世博会宣传周”活动，共举办36站活动，通过大型展览、新闻发布会、论坛、系列讲座、网上知识竞赛、投放公益广告、活动进社区等各种形式的活动，海内外现场观众近300万人次到场参观，覆盖中国31个省、自治区、直辖市和港、澳、台地区。在我国香港、澳门、台湾地区，以及日本、韩国、美国、加拿大、东南亚、英国、法国、德国等世博会目标市场，以一系列推广活动，不断向民众推出世博会的主要看点和筹备进展。上海中心城区通过灯箱、展板、海报、视频等方式进行世博公益宣传。临开幕之前，在各大媒体上启动世博专栏，做好世博会开幕、开园报道。世博会运行期间，新闻中心新闻发布厅共举行150次新闻发布会，满足了记者和媒体对精彩场馆的采访报道需求。

组织方共编辑出版了世博出版物40余个品种，发行数达300多万册，语言种类覆盖中、英、法、日、韩等。《中国2010年上海世博会官方导览手册》和《中国2010年上海世博会官方图册》在世博会运行期间全国发行总量达到200万册。协助电视媒体拍摄了《走向2010》、《走进世博会》、《世博纪事》、《创意世博》、《盛会2010》、《百年世博梦》、《科技世博年》、《建筑奇观：上海世博园》、《上海大观》、《世博的记忆》等近200集（部）影视节目。

组织方还设立了面向全球的世博官方网站——世博网，设资讯、展馆、活动、论坛、服务、志愿者、地图等7个频道，分中、英、日、法四个语种提供园区各类即时信息和视频直播服务。世博开幕后，世博网累计页面浏览量超过3.8亿人次，用户数达7100万。

网上世博会是上海世博会的一大创新和亮点，为参展者提供全新的推介与交流的平台，并通过对实体世博会的延伸和拓展，使世博会成为开放、无障碍、鼓励全球公众共同参与的盛事。所有参加实体世博会的国家和国际组织、44个城市最佳实践区案例，31个省、自治区、直辖市、港澳台及企业参展方都以不同形式亮相网上世博会。截至2010年10月31日，网上世博会入“园”人次为8234多万。

**6. 保障支撑——从资金、人力资源、法律、监察、科技等方面提供保障**

世博会资金来源主要包括门票收入、品牌赞助、特许经营、商业租金及提成、捐赠等。按照项目规划，上海世博会建设资金180亿元，运行资金106亿元。世博会运营资金实现平衡目标，门票收入，13家全球合作伙伴、14家高级赞助商、31家项目赞助商，以及特许经营、商业租金等都超过预期。

在会计核算上，制定专门办法，创新和完善了我国大型活动项目会计核算制度，确保了世博会项目管理规范和资金安全。同时，围绕廉洁办博的目标，对重大资金、重大项目加强监察审计力度，确保了资金安全。

办博队伍十分庞大，组织者充分利用全市人才资源，开拓多种渠道，充实办博骨干队伍。通过组织借调方式、社会公开招聘，结合专业猎头公司定向推荐等，选拔社会各行业优秀人才充实办博队伍。同时，还采用了租赁、返聘、临聘等多种灵活的用工形式，进一步充实办博所需各层面人员。进入运行期后，以服务团队形式满足用人需求较大这一问题。在干部任用方面，不拘泥于干部任职年限和资历，不受限于岗位职数，加大选拔使用力度，夯实配强现场运行部门领导力量，加强充实配备专职党建干部。在人员的后续安置使用上，关心办博队伍，做好办博人员职业生涯发展规划。

上海世博会选拔、培训了近8万名园区志愿者，分13批次向游客提供了129万人次、1000万小时的志愿服务。志愿者提供的问讯、媒体服务、秩序引导、文明劝导、游客协助、语言翻译、贵宾接待等服务工作，展示了东道主热情友好形象，被大家昵称为“小白菜”的世博志愿者已经成为世博会一道亮丽的风景线，受到境内外游客的一致好评，获得了来自社会各界的称赞。

上海世博会是一届科技先导的世博会。在国家科技部牵头下，“世博科技行动计划”集合了全国近千家单位、上万名科技人员，紧紧围绕世博主题，利用科技创新、技术集成和突破，在建设规划、能源、环境、运营、展示及安全等六大领域，实施科技攻关项目140项，取得了1100多项具有自主知识产权的科研新成果，包括太阳能发电、新能源汽车、RFID、第四代移动通信等技术在园区内集成应用或直接应用，推动世博园区成为代表我国先进生产力发展方向的前沿阵地。

## 三、上海世博会的举办过程

### 1. 举国办博的体制优势

党中央、国务院对世博会工作高度重视。2010年新年伊始，胡锦涛总书记亲临世博园区视察，明确提出了“六个确保”的要求，发出了举全国之力、集世界智慧办好世博会的总动员令。中央领导先后视察世博筹办、运行工作或出席相关活动，指导办博工作。

按照中央部署，国家成立了上海世博会组委会，由有关部委和上海市共约40家成员单位组成，召开了十一次全体会议，全面部署和推进世博会筹办和运行工作，推动了世博会相关法规的制定，落实了一系列支持政策，推动各地区各部门积极参与办博事务。中央还批准成立了世博会安保、外事、宣传等工作协调小组，充分调动各方力量，为筹办世博提供强有力的支持和保障。

上海市委、市政府建立健全了工作领导机构和五个指挥部。市委、市政府领导高度重视园区运行工作，时刻关注、及时指导。各区县、各部门、各单位的紧密通力合作，为园区工作提供了有力的支持。水、电、气、通信、交通、医疗卫生、金融保险等单位充分利用各自的网络资源和专业力量，为园区提供了可靠的保障。

各省、自治区、直辖市讲大局、讲风格，先后成立了参与上海世博会的领导机构，统筹资源，积极参与展示、论坛、文艺活动、宣传推介、门票销售等工作。特别是上海周边各省、自治区、直辖市，积极为世博会安全保卫、交通保障、旅游接待等提供全方位支持。上海与全国兄弟省区市一起，共同当好世博会东道主，热情服务各地参展。

香港、澳门各建了1000平方米左右的自建馆参展，并参加城市最佳实践区的展示。港澳各界或积极向中国馆捐赠，或成为世博会赞助企业，参与世博会建设和运营保障。台湾建了台湾馆、震旦企业馆，并有两个案例参与城市最佳实践案例展示，这是台湾第一次如此全面地参与世博会。

全国各行各业自觉服从和保证世博大局，主动把困难留给自己，把方便让给世博，凝聚成办好世博的强大合力。全国人民对上海世博会倾注巨大热情、给予强大支持。世博会志愿者招募启动以来，全国60余万人报名参加园区志愿服务，近百万民众在世博会期间参与城市文明志愿服务行动。作为东道主的上海市民，识大体、顾大局，为上海世博会的筹办举办做出了突出贡献。13亿中国人民发自内心的支持和对世博会的热情令世界各地的参展方深受感动。

广大华人华侨与祖国同呼吸、共命运，以各种方式支持上海世博会，充分彰显了中华民族的强大凝聚力和向心力。

### 2. 以人为本的管理理念

为参观者和参展者服务是办好世博时刻不能忘记的中心任务，上海世博会是否成功，归根结底，是由参观者、参展者以及社会各界来判断的。所以，在工作中组织方始终坚持以人为本，精益求精，真正把参观者、参展者的需求放在第一位，想其所想，急其所急，竭尽全力为他们排忧解难，将以人为本融入服务管理细节之中，想方设法为他们参展、参观创造更便利、更舒适的条件。

在为参观者服务中，组织方始终坚持“用心思考、用情待人、用诚服务”，认真听取参观者的各种意见，从小事做起，从点滴改进做起，做到“参观者有所想、组织方有所谋，参观者有所呼、组织方有所应，参观者有所求、组织方有所为”，努力做到了每天都有新的进步，从而赢得了越来越多的参观者的欢迎。

在为参展者服务中，建立了与参展者定期沟通的机制，平等协商，不强加于人，并坦诚地对待工作中的不足，及时加以改进，赢得了参展者的理解、支持和信任，使他们更加热情地投入到办博工作之中。

为了真正将以人为本理念落到实处，组织方在“坚持、细节、改进、落实”上下足了功夫：一是在“坚持”上下功夫。将好的做法、好的经验、好的制度坚持下去，让这些做法、经验、制度发挥更大的效应；二是在“细节”上下功夫。组织方始终坚持精益求精，牢固树立细节决定成败的意识，于细微处见精神，做到细之又细，为参展者、参观者提供更加细致入微、体贴周到的服务；三是在“改进”上下功夫。坚持世博184天，天天有改进，天天有进步，做足了“改进”文章。四是在“落实”上下功夫。任何措施、任何工作不落实都是空中楼阁，都是纸上谈兵，任何事情不想做都是有理由，想做都是有办法的，要切实将各项制度、工作措施、活动方案落到实处，切实提高执行力，做到实之又实。

### 3. 安全有序的组织运作

建立服务园区实际的管理架构。组织方在世博园区设立了10多个片区和场馆部，建立了以“片区为基础、展馆为重点，条线作支撑”的园区管理体制，并与驻园军队、武警、公安管理体制有效整合，紧密合作。同时，根据运行情况，明确片区部门和条线部门的职责分工，做到既赋予责任，又明确授权，使片区的管理任务真正落地。

运用现代先进信息技术，建立了园区运行指挥中心，实现一体化、扁平化、专业化的指挥。一体化，即园区运行、安保、服务统一决策、统一指挥，并为军警民在处置突发事件时提供共同研究、同时下令、统一执行的指挥平台。扁平化，即建立片区、场馆和执行单元的二级指挥平台，使园区指挥部的指令能够快速下达到第一线，第一线的信息又能够及时、迅速上传至指挥部。专业化，即进入指挥中心的指挥员必须经过专业的训练，具有专业指挥的能力，能够严格执行指挥中心建立的指挥程序和行动序列。这样的指挥体系，号令畅通、运转高效，确保了园区运行期间，第一时间发现问题，第一时间协调问题，第一时间解决问题。

建立密切配合、运转高效的园区内外联动管理机制。园区管理涉及方方面面，需要全市相关部门的参与。组织方通过园区指挥部这个平台，让全市相关部门参与园区管理和服务工作，建立了园区内外联动的工作机制，实现园区内外交通的联动，实现客流控制的联动，实现园区运营和城市运行的联动。组织方还紧紧依靠各指挥部，与全市各部门、各区县紧密联动，实施好交通、宣传、观众接待、安保、应急处置等各项演练方案。

此外，工商、税务、城管、劳动监察、食药监、气象等部门都进驻园区，利用已有的机制，依托全市资源，与园区实行紧密联动，支持园区工作，使园区餐饮、卫生、环境、市场管理、医疗保障、金融服务以及各种外事活动正常有序进行。各地区、各单位主动担责、各司其职，心往一处想、劲往一处使、事往一起做，遇到问题加强沟通，发现疏漏主动补台，共同应对可能遇到的各种困难和挑战。这种内外联动的管理机制，确保了园区安全稳定有序运转。

## 四、上海世博会对上海城市发展的影响

### 1. 夯实经济发展的基础

在基础设施方面，对浦东和虹桥两个机场进行扩建，形成了 8400 万人次的年吞吐能力；建成轨道交通基本网络，运营里程达到 400 公里；新建、改建了道路、隧道、桥梁、电力、通信等一系列市政工程。这些设施的建成，完善了城市功能，使整个城市基础设施规划提前 5 ~ 10 年实现。

加快了会展、旅游、文化创意、金融服务、现代物流等产业的发展，促进以服务经济为主的产业结构升级，推动经济发展方式的转变。

世博园区选址是中国近代工业的发祥地，虽处城市中心，但老旧工厂林立，环境负担沉重，产业布局和城市功能亟待调整。通过开创性地将旧城改造与未来城市功能规划有机结合，以世博园区规划选址推动全市产业结构升级和产业布局调整，加快了旧区改造，淘汰了落后产能，促进了技术升级，改善了生态环境，为企业迁建和产业升级创造机会，推动了区

域功能转型和可持续发展。

**2. 提高精神文明**

世博会对于青少年教育有着不可小觑的意义。世博会不仅打开了青少年的眼界，开阔胸襟，接触到全世界的先进理念和智慧，更能使他们跳出一个国家的角度，以国际视野来看整个世界。参观过世博会的中国青少年，在其成长过程中有机会亲身经历千百万中外游客的交流场面，不出国门便能看到世界各国的风土人情，对他今后的成长会产生深远影响，使其更自觉地以国际责任感来思考问题，以此重塑自己的人生。

世博会还是一场极好的科学和人文素质教育实践。通过参观世博会或者参与世博志愿者活动，老百姓能真切感受到国家的进步与发展，增强以科学发展观来建设和谐社会的责任感。作为志愿者亲身参与推广宣扬世博会的理念，也能使他们站在第一线为世博做贡献，为培养市民的文明行为作出榜样，从而提升整体精神文明素养。

世博之后，将志愿者精神从世博园区扩展到园区外，从世博中延续到世博后，使志愿者活动规范化、程序化，将上海世博精神作为上海师资培训、公民教育和干部教育的重要资源，为上海的长远发展提供精神力量来源，将会成为促进人民精神文明的推动力。

**3. 推动科技产业**

世博会是科技创新的展示舞台。它对科技发展具有重大推动作用，是引领科技文明发展的风向标。上海世博会在新能源利用、节能设备和生态建筑技术、智能化技术、新材料技术方面，用最新科技成就来演绎“城市，让生活更美好”的理念，包括太阳能飞机、万能相机、透明水泥、可发电地板等新鲜事物都亮相上海世博会。这些科技成果大大改变了当时人们的沟通方式、出行方式、娱乐方式以及生活方式，大幅提高了人们的生活水平以及社会生产力，促进了经济的发展及社会文化内涵的提升。

上海将世博会主题聚焦到低碳经济和低碳城市，期间涌现的低碳环境、生态之家、智能低碳厨房、回收雨水、空调革命、清洁汽车、降温高招、零碳建筑、低碳餐具和食品、太阳能源这些创意理念将深刻改变我们的生活方式。这种低碳理念必将对社会经济文化内涵的提升发挥重要作用。对于上海而言，“低碳”早已不仅仅局限在世博园区，而是成为整个城市共同奋斗的目标。超过420公里的轨道交通网络和更加完善的巴士交通网络的建成，新能源汽车在公交路线的投放，还有综合环境的治理、市民低碳生活方式的推广，都让上海这座城市焕发出新的活力。

世博会作为人类文明的盛会，既是各国传统文化与民族风情展演的舞台，更是各国发展理念和最新科技成果比拼的场所。在上海世博会参观，感受到的不仅是多元文化交流与融合，更是人类文明进步的理念和实践。在世博会的各个场馆，从建筑设计、布展规划、互动演示到每一个实物模型和每一块展示平台，都传递着参展方对文明进步理念的独特思考和在技术研究方面的最新成果。世博会对上海科技发展的影响，不仅仅是已有技术创新成果的应用和推广，更是技术创新理念和路径的优化创新，这将不仅仅有助于上海更好地依托技术进步成果提升城市发展的水平和能级，更刺激了上海的微观经济主体更好地从事技术创新活动，从而使整个城市"创新无处不在"。世博会展示出丰硕的技术创新成果，是当今人类解决生存危机的宝贵财产。在吸取世博会成果的过程中，上海积极推进消化、吸收和集成创新，将各国的技术成果通过逆向工程等进行解构，并结合上海的实际进行集成和创造，从而提高上海技术创新的基础平台和研发效率。同时，世博会的不少技术还处于实验室和展示阶段，上海还将借东道主之利，充分考察这些技术的中试和产业化可行性，力争将适宜在上海进行产业化的技术真正转化为推进上海新兴战略产业发展的动力。

**4. 创新社会管理**

上海世博会中形成、凝练的管理创新，是推动上海城市建设和城市管理的新资源。

在交通管理领域方面，将围绕综合交通系统的管理和创建新型交通服务，进行科学技术的系统整合与创新。围绕管理整合和服务创新两大需求领域，融合交通信息技术、新能源汽车技术、交通工程技术、物联网技术、计算机技术等，在现有技术系统基础上，配合城市交通系统建设，采用逐步渐进的方式推进综合交通管理系统和新型交通服务体系的构建。特别是在几个技术整合方面取得突破性进展，包括交通信息技术与交通管控技术的整合，车载信息技术、新能源车辆技术及物联网技术与交通服务技术的整合，交通信息技术与综合交通运行管控技术的整合。

在世博管控系统经验的基础上，针对虹桥枢纽及虹桥商务区、外高桥枢纽地区、闵行新城及西南入城通地区的情况，逐步建立交通集聚区域管控系统。虹桥枢纽及虹桥商务区交通管控、虹桥枢纽积聚的大量交通、虹桥商务区大规模开发所带来的交通负荷，加上正在建设的会展中心，这一带所遇到的交通压力和挑战不亚于世博会。因此，充分利用该地区正在建设的强大公共服务体系，采取引导、疏导、服务等手段，确保该区域正常运战，使上海综合交通管控所面临的一个重要课题，也是上海世博交通管控经验的一个很好的拓展应用。

通过有效的产学研链接机制、现代市场运作模式创新等手段，特别是在城市规划、产业布局、现代服务业发展、区域合作等领域，实现世博资源和城市硬件的有机结合。上海将把握世博后城市建设和国家建设的新资源和新机遇，把上海世博精神落实到城市建设中去，使之成为城市建设的思想指导。弘扬"天人和谐、师法自然、取之有道、用之有节"的中国文化理念，用以引领城市生活方式的现代转型，发展体现世博精神的低碳经济和文化产业，设计体现世博精神的特定产品和建筑，提升上海与长三角资源共享的质量能级等，将世博会展示的未来城市理念付诸实践。尤其是在处理经济快速发展与环保的矛盾时，真正做到坚持将人类长远利益和未来城市的环保理念放在首位。

（作者：朱航，上海世博会事务协调局主题演绎部/研究中心，助理部长/助理主任；刘骁，上海世博会事务协调局办公室助理主任，高级经济师）

# “信息化与城市发展”主题论坛综述

2010年5月15—16日，由国家工信部、上海世博会执委会、国际电信联盟和宁波市政府共同主办的中国2010年上海世博会“信息化与城市发展”主题论坛在宁波举办。本次论坛聚焦经济全球化背景下的城市管理、城市生活和城市融合中的相关问题，展望信息通信技术发展下的城市未来图景，进行了深入广泛的交流和探讨，碰撞出大量思想火花，带来了很多启迪，形成了许多共识。

国家工信部部长李毅中，浙江省委书记、省人大常委会主任赵洪祝，上海市委书记俞正声，国际电信联盟秘书长哈玛德·图埃，菲律宾副总统诺利·德·卡斯特罗出席论坛开幕式。来自国际组织、相关国家和地区以及国内各省、自治区、直辖市的政府官员、企业管理者和专家学者以及上海世博会参展方代表和中外记者近800人参加了论坛。

## 一、论坛背景

当今社会高速发展，已进入了一个全球化、信息化的时代，信息技术正在日益改变着我们的城市生活，不断影响着我们的行为方式。人们在享受更多便利、更美好生活的同时，也遇到了信息安全、网络犯罪、数字鸿沟等问题。在这种背景下，“信息化与城市发展”主题论坛依托2010年上海世博会“城市，让生活更美好”的主题，探讨如何更好地运用信息手段造福人类，促进城市的可持续发展，关注信息机遇的平等共享，让更多的人分享到信息技术进步带来的好处。

## 二、主要议程

“信息化与城市发展”主题论坛会期两天，主要从城市建设和管理、城市生活、全球化、现代物流与航运中心建设、产业、教育、社会责任等方位展开7个有关联的平行分论坛，深入探讨信息化下城市发展所面临的机遇和挑战，广泛交流信息化与城市发展的经验和道路，为今后世界各国的城市发展提供了参考意见和借鉴作用。

（1）“信息化与城市建设和管理”平行分论坛关注未来城市信息化管理的发展、国际化大都市信息化管理的困境。城市作为社会、经济发展的中心，是各类信息的交换、中转和辐射的神经中枢。随着信息社会的到来，城市的发展逐渐呈现出不同于以往的新态势。世界性大都市的建设与管理日益复杂，对综合管理水平和风险应急能力的要求也越来越高。该分论坛从理论上以及各国各地区范例中，对信息化助力城市建设和管理水平的升级，提高社会经济发展效率的运用和创新进行了广泛的交流。

（2）“信息化与城市生活”平行分论坛关注如何更好利用信息技术提高生活便利，提高公众社会参与。信息革命带来的不仅仅是产业的转变，人类的生活方式也日益向信息化、数字化、网络化转变。该分论坛探讨信息化给城市生活带来更多更丰富的内涵和意义，并提醒关注由此引发的社会心理学、儿童网络安全等新问题。

（3）“信息化与全球化”平行分论坛关注如何利用信息技术应对全球性危机和风险，如何通过信息技术的普及推动全球范围的公平与合作。联合国《千年宣言》颁布已有10年，但贫富国家之间的数字鸿沟还在不断加大。该分论坛探讨了利用信息科技的具体做法推动欠发达地区的经济与社会发展，缩小由信息鸿沟所造成的社会发展不平衡，帮助人民获得信息获取与传播的途径，让更广大的人民都能分享科技进步所带来的福利。

（4）“现代物流与航运中心建设”平行分论坛关注信息技术对现代物流业的改变；物流信息化对现代城市发展的重大意义。建设国际航运中心应认识到“信息化”的战略价值。信息技术的发展使“物流”由企业内部的管理概念转变为一种产业观念，催生了现代物流业。物流业信息化建设是现代化建设的重大课题，也是该产业生存和发展的关键所在。分论坛探讨交流运用信息技术手段，解决现代物流业存在的矛盾和问题，提高物流效率和企业服务水平，加快国际航运中心建设和城市的竞争力。

（5）“产业信息化”平行分论坛关注产业应用信息技术的基本路径和方式、信息化技术与传统产业创新、信息技术创新与企业活力。现代社会，信息的创造、分配、传播、使用和管理不仅是一项经济产业，更为重要的是它已经成为推动工业与农业发展的引擎。可以说，信息化已深深植入了产业发展的各个领域、各个环节，特别是当前金融、钢铁与汽车等产业的快速发展，在相当程度上是以信息为主导的。掌握了对信息的获取、运用与传播的能力，就掌握了产业发展的自主权。分论坛探讨了信息化给传统行业带来创新和活力，以及由于信息技术的创新又为各相关企业界带来的新的机遇。

（6）“教育信息化”平行分论坛关注如何利用信息技术革新教育模式，如何利用信息技术提高学习能力。当代信息技术使得教育从内容、形式、方法和组织等方面都发生了根本性的变革。现代社会要求人人都应具有运用多媒体和网络技术进行学习和工作的能力，这也使得跨越了时空障碍的远程教育等新的学习形式成为可能，从而为真正实现人的终身学习提供可能性。与教育一样，世界各国的科学研究事业更是与信息技术的发展相辅相成。分论坛探讨如何通过实现教育的信息化，从而实现教育的终身化。

（7）“信息化与社会责任”平行分论坛关注在信息社会中，政府和企业如何关注弱势群体并促进社会包容性。信息通过多点、多元的方式进行交换，与普通商品的“给予”和“获取”不同，信息的特殊价值在于“分享”。以信息化为基础的商务、教育和其他各项活动均是在这样一种平等互动的环境中创造财富与价值。创造社会价值与担当社会责任的核心理念是一致的。如果说过去20年中我们着重于运用信息技术创造物质财富，那么今后，我们需要探索更多更广的新途径来发挥信息技术为国家、城市、企业与个人创造社会价值，担当社会责任的核心作用。分论坛探讨了中外政府和企业在利用信息化创造财富的同时，体现出对社会环境的爱护、资源的珍惜、民众个体的包容。

## 三、主要论点

国家工信部部长李毅中代表工信部致辞，对本届论坛的举办表示热烈的祝贺。他说，众所周知，信息化对城市的发展、建设和管理都具有积极的促进作用，信息技术在城市的应用加快了城市化的进程和发展。与此同时，城市化的进程也带动了信息化与信息产业的快速发展，居民消费结构的升级、城市基础设施的建设，为信息化提供了广阔的发展空间。回顾中国城市的发展，我们深切地体会到信息技术的应用和信息化的深入推进，提高了城市的通信效率，便捷了居民的沟通和交流，加强了城市的交通管理，加快了物流业的发展，增强了城市的公共服务能力和应急反应能力，改善了城市的综合发展环境。需要指出的是，信息技术的应用在带来便利的同时，也带来了数字鸿沟、网络信息安全等问题。在信息化发展过程中，我们倡议各国加强合作，兴利除弊，发展与管理并重，健全法律法规，加强行业自律，共同促进信息化的健康发展。

上海市委书记俞正声在致辞中代表中国2010年上海世博会组委会和执委会，向论坛的举行表示热烈的祝贺。他说，信息技术不可或缺地推动着城市的发展，承载着创造更加美好生活的希望。这是我们的信念也是本次论坛的意义所在。这次论坛选择“信息化与城市发展”为主题，通过聚焦经济全球化与信息技术进步双重背景下的城市管理和城市生活中的相关问题，进行广泛而深入的研讨。对诠释演绎世博会主题内涵具有重要意义。

浙江省委书记赵洪祝在致辞中说道，信息化是当今世界推动社会变革的重要引擎，特别是新一代移动通信、物联网、智慧地球、智慧城市等新技术，层出不穷，向我们展现了信息化的广阔前景和美好的蓝图。学习和借鉴做好本次主题论坛研讨成果的转化、运用工作，促进信息化与城市化的深度融合，必将为城市发展注入更多的智慧和活力，为城市生活增添更多的色彩，让更多的城市居民分享信息化带来的便捷和快乐。

国际电信联盟秘书长哈玛德·图埃在开幕致辞中指出，在过去的100多年中，全世界经历了史无前例的城市化的进程，城市将会进一步发展和扩大，同时也会在未来国家的经济和社会发展方面发挥更加重要的作用。我们必须利用各种工具，特别是信息通信技术，使城市生活更加美好。未来的城市环境必将更健康、更清洁、更安静、更人性化。

中国科学院副院长江绵恒在“城市化与信息化——中国发展的时代机遇”主旨演讲中指出，所谓信息化，是指信息技术在材料、器件、系统的发展，使信息的传输、存储、应用形成了一个系统。信息技术的发展催生了以信息化为主要特征的新产业，包括信息制造业和信息服务业。当这样的新产业成为社会生产力的主要方面，我们则进入了信息社会。信息化是人类文明下一个发展阶段的主要特征。物联网在中国刚刚起步，具有巨大的发展空间和潜力，且技术上已经没有大的障碍了。再提一个新的概念，就是新三网融合，即人与社会、人与自然、自然与社会的融合。这一融合不光是技术上的新的挑战，还要有新的标准。同时也给新兴的信息产业带来了巨大的发展商机。中国是世界上人口最多、最大的发展中国家，城市化进程速度飞快。我们面临着一个历史性的机遇，那就是要通过城市化、工业化、信息化，三化协同发展，齐头并进，来解决我们发展的问题。

美国国家研究创新联合会总裁兼首席执行官罗伯特·卡恩在“下一代互联网与未来生活”主旨演讲说道：信息化对于教育、健康、卫生、政府服务、经济增长、商约机会的发展是非常重要的。因特网能够给发展中国家和发达国家带来很多机会。移动互联网的能力是无穷的，未来人们可以获得更多的信息，可以了解最新的经济发展动态、政治发展动态，在天气、交通、建筑设计各个方面，这些技术都可以帮助他们工作。未来的信息通信技术，可能最大的一个挑战，就是如何来部署一个有效的信息基础构架。需要我们以最好的工程技巧和各个城市、各个国家之间的合作，确保它更好地发展，就能够对未来有更好的把握，同时也能够帮助我们更好地应对无法预测的未来。

中国移动通信集团公司总裁、中国移动有限公司董事长兼 CEO 王建宙在“物联网和无线城市”的主旨演讲说道：物联网实现了人与物、物与物之间的沟通，让物体也具有智慧。这里的物可以包括机器、设备、装置，也可以包括动物甚至植物。物联网的结构有三个不可缺少的部分：第一个是感知部分；第二个部分是传递层；第三个部分是处理层。利用云计算的技术、模糊识别的技术，可以在短时间内进行海量的处理。把从物体取到的第一手信息经过处理以后变成对我们的生产、生活、工作有用的信息。无线城市，是指利用各种无线接入的技术，为城市提供随时随地随需的无线网络的接入，无线城市从强调网络覆盖到现在强调应用。通过无线城市的发展，促进城市产业结构的优化，提高政府服务市民的效率。他认为信息通信技术有三个方面的变化： 是应用的趋势日益明显，技术应用于技术本身融合的趋势越来越明显；二是信息通信技术产业价值链结构也发生了变化；三是信息通信技术除了自身的结构发生变化以外，还接入了许多延伸的领域。他指出，企业要加强行业之间的合作，比过去以往任何时候都显得重要。

中国工程院副院长、国家信息化专家委员会副主任邬贺铨在“网络技术与智慧城市”的演讲中指出：有人说物联网是互联网的演进。这种说法不准确。互联网是全球性的，而物联网是行业性和区域性的。与其说物联网是网络，不如说物联网是业务和应用。什么叫智慧城市？也没有明确的定义。一个咨询公司的定义是：用智能技术，使得城市的关键基础设施，通过组成服务，使城市的服务更有效。为市民提供人与社会、人与人的和谐共处，智慧城市本身就是一个网络城市。物联网是互联网的应用拓展，因此物联网是智慧城市的重要标志。物联网本身主要应用首先是在工业部门，资产管理、生产自动化，还有产业等，包括销售的管理。更多的应用是在物流系统。此外，还有移动电子商务、移动支付、远程医疗、移动医疗、电子医疗、电子病历等。总的来说，互联网宽带化、移动化、泛载化发展，智慧城市使人们工作和生活更安全、更有效、更舒适。

国际电信联盟 2009 年度世界电信和信息社会奖得主、美国联邦通信委员会前任委员德博拉·泰勒·泰特在“儿童网络安全”的主旨演讲中说：网络是一把双刃剑，在给我们带来很多利益的同时，也产生了很多问题，其中很多影响到了儿童。除了网瘾、自杀模拟、网络犯罪之外，在美国，有43%的孩子表示受到过网络欺凌，但只有9%的孩子会站出来述说。网络欺凌会影响到数以百万计的儿童的心理健康，这种影响不仅仅是一时的，甚至会是一生的。在美国，十几岁的孩子75%拥有手机，70%的年轻女孩都会参与发送淫秽短信，这是非常令人不安的。现在很多的国家都意识到了这个问题，并在学校注重加入了一些加强网络认识的课程。除了政府部门，企业和很多的私人机构也应该共同合作，用学习到的各种声音，用分享到的各种信息，建立起一套原则，并且能够采取协调一致的行为保护网络世界中的儿童，去解决网络对儿童负面影响的问题。

腾讯控股有限公司董事会主席兼首席执行官马化腾在“在线精彩，生活更精彩——腾讯眼中的信息化与城市生活”主旨演讲中说道，以个人为中心的社会化网络的形成是今后互联网的发展趋势。随着手机的普及，人们通过社交网络进行沟通的趋势日益明显。未来互联网发展的另一个趋势是移动互联网。作为服务提供商，我们感觉到变化越来越快。未来移动互联网将把人们的碎片时间运用得更好，提高人们的单位时间效率。互联网向企业方向延伸是又一大趋势。随着企业信息化进程的加快，它将把企业的内网与互联网结合起来，大大有利于帮助企业提高效益。

国家工信部信息化推进司司长、国家信息化专家咨询委员会秘书长徐愈在“信息革命和数字鸿沟”的主旨演讲中讲到：信息革命带来了不同国家、地区、行业和人群在信息获取、利用能力方面的巨大差异，这就是数字鸿沟。它的实质是经济和社会发展水平在信息化条件下的客观反映。造成国家间数字鸿沟的主要成因有经济技术、教育、战略方面，而一国内部不同地区、行业人群中的数字鸿沟还会因历史、文化、地理位置、种族性别等差异有不同的表现。经济差距是数字鸿沟的核心，只要经济差距存在，数字鸿沟就不会完全消除。过大的数字鸿沟对社会发展存在较大的危害，同时缩小数字鸿沟也会成为经济社会发展的新动力、新机遇。缩小数字鸿沟的过程也就是加速信息知识传播和信息技术普及应用的过程。这方面，中国近年来作出了很大努力，在消除城乡和地区发展的不均衡性方面进行了积极探索。希望通过国际间合作，在这方面取得更大的成效。

宁波市委副书记、市长毛光烈在“物流信息化过程中的关键问题：以宁波为例”的主题演讲中指出，港口城市应把国际航运物流业的信息化摆到更突出的位置。结合宁波的实践，他有五点体会：（1）国际航运物流信息化的基础，是物流各环节单个企业的信息化。现代物流的信息化，是基于企业的信息化。（2）国际航运物流业信息化是整合众多中小物流企业的信息化。宁波启动第四方物流市场建设，信息化、市场化和制度化这三种手段有机地组织各中小企业的共同合作，形成了有序整体的物流体系。（3）国际航运物流业信息化是各物流企业行为规范、标准的信息化。只有众多中小物流企业经营行为的统一，才有可能在此基础上实行社会范围内物流企业的系统化和标准化运作。（4）国际航运物流业信息化是物流产业基地的信息化。只有加快物流产业基地的信息化，提升物流专业贸易市场的信息化水平，同时配套推进口岸服务，政务服务公共平台建设，才能形成物流产业供应链整合的强大合力。(5) 国际航运物流业信息化是国内外城市物流业之间开放合作的信息化。以物流信息公共平台和口岸大通关为载体，积极推进跨区、跨部门的合作发展，加快与国内外城市物流业信息化的开放合作。

交通银行首席信息官、中国银联技术管理委员会主任委员侯维栋在"金融服务创新与城市发展"的主题演讲中说，信息化是城市发展的重要推动力，是目前城市发展中面临的一系列问题和挑战的重要解决途径。对金融行业来说，信息技术同样是业务创新、服务创新的重要手段和推动力。以技术改良为载体的金融服务创新不仅是现代商业银行提升核心竞争力的重要手段，也体现了城市生活发展进步的历程。以技术改良为载体的金融服务创新改变了城市生活方式。基于互联网、通信、语音等技术的新兴金融服务方式的出现，改变了居民的生活、消费习惯，使金融服务更为方便快捷。以技术改良为载体的金融服务创新促进了城市文化繁荣。金融服务的创新以先进技术为载体，展示了先进的金融服务理念，拓展了金融文化传播途径，促进文化产业发展。

通用汽车中国公司总裁兼总经理甘文维在"车联网——未来城市个人交通的美好愿景"的演讲中讲到，借力于信息技术，改变汽车的驱动方式，实现车辆的电气化，并实现车联网。电气化和车联网技术的完美融合，重新定义了汽车 DNA，将这一未来城市交通愿景变成现实。这两项技术将使未来的汽车依靠纯电力驱动，以纯电力或氢气作为燃料，由精密电子设备和软件进行整体操控，并且通过无线通信实现车与车之间，车与建筑物之间，以及车与城市基础设施之间的互联。利用 GPS 技术，2030 年的汽车可以被精确定位。车辆将有能力感测到车身四周的物体，并利用无线通信系统与其他车辆或道路基础设施进行沟通和互动。最终，这些汽车将实现自动驾驶。通过车联网技术，汽车将拥有收集、处理和共享大量数据的能力，因此道路的有限资源可以得到最优化的配置，行驶时间得以大幅缩减且更具可预测性。它还将大幅减少交通事故，驾驶者将得以与他们的社交网络时刻保持互联。这将彻底改变我们的驾驶方式。

东软集团股份有限公司董事长兼首席执行官刘积仁在"信息化与健康城市"的演讲中说道，医疗服务形式的过度单一和医疗资源配置的不合理，导致了优质资源只被少数人使用，而无法有效地覆盖到偏远地区和低收入的人群。政府和个人更关注的是医疗，而不是健康的日常维护，这使得在医院不断扩大规模的同时，病人的数量还在不断增多。对于中国，建立健康服务体系应该是比对医疗的投入更为重要，社会需要通过更完美的健康服务体系来使人们有更健康的生活方式。

全国人大常委会委员、同济大学教授、博导吴启迪在"信息社会中的终身教育"的主旨演讲中表示，教育信息化是教育发展的重要趋势，也是教育现代化的强大推动力。同时教育信息化也是推进教育公平，实现教育跨越式发展的重大举措。教育信息化使终身教育或终身学习成为可能。推进信息社会的终身教育健康发展，关键是构建完备的全民终身教育体系。终身教育是纲，是蓝图，纲举目张，促进各类教育纵向衔接、横向沟通，搭建终身学习的"立交桥"。重点是加强教育信息化建设，这其中，远程教育应当发挥更积极的作用，要建立开放式的教育机构，特别是开放大学。

微软在线服务集团总裁陆奇在“信息化和软件服务经验”中指出，云计算带来了新的商业模式、新的业务，不管是电子商务、数字商务、移动支付、移动商务都给我们带来了重大的机会，让我们能够产生新的企业、新的业务模式，同时这也意味着我们所有人的责任更加重大。因为更多的数据是在云里面移动的，安全性、私密性都需要担起责任来。

上海市常务副市长杨雄在论坛闭幕总结大会上作总结发言说道，信息技术和信息产业的发展正推动着城市各类要素资源的优化配置以及城市建设和运行管理的不断完善。信息技术仍将引领全球的科技创新，信息化给城市和社会发展带来的深刻变革，将延续和扩展。城市是人类生活的美好家园，信息化不仅为城市发展增添了新的载体和动力，更为城市的美好明天创造了无限可能。

## 四、小结

中国2010年上海世博会信息化与城市发展主题论坛，通过一个全体大会、一个对话会、七个平行分论坛，就城市化育信息化、信息化与城市发展这一历史性的主题作了全新的诠释和注解。

此次论坛在信息技术及产业创新发展趋势、信息化应用促进城市和社会进步以及如何缩小数字差距等方面，形成了许多重要共识。

共识一：全球信息通信技术加速创新发展，并通过经济社会各领域的渗透应用，产生了更加广泛的影响。下一代互联网、移动互联网、三网融合、物联网和云计算等信息技术，正在催生新的信息化浪潮。智能城市、无线城市、3G与4G时代的便利生活服务等，推动信息化应用进入新的发展阶段。信息化促进产业升级发展，信息技术在产业各个领域的广泛应用，及信息化与工业化的融合发展，带动企业生产和经营管理方式的革新，提升产业技术创新能力和发展能级，信息化有力支撑金融、航运、物流、贸易等服务业的发展。促进商业模式的创新，形成产业发展的新动力。

信息化推动了经济发展方式的转变。通过信息技术的深化应用，提高资源、能源的利用效率和劳动生产率，促进了产业向高端化和低碳化方向发展。推动了电子商务、互联网服务、节能环保等绿色新兴产业的发展。

共识二：信息化为城市的可持续发展提供了新的机遇和路径，也创造了人类更加美好的生活。信息化助推城市化进程，当前，信息化与城市发展更加紧密地结合在一起，提供了解决城市规划、交通与物流、资源节约和环境保护等问题的手段，推动了城市管理和服务向智能化、精细化和便捷化方向发展，提高了城市的运转效率，促进了城市的可持续发展。

信息通信技术为实现以人为本的目标，创造了无限空间。信息化以满足人的实际需求为导向，通过电子政务缩短政府与公众之间的距离以及服务时间；通过教育信息化应用，构建全民终身教育体系；通过社区的智能服务，使家居生活更加安全、舒适和高效；通过数字医疗提高医疗服务的质量等。

信息化为人类社会进步和发展提供了强劲动力，推动人力、资金、技术等要素资源的优化配置，促进了经济与社会、人口资源与环境的协调发展，使城市更加宜居，生活更加美好。

共识三：我们要更加关注缩小区域和人群间的数字差距，体现信息化开放、合作、共赢的特性和理念。在推进信息化进程中，建立和完善更加密切的国际交流合作机制，帮助欠发达国家和地区，以及各国、各地区内弱势群体公平享受信息化成果，符合各参与者的共同利益，也是我们需要承担的责任。

积极探索缩小数字差距的现实路径，通过推动宽带网络建设，缩小沟通成本，增进人们之间的交流合作；利用创新的信息技术，使弱势群体能够掌握信息化的基本技能；创造公平的信息化应用机会，实现公众在信息社会进程中的普惠发展。持续推动信息化的开放和健康发展，加强各领域的技术合作、研发以及产学研用的结合。倡导信息技术兼容和标准的普适性，努力促进信息通信技术更加高效、低耗、低成本和人性化。增加沟通与协作，减少网络犯罪、不良信息传播等负面因素，创造健康的网络生态环境，促进信息社会的和谐发展。

（作者：吴素芝，广州市城市规划勘测设计研究院城市地理信息中心副主任）

# “城市更新与文化传承”主题论坛综述

2010年6月12—15日，由文化部、国家文物局、上海世博会执行委员会、联合国教科文组织、苏州市人民政府联合主办的“城市更新与文化传承”主题论坛在苏州太湖国际会议中心、上海世博园区举行。本次论坛倡导多元文化的共生与融合，主张在提升城市硬件的同时保持对文化的传承与创新，对当前大规模城市化浪潮进行探讨和反思，对影响城市建设与发展的文化热点问题进行广泛的探讨。

全国政协副主席厉无畏，文化部部长蔡武，江苏省委书记梁保华，上海市市长、上海世博会组委会副主任委员、执委会执行主任韩正，江苏省省长罗志军，联合国副秘书长沙祖康和联合国教科文组织副总干事汉斯·道维勒出席论坛开幕式。上海世博会参展方代表、中外专家学者、国内各省、自治区、直辖市代表和中外记者近800人参加论坛。

## 一、论坛背景

当今时代，文化在综合国力竞争中的地位和作用越来越突出，文化的力量深深地熔铸在民族的生命力、创造力和凝聚力之中。文化是城市的内核和灵魂，城市居民不仅需要便捷的交通、功能齐全的基础设施、丰富的物质财富，还需要绚丽多彩的文化。随着城市化进程的加快，城市数量急剧增加，城市规模不断扩大，城市在发展的同时，也面临着自身成长和文化传承的矛盾。在这种背景下，“城市更新与文化传承”主题论坛依托2010年上海世博会“城市，让生活更美好”的主题，探讨如何将文化与城市有效融合，为城市化进程注入全面、协调、可持续发展的动力，寻找“城市，让生活更美好”的文化之路。

## 二、主要议程

“城市更新与文化传承”主题论坛会期一天半，主要从物质文化传承和非物质文化保护、城市多元文化融合和跨文化交流、创意文化和文化生态等角度展开6个有内在联系的平行分论坛，深入探讨城市更新环境下文化传承的意义以及面临的机遇和挑战，广泛交流城市更新中文化传承的经验和教训，为包括中国在内的广大发展中国家的城市更新和文化建设提供参考与借鉴。

(1)"物质文化遗产保护：寻找城市个性与标识"平行分论坛关注城市发展与文化遗产保护的平衡关系及其可操作性。在社会发展的历程中，人类创造了丰富而珍贵的物质文化遗产，并形成了独特的城市风景和文化特征。然而，近一个世纪以来，随着城市化进程的加快，大量物质文化遗产在这个过程中渐渐消失。如何在兼顾城市发展和物质文化遗产保护的双向要求中找到一条平衡发展的道路，如何从理念和手段方面实现城市物质文化遗产的保护和传承，这些问题将从根本上决定城市物质文化遗产的未来命运，也决定着城市独特个性的形成与确立。该分论坛从理论到范例对物质文化遗产的保护要素、手段和理论创新进行了全方位的探讨。

(2)"城市多元文化的融合与共生"平行分论坛关注城市多元文化的繁荣与发展问题。多元文化融合与共生是城市发展中突出的文化现象，也是城市开放程度和国际化程度的一个重要衡量指标。城市更新过程中对主流文化之外的文化多元现象有更多的宽容和支持，将为城市文化的繁荣和发展提供更多选择。该分论坛从城市管理的角度探讨文化的多元性和多样性，对城市更新本身的内涵进行归纳与总结，为全球化背景下的城市发展与融合提供文化角度的思考和支撑。

(3)"城市文化创新与实践，创意产业与文化旅游"平行分论坛关注新时代下，传统文化的适应性与创新能力。在社会的发展过程中，传统的城市文化环境在不断变迁，其文化基因被重新组合入新的文化系统中，并继续发挥作用。该分论坛旨在讨论在城市快速更新过程中，如何通过创意的形式使文化思想更新与传承，再用现代都市所具备的大众传媒和产业营销手段整合人当代城市文化发展体系当中，使其成为新的城市文化符号。

(4)"非物质文化遗产保护：延续城市的历史脉络"平行分论坛重点寻求在城市时代中非物质文化遗产更有效的保护途径。非物质文化遗产是反映民族个性、民族审美习惯的活化石，它是人类历史脉络的延续，也是城市文化传统中最脆弱的部分，因此需要政府、社会、民众的共同努力，才能得以传承和发展。该论坛对各国非物质文化遗产保护的经验进行交流与回顾，以促进非物质文化遗产的保护与传播。

(5)"跨文化交流与城市文化变迁"平行分论坛关注发生在不同城市间和城市内的跨文化交流现象。随着全球化时代的到来，这些现象深刻地改变着城市居民的价值观和生活方式，并影响城市的文化变迁。国家文化与地区文化、本土文化与外来文化、主流文化与亚文化，以及对社会政治和经济产生很大影响的文化冲突、文化认同等概念和文化现象，都是该论坛的关注焦点。

(6)"文化生态：城市文化要素的继承与演进"平行分论坛关注城市人文空间的建设，并对城市更新提出更高的要求。城市是一种以人为主体的复合生态系统，文化变量是城市生态的有机组成部分。人类建设城市的目的是为了追求更美好的物质和精神生活。该论坛关注如何在城市建设中继承传统文化元素的精华，使城市的文化生态既符合现代人的生活习惯，又充满传统文化的神韵，使人们在紧张的城市生活中寻找内心的安宁，守护精神家园。

## 三、主要论点

文化部部长蔡武在致辞时代表文化部对世博主题论坛的举办表示热烈祝贺。他说，当今时代，文化在综合国力竞争中的地位和作用越来越突出，文化的力量深深地熔铸在民族的生命力、创造力和凝聚力之中。文化是城市的内核和灵魂，城市居民不仅需要便捷的交通、功能齐全的基础设施、丰富的物质财富，还需要绚丽多彩的文化。文化是保证城市居民生活品质和提高幸福指数的重要因素。本次论坛提供了一个广阔的平台，来自世界各国的专家、学者和有识之士就文化遗产保护、城市多元文化的融合与共生、城市文化创新与实践以及文化生态等问题进行广泛交流，进而达成共识，形成成果，指导实践。

上海市市长韩正代表中国2010年上海世博会组委会和执委会，对论坛的举行表示热烈祝贺。他说，城市化的过程，不只是城市经济社会发展和经济结构升级的过程，不只是现代化城市景观和建筑拔地而起的过程，而且还是城市历史文化积淀和历史文脉延续的过程，是城市多元文化互动交融、文化内涵和形式不断创新的过程。本次论坛围绕深化上海世博会主题，聚焦新形势下城市发展更新中的文化传承创新，一定会有利于我们对共同维护好人类文化的丰富遗产，推动城市可持续发展形成更加广泛的共识。

江苏省省长罗志军在致辞时说，本次论坛从多个角度深入探讨城市更新环境下文化传承的意义以及面临的机遇和挑战，广泛交流城市更新中文化传承的经验和教训，充分体现了“城市，让生活更美好”的世博主题，对于推动世界各国加快城市化和城市现代化步伐，共同保护好人类丰富的文化遗产，必将产生积极和深远的影响。

联合国副秘书长沙祖康表示，联合国一直在积极应对城市化挑战，致力于保护世界物质和非物质文化遗产。联合国大会宣布2010年是国际文化年，期待大家在世博论坛上畅所欲言，对城市发展以及认识和保护文化遗产提出新的思路。

联合国教科文组织助理总干事汉斯·道维勒代表联合国教科文组织向世博主题论坛的顺利召开表示祝贺。他说，我们可以在论坛上从不同角度探讨和交流城市更新和文化传承的主题，呼吁大家在城市化的过程中更加重视文化起到的重要作用。上海和苏州在城市更新和文化传承上都是非常好的例证，联合国教科文组织愿意与不同国家和各相关方面加强合作，使我们的城市实现可持续发展，保持文化的多样性。

全国政协副主席厉无畏在“创意产业——城市文化的创新与实践”的主旨演讲中认为，创意产业在促进城市文化创新当中，主要体现在内容、形式、载体、体制、传播手段这五个方面，在整个发展中不仅是精神方面的支柱，同时也带动整个经济的发展。发展创意产业，能够促进城市经济的转型和文化的创新，可以让人们分享创意成果，让生活变得更加轻松、愉快。创意产业的发展满足了人们多元化的精神需求，也挖掘和拓展、提升了人们对精神文化方面的需求。所以，人们的精神文化需求越丰富、越多样，创意产业的发展就越具有深厚的社会基础和广泛的市场空间，从这个意义上说，创意产业也让城市的生活更美好。

全国政协委员、国家文物局局长单霁翔在“文化遗产，让城市更美好”主旨演讲中总结了中国文化遗产保护的六大趋势：一是文化遗产保护要素方面，从文物保护重视文化要素的保护，向今天文化遗产保护要同时注重由文化要素和自然要素相互作用形成的混合遗产、文化景观的保护发展；二是从重视静态遗产保护向重视动态遗产的保护方向发展；三是在文化遗产保护的空间尺度方面，从重视文化遗产的点、面的保护，到今天同时注重大型文化遗产和线性文化遗产保护；四是文化遗产保护的时间尺度方面，从过去文物保护重视古代文物，到后来重视近代史迹，今天还要同时重视20世纪遗产、当代遗产保护；五是从重视过去宫殿、寺庙、教堂、纪念性建筑，到今天重视反映民间普通民众生活的建筑的保护；六是在文化遗产保护形态方面，从重要物质要素的文化遗产保护，向今天同时重视物质要素和非物质要素的方向发展。他总结说，文物保护走向文化遗产保护，是在原有认识上的继承与发展。从古物到文物到文化遗产，反映出人类认识由注重物质财富向注重文化内涵，再向注重精神领域的不断进步。同时，文化遗产更加演绎出城市迷人的底色，使城市更加美丽，与民众生活密切相关，也使城市更加美好。

北京大学高等人文研究院院长杜维明在“城市化与核心价值的文明对话”主旨演讲中说道，世界上各种大都会，因为物欲的充分释放，造成了大家熟悉的环境的破坏、交通堵塞、贫富不均，乃至农村里祖祖辈辈积累的诚实、朴素的价值观念，被城市化解构，甚至成为一种反面价值。我们不应该说“你们发展过了，污染过了，没有权力不让我们发展”之类的蠢话。我们应该踩在纽约、巴黎、伦敦的肩膀上，取其长，避其短，做长程计划，把后发展变成一种优势，把我们的城市建成一座座符合未来人要求的绿色新城。至少我们在积累经济资本的过程中，也要回避前人在建设现代化都市时破坏自然生态的粗鲁，充分利用自然能源，这也是积累社会资本的一种方式。除了发展、培养科技资本以外，很重要的是发展文化的能力，也就是培养对于文学历史哲学，对于宗教信仰的尊重赏识的能力。如果一个城市只有集聚经济资本的能力，没有集聚文化资本的能力，这个城市一定是残疾的，粗鲁的。思想智慧和文化艺术是城市的血脉，也是城市的魅力。举世闻名的大都市，大多具有这些魅力。

苏州市市长阎立在“物质文化遗产保护：寻找城市个性与标识”分论坛发言中指出，只有加强古城保护才能实现文化传承。祖先留下的遗产并非只为今日的人们所独享，更要求将其留给后代，传之永远，这正是我们不遗余力地保护古城、传承文化的宗旨所在。保护古城，更应当推动古城的复兴，在保护中利用古城的历史文化资源，在发展中实现古城文化、经济的全面复兴。也就是说，不但要做古城的守望者，更要做价值的发现者和历史的缔造者。只有推动古城的复兴，才能在永不消散历史印迹的同时，实现古城的永续发展。

同济大学建筑与城市规划学院教授、国家历史文化名城研究中心主任阮仪三教授在该论坛中发表讲话指出，中国有众多的历史古城，都有丰富的文化内涵，并且各具特色，风格迥异。但由于缺乏正确的保护理念，多年来遭到建设性严重破坏。新城建设由于求快、求新，造成了千城一面、万屋一貌。有些比较好的古城保护发展模式值得肯定，保护了旧城、开拓了新区，发展了旅游、振兴了经济的有苏州、平遥、丽江和江南六镇等；保护好历史地段和街区，并根据实际需求合理地利用和创造性发挥的有扬州、绍兴、上海外滩和上海的老洋房地区、旧厂房地区等。城市遗产保护就是重视城市生态，就是城市和谐的问题。“城市，让生活更美好”，新城要美好，老城也要美好，城市要有自己的传统、自己的特色、自己的文化，才能真正更加美好！

当代著名作家、学者王蒙在“城市多元文化的融合与共生”分论坛中，以大众文化与精英文化为主题，指出文化、文艺不仅仅是品牌名片。文化和文艺首先是对于人类的物质与精神的满足，对人类生活的质量提高，是人性的拓展、积累和升华，是人生的魅力，生活的多彩，是历史的庄严与世界的光明。一个有志于从事文化、文艺的人应该有自己的品位与追求，有自己的境界与底线。

肯尼亚内罗毕市市长杰弗里·马基瓦在该分论坛中以“多民族城市中多元文化的繁荣与发展”为主题，指出，如果城市生活的标准是好的，大家就会有凝聚力，所以城市必须制定好的政策，促进文化的竞争，这也是发展的一个根源。不仅仅是经济发展，在知识方面，情感方面，精神方面能够得到更好共存的状况在我们的城市里面有好的例子。我们曾经是一个殖民国家，他们希望把本地的文化吸收进来，在他们离开以后我们人民继承了他们的权利，其文化的特点在改变我们的城市认同，大家谈到城市想到的是好的生活，所以城市应该更好地去弥补差距，缩小不同种族的差距，需要保护自然的环境，这样才能够让人类更好地生活。如果能够实现这一目标，繁荣和发展也是指日可待的。

上海图书馆馆长、2010 年上海世博会主题演绎顾问吴建中在“城市文化创新与实践：创意产业与文化旅游”分论坛中指出，如何保持创意产业可持续进步，是摆在我们面前的一个重要课题。第一，我们要充分挖掘个人的创造力，让更多的人将自己的聪明才智释放和奉献出来，改变由少数人主导产业发展的精英化倾向，使创意产业成为激活每一个人的灵感和活力的智慧产业。第二，要不断挖掘体现民族和区域个性特色的文化积淀，继承传统艺术的精髓，提高民族品牌的影响和竞争力，让传统文化成为创意产业持续发展的不竭源泉。第三，要着力挖掘艺术对经济的渗透和贡献力，艺术不仅是人们精神生活的一部分，而且是经济生活中最具活力的一方面。积极探索新的发展模式，努力从传统文化中、从大自然中寻找人类已经有过的智慧和答案，将那些环境友好的传统手工艺融入创意经济之中，在拓展就业机会的同时，促进社会经济文化的和谐发展。

伦敦城市大学城市学院院长、联合国教科文组织创意城市专家格雷姆·埃文斯指出，我们已经开始从城市文化的概念步入 21 世纪新的理念，文化旅游业在过去大量依赖于政府补贴，处于被动的地位，通过创意产业，我们希望能够有更好的发展。我们创造那些创业集群区实际上并不是只有一个或者两个，我们采取多种多样的发展才略，比如在创造产业区的时候，可能涵盖了艺术家和研究机构，看上去他们之间并不关联，但是实际上有紧密的联系。而所有的这些集群集合在一起，能够创建文化角色和实现文化价值，很重要的一点就是，我们不是一个城市的拯救者，而是以我们的努力激发一个城市的活力，以城市社区和居民能够接受和乐于接受的方式来改变城市。

文化部非物质文化遗产司副司长屈盛瑞在“非物质文化遗产保护：延续城市的历史脉络”分论坛中说道，历史文化名城的保护事关一个城市的人文态度、人文素养。这是事关一个城市的整体文明和我们后代回家的路的问题。保护非物质文化遗产已经成为时代赋予我们的使命和义不容辞的责任。

美国爱达荷州立大学人类学系中美洲研究所高级研究员理查德·汉森认为，非物质文化遗产要和物质文化遗产紧密联系在一起，因为有很多物质文化遗产其实就是非物质文化遗产产生的，它们之间有紧密的联系。如果不把两者紧密连接起来，我们就无法很好地理解非物质文化遗产了。非物质文化遗产和物质文化遗产都要得到足够的重视，要同样重视地去进行保护。当然，在遗产保护的方法上，必须采取一个全面的、全国性的努力，我们要在全国的范围内建立这样一种认同感。很多的社区、政府机构、非官方的机构，都要作出这方面的努力。

复旦大学特聘教授葛剑雄在"文化生态：城市文化要素的继承与演进"分论坛中指出，今天的城市一定胜于以前的城市，那是我们还没有了解先人在城市方面的智慧。如果我们轻易地更新了，就可能造成不可挽回的损失，这个损失不是一座城市的，是我们整个人类的，而这样的损失已经发生了不少。我们从可持续发展的原理出发，也不是所有的旧的城市设施都必须采用彻底消除的办法才能够更新。在一定程度上，我们守旧并使它保持原来的样子或者是保持原来的模式，那恰恰是一种比较有利的发展方针，恰恰是符合今天环保的理念、可持续发展的理念。我觉得在飞速发展的情况下，应该给旧的留下一定的空间，应该神圣地对待我们以前曾经称之为保守落后的观念。城市也必须创新，因为人的生活生产方式总是在发展的，特别是年轻一代要追求新的生活方式。我觉得一座城市应该怎么样创新，起决定作用的是其管理者。

同济大学副校长伍江教授从五个方面来探讨城市文化生态。第一个方面是城市文化生态有一个整体性的特征。任何一个生态系统都是一个完整的系统，如果这个生态系统健康的话，那么其中有自身的相互依存的平衡规律，各种组成部分的平衡一旦被打断，这个生态系统就会崩溃，所以，城市文化的重要特征就是整体。第二个方面是多样性的特征，物种多样性是我们的美丽所在，城市的多样性同样是人类城市文明的灿烂光辉所在。第三个方面是城市文化生态特征的延续性特征。人类文化是一个连续不断的过程，人类文化的连续性是人类自身充满生命力的标志。第四个方面是城市文化生态的道德观，今天人类的道德观发生了很大的变化，如果说我们自身的道德水平有什么进步的话，这个进步就是从人类社会的层面上升到了自然宇宙的层面。我们中国传统文化就是人与自然之间的关系，不是相互冲突的关系，更不是人定胜天的关系，而是天人合一的关系。第五个方面是城市文化生态系统同样也有它的进化，城市从来就不是一成不变的，城市是一个有生命力的载体，其最大的特征是对过去延续，同时还有对新的创造力的要求。

上海市政协副主席、上海世博会执委会副主任周汉民在论坛闭幕总结大会上作总结发言时说道，在城市迅速发展的时代，文化遗产的保护需要汇集全球各方的经验和教训，从而提炼出有现实意义和可操作性的实践指南，这考验着当代人类的智慧。文化多样性，是城市文化传承和发展的基本样态，是人类生存状态的本来面貌。无论保护文化遗产还是繁荣多样文化，都需要文化的继承、演进与创新。上海世博会是跨文化交流和讨论的伟大平台，来自世界各地的人们将共同分享彼此的愿景和目标。

## 四、小结

中国2010年上海世博会城市更新与文化传承主题论坛，通过一个全体大会、六个平行分论坛，就城市更新与文化传承诸方面问题，进行了讨论。面对城市更新对文化传承所造成的困境，面对城市更新对文化多样性产生的冲击，面对城市更新对文化繁荣、文化产业提出的新要求，此次论坛得出了一些对未来城市具有重大启示意义的结论，也形成了一些兼具现实性、可操作性的政策主张。

(1) 文化遗产保护，既包括对物质文化遗产的保护，也包括对非物质文化遗产保护，涉及政治、经济、文化生态等多方面的内容，是一个系统工程，需要持续不断的政策措施和手段。虽然物质文化遗产和非物质文化遗产在具体行动和保护方法上存在相当差异，建筑和人文景区等物质文化遗产更多依赖持续不断的资金投入，而像京剧、歌剧等非物质文化遗产更多依赖特定文化生态的滋养。这两者归根到底都必须返璞归真，从提升民众日常生活化的嗜好和审美情趣入手。否则，无论是物质文化遗产还是非物质文化遗产，就必将失去其遗产的活态性和生存基础，沦落为历史遗存，而失去历史文化遗产的桂冠。

文化遗产保护要取得良好成效，就必须对其存在前提——文化生态，进行深入的修复和架构。有人提出，文化遗产，无论是有形还是无形的，无论是物质还是非物质的，在市场经济条件下都应当成为一种经济资源，要将其与市场结合，并以此作为保护工作的主要方向。但我们同时应当看到，过度强调文化遗产的经济效益，也可能给遗产本身带来灾难性的影响。必须平衡、把握、引导好遗产保护与未来发展的关系。

(2) 文化多样性，是城市内外文化传承和发展的基本样态，是人类生存状态的本来面貌。从跨文化交流与城市文化变迁的互动关系中，我们认识到保证和繁荣文化的多样性，对推动城市发展提升城市居民心灵境界和幸福指数，极为重要。正如世界充满着各种活跃的民主一样，城市中也存在信仰多种价值、多种文化的社会群体。这些群体默默融合成城市文化创造的源头活水。一座城市既有横向文化，也有纵向文化。从横向来看，不同国家与地区之间，本土与外来之间，主流文化与亚文化之间，不同文化背景的人都能彼此尊重、相互包容。纵向来看，现代文化从传统文化中汲取养分，以旧养新、新旧交融，迸发出新的活力。城市文化在纵横交错中不断演进，并显示出多样的繁荣。城市多元文化繁荣，显然不局限于自身，与其他文化的互动也异常重要。

通过本次论坛，我们认为，文化确实可以汇聚成国际政治新的力量，某种程度上推动着经济全球化、政治多极化进程，但文化本身不是也不应成为冲突根源，因为文化的本质在于让生活更美好。我们应当看到，目前更令人担忧的并不是文化多元、多样造成的冲突，而是日渐明显的全球文化趋同的趋势。在这一趋势下推动什么样的文化价值，实行什么样的文化政策，考验着城市文化管理者和经营者的智慧。

(3) 无论保护文化遗产还是繁荣多样文化，都需要文化的继承、演进与创新。需要在适宜的文化生态中推动文化产业成长。通过创意产业积极创造历史城市的文化身份，已经不仅仅是文化命题，更已经成为经济命题。

城市的生长、繁荣，需要数百年乃至千年的历史，而城市也承担着一系列相互交错的功能，它们既是社会包容与融合的载体，也是经济发展驱动力、知识和革新中心。文化产业具有满足人的精神体验和推动经济成长的双重功能，在“城市，让生活更美好”的进程中，作用日益凸显。

威尼斯市市长就威尼斯如何保护文化遗产的介绍，让我们了解到，时代变迁、东西方文化交汇、居民生产和生活方式不断变迁，城市更新，也成为城市历史中永久的现象。因而，怀旧与更新会产生紧张和冲突，处理这种紧张和冲突需要源自城市居民本身的创意。创意和创意社会建设，已经成为城市生活的本质内容。

然而，创意社会离不开创意产业，创意产业也离不开创意经济，而要发展创意经济，更离不开文化、风格、语言等方面的多样性所构成的生态要素，也离不开高度的变化、学习的机会以及适应回报等基本制度框架。未来的政策重点、资源配置应当更加关注城市文化发展的创意要素，及时将城市发展过程中出现的新鲜要素、新鲜现象归纳出来，实施创造性的创意计划，并从更广阔的领域加以推广。无论是国家还是城市，都应当把创意产业列入创意计划，加强人才培养，最终使文化产业成为“城市，让生活更美好”有力的支柱之一。

（作者：冯萱，广州市城市规划勘测设计研究院区域与交通规划设计所工程师）

# “科技创新与城市未来”主题论坛综述

2010年6月20—22日，无锡成功举办2010年上海世博会六大主题论坛之一——“科技创新与城市未来”主题论坛。该论坛由中华人民共和国科学技术部、2010年上海世博会执委会、联合国贸易和发展大会以及无锡市人民政府共同主办。全国政协副主席、科技部部长万钢，江苏省委书记、省人大常委会主任梁保华，上海市市长、上海世博会组委会副主任委员、执委会执行主任韩正，江苏省省长罗志军，联合国贸易和发展会议秘书长素帕猜·巴尼巴滴和上海世博会执委会专职副主任钟燕群等出席论坛。江苏省委常委、无锡市委书记杨卫泽主持开幕式，李政道、巴里·马歇尔、袁隆平、无锡市市长毛小平等40余位中外嘉宾在论坛上进行了演讲和讨论。上海世博会参展方代表、中外专家学者、国内各省、自治区、直辖市代表和中外记者近800人参加论坛。

## 一、论坛背景

当今世界面临气候变化、水源匮乏等威胁，呼唤着新的城市发展模式。科技创新已成为推动经济社会发展的主导力量。城市作为经济社会发展的重要载体，也是创新要素的主要集聚地，科技创新在城市发展中的作用日益突出，将引领城市未来的发展。

在此背景下，“科技创新与城市未来”主题论坛，着力探讨如何将科技创新与城市未来有效融合，寻求未来城市可持续发展的科技对策，并在相关领域达成重要共识，形成了一些对城市未来发展有启示作用的思想成果。

## 二、主要议程

本次主题论坛通过一个全体大会、四个平行分论坛、一个圆桌讨论和闭幕总结大会，从安全、发展、教育、竞争力和生活等五个方面，对城市安全保障与可持续发展中的科技创新问题、科技创新如何提升城市综合竞争力，以及科技如何创造未来美好生活等热点问题进行了广泛的讨论。

**1. 全体大会：科技创新与城市未来**

城市是人类文明的结晶和象征，科技进步为城市发展提供了强劲动力，有力推动了城市的变革，日益改变着人们的生活方式和生产方式；随着技术的进步和社会的发展，将带给人们更美好的生活和更繁荣的经济。面向未来，中国政府将着眼于城市的可持续发展，继续加大科技创新力度，加快发展方式转变，让科学技术引领城市未来发展。

**2. 平行论坛一：科技创新保障城市安全**

在自然或人为灾害面前，城市往往显得比农村更加脆弱，特大型城市所面临的压力尤为巨大。世界各地的城市管理经验均表明，科学技术在保障城市安全尤其是应对灾害的过程中意义重大。从城市规划、公共设施配置到公共卫生和灾害应急系统的构建，科技处处发挥着重要作用，保障着城市安全。在本平行分论坛，来自美国、日本、印度、中国的科技专家介绍了城市安全领域的科技创新前沿趋势，展望更安全、更美好的未来城市生活。

**3. 平行论坛二：科技创新引领城市发展**

在21世纪，资源环境与可持续发展问题是人类会面临的最大挑战。未来的城市需要探索可持续发展的解决方案，而科技创新是推动这种探索的主要动力。能源、环保、通信、控制、计算机等前沿技术综合应用于城市发展，将有效缓解能源、资源和环境压力。本平行分论坛聚焦这一领域，探讨科技创新对城市可持续发展的引领作用。

**4. 平行论坛三：科技创新提升城市竞争力**

近年来，随着各国经济发展和社会不断进步，科技对经济的引领作用日益凸显。科技创新能力不断地加强，决定着城市竞争力得到更大提升，经济更加繁荣，社会更加和谐。提升城市综合竞争力必须进一步增强自主创新意识，健全专业技术人才培养体系，优化科技管理体制，壮大高新技术产业，培育新的经济增长极，健全知识产权保护体系以及加强科普建设工作，提高全民科学文化素养。

**5. 平行论坛四：科技创新创造美好生活**

创新引领科技，科技创造未来。未来的时代，是一个科技革命的时代，一个富有创新的时代。该分论坛聚焦未来科技发展的创新点及亮点，选取信息技术、新材料技术、纳米技术、生命科学和生物技术等典型领域，以此展示未来科技的灿烂成果，保证各种需求人士享用平等发展机会和生存权利，以及先进科技带给人类的美好图景。

**6. 圆桌对话：教育与人才培养**

一个国家，一个城市能否可持续发展，能否在国际竞争中具有竞争力，关键在人才，根本在教育。任何一个社会的科技创新都离不开该社会的科普教育底蕴。在全球科技革命浪潮中，科技人才资源竞争必然加剧，因此，引导、鼓励和支持培养科技创业人才和领军人物极为重要。专家们认为要坚持终身教育、全民教育、实践教育、多元教育来培养人才，同时要强化基础性教育和国际化教育，使我们培养的人才具有独立的科技创新能力、符合社会的真正需求。

## 三、主要论点

联合国贸易和发展会议秘书长素帕猜·巴尼巴滴在开幕致辞上剖析了科技与城市问题的关系。他认为，城市在解决环境问题上的最好方法，就是通过一个可以实现国家和地方层面的合作和交通的规划体系，城市的规划者可以让城市更加高效、宜居，可以通过规划和投资建筑、交通、能源、沟通、水管理和卫生系统，而挑战在于如何结合新技术、城市设计以及基于社区的创新。

江苏省省长罗志军认为，科技进步为城市发展提供了强劲动力，有力推动了城市的变革，日益改变着人们的生活方式和生产方式。面向未来，我们要坚持以科技创新引领城市发展，推动城市转型，加快建设创新型城市、活力城市，使城市成为新兴产业的集聚地、科技创新的主阵地、文化创造的新高地，始终保持旺盛的发展生机。

上海市市长韩正认为，科技创新是推动人类社会文明进步的强大动力，也是驱动城市化进程、促进城市可持续发展的强大动力。现代世界城市的发展史，很鲜明而又突出的一个特征，就是城市是科技创新的摇篮、是推动创新扩散的中心，科技创新是破解城市发展难题的利器、是引领支撑城市发展的引擎。

全国政协副主席、科技部部长万钢认为，城市是人类文明的结晶和象征，随着技术的进步和社会的发展，城市发展正处在一个转型期。城市的发展动力、发展方式、发展模式等的转变，将带给人们更美好的生活和更繁荣的经济。而上海世博会正提供这样一个平台，并展示出这样一个愿景。面向未来，中国政府将着眼于城市的可持续发展，继续加大科技创新力度，加快发展方式转变，让科学技术引领城市未来发展。

诺贝尔物理学奖得主、美国哥伦比亚大学教授李政道的演讲“世搏始博”中有很多精彩的言论。他认为“世搏”是世世代代和大自然的搏斗，“世博”是世世代代我们成功的博览，正是人类与大自然世世代代的搏斗才开始产生了今日如此宏伟的世博会。“昔时矿山已无锡，今日科技可博世”。也正是因为这些科技的“搏斗”，我们这个黄土蓝水的地球才比宇宙其他部分有特色、有智慧、有人的道德。

当有些人怀疑科技和城市发展给我们带来的是灾难时，巴里·马歇尔持有反对的观点：只要保持经济的繁荣，应用新的科技来解决现代城市生活中的问题，我们就可以继续过上美好的生活，而不需要作出太多的牺牲。而现代城市的成功是因为人们改善了他们的生活环境，使更多的人可以有一个健康的生活。由此带来的不仅仅是科技的规模化，同时也使得社会分工更加的专业化，更加的全球化，也使得我们更加需要彼此。

中国工程院院士、“杂交水稻之父”袁隆平介绍了研发杂交水稻的意义所在。袁隆平用数据说明了在世界范围内大力发展杂交水稻，必将对保障世界粮食安全和为发展中国家解决粮食短缺发挥重要作用。

国务院参事、国家减灾委专家委副主任闪淳昌认为我国的城镇化和城市现代化取得重大进展。但是，城市公共安全面临着许多新风险、新情况、新问题、新挑战。必须贯彻落实科学发展观，统筹做好城市规划、建设和管理等各项工作，加快防灾减灾体系建设，建立健全城市的应急体制机制，坚持以人为本，建设安全宜居城市。必须把城市公共安全状况的根本好转，建立在依靠科技进步、加强科学管理的基础上，提高城市应对危机和风险的能力，让城市更加安全和谐。

美国华盛顿大学生物工程系荣休教授艾伦·S·霍夫曼指出，从全球的角度来看，细菌和病毒将持续不断地挑战未来的城市安全。他总结了目前及发展中的定点照护诊断分析报告，并介绍了华盛顿大学的新型测试方法，比如根据智能聚合磁性和金纳米粒设计和开发的微流体免疫测定，可快速直接地对细菌和病毒进行检测。

中国高等科学技术中心学术主任叶铭汉的报告指出，紧凑型荧光管（或称之为“节能灯”）废弃的灯管如果处理不当，将会造成环境污染。最好的办法是利用科技创新来保障城市安全，用更省电、更环保的光源来替代这种不十分理想的紧凑型荧光灯（节能灯），如正在发展中的发光二极管（LED）是极有希望的新光源。

印度计划委员会共享性增长低碳战略专家组主席、印度计划委员会前委员基里特·帕里克认为，印度和中国一样，面临着城市化突飞猛进的问题。在很多问题上，印度和中国具有相似性，比如建立公共交通系统、提供干净的生活用水、固体废弃物处理、建设排水设施、提高污水处理能力、提高能源使用效率、提供干净的居住环境等对一个可持续的、宜居的、舒适的城市而言都至关重要。如果没有发生重大的技术变革，这些是很难，甚至是不可能实现的。中国和印度可以在这些问题上共同探讨，互相借鉴。

军事工程专家、教育家、中国工程院院士钱七虎认为，中国交通困境可以通过探索未来的城市交通和城际交通来解决。他认为发展地下磁悬浮交通是缓解我国城市化难题的有效手段和未来交通的必然发展趋势。必须进行地下磁悬浮试验研究，从而实现客运交通以地下轨道交通（地铁）为主，货运交通以地下货物运输系统为主的未来交通。

日本关西学院大学综合政策学部教授室崎益辉针对日本多自然灾害的特点，介绍了日本在灾后重建中所遇到的问题和解决经验。他认为大规模灾害发生之后，重建的目的应该是在灾害前的状况上进行提升，而不是照实恢复原有状态。要从灾害经验中学习，就一定要完善脆弱的城市结构，因为只有这样才能避免同样的灾难重演。在利用资源方面，理想的情景是建立这样一座城市：在这里，若需要灾后重建，就可以调动众多的资源和人力，并能得以有效利用。

北京大学原常务副校长王义遒认为，作为城市安全管理工作处在城市管理的顶层，在开展常态与突发态安全管理工作时，需要掌握城市运行相关的大量信息资源并对相关信息资源进行快速分析研判，为应急处置提供准确翔实的决策辅助信息，并需要全面的信息化支撑服务。数字城市的相关建设工作成果，包括基础网络、安全设施、信息资源共享平台、空间地理信息系统等，都能够为城市安全管理应用系统的建设和使用过程提供支撑，为相关系统的快速搭建和高效应用打下信息化基础。

江苏无锡市委副书记、市长毛小平回顾了近几年以科技创新引领无锡城市转型之路。科技创新绝不是单一的经济驱动，它需要创新氛围的感染、创新文化的熏陶和创新理念的支撑。以科技创新引领城市转型，产业优化是基础，人才引育是关键，环境改善是保障，文化提升是核心。这几点对于我们其他城市转型都具有很好的指导意义。

国际科学理事会副主席、东京大学教授、行政理事会成员黑田玲子介绍了国际科学理事会应对城市问题的方法。在一个全球化的时代，知识型的经济、知识的竞争专业化就是我们所处的这个时代的特征。那么如何运用科技来解决我们所面临的问题，或者说来预防城市化当中出现的问题，如何改善科技创新，更好地解决城市化当中遇到的种种问题就成为亟需深思与解决的难题。国际科学理事会综合各个区域、各个领域的人才来共同着手解决这些问题。

国际交通论坛总干事科林·斯泰西介绍了科技创新在交通领域是如何引领城市发展的。要解决车辆、燃料、管理网络等方面的问题。此外，城市交通发展面临的最大挑战，就是公众对于改变的接受程度。这涉及我们现在的认识。由于城市人口的增长，交通的增长可持续性就成为一个重要的问题，必须要在所有的模式当中增加可持续性，同时需要框架方面的配合。

英国曼彻斯特大学可持续化学工程教授阿迪萨·阿扎帕吉克的报告针对城市人类活动碳足迹测量提出了一些想法。从政府、工程师或者消费者来讲，该如何减少温室气体的排放呢？第一种方式就是适应气候变化，然后开始采取一些防御措施，保护自己；另一种方式可以利用技术上的更新或者说改变我们的生活方式从而减少气候变化。但是哪一种技术和活动本身是低碳的就需要对碳排放进行测评，其手段就是计算碳足迹。

英国苏塞克斯大学科学与技术政策研究部主任戈登·麦克伦介绍了科技管理方面的内容。他认为，现在的技术虽然说不上完美，但是已经足够好了，真正的问题是有没有很好的政策系统把这些技术充分的利用发挥作用，所以主要的障碍在于技术能不能被利用起来。这个障碍存在于治理结构当中，如何在城市治理的不同系统当中更好地利用技术，让我们的城市发展有更高的可持续性，才是挑战所在。

国家自然科学基金委员会副主任、中国科学院上海分院院长、上海市科协主席沈文庆介绍了三个教育观点。首先，继续教育、终身教育是人才培养的一个重要理念。其次，要在科学实践中培养人才，同时也只有在科学实践当中才能推动城市科技的创新。最后，全民科学素养是城市发展的基础，是涌现人才的源泉。

西澳大学生命和物理学院院长修权治谈到了“教育和研究的国际化”。想要改进城市的质量，就必须要改进这个城市大学的质量。目前中国大学碰到了一个挑战，就是如何把地方大学变成全球大学。虽然在地方一级已经有了一些国际合作，但在学生之间的国际交流方面受到先行教育体制的限制。我们要跨越这样的局限，使我们21世纪的大学生能够成为全球的公民，能够具有真正的全球视野。

美国宾夕法尼亚大学教育研究生院副院长严正认为，better city 应该有最好的教育，有了好的教育才能 make better city 和 better life。教育与人才培养不完全是以钱为主，也不一定以学位为主，而是要以质量为主。这个质量是要由各个城市和各个学校的教授去鉴定的，而且需要城市来承认它。教育质量要看的是交给学生的是什么东西，要让学生成为终身的学习者，交给他 tool，教给他怎么学习，这才是教育最成功的地方。

美国斯坦福大学荣休教授、美国斯坦福创新与创业地区项目（SPRIE）联席主任威廉·米勒谈到了创业精神的培养。对于一个城市、一个地区，如果想成为一个充满活力的企业家的天堂，它必须有下列的一些特征：第一，必须要有研究能力，要有很多的工程师在这个地区；第二，也要企业家自己把这些创新成果产业化，有时候有了研究成果不一定可以转化为现实；第三，还必须有一个很好的商业社会的气氛来鼓励创业。

同济大学党委副书记、上海市科学技术委员会世博科技促进中心副主任姜富明认为，大学如同人、城市、地球这个生命共同体的大脑一样，它实际上是一个城市发展中的思想库和智慧谷。如果大学的功能发挥好，那么相信在城市化的进程中，我们就可以避免很多不应该出现的污染和不应该出现的生态破坏等等。要培养可持续发展的人才，我们也不能以过去传统的方式来传授知识，可能更需要注于培养具有绿色智商的人才。

江南大学校长、国家教育部科技委委员、中国轻工联合会理事会副会长陈坚认为，大学与城市应该有彼此的责任感。一方面，大学当然应该主动融入城市，强化服务和引领城市的经济社会发展的理念。服务和引领，这是大学的责任，并且付诸行动。另一方面，通过制度化的投资和项目引导，让大学和城市共生、共赢。

俄罗斯联邦国务秘书、俄罗斯联邦工业和贸易部副部长斯坦尼斯拉夫·瑙莫夫介绍了俄罗斯是如何利用技术创新解决城市问题的。他认为技术创新和发展，在改变现代城市环境中发挥着重要的作用，技术对于改进生活质量和城市居民的生活品质有着重要的意义，这一点在能源领域得到了充分的体现。技术创新可以极大地改进电力使用的有效性，对于传统能源和可再生能源来说都是如此。同时它也可以提供有效的方法，建立预测系统，让我们能够更好地抵御技术和自然的灾害，可以让我们城市的交通可及性更加便捷，同时让我们的医疗服务更便宜，生活品质更好。

国家自然科学基金委员会副主任、中国科学院上海分院院长、上海市科协主席沈文庆就基础研究对引领城市创新的作用进行了解说。他认为，基础研究是自主创新的活力之源，基础研究的文化功能就是提升全民科学素养，同时要发挥支撑引领作用，依靠创新来驱动城市发展。

芬兰阿尔托大学校长图拉·泰里介绍了大学在提升城市竞争力中的作用，她认为人才的培养要多方面来考虑。谈到创新，大家可能想到的就是技术方面的专长，当然你也需要经济学方面领域的专业知识。但是除此之外，你还需要有设计和艺术方面的才能，来激发创新的热情，这样才能够在社会上进行创新。所以最重要的问题在于我们能够找到什么样的人和我们一起工作。我们必须找到人才，要用最好的人才，在社会上最重要的问题上工作，同时我们要能够留住人才，这些问题对于大学和社区来说同样的重要。

美国斯坦福大学荣休教授、美国斯坦福创新与创业地区项目（SPRIE）联席主任威廉·米勒指出，对于一个城市和对于一个地区来说，要成为一个有活力的高技术的地区，第一，要有基本的资源，比如说研究的人员、工程师，他们能够创新。第二，要有企业家，他们能够将这些创新变成商业机会。第三，还需要一种生存环境，那是社会、政治、经济的环境，能够推动企业家精神，并且培养企业家。要特别关注创新人才的培养，创新人才在所有的劳动力当中，他们所得到的回报比例是最高的，而且创新人才越多，地区的增长速度也越快。

意大利的里雅斯特大学代数学教授、生物医学产学研联合体（CBM）总裁玛利亚·克里斯蒂娜·佩迪奇奥介绍了意大利关于研究、创新和人才方面的问题。她指出，欧洲倡导的是开放性的创新，所谓开放性是指各个方面都能够进行自由的思想、资本、技术和才能的交换。因为这些市场和研究行为是相互影响，相互推动，相互激发的，所以必须建立公共部门和私营部门之间的密切合作。这对于重大的经济社会挑战来说，是一个非常有效的措施。

Discovery 国际电视网总裁兼首席执行官马克·霍林格介绍了 Discovery 的节目宗旨。他说今天的世界已经不可以按照东西方来区分，而是一个地球村，Discovery 讲述的故事是关于这个世界的，是为这个世界讲述的。一个国家发生的事情不可避免都会影响到其他国家，Discovery 要把这个故事讲出来。

世博会总代表联席会议主席、世博指导委员会主任、世博日本政府总代表塚本弘介绍了日本的科技创新及未来生活模式——未来社会如何使用机器人。在世博会的日本展馆，它的主要宗旨就是能够很好地利用机器人，而且尽可能多地利用它们创造更美好的生活。包括清洁工作的清洁机器人、机器人金鸡独立、见面机器人、搬运工机器人，以及为一些老年人、残障人士提供帮助的机器人，这些机器人会对未来的生活起到很大的作用。

同济大学科技处副处长，上海市世博科技促进中心副主任李光明认为，世博会是利用科技创新来引领未来美好生活的，而世博会最大的魅力就是看科技。以往的世博会已经能感受到很多新的产品、新的科技应用改变我们的生活。上海的世博会对我们的城市话题产生什么样的影响呢？世博会的各个展馆都在讨论城市话题，城市最佳实践区更是展望了未来的城市生活，同时在世博会的各个角落都存在着科技亮点，体现着科技魅力。

尚德电力控股有限公司董事长兼首席执行官施正荣介绍了从世博样本看太阳能的发展前景，比如中国馆的最顶端采用了光伏的组件，同时也应用了制冷技术，可以使中国馆不仅成为非常好的中国文化的展示之地，也能够在夏天成为非常舒适的地方。主题馆在屋顶上同样应用了太阳能组件，这种 BIPV 的技术，也就是和楼宇一体化的太阳能技术。中国在太阳能使用方面还是初步的，但在 21 世纪末之前，70% 的电力将会由太阳能来提供。

## 四、小结

“科技创新与城市未来”主题论坛，通过一个全体大会、四个平行分论坛，一个圆桌讨论和闭幕总结大会，阐述了城市与科技之间相互促进、互为依托的关系，为寻求未来城市可持续发展的科技对策提供了大量丰富而精彩的素材，也为国际间各领域的交流提供了一个很好的平台。

**共识一：科技创新是城市未来发展的动力和保障**

科技进步和创新为城市发展提供了强劲动力，有力推动了城市的变革，日益改变着人们的生活方式和生产方式。

科技发展不仅从城市规划、公共设施配置到公共卫生和灾害应急系统的构建等方面，保障着城市安全，而且，通过能源、环保、通信、控制、计算机等前沿技术综合应用于城市发展，将有效缓解能源、资源和环境压力。

科技发展在未来对城市经济发展的贡献将越来越大，将壮大高新技术产业，培育新的经济增长极，提升城市综合竞争力。而且，科技的发展特别是信息技术、新材料技术、纳米技术、生命科学和生物技术等典型领域的技术突破，能保证未来各种需求人士享用平等发展机会和生存权利，带给人类更好的生存环境。

**共识二：城市要为科技创新创造良好环境和提供支持**

城市发展要为科技创新提供制度支持，建立鼓励、支持创新的氛围；实行开放性的创新，在社会各个方面都能够进行自由的思想、资本、技术和才能的交换。

要注重创新人才培养。坚持终身教育、全民教育、实践教育、多元教育，同时要强化基础性教育和国际化教育，使我们培养的人才具有独立的科技创新能力。在提高创新人才在劳动力当中比例的同时，注重培养创新科技的领军人物。

（作者：李少云，广州市城市规划勘测设计研究院城市与建筑设计所所长，高级规划师）

# “环境变化与城市责任”主题论坛综述

2010年7月3—4日，由环境保护部、中国气象局、国家能源局、上海世博会执行委员会、联合国环境规划署和南京市政府共同主办的中国2010年上海世博会“环境变化与城市责任”主题论坛在南京举行。

中共中央政治局委员、上海市委书记俞正声，全国政协副主席厉无畏，江苏省委书记、省人大常委会主任梁保华在开幕式上致辞。环保部部长周生贤，国家发改委副主任、能源局局长张国宝，中国气象局局长郑国光，联合国副秘书长、环境规划署执行主任阿希姆·施泰纳和联合国政府间气候变化专门委员会主席拉金德拉·帕乔里在全体大会上作主旨演讲。上海世博会参展方代表，中外专家学者，国内环保、气象系统代表和中外记者700余人出席论坛。

## 一、论坛背景

城市汇聚了人类文明进步的精华，创造了巨大的物质财富和精神财富，越来越多的居民享受着城市现代生活。但是，城市的发展也带来了人口膨胀、交通拥挤、环境污染等严峻困扰和挑战。特别是资源环境问题日益突出，气候变化、资源枯竭、生态破坏已成为人类社会必须面对的重大课题，也在很大程度上挑战着我们既有的城市发展理念、发展模式和生活方式。城市作为人类生活的重要空间载体，既产生环境问题，也受害于环境的恶化，更应该是环境问题解决方案的重要提供者和执行者。

2010年上海世博会是一届以城市与生活为主题的世博会，其主要目的是通过展览展示和论坛研讨，来探索和思考“更好的城市，更美的生活”。上海世博会担负起着实践和传播可持续发展理念的重要角色，荟萃全球绿色环保城市的先进案例、成功经验和无限创意，充分展示城市文明成果，交流城市建设经验，传播先进城市发展理念；致力于探究什么样的城市才能让生活更美好，致力于办成一届低碳环保的全球盛会，致力于成为低碳环保理念重要的倡导者、实践者和传播者，从而为人类可持续发展留下一份丰厚的精神遗产。

世博会期间共举办了六个主题论坛。作为汇聚全球环境领域前沿思想的舞台，本次南京论坛选择了“环境变化与城市责任”为主题，围绕环境保护、低碳发展、绿色创新等热点话题进行交流，分享应对气候变化、实现可持续发展的经验，加强政府、企业、公民的环境责任意识，共同探讨城市未来的发展模式和相关各方的环境责任，应对环境变化的挑战。

## 二、主要议程

“环境变化与城市责任”主题论坛包括一个全体大会、六个平行分论坛和一个闭幕总结大会。六个平行分论坛分别为：低碳发展与气候变化应对；产业发展与绿色创新：公众参与绿色城市建设；城市环境综合治理与清洁能源发展；产业发展与绿色创新：可持续建筑；可持续的生产和生活模式。

“低碳发展与气候变化应对”平行分论坛：气候变化是全球共同面对的巨大挑战，需要全球城市为此展开合作，尤其是围绕技术资金开展的合作。国际城市间的合作、环保经验分享和技术转让等都是应对气候变化的重要支撑。而全球低碳未来和低碳核心技术的勃兴将在世界范围内提升能源产业及其装备制造业的战略地位，城市既面临空前的竞争压力，又存在跨越式发展的机遇。在这一过程中，要积极加强城市低碳政策和管理机制建设，为低碳发展营造良好的环境。

“产业发展与绿色创新”平行分论坛：企业绿色创新是应对环境变化的重中之重。能源危机、金融危机和全球变暖，给世界产业经济带来巨大的挑战，也带来重大发展机遇，发挥绿色产业已经成为发达国家和发展中国家的共识。绿色产业采用清洁生产，即采用无害或低害的新工艺、新技术，大力降低原材料和能源消耗，实现少投入、高产出、低污染，尽可能把对环境污染物的排放消除在生产过程之中。

“公众参与绿色城市建设”平行分论坛：2010 年世博会是一次环境友好的绿色盛会，是一次弘扬绿色理念的盛会。政府、公民和企业都是弘扬绿色环保理念的主要行为体。在教育宣传和媒体层面上，世界城市可以引导和鼓励社会公众参与绿色城市建设，推动全社会有效参与环境保护。

“城市环境综合治理和清洁能源发展”平行分论坛：城市作为解决环境问题，倡导可持续发展的行为主体，应当以重大活动为契机，提升活动举办城市的环境行为，充分发挥示范带动效应。本论坛探讨城市的产业发展模式、环保政策、城市环境规划、绿色能源与交通等。传统化石燃料威胁到日益脆弱的地球生态系统，对清洁能源的利用则是大势所趋，走可持续的低成本的清洁能源发展之路成为未来城市的首选。

“产业发展与绿色创新：可持续建筑”平行分论坛：“绿色建筑”是指按照可持续发展理念设计规划的建筑。绿色建筑的设计所涉及的内容包括建筑材料、建筑物、城市区域规模大小等等，设计中必须考虑同时兼具功能性、经济性、社会文化和生态等诸多要素。绿色建筑倡导“高效率地利用资源、最低限度地影响环境”，以此为目标营造“健康、舒适、安全”的居住和商业环境。绿色建筑的推广使用是解决城市发展所造成的诸多环境问题的一大途径，其系统应用也因此成为了未来城市的必然选择。在这一过程中，学者、建筑师、企业、政府都有责任推动这一变革，以尽量降低城市化发展对环境造成的不良影响。

“可持续的生产和生活模式”平行分论坛：联合国《21 世纪议程》明确提出：“全球性

环境持续恶化的主要原因在于不可持续的消费和生产模式。”实现环境可持续，必须实现物质资料的生产、人类自身的生产和环境生产三者的协调。而这一协调既需要正确的理论和准则作为指导，也需要依靠方法和技术进行操作。在这一过程中，政府的作用就在于把各种手段结合成一个系统的整体行为，去提高公众的可持续发展意识；而公民，作为解决环境问题的重要行为体，需要通过可持续消费等行为来实现可持续发展、解决城市环境问题。以绿色消费为主要内容的可持续消费观念、可持续消费机制以及城市的可持续消费行动，均是本次论坛研讨的重点。

## 三、主要论点

上海市委书记俞正声在致辞中表示，以“城市，让生活更美好”为主题的上海世博会担负着实践和传播可持续发展理念的重要角色。以筹备和举办世博会为契机，上海进一步加大了节能减排和环境保护力度，推动经济社会持续快速发展和城市环境同步改善。此次论坛通过聚焦全球化、城市化进程中的环境问题，共同探讨城市未来的发展模式和相关各方的环境责任，相信一定能为应对全球环境变化的挑战和促进城市可持续发展带来有益启迪和帮助。

全国政协副主席厉无畏在致辞中表示，此次世博论坛旨在从环境角度探索人、城市和地球的关系，揭示城市与自然环境的相互影响，以及城市在全球环境治理中的重要地位和责任，相信对于城市如何更好治理环境、实践低碳经济，构建更有效的国际城市间环境合作机制，更好发挥城市在全球环境治理中重要载体和平台的作用具有重要意义。节能减排和低碳发展已在中国成为热点话题和大势所趋，相信本次论坛一定会为城市管理者提供有指导性的理念和实践主张，对企业清洁生产机制提出更明确的战略方针，对公众低碳生活方式的养成提供清晰指南。

江苏省委书记、省人大常委会主任梁保华在致辞中表示，江苏正处在加速推进城市化和城市现代化的关键时期，我们坚定不移走科学发展之路，坚持环保优先、节约优先，致力于建设环境友好型、资源节约型生态城市。江苏将以本次论坛为契机，学习借鉴世界环保先进理念和成功经验，积极开展城市环保的国际交流与合作，努力把城市建设得更美好，让人民的生活更幸福。

环保部部长周生贤表示，中国政府高度重视环境保护工作，把环境保护确定为基本国策，把实现可持续发展作为国家战略。我们必须深入贯彻科学发展观，在生态文明的视野下，在新型工业化和快速城镇化的进程中，立足于中国国情，借鉴世界各国的经验教训，不断改革创新，积极探索一条代价小、效益好、排放低、可持续的环境保护新路。

联合国副秘书长、环境规划署执行主任阿希姆·施泰纳表示，联合国环境规划署一直关注中国的可持续发展。今天的城市是创新的前沿，同时也是实现可持续发展目标的重要对象。我们谈论绿色经济，谈论城市发展，中国也在讨论下一个五年规划。希望中国的愿景和志向得以实现，使中国将自己的发展模式进行转型，最终也鼓励世界上更多的国家和地区向中国学习。

国家发改委副主任、能源局局长张国宝表示，中国政府高度重视城市和环境的协调发展，并在建设低碳城市、减少环境污染方面，开展了大量卓有成效的工作。建设低碳城市，应对环境变化，需要城市领导者和居民的共同努力，坚持科学发展，促进城市和环境和谐。要大力发展低碳能源、促进城市低碳发展、倡导低碳的消费方式和生活方式并开展国际交流与合作。

联合国政府间气候变化专门委员会主席拉金德拉·帕乔里表示，今天世界一半以上人口居住在城市中，城市面临的挑战之一是要找出一个可持续的城市化方式，避免对自然资源的滥用。我们必须走"低碳"之路，只有这样才能维系可持续发展。气候变化是人类面临的最大挑战，我们必须朝着绿色增长的方向发展。上海世博会的实践和建设，向全世界传达了低碳环保的信息。这个信息非常重要，而且做得很有成效。

中国气象局局长郑国光表示，气候变化既是环境问题，更是发展问题。上海世博会的主题阐述了城市发展与人类生活和谐统一的理念，为了实现这一理念，需要把应对气候变化与城市可持续发展紧密结合起来，把减缓气候变化和适应气候变化紧密结合起来，把法律制度和社会行动紧密结合起来，以发展经济为核心，以节约能源、优化能源结构、加强生态保护和建设为重点；以科学进步为支撑，以市民整体素质提高为基础，努力控制和减缓城市温室气体的排放，不断提高城市适应气候变化的能力。

清华大学公共管理学院教授胡鞍钢表示，国家"十二五"规划将成为中国第一个绿色发展规划，将成为中国实现绿色现代化的历史起点。全球气候变化不仅是全球的最大挑战，也是中国未来发展的最大挑战；中国需要积极地参与第四次工业革命，即绿色工业革命；要积极促进绿色合作。

上海市常务副市长、上海世博会执委会常务副主任杨雄表示，本次论坛围绕"环境变化和城市责任"的主题，从应对气候变化与低碳发展、城市环境治理、绿色产业发展、可持续交通和建筑、可持续的生产和消费模式、公众参与等方面，重点探讨了城市如何承担环境保护的责任和义务，就如何选择符合城市特点的可持续发展道路，如何通过技术、政策创新落实全社会环境责任等问题，形成了一系列共识和主张。本次论坛汇集了世界各地专家学者和城市管理者的智慧与实践成果，这是上海世博会留给世界的一笔重要精神财富，必将对进一步推动城市和全球可持续发展发挥重要作用。

联合国环境规划署前执行主任克劳斯·特普费尔表示，本次论坛邀请了来自全球的建筑设计师、城市规划者、政策制定者和企业家，共同探讨城市化进程中面临的挑战和可持续发展模式，听取各自的经验和做法，是一个真正的互相学习的好平台。上海世博会传递了一个非常清晰的信息，那就是面对全球环境挑战，必须马上采取行动。我们必须清醒地意识到，低碳经济、低碳城市的成功是实现经济和城市可持续发展的重要前提。

## 四、小结

"环境变化与城市责任"主题论坛，来自世界各地的专家学者，对世博会主题"城市，让生活更美好”隐含的三个理念基于环境视角给予充分诠释：“只有人与环境和谐的城市才能让生活更美好；只有积极应对环境变化的城市才能让未来更美好；只有资源节约、环境友好的城市发展模式才能让地球家园更美好。”根据各位参会人员发言的观点，未来城市围绕环境变化，主要呈现以下趋势：

（1）城市将成为应对全球气候变暖和环境变化的主战场。据联合国副秘书长阿希姆·施泰纳的报告，当今城市消耗了75%以上的世界资源，城市居民大概产出了60%～80%的温室气体；而且城市也应该意识到：城市不再是孤独的存在，而是处在一个经济和生态的大环境当中。俞正声认为，城市的可持续发展离不开全球的发展环境，同样，全球的可持续发展必须落实到地区和城市的行动当中。上海市要坚持气候变化等全球环境问题与城市当地环境污染问题协同解决的观点，在解决城市环境问题中为全球环境问题的解决作出贡献。郑国光指出，城市化的快速发展造成了城市温室气体排放的显著上升，城市也是受气候变化影响的脆弱地区。在全球气候变暖和城市化快速发展的背景下，台风、局部暴雨、高温热浪、低温冷害等极端气候现象频繁发生，并与城市环境状况和城市居民活动交织在一起，诱发了一系列次生灾害，形成灾害链事件，对城市安全运行产生了重大影响，如2005年肆虐美国新奥尔良城的“卡特里娜”飓风。在全球气候变暖的背景下，过去认为是较小程度的波动也会对当今城市的某些方面造成很大的影响。一场暴雨可以使一座现代化的城市全面瘫痪，复杂的气候异常容易导致流行疾病的传播和现代城市人心血管、呼吸道等疾病的发生率增加。城市经济相对发达，公众科学素质相对较高，生产能力和消费能力都比较大，对于生命财产安全和良好的生存生活环境有着深刻的诉求，对于科学应对气候变化和促进城市和谐发展有着紧迫的压力，对于减轻温室气体排放强度和保护全球气候有着不可推卸的责任。积极应对气候变化是城市应尽的职责，是实现让城市更安全、让生活更美好的重要基础。

（2）积极转变城市建设理念和发展方式，构建以低碳发展为中心的城市发展体系。郑国光认为，应当面对资源环境约束条件下城市化面临的现实矛盾和未来的挑战，通过明确城市发展的资源消耗和环境影响的目标要求，来实现城市的可持续发展。要对城市经济发展阶段发展模式开展充分的战略评估，结合城市的特征，确立低碳、绿色的发展战略。要科学系统地分析城市温室气体排放的结构和特点，制定合理的低碳绿色发展的规划。要挖掘新能源利用、建筑节能、新能源交通、绿色消费等领域温室气体减排的潜力，实现城市节能减排降耗的目标，达到城市可持续发展。在城市规划和建设领域，张国宝认为，要贯彻低碳理念，着力推进交通、建筑和照明节能，推广太阳能光热一体化建筑。要鼓励使用新能源汽车，优先发展公共交通和轨道交通。要加强城市智能电网和分布式能源建设。要推动能源技术进步，提高城市能源利用效率。

（3）创新绿色技术、发展绿色产业，是推进可持续发展的产业必然选择。城市是人们生活的空间，也是市民共守的家园。政府的一个重要责任，就是要在产业发展、城市建设与管理中，坚持绿色发展理念，推进绿色产业发展。南京市市长季建业认为，重点应该推进产业“五个化”的发展，即低碳化、智能化、集约化、生态化和循环化。其中，低碳化就是加快产业转型升级步伐、发展方式转变和运用低碳技术改造提升传统产业，广泛推广环保新技术、节能新产品，对重点节能项目予以专项资金支持和奖励。在能源应用中合理调整煤电油气使用比重，积极发展利用太阳能发电、风力发电，推进能源结构的多元化、清洁化、可持续化发展。智能化，重点实施智能工业、智能环保、智能交通、智能灾害防空、智能农业、智能公共安全、智能医护、智能物流、智能电网和智能家居等物联网应用十大示范工程，力争把南京建设成为智慧之都。集约化就是明确城市主体功能区，优化产业布局；发展新兴产业集群，重点是围绕绿色新能源、电力自动化与智能电网、现代通信、节能环保、生物医药、新材料、轨道交通和航空航天产业，着力打造新兴产业集群；推进绿色集聚区建设。生态化就是在产业发展中，设置绿色门槛，增加绿色标准，大力发展高端制造业和高端服务业，坚决淘汰落后产能；强化生态修复与环境工程治理。循环化就是大力推进循环型企业和循环生态园区建设。

（4）构建以公众参与为目的的城市人文体系，推动生态文明建设和绿色发展。中国气象局局长郑国光指出，要充分发动城市各阶层的力量，利用各种资源开展应对气候变化和防灾减灾的科普教育和宣传，把气候变化的事实、影响的科学的阶段、适应和减缓气候变化的科学措施以及气候变化的不确定性，告诉给公众，提高应对气候变化和防灾减灾的科学认识。要鼓励城市居民积极参与应对气候变化的行动，倡导绿色消费、节能环保的理念，不断增强全社会节约资源和能源、保护生态环境、应对气候变化的意识，使低碳生活成为城市百姓的自觉行动。环保部部长周生贤指出，弘扬城市绿色发展理念，就是弘扬城市生态文明理念；推进城市绿色发展，就是推进城市生态文明建设。环境意识的广泛宣传和环保知识的教育普及，是实现国家环境保护意志的重要方式。要弘扬绿色发展，倡导生态文明观念，以环境友好促进社会和谐，以环境文化丰富精神文明。当然，公众参与，离不开政府引导。中国环境保护部环境发展中心主任唐丁丁介绍，中国实行环境标志认证制度，引导居民选择低能耗产品，政府采购更要求优先选购绿色产品。联合国规划署前执行主任克劳斯·特普费尔表示，通过政府引导，说服公众信任绿色产品与自身利益息息相关，从而引导公民环保意识提升，自觉督促政府绿色政策，才能形成良性循环。

（作者：肖纽浮，广州市城市规划勘测设计研究院高级工程师）

**参考文献**

[1] http://www.expo2010.cn/zt/2010/hjbhcszr/index.htm

[2] http://www.chinadaily.com.cn/dfpd/shanghai/2010-07-04/content_533321.html

# “经济转型与城乡互动”主题论坛综述

2010年9月9—10日，由国家发展和改革委员会、上海世博会执行委员会、世界银行和绍兴市政府共同主办的“经济转型与城乡互动”主题论坛在浙江省绍兴市举行。论坛是上海世博会六个主题论坛之一，重点剖析转型期城乡经济发展面临的机遇和挑战，展望城市化时代经济可持续发展的远景。

中共中央政治局委员、上海市委书记俞正声，浙江省委书记赵洪祝，国家发展和改革委员会副主任张晓强，世界银行副行长詹姆斯·亚当斯，德国前副总理、前外交部长约施卡·菲舍尔，欧盟委员会前主席、意大利前总理罗马诺·普罗迪，浙江省领导陈敏尔、李强、陈加元，上海市领导朱晓明、钟燕群，绍兴市委书记张金如等出席了开幕式。

## 一、论坛背景

2010年上海世博会是一届以城市与生活为主题的世博会，旨在从全球视角审视“城市”这一主题，共同探索在21世纪全球化进程中城市发展所面临的新挑战，寻找城市发展使人类更幸福的新道路和新模式。

在经济全球化、政治多极化、社会信息化和文化多元化的新形势下，城市已成为全球经济系统的中枢、增长极和世界治理体系的组织结点。在追求增长和创新的市场制度框架下，城市规模日益增大，实力迅猛增强，基于创新的先进生产力层出不穷，居住环境也日益朝着更加人性化的方向改善；但与此同时，自然资源的大量消耗和环境的不断恶化使城市生态脆弱性进一步凸显，消费和积累不平衡致使过度依赖投资的经济增长方式遭遇极大挑战，货币体系和虚拟经济监管体系的缺失更造成了金融危机的泛滥，经济转型由此成为经济理论与实践中的一个世界性命题。

全球经济失衡要求人们必须从人文发展水平角度关注经济。虽然经济增长是实现人类发展的重要途径之一，但经济增长本身并不足以反映全球美好生活的概念框架，因此必须纳入更为广阔的发展框架。从国际经验看，无论是发达国家还是新型工业化国家，在经济发展到一定程度之后，都需要实现经济转型才能保持经济的持续快速发展。作为一种经济运行状态向另一种经济运行状态的转变，经济转型是国家或地区的资源配置和经济发展方式在一定时期内发生的根本变化，主要体现在“经济体制的更新、经济增长方式的转变、经济结构的提升、支柱产业的替换"四个方面。

然而，如何成功实现经济转型，却无普遍行之有效的经验，对发达国家和发展中国家等处于不同国情的国家来说也有着不同的适用政策和前景。与传统发达工业国家只是在减少消费，增加储蓄，产业结构升级和寻找新生增长点的挑战相比，以中国为代表的发展中国家则面临着经济转型、产业升级、部门平衡和社会结构转变的多重压力。在实现从农业为主的经济向工业、服务业为主的经济转型同时，许多发展中国家还需要实现从传统农业社会向现代工业社会、从乡村社会向城镇社会、从农村人口向城市人口迁移的转型。

城乡互动的实质是要求资本、劳动力、物质、信息等社会经济要素在城乡空间的双向流动与优化配置。城乡之间的互动和关联发展突破了城乡隔离体制下单向流动格局，将最终有利于城市和乡村的共同发展和区域空间结构的整体优化。对仍处于二元结构的发展中国家而言，城乡互动最重要的前提是构建城市—乡村的联动机制，找寻将这种联动机制与可持续发展联系起来的途径和方式。对正处于城市化的发展中国家来说，"城乡互动"的最终目的是"城乡一体化"，这种"一体化"不仅是经济的一体化、形态的一体化，更是文化和社会生活的一体化。

## 二、主要议程

"经济转型和城乡互动"按照经济转型、社会融合和城乡互动的角度设置了6个板块，分别为：城市化、经济转型与企业应对；城乡互动与公共服务均等化；增长模式转变与经济可持续发展；人口流动与社会融合；全球化背景下的城市群经济整合；全球视野中的村镇与小城市。论坛结构顺序上由一个全体大会、一个主题对话会、一个圆桌论坛、四个分论坛和大会闭幕式等构成。这几个分论坛紧密关联，并与"城市，让生活更美好"的经济和社会维度整合在一起。

大会主旨发言围绕论坛主题"经济转型与城乡互动"来展开。面对气候环境变化和金融危机的双重驱动，经济转型是当今世界经济理论与实践中的一个前沿性命题，也是大多数国家如何重塑核心竞争力的重要机遇。经济转型需要技术，更重要制度和结构的变革。传统发达工业国家主要面对的是产业结构升级和寻找经济新增长点的挑战；而更多的发展中国家则面临着经济结构和社会结构转变的双重压力。伴随着城市化迅猛进展和从传统农业社会向现代工业社会的转变，发展中国家越来越多人口迁移城市，城乡互动和经济发展的关系、因果逻辑也变得越来越重要。城市化进程既是经济增长的动力，也是城乡互动的关键所在。

"城市化、经济转型与企业应对"主题对话会涉及几方面的要素，核心在于企业。在资源环境和金融危机的双重压力下，经济转型已成为全球各城市的共同心声，然而，如何对传统发展方式进行改革以实现顺利转型，目前仍无现成的答案可循。经济转型意味着政策环境和市场环境的转变，这将对企业的生产与经营带来诸多现实挑战，更对企业的未来发展产生重大的影响。如何应对这些挑战和变化，是对话会主要关注的内容。对话会主要聚焦两个话题：其一，城市化与经济转型的相互影响；其二，经济转型对企业所带来的挑战和机遇。

“城乡互动与公共服务均等化”平行分论坛聚焦城乡不同的公共物品。在经济发展过程中，城市与乡村的经济发展在一定时期内出现显著的不平衡，这既是发达国家的历史经验，也是广大发展中国家普遍面临的现实，更是中国近几十年发展中的突出问题。相对于乡村，城市具有制度、政策、资本、公共服务等诸多优势，而公共服务的不平等又是其中一个尤为关键的症结。该分论坛就聚焦于如何以公共服务均等化和其他政策，推动城乡互动，促进城乡经济均衡发展。

“增长模式转变与经济可持续发展”平行分论坛聚焦城市经济模式。随着城市经济活动的迅速扩张，资源、环境等方面的压力变得日益突出，反过来制约城市的发展。因此，转变增长模式，实现可持续发展，已经成为城市进一步发展的关键。如何使生产、消费、流通符合可持续发展和现代化城市的要求，是大多数城市管理者面临的挑战和机遇。

“人口流动与社会融合”平行分论坛聚焦城乡人口迁移和城市内部人群融合。随着农村劳动力释放并向城市转移是工业化进程中必不可少的环节，对于大部分发达国家来说，这一阶段已经基本完成，而发展中国家劳动力和移民人口流动的大潮正在持续，并引发了许多社会问题。因此，这一议题更多地能引起社会各阶层的共同关注。在当前金融危机的形势下，流动人口就业和社会稳定等问题，已经成为当前困扰包括中国在内许多发展中国家城市管理者的重要议题。

“全球化背景下的城市群经济整合”平行分论坛聚焦城市群。随着全球化的深入推进，世界经济领域的竞争正在从国家之间逐步发展为城市之间，而单一的城市在全球性的竞争中也越来越难以取得优势。经验表明，全球城市的崛起更多地依赖与其毗邻地区所建立的密切的内在经济联系与资源整合，因为在代表整个区域参与国际竞争的过程中，无论是何种意义上的“中心”的建设，归根到底都是城市及其周边地区服务功能的提升和各种资源的有效配置与流转。

“全球视野中的村镇与小城市”圆桌对话重点围绕村镇和小城市而展开。当代经济活动在全球范围内进行，其末梢关系着无数村庄、市镇和小城市。作为全球经济的细胞，村、镇、小城市往往是被忽视的群体，但他们的繁荣与萧条，却影响着全球经济的阴晴冷暖。

## 三、主要观点

中共中央政治局委员、上海市委书记俞正声在致辞中说，经济转型与城乡互动，是世界各国在经济全球化背景下、快速城市化进程中所面临的共同课题。中国在经历了长期高速增长后，发展中不平衡、不协调、不可持续的问题日益突出，资源环境约束、外部市场需求约束越来越大，城乡二元矛盾依然突出。本届世博会以“城市，让生活更美好”为主题，为我们展示了未来城乡和谐互动的全息画卷，给我们带来了从发展理念到实践案例的多方位启迪。本次论坛选择“经济转型与城乡互动”为话题，通过聚焦转型中的经济发展困境、城乡二元等问题，进一步深化演绎世博会主题，共同探讨城市可持续发展和城乡融合协同发展的行动路径，意义重大。

浙江省委书记赵洪祝在致辞中说，经济转型是当今世界经济理论与实践中的一个前沿性课题，也是大多数国家和地区共同面临的一个发展问题。追求绿色、环保、可持续，强调人与自然相和谐，加快城乡一体化发展，则是经济转型的重要方向，也是现代文明向更高层次发展的重要途径。

国家发展和改革委员会副主任张晓强在致辞中说，新世纪以来，根据发展的新形势、新任务、新要求，中国政府及时作出了统筹城乡发展、建设社会主义新农村的重大战略决策，实行工业反哺农业、城市支持农村的方针，建设现代农业，繁荣农村经济，增加农民收入，促进城乡经济社会良性互动、共同发展。经过不懈努力取得了显著成效。但是，由于中国农业人口仍然有7亿多，农村基础差，城乡二元结构造成的深层次矛盾依然存在，因此，中国将继续把解决好农业、农村、农民的问题作为全部工作的重中之重，着眼于巩固农业基础地位，改变农村落后面貌，加快城乡二元结构，努力在城乡经济社会发展一体化方面迈出更大的步伐。

世界银行副行长詹姆斯·亚当斯在致辞中说，很多年以来，城乡发展是相互争夺资源，但是今天已经看到了，城乡之间是相互依存的，所以需要有统筹兼顾。一方面，要统筹增长、统筹发展，需要政策的保护。这些政策要保证在城乡提供同样均等的服务，这种均等就包括城市设施的提供，以及高效的农业生产，以及流通措施；另一方面，通过城市群的构建形成一种合力，能够让城镇之间相互依存。

诺贝尔经济学奖得主、美国普林斯顿大学教授埃里克·马斯金说，中国的成功跟世界全球化有绝对的关系，和各国的经济上的互动表现了中国的成长性。在成长中，也有很多的特殊现象，特别是收入差距的扩大，这个差距特别是在乡村和城市之间。这个差异可能是生产模式的不同，生产的因素包括了劳动力、资金、土地，在这里讨论的主要是围绕劳工的问题。认为贫富不均只是暂时的现象，透过技术培训、技能提高，低技能的工人（也就是农村的工人）就可以在全球化的进展中获得好处。从长期的发展来看，全球化的的确确可以减少城乡之间的贫富差距。

欧盟委员会前主席、意大利前总理罗马诺·普罗迪说，世界上五大洲，有些国家已经在享受着繁荣，享受着增长，享受更好的生活，而有些还没有完全享受到我们今天的美好生活，还在争取当中。我们已经进入了一个新的时代，经济社会、技术等方面的发展就要齐头并进。新时代的发展必须要有社会的统筹发展，必须是更加公正。正是基于这样的原因，必须有统筹发展的方法，包括社会财富的结构，包括教育，包括养老制度等。

德国前副总理、前外交部长约施卡·菲舍尔说，经济转型必须从高碳转为低碳，或者零碳排放。投资更好的智能交通系统网络，同时水资源的利用最优化、能源优化，这样这座城市就会变成全球领先的城市。欧洲今天一部分达到稳定的原因，也就是社会的稳定，就是一个平衡的政策。富民政策是非常重要的，居民都应该享受同样的生活水平，这就意味着大部分的投资转移，还有基础设施，还有教育体制，还有社会福利。绿色战略、农村建设，还有富民政策，这都是应该积极面对的。

中国社会科学院副院长李扬说，中国经济发展是相当快的，与此同时，一个副作用就是收入分配的差距在扩大。政府理所当然地顺应民意，把调整国民收入分配作为我们的重要任务。也就是说，在中国进入一个新的时期，进入经济发展方式转变的新时期，我们的一个重要任务就是要调整收入分配方式，要缩小贫富差距。城乡收入差距、地区收入分配差距是造成贫富差距的主要原因。

上海市政协副主席、上海交通大学经济与管理学院名誉院长朱晓明说，世界在城市化，亚洲在城市化，城市化的水平迅速上升，交通越来越便捷。长三角一小时的城市圈指日可待，商务越来越便捷，通信越来越便捷，生活越来越便捷，城市真的比过去的年代美好了。但是，城市化的城市群有3个趋同：规划趋同、产业趋同和形象趋同。我国100多个城市都将建国际大都市、国内大都市，大部分省份的产业结构是趋同的，趋同率达到90%。国内600多个大、中、小城市，它们的形象千城一面。城市不转型，企业不转型，过度的开发会带来很多问题，比如像劳资纠纷、气候异常、交通堵塞、城市污染，这种无穷的烦恼、灾祸、隐患接踵而来。当然要寻求解决办法，政府推动、政策驱动的确是非常重要的。但是，我们千万不要忘记市场驱动或许也非常重要。这是因为世界在细分重构，这种不由自主的细分重构是一种经济规律。

清华大学中国与世界经济研究中心李稻葵说，中国经济未来10年增长的最大潜力就是来自于城市化，如何挖掘中国经济城市化这座金矿呢？有三个重要的瓶颈需要突破。第一个瓶颈就是制度瓶颈，各地仍然实行的以不同的程度、力度来实行的户籍管理制度；第二个瓶颈，特大型城市的公共管理方面的改革；第三个瓶颈，土地价格的问题，只有解决了这些瓶颈，才能使得城市化进程潜力真正释放出来，带动整个中国经济的转型。

中国经济改革研究基金会国民经济研究所所长樊纲说，要承认城市化进程不是一个只有幸福没有痛苦的过程。城市化进程是一个社会发展进程，有经济的发展过程，也有社会的发展过程。其中要应对各种经济的问题、经济的转型当中的各种矛盾，包括农民市民化的进程，包括在一个城市里面收入差距越来越明显的时候，怎么能使低收入阶层、高收入阶层安居乐业、相得益彰，社会和谐。这就需要一系列的公共政策。城市化需要一系列的公共政策来配合、来应对，包括医疗、社保、教育、环境、住房、土地等。

中国农业大学校长柯炳生说，改革开放以来农村发展取得了巨大成就，也取得了巨大进展，但是城市发展更快，因此城乡差距有些地方变得更大、更显著了，但是更主要的是变得显性化。城乡差距有很多表现，粗略地归纳为三个方面：收入、基础设施、社会权利。如何解决城乡收入差距问题，从长期看根本无法用价格办法提高农民的收入，补贴更是有限。从长远看应当是转移，就是让更多的人从农业中、农村中转移出去，从事农业或者农村的劳动力要减少，这样使每个从事农业的农民经营规模不断扩大，生产产品数量不断增加，质量不断提高，才能获得更多的收入。农村基础设施之所以差，最根本的原因很简单，就是政府的投入不足。缩小城乡差别的根本途径在于统筹城乡发展，首先政府要做的就是规划，加强基础教育非常重要。解决城乡差距是一个长期性的历史任务。实际上，城乡差距的解决过程是我国城市化和现代化的进程。

世界银行学院首席城市专家、城市与地方政府主任韦胜利说，对中国来说，克服城乡之间的差距是一个非常大的挑战。我们一直在说，这是一个转型期，实际上它是一个非常艰苦的阶段，很多国家都还没有经历这样的转型期。我们要是没有好的政策，就不可能进行成功转型。这里不能靠市场，必须靠政策很好的执行。说到差距，不光收入的差距，还有教育的差距。中国经常会从实践当中学习，可能外国人对中国提供建议并不完全有效果，中国人喜欢从自己的实践中总结经验。我们可以通过实践来总结经验，有了好的效果后再把它拓展到社会其他方面。我们要进一步发展我们的中产阶级，我们都知道中产阶级最主要的支撑就是他们的技能和教育。另外，我们针对的挑战就是价格的巨大波动。

上海社会科学院常务副院长左学金说，追求城乡均衡发展的政策重点是要让城乡居民享有同等的发展机会，尤其是接受义务教育、公共卫生和基本医疗服务，以及通过劳动力的自由流动来寻求就业创业的机会，在工资收入、劳动保护、社会保障以及金融服务等方面都享受公平待遇。中国准城市人口有2亿多，6.3亿城市居民中大概1/3是准城市人口。有这么多的准城市人口，这个现象是“浅度的城市化”。绝大多数都是没有户籍的城市人口，解决这样的问题就变得非常迫切。解决浅度城市化的措施应该包括转变地方政府观念，积极向进城农民工和他们的家属提供平等的公共服务。

上海市发展和改革委员会副主任兼上海发展改革研究院院长肖林说，“城市，让生活更美好”的世博主题，深刻诠释了社会发展的理念和发展模式。这次世博会的主题给我们一个新的城市发展的理念，就是系统发展的理念。这种系统发展理念，就是人文关怀的理念。城市与人的关系，城市发展应当以人为本，绿色发展理念即是城市与自然的关系，城市发展应当追求低投入、高产出的绿色经济。城市与历史的关系，城市文化应当兼容并传承历史。协同发展的理念，即是城市与城市的关系。上海世博会深化了我们对于未来城市发展的思考。要实现历史与未来、人与自然、人与人的和谐，走出一条可持续的发展之路。我们的发展是要追求历史与未来的和谐，城市发展既要求注重新理念、新技术的运用，也要注重历史文脉、传统文化的传承。

世界银行东亚和太平洋地区首席经济学家维克拉姆·尼赫鲁说：第一，城镇化进程对于城镇发展来讲是至关重要的。第二，城镇化进程随着其进展的过程增加，它的复杂性也会增加。第三，我们的城镇化进程并不是一个完全清洁而有序的过程，实际都会有贫民窟这样的现象存在，但随着时间的推移将会进一步改善这一现象。

中科院科技政策与管理科学研究所副所长、研究员王毅说，中国21世纪以后，经过了快速的城市化进程。同时我们也面临结构的矛盾，无论是城乡还是城市化，同时还有金融危机的影响，也是面临着短期的经济复苏和长期结构性的矛盾和持续发展的冲突。中国也面临着绿色增长和转型的阶段，特别是未来10年。未来5到10年中国可能面临着五大挑战。第一个是绿色新兴产业的技术，比如说新能源、电动汽车和节能环保产业。但是我们在这些产业当中并不完全掌握它的核心技术。第二个我们现在没有建立起一个长期的价格信号与经济激励制度。第三个挑战就是结构性调整是需要时间和成本的，不是一蹴而就的。第四个就是培育国内绿色消费市场。第五个就是国际气候机制的不确定性。未来5年可能我们要以提高能效和政策驱动为主，并不是把结构性的减排放在第一。2011到2015年“十二五”期间，我们要把提高能效和结构性减排并重。我们未来5年可能主要是制度和政策的制定，为“十二五”奠定一个更好的结构性变化的基础。

清华大学人文社会科学院院长李强说，中国在流动人口的政策上，2003年是一个关键年。那年6月国务院宣布废止收容法。中央开始调整人口政策，也就是说采取了城市比较接纳、融合的办法。因为我们今天的主题是社会融合。这个社会采取了比较多的社会融合政策，强调改善就业环境、提高工资、解决拖欠工资。2007年很重要的一个法律是《中华人民共和国劳动合同法》，它加强了劳动的稳定性。

清华大学公共管理学院教授、重庆市国资委主任助理崔之元说，重庆是在2010年8月15日开始进行户籍改革的，这次改革的目的是通过户籍这个制度，能够让居住在重庆市的330万进城的农民工兄弟们，拿到城市居民的户口。户籍制度的改革不仅仅是一纸空文、一张纸，或者一纸户籍的说明。这里的关键问题是在中国户籍登记，身份证跟你的口粮有很大的关系，拥有一个户口就基本拥有五个权利，包括了医疗保险、住房、教育、就业福利和养老基金。这五个权利就需要很多的资金，需要政府很大的经费来执行。每个农民在中国有三个权利：第一个权利是他有土地承包权，第二个权利就是他在农村拥有宅基地，第三个权利是林权，他可以租到林地。所以，整个户籍改革制度就是怎么样使得农村的户口能够顺利的转型，把三个权利转换成五个权利。

## 四、小结

“经济转型与城乡互动”主题论坛从经济转型、城乡发展、城乡互动等方面入手，选取转变经济增长方式、社会融合、人口流动、服务设施均等化、户籍制度等具体的热点问题作为议题，通过国内外的著名学者、企业家、城市管理者的踊跃发言和探讨，分享了城市规划和建设的成功经验，涌现了许多思想创见和精彩观点，对未来城市发展具有重要启示意义。

1. 中国将面临着绿色增长和转型的阶段。绿色增长将以提高能效、发展清洁能源为核心，以转变发展方式、创新发展机制为关键，以经济社会可持续发展为目标的低碳发展，应该是今后我国经济社会发展的必然战略取向。其中重点实施能源结构调整、绿色能源开发利用、绿色建筑、公共交通等重大行动计划。

2. 解决城乡差距是一个长期性的历史任务。如何解决城乡收入差距问题，从长期看，根本无法用价格办法提高农民的收入，补贴更是有限。从长远看应当是转移，就是让更多的人从农业中、农村中转移出去，从事农业或者农村的劳动力要减少，这样使每个从事农业的农民经营规模不断扩大，生产产品数量不断增加，质量不断提高，才能获得更多的收入。

3. 促进社会融合，实现真正的城镇化。据有关学者统计，中国准城市人口（即没有户籍的城市人口）有2亿多，这个现象是“浅度的城市化”。从广大农村地域转移出来的农村人口为城市建设做出了贡献，但在城市中享受不到城市待遇。城市需要从体制创新方面作出调整，重庆的户籍制度改革是一个很好尝试。

4. 加快设施均等化建设，促进城乡统筹发展。追求城乡均衡发展的政策重点是要让城乡居民享有同等的发展机会，尤其是接受义务教育、公共卫生和基本医疗服务，以及通过劳动力的自由流动来寻求就业创业的机会，在工资收入、劳动保护、社会保障以及金融服务等方面都享受公平待遇。要破解二元结构，把医疗问题解决了，教育问题解决了，养老问题解决了，把残疾人、孤寡老人的问题解决了，把残疾儿童的问题解决了，二元结构不言而喻就破解了。

5. 转变经济增长方式、追求可持续发展正日益成为世界各国的共同诉求。本次论坛所汇集的关于经济转型、城乡互动的智慧与实践成果，必将为全国的城市经济发展和城乡一体化战略提供思路，也将为全球城市的经济转型带来更多启示，有助世人建设更好的城市，实现更美的生活。

（作者：廖远涛，广州市城市规划勘测设计研究院规划研究中心副总规划师）

# “和谐城市与宜居生活”主题论坛综述

2010年10月6—7日，由住房和城乡建设部、上海世博会执委会、联合国人居署和杭州市政府共同主办的上海世博会“和谐城市与宜居生活”主题论坛在杭州举行。该论坛是上海世博会六个主题论坛之一，主要探讨和谐城市和宜居生活之间的关系。

全国人大常委会副委员长、中国科学院院长路甬祥，住房和城乡建设部部长姜伟新，浙江省委书记、省人大常委会主任赵洪祝，上海市市长、上海世博会执委会执行主任韩正，浙江省省长吕祖善，联合国助理秘书长、联合国人居署代理执行主任英格·比约克·克莱弗比，国际展览局秘书长文森特·冈萨雷斯·洛塞泰斯等出席了开幕式。多国城市规划、城市生态经济、城市管理领域的专家和官员，上海世博会参展方代表，国内各省、自治区、直辖市代表和中外记者近800人出席论坛。

## 一、论坛背景

2010年上海世博会是一届以城市与生活为主题的世博会，其主要目的是通过展览展示和论坛研讨，来探索和思考“更好的城市，更美的生活”。

随着发展中国家的城市化进程的加速，全球越来越多的人口居住于城市。作为衡量城市化水平通用标准的城市化率，已不足以全面反映幸福生存和发展所需的基础前提和条件，也不足以充分反映城市化质量尤其是城镇化对生活的影响。“和谐”、“宜居”已成为21世纪城市和区域发展的重要宗旨和主要目标，决定了城市发展方向、内容和持久力，并与城市前景深刻紧密联系在一起。和谐的城市本质上是指城市经济、社会、文化、环境协调发展，人居环境良好，能够满足居民物质和精神生活需求，适宜人类工作、生活和居住的城市。城市发展的重要目标，应该在于为居民提供宜居的生活。

“和谐城市与宜居生活”主题论坛重点探讨和谐城市的决定要素和发展障碍，并就城市建设所需的技术基础、政策目标、战略规划等层面进行深入探讨，分享全球经验和智慧，展望什么样的城市才能使21世纪的生活更美好。

## 二、主要议程

“和谐城市与宜居生活”主题论坛按照区域、政策、主体和制度设置为6个部分，结构顺序上由开幕式和全体大会、圆桌讨论会、6个分论坛和闭幕总结大会组成。6个平行分论坛分别为“区域协同与城乡和谐”、“和谐城市与支撑系统”、“和谐城市与女性智慧”、“城市治理与社区参与”、“建成环境与宜居生活”、“社会保障与宜居生活”，圆桌讨论会为“住房政策与宜居生活”。

“区域协同与城乡和谐”平行分论坛关注经济发展的区域化，以及城市化过程中如何实现与周边区域紧密结合，主要探讨了在中国城镇化快速发展的进程中，如何兼顾城镇化的质量；在城乡差异背景下，如何从和谐城市的角度推动区域的和谐发展；和谐城市建设和新农村建设如何实现区域协同；城市和乡村是否可以同样享有宜居的生活等议题。

“和谐城市与支撑系统”平行分论坛关注城市建设的基础设施，包括诸如城市交通、公共安全危机处理、环境保护以及水、电、暖、气和能源循环等系统。主要探讨了在和谐城市的理念下，如何提高城市空间的可达性，实现公共资源的公平分配，保障社会安定，减轻自然灾害损失，减少环境污染和能源消耗等议题。

“和谐城市与女性智慧”平行分论坛重点聚焦城市发展过程中的女性角色和女性作用。主要探讨了在和谐城市的理念下，如何看待社会性别意识主流化和性别和谐对推动城市和谐的积极作用；如何评价女性在参与经济、政治、文化、社会和生态文明中的独特作用；如何让作为人类智慧不可或缺的女性智慧充分涌流、男女两性携手建设和谐城市等议题。

“城市治理与社区参与”平行分论坛聚焦和谐城市构建过程中的面对利益主体多样化条件下的多元治理。主要探讨了在和谐城市建设的进程中，城市管治发挥着怎样的作用以及其权力的分配机制和影响效果如何；社区的居民如何积极参与到城市管治的实践当中；发达国家和发展中国家在城市管治与社区参与方面的经验和教训如何互相借鉴等议题。

“建成环境与宜居生活”平行分论坛聚焦于城市物质环境与居民生活满意度的关系。主要探讨了在和谐城市的理念下，如何通过高质量的设计和有力的政府行动提升建成环境的质量，为居民提供多样化的城市空间、具有归属感的社区和令人满意的住区环境等议题。

“社会保障与宜居生活”平行分论坛关注的是社会保障与城市内部和谐度的关系。主要探讨了在全球新的发展环境下，如何通过城市社会保障系统积极应对经济全球化的挑战；如何解决人口老龄化趋势等社会转型对社会保障制度带来的压力；如何通过建设多元化的社会保障模式、扩大社会保障覆盖面，从而促进城市社会保障的可持续发展等议题。

“住房政策与宜居生活”圆桌讨论会重点聚焦宜居生活核心的住房，讨论其可承受性和便利性。主要探讨了如何制定和执行合理住房的法律和规章制度，使住房发展计划为公众提供均等的机会，并向无家可归者、残疾人和低收入家庭提供住房援助；如何使住房政策更加适应老龄化社会的发展趋势；如何促进房地产业的健康发展等议题。

## 三、主要论点

全国人大常委会副委员长、中国科学院院长路甬祥在致辞中说，上海世博会“城市，让生活更美好”的主题，体现了人类对未来城市美好生活的共同向往和追求。上海世博会为世界城市多元文化和多元化的发展提供了相互交流的平台，展现了和谐城市和宜居生活的未来城市多彩多姿的范本。我们要依靠科技创新，走建设绿色智能、平安和谐、布局合理、繁荣宜居而有特色的城镇化文明发展之路，加快实现“城市，让生活更美好”的共同愿景，为中国的现代化，也为人类文明做出无愧于时代的贡献。

住房和城乡建设部部长姜伟新在致辞中指出，城市化是经济发展的必然过程，也是人类社会文明进步的重要标志。今后数十年，尤其在发展中国家，城市化将是主要的发展趋势。如何促进人与人、人与自然、人与社会、人与城市之间的和谐发展，一直是世界各国政府和人民关注的话题。和谐是中国文化的重要内涵，实现和谐的城市发展和宜居的城市生活，是中国人民孜孜以求的愿景。我国将积极发展和谐城市，创造宜居生活。今后一段时期，中国城市化进程仍将保持较快的发展势头，我们将坚持科学发展理念，更加积极稳妥地推进城镇化。住房和城乡建设部与各有关部门、各个城市，将继续统筹城乡规划，促进城市基础设施建设，推进绿色建筑、建筑节能、城市垃圾和污水处理，促进节约能源资源，建设生态城市，改善城市交通和地下空间管理，保护历史文化遗产、完善文化设施、提高人的精神文化素质。相信本次论坛会对建设和谐城市、创造宜居生活，在理论与实践上起到积极的促进作用。

上海市市长、上海世博会执委会执行主任韩正说，上海世博会的六个主题论坛分别由长三角六个城市举办，体现了长三角兄弟城市共办世博、共享世博的合作精神。我们对长三角兄弟省市的大力支持和热情参与表示衷心的感谢。城市是人类文明的结晶，也是人类文明的象征。城市化的迅速发展，使越来越多的人享受到城市的繁荣和便利。与此同时，城市扩张也带来人口膨胀、交通堵塞、环境污染、资源紧缺、城市贫困、文化摩擦等诸多问题。应对这些挑战，建设生活更加美好的城市，成为全世界共同关注的课题。创造和谐城市、宜居家园，让蓝天白云长驻城市，让花园绿地遍布街头，让全体市民居有所住，让交通出行畅通便捷，让人们在城市中更加幸福美满的生活，已经成为世界各国城市的共识。上海世博会上，各国的展馆展示生动描绘了人类对美好城市生活的向往追求。在城市最佳实践区，世界各国城市精选报送的案例，深入展现了人类营造宜居生活、建设“和谐城市”的不懈探索。

浙江省省长吕祖善说，“和谐城市与宜居生活”是当今世界城市发展的理论与实践的重大课题。浙江是中国改革开放前沿地带和市场经济的先发省份，在推进城市建设和发展过程中，要着力打造富饶秀美、和谐安康的生产生活环境，努力实现经济社会的可持续发展，不断提高浙江人民的生活品质。浙江将以这次主题论坛为契机，进一步探索新型城市化的道路，进一步推进统筹城乡经济社会的发展，以安居促乐业，以宜居促和谐，使人民的生活更加富裕，环境更加优美，社会更加和谐。

联合国助理秘书长、联合国人居署代理执行主任英格·比约克·克莱弗比表示，联合国人居署一直把和谐城市作为其城市工作的一个主要框架。我们一定要有更好的城市、更聪明的城市、更智能化的城市。上海世博会提供了一个非常好的范例，告诉我们怎么创造更好的城市未来。只有我们对全世界的城市化采取更积极的态度，才能够达到现在还没有达到的和谐。

国际展览局秘书长文森特·冈萨雷斯·洛塞泰斯说，上海世博会主题论坛对世博会起到了非常重要的作用，已经成为上海世博会在教育、合作和交流过程当中一个非常重要的支柱。在这届世博会上，通过不同的展馆以及城市最佳实践区的各种展示，我们看到并体验到了不同的地点、不同的人物、不同的政策而构成的不同类型的城市。城市在发展过程中的确遇到了很多挑战，但是我们相信，通过包括今天"和谐城市与宜居生活"主题论坛在内的系列世博论坛，可以更好地加深我们对和谐社会的理解，为"城市，让生活更美好"提供新的内涵。

加拿大不列颠哥伦比亚大学城市与区域规划学院荣誉教授约翰·弗里德曼认为，社区才是人们真正生活的地方，宜居应从有归属感的社区起步。中国正经历着城市改造的热潮，数百万人因拆迁而离开原来的居所，但这种由速度、规模、扩张、割离构成的城市新景观，并非真正的宜居城市所需要。作为宜居的场所，无论是在哪里，最重要的就是打造一个有归属感的社区。一个优质的社区至少应该符合以下几个标准：一是充满活力、生机勃勃；二是以一个到多个集会和社交场所为中心；三是有集体意识；四是拥有一个可以促进社会和人文氛围的硬件环境；五是能被生活在其中的人所珍惜。很多来到城市建设的外来务工人员，却往往被城市的规划者所忽视，这也是一个宜居城市所需要考虑到的。

英国社会科学院院士彼得·霍尔认为，创意城市与宜居城市，两者是可以兼得的。对于创新城市、宜居城市，其实没有 个既定的公式。在各个不同的地方，比如新的城市或者老的工业城市，其实都可以创新出新的城市，关键是一定要创造必要的条件，能够真正地塑造技术、环境、社会的必要的条件，才能够真正把宜居性和创新型完美结合。创新城市有三种类型：第一种，历史悠久的大都市，如伦敦、巴黎、纽约、上海等。第二种，人们非常喜爱的阳光地带的城市，如旧金山、温哥华和悉尼。第三种，文艺复兴类型的城市，不仅有老的制造行业，还有深厚的文化底蕴，有大量的博物馆、很多的高校和其他的展示会。这些城市中老的历史街区和新的技术结合产生了新的魅力，成为城市发展的推动力。

中国科学院院士郑时龄教授说，2010 年世博会对于上海的历史而言，已经成为城市发展的一个里程碑。它在城市空间和环境方面将推动上海成为一座可持续发展和宜居的城市。在准备以及举办世博会的期间，上海城市环境已经大大提升，上海将重塑城市空间，构建并完善城市结构组成。上海在规划并实施一系列的发展规划，既考虑后世博园区的发展，也考虑到整个城市的发展。上海城市未来的发展必须适合人口众多、土地资源和水资源稀缺的特点。在主办世博会和后世博时代，我们建设适合上海的理想城市模式，这已经成为城市空间发展战略的核心理念。2010 年世博会已经使上海成为一座宜居的国际大都市，从黄浦江畔一直到城市空间，都把上海领入了新的时代。在快速城市化或者再城市化过程中，要优化我们的城市环境，建立一个有创意的经济和产业，提升我们的工业结构和城市的结构。处理好城乡之间的关系，达到平衡的城乡发展。要逐步消除资源分配的不平衡和城市区域之间的不平衡，同时提升服务的水平和人们的创意水平。

新加坡国立大学东亚研究所教授、所长郑永年指出，建设和谐城市不光是技术层面，城市的和谐就是人的和谐，技术上的基础设施很重要，但是还是要以人为本，要考虑各个社会群体的需要。中国和谐城市建设中应注意四点：第一，在经济结构中要处理好国有企业和民营企业之间的关系；第二，要关注劳动收入分配的情况；第三，要建立社会保障制度；第四，要注重城乡整合。

中国2010年上海世博会园区总规划师、同济大学校长助理吴志强指出，中国过去60年的发展历史告诉我们，城镇化是中国总能量消耗的更关键的要素。要谈城市化，谈城市问题，就牵涉到整个中国的能源方向怎么走，抓住城镇化比抓住GDP更重要。今天我们如何做到“城市，让生活更美好”？第一，不能把人分成城里人和乡下人，不能把人分成市中心人和边远人。所有人都一样，这是前提条件；第二，我们对待城市要改变态度，只有有尊严的城市，有爱的城市，城市才会回馈你更美好的生活；第三，城市这个生命体不能离开它所处的环境，它需要地区的生态条件，地区的劳动力、传统和资源。要从单个城市走向区域协同来认识城市这个生命，这就是我们最重要的一个想法。

加拿大不列颠哥伦比亚大学亚洲研究院前院长、亚洲研究和地理学荣休教授特里・麦吉指出，绿色城市要保持生态体系，农业是一个重要的环节。在城市化过程中，要关注城乡融合，关注特大城市区域的乡村发展。各级政府要有非常好的沟通机制，推进整个生态系统的发展，在制定政策的过程中，将城市融入到区域发展中，未来的发展必须依靠农村和城市的有机合作。

清华大学建筑学院副院长、教授毛其智提出，真正的城市规划必须是区域规划。要促进城市的平等，建设包容性的城市。建立覆盖全民的社会保障体系，注重解决教育、劳动就业、医疗卫生养老等民生问题，取得区域协调发展和人居环境的发展。

国家环境保护部环境规划院副院长、总工程师、研究员王金南指出，要从经济、社会、环境三个维度，来构造整个城市环境宜居指数。总体上看，中国南方城市的环境宜居指数普遍高于北方城市，东部沿海地区、经济发达地区的城市指数高于西北地区。大气环境方面宜居指数上，南方城市高于北方城市，工业化、资源性城市的大气环境指数相对比较低。

杭州市委副书记、代市长邵占维指出，在城市飞速发展的今天，工业化和城市化的加速推进，使城市面临一系列的挑战，交通拥堵、房价上升、资源短缺、污染排放、文化冲突。杭州市在建设和谐城市方面的经验主要有五点：一是实施城市国际化、服务业优先、软实力提升、民主民生六大战略，实现经济的和谐发展；二是以完善城市功能，方便居民生活，优化人均环境，扩展生活空间为目标，完善城市基础设施，特别是公共服务设施，实现城市的和谐建设；三是引进资本创新创业，实现城市和谐创意；四是弘扬和谐、开放、大气的城市文化，加强文化名城建设，实现文化的和谐繁荣；五是大规模推进绿化建设，保护物种的多样性，加强自然保护区森林公园、湿地公园的建设和养护，注重垃圾处理、污水处理等环保基础设施的建设，实现生态的和谐共生。

上海市城乡建设和交通委员会主任黄融认为，当前国家之间的竞争突出地表现为城市层面的竞争，基础设施的建设是提高城市竞争力的基础。一是积极推进节能减排，完善生态基础设施系统；二是努力提高公用服务质量，完善城市保障体系建设；三是努力转变发展方式，城市建设重心由中心城区向郊区转变，城市空间布局由单核中心向多核多极转变。

世行东亚与太平洋地区可持续发展部部长约翰·鲁姆认为，更好地预防自然的灾害和气候的变化，对城市的可持续发展有着重要影响。一是要将应对气候变化政策融入到城市中；二是做好软实力投资，如建立早期预警系统、更系统性的防水防洪系统等；三是关注住宅提升，了解洪水、地震带来的一些负面影响，在城市的建筑物的建设中考虑到对自然灾害的应对，尤其是学校和医院等场所；四是建立相关机构和机制进行系统化风险检测和管理，找到城市中最为薄弱的地区和区域，制定相关的措施和手段来应对。

国务院参事、中国科学院可持续发展战略研究组组长、首席科学家牛文元指出，一个城市是多元网络的结合，电网、水网、通信网，以及物流网构成城市运行的基本网络运行的形态，通过网络的完善健全形成一个绿色城市的支撑。为实现绿色和谐城市的目标，第一，从传统的业态向现代型业态革命性转移；第二，从传统的经济向生态经济的革命性转移；第三，从末端的产品向源头绿色产品革命性提升；第四，从打造名牌向创造绿色标准的革命性提升。

浙江省妇联主席厉月姿指出，和谐城市，宜居生活城市再现了女性创造力。女性平等接受教育的制度保障，极大提升了女性立足社会的能力。随着长三角都市圈内经济社会的一体化发展，政策框架的逐步建立，体制机制的创新，乃至户口、教育、医疗和社会保障等等方面的壁垒被打破。在经济结构调整中，长三角地区的金融业、现代服务业、高新技术产业将快速发展，女性参与长二角发展的视野更加宽广、空间更大、层次更高、机遇更多。

泰国亚洲理工学院性别与发展研究副教授贝尔纳黛特·雷苏雷桑认为，要把女性的参与，从传统的机构转到一些与战略、策略以及国家发展相关的机构中；要将性别平等的教育融入到个人发展中去；在组织架构上促进一些变化，建立妇联或者其他组织，让女性有更多的话语权，提供女性能力发挥的机会。

上海市妇联主席张丽丽认为，如果女性智慧用于社区，社区一定充满活力和谐。女性社团和女性人才的参与，社区参与，能充分发挥女性在家庭、社会中的作用，通过家庭美德，文明家庭的创建不断促进社会和谐。

联合国人居署全球司司长、上海世博会联合国馆馆长拉尔斯·雷乌特斯韦德指出，城市治理中的一个关键点在于要确保管理制度可行，并且让所有人都参与其中，让每个人承担起自己的责任。城市的地位越来越高，很多的城市发展过程中，发现以前需要国家政府管理的事情，需要由城市来管理。社区参与会对城市规划或者城市治理发挥越来越重要的作用。

中国科学院院士、香港大学城市规划与设计系主任叶嘉安指出：在城市规划领域，公众参与不是一个单一的东西，而是涉及市民的需求。不同的社会背景有不同的规划参与模式。西方城市规划公众参与的方式有通知、知会、咨询、参与、协作等，到最后的最高层次参与决策，不同的层次有不同的方式。

美国伊利诺斯大学城市规划系教授、大城市研究所亚洲及中国研究中心主任张庭伟认为，中国现在的参与，是一种新形式的民主，一个是分权，很多和经济事务有关的决策权下放给地方政府做。同时再集权，中央政府对和经济没有直接关系的其他事务的管理更加严格，这两个不同的过程同时发生。目前，中国的很多城市都提出了一定要有公众参与城市规划；新一版《城乡规划法》把公众听证会作为城市规划必定要经过的过程，这是一个巨大的进步。

杭州市副市长张建庭在“建成环境与宜居生活”分论坛的发言中指出，宜居城市的内涵包括五点：一是具备良好的自然环境和区位条件，拥有宜人的气候、新鲜的空气、清洁的水、高频密的绿化、宽敞的城市公共空间、宁静的生活环境等；二是具备良好人文环境与城市文明拥有发达的教育，完善的公共文化服务设施，和谐的社区文化等；三是具备良好健康安全与生活便利条件，拥有健全的法制秩序、完善的医疗系统、安全的生活设施、便利的交通出行等；四是经济发展与国际化程度较高，拥有较为发达的经济充足的就业机会，具有国际知名度和美誉度等；五是社会和谐与可持续的城市，具备完善的公共安全文化、宗教、可持续的发展方式等。杭州通过强化公共决策、公共管理和公共服务，从客观评价和市民意见中人居环境较弱的地方改起，逐步完善生态建设、人文共建、居住改善、公共空间、交通出行、社区服务，提高城市宜居水平。

加拿大女王大学城市与区域规划学院前院长、教授梁鹤年认为，建立和谐社会，首先重视社区建设。社区的自治性高，城市的服务水平就能提高，和谐城市就会出现。居民的记忆是经过他们对城市的感受而累计起来的，集体记忆是公民精神和他们对城市向心力的传承。要组织居民集体互动、使用社区的公共空间、建设基层民主和社区环境。

上海大学社会学教授、上海社会学会会长邓伟志指出：第一，政府是为弱势群体而设立。第二，在“居者有其屋”不可能全部实现的情况下，要提倡“居者租其屋”；第三，要让全体人们都有城市居住权；第四，社会政策要把公平正义作为核心价值观。

上海市政协副主席、中国2010年上海世博会执委会副主任周汉民指出，在经济全球化的背景下，人类的城市化进程已经不可逆转。城市化带来文明进步，也带来极大的压力和挑战。最核心的是两大挑战：一个是城市人口老龄化问题，一个是贫富差距日益扩大的问题。社会保障制度在城市化进程中应当不断地创新，国际社会公认的社会保障制度应当包括三大制度：针对贫困和灾害的社会救济制度，应当包括针对养老医疗、工伤和失业的社会保险制度，应当保护针对老年人、残疾人、妇女儿童的社会福利制度。因此，这三大制度需要不断地更新，这就是可持续发展社会保障给我们提出的重要命题，也就是：保障制度既要保障当代人的需求，但是又不危及后代人的发展。上海世博会城市最佳实践区中，有三个关于社会保障的案例值得借鉴：一是马德里案例中建立在普遍性、公正性和可持续性上的公共住宅政策。二是印度艾哈迈德巴德案例对于解决城市贫困人口和随之而来的资源环境困难问题。三是巴西阿雷格里港案例中，政府如何统一长途和短途的公交票价，实行统一账户，按照运营成本在公交成本中进行比例分配，使居民和公交公司都能够共享公平的计划。

美国白宫城市政策办公室高级政策顾问江慕致认为，要确保社会保障政策统一化和协调化，让私营部门、公营部门、州政府和联邦政府一起合作。第一是持续发展社区，第二是社区重新复兴，第三是降低污染。要为城市的中心以及城市边缘地带提供同样的机会，使他们能获取一些相应的资源，这样社会才会变得更加有活力，更加宜居。

马德里市政府国际战略总协调员，中国2010年上海世博会城市最佳实践区马德里案例馆总协调人伊格纳西奥·尼诺·佩雷斯提出，在公共住房政策中，最重要的一个原则就是利用再生能源，另外一个原则就是为居民带来友好的、宽敞的空间。马德里公共住房吸引大家的注意力的原因在于：第一，在住房项目中，除了对房屋稠密度进行控制之外，还在这个区域中配上了相关的公共空间；第二，马德里公共住房最大特色在于平等，吸引各个阶层、各个人群居民居住，不管是年轻的还是年老的、有钱的还是没钱的；第三，在同样的地理区域，用50%的土地建保障性住房，让不同的人群分享共同的土地。

中国社会科学院常务副院长王伟光认为，城市化已成为中国经济持续较快增长和社会进步的强劲动力。城市化在加速推进经济快速发展和社会快速进步的同时，也滋生了较为严重的城市病，引发了较严重的发展失调问题，给人们的生存环境带来巨大挑战。破解这些挑战和问题，需要树立以人为本，全面、协调、可持续的城市科学发展理念。构建社会和谐、创造美好生活，是人类共同的理想和追求。大力推进宜居城市建设，是实现这一理想和追求所面临的一个重要而紧迫的命题。

## 四、小结

“和谐城市与宜居生活”主题论坛从城市空间、城市社会和城市环境三个方面入手，选取区域协同、支撑系统、城市社区、住房政策、社会保障等具体的热点问题作为议题，通过来自国内外的著名学者、企业家、城市管理者的踊跃发言和探讨，分享了城市规划和建设的成功经验，既展现了城市规划与区域治理方面的经典智慧，又汇聚了全球城市实践中的许多创意经验，涌现了许多思想创见和精彩观点，进一步丰富了和谐城市、宜居城市的建设理论，对未来城市发展具有重要启示意义。根据各位专家在论坛上的观点，未来城市发展主要有以下趋势：

（1）城市化仍然是未来数十年主要的发展趋势，解决快速城市化带来的城市病和发展失调问题，是建设宜居城市、和谐城市的重点。住房和城乡建设部部长姜伟新认为，城市化是经济发展的必然过程，也是人类社会文明进步的重要标志。今后数十年，尤其在发展中国家，城市化将是主要的发展趋势。城市的和谐发展，一直是世界各国政府和人民关注的话题。上海市市长、上海世博会执委会执行主任韩正认为，城市化的迅速发展，使越来越多的人享受到城市的繁荣和便利。与此同时，城市扩张也带来人口膨胀、交通堵塞、环境污染、资源紧缺、城市贫困、文化摩擦等诸多问题。应对这些挑战，建设生活更加美好的城市，成为全世界共同关注的课题。上海市政协副主席、中国2010年上海世博会执委会副主任周汉民认为，在经济全球化的背景下，人类的城市化进程已经不可逆转。中国社会科学院常务副院长王伟光认为，城市化在加速推进经济快速发展和社会快速进步的同时，也滋生了较为严重的城市病，引发了较严重的发展失调问题，破解这些挑战和问题，需要树立以人为本，全面、协调、可持续的城市科学发展理念。

（2）城市发展将更加关注人的需求。上海市市长、上海世博会执委会执行主任韩正认为，让全体市民居有所住、让交通出行畅通便捷，让人们在城市中更加幸福美满的生活，已经成为世界各国城市的共识。加拿大不列颠哥伦比亚大学城市与区域规划学院荣誉教授约翰·弗里德曼认为，社区才是人们真正生活的地方，作为宜居的场所，无论是在哪里，最重要的就是打造一个有归属感的社区。新加坡国立大学东亚研究所教授、所长郑永年认为，建设和谐城市要以人为本，要考虑各个社会群体的需要。中共杭州市委副书记、代市长邵占维认为，完善城市基础设施，特别是公共服务设施，方便居民生活，优化人均环境，扩展生活空间是建设和谐城市的重要内容。杭州市副市长张建庭认为，具备良好人文环境与城市文明拥有发达的教育，完善的公共文化服务设施，和谐的社区文化是宜居城市的重要内涵。

（3）城市发展将更加关注和维护弱势群体的利益。加拿大不列颠哥伦比亚大学城市与区域规划学院荣誉教授约翰·弗里德曼认为，很多来到城市建设的外来务工人员，却往往被城市的规划者所忽视，这也是一个宜居城市所需要考虑到的。浙江省妇联主席厉月姿认为，和谐城市，宜居生活城市再现了女性创造力。女性平等接受教育的制度保障，极大提升了女性立足社会的能力。上海市政协副主席、中国2010年上海世博会执委会副主任周汉民认为，宜居城市应建设三大制度保障弱势群体利益：针对贫困和灾害的社会救济制度，应当包括针对养老医疗、工伤和失业的社会保险制度，应当保护针对老年人、残疾人、妇女儿童的社会福利制度。瑞安集团主席、瑞安房地产有限公司、瑞安建业有限公司主席罗康瑞认为，住房是来改善民生的，让市民能够安居乐业，这也是社会的一个基础，政府应负责为低收入的群体提供公共的廉租房。

（4）城市发展将更加重视公众参与制度。联合国人居署全球司司长、上海世博会联合国馆馆长拉尔斯·雷乌特斯韦德认为，城市治理中的一个关键点在于要确保管理制度可行，并且让所有人都参与其中，让每个人承担起自己的责任。杭州市副市长张建庭介绍杭州的经验时说，杭州通过强化公共决策、公共管理和公共服务，从客观评价和市民意见中人居环境较弱的地方改起，逐步完善生态建设、人文共建、居住改善、公共空间、交通出行、社区服务，提高城市宜居水平。

（作者：王鹰翅，广州市城市规划勘测设计研究院规划二所所长，教授级高级规划师；李晓军，广州市城市规划勘测设计研究院规划二所工程师）

# “城市创新与可持续发展”高峰论坛综述

2010年上海世博会“城市创新与可持续发展”高峰论坛于10月31日上午在上海世博中心开幕。中共中央政治局常委、国务院总理温家宝出席开幕式并发表了题为《让世博精神发扬光大》的主旨演讲。论坛开幕式由中共中央政治局委员、上海市委书记、上海世博会组委会第一副主任委员俞正声主持。联合国秘书长潘基文和国际展览局秘书长洛塞泰斯分别在开幕式上致辞。国际展览局主席蓝峰、联合国副秘书长沙祖康、俞正声作闭幕演讲。部分国家元首和政府首脑、诺贝尔奖获得者、国内外城市市长、国际组织代表、专家学者、企业家、妇女青年代表和媒体代表等2000人出席论坛。

## 一、论坛背景

2010年上海世博会共有246个国家和国际组织参加，自5月1日开幕以来，在184天的展会期间，接待了超过7000万人次的海内外游客，创造了世博会历史上新的纪录，成就了一届成功、精彩、难忘的世博会。温家宝总理在高峰论坛开幕式上发表主旨演讲时表示，本届世博会谱写了世界博览史的辉煌篇章，并重申中国将坚定不移地走和平发展和开放兼容的道路，继续深化同各国的互利合作。

展示、论坛与活动是2010年上海世博会的三大组成部分，三者都围绕“城市，让生活更美好”这一核心主题展开。其中论坛是与世博会主题理念、思想成果有着紧密联系的一个板块，它直接演绎世博会主题，既是世博会精神遗产的集中体现，也是展望世博会未来的重要平台。本届世博会除高峰论坛外，另举办了六场主题论坛和数十场公众论坛。其中高峰论坛对全球共同面临的城市发展问题进行宏观探讨，是世博会系列论坛中级别最高的论坛。高峰论坛上发布的《上海宣言》，是建立在上海世博会各参展方对世博会成果总结和全球城市可持续发展问题共识基础上的一份重要文献。

可持续发展是世界各国共同关注的热点问题，城市创新是城市可持续发展的根本动力，是提高城市竞争力的关键，也是实现“城市，让生活更美好”的根本途径。本次世博会高峰论坛以“城市创新与可持续发展”为主题，是在我国贯彻落实科学发展观、努力构建和谐社会的大环境下举办的。倡导通过创新来寻找城市可持续发展途径、通过与广大发展中国家和发达国家开展广泛而深入的交流，共同探索和解决城市发展中所面临的各种现实问题，努力为世界城市未来和人类自身的发展留下有益的精神遗产，是本次世博会高峰论坛所承担的重要历史使命。

## 二、主要议程

高峰论坛由上海世博会组委会、联合国和国际展览局共同主办。论坛会期一天，包括开幕式、全体大会、7个平行论坛和闭幕大会。其中7个平行论坛分别围绕“信息产业与数字城市”、“知识创新与文化城市”、“绿色发展与生态城市”、“科技进步与创新城市”、“经济转型与永续城市”、“社区治理与宜居城市”以及“青年创造力与未来城市”等主题展开讨论。

随着以信息产业为代表的高新技术革命的飞速发展，全球城市自20世纪90年代之后开始步入数字时代。“信息产业与数字城市”平行论坛聚焦广泛应用的信息通信技术对于提升城市管理水平和改善民众生活质量带来的深层次挑战，以及信息化背景下数字城市、无线城市、物联网和消除数字鸿沟等未来城市发展与合作的热点话题。

文化是城市发展战略的维系核心，现代城市发展不仅要靠功能分区，更需要文化的有力支撑。“知识创新与文化城市”平行论坛关注在全球化和城市化的浪潮中，如何围绕文化传承深入探讨和反思，不断发展和完善城市规划理念，在总结世界历史经验的基础上实现对城市文化的包容和超越；同时探讨如何依靠知识创新与变革，解决文化传承和文化冲突等问题；如何依靠城市管理者和社会各界的力量，共同建设有文化特色的和谐城市。

作为全球半数以上人类聚居之所，城市在不断创造现代文明的同时，也正大量消费地球资源，并受到愈演愈烈的环境灾害和能源匮乏的影响。为实现全球可持续发展，国际社会正积极开展最广泛的合作，并将应对气候变化和绿色发展作为重中之重。在这一进程中，城市也扮演着不可或缺的角色。“绿色发展与生态城市”平行论坛邀请相关领域的权威专家和学者，积极探讨事关人类未来的绿色和低碳发展道路，并就城市的生态环境建设经验进行交流。

科技是人类社会进步的阶梯，也是历届世博会的核心展示内容。工业革命以来，城市化的飞速进展和居民生活方式的巨大改变离不开科技的创新、应用与发展。历史证明，只有自然科学和人文科学协调发展才能推动人类社会不断进步，引领城市文明不断走向和谐与繁荣。“科技进步与创新城市”平行论坛聚焦科技与城市的关系，探讨教育、政策和创新对科技进步的影响，并对创新城市的内涵进行讨论。

金融危机、粮食安全和气候变化等现象对世界经济结构和制度提出了严峻挑战，更强烈冲击着工业革命以来的传统经济发展模式。“经济转型与永续城市”平行论坛为城市管理者们和经济领域专家们提供就经济转型和生产方式转变进行探讨的平台，为实现经济的顺利转型和城市的永续发展提供契机。

当人们在享受城市文明成果的同时，也承受着不同阶段城市化进程所带来的诸多困扰。

社区连接着城市和居民，社区治理在城市管理中扮演越来越重要的角色。社区居民的广泛认同和积极参与，将提升社区活力，从而使整个城市和谐有序发展。"社区治理与宜居城市"平行论坛关注如何综合规划、设计、治理等功能，提升社区的满意度和归属感，打造和谐健康的生活，为居民提供多元、舒适、开放和公平的城市宜居空间。

城市发展离不开青年的发展和参与，青年发展又与城市发展息息相关。城市化进程的不断加快，在带给青年发展机遇和空间的同时，也给青年带来新的压力和挑战。实际上，青年发展与城市发展能否相互促进已经成为影响未来城市可持续发展的重要因素。青年友好型城市作为一种城市的未来形态，通过为青年提供更加友好的发展环境，在推动青年和城市的同步发展和良性互动方面具有示范意义。"青年发展与城市未来"平行论坛探讨青年发展与城市发展的内在关系，共同展望有利于青年发展的城市形态和发展模式，为打造和谐、创新、可持续的未来城市献计献策。

高峰论坛闭幕时发表《上海宣言》。这份宣言凝聚了上海世博会各参展方对全球城市可持续发展问题所形成的共识，集中体现了上海世博会的重要成果。

## 三、主要观点

温家宝总理在开幕式上发表主旨演讲时表示，本届世博会以"城市，让生活更美好"为主题，充分展示了丰富多彩的当代文明成就，汇集了人类探索城市发展的共同智慧，创造了多项世博会的新纪录，谱写了世界博览史的辉煌篇章。上海世博会首次以城市为主题，对解决人类共同面临的难题进行开创性的探索。我们要认真总结上海世博会关于城市发展的宝贵思想成果，创新城市发展模式，建设经济集约高效、社会公平和睦、文化多元包容、生态环境良好的和谐城市，努力创造更加美好的城市生活。温家宝总理还表示，上海世博会是在国际金融危机的背景下首次来到发展中国家，首次在一个特大城市的中心城区举办，这对中国是严峻的考验。世博会的成功举办，更加坚定了中国推进改革开放的信心和决心。中国将坚定不移地走和平发展和开放兼容的道路，学习和借鉴世界各国的优秀文明成果，深化同各国的互利合作。

联合国秘书长潘基文在开幕致辞中称，如今的城市面临着巨大压力，上海世博会为世界带来信心和希望，向我们展示了宝贵的理念，帮助我们应对城市化时代日益涌现的挑战。"城市，让生活更美好"的主题独具创新且昭示未来，让数以千万的人民知道，城市是有可能变得更加健康、更加安全的，城市能够更好地把自然和技术融合在一起。潘基文指出，在解决城市贫民窟的挑战的问题上，在利用推广绿色技术、可再生能源以及绿色业务模式发展方面，中国已经走在了最前沿。我们期待着在可持续发展方面与中国进行更密切、更广泛的合作，更加有效地、明智地利用自然资源，将可持续的发展方式贯穿于消费、贸易的各个环节，从政策制定和企业运营方面全面践行。

国际展览局秘书长洛塞泰斯在开幕式上高度赞赏上海世博会在推动创新与合作方面的卓越贡献。本届世博会创造了一个世人共享城市未来实验室，让我们以互不冲突的、建设性的、实用和可广泛应用的方式进行交流、探讨和实验。本届世博会也是国际展览局和联合国首次携手合作，强调了协同作用的重要性，能够加强未来世博会对公民乃至地方和世界领导人的启示和影响。上海成功地证明了世博会能提供一个核心场所，将各国民众与全球机构凝聚到一起，本着和平、创意与团结的精神，为应对人类共同面对的挑战做出积极的、建设性的贡献。

芬兰总理玛丽·基维涅米在全体大会上发表主旨演讲，指出建筑物以及建设行业所使用的能源占全球最终能源消耗的百分之四十以上，因此改善人工环境对于合理使用能源具有举足轻重的意义。欧洲新近实施的建筑物能源绩效指令为欧盟各国所有新修建筑和主要维修工程规定了严格的节能要求。作为欧盟的一员，芬兰正逐步改进其能源效率要求，向低能耗和被动式节能房屋标准转变。达到该目标的方法之一就是在土地利用规划中提高能源效率，减少排放。排放将被计算在土地利用规划评估中。另一种方法则是监督建设行业，以确保其支持节能低能耗建设环境的创建。其中的关键工具将是建设标准、能源证书和财产税。

匈牙利总理维克托·欧尔班在主旨演讲中阐述了传统文化在劳动力价值的创造方面的重要意义。他认为，过往关于经济危机和社会危机的话题其实是一种世界经济历史性洗牌的副产品，它决定了未来世界的秩序、世界权力的分配以及文化等因素在其间的作用。一个社区的努力必须基于其传统和文化之上，才能创造出有意义的工作。城市未来、文化传统、合作以及务实的作风，都对我们未来的幸福生活有着重要的影响。

莱索托王国首相帕卡利塔·莫西西利在主旨演讲中说，莱索托对“城市，让生活更美好”这一主题的演绎方式，就是关注城市以及乡村结合处的平衡、文化和现代的平衡、自然环境与人为成就的平衡。农村的产业要进一步发展，进一步加强，这样才有助于提高农村社区人们的生活质量，也能够提高城市居民的生活标准。同时，也有必要进一步提高在农村的服务行业的发展水平，从而能够让农村向城市的人口转移这个过程进一步优化。和这一点有关的就是如何更好地维护历史以及文化的传统，并且进一步推广在城市的文化多样性。这些要素都应该整合在城市规划的全过程中。

波兰众议院议长格日高什·斯赫蒂纳指出，特大型城市对全球的经济、文化，甚至对于世界的政治来说都扮演着重要的角色，但同时城市中很容易出现迷失和孤独感。我们希望城市成为居民友好型的城市，希望城市没有污染，同时推进科技和产业的创新，从而为城市越来越多居民居住的郊区提供安全、生态的环境。所有的国家都希望解决城市化所带来的一系列的问题，而且根据各自的历史文化特征采取了不同的经济发展方式。只有通过经济强市，才能在全球的竞争中实现强国。

全国人大常委会副委员长、中国科学院院长路甬祥教授指出，城市的兴衰记载了一个国家和民族孕育、成长、创造、发展的历史，记载了人类文明的历史进程。21 世纪，世界各国尤其是新兴发展中国家的城市化进程进一步加快。未来 40 年，包括中国在内的 20 亿 ~ 30 亿人将进入基本现代化行列。世界大多数人追求现代化生活的强烈需求，为城市化和人类文明进程注入了新的动力和活力，也对地球有限的资源和环境承载力带来新的挑战，决定了这一进程不可能沿袭传统的无节制的耗用自然资源的模式。展望未来，知识将成为人类永不枯竭、可持续的主要资源。知识创新及应用，将成为经济发展社会进步的主导因素，以知识为基础的产业将成为社会的主导产业，将影响和渗透到各个领域，将成为城市规划、建设、运行、管理、健康发展的主要基础和根本动力，将引领人类社会从工业文明时代进入知识文明时代。

英国社会科学院院士斯特恩指出，中国已经让几亿人口脱离了贫困，可以说，这是人类历史上最伟大的发展之一。但是，如果发展得不到管理，可能会导致过去取得的巨大进步停止甚至倒退。我们今天所面临的最大的挑战就是更好地管理气候变化。中国已经在现有的低碳市场中占有了很大份额，并且会进一步增长。这些低碳市场很可能到2020年的时候实现每年50万亿~60万亿的市场规模。那些将低碳经济的增长视为经济发展负担的认识是完全错误的。必须承认历史必然是不公平的，发达国家经过高碳方式发展起来，而发展中国家却最容易受到气候变化的影响。中国的发展速度意味着中国无法从全球气候控制中全身而退，所以，一个重要的方式是转型到低碳经济的增长。在全世界没有一个比中国更重要的国家来引领全世界实现经济低碳增长的转型。

美国加州大学戴维·格罗斯教授指出，科学是终极革命，只有完善对基础科学的研究才能带来解决可持续发展问题的技术创新。但解决这些问题最真实的挑战并不在于科学家，而是在于我们的政策制定者、经济学家和政府。我们最终必须要建立一个可持续消费和增长模式的经济和政治体制，实现全球治理，建立"全球政府"。

第十届全国政协副主席、中国工程院主席团名誉主席、中国美国人民友好协会会长徐匡迪在"信息产业与数字城市"平行论坛中指出，通过物联网在智能电网、智能交通、智能建筑等领域的应用，可以实现对城市的"巧妙管理"。日本在很多CBD地区的建筑里面用了大量的物联网传感器，实现节能30%。我们国家的建筑能耗比较高，因此这个技术非常重要。

中国文化部部长蔡武在"知识创新与文化城市"平行论坛指出，传统文化在塑造城市个性特色、提升城市生活品质、维护文化多样性、保持代际延续性、维持居民对社区和城市的认同感等方面具有举轻若重的作用。文化本身的发展也是一个传承与创新交融的过程。任何一种优秀文化的传统，只有随着时代的前进、不断的扬弃、改造和更新，才能保持其旺盛的生命力。随着科学技术的进步和文化的创新，传统物质生产的产品、传统的服务业获得了提升其自身文化内涵和高附加值的动力。创意产业日益成为城市经济新的支柱，成为传统产业结构调整的最佳切入点。后工业化时代的经济，只有与文化相结合才能实现自身的价值及其增值。

德国波茨坦可持续发展高级研究所科学主任、1984年诺贝尔物理学奖获得者卡罗·卢比亚在"绿色发展与生态城市"平行论坛中指出，新能源的创新需要很长的周期。在实现一定市场规模之前，投资和创新、监管框架的更新都需要很长时间。由于面临着基础设施投资以及利益相关方、能源价格限定、监管框架改变、网络连通性等方面的挑战，新技术肯定是更为昂贵的，而且还不一定带来立竿见影的效果，在社会接纳方面也会有障碍，确实面临很大的挑战。虽然目前无法完全实现"去碳"，也要加大科研投入，最大限度地实现“脱碳”。

剑桥大学校长莱谢克·博里塞维奇在“科技进步与创新城市”平行论坛上强调，大学是一个城市未来的关键一环或者研究中心。一个城市的发展是多面性的，必须通过多学科、国际性的合作。而寻找解决问题方法的最好地方就是大学。通过各种学科的努力和智力资本来解决问题正是大学的强项。大学可以提供一个智力方面的框架，让社会了解什么是可持续性。本届世博会的主题对于大学来说提出了一个新的课题，通过我们的员工、通过我们的学生、通过我们的研究项目，我们一起合作，是可以解决全球面临的问题的。

2001 年诺贝尔经济学奖获得者迈克尔·斯彭斯在“经济转型与永续城市”平行论坛中指出，经济结构的转型在中国广为人知，中国政府对经济转型的重要性非常了解。但在发达国家，对经济转型的重要性可能并没有认识那么深，带来一些深层次的问题。中国的增长和发展的转型过程非常复杂，必须平衡两个问题：一是持续高增长与收入和机会公平、能源使用效率和能源安全目标的协调；二是自身发展与在国际上维持全球经济可持续增长两种角色的协调。亚洲、拉丁美洲、非洲以及其他一些地区的增长都依赖于中国的经济增长和转型。世界经济是否向好，很大程度上要看中国的经济转型是否成功。

清华大学人居环境研究中心主任，中国科学院院士、中国工程院院士吴良镛在“社区治理与宜居城市”平行论坛中指出，社区本身是一个社会学概念，人是城市的核心，社区是人最基本的生活场所，社区规划与建设的出发点是基层居民的切身利益。这不仅包括住房问题，还包括服务、治安、卫生、教育、对内对外交通、娱乐、文化公园等多方面因素，应是一个“完整社区”（Integrated Community）的概念。在社会整体转型的今天，建设“完整社区”正是从微观角度出发，进行社会重组，通过对人的基本关怀，维护社会公平与团结，最终实现和谐社会的理想。

世界银行东亚地区人类发展局局长埃曼努埃尔·希门尼斯在“青年发展与城市未来”平行论坛中指出，增加对青年人的投资，可能是政府，包括国家层面和城市层面的政府最为重要的一个任务。第一，要确保青年人有更多的机遇，增加对于人力资本的投资；第二，要帮助青年人有能力作出明智的选择；第三，一旦作出错误选择的时候，我们要再给青年人一次机会，让他们重新来过。

联合国副秘书长沙祖康在高峰论坛闭幕式上指出，与以往世博会不同的是，上海世博会首次展示了破解城市挑战的各种方法，最佳城市实践区重塑并展示了其他城市已经在践行的方法。科学技术的应用是提高城市居民生活质量的必经之路。我们必须推广这些令人惊叹的科技成果，以实现人与自然的和谐共存。这才是建设和谐城市的答案。这也是城市可持续发展的核心理念，是“城市，让生活更美好”的真谛。

上海市委书记、上海世博会组委会第一副主任委员俞正声在闭幕辞中说，居民是城市的主人，人们来到城市是为了更加有尊严地生活。我们必须坚持以人为本，促进社会的公平与正义，缩小贫富差距。这是构建宜居社区、和谐城市的要义所在。

论坛闭幕大会发布了《上海宣言》。这是建立在上海世博会各参展方对全球城市可持续发展问题共识基础上的一份重要文献，表达了城市时代全球公众对和谐美好城市生活的共同愿景。《上海宣言》提出了创造未来的生态文明、追求包容协调的增长方式、坚持科技创新的发展道路、建设智能便捷的信息社会、培育开放共享的多元文化、构筑亲睦友善的宜居社区、促进均衡协调的城乡关系等理念。宣言呼吁将10月31日上海世博会闭幕之日定为世界城市日，让上海世博会的理念与实践得以永续。

高峰论坛还发布了《中国2010年上海世博会青年倡议》，号召全球青年行动起来，积极传播和实践和谐、可持续的发展理念，共同保护我们的地球家园；努力推动不同文明间的理解和对话，共同倡导开放包容的时代文化；继续发扬友爱互助的志愿精神，共同建设一个持久和平、共同繁荣的和谐世界。

## 四、小结

在闭幕之际，上海世博会以一次前所未有的强强对话和脑力激荡，盘点丰硕的世博精神财富，并展望世博会及人类社会的美好未来。"城市创新与可持续发展"的议题既能体现全球关注的热点问题，又与本届世博会主题相切合；既契合上海世博会围绕人与自然和谐相处和可持续发展的主线，又彰显了人类追求永续发展的长期目标。论坛倡导通过创新来寻找城市可持续发展的途径，通过对话与交流来寻求解决城市发展中所面临的现实问题，不仅与全球的发展目标相吻合，而且将进一步丰富世博会的内涵。

（1）《上海宣言》汇聚了本届世博会的思想成果。《上海宣言》再次提醒我们注意粗放式城市化带来的各种后果，包括不安全感、气候污染、交通堵塞、人际疏远、贫富分化等。《上海宣言》同时告诉我们，所有这些挑战都是可以战胜的，科技进步能帮助我们找到补救的方法。但要取得进步，需要我们每一个人都拿出政治意愿。只有重视《上海宣言》并持续跟进，才能确保实现其价值。正如国际展览局主席蓝峰在闭幕演讲中所言，过去达成的太多宣言最终都成了一纸空文，许多既定目标也由于在执行过程中困难重重而无法实现。他建议以国际展览局的名义，希望能与中国有关部门一起，根据有待进一步确定的各项办法，与基层工作者、各大城市市长、建筑设计师、城市规划师、社会学家和非政府组织开展经常性交流，对《上海宣言》在各国的实施情况进行定期评估。

（2）中国城市化成就举世瞩目。论坛演讲嘉宾不约而同地提及本次世博会的规模。246个国家和国际组织参展，超过7000万人次观展，首次在发展中国家举办的世博会成功吸引了全球的目光。联合国秘书长潘基文在开幕致辞中称，在解决城市贫民窟的挑战的问题上，在利用推广绿色技术、可再生能源以及绿色业务模式发展方面，中国已经走在了最前沿。芬兰总理玛丽·基维涅米在主旨演讲中指出，上海世博会展示了城市创新和城市发展在实现全球可持续发展方面的重要作用，中国成为建设可持续发展生态城市的真正先锋。匈牙利总理维克托·欧尔班认为，整个世界正在经历一场深刻的变革，中国在其中发挥着重要作用。英国社会科学院院士斯特恩指出，在全世界没有一个比中国更重要的国家来引领全世界实现经济低碳增长的转型。2001年诺贝尔经济学奖获得者迈克尔·斯彭斯认为，世界经济是否向好的关键，很大程度上要看中国的经济转型是否成功。

（3）低碳成为未来城市发展之路。论坛呼吁规划并建设更多的生态城市，来帮助我们拯救地球，减少贫穷和社会问题，维护社会稳定，为良好的经济发展打下基础。英国社会科学院院士尼古拉斯·斯特恩认为，我们今天面临的最大挑战是更好地应对气候变化，在2050年，世界经济主要部门都应接近到零碳排放，这样才可能把全球气候变暖控制在2度以内。美国加州大学教授戴维·格罗斯认为，环境的灾难甚至比核威胁更严重，这是一个真正的全球性问题，要解决它就必须要所有的国家共同努力。联合国贸易和发展会议秘书长素帕猜·巴尼巴滴希望找到气候变化和发展之间的平衡，找到一种新的发展模式、发展路径，找到一条低碳发展之路，可以减少二氧化碳的排放，还可以帮助经济增长，创造就业，并改善人类的生活。

（4）经济转型是未来城市发展关键。金融危机、粮食安全和气候变化等现象对世界经济结构和制度提出了严峻挑战，更强烈冲击着工业革命以来的传统经济发展模式。无论是发展中国家还是发达国家的领导人，无论是大城市、中等城市还是小城市的管理者和专家学者，都把如何将应对危机、促进经济结构调整和各城市可持续发展有效结合起来，当成是需要认真思考并寻求解决之道的重大命题。“和谐城市”是高峰论坛上专家们的共识，是建立在可持续发展基础之上的合理有序、自我更新、充满活力的城市生命体，是生态环境友好、经济集约高效、社会公平和睦的城市综合体。

（作者：曾文清，广州市城市规划勘测设计研究院）

# 案例篇

# 将规划从地区意愿上升到国家战略

## ——横琴的“谋”与“动”

长期以来，横琴岛的开发建设深受中央、广东省、珠海市及澳门特别行政区的高度关注。追溯其开发的历史，从1992年横琴岛被广东省定为扩大对外开发的4个重点开发区之一，到2006年“泛珠三角横琴经济合作区”的设想，再到2009年8月14日国务院正式批准通过《横琴总体发展规划》（以下简称《规划》），横琴新区已成为继上海浦东新区、天津滨海新区之后第三个由国务院批准的国家级新区。2005年9月，温家宝总理视察横琴岛时指出，横琴开发“要谋而后动，争取最大的经济社会效益”。如何谋？谋什么？如何动？动什么？这是横琴开发最终从地区意愿得以上升到国家战略的关键所在。

### 一、区域发展之“谋”：发挥横琴的“+”号作用

“不谋全局者，不足以谋一域；不谋万世者，不足以谋一时。”对于一个地区发展的谋划，首先也是最为关键的就是进行精准的区域定位谋划，其目标是在把握地区发展真实意愿的前提下，通过加强自身与外部区域特别是周边地区的紧密合作，共同承担区域发展的责任，解决国家层面所关注的核心问题。

#### 1. 珠三角发展困局：发展腹地受限与核心竞争力弱化

过去30多年来，偏居一隅的珠三角地区依靠毗邻港、澳的区位优势和先行先试的政策优势，迅速发展成为我国经济社会发展的重要引擎。然而，随着外部市场环境萎缩和原有优惠政策普适化，珠三角制造业的低成本优势在逐步弱化，发展腹地受限引发的内需市场不足的问题显得尤为突出；而以金融、国际贸易和现代物流为主体的高端生产性服务业所代表的核心竞争力，也受到长三角、环渤海以及新加坡等周边地区的有力挑战。珠三角地区由腹地不足和核心竞争力弱化所造成发展困局亟需寻找一个突破口来破解。

#### 2. 横琴发挥“+”号作用破解困局

(1) 第一轮“谋”：横琴作为泛珠三角（“9+2”）合作基地，力图破解腹地受限困局

始自2006年的横琴规划立足于泛珠三角合作。第一届泛珠三角合作论坛后，为使“9+

2”合作有更加实际的联系和内容，广东提出将珠海横琴作为“9+2”泛珠三角合作的空间载体，由“9+2”政府共同开发，由此破解珠三角及港澳发展空间腹地受限的难题（见图1）。在此背景下开展的《泛珠三角横琴经济合作区规划设计》提出横琴的区域定位，是将其打造成为服务港澳、辐射泛珠、区域共享、示范全国、与国际接轨的复合型、生态型的创新之岛。然而，尽管泛珠三角区域合作符合国家区域协调发展战略的要求，但与国家实践“一国两制”和提升国际核心竞争力的需求存有一定差距，因此这一轮的“谋”最终没能获准。

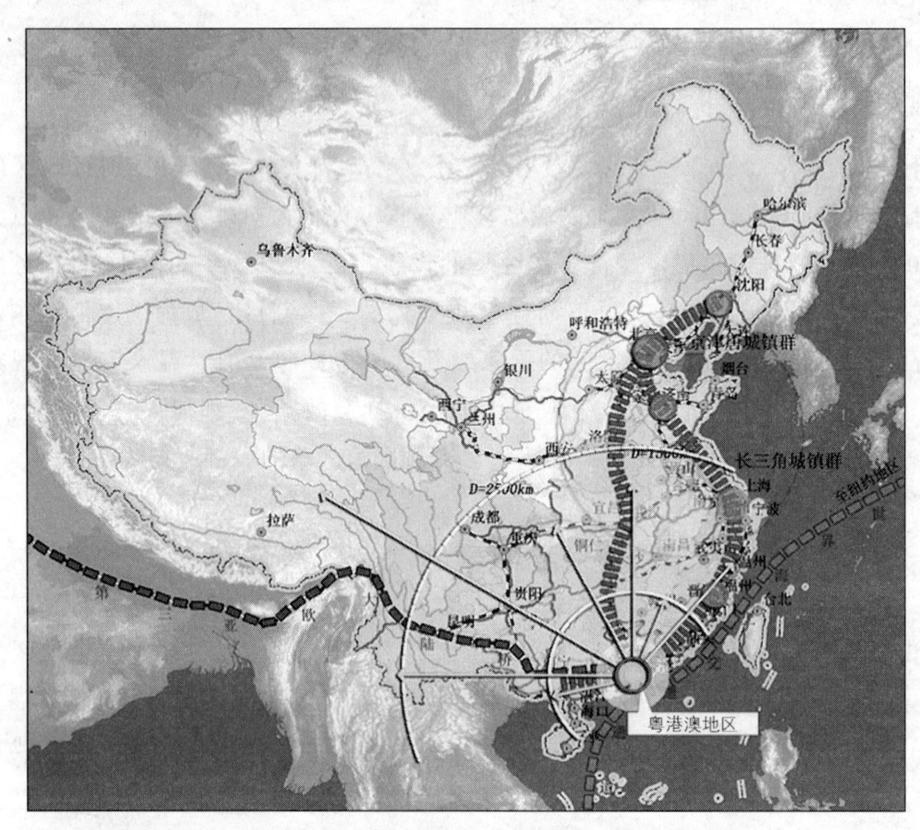


图1 粤港澳与全国联系图

(2) 第二轮“谋”：横琴是粤港澳（“9+2”）合作示范区，破解核心竞争力弱化困局

自2008年开始的横琴新一轮谋划着眼于粤、港、澳三地合作。粤、港、澳地区的发展融合了“一国”的共同优势。在金融方面，广东有整合内地资本和大量融资需求的优势，而港、澳有引进国际资本和开展国际化融资服务的优势；在研发方面，广东的基础性研发优势突出，而港、澳拥有面向市场转换的商业性研发优势；在航运方面，广东有连通内河和内地市场的航运优势以及大量需要外销的产品优势，而港、澳建立了国际化的船务网络，有自由港运转国际资源的优势；在营销方面，广东有运转内地市场的营销优势，而港、澳拥有国际性的营销网络。粤、港、澳三地，对内连通泛珠三角，连通全国，对外联系东南亚和全世界，是中国参与经济全球化的重要战略平台。

然而，在金融危机的背景下，粤、港、澳地区面临的核心竞争力弱化的问题日渐突出。

一方面，珠三角地区的现代服务业发展滞后，制造业仍处于全球产业链和价值链的低端，传统发展模式难以为继。另一方面，港澳地区虽拥有人才、技术以及连通国际的自由港优势，能够为广东的创新发展提供支持，但也存在着发展空间不足、产业空洞化和与内陆腹地联系不畅等问题，成为制约核心竞争力提高的短板。此外，粤、港、澳三地传统优势的弱化主要是由于有关制度性障碍导致的三地产业优势融合不够。首先，粤、港、澳三地之间由于通关制度、交通体制等方面的障碍，往来的时间和交易成本较高；其次，技术标准的差异，使港、澳研发成果的转换效率以及三地基础设施对接方面受到影响；最后，福利体制的差异，使港、澳高端服务人员难以“扎根”内地，提供更多“面对面”的服务。

推进横琴开发是“一国两制”下探索内地与港、澳合作新模式、破解珠三角发展困局的重大战略举措。横琴与澳门一桥相连，最近处相距不足200米，可通过在建的港珠澳大桥、京港澳等多条高速公路、广州至珠海城际轨道交通等加强对外联系，实现与港澳及珠江口西岸地区紧密相连，是唯一一个直接连通粤、港、澳三地的重要战略通道（见图2）。为推进粤、港、澳紧密合作，利用横琴地处粤、港、澳交汇点的区位优势，《规划》提出将横琴建成“粤、港、澳紧密合作示范区”。横琴将通过政策创新促进发展创新，既能充分发挥珠海的特区优势，又能延展港、澳国际自由港优势；既能与内地自由连通，又能与港、澳更紧密合作，融合三地的整体优势，极大地吸引国内外高端人才，以及物流、资金流、信息流的高度集聚和高效流动，破解该地区核心竞争力弱化困局。

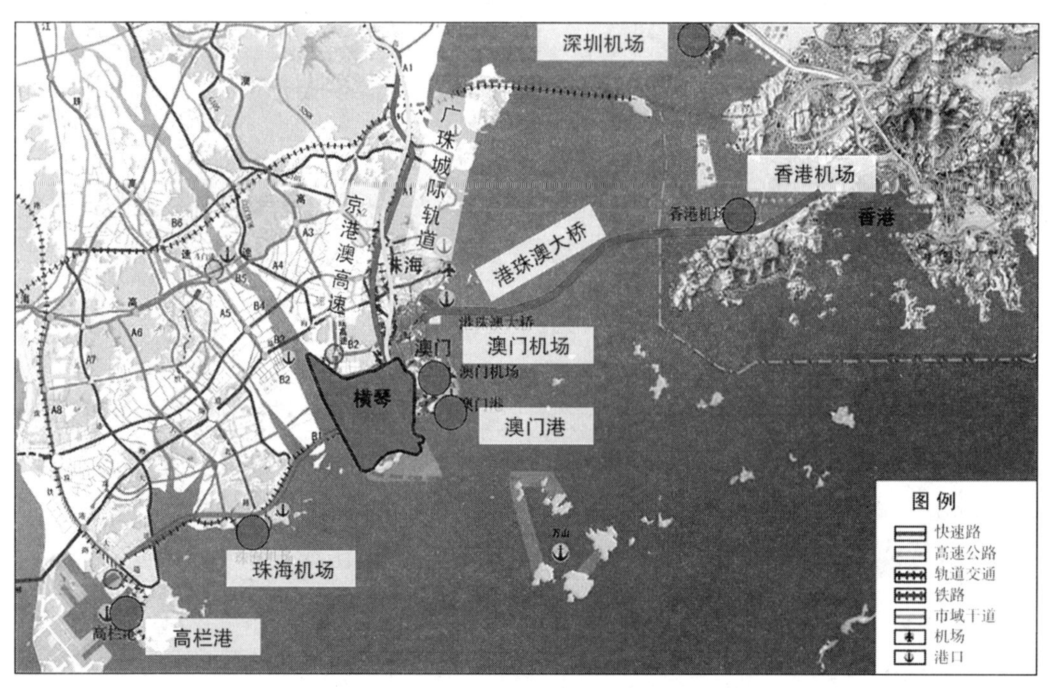


图2 横琴区位图

2009年1月初，国家副主席习近平视察澳门，在会见澳门各界人士时表示，中央已决定开发珠海横琴岛，标志着这一轮“谋”成功了。

## 二、横琴前景之“谋”：“特区中的特区”

### 1. 设立横琴新区，成为连通粤、港、澳的战略通道

2008年年初，广东省委书记汪洋同志提出：“要通过加强粤、港、澳合作，全面提升粤、港、澳地区在全国乃至整个东南亚发展格局中的战略地位。”2008年年底，国务院审议通过《珠江三角洲地区改革发展规划纲要（2008—2020年）》（以下简称《纲要》），明确提出“规划建设横琴新区等粤、港、澳合作区域”，横琴新区被正式赋予开展粤、港、澳更紧密合作的新的历史使命，也迎来新的历史发展机遇。

未来，横琴将承担最便捷地连通粤、港、澳三地，连通国内、国际两大市场的重要甚至唯一的战略通道地位（见图3）。

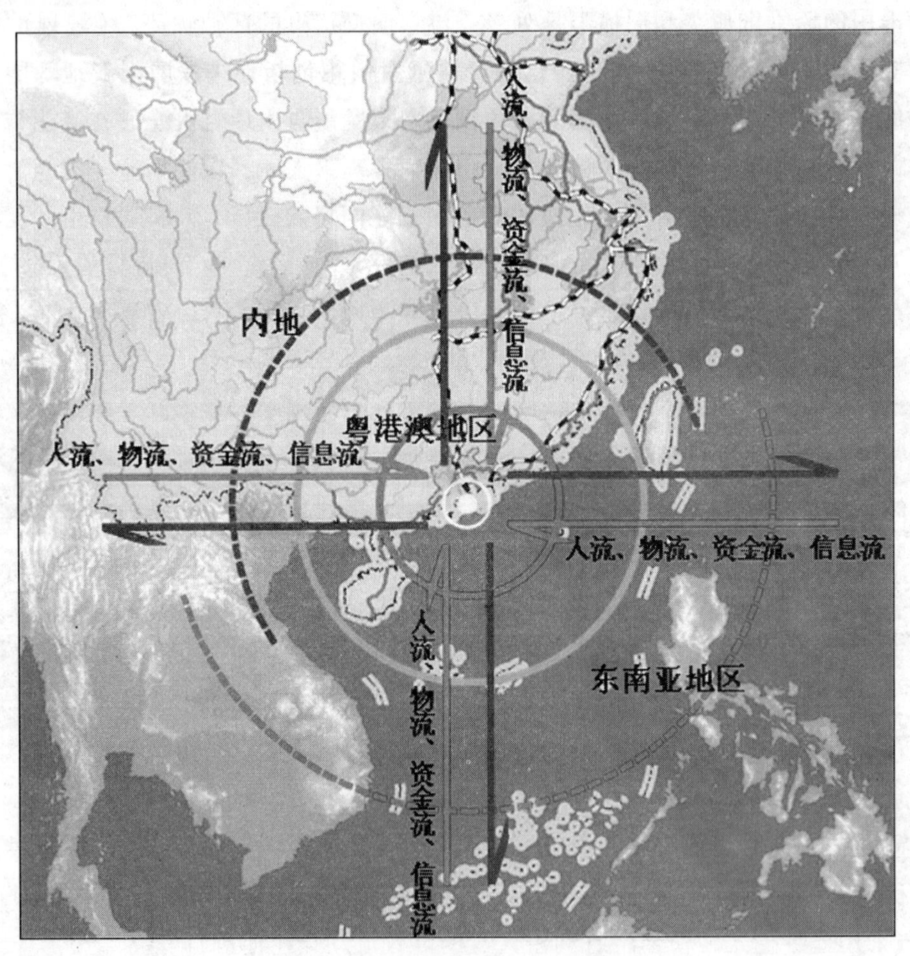


图3 横琴连通国内、国际示意图

**2. 两项体制突破：延伸港、澳自由港优势，成为特区中的“特区”**

（1）纳入经济特区范围，享受财税和立法权等优惠

对于地区发展而言，争取到由相关体制突破带来的政策是关键。横琴纳入珠海经济特区范围后，在财税方面，能够享受五年过渡期限定于高新技术企业的“两免三减半”的优惠财税政策，以及五年过渡期的企业15%所得税税率，有利于横琴吸引国内外投资和高新技术产业的发展。在立法权方面，根据《立法法》第八十一条，经济特区法规在经济特区内具有最高的法律效力。如果横琴仅适用一般的地方性法规，就会存在相互之间没有约束力的问题，而且地方出台的一般性地方性法规不能约束海关、商检、国税等垂直管理的部门。而纳入经济特区，其立法将成为各相关部门、单位和人员均必须普遍遵守的法规，其效力等级高于一般地方性法规和部门规章。

（2）延展国际自由港优势，促进各要素的高效流动

横琴采用的监管区域类型是在比较研究国际自由贸易区和国内保税区基础上的探索创新。它不同于国际上的自由港（狭义自由贸易区）。自由港指在主权国家或地区的关境以外划出特定的区域，准许全部或绝大多数外国商品可以免税进出，并且允许在港内或者区内开展商品自由储存、展览、拆散、改装、重新包装、整理、加工和制造等业务活动的区域，以中国香港、新加坡为典型。自由港是海关管辖区之外的特殊区域。它采取自由和便捷的管理措施，其开放度全面体现在关税免税、人员出入境、自主投资企业和自由汇兑的货币等优惠政策上。与自由港相比，横琴仅是一个国家内部多个地区之间的自由贸易区，而不是对其他国家的人、货物、资金均实行自由进出的自由贸易区。

横琴监管区域类型也有别于国内的普通保税港区。我国的保税港区是经国务院批准设立的，在特定港区专门发展现代国际物流业和出口加工，实行一体化封闭管理，并由海关统一监管的特殊功能区域，如上海洋山保税港区、天津东疆保税港区等。保税港区是海关按照我国国情实际需要，与国际通行做法相衔接的新兴监管区域，为我国目前开放层次最高、政策最优惠、功能最齐全、区位优势最明显的监管区域，采用“一线放开、二线管住、区内自由、入港退税”的管理方式，其开放度主要体现在税收政策上。保税港区是狭义的自由贸易区，是一个国家内部设置的对世界其他地区开放的地区。与之相比，横琴是三个独立关税区之间实行开放的自由贸易区。保税港区仅对货物实施自由进出，而横琴对人员、货物、资金均实施自由进出。

准确而言，横琴更符合广义自由贸易区的概念。然而，鉴于横琴是处在一个国家内的三个独立关税区之间的自由贸易区，而非两个或多个国家之间，所以称之为“特别自由贸易区”。通过采用此种模式，横琴将有利于人员的高效流动，在促进自身高端服务业发展的同时，拓展港、澳服务业的发展空间；有利于吸引从澳门直接进入横琴的巨大潜在客流量，获得国际化特色更突出的旅游业发展地位；有利于发挥港澳原产地、知识产权保护的优势，把主要工序放在港、澳，把配套工序放在横琴，吸引更多的国际高新技术产业转移；有利于吸引港、澳教育资源入驻，发展科教研发产业或为珠三角提供科研服务的重要相关产业。横琴

将发展成为“内地开放度最高、体制宽松度最大、创新空间最广”的地区。

表1　国内外监管区域类型比较

| 类型 | 境外自由贸易区 | | 国内保税港区 |
|---|---|---|---|
| | 自由港(狭义自由贸易区) | 自由贸易区 | |
| 定义 | 在主权国家或地区的关境以外划出特定的区域,准许全部或绝大多数外国商品可以免税进出,并且允许在港内或者区内开展商品自由储存、展览、拆散、改装、重新包装、整理、加工和制造等业务活动的区域 | 两个或两个以上的国家通过达成某种协定或条约取消相互之间的关税和与关税具有同等效力的其他措施的国际经济一体化组织 | 经国务院批准设立,在特定港区专门发展现代国际物流业和出口加工,实行一体化封闭管理,并由海关统一监管的特殊功能区域 |
| 管理方式 | 境内关外 | 境内关外 | 一线放开、二线管住、区内自由、入港退税 |
| 主要政策 | 关税免税;人员出入境自由;企业自主投资;货币自由汇兑等 | 原产地原则;区内取消关税和其他非关税限制,区外实行保护贸易 | 税收、金融、外汇方面优惠;投资经营自由;货物进区自由;外汇管理相对放宽等 |
| 代表地区 | 中国香港、新加坡 | 北美、中国—东盟 | 上海洋山、天津东疆 |

### 3. 三大发展定位、四大城市功能、五项配套政策

(1) 三大发展定位

《规划》实现了从“策划”到“规划”到“运营”的整体开发。横琴首先从发展方向开始策划,将发展定位作为规划的核心,提出了下述三个定位:①“一国两制”下探索粤、港、澳合作新模式的示范区。以横琴为载体,率先探索建立合作方式灵活、合作主体多元、合作渠道畅顺的新机制,为推进粤、港、澳更紧密合作提供示范。②深化改革开放和科技创新的先行区。以横琴为载体,进一步在深化体制改革和提升开放水平方面率先突破,为珠三角“科学发展,先行先试”创造经验。③促进珠江口西岸地区产业升级的新平台。以横琴为载体,共同培育珠、澳国际都会区,形成珠江口西岸地区新的增长极,促进珠三角地区协调发展,为全国区域协调发展发挥更加重要的作用。

(2) 四大城市功能

《规划》逐层推进,落实到城市功能及空间安排,保证了规划的连续性和整体性。产业发展既注重适当多元化,又非面面俱到,坚持高门槛、高层次和高附加值的配置原则。未来,横琴将重点发展商务服务、休闲旅游、科教研发和高新技术四大功能(见图4),逐步建设成为粤、港、澳地区的区域性商务服务基地,与港、澳配套的国际知名旅游度假基地,珠江口西岸的区域性科教研发平台和融合港、澳优势的国家级高新技术产业基地,巩固香港国际金融中心地位,促进澳门经济适度多元发展。

(3) 五项配套政策

推进横琴开发,配套政策是关键。《规划》真正体现了空间规划和政策规划的融合,成为政府提供公共政策与公共服务的重要依据与手段。在《纲要》及CEPA框架下,《规划》

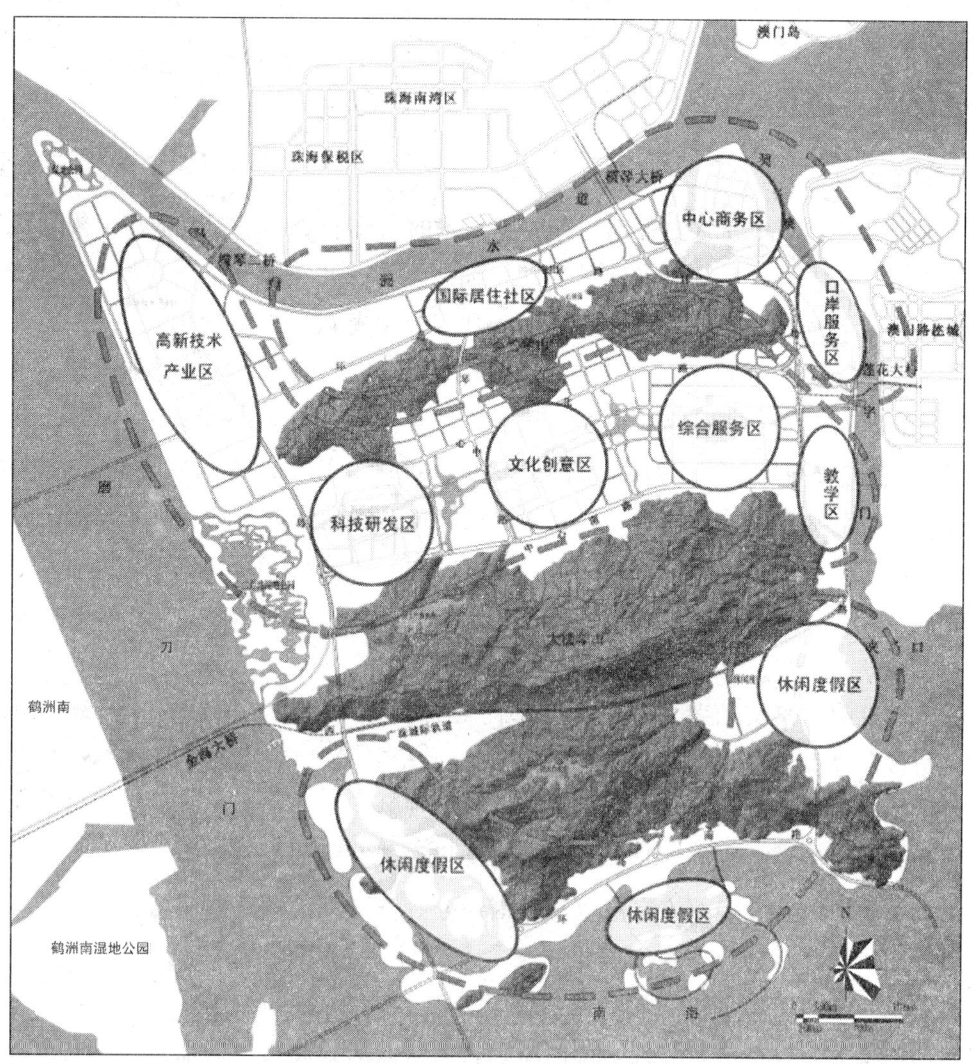


图4　横琴功能布局图

建立了与香港、澳门自由港政策相适应的粤、港、澳创新合作机制，将发展目标和主要内容转换为支持横琴开发的具体政策，包括将横琴纳入珠海经济特区范围、创新通关制度、鼓励金融创新、实行更加开放的产业和信息化政策和支持进行土地管理制度改革等。

## 三、转化为公共政策之“动”：上升为国家战略

### 1. 上下联动，争取国家支持

在横琴规划过程中，经过国家层面和省、市、区各层面的共同努力，进行了不同层面约30次的协调会议，多次征求国家部委、省直部门、珠海市的书面意见，最终使规划得到了国家层面就相关政策实施、项目安排、体制机制创新等方面的积极支持，也使其更加符合实际，更易于操作。《规划》成为中央和省、省和市、规划部门和相关部门、政府和社会反复

协商、共谋发展的一次卓有成效的实践。

**2. 部门合作，形成公共政策**

（1）推进规划编制

横琴规划编制过程中，省内各部门开展了有序的合作与分工，有效推动了规划从谋划上升为公共政策。具体由省发改委负责《规划》编制工作，并在国务院正式批准《规划》后，又牵头组织编制了《横琴产业发展专项规划》和《横琴基础设施专项规划》，为实现横琴产业又好又快发展，以及为下一步道路交通、市政公用设施、建筑和环境详细设计寻求项目支持和提供技术指导；省住房和城乡建设厅负责规划层面的技术指导，并牵头组织编制了《横琴新区控制性详细规划》，为开发建设提供更为准确和详细的空间方案，包括用地布局、开发强度、各项基础设施及公共服务设施的建设安排；省港澳办负责相关政策制定及制度设计，并由其牵头和会同有关部门在进一步深化、完善《规划》有关政策的基础上，明确规划实施的工作部署和机制保障。

（2）落实政策细化

每一个政策细化落实的背后都是多个部门通力合作的成果。横琴的“一线放开、二线管住”的分线管理制度，经过海关、口岸、出入境检验检疫等多个部门的多轮联合政策研究，并对出入境人员及其携带的行李物品和本外币现钞、交通运输工具、进出境货物、口岸基础设施和边防设施等分别开展具体实施办法和操作细则的研究和制定。

澳门大学管理是粤、澳双方在发改委、港澳办、教育部门以及澳门运输工务司等部门通力合作的一次成功实践，成为在“一国两制”框架下澳门借地发展、广东借人才和经验发展的经典示范。2009年6月，全国人大常委会决定澳门大学迁建横琴并授权澳门特别行政区按照澳门法律对新校区进行管理，澳门特别行政区政府以租赁方式取得横琴岛澳门大学新校区的土地使用权。校园的边防管理采取“相对岸边开放，陆地有效隔离”的方案，边防设施本着既有效隔离、又有利于创造文明美观、和谐祥和城市氛围的原则建设，河底隧道连接和封闭式校园管理是对现行通关设计的优化和提升。这对澳门拓展发展空间、优化产业结构、完善管理体制等都具有重要意义，开创了粤澳合作的新模式。

**3. 多方参与，达成行动共识**

规划是对社会各项利益的平衡，是在协商和合作的基础上所形成的社会共识。横琴规划充分体现了“协同规划”、“互动规划”的鲜明特色，尤为尊重内地和港澳各自的利益诉求和行为原则，妥善处理好各方面在横琴开发中的关系，形成互动合作的良好局面。规划过程中，反复征求了国家宏观经济院、中咨公司、中国开发区管理等专家意见以及社会公众的意见。就澳门大学迁建横琴的选址、用地规模、边防管理、项目建设实施等事宜，广东省、珠海市与澳门方面多次协商并最终达成共识。横琴开发的细化方案也正在抓紧研究之中，将鼓励港、澳有关机构积极参与进来，加强粤、港、澳三方的沟通协调，根据各自的需求和实际情况，寻求适宜的合作内容和有效的合作方式，逐步形成有利于港澳参与横琴开发最便利、最灵活、最富效率的长效机制。通过多方参与，《规划》现已成为政府和社会各界推动横琴开发的共同行动纲领。

## 四、落实到实施安排之“动”：“十年三步走”

### 1. 建立、健全实施规划的常设机构

建立、健全实施规划的常设机构有利于明确分工、完善机制及落实责任，保障实施工作的顺利开展：（1）为推进政府事务综合管理与协调，横琴按政府综合管理职能合并政府部门，组成大部制的政府组织体制，建立横琴新区管理委员会。（2）为使政府部门专注于公共管理和服务，同时保障横琴开发过程中公共资产的有效经营，通过政府控股的形式建立横琴开发运营公司。（3）为广泛吸纳社会力量共同推动开发，探索粤、港、澳合作创新，将成立粤、港、澳合作战略顾问小组或粤、港、澳合作研究机构，促进三地合作开发横琴的研究和规划协调工作。

### 2. 分阶段实施，指导基础设施建设和土地整备工作先行展开

宏观规划下，更需要提出从长远安排到短期建设的分阶段目标，制定土地开发计划和分期建设重点，为决策人员提供各阶段的操作依据。近期内把完善市政基础设施及公共服务设施建设作为公共投资的优先重点，形成完善的城市机能以快速引导人口、资源及产业的集聚，并先行开展土地空间整备工作，释放土地的潜在价值。截至 2012 年，横琴将初步完成岛内市政基础设施建设（全岛的 BT 项目），包括快速道、环岛路和中心南、北路等主干道和岛内次干道，海堤与环境工程，对外交通初步建成广珠城际轨道延伸线、广珠西线高速延长线等项目，澳门大学、横琴总部大厦、长隆国际海洋度假城、十字门商务区、多联供燃气发电等按计划推进建设。截至 2015 年，港珠澳大桥将建成，口岸服务区、中心商务区、国际居住社区、教学区、综合服务区、文化创意区、科技研发区、高新技术产业区、红树林保护区、休闲度假区等初步建成，将成为充满活力的粤港澳合作示范区。截至 2020 年，横琴将全面建设成连通港澳、区域共建的“开放岛”，经济繁荣、宜居宜业的“活力岛”，知识密集、信息发达的“智能岛”和资源节约、环境友好的“生态岛”。

### 3. 制定行动计划，逐项落实主体、资金和规模

进行重点项目的储备，并制订行动计划指导建设，通过项目审批制度落实年度行动计划的相关要求，建立年度核查制度对项目实施情况作出评价，并明确责任主体加强对项目实施的监督检查。如：横琴项目库由横琴管理委员会对项目分类入库集中管理并监控项目的运作状况；由开发运营有限公司站在高起点，着眼于粤港澳地区进行招商引资；各项目按照休闲旅游、教育科研、高新产业、市政公用设施等类别以及建设主体、资金和规模等方面进行管理。目前《规划》实施效果已初步显现，依据规划，横琴启动了教学区、中心商务区、口

岸服务区、综合服务区、高新技术产业区和休闲度假区内的六个重大项目的前期工作，包括珠海长隆国际海洋度假城、十字门中央商务区会展商务组团、横琴多联供燃气发电工程、横琴新区总部大楼、横琴岛基础设施建设项目以及澳门大学新校区等。近期重点建设项目的启动标志着横琴已经进入实质开发阶段，并为今后稳步推进开发做好了准备。

## 五、小结

从“谋”到“动”，横琴借助良好的开发时机，将自身的发展意愿与珠江口西岸、珠三角乃至粤、港、澳地区发展的区域责任相结合，谋准区域定位、功能与政策，由此成功地上升为国家战略，成为粤、港、澳三地政府和社会各界共同关注的开发焦点。2009 年 12 月，澳门回归 10 周年之际，胡锦涛总书记听取规划汇报后强调：“开发横琴岛是中央的重要决策，广东省和珠海市要加强对横琴岛总体规划实施的组织领导，抓紧推动各项任务落实。”

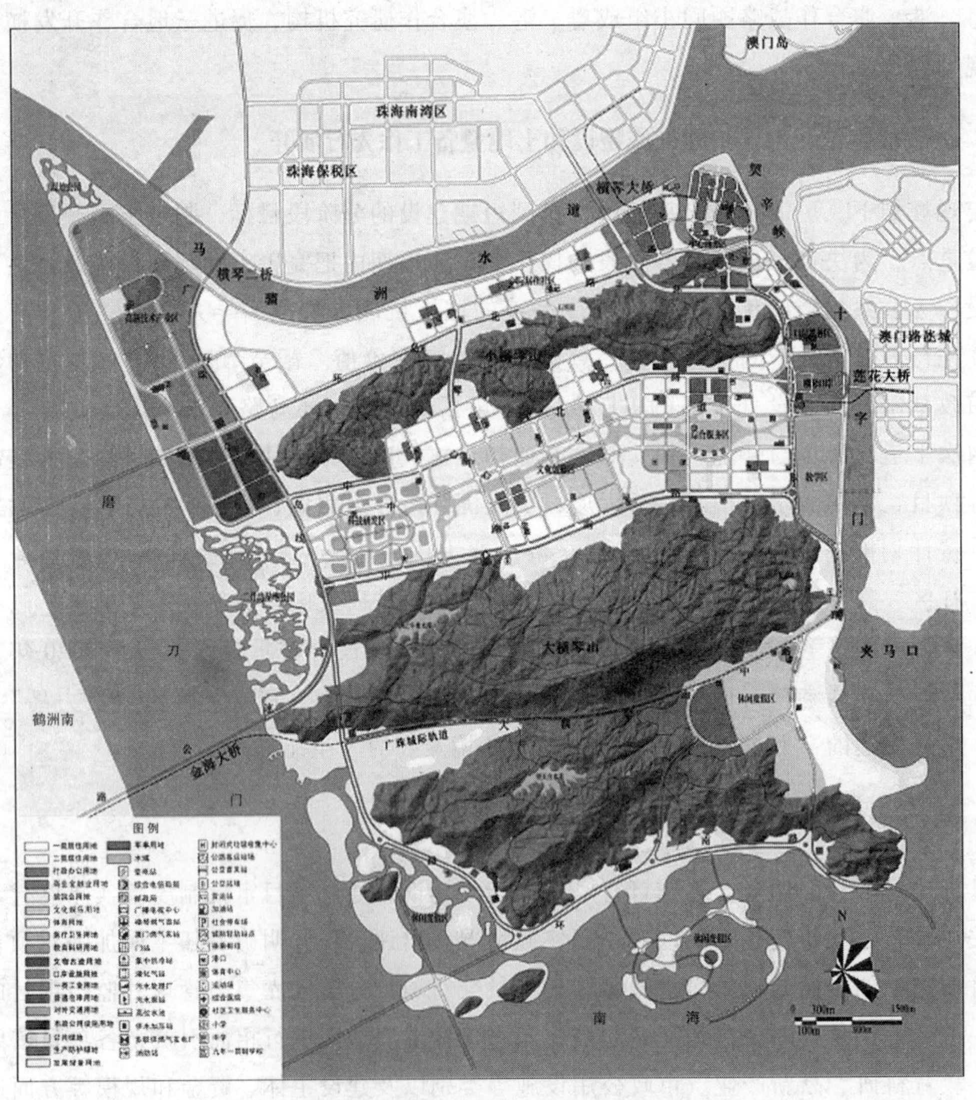


图 5　横琴岛土地利用规划图

目前，横琴的开发建设正在规划的指导下紧锣密鼓、有条不紊地展开。

（作者：宋劲松，广东省城市发展研究中心主任，教授级高级规划师；罗勇，广东省城市发展研究中心副主任，高级规划师；龚蔚霞，广东省城市发展研究中心项目总监）

### 参考文献

[1] 国家发展和改革委员会．珠江三角洲地区改革发展规划纲要（2008—2020 年）. 2008

[2] 国家发展和改革委员会，广东省人民政府．横琴总体发展规划 . 2009

[3] 广东省建设厅．粤港澳空间发展战略规划研究 . 2008

# 特色城镇化道路促进拉萨健康发展

## 一、特色城镇化道路的内涵

“中国特色”城镇化发展道路是特色城镇化理论研究的总纲，从城镇化概念引入中国开始，学界就开始将中国国情与城镇化发展的理论相结合，就特色城镇化的内容、动力、实现方法、理论框架等进行了研究和探索。笔者认为，特色城镇化道路就是指从城镇化发展的实际出发，总结实践经验，贯彻科学发展的理念，遵循城镇化发展的一般规律，制定出符合当地发展条件需要和资源与生态环境相适应的发展道路。

### 1. 基本原则

（1）体现综合效益

城镇化的效益是综合多方面的，包括经济、社会和环境效益的统一。这里有两层含义：一是特色城镇化发展需要从过去单纯注重经济效益向注重综合效益的转变；二是某些地区和城市的发展可能更多的需要关注社会效益和环境效益，例如，社会冲突问题严重的地区、生态环境脆弱的地区等。

（2）强调因地制宜

各地区和城市自然条件、经济发展阶段以及工业化水平和产业结构状况等条件差异较大，城镇化也处于不同阶段，因而难以用固定模式来指导发展。因此，城镇化发展中更应注重因地制宜，采取适合于实际情况和特点的发展战略，建立充分体现地域特色的城镇体系，优化城乡空间布局。挖掘地方历史文化和人文景观资源，注重传统手工业和旅游业的相结合，丰富和特色化城镇化内容。

（3）协调与统筹发展

主要体现在三个方面：首先，城市发展要同经济发展水平相适应，与工业化进程相协调，这是城镇化的基本规律；其次，各规模等级城市之间要相互协调，做好产业分工和产业结构调整、基础设施布局和建设工作，促进区域经济发展；最后，区域和城乡发展必须协调与统筹，充分发挥中心城市对于区域的带动作用，建立城乡统筹的一体化发展机制。

(4) 数量和质量并重

虽然东、中、西部地区由于经济社会发展水平的差异，城镇化发展阶段也不尽相同，但城镇化发展都已逐步注重城镇化质量提高和城市现代化等问题。对于西部地区城市，外延式扩张不可避免地会成为城镇化的主要趋势。但未来发展必须对城镇化内涵质量给予足够的重视，注重城乡统筹发展，注重城乡公共服务和基础设施建设。

**2. 实现路径**

特色城镇化道路需要依靠相关的制度建设和政策设计加以实现。特色城镇化实现路径关键是要从实际出发，从效益出发，发挥市场机制在人口向城镇迁移、要素向城镇集聚以及城镇内部结构调整和外部扩张等方面的基础性和主导性作用（朱铁臻，2003）。住房和城乡建设部副部长仇保兴（2002）认为，在指导思想上，要把可持续发展放在突出地位，要采取不均衡的发展策略，以现有的县城和有条件的建制镇为基础，科学规划，合理布局。消除不利于城镇化发展的体制和政策障碍，引导农村劳动力合理有序流动，强化规划对城镇化的调控作用，确保城镇化的健康发展。笔者认为，西部地区还需要重点抓好基础设施和生态环境建设，特色城镇化的路径选择是为了实施城镇化发展战略，是为了保障可持续发展，其目的在于切实促进人口和产业的城镇化转移，实现集聚发展，引导城镇集约发展，优化城乡与区域空间布局，提高公共服务和基础设施服务水平，以实现城乡统筹发展和同步现代化。

## 二、拉萨城镇化发展概况

**1. 城镇化发展的本底条件**

拉萨生态环境总体比较脆弱，虽然生态资源和条件丰富，但随着人类活动加剧，引起区域生态环境质量退化现象，威胁拉萨的生态平衡。特别是近十多年来大气综合污染指数逐年增加，总悬浮颗粒物污染逐年增加，水环境质量也有恶化趋势。主要表现在：

(1) 草原退化

拉萨地区牧草地净面积 138.65 万公顷，是土地利用类型中面积最大、分布最广的一类，占土地面积的 73.15%。据统计，拉萨市有 39.67 万公顷的草地发生了不同程度的退化，占草地总面积的 27.85%，大约有一半是中度或重度退化。据估算，截至 2003 年，拉萨全市有 5.53 万公顷草地出现了严重的沙化和退化现象，造成年经济损失约 400 多万元。

(2) 土地沙化

受旱寒多风气候、河谷沙源丰富等自然条件的影响，耕地表土层风蚀严重，并且流沙、沙尘时常掩埋耕地和牧场，土地沙化成为拉萨地区的主要环境问题之一。根据土地沙漠化普查结果显示，各种类型的沙漠化土地共 16.95 万公顷，占全市土地面积的 5.74%。

(3) 灌木林破坏严重

由于拉萨农村地区能源短缺，能源消耗以生物质能源为主，导致有限的灌木林遭到严重破坏。在近居民点的山坡地，灌木林地破坏严重，并且灌木林的破坏范围仍在继续向外扩展。拉萨地区共有8.9万公顷灌木林，并且都位于生态环境脆弱的坡地上，其生态效益和生态屏障作用十分突出，灌木林的砍伐，加剧了水土流失、土地沙化等问题。

(4) 湿地退缩

有“拉萨之肺”之称的拉鲁湿地以及拉萨河河谷湿地是拉萨河流域重要的生态系统，生物多样性十分丰富，并且是黑颈鹤冬季的越冬场所。但在拉萨市城市快速扩张、农牧业综合开发等影响下，湿地被大片占用，面积迅速锐减，所剩湿地的生态环境因子也发生了巨大变化，湿地旱化、沙化问题严重，生物多样性遭到破坏。

(5) 城镇工业和生活污染加剧

由于认识的误区和经济实力薄弱，拉萨环境保护措施、投入强度十分有限，人口和工业集中的城镇地区“三废”污染逐年增加，拉萨市的“三废”排放量占全自治区的90%以上，每年约有100万吨以上的未经处理的工业废水和近1000万吨的生活污水排入拉萨河。

**2. 现状人口与城市化水平**

2007年年底，拉萨市域总人口约为60.4万人。其中：户籍人口46.5万人，外来人口13.9万人，城镇人口为34.8万人。市域人口密度约为每平方公里20人。同期，西藏自治区人口密度为每平方公里2人，全国人口密度为每平方公里137人。拉萨城镇化水平为57.6%，1995—2007年城镇化水平年均增长1.7个百分点。

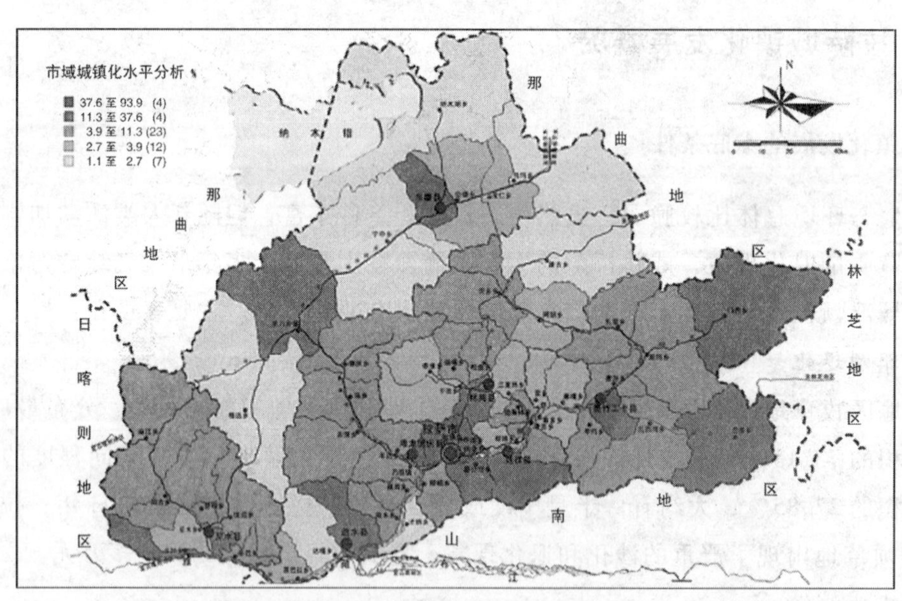


图1 拉萨市域现状城镇化水平分析（2007年）

**3. 拉萨城镇化发展特征分析**

(1) 从城镇形成过程看，城镇发展动力已经发生变化

历史上，宗教直接影响着拉萨城镇的兴衰。公元7世纪大昭寺和小昭寺的兴建，促进了

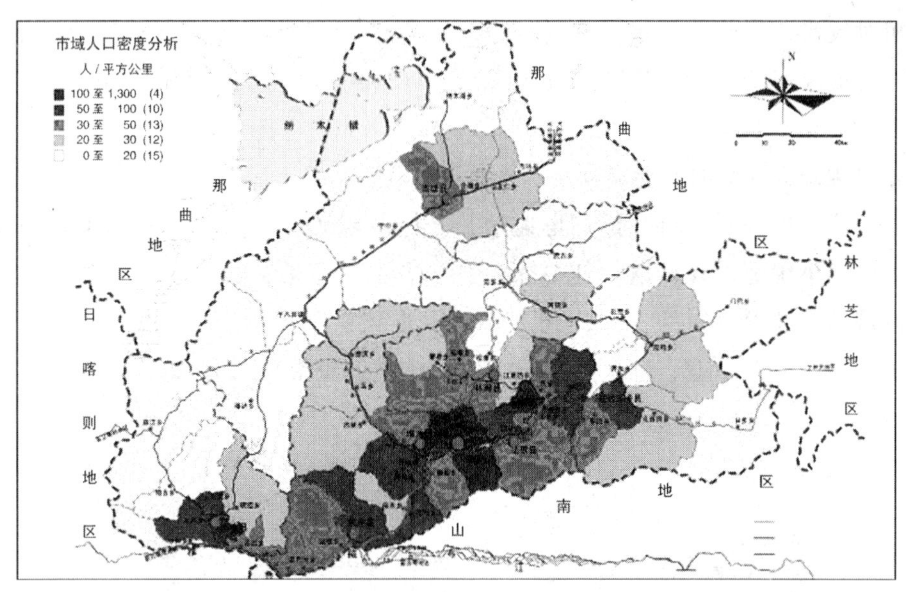


图2 拉萨市域人口密度分析（2007 年）

八廓街的形成和拉萨城的兴盛。公元 15 世纪，三大寺相继修建，使拉萨城再度扩展、繁荣（王小彬，2002）。宗教对城镇形成的影响成为拉萨城镇化不同于其他地区城镇化的一大特点。和平解放以来，宗教的作用对城镇化的影响逐渐减弱。行政中心、交通要冲、商贸中心、旅游等在拉萨城镇发展中起着越来越重要的作用。

（2）市域城镇化水平差异较大，城镇规模偏小，结构不尽合理

2007 年，拉萨市域城镇化水平为 57.6%，但是所辖各县区差异较大。城关区城镇化水平最高，达到 96.4%，其他各县城镇化发展水平较低。其中，堆龙德庆县达到了 27%，其余各县城镇化水平在 13% 以下。除中心城市人口规模达到 30 万人以外，7 个县城和其他乡镇城镇人口都在 5000 人以下，且其他多数乡镇城镇人口不足千人。这种状况必然影响拉萨地区经济社会的有序发展。

（3）城镇及人口分布主要集中于青藏和川藏公路沿线

自然地理环境是拉萨人口和城镇空间分布格局形成的基底，地形地貌条件和气候条件适宜的地区是人口密度较高的地区。山谷和河谷等地势平坦地区成为城镇集中分布的地区，也是人口较为稠密的地区，即青藏和川藏公路沿线地区。拉萨地区人口绝对数量少，致使城市规模的扩大、城市人口的增加和新城市的形成缺乏一定的人口基础，成为制约拉萨城镇化发展的重要因素之一。

（4）城镇发展的内在动力不足

主要表现在四个方面：一是农牧业劳动力占比远远高于全国平均水平，但农牧业产值远低于全国，说明农牧业效率极低，不能对城镇化的发展形成推力；二是工业化发展水平滞后，且重工业比重过大，很难吸收剩余劳动力就业，对高原经济增长缺乏牵引力，不能对城镇化的发展形成拉力；三是目前工业化水平较低，限制了农业产业化的进程；四是第三产业发展层次较低，城镇化的后续动力不足（马玉英，2006）。拉萨地区尽管第三产业特别是旅

游业发展相对较快，但其总量很小。2007年，拉萨第三产业增加值占全部地区生产总值的68.3%，该比重仅低于北京市位居全国第二位，但其规模只有北京市第三产业总值的1.3%。

(5) 新时期外来人口对拉萨城镇化水平的提高作用明显

近年来，拉萨市外来人口数量在迅速增长。拉萨城镇外来人口达到了13.9万人，外来人口几乎主要都集中分布在城镇。其中拉萨中心城区13.3万人，占全部外来人口的95.6%，外来人口占城镇常住总人口的比例达到23.2%。进藏的外来人口希望在拉萨谋求更多的就业机会和更理想的经济效益，已经成为拉萨城镇化中的重要推动力量。

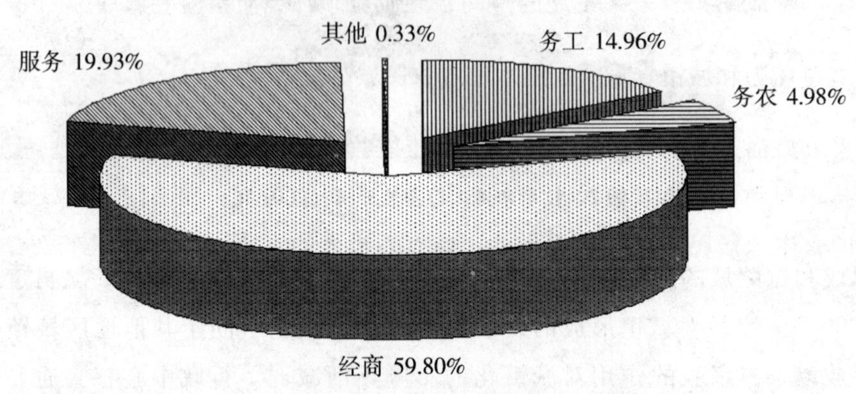


图3　2007年外来人口就业结构

## 三、拉萨城镇化发展路径分析

### 1. 城镇化战略路径的形成原因

改革开放以来，拉萨的经济社会发展已经取得了翻天覆地的变化，三次产业的比重已恢复到较为正常的水平，但其背后是生产力发展水平极低的第一产业、产业层次和技术含量较低的第二产业，以及在二者基础上形成发展的第三产业，且区域间经济发展极不平衡。可以判断，由于社会经济自然发展可能难以实现城镇化与现代化的发展目标，且拉萨地区目前自身尚不具备较完善的自我“造血”能力，难以实现城镇化与现代化的战略目标。因此，拉萨的城镇化道路选择了由政府主导、市场辅助的路径。

### 2. 当前城镇化战略路径的实施评价

虽然拉萨的城镇发展取得了令人瞩目的成就，但由于区域城镇化缺乏行之有效的统筹规划，在市域城镇体系中城镇定位不清、功能雷同，不同类型的城镇之间难以形成有效的分工协作关系，难以提高市域城镇体系的综合效益，难以有效促进市域城镇化的协调发展。

## 四、拉萨可持续城镇化发展的影响因素和主要问题

### 1. 人口和产业集聚使得城镇环境容量压力加大

受资源环境基础的约束，城镇发展应有一个合理的容量。拉萨虽然地域辽阔，但适宜城镇化的空间十分有限。人口和产业的集聚产生两个严重的问题：一是适宜人口产业集聚的拉萨河平原现有的城镇、人口、产业密度较高，其能够承载的容量毕竟有限；二是已有城镇的环境污染还在不断地缩小着未来发展的空间，导致城镇环境质量受到威胁。

### 2. 就业竞争压力和城镇容量限制给本地农牧民城镇化带来很大压力

大量外来人口涌入拉萨务工经商，使得本土农牧民城镇化进程缓慢。长远看，由于城镇发展规模将趋于饱和，本土农牧民未来城镇化进程将更趋艰难。同国内其他城市的外来劳动力往往从事的是本地居民能做而不愿做的工作有着极大的不同，在拉萨，外来人口与当地从业者相比，因人口综合素质较高而具有明显的就业竞争优势，进入的是本地劳动力目前尚未能胜任的技术岗位、管理经营和服务领域（朱玲，2004）。大量外来人口在为拉萨经济繁荣做出贡献的同时，对当地人口的就业和发展机会产生了一定的压力。

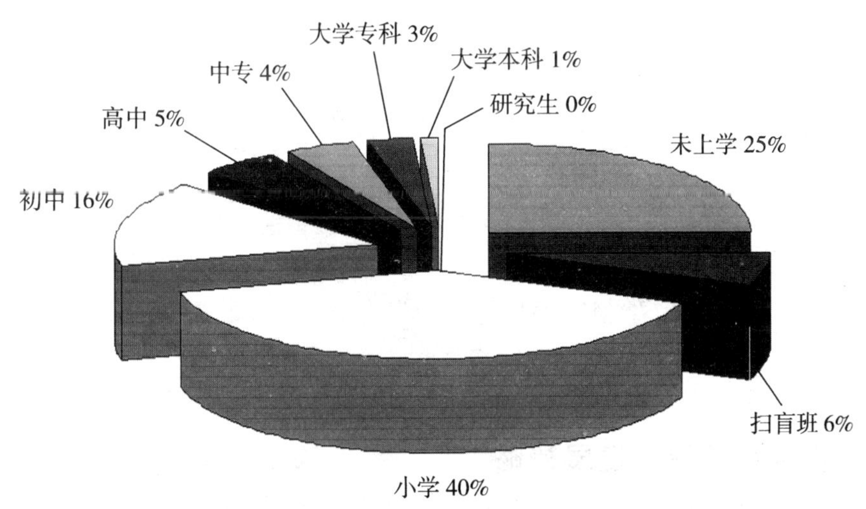


图 4　拉萨市 2000 年 6 岁以上受教育人口构成

### 3. 农牧民滞留于土地上将加剧资源环境的负荷

本土农牧民的城镇化在减轻农牧区的生态环境压力、实现多文化融合与转变农牧民思想观念等方面，有着不容忽视的作用（李陪祥等，2003），但目前的城镇化过程在这些方面尚未收到理想的效果。拉萨 45% 的从业人员禁锢于农业生产，大量的农牧民滞留在土地上，对土地、草场等农牧业资源的直接作用强度日趋加大。受开发利用方式和技术水平的限制，

这种高强度的作用往往表现为对土地、草场等的过度利用，加重了资源环境的负荷，进而使原本脆弱的生态环境压力日益增大。因拉萨地区的原生态系统有其自身的特殊性，一旦被破坏，再度恢复将十分漫长和艰难，其反馈作用是农牧民进一步扩大再生产和提高经济收益的难度增大，从而导致农牧民增收的难度加大与资源环境恶化的非良性循环，影响拉萨经济社会的整体协调发展。

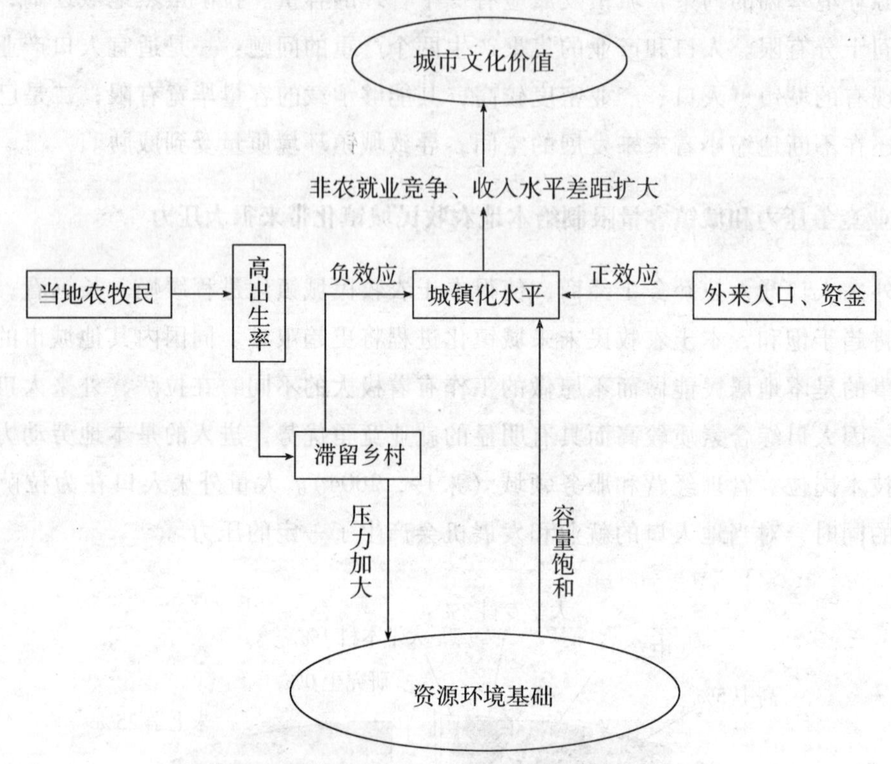


**图5　拉萨人口增长、城镇化与资源环境的相互作用关系**

资料来源：樊杰，等.西藏人口发展的空间解析与可持续城镇化探讨［J］.地理科学，2005（8），25（4）：389

## 五、拉萨特色城镇化发展战略

### 1. 基本思路

实现可持续的城镇化是拉萨人口发展和城镇化进程中需要努力实现的目标，其可持续城镇化的深刻内涵有两个重要方面：一是城镇化应有利于拉萨经济发展同生态环境保育、社会文化传承的协调；二是有利于同当地非农化相匹配，切实为提高当地人民的生活水平做出重要贡献。因此，拉萨特色城镇化的基本思路是：基于生态保护、利于文化传承的特色城镇化道路；提高本地人口素质、促进农牧民增收的本地城镇化策略；国家帮扶与自主发展并举，提高城镇化质量。

### 2. 拉萨城镇化发展战略

(1) 旅游带动

旅游产业是拉萨目前的支柱产业和龙头产业。拉萨具有独特而丰富的自然资源和历史文化资源，旅游产业发展前景广阔。随着交通条件的改善，拉萨旅游接待量已经迅速增长，2007年拉萨游客接待人数274万人次，是2004年的6倍以上。同时，旅游产业比较适宜于拉萨特殊的高原生态环境条件，在合理的接纳容量下，能够较好带动拉萨市域的城镇化进程。拉萨城镇发展应结合自身特点和市域内部的地区间差异，以旅游产业等特色产业的发展积极推进城镇化进程，优先发展基础较好、条件优越、具有良好发展前景的城镇，使这些城镇尽快发展起来，以带动其他地区的发展。一方面，旅游产业的发展能够提高当地群众的收入水平，另一方面，旅游产业发展将带动相关产业，特别是旅游产品加工制造业和拉萨传统手工业的发展。

(2) 强化中心

作为西藏自治区首府的拉萨，是西藏经济建设和社会发展的龙头，特别是在西藏的城镇化、现代化进程中，拉萨的带动作用举足轻重，其发展情况直接关系到整个西藏的城镇化和现代化进程。拉萨城镇化进程中必须突出拉萨中心城市在全市乃至全区城镇化发展中的核心地位和示范作用，努力提高城镇发展的整体质量和综合效益，完善中心城市的公共服务功能，辐射和带动市域和全区的发展。

(3) 区域统筹

拉萨的城镇化道路必须坚持区域统筹的发展战略，在城乡统筹发展的基础上，协调周边地区发展，真正体现拉萨城镇化进程在全区城镇化发展中的核心地位和示范作用，带动全区的发展。

(4) 特色取胜

自然地理环境是拉萨人口和城镇空间分布格局形成的基底，这种独特性决定了拉萨的城镇化道路不能复制其他地区，必须因地制宜、尊重客观实际，特色取胜。拉萨必须走一条由健康经济社会发展、独特资源禀赋、特色产业支撑、合理城镇空间布局相结合的具有拉萨特色的城镇化道路。

### 3. 基于城乡统筹的空间发展格局

按照城镇化发展战略，在拉萨市域形成“一心、两线、多点”的城镇空间格局。一心：拉萨中心城市。两线：青藏线（包括青藏公路和铁路）和川藏线，是拉萨市域城镇分布相对较为密集的地区。多点：指在市域范围内优先选择县城和特色乡镇，形成产业特色明显、人口较为集聚、服务功能完善的辐射周边的城镇职能中心。同时，根据“生态优先、依托城镇、因地制宜、保障安全、体现特色、合理配套”的原则，对农牧业发展和农牧民安居点规划布局进行统筹安排。

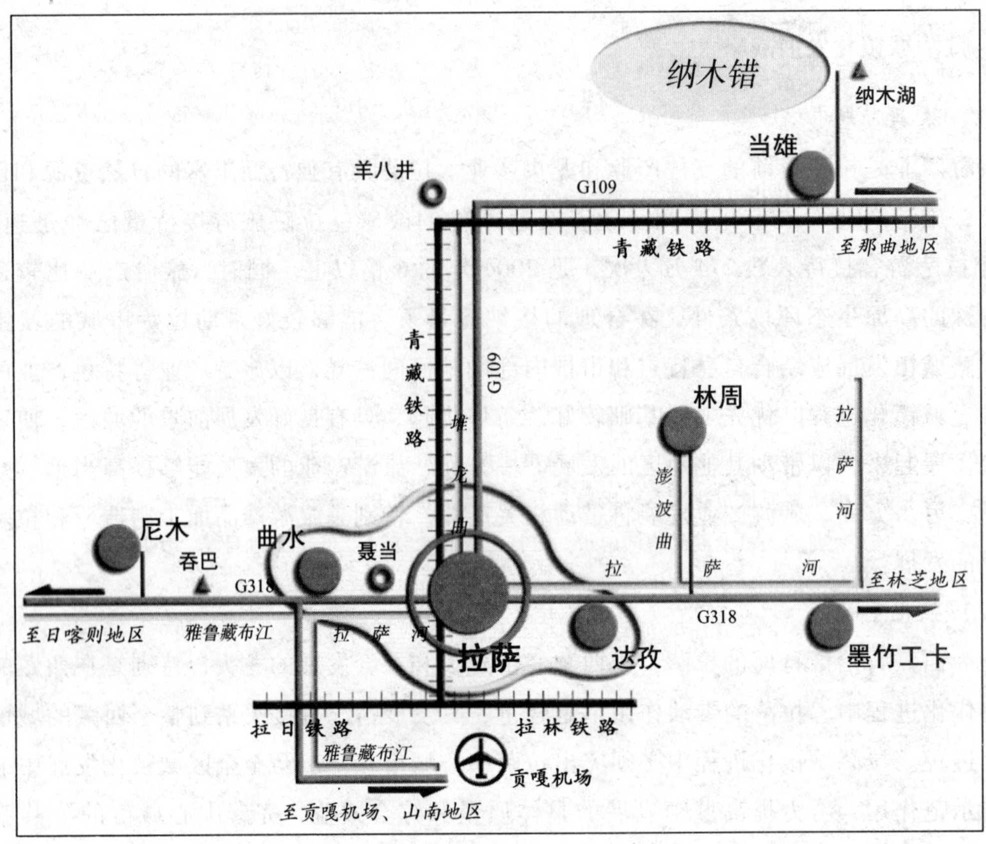


图6 拉萨市域城镇空间发展格局

## 六、小结

当前，城镇化发展道路已经与城市经济社会发展转型密切联系起来，在科学发展的背景下，高度重视生态环境与社会人文发展问题。特色城镇化的内容、方法、体系、保障等多个方面都需要做多样性的探讨和总结，这将为丰富和完善具有“中国特色”的城镇化内容体系，为西部地区城市发展提供一些借鉴。

（作者：袁锦富，江苏省城市规划设计研究院总规划师，教授级高级规划师；胡海波，江苏省城市规划设计研究院副总规划师，教授级高级规划师；丁志刚，江苏省城市规划设计研究院工程师）

**参考文献**

[1] 侯捷．走出一条具有中国特色的城市化道路［J］．城市发展研究，1996（6）：13

[2] 赵宝江．积极探索具有中国特色的城市化道路［J］．城市发展研究，2000（5）：19

[3] 姚士谋．中国特色的城市化问题［J］．长江流域资源与环境，2001（9），10（5）：401

[4] 仇保兴．中国特色城镇化道路“特”在何处［N］．南京日报，2002－12－09
[5] 汪光焘．关于中国特色的城镇化道路问题［J］．城市规划，2003（4），24（4）：11
[6] 朱铁臻．城市现代化问题研究［EB/OL］．http://www.121nong1.com/2003news/shownews1asp?newsid=117
[7] 朱铁臻．城市现代化发展的几个理论问题［N］．中国经济时报，2002－12－21
[8] 周干峙．走具有自己特色的城市化道路［J］．城市发展研究，2006（4）：13
[9] 肖金成，等．中国特色城镇化道路的内涵和发展途径［J］．宏观经济管理，2008（11）：19
[10] 仇保兴．中国特色的城镇化模式之辨——“C模式”：超越“A模式”的诱惑和“B模式”的泥淖［J］．城市发展研究，2009（1）：16
[11] 简新华．论中国特色的城镇化道路［N］．光明日报，2003－08－05
[12] 王小彬．西藏城镇发展研究［J］．小城镇建设，2002（6）：67
[13] 马玉英．青藏高原城市化的制约因素与发展趋势分析［J］．青海师范大学学报，2006（4），117：22
[14] 樊杰，等．西藏人口发展的空间解析与可持续城镇化探讨［J］．地理科学，2005（8），25（4）：389
[15] 朱铃．西藏经济市场化进程中的劳动力流动［J］．中国人口科学，2004（1）：50－56
[16] 李培祥，李诚固．论城乡互动：解决“三农”问题的机制与对策［J］．地理科学，2003，23（4）：408－413

# 长株潭城市群“两型社会”规划与建设

2007年12月14日，长株潭城市群获批全国资源节约型和环境友好型社会建设综合配套改革试验区，揭开了以“两型社会”建设为主题的发展改革序幕。为落实国家战略，湖南省为“两型社会”建设制定行动路线图，现已基本形成全方位、多层次的规划体系，规划的统领作用不断增强，试验区建设已取得实质性进展。

本文从四个方面对长株潭城市群“两型社会”建设试验区进行介绍。第一部分，介绍试验区基本情况；第二部分，介绍试验区规划体系的形成、地位与意义；第三部分，介绍试验区建设阶段性进展；第四部分，介绍试验区未来前景。

## 一、长株潭城市群“两型社会”试验区基本情况

长株潭城市群是以长沙、株洲、湘潭三市为核心，辐射周边岳阳、常德、益阳、衡阳、娄底五市的区域（又称长株潭“3+5”城市群），总面积9.68万平方公里，占全省45.8%；城市群人口4125.5万人，占全省59.8%。其中，长株潭三市沿湘江呈“品”字形分布，两两之间半小时车程，总面积2.8万平方公里，人口1325.7万人。

2008年12月，国务院批准《长株潭城市群资源节约型和环境友好型社会建设综合配套改革试验总体方案》，明确要求湖南“加大力度推进重点领域和关键环节的改革试验，推进经济结构调整和发展方式转变，在长株潭城市群形成有利于能源资源节约和生态环境保护的体制机制，不断增强区域综合实力和可持续发展能力，使长株潭城市群在促进中部地区崛起和区域协调发展中发挥更大的作用，为全国深化体制改革、推动科学发展和促进社会和谐提供经验和示范”。根据国务院批复，长株潭“两型社会”改革试验区的总体要求是“三个率先”，即：率先形成有利于资源节约和环境友好的新机制；率先积累传统工业化成功转型的新经验；率先形成城市群发展的新模式。具体目标是“四个定位”，即成为全国“两型社会”建设的示范区，中部崛起的重要增长极，全省新型工业化、新型城市化和新农村建设的引领区，具有国际品质的现代化生态型城市群。改革试验分“三个阶段”进行，2008—2010年为第一阶段，打好基础，重点突破；2011—2015年为第二阶段，纵深推进，初见成效；2016—2020年为第三阶段，基本完成“两型社会”建设综合配套改革任务，取得较好的“两型”示范效果。

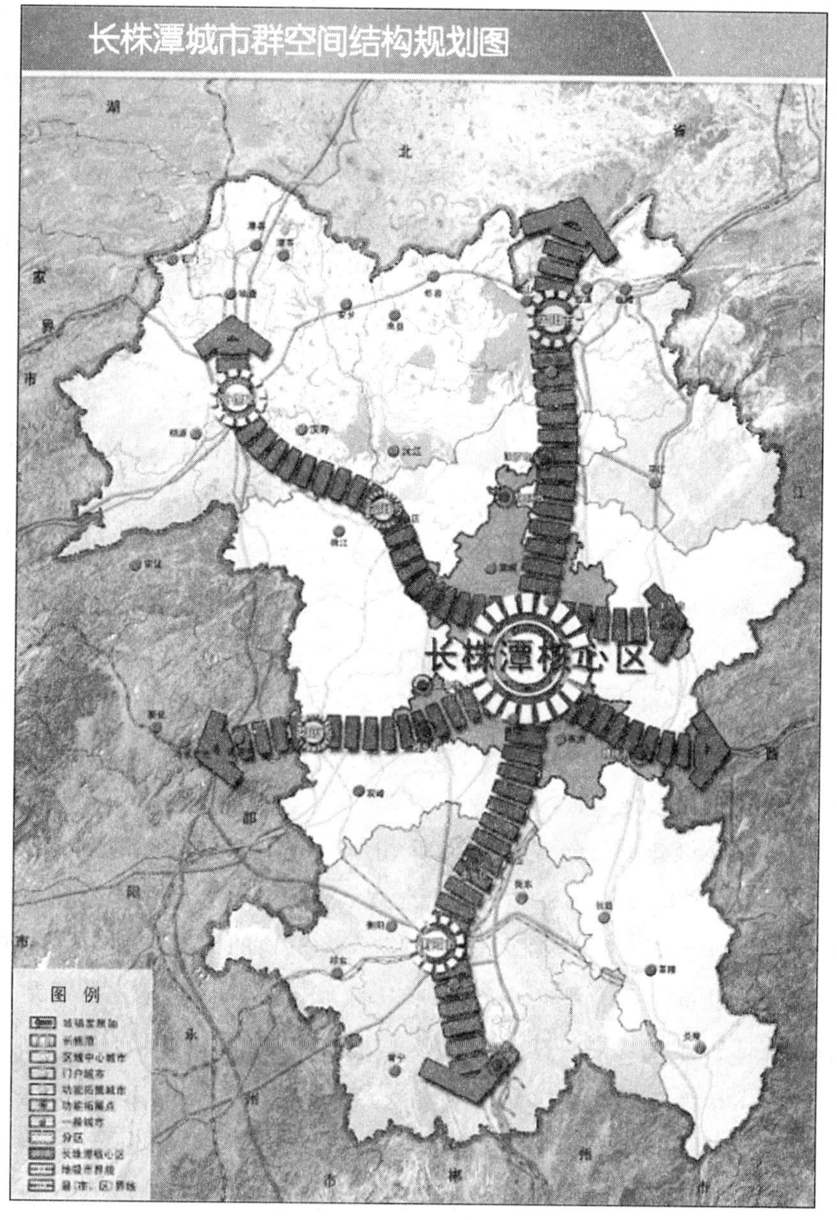


图 1　长株潭城市群空间结构规划图

自试验区获批以来，长株潭城市群试验区初步步入科学发展、率先发展的快车道。(1) 核心增长极作用显现。2009 年，长株潭城市群实现 GDP 10347.5 亿元，占全省 80%，是 2007 年的 1.5 倍；长株潭三市实现 GDP 5506.7 亿元，占全省 42.6%，提前实现“十一五”发展规划目标。(2) 经济结构进一步优化。2009 年，长株潭城市群三次产业比为12.5:48.7:38.8，呈现出“二三一”的结构，与 2007 年相比，第一产业所占比重降低 3.4%。城市群工业化率、城镇化率和高新技术产业增加值占 GDP 比重在 2007 年的基础上，分别提高 3.4%、2.4% 和 3.9%。(3) 资源环境承载能力切实增强。与 2007 年相比，2009 年，“3+5”八市城镇生活垃圾无害化处理率和城镇生活污水集中处理率分别提高 12.5%、17.6%，万元 GDP 用水量减少 62.4 吨，湘江流域重点断面功能区水质达标率提高 2.5%，人均城市公共绿地面积提高0.7平方米，二氧化硫提前一年完成“十一五”削减目标任务，试验区带动全省单位GDP能耗下降5.1%。(4) 社会民生明显改善。2009年，城市群地方一般预算收入、城镇居民人均可支配收入和农民人均纯收入分别是2007年的1.4倍、1.24倍和1.28倍；(5) 城乡社会保障更加健全，就业更加充分。2009年，城市群城镇登记失业率控制在4.2%以内，比2007年降低0.4%。

## 二、规划统领试验区发展

### 1. 规划体系逐步形成

湖南省长株潭“两型社会”建设规划体系的形成，经历了以下两个阶段。

第一阶段：“两型社会”顶层设计阶段（2007—2008年）

湖南省广泛借鉴国内外先进地区经验，对长株潭试验区科学论证、高端定位，编制了《长株潭城市群资源节约和环境友好型社会建设综合配套改革试验总体方案》，提升了《长株潭城市群区域规划（2008—2020年）》，于2008年12月获得国务院批准。在此基础上，启动编制专项改革方案和专项规划编制和提升工作。

第二阶段：规划体系形成阶段（2008—2010年）

完成了城市群核心区建设管治规划等18个由省直有关部门负责的专项规划的编制、评审及报批工作。其中，“3+5”城市群综合交通规划、信息同享规划经省政府批准实施。湖南省政府确立的五大示范区、18个片区全面完成片区规划的编制与评审，上报省人民政府审批。在区域规划的指导下，自2009年起，长株潭城市群各市、县开始编制下位规划，至今已完成长沙市生态控制性规划、株洲轨道城规划、湘潭市现代物流产业规划、益阳市环境卫生保护专项规划、娄底市两型产业发展规划等80多个市域规划、上百个工程规划，规划体系建设进一步加强。同时，启动长株潭城市群八市城市总体规划的同步修编，预计3年内完成。

### 2. 规划管理机制不断完善

为切实增强规划的统领作用，湖南省加强了规划的法制保障力度，把顶层设计纳入法制体系。根据“两型社会”建设的新形势、新要求，2009年9月27日，湖南省十一届人大常委会第10次会议通过了《长株潭城市群区域规划条例》，对区域规划的法律地位、区域规划实施的事权划分、区域规划的编制和调整、具有区域性影响的建设项目的管理、城市群空间管治等进行系统规定；进一步从法律上确定了长株潭城市群区域规划的权威性和强制性，为长株潭“两型社会”建设提供了法制保障。同时，省政府拟出台《长株潭城市群区域规划条例实施细则》，通过程序性规定，使规划实施进入各部门、各市的工作程序。不断加强对城市群区域规划实施的监督，建立长株潭城市群核心区动态监控系统，规划的统领、指导功能不断强化。

### 3. 评价指标标准体系逐步形成

在构建规划体系过程中，湖南省对制定"两型社会"建设指标体系进行了积极探索。区域规划的指标体系，共有70个分阶段实现的指标，分为三大类：一是环境友好型指标；二是资源节约型指标；三是社会经济和人文建设指标。各专项规划、市域规划又均依据区域规划的指标体系和各自的特点建立了自己的指标体系。2010年7月，出台长株潭"两型社会"建设试行标准，涉及"两型"产业、企业、园区、县、镇、农村六大类。

### 4. 规划引领试验区空间布局

在规划的引领下，试验区生态优先、优势互补、整体推进、率先突破的新格局正在形成。

科学划分功能区，优先保护生态。《长株潭城市群区域规划》将试验区分为禁止开发区、限制开发区、优化开发区和重点开发区四类功能区，《长株潭城市群区域规划条例》进一步对四类功能区进行了界定。针对位于长株潭三市结合部的"绿心"，编制了《长株潭城市群生态绿心地区总体规划（2008—2020年）》，明确遵循"生态保护优先"原则，将规划面积522.87平方公里的生态绿心地区划分为禁止开发区（面积262.21平方公里）、严格限制开发区（面积155.24平方公里）、一般限制开发区（面积47.3平方公里）和建设协调区（面积58.06平方公里），对不同分区实施不同的空间管制。

整体优化提升，实现错位发展。对长株潭城市群的空间格局和目标定位进行统筹规划，统一规划跨区域的资源开发、产业布局、设施配套、市场体系等重大问题。力图打破行政体制障碍，创新合作机制。大力推进城际铁路、机场、长株潭组合港和岳阳港等现代交通网络建设，推动人口、产业、技术、资本和市场的聚集与融合，放大同城效应。重视建立优化产业布局的协调促进机制，建立分类引导的产业发展导向机制，加快长沙、株洲、湘潭、衡阳等老工业基地振兴。推动城市群各市发挥各自优势，对产业进行有差异的、功能互补的布局，实现错位发展。

大胆设立示范区，力争率先突破。为集中力量，先行先试，长株潭试验区选择大河西、云龙、昭山、天易、滨湖五大示范区的"五区十八片"先行启动"两型社会"建设改革探索，提供示范，成为推动城市群"两型社会"建设的强大引擎。

## 三、长株潭"两型社会"建设取得实质性进展

### 1. 生态环境治理

生态方面，摒弃"摊大饼"式的城市发展模式，建设"山中有城、城中有山、山水相宜"的生态城市群。突出湘江生态经济带建设，建设集生态、文化、防洪、景观、交通、旅游于一体的绿色长廊，强化湘江两岸以及洋湖垸等六大湿地保护，推进法华山、金霞山、

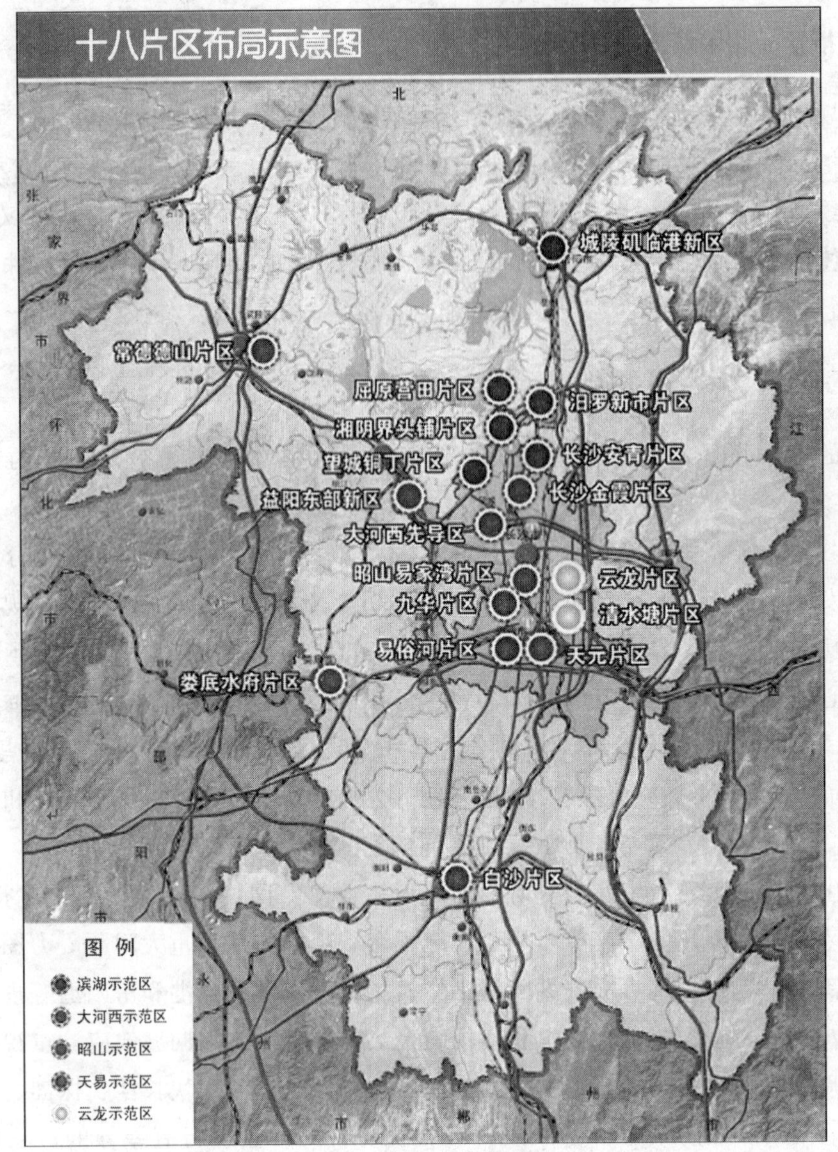


图2　十八片区布局示意图

昭山等20多个森林公园建设，突出城市群“绿心”保护与合理利用，构筑生态隔离、绿色屏障。连接长株潭的沿江防洪景观道路建设进展顺利。环境方面，积极推进治污减排基础设施建设，实施重污染区、湘江和洞庭湖综合治理工程，加强城乡环境整治。加强治污设施建设。实施全省城镇污水和垃圾处理设施建设三年行动计划。2008—2010年，全省共新建城镇污水处理厂119座，新增污水处理能力420万吨，实现设市城市和县城污水集中处理设施全覆盖。株洲冶炼厂铅烟气治理、株洲霞湾污水处理厂建设、潭钢高炉废水治理、湘潭电化废水治理、长沙垃圾卫生填埋厂等一批环保项目相继建成。重污染区实现重点整治，长沙坪塘老工业基地两年内共有20家污染企业全面退出，26家非煤矿山全面关闭，35家工业企业清洁能源改烧工程全面完成，核心区落后产能淘汰率达到100%。湘潭竹埠港启动实施了现有重污染企业逐步退出计划，化工企业已由5年前的37家减少到了26家。株洲清水塘2010

年减排 COD 133 吨、$SO_2$ 10714 吨，空气质量良好率达 98.7%，创历史同期最好水平。实施湘江水污染整治三年行动计划和重金属污染专项治理，推进工业源头治理、农业面源治理等工程。实施洞庭湖污染治理。2006 年以来，关停环洞庭湖 236 家造纸厂中的 234 家，洞庭湖水质由局部Ⅴ类整体转为Ⅲ类。

**2. 基础设施建设**

打造以轨道交通为核心、水运、公路等各种运输方式协调发展的“两型”综合交通运输体系。截至 2010 年年底，全省在建和通车高速公路近 6447 公里，省会长沙与 13 个市州全部高速连接、4 小时可达，全省等级公路达 148180 公里，占公路总里程的 77%。2010 年年底，全省铁路营运里程 3693 公里，其中电气化里程 2123 公里，占 57.5%。目前有沪昆高铁、石长铁路复线、衡茶吉铁路等 6 个项目在建，建设里程 1362 公里。到 2015 年，全省铁路运营里程将达到 5000 公里。长沙黄花机场旅客吞吐量 2010 年达到 1400 万人次，居中部第一。打造以洞庭湖为中心、四水干线为主通道、沟通全省大部分城市、通江达海的航道网。2009 年，湖南省内河航道里程 11968 公里，居全国第三。建设高铁、地铁、快速公交和长途客运、城市公交零换乘的综合交通枢纽，方便居民出行。能源保障体系建设力度加大，电网建设加强，新能源和清洁能源大力发展。积极开展节水型社会建设试点，水库、灌区、堤防建设大力推进，水利基础设施不断完善。信息化建设加速。2009 年 6 月，长株潭三市通信实现并网升位，成为全国首个通信一体化的城市群。2010 年，长株潭成为全国首批三网融合试点中唯一的城市群。目前，3G 网络已覆盖长株潭全部县城以上区域，90% 以上的农村实现宽带通。积极发展新一代网络技术，加快数据中心、呼叫中心等基地建设。开工建设超算中心。

**3. 产业发展**

获批全国综合性国家高技术产业基地。先进装备制造、新能源、新材料、生物医药、节能环保、文化创意等产业快速发展。2009 年，高科技产业增加值占 GDP 的比重达 13.5%。工程机械行业国内市场占有率近 30%，新材料销售收入居全国第三。改造提升制造业，推动钢铁、有色、化工等资源型产业向精、深加工发展。做大做强工程机械、轨道交通、汽车及零部件等优势装备产业。加快纺织、食品、卷烟、烟花、陶瓷等传统特色产业提质升级。对落后产能和污染企业分批次实行关、停、并、转和产业整体退出，2009 年，试验区六大高耗能行业增加值占地区工业增加值下降 4.4%。发展战略性新兴产业，突出先进装备制造、新材料、文化创意等三大支柱产业和新能源、信息和节能环保等四大先导产业，打造新能源示范、电动汽车产业、航空航天产业等战略性新兴产业基地。湖南列入国家战略性新兴产业创投计划首批试点省份，信息、生物医药、新能源等三只战略性新兴产业创投基金落户长株潭试验区。加强自主创新，2009 年全省专利授权量 8309 件，居中西部第一；取得国家科技成果 30 项，居全国第三；承担国家“863”计划项目 191 项，高新技术产业发展项目 48 项；取得省部级以上科技成果 982 项；完成省级及以上新产品开发目录 2841 项。组建了电动汽车、风力发电装备等四大产业技术创新战略联盟，为促进产学研的结合提供了重要平台。在2009年全省科学技术获奖项目中，产学研结合的成果占近29%。

## 四、前景：长株潭“两型社会”建设加速推进

进入“十二五”时期，国家已将“两型社会”建设作为转变发展方式的重要着力点，湖南省将“四化两型”作为重大战略，长株潭试验区“两型”社会建设也转入第二阶段。在已有基础上，长株潭试验区将全力推进“八大工程”建设，加快推动“十个一体化”。

### 1. 八大工程

“两型”产业振兴工程，淘汰提升落后产业，大力发展新兴战略产业，以信息化带动工业化，构建特色突出、结构优化的“两型”产业体系；基础设施建设工程，加快打造以轨道交通为核心的综合交通体系，形成“布局合理、功能完备、特色鲜明、承载力强”的城市基础设施体系，加速城市群对接融合；节能减排全覆盖工程，建立健全考核评价体系、行业标准体系、用能标准和设计规范体系，实行节能减排在线管理，与国际国内碳交易市场对接，率先在全国形成系统管理的体制机制；湘江流域综合治理工程，以重金属治理为重点，削减源头工业污染排放总量，提高城镇污水垃圾处理率，强化科技攻关，健全保护机制，加强两岸生态和涉江基础设施建设；示范区建设推进工程，以“两型”规划为龙头，积极推进体制机制创新、基础设施建设、产业发展、招商引资，努力打造改革创新、加快转变发展方式的示范区、引领区，成为试验区崛起的核心增长极；城乡统筹示范工程，统筹城乡建设用地、就业、养老、医疗、最低生活保障和社会救助体系，打造一批“两型”村镇，加速推进新型城镇化；长株潭公交一体化工程，突出以长株潭三市城际公交一体化运营、公共交通资源共享、城乡公交一体化、同城公用事业缴费一卡通及干道站场建设为重点，实现三市公交出行同城同享；三网合一工程，突出电信、广电、互联网之间的互联互通、资源共享，加快网络基础建设，促进新型通信信息、广播电视、文化生活服务的开发应用，带动试验区战略新兴产业发展。

### 2. 十个一体化

示范区管理一体化，加大领导协调力度，在规划、项目建设、土地、投融资、产业布局、招商引资、体制改革等重点领域，统筹安排；重大基础设施建设一体化，统一规划，促进长株潭三市基础设施延伸对接，在联合中共建、在联网中共享、在联营中共管，发挥整体效应；通信信息建设一体化，加快三网融合进程，促进信息共享；公用事业建设一体化，对公交、自来水、环卫、教育、医疗和文化等设施科学布点，统筹建设，全面覆盖，综合利用；湘江综合治理一体化，突出重点，综合治理，一江同治；金融服务一体化，加快金融系统的电子化、网络化，实现统一互联、同城共享，实现存贷一体化和征信体系建设统一化；能源管理一体化，统一调度，科学安排，一体运转；价格工商管理一体化，统一工商管理政

策，建立三市价格协调机制，统一准入门槛，统一执法；户籍社保一体化，打破区域、城乡限制，统一户籍和社会保障标准，逐步提高“五险”统筹层次；环保执法一体化，统一监测体系，整合执法力量，统一标准，加强执法联动。

湖南将充分利用长株潭“两型社会”试验区先行先试的优势，加快推进长株潭“两型社会”试验区建设，切实走出一条有别于传统模式的工业化、城市化发展新路，为全国“两型社会”建设积累新经验。

（作者：徐湘平，湖南省长株潭两型办主任，湖南省发展和改革委员会副主任；夏安桃，湖南师范大学资源与环境科学学院副教授，博士）

# 中国首个新能源示范城区

## ——吐鲁番市新区规划建设

近年来，随着全球气温的不断上升，气候与能源问题成了人们日益关注的问题。哥本哈根气候会议之后，低碳生产生活模式已成为世界各国追求的方向。面对气候变化的严峻挑战，国家要建设资源节约型和环境友好型社会，力争到2020年我国单位国内生产总值二氧化碳排放比2005年下降40%～45%。在新能源的综合利用中，中国开始在太阳能和风能富集的西部干旱地区探索可再生能源综合利用的发展之路。

在此背景下，吐鲁番市开展了新区的规划建设，结合吐鲁番独特的地理气候环境与人文特点，采用科学适宜的建造技术，建设特色鲜明的、适合人居、充满活力的和谐生态城区与城乡一体化建设示范区，对新能源综合利用方式以及荒漠化地区和谐城市发展模式进行了有益探索。

### 一、规划背景

2008年10月，原住房和城乡建设部部长汪光焘来吐鲁番地区考察，与新疆维吾尔自治区王乐泉书记、努尔·白克力主席谈了吐鲁番市新区的建设工作。之后，在自治区各级领导的支持下，以建设一个适合西部气候条件的可持续城市新区的思路开始了吐鲁番市新区的规划工作。

随后，由国际欧亚科学院中国中心城市科学学部、广州市城市规划勘测设计研究院、北京市建筑设计研究院、新疆建筑设计研究院、北京市城市规划设计研究院共同组成的吐鲁番市新区规划联合工作组，开展了吐鲁番新区可持续发展的研究、规划工作。

吐鲁番市新区规划采用“专题研究——概念规划——总体规划——控制性详细规划”的工作思路。在《吐鲁番市总体规划（2004—2020年）》的基础上，联合工作组从2008年10月底着手新区的概念性规划工作。工作组在经过实地考察、收集资料、部门访谈的基础上确定了“新区产业发展研究”、“新区绿色交通系统发展研究”、“基于生态的城市空间发展策略研究”、“地域性生态建筑研究”4个专题研究，在此基础上完成了《吐鲁番市新区概念规划》，提出规划的原则和理念，并完成规划初步方案。

《吐鲁番市新区概念规划》进一步明确新区规模与定位，并在城乡一体化协调发展、综合交通、绿地系统与水系、城市景观与建筑风貌、地下空间综合利用、资源节约、综合防灾、数字化城市建设等方面，提出目标、原则及相应策略。根据当地建设实际情况，新区规划将 8.81 平方公里的新区分为三期建设：一期（起步区）2.86 平方公里，二期 3.86 平方公里，三期 2.09 平方公里。起步区的控制性详细规划进一步划分地块，明确地块基本情况及各种强制性和引导性控制要求。在控制性详细规划的基础上对起步区的城市风貌、建筑高度、色彩、重要建筑、建筑细部与材料指引等方面进行城市设计。

目前，吐鲁番市新区一期起步区已经完成了进一步的修建性详细规划，开发建设范围为 1.43 平方公里。规划总建筑面积 75.39 万平方米，容积率 0.97，绿地率 36%，规划总户数 7016 户，居住人口 24556 人。规划以低碳发展为导向，以太阳能综合利用为核心，建设一个特色鲜明、适合人居、充满活力的和谐生态城区和城乡一体化建设示范区。

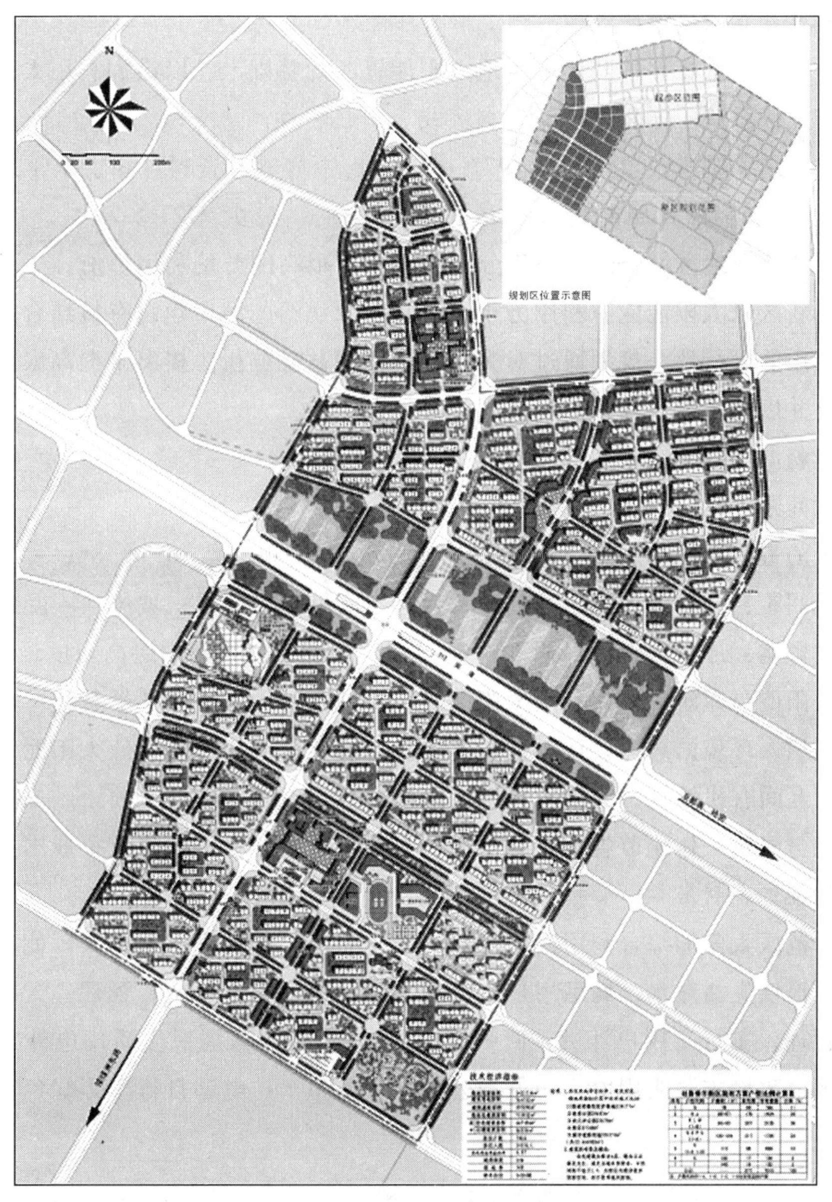


图 1　吐鲁番市新区起步区一期修建性详细规划总平面图

## 二、规划理念与策略

生态与低碳是贯穿吐鲁番新区规划建设的重要理念。吐鲁番市新区规划根据我国西北荒漠化地区城市发展的生态特征和当地的生态本地特征，提出了新区规划应采用的生态理念和策略。其中新能源利用、推行“公交+慢行”的绿色交通、打造地域特色的建筑空间环境等规划策略，在新区建设实践中集中体现了新区生态与低碳的规划理念，实现了将吐鲁番市着力打造为富有地方特色的和谐新城的目标。

### 1. 新能源利用

(1) 太阳能建筑一体化设计

这是吐鲁番市新区在评估吐鲁番当地太阳能资源的基础上，以最大利用太阳能资源为目标，对建筑与光伏系统一体化设计的一次实践。

根据吐鲁番国家基本气象观测站1971—2000年30年观测资料可知，全年总日照时数平均为2912.3小时，年总日照时数最多达3126.3小时，最少2721.8小时，年日照百分率69%。可见，吐鲁番地区太阳能资源十分丰富，具有很高的开发利用价值。

吐鲁番市新区以太阳能能源利用为重点，将能源供给与城市建设有机结合起来，改善了城市新能源应用的可行性。规划通过对太阳能利用的基础分析，提出了提高太阳能利用效能的最佳条件，并以此指导设计：

建筑最佳朝向：南偏东3°；

建筑日照间距：L≥1.7H；

太阳能板的最佳朝向：正南到南偏东10°，最佳壁面倾角是30°到38°；

太阳能板间距：两排阵列间距达到1.8米基本能够满足要求，坡屋面不受此限；

规划条件影响：居住区合理容积率0.8~1.0。相同容积率，低层高密度最佳。

示范区太阳能与建筑一体化利用太阳能光伏电池板和太阳能集热器替代屋顶覆盖层，把太阳能的利用纳入环境的总体设计，把建筑、技术和美学融为一体，使太阳能设施成为建筑的一部分，相互间有机结合，取代了传统太阳能的结构所造成的对建筑的外观形象的影响，同时，太阳能与建筑一体化节省了土地资源，也避免了重复投资，降低了成本。

(2) 太阳能综合利用

吐鲁番示范区太阳能综合利用采用光热与光电相结合的原则。利用太阳能光热产生的热水为小区居民提供生活热水，满足用户自身需求的原则，不进行统一管理。太阳能光伏发电将进行统一管理，实行“用户计量、回归使用”。除满足小区居民生活用电外，余量生活用电将用地新区市政设施照明用电，为电动公交车、出租车、电动自行车等绿色交通工具提供充电。

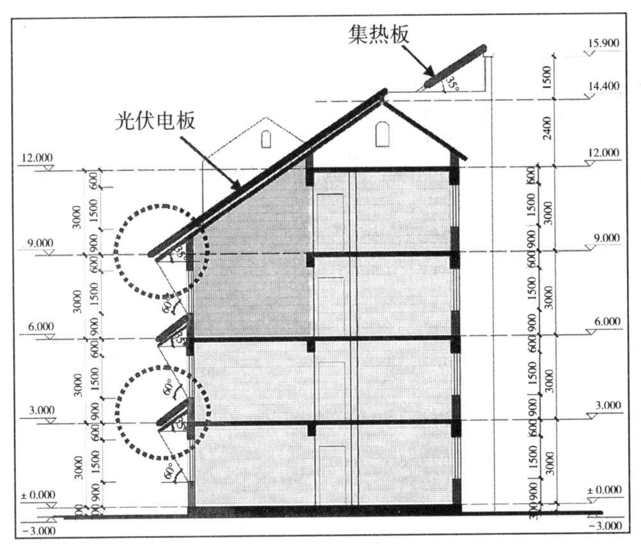

图2　太阳能板与建筑结合模式示意图

吐鲁番示范区的太阳能运用了智能微电网技术。由于太阳能光伏发电属于能量密度低、调节能力不高的能源，因其特殊的不稳定性，并网发电后可能会对电网安全稳定运行以及电网供电质量造成一定影响。智能微电网的采用可以有效控制太阳能光伏发电，实现太阳能发电和用电的相对平衡，解决太阳能光伏发电与地方电网并网的难题，使得太阳能成为示范区安全、持续的主导能源。

此外，吐鲁番示范区把公交、出租、电动车储能与智能微电网、低压侧并网三技合一，实现对太阳能光伏发电电能的充分利用，尽可能把太阳能转化出的电能直接应用到新区居民生产、生活中，达到节能、绿色、生态、环保的目标。

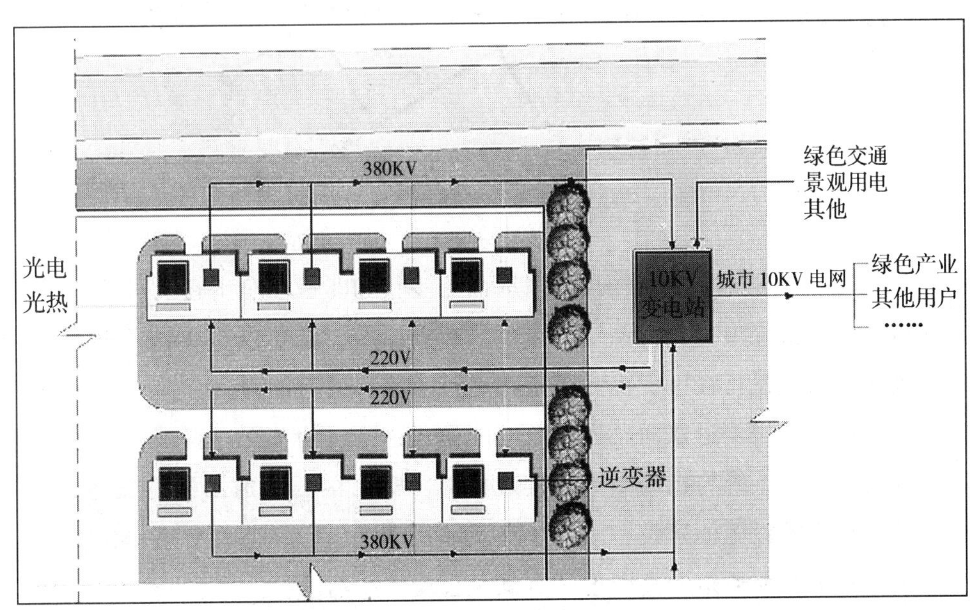


图3　太阳能用能管理模式示意图

### 2. “公交+慢行”的绿色交通

(1) 干道双行，支路单行的道路网系统

吐鲁番市新区规划改变传统以机动化方式为主导的四级道路等级体系，采用面向慢行、公交、全部车辆使用的三类使用功能的道路分级体系，将道路分为干道、支路、慢行廊道三个等级。干路是机动车主要道路，主要承担过境和出入境交通功能，是新区与老城区、新站区以及外省市联系的主要通道，红线规划30米。支路是公交廊道和社区内部主要道路，沟通干路，承担区内组团间的机动化联系功能。支路分为两级：一级支路规划红线20米，采用三车道设计，中间车道作为一般机动车单行车道，两侧为公交车道；二级支路规划红线12米，主要组织单向交通和慢行交通。慢行廊道是慢行交通专用道路，采用葡萄绿廊的建设模式，同时可作为应急情况下的绿色通道，规划红线为12米。

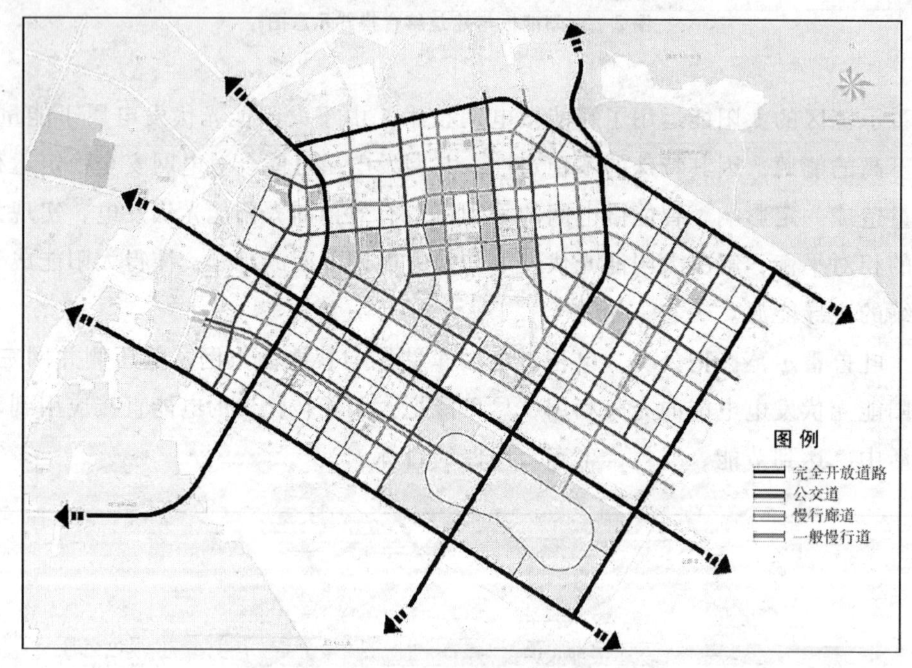


图4 吐鲁番市新区道路网系统规划图

从新区绿色交通发展要求出发，规划采取面向步行和非机动车出行及可达尺度的道路网格设计，并以步行+公交出行作为系统可靠性的衡量标准，建立以150m×150m为基准路网间隔的高密度、小尺度慢行社区，提高了道路通行效率和通行能力。

交通组织方面，采用干道双向，支路单向的模式进行机动车交通组织，以提高道路通行效率和通行能力；慢行系统与机动车系统实现相对分离，区内交通以慢行交通为主导方式，通过优先保障慢行系统设施的建设，提倡步行及非机动车出行；公共交通作为慢行交通的补充和延伸，通过环形公交通道和高密度站点满足公交出行需求。

(2) 基于太阳能利用的公交系统设计

新区公交系统建设强调公交系统的便捷、直达以及与慢行系统、停车系统的良好衔接，

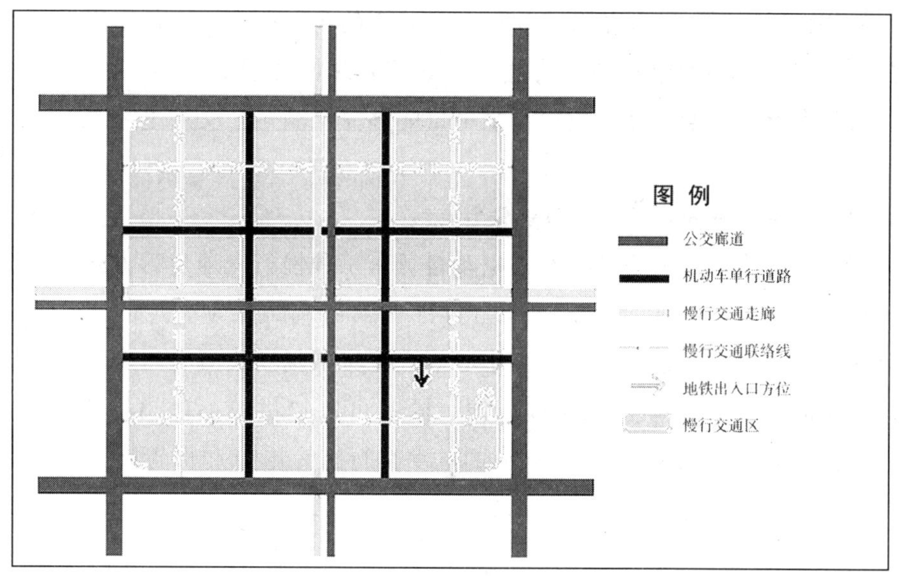


图 5 新区绿色交通组织模式图

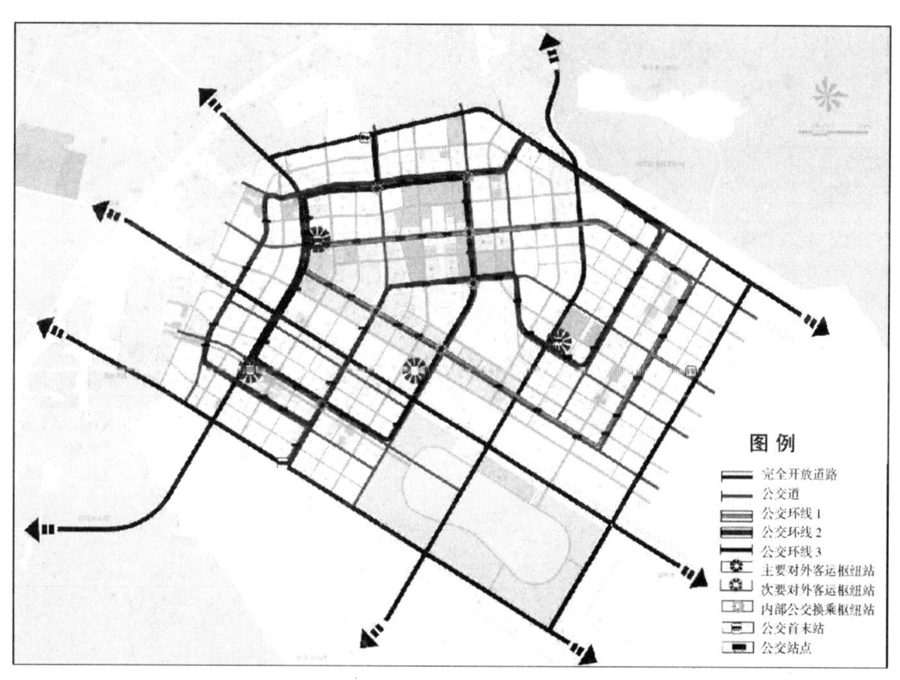


图 6 吐鲁番市新区公交系统规划图

作为慢行系统的有力补充。

根据新区公共交通的功能定位，规划新区公交系统主要分为跨区公交和区内公交两类：跨区公交为联系新区与老城区和新站区，线路设计保证较高直达性，控制运行时间，与新区内部公交线路换乘衔接。区内公交以环线为主串联各发展组团，站点固定。

新区公交系统改变传统的在机动车道路交叉口设置服务及活动中心的思路，深入到社区中心，并在中心商业区、社区中心等城市客流集中处设置公交首末站或换乘枢纽，采用高密度、小站距的公交组织方式，尽量减少居民乘坐公交的步行距离，方便居民出行。

新区公交车型以中小型电动车辆为主。公交首末站同时设置充电站，方便公交车辆使用。同时，新区内近、远期的光伏发电富余电量能够完全满足公交用电需求，实现真正的绿色交通。

(3) 与机动车系统相分离的慢行系统设计

新区内主要考虑步行、人力自行车、电动自行车三种慢行交通出行方式。步行为新区居民短距离出行和换乘公交的主要方式。人力自行车以私人拥有为主，同时结合机动车停放点、主要公交站点、交通枢纽和公共服务中心等人流集散场所设置自行车租赁系统。电动自行车能充分利用吐鲁番地区丰富太阳能资源，同时可以提供较高的出行服务质量（灵活、省力、时效有保证）。沿慢行廊道建设相应的电动自行车充电点和保管站，为电动自行车的推广使用提供设施方面的保障。

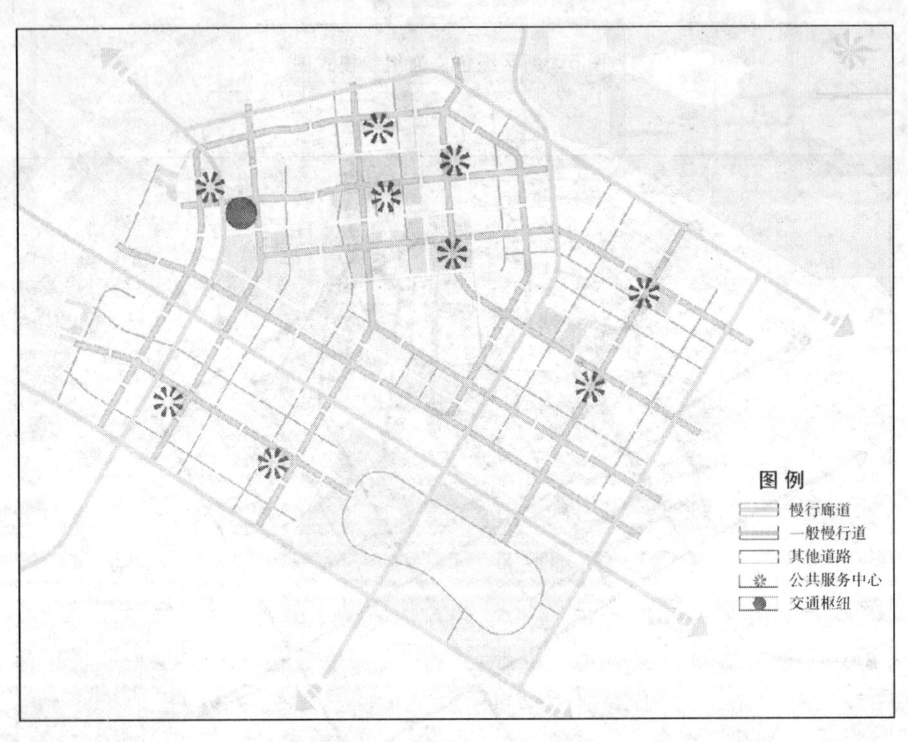


图7 吐鲁番市新区慢行系统规划图

交通线路的设计充分利用具有地方特色的葡萄绿廊、沟渠（坎儿井）建设庭院式的慢行街道，设置空间上独立的城市慢行廊道和社区二级慢行系统。慢行廊道将各公服中心、主要景观节点和主要居住带串联起来，次级慢行系统深入到社区。慢行系统空间内，禁止除应急救灾情况下的一切机动车使用，为步行交通和自行车交通创造良好的出行环境，引导慢行交通出行方式成为居民内部出行的首选。

### 3. 地域特色的建筑空间环境

(1) 延续传统的空间结构

街巷是吐鲁番聚居区中极为重要的空间。通过对选取街区的分析可见，虽然空间肌理不尽相同，但仍能看出同一的居住模式——以院落组合为单元、以步行廊串连院落、以平行街巷为骨架构建基本的居住空间模式。在对传统地区街巷结构的抽离、变异变化后，这样一种空间组织方式在新区的居住空间中仍具有较强的适应性。

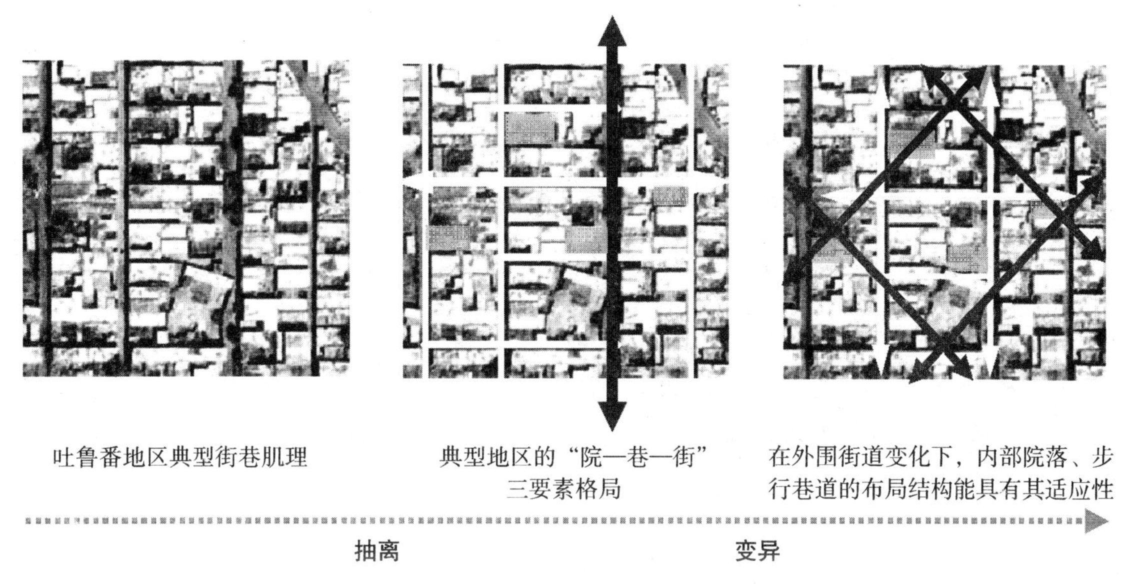


图 8　空间模式分析图

因此，吐鲁番市新区规划对传统的“院落—街巷”空间模式进行了演进，使其更能满足现代生活的功能需求。由于吐鲁番地区日照间距大，除去每户的院落用地，南北住宅之间的空间亦可作为小型的公共环境，提供了一个公共活动的场所。通过住宅围院式的建筑布局，形成一个小院围大院的组团单元。步行走廊代替了传统巷道的功能，串联起各个组团和街区内的绿化及公共空间。而内街则建立起街区与街区的联系，并满足了住区车行及停车的功能。住宅院落、组团围院、步行走廊和内街形成了“封闭—半封闭—开敞”的空间序列，正是对传统的“院落—街巷”空间模式的一种发展和演绎。

将这样一种单元模式运用到每个街区，通过步行走廊加强街区之间的联系，并在居住区设置社区公园等公共空间，由此形成了一个整体的“院落—街巷”的空间结构。

(2) 借鉴民居的建筑风格

地理和气候也使得吐鲁番民居表现出独特的建筑特征。注重环境、因地制宜的吐鲁番传统民居给设计者提供了十分丰富的建筑创作素材。本次规划在居住建筑的设计上沿用了现代户型，也同样借鉴运用了吐鲁番传统民居的众多因素。

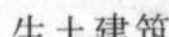

生土建筑

小而密的采光通风口

拱券柱廊

图9　吐鲁番地区传统民居的建筑特征示意图

图10　规划住宅的典型立面形式

在建筑功能上，注重延续地域建筑对环境的适应性。设计吸取提炼了传统建筑中庭院、檐廊、晾房等生态空间形式。建筑空间的围合创造出有遮阴的内部庭院，在其内部配以植物，形成相对舒适的微气候环境。檐廊作为户外到室内的灰空间，起到了遮阳作用，沿街的檐廊还可为行人提供阴凉的步行空间。在住宅的顶楼保留了晾房的功能，也丰富了住宅建筑的造型。

在建筑形态设计上，融入吐鲁番历史多元文化，创造时代感和地方特色兼备的吐鲁番现代建筑，建立风格多样而不混乱的居住建筑。提炼传统建筑中的建筑元素，设计融入传统建筑中的彩绘、花砖搭砌、密致镂空木窗棚、拱形结构等元素，形成错落、凸凹的建筑体型和阴影丰富的建筑形态，唤起传统回忆，突出地方特色。

建筑色彩采用大地色系作为建筑的主色系，以土灰、土黄、土红为基色，辅以蓝、绿、灰色。建筑材料的色彩融入当地环境，体现地域性建筑特色。

（3）因地制宜的特色环境

葡萄是吐鲁番地区的特产之一，在建筑庭院、屋顶、阳台及墙面设置葡萄架可在短时间内使建筑外部绿化成荫，还可通过葡萄的光合作用和叶面水分的蒸发吸收大量的热量，调节建筑微气候。同时，特色的葡萄绿化为新区的建筑空间增加了新的景观。

坎儿井是新疆地区特有的地下运河体系，规划拟将其引入到建筑之中，结合“现代坎儿井”地下水系开发地下广场、地下商业服务设施，地下休闲娱乐设施等，不仅仅是一种地域特色环境的展现，也是一种利用水进行低温辐射及蒸发降温的有效手段，可有效提高空间环境的舒适性。

## 三、小结

2010 年 5 月 5 日，国家新能源示范城市暨自治区和谐生态城区和城乡一体化吐鲁番示范区举行了开工典礼仪式。目前，新区规划建设后续研究工作正在按计划进行，包括新区修建详细规划的确定与完善、住宅方案实施与完善、新能源汽车方案的选择与充电站建设、光伏工程与微电网建立与试运行等。

吐鲁番市新区建设积极应对干旱炎热气候，因地制宜，立足特有的环境条件，以太阳能利用为突破口，探索实现低能耗、低排放的城市可持续发展新模式，实现低碳城区、绿色交通和太阳能光热、光电等可再生能源在示范区建筑、交通、数字化管理等方面的利用。同时，新区规划注重城市空间环境的地域特色的传承，实现了传统与现代的和谐。吐鲁番市新区建设对我国西部地区的和谐城市发展具有重要的指导意义和示范效应。

（作者：吴天谋，广州市城市规划勘测设计研究院规划研究中心副总工程师；李文龙，广州市城市规划勘测设计研究院规划研究中心工程师）

### 参考文献

[1] 欧亚科学院中国中心城市科学学部，广州市城市规划勘测设计研究院，新疆维吾尔自治区建设设计总院，北京市建筑设计研究院，北京市城市规划设计研究院．吐鲁番市新区总体规划（2009—2020 年）[R]．2009

[2] 广州市城市规划勘测设计研究院．基于太阳能应用技术的绿色交通发展研究 [R]．2009

[3] 北京市建筑设计研究院．太阳能应用技术与地域性建筑的有机结合研究 [R]．2009

[4] 广州市城市规划勘测设计研究院．吐鲁番市新区起步区一期修建性详细规划 [R]．2010

# 浙江嘉善县建设低碳示范新区的规划实践

## 一、嘉善新区的发展条件

### 1. 区位优越

嘉善地处太湖流域杭嘉湖平原，位于浙江省东北部、江浙沪两省一市交会处，东邻上海（80公里），西依杭州（98公里），北靠苏州（90公里），南临乍浦港（35公里），是国务院批准的首批对外开放县市之一，素有“接轨上海第一站”之美称。

城市新区（南区）规划区位于嘉善县城南部，沪杭高铁西北，白水塘以南，杭州湾跨海大桥连接线以东，规划面积12平方公里。

长三角区域规划确定的“一核九带”的总体布局结构中，上海作为长三角发展龙头的区域地位进一步得到强化，上海对周边地区的要素吸引能力和辐射能力进一步增强，形成多层次的“核心—边缘”的空间关系。在此背景下，嘉善在城市发展中制定了“接轨上海”的发展战略，努力实现与上海的同城化发展。因此“城市新区南区”的发展动力将来自于由同城化产生的上海的外溢效应、长三角高端功能的重新布局所产生的新经济增长。嘉善具有从边缘到门户，实现沪嘉同城，接轨上海的有利区位。

### 2. 沪杭高铁对嘉善新区发展发挥带动作用

沪杭高速铁路是我国“四纵四横”客运专线网络中沪昆客运专线的一个组成部分。由上海虹桥站引出，经松江南——金山北——嘉善南——嘉兴南——桐乡——海宁西——余杭南引入杭州东站，全长160公里，设计时速为350公里。2010年10月26日已正式通车营运。

对于嘉善而言，由高速铁路带来的同城化效应、一体化效应和负溢出效应将对嘉善城市以及新区的未来发展产生带动作用。首先，高铁嘉善站是从上海进入浙江的门户，嘉善成为上海外溢效应的受益者和区域高端功能的接纳地。其次，高铁开通，有利于浙江优质民营资本趋近在上海周边地区投资，为企业接轨区域发展提供了更高的平台。由于沪杭高铁嘉善站的设立，城市新区不再是南扩形成的“边缘区”，而成为嘉善与长三角地区接轨的“门户区”。新区的开发建设对加快嘉善县发展，增强综合实力，融入区域，具有战略意义。

### 3. 区域一体化赋予新区新功能

新一轮《嘉兴市域总体规划》和《嘉善县“十二五”规划基本思路》都对嘉善县产业发展提出明确的目标，提出推进区域经济联动发展，推动上海总部型企业、研发型企业、科技孵化型企业向嘉善延伸创业。围绕上海“四个中心”建设，加大新兴产业和现代服务业发展力度，围绕节能环保、数字新技术、电力电子（物联网和智能电网）、生物医药等新兴产业加快发展。区域性高端服务业也趋向于选择在交通便利的高铁站地区。城市新区将成为新产业、新功能的空间载体，并为区域一体化带来的新功能提供发展空间。

## 二、嘉善城市新区的定位与概念设计

### 1. 选择与被选择：新区定位的基本判断

基于新区发展条件和发展目标导向，新区的功能定位能否成立，需要回答两个关键性的问题：第一是选择：新区可能引入的现代服务业类型和其产业支撑是什么？第二是被选择：新区在区域竞争中比较优势是什么？

（1）选择：现代服务业的可能选项

高铁站点对地方现代服务业的影响分为两个层面：一是对于服务对象为本地的生产性服务业，在降低经营成本和扩大服务市场的同时，将面对来自区域的竞争；二是由于交通条件的改善，为地区承接区域内相关产业链的转移带来机遇，将壮大地方生产性服务业的规模和区域影响力。同时，生产性服务业的发展也必将带来非生产性服务业的繁荣。

“接轨上海”是嘉善县发展的战略选择，也是区域发展的趋势。嘉善县现代服务业的发展除了自身资源的整合利用外，更大的动力和机遇来自于区域，具体来说，就是上海市相关产业的功能外溢。因此，对于嘉善县现代服务业的选项分析，主要立足于对上海市的产业集聚和现代服务业的发展和外溢。

结合上海的产业发展趋势，上海未来发展的服务业类型中生产要素流动弹性强的、对环境品质敏感的，以及对地租敏感的服务业类型有可能向外扩散，当然还要考虑服务对象和交通运输成本。在高速铁路便捷的交通优势下，以下类型服务业可能外溢：

①人力密集的新兴产业。此类服务业的资源要素主要是人的智力，高铁的快速便捷使人的流动弹性增强。相对于上海而言，如果具有环境优势和地租成本优势，此类企业可能向外扩散。如软件开发、信息服务、动漫产业、新媒体、新娱乐、管理咨询等。

②公共卫生、医疗服务。公共卫生和医疗服务对于环境的要求很高，同时对土地、成本等要素的要求也较高。城市新区（南区）相比于上海具有更好的环境品质，有适合公共卫生、医疗服务发展的土地资源，适宜引进大型医疗卫生设施；同时土地、人力成本具有竞争力，具有发展医疗卫生产业的极大优势。

③教育培训业。教育培训业受众面广，需要办公场所大，对地租比较敏感。与新兴产业相关的企业培训、再就业培训、职业教育、技术职业教育等面向个人消费的服务业，可能外溢抢占区域市场。

④结合地方资源的文化创意产业和旅游业。在区域资源配置一体化的趋势下，地方的文化资源和旅游资源就是区域的共享资源，地方的服务设施也是区域共享的服务设施。具有特色文化和旅游资源的地区将会吸引上海的文化创意产业和旅游业外溢。

（2）被选择：区域竞争的比较优势

对于上海市外溢的服务业类型在区域范围内的空间选择是通过市场机制进行的，地方政府可以通过政策引导来增强地区发展的区域竞争优势，但最终还是一个“被选择”的过程。对嘉善城市新区（南区）的比较优势分析分为两个层面：一是与沪杭线两端的中心城市比较；二是与上海市周边的同级别城市比较。

①与上海、杭州等一线城市相比。嘉善在运输、储存、租金和劳动力等方面，均具有低成本优势。比如，完成“八通一平”的土地出让价格远低于上海地区，建筑成本每平方米比上海地区低150~200元，劳动力的附加工资比上海地区低30%~50%，这都有利于嘉善承接上海的产业转移、服务业转移和服务消费转移。同时，嘉善的生活成本与日渐飙升的上海、杭州等大城市相比，明显低廉很多。仅房价而言，2009年嘉善出售的新建住房均价不到上海、杭州的1/3，这就为承担大城市的居住功能外溢提供了有利条件。

②与上海周边区县相比。首先，嘉善具有政策优势。在《长江三角洲地区区域规划》中，嘉善县被确立为唯一的“县域科学发展示范点”。这是对嘉善县科学发展示范点建设的充分肯定，有利于嘉善县向上争取相关政策扶持，开展综合配套改革，推动科学发展，实现经济社会全面转型。其次，嘉善处于我国经济活动高密度的长三角地区的中心位置，是浙江省唯一与上海市和江苏省共同接壤的县。沪杭高铁在此设站，更是进一步提升了嘉善在长三角中的地位，其与上海的郊区金山、松江、青浦、嘉定、宝山等取得了类似的区位条件，也成为接受上海辐射的第一阵地。高速铁路建成通车后，以本区域为中心的“一小时交通圈”将覆盖“长三角”内的主要城市。最后，嘉善旅游资源丰富，水乡如梦，古镇入画，田园可诗。国家4A级景区西塘古镇、十里蓉溪水乡游——大云生态旅游区、吴越名湖江南情——汾湖旅游度假区，每年都吸引国内外大量游客。嘉善县的旅游业发展潜力巨大。

**2. 新区定位与发展策略**

（1）新区定位

①现代健康产业基地。依托上海优质医疗服务体系，应对长三角乃至全国对上海医疗服务的巨大需求，打造服务长三角区域的健康产业基地和医疗服务中心。嘉善城市新区（南区）的建设需要走特色化、专业化路线，与区域内其他城市、嘉善县其他片区展开错位竞争。健康产业是集医疗、旅游、地产等为一体的新兴现代服务业。在长三角地区尚处于初步发展阶段。这为嘉善县率先进入这一领域，快速奠定竞争优势提供了契机。

②技术转移与创新基地。充分吸引国际国内技术转移，利用国家鼓励技术创新的技术

优势，建立技术转移中心，引进、鉴定、转移国际先进技术，促成民营企业技术更新、技术创新与技术再造。在新一轮国际国内技术转移大潮的背景下，浙江的民营经济不断遭遇出口壁垒，急需在成本优势的基础上提升技术创新能力。《长江三角洲地区区域规划》提出要加强“自主创新与创新型区域建设”，嘉善应抓住机遇，利用上海的平台和窗口优势，发挥环境、交通和级差地租优势，主动对接技术转移需求，为经济进一步提升积蓄能量。

③优质低碳生活社区。建设高标准的完善配套设施，利用先进的低碳建设技术，凸显独特的水乡风情，打造优质生活圈，成为上海第十镇。随着沪杭高铁开通，传统的地缘优势得到进一步的巩固，城市新区（南区）已经成为嘉兴市乃至浙江省接轨上海的桥头堡。结合大云镇旅游资源的开发，整合嘉兴市东部地区的其他旅游资源，城市新区（南区）可以打造成为集中体现城市形象的低碳生活的样板区、吸引高端人才的上海生活圈。

（2）发展策略

①实现沪嘉同城，承接上海产业转移。嘉善城市新区（南区）临近上海，区位优势明显。应依托临沪发展带，主动对接上海，承接上海产业转移。随着生物医药高新产业不断由单纯的制造业向研发提升转型，目前落户上海的高新制造业和研发需要向外转移；健康管理产业在发展成熟后也急需向外拓展市场；优质医院提供的医疗服务供不应求，但受限于发展空间无法扩大规模。新媒体产业尚处于形成阶段，上海集聚的是研发等高端类型产业，还有大量的用地需求更大的制造和服务外包需要向外转移。嘉善城市新区（南区）具备了优越的区位条件，并能提供发展上述产业发展所必备的土地资源，应当抓住机遇，大力招商，承接转移，打造健康产业集群，率先形成产业高地，构筑竞争优势。

②打造沪浙门户，引进浙江优质民资。浙江民营资本实力雄厚，且发展活跃。近年来，原有的小商品制造业受到技术水平较低、劳动力成本高的影响，发展缓慢，加之金融危机影响，渐入困境，不得不考虑转型。民间资本正积极寻找新兴产业和重点项目。嘉善应充分抓住浙沪门户这一优势，使城市新区（南区）作为浙江民资北上进入上海的桥头堡，引进若干具有实力的上市公司投资嘉善健康产业和新媒体、新娱乐，以快速形成产业集群和规模。

③保持规划弹性，适应城市多元发展需求。健康产业和新媒体、新娱乐产业规划必须要保持弹性：一是因为产业本身具有不确定性，招商过程中可能引进占地规模较大的企业，也可能引进占地规模较小的企业，不同的产业门类实际招商规模与规划目标可能存在差异；二是需要留有竞争力提升空间，当出现新的发展趋势时，能够有充足的土地引进和发展新兴的产业方向，保证产业持续的竞争力。

规划的弹性主要体现在用地规模的划分，确定用地规模弹性范围，根据投资规模大小给予相应的用地规模。集约现阶段发展用地，保留发展备用地，便于调整产业发展方向，为可能出现的新兴产业保留发展空间。

④建设低碳新区，凸显水乡风情。建设低碳城市是实现城市可持续发展的必由之路，是发展高端服务业和新兴制造业的必然要求，也是当前国家鼓励的城市发展方向，是科学发展的应有之意。城市新区（南区）作为嘉善县城市发展的重心，提供了发展低碳新区的绝佳机会。因此，建设低碳新区，构筑新型城市，成为长三角地区低碳城市样板。低碳城市与

城市特色结合，更能彰显城市魅力，增强城市对于新兴产业、人才的吸引力。嘉善县最大的城市特色是以西塘为代表的水乡风情。在城市新区（南区）建设中，应传承传统水乡风韵，延续水网、路网、建筑有机结合的城市肌理，营造富有地方特色的人文、生态气息。

**3. 概念规划设计**

(1) 规划愿景

嘉善新区（南区）将糅合江南水乡与吴越文化特色，打造水乡故里的嘉善门户区。以健康产业为主导方向，配套完善高端休闲娱乐设施，打造长三角健康、新媒体创意产业与优质生活共核发展的生态、低碳、高效的示范区。

愿景一：展现传统水乡与现代新城融合的城市门户。

愿景二：追求工作、生活与自然平衡的健康生活模式。

愿景三：倡导低碳技术实践，引领低碳生活潮流。

愿景四：体验吴越水乡文化魅力的活力新城。

(2) 设计构思

① 延续总体路网格局，建立高铁站地区与西塘、主城、大云的高效联系。在延续南北向主干道网络基础上，提升次干道等级，增加一条连通南北的主干道，远期建设途经主城至西塘的轻轨线路；理顺嘉善大道、新增主干道与高铁站的交通流线组织；完善区内东西向道路与善江公路的对接，加强高铁站地区与西塘、大云镇的便捷联系。

② 对接总体规划“绿网”布局，完善新区绿地开敞空间体系，打造两大标志性生态公园，凸显地区优越的生态景观资源。

③ 尊重现状及水网格局，延续独具特色的江南水乡肌理，通过合理改造，提升区内防

图1　嘉善新区鸟瞰图

洪能力。形成“五主、四次、多分支”的水系网络；贯通南部中心河，结合区内“毛细血管”状的水系网络，提升本地区的防洪排涝能力。

④打造富有江南水乡韵味的“公共活力环”，串联“四大公共核心区”。公共活力环——依托主要水道布置慢行系统，串联城市主要的公共核心并承载多种公共职能的开敞空间环路。四大公共核心区分别为高铁站前门户区、水乡购物公园区、湿地公园区、产业研发区。

⑤打造一条连通新旧城区、功能复合、建筑特色鲜明的“V型”新区形象展示带。与旧城公共服务带对接，共同构成嘉善公共服务、产业发展及城市形象展示的主轴线。展示带与景观有机融合，打造医疗技术产业群岛、高铁站前门户区、低碳示范岛、综合产业中心、水乡购物公园等几大形象展示节点。

⑥解读江南水乡地区肌理特征，结合现状水网，对水乡风貌进行分区指引。江南水乡地区典型的形态肌理可大致总结为网格状、梳状、龟裂状、岛状四类，本方案结合现状水网形态特征，通过梳理及改造，对不同区域进行水乡风貌控制及引导，凸显嘉善南区（新区）的水乡意象。

⑦借鉴江南水乡传统的空间断面形式，营造可感受的新区水乡意象。江南水乡古镇传统的空间布局特征主要体现在建筑与公共开敞空间的断面关系上。公共开敞空间主要是指水网、道路及沿河分布的码头广场等；江南水乡古镇传统的空间断面形式可大致分为沿河开敞型、半公共型、私密型三类。上述三类传统断面满足了不同使用功能的需求，与本方案根据使用功能划分水网类别及断面形式的构想相一致。

⑧倡导产业、居住、配套混合利用的土地开发模式。方案用地布局采用产业、居住、配套相结合的土地开发模式，避免了单一功能开发可能导致的地区活力不足问题，提升了土地开发的合理性。混合的土地开发模式将有效降低通勤需求，体现了低碳规划的设计理念。

⑨尊重市场发展需求，为地块的开发预留足够的弹性空间。嘉善新区（南区）规划预留了功能弹性发展用地，可根据市场发展的需求，转化为居住功能或产业功能，保证了新区发展的弹性空间。方案采取灵活的支路网布局方式，可根据市场发展的需求，调整地块规模大小，为地块“可分可合”的开发模式提供足够弹性。

⑩进行低碳规划，应用低碳技术。产业、居住、配套紧凑混合的布局模式体现了低碳规划的核心理念；打造一个慢行系统主环路，融合自行车、电瓶船、步行道等流线，预留远期发展环保轻轨的可能，提倡低碳交通方式。打造三个低碳示范点（产业低碳示范岛、商业低碳示范点、水乡低碳居住示范点），积极推进新低碳技术的应用。

(3) 规划结构——“一带、一环、四心”

“一带”——联系新旧城区的城市形象展示带。

“一环”——依托主要水道及开敞空间，联系主要的公共节点，承载主要公共活动的城市活力环。

“四心”——串联于活力环上的重要节点，包括站前商务文化中心、水乡购物公园、湿地公园、医学技术研究中心。

图2 嘉善新区核心区透视图

## 三、建设低碳示范新区的技术体系

### 1. 低碳生态建设的目标

(1) 发展目标

本次规划围绕建设生态低碳新城，提出了四大发展目标，并形成了一系列相应的子目标。管理标准的制定将以这些目标为导向。

表1 四大发展目标及其子目标

| 发展目标 | 子目标 |
|---|---|
| 发展低碳产业，建设创新活力之城 | 发展资本密集型、智力密集型的服务业；<br>发展高端文化、创意产业，吸引高素质人才集聚；<br>混合布置城市功能，营造有利于经济和文化发展的创新性环境；<br>规划城市创新节点，并配套高端商业、商务和文化设施。 |
| 发展低碳交通，打造便捷高效之城 | 实行公交优先，鼓励绿色出行；<br>城市公交系统与高铁高效接驳；<br>体现江南水乡特色的路网系统；<br>与绿色开放空间结合的人行及自行车慢行系统；<br>BRT交通环与电动公交车。 |

续表 1

| 发展目标 | 子目标 |
|---|---|
| 建设低碳社区，打造生态宜居之城 | 相对紧凑、混合使用的街区；<br>完善公共空间、半公共空间、半私密空间和私密空间体系，满足人们不同活动的空间需求；<br>步行可达的社区服务中心，满足不同年龄、层次人群的生活需求；<br>完善的绿色基础设施网络；<br>采用适宜节能技术的绿色住宅。 |
| 采用低碳技术，打造绿色健康之城 | 基于太阳能、风能、地能等可再生能源的能源供应系统；<br>分布式能源供应体系；<br>分质供水与再生水利用系统；<br>基于自然生态的雨洪管理系统；<br>垃圾分类、真空管道收集与回收利用系统；<br>集中设置的能源监控与管理中心。 |

（2）总体构架

生态城市建设管理通过设置管理标准来实现。管理标准的设立以生态城市规划的目标体系作为导向，以生态城市的技术体系作为支撑，形成既能满足生态城市发展需求，又具有很强实施性的标准。其中，不能量化考核的标准以定性的规定设置作为技术导则，可量化考核的标准以定量的指标设置作为指标体系。

### 2. 低碳生态建设的技术导则

技术导则是定性的技术指引。依据低碳生态建设目标，结合低碳技术要求，提出非强制性的指引性建设导则。建设导则是从技术角度出发，定性设置的技术要求。

技术导则构建从两个角度出发。第一个角度是城市发展目标和子目标，并以目标为引导；第二个角度是构建生态低碳城市的技术支撑，包括水资源循环与利用、节能、废弃物利用、交通指引、生态社区建设等五大方面的技术。技术导则的确定是从技术角度出发，提出一系列定性的导则体系，既是建设低碳生态新城的技术准则，也作为建立指标体系的技术基础。

表 2　技术导则体系

| 技术体系 | 技术导则 |
|---|---|
| 水资源循环与利用 | 保持自然水体循环：增加植被和透水性路面面积，加快地面排水。<br>雨水收集利用：城市建筑安装雨水收集系统和存水设施，将雨水集中储存，提供自然通风、消防和植物灌溉的功能。<br>污水处理：提高污水处理率，从废物及污水中回收资源，实现水资源最大限度的再利用。<br>节水设备：推广家庭节水设施，推进工业节水和中水回用，而在城市设计相关节水装置，如防火用雨水储存、中水利用系统、真空下水系统等。 |
| 节能设计 | 推广绿色“零能耗”建筑：通过对分布、朝向、采光、结构、体量、外立面等设计，减少能源需求。<br>鼓励使用节能电器：如节能灯具、节能空调等，降低家庭用电量。<br>大力发展新能源：利用太阳能发电、垃圾焚烧发电、风力发电，减少对煤电依赖。<br>自然采暖制冷：利用太阳能提供热水，利用风，水体降温制冷。<br>发展新能源交通：推广电动公交车、电动小汽车、电动自行车。 |

续表 2

| 技术体系 | 技术导则 |
| --- | --- |
| 废弃物利用 | 废弃物:实现工业废弃物再利用,变污染物为原料。<br>废热:建立工业废热回收利用机制与设施。 |
| 交通指引 | 确立公共交通的主导地位,公交出行分担率达到50%以上。<br>创造适宜步行和非机动交通的设施环境,步行和非机动交通分担率不低于35%;个体机动交通分担率低于15%。<br>城市内部公交系统发达,通过公交半小时内可达城市任何地点。 |
| 生态社区建设 | 建立社区级"能量—物质"循环系统:利用太阳能为住宅提供所需要的能源。夏季利用太阳能加热地下水;冬季保存部分蓄水层的冷水,夏季为温度较高的居住空间降温。利用社区废弃物中产生沼气,生产电和热水。<br>社区建筑布局控制微风廊道畅通,引导夏季主导风进入,创造良好区域微风环境。居住组团内北高南低的空间布局,以利于阻挡西北风,引入东南风。利用主要道路布局构筑通风廊道。 |

### 3. 低碳生态建设的管理与指标

指标体系是定量化的指标体系。根据特定的目标情景，制定相应的指标，并可以根据政府部门的统计对指标进行考查。

指标体系由建设低碳生态城市核心指标组成。指标体系的构建以城市功能为主导维度，综合时间维度、管理次序维度、空间维度、主体维度，形成多维的指标管理体系。指标落实到具体的政府部门、企业或个人，形成可考核的体系。

城市功能维度包括自然环境、人工环境、人居、能源、资源、经济等层面。

(1) 自然环境指标

控制最基本的自然条件，从大气、水、噪声、林地和碳排放量等角度控制自然环境的保育程度。

(2) 人工环境指标

控制与自然环境紧密联系的人工建筑对自然的影响，包括人工植被、水循环、基础市政设施等。

(3) 人居指标

关注与居住紧密联系的指标，包括住房、水、垃圾、交通、公共服务、通信等方面。

(4) 能源指标

强调新能源和节能两个方面，包括建筑节能、生活节能、交通节能、新能源使用、能量回收利用等方面。

(5) 资源指标

重点关注资源回收利用，包括垃圾、水循环利用。

(6) 经济指标

重点关注产业层级，包括研发能力和现代服务业和先进制造业发展水平。

在主导维度之外，时间维度控制指标的达成日期，分为近期（2015 年）、中期（2020

年）和远期（2030 年），以近期和中期控制为主。

管理次序维度分为规划控制和管理控制。规划控制是指在规划建设过程中即可确定的指标，例如人均绿地面积；管理控制需要建成之后的管理调度的配合，例如公交运行时间。

空间维度控制指标落实的具体空间范围有所区别：有些指标适用于城市范围，如大气环境指标；有些指标需要落实到街区，在城市范围内平衡，例如考虑到居住混合的需要，经济适用房在街区范围内平衡；还有的指标可以落实到地块，例如无障碍设施指标。

主体维度控制指标的达成与考核主体予以明确，例如城市范围的公共服务主体为政府，涉及产业的指标主体为企业，而需要末端管理的人均指标主体为个人。

（作者：张明超，浙江嘉善县委书记）

# 从生态政策到民生工程

## ——珠三角绿道建设模式初探

改革开放30年来，珠三角成长为中国经济最活跃的“中心”的同时，日益严重的生态环境问题逐渐成为持续发展的一大隐患。《广东省珠江三角洲城镇群协调发展规划实施条例》提出：珠三角环状区域生态屏障、近海生态防护带、区域绿核、网络状生态隔离廊道等关系到区域生态稳定、健康的重要区域必须划入一级空间管治区，实行强制性监管。对区域生态系统完整性起重要作用的生态廊道，往往由于缺乏保护专业主管部门，已经渐渐成为生态管治政策实施过程中最为薄弱的环节。虽然自然保护区等重要生态绿核大都有专门机构实施监管，但其中绝大多数属于“散点状”布局，犹如汪洋大海中的片片“孤岛”，城市建设用地的持续扩张，使这些“孤岛”越来越分散。近年来，珠三角通过不断摸索，借鉴国外绿道建设经验，将生态保护与绿道休闲游憩功能相结合，逐步探索出了一套区域生态廊道的保护方法与模式，旨在使珠三角生态保护不仅是一项生态工程、环境工程，而且能成为惠及老百姓的经济工程、民生工程。

## 一、发展困境

### 1. 城市发展中的现实问题

珠三角在城镇化过程中呈现两大矛盾：一是城乡建设快速扩张、无序蔓延与自然生态空间总量逐年减少的矛盾。2005年，深圳、东莞两市建设用地占市域总面积已达40%，超出30%的安全底线，广州与佛山之间、深圳与东莞之间已无大面积绿带进行有效生态隔离。二是生态绿地少而零散，与城市居民提升生活品质、对休闲生态绿地的需求不断增长的矛盾。世界发展历史证明，当人均GDP 3000美元以上，社会对休闲消费就会产生强烈需求。2009年珠三角人均GDP逼近1万美元大关，珠三角城乡居民对休闲游憩活动的需求日益强烈。

### 2. 生态保护管理中的问题

(1) 保护与利用未能有效结合

珠三角生态绿地保护出现了两种极端：一种是以开发为主导，导致保护失效，表现在许多风景名胜区过度开发，使景观环境质量显著下降；二是从保护出发，普遍重视对于生态要素的保护，而忽视生活功能，忽视提升生活品质、增强居民幸福感等软性要求。

（2）生态绿地界线不清晰

国外通过划定明确的增长界线来对城市发展进行控制和管理。而我国目前除了划定自然保护区的核心区、基本农田保护区外，绝大部分从城市可持续发展角度应禁止建设的区域并没有划定清晰的界线来对其进行管理或保护。

（3）政府对城市开发与管理的关注重点有偏差

珠三角生态保护没有真正获得地方政府和政治家的有力支持。由于政绩考核等相关政策制度以及所处发展环境与阶段的影响，以经济建设为中心成为了地方政府的基本政策。

## 二、国外经验与绿道理念

### 1. 相似的困境——19 世纪末的伦敦

19 世纪末的伦敦，处于工业化快速发展的阶段，出现了城市无序蔓延、生态环境破坏等诸多问题。面对这些问题，当时伦敦郡的议长罗斯伯里伯爵感叹：“非常严酷的事实是，几百万人在这条壮丽的河边犹如遭受灾难般的沮丧……住房非常拥挤，城市被毫无顾忌地糟蹋，变得肮脏、污水横流，日复一日地变成人类的坟墓。”

### 2. 解决之道——从花园城市到绿道

伦敦的城市问题引起了许多有识之士的担忧和关注。现代城市规划思想的先驱——霍华德先生提出了“城市—乡村”结合的“花园城市”模式，试图解决这些问题。“把 切最生动活泼的城市生活的优点和美丽与愉快的乡村环境和谐地组合在一起”，“人民自发地从拥挤的城市投入大地母亲的仁慈怀抱——这个生命、快乐、财富和力量的源泉”。这为伦敦创造了“新的希望、新的生活、新的文明”。

根据他的理念，20 世纪 40 年代，大伦敦规划建设了环城绿带及与之相联系的绿色通道网络，之后逐渐发展成为目前国外正在大规模建设的“绿道”。(见图 1)

### 3. 绿道理念

绿道（greenway）是一种线形绿色开敞空间，通常沿着河滨、溪谷、山脊、风景道路等自然和人工廊道建立，内设可供行人和骑车者进入的景观游憩线路，连接主要的公园、自然保护区、风景名胜区、历史古迹和城乡居民居住区等。

绿道主要由人行步道、自行车道等非机动车游径和停车场、游船码头、租车店、休息站、旅游商店、特色小食店等游憩配套设施及一定宽度的绿化保护带构成。根据需要，绿道外围还可以划定一定范围的绿化缓冲区作为城市生态廊道或组团隔离带。(见图 2)

绿道具有如下特点：

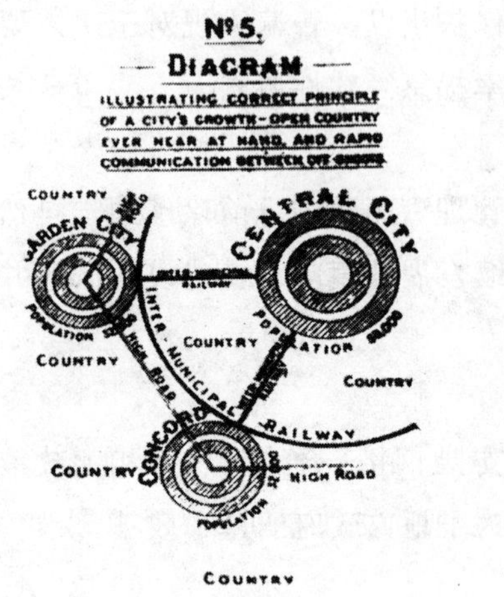

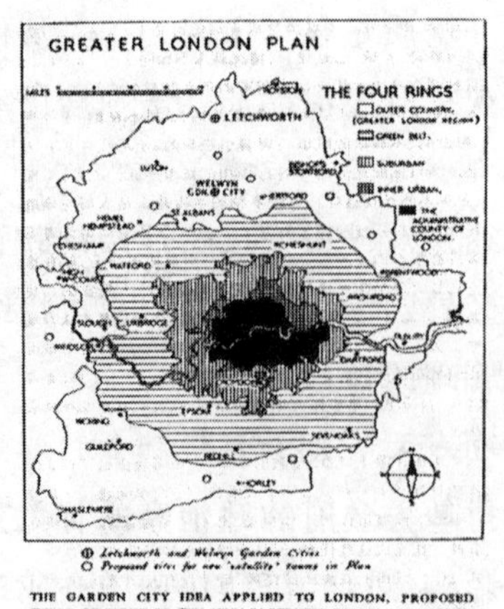

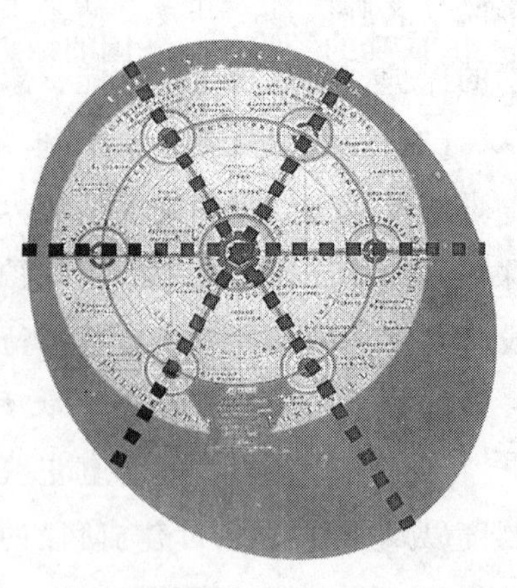

图1 “花园城市”理念

图2 绿道典型断面

(1) 绿道从乡村深入城市中心区，具有生态联系功能，可减缓城市热岛效应，改善人居环境，是城市的“风道”，符合建设低碳城市的发展要求。

(2) 绿道是城乡联系的纽带，可为人们提供便捷的户外交往空间，增加城乡居民彼此交流的机会，有助于城乡统筹及和谐社会的建设。

(3) 绿道除了设置游径、休息站、零售和简易餐饮服务等必要设施外，还可以在绿道周边结合旅游业的发展，建设酒店、度假村、运动俱乐部等设施，扩大内需，刺激经济增长。

(4) 绿道建设基本不需要占用建设用地指标，具有投资少、见效快的特点。

总之，绿道是提高城市化质量的有效途径，可以全面提升城乡居民的生活质量，完善城市功能，强化地方风貌特征，提升发展品位。

### 4. 成功的经验——各国的绿道建设

(1) 日本：通过绿道打造具有地方特色的自然景观

日本对国内主要河道一一编号加以保护，通过滨河绿道建设，为植物生长和动物繁衍栖息提供了空间；同时，绿道串联起沿线的名山大川、风景胜地，为城市居民提供了体验自然、欣赏自然的机会和一片远离城市喧嚣的净土。

(2) 新加坡：通过绿道扩大户外交往空间，促进社会和谐

新加坡于1991年开始建设一个串联全国的绿地和水体的绿地网络，通畅的、无缝连接的绿道为生活在高密度建成区的人们，提供了足够的户外休闲娱乐和交往空间，为多民族社会的和谐融合创造了物质基础。

(3) 美国：通过复合功能的绿道建设，刺激经济增长

美国东海岸绿道全长约4500公里，是全美首条集休闲娱乐、户外活动和文化遗产旅游于一体的绿道，可为沿途各州带来约166亿美元的旅游收入，为超过3800万居民带来巨大的社会、经济和生态效益。

(4) 德国：绿道成为推动旧城更新、提升土地价值的重要手段

德国鲁尔区将绿道建设与工业区改造相结合，通过七个“绿道”计划将百年来原本脏乱不堪、传统低效的工业区，变成了一个生态安全、景色优美的宜居城区。在改善居民生活质量的同时，也提升了周边土地的价值。

### 5. 绿道建设的现实意义

国外绿道建设的成功经验，对珠三角地区城市建设具有较强的现实意义。首先，绿道建设是落实科学发展观、建设宜居城乡的重要内容。其次，绿道建设是提高城市化质量的有效途径。最后，绿道建设是促进消费扩大内需的创新手段。绿道成网后，集环保、运动、休闲、旅游等功能于一体，是城乡、区域生态网络系统的重要组成部分，是能将保护生态、改善民生与发展经济完美结合的有效载体。

## 三、探索与实践

### 1. 生态政策与规划的制定——为绿道建设提供技术与理论支持

为实现区域资源有效配置，保障社会、经济和环境协调发展，广东省于2003年颁布了《广东省区域绿地规划指引》，探索“绿线管制”政策。同年11月颁布了《广东省中心镇规划指引》，提出“三区六线”的空间管制体系。2004年，《珠江三角洲城镇群协调发展规划(2004—2020年)》将区域绿地和区域性交通廊道纳入一级空间管制区。2008年年底，《珠江三角洲改革发展规划纲要》出台，提出“优化区域生态安全格局，构筑以珠江水系，沿海重要绿带和北部连绵山体为主要框架的区域生态安全体系”的要求。2009年印发《珠江

三角洲区域绿地划定及管理工作方案》，在珠三角地区先行开展区域绿地的划定工作。

区域绿地为绿道的生态基底，珠三角这些基础性、先导性的探索为目前大规模绿道建设提供了重要的技术和政策支持。

**2. 生态建设计划与行动——为绿道建设提供实施基础**

面对日益严峻的生态环境问题，珠三角各市近十年来实施了一系列生态环境改善工程。如广州从1998年开始实施“青山碧水蓝天工程计划”，结合第16届亚运会城市生态环境整治，2010年广州环境面貌实现“一大变”。

绿道与绿网、水网、路网相互因借，互联互通。绿网水网是绿道的生态和环境基础，城市生态环境整治工程为绿道建设提供了载体，绿道又为生态工程注入了休闲、健身、慢行等新内涵。

**3. 先行先试的示范点——为绿道建设提供实践经验**

(1) 基本生态控制线划定

2005年，深圳市推出的“基本生态控制线”制度为绿道控制线的划定提供了实践经验，为更加切实有效地保护绿道绿廊系统提供了可借鉴的空间管制政策。

(2) 自行车道建设

近年来，珠三角一些城市已在一定范围内开展了绿道前期建设的探索，成效初显。如广州增城已建成全长80公里连接城乡的休闲健身自行车道，深圳市在盐田区打造一条长达19.5公里的步行廊道和自行车道。广州拟沿着道路、河涌、江岸用生态廊道联系各个城区，实施环境整治与改造，建成11条总长约145公里的富有特色的步行生态连廊，贯穿中心城区。

## 四、统筹规划

**1. 规划组织**

2010年1月召开的广东省委十届六次全会，正式提出建设珠江三角洲绿道网的工作部署，将绿道建设纳入到今后三年的城市建设计划中，要求“一年基本建成，两年全部到位，三年成熟完善”。3月，广东省住房和城乡建设厅组织编制和制订《珠江三角洲绿道网总体规划纲要》、《珠三角区域绿道规划设计技术指引（试行版）》等相关技术标准也先后出台。珠三角九市纷纷根据《珠江三角洲绿道网总体规划纲要》的要求制订各市的绿道网规划。(见图3)

**2. 规划制订**

(1) 规划原则

珠三角绿道建设遵循“生态化、本土化、多样化、人性化”的原则，以支持构建区域

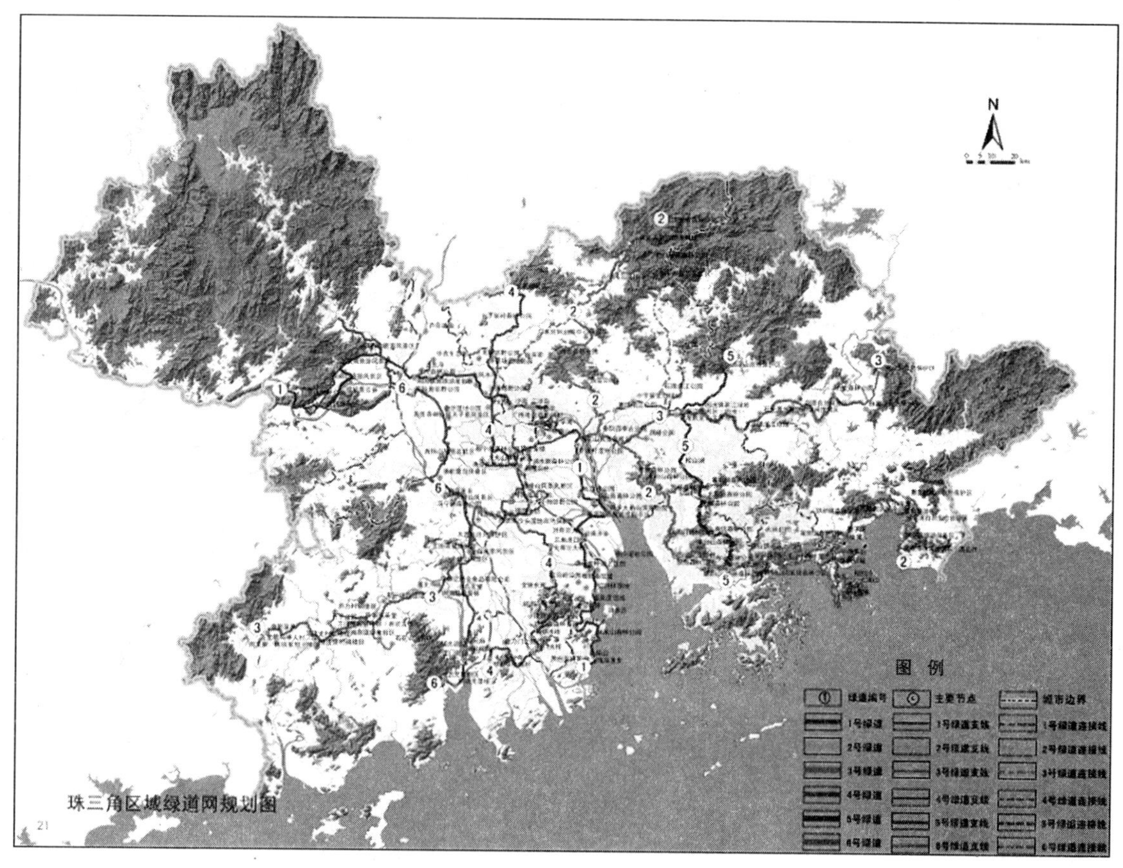


图 3　珠三角区域绿道网规划图

生态安全格局、优化城乡生态环境为基础，充分挖掘地方特色和人文内涵，以人为本，打造形式多样、功能各异的绿道。

（2）*布局考虑要素*

资源本底、政策要素、地方意愿等是珠三角绿道网总体布局考虑的主要要素。自然生态要素、人文要素、现状道路和城镇布局等为绿道建设的资源根本要素，上层次规划及相关规划等为政策要素。绿道网总体布局方案充分遵循了各地政府和自行车运动协会、登山协会等民间组织及公众的意见。

（3）*绿道网整体布局*

根据绿道网规划原则，综合考虑相关要素，结合各市的实际情况叠加分析，综合优化形成由“6 条主线、4 条连接线、22 条支线、18 处城际交界面和 4410 平方公里绿化控制区”构成的绿道网总体布局结构。

①6 条主线。珠三角 1 ~ 6 号区域绿道主线全长约 1690 公里，串联 200 多处主要森林公园、自然保护区、风景名胜区、郊野公园、滨水公园和历史文化遗迹等发展节点，连接广佛肇、深莞惠、珠中江三大都市区，服务人口约 2565 万人。

②4 条连接线。为促进区域绿道主线的有效衔接，规划四条连接线，建立起 1 号—2 号—4 号、2 号—4 号、1 号—3 号、2 号—3 号绿道的联系，总长约 160 公里。

③22 条支线。为实现主线与主要发展节点之间的有效联系，共规划 22 条支线，全长约

470公里。

④18处城际交界面。绿道建设跨市之间的交界面共18处。城际交界面建设的主要任务是通过统筹规划，协调各市绿道的走向和建设标准，将各市孤立的绿道通过灵活的接驳方式有机贯通起来，形成一体化的区域绿道网络体系。

⑤4410平方公里绿化控制区。绿化控制区起到维护区域生态系统健康稳定，营造生态环境优异、景观资源丰富的游憩空间的作用。绿化控制区总面积约4410平方公里，占珠三角总面积的8%。

## 五、绿道建设

珠三角绿道建设从策划到全面实施，基于“从规划到政治家的行动，从公共政策到建设项目”的理念与转变。如何将公共政策落实到建设项目，如何将区域绿道这一建设项目统筹珠三角九个地市共同展开，是切实推进珠三角区域绿道建设的关键。

### 1. 组织管理

以“省建设宜居城乡工作联席会议制度”为统筹协调机构，下设绿道建设办公室，负责珠三角区域绿道建设统筹、专项资金管理、验收等工作。省市具体分工为“省统筹协调、市具体实施”。(见图4)

### 2. 建设资金

绿道属城市新型的公用服务设施，因此应纳入城市规划建设的总盘子中统筹考虑。绿道项目的建设资金，以珠三角各市财政投入为主，社会资金投入为辅。

### 3. 土地来源

绿道网可结合防洪堤坝路和栈道、公路防护林带、山边小路、机耕路等进行连通、改造、提升和美化，基本不需新增建设用地。绿道建设用地可通过土地协议、土地租赁、土地捐赠、土地征用等四种方式获取。

### 4. 验收与考核

区域绿道建设任务完成三个月内，由各市绿道办完成建设项目的竣工验收工作，并将验收结果纳入绿道建设工程年报。省住建厅根据年报内容适时组织领导和专家对绿道进行监督检查。绿道建设项目综合考评结果与领导政绩考核直接挂钩，纳入各市创建宜居城乡工作绩效考核的指标体系。

## 六、长效机制

绿道建成后将面临着管理和维护的问题，从已建成绿道的管理和维护现状来看，各地尚

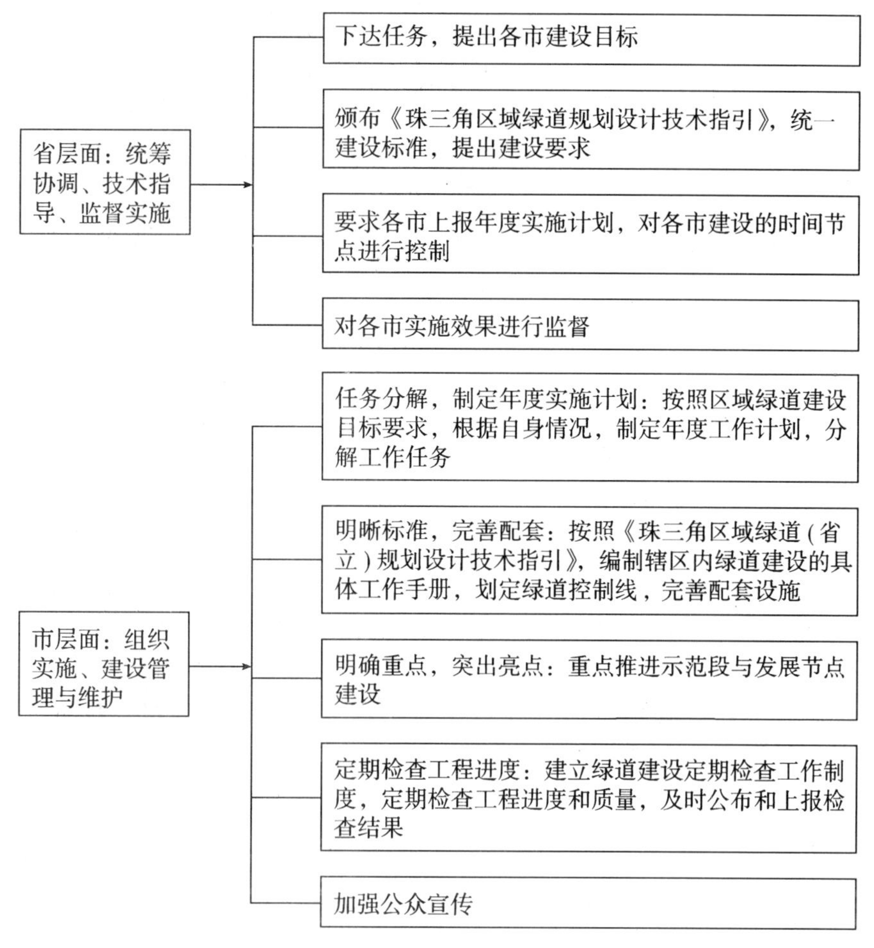


图 4　省市绿道建设职责分工

未形成系统的绿道管理和维护方法。因此，进行绿道建设管理与维护长效机制探索与研究尤为必要。

### 1. 管理与维护模式

根据绿道建设属于生态工程、市政工程的特点，绿道建设、管理与维护的长效工作，宜采用属地管理和分级管理相结合的模式，条块结合，以块为主。属地管理可以放到珠三角各市的区（县、县级市）一级，有条件的可到镇（街道）一级。

公众参与是绿道管理与维护模式的必要补充，有利于保证绿道的长效运营和维护，形成政府部门和社会各界共同参与管理与维护的良性格局。（见图 5）

### 2. 建设管理

各级绿道建设办公室制定管辖范围内的绿道年度建设工作计划，并上报本级人民政府和上级绿道建设办公室备案作为年度考核的依据。省级以下绿道建设办公室通过年报、月报等制度向本级人民政府及上级绿道建设办公室汇报绿道建设进度。市、县、镇（街道）的绿

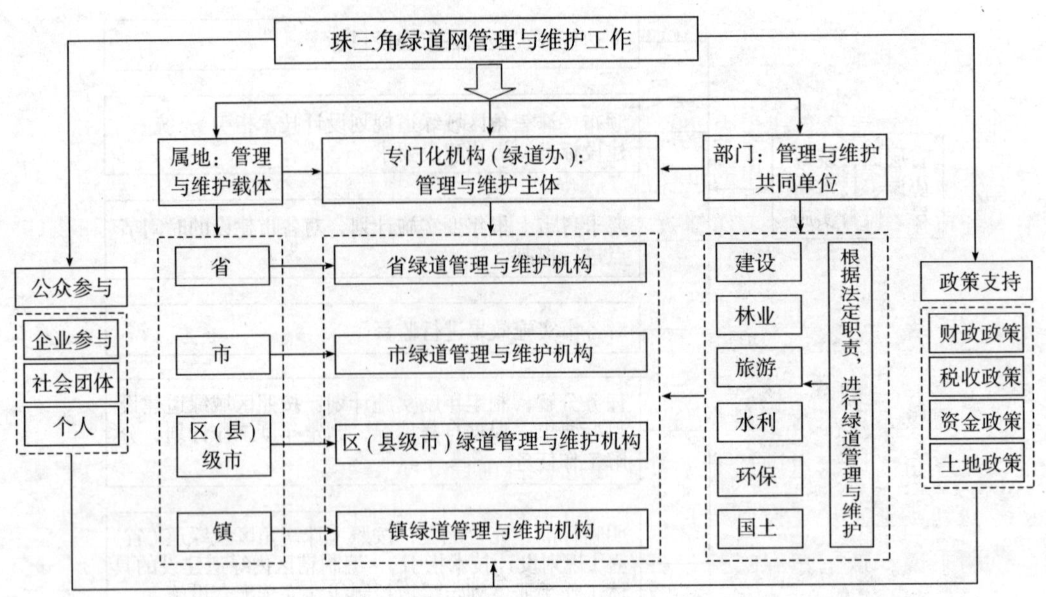


图5　珠三角绿道网管理与维护总体框架图

道建设办公室是绿道建设管理机构和项目法人，对工程建设的质量、投资、进度等全面负责。

### 3. 经营管理

绿道网经营管理可根据具体情况，采取“公园经营”、“旅游公司经营”、“政府部门+个体经营”三种模式。都市型绿道可采取公园经营管理模式，由属地园林或绿道管理专门机构负责日常经营。鼓励旅游公司、私人承包商竞投绿道的特许经营权。各地政府或绿道管理专门机构应积极向社会公众、经济组织宣传推广绿道项目。

### 4. 维护机制

各地应组织编制绿道网维护计划，明确维护机构及责任人、维护操作程序指南和维护成本测算等内容，保障绿道网日常维护工作顺利推进。绿道网硬件系统以属地维护为基础，由地方绿道建设办公室牵头，相关行政主管部门按照各自职责配合，同时鼓励公众参与，共同做好日常维护工作。绿道网软件系统建立与维护宜由旅游行政主管部门牵头，相关行政主管部门按照各自职责配合，保障绿道网网络查询系统、宣传系统等软件设施的正常运作与使用。

### 5. 安全管理

绿道建成后，一方面要制定绿道使用指南，告知使用者安全使用绿道的信息和方式；另一方面要建立绿道设施定期安全检查与安全巡查制度，现有的安全制度和安全巡逻网络要尽量涵盖绿道使用区域，鼓励各类经济组织、社会团体、单位或个人参与绿道的治安巡逻。

**6. 监督检查机制**

为推动全省宜居城乡建设，2009年《广东省创建宜居城乡工作绩效考核办法（试行）》出台。绿道建设是宜居城乡工作的重要抓手，广东适时将绿道建设效果与领导政绩挂钩，并将其效果纳入各市创建宜居城乡工作绩效考核的指标体系，根据综合考评结果进行排名和奖惩。

## 七、小结

绿道网建设是广东落实科学发展观，建设生态文明和宜居城乡的创新之举。通过一年多的建设，珠三角区域绿道网络骨架基本建成，目前已正式开展城市绿道、社区绿道的建设工作。从策划到实施、从建设到维护，珠三角先行先试，初步探索出了一套中国绿道建设的新模式。总的来说，珠三角绿道建设具有以下特点：

**1. 把握绿道的核心要义：联系**

自始至终把绿道建设作为一项系统工程，将绿道生态功能与民生、环境、经济功能紧密联系起来。不将绿道看成孤立的建设项目，而是与农林、水利、园林、交通等项目相结合，叠加绿道使用功能，从而提高土地利用和资金使用效率。绿道管理与维护并未新设机构，各项职责在现有部门职能基础上就近延伸。

**2. “一把手”参与加强了项目推进**

珠三角绿道建设各地领导“一把手”亲抓，与绩效考核、执政能力和执政水平挂钩。这种具有中国特色的项目推进模式，为绿道建设建立了“绿色通道”，大大提高了项目推进速度。

**3. 统筹协调，上下联动，使绿道建设各具特色**

省的工作重点是目标分解、技术指导、跨界协调、监督检查、信息交流，地方政府负责具体建设事务，各显其能，积极实施，使各地绿道呈现不一样的精彩。

最后，需要引起我们重视的是：通过民众使用，绿道为生态廊道的保护增加了一道新的屏障，但也并非不可逾越。今后，珠三角将继续开展后续工作，如划定绿道控制区，推进基本生态控制线的立法等。不断完善的珠三角绿道建设模式是可复制、可推广的。目前，广东绿道建设正逐步由珠三角向全省延伸，并谋划与港、澳绿道的对接。浙江、山东等省正在借鉴广东经验开展绿道建设的前期工作。

（作者：蔡瀛，广东省住房和城乡建设厅副厅长；蔡云楠，广州市城市规划勘测设计研究院副院长，教授级高级规划师；方正兴，广州市城市规划勘测设计研究院规划专业副总工程师，高级规划师）

## 参考文献


[1] 广东省住房和城乡建设厅．绿道——广东宜居城乡建设的希望之路．2010－1

[2] 广东省住房和城乡建设厅．珠三角绿道网总体规划纲要．2010－3

[3] 广州市城市规划勘测设计研究院．珠三角绿道网管理与维护机制研究．2010－10

[4] 许学强，李郇．珠江三角洲城镇化研究三十年．人文地理，2009（1）

[5] 汪劲柏，赵民．论建构统一的国土及城乡空间管理框架．城市规划，2008（12）

[6] 王富海，谭维宁．更新观念，重构城市绿地系统规划体系．风景园林，2005（4）

# 新一轮武汉城市总体规划

## ——低碳发展研究

随着城市化和全球化的深入推进，气候变化已经成为中国城市发展不能回避的问题和中国城乡规划所面临的最新挑战，以"低碳"为导向的城市发展越来越受到广泛的关注和重视。在此背景下，武汉新一轮城市总体规划（2010—2020年）以其"低碳城市"的规划理念获得了2009年国际城市与区域规划师学会（ISOCARP）"全球杰出贡献奖"（见图1）。

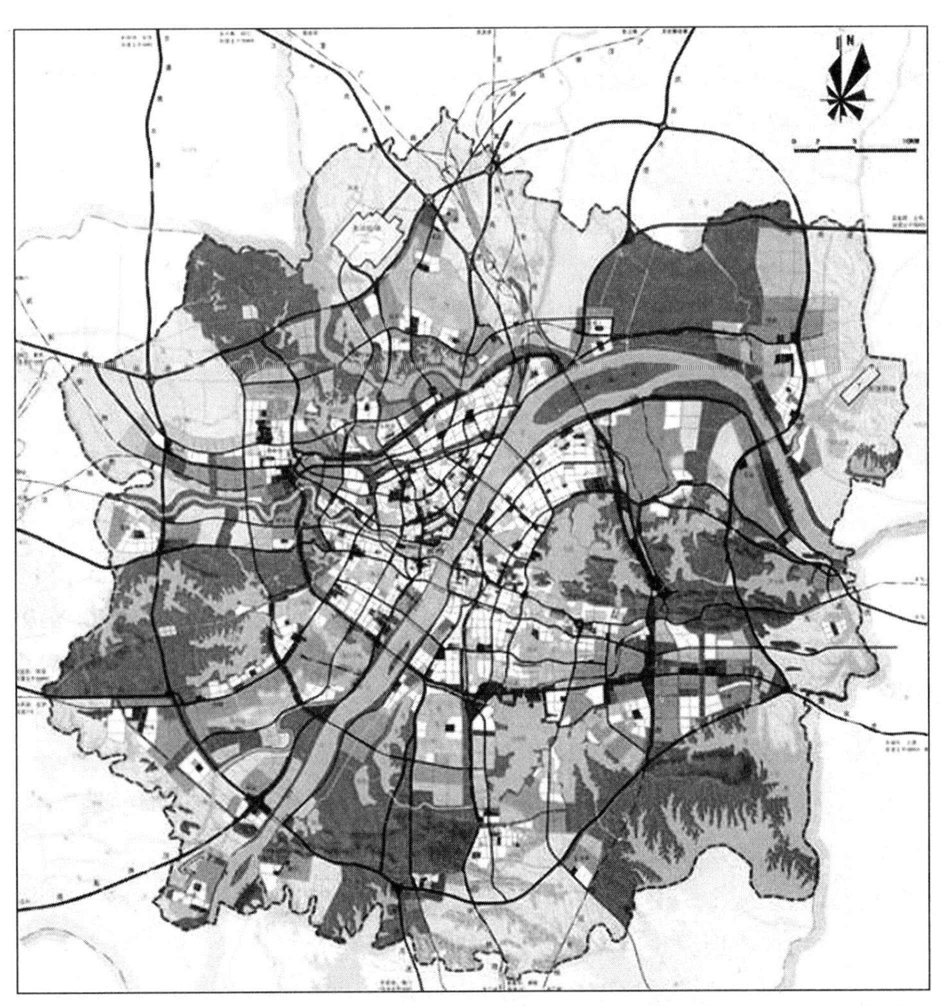

图1　武汉城市总体规划都市发展区规划图

本文从“低碳”角度对武汉的规划和实践做一个简要的介绍。

## 一、当前国内外低碳发展导向的规划探索

低碳概念是在应对全球气候变化、提倡减少人类生产生活活动中温室气体排放的背景下提出的。而在城市领域，低碳城市则是从生态城市概念逐步演变而来，并在实践中并行不悖。低碳城市的内涵，也随着最初的以减少碳排放为主的环境课题演变为现在包含社会、文化、经济、环境的综合课题，低碳城市已经成为综合低碳技术、低碳生产及消费方式和低碳城市运行方式的一个巨系统，最终放大到生态城市的整体层面。推行低碳城市建设有着深刻的时代背景和实践意义，正如英国卡迪夫大学于立教授所总结的，至少包括三个方面：一是通过创建生态城镇，减少碳排放，回归人与自然和谐发展的生活方式；二是各国通过生态城镇技术、理念和发展模式的探索，希望获得创新的领导地位，从而引领下一代可持续城镇的建设；三是在解决“全球暖化”问题的同时，解决本国和本地区所面临的主要问题。

从全球低碳城市建设的理论探索来看，规划和空间策略的作用得到日益突出的重视。1996年理查德・雷吉斯特（Richard Register）所领导的“城市生态”组织提出生态文明城市十项原则，第一条是“修改土地利用开发的优先权，优先开发紧凑的、多种多样的、绿色的、安全的、令人愉快的和有诱惑力的混合土地利用社区”。2009年，英国的Chris Gossop在第45届世界规划大会上提出“低碳城市七大关键要素声明”，其中第五项为“城市、区域和人类聚落系统的集成包容性规划，即将土地利用、交通、能源和废弃物规划整合到空间规划中”。

从实践层面来看，不同规模尺度的城市地区也都对适应气候变化的空间模式进行了积极的探索。例如，在大都市区的规划政策制定中，纽约《2030年城市规划战略》将未来20年城市发展所面临的挑战进行了不同的规划路径图示，提出了适应气候变化的专门战略内容。而新加坡、库里蒂巴、伦敦等城市也在规划的整体应对、公共交通的创新性发展以及维护具有地方特色的城市空间布局方面提出了前瞻性的战略。在中观尺度的城市区域发展中，蓬勃兴起的生态城成为低碳规划实践的亮点，这既有以英国“生态城镇（Eco-town）”为代表的生态新城建设模式，也有以法国“生态城市”为代表的现有城镇区扩展的发展模式，还有以丹麦凯隆堡（Kalundborg）和日本北九州为代表的生态产业园区模式。在微观的尺度上，低碳城市社区的建设则取得了更具有操作性的成果，如1980年竣工的丹麦Beder的太阳和风社区（Sun & wind community），2002年建成的英国伦敦南郊的贝丁顿社区（Beddington zero energy development，BZED），将众多节能减排的措施集中于一个小的生态社区中，切实有效地减少了二氧化碳的排放量。

无论何种模式和尺度，既说明了在全球气候变暖的形势下，城市规划和空间模式对于城市发展的长期、结构性作用，我们需要反思和改变工业革命以来近300年的传统的“高碳”城市空间模式，也证明了低碳规划作为低碳城市建设技术融合的集成作用。

中国“低碳城市”的建设方兴未艾，说明快速城市化过程中中国城市对环境约束已经

做出敏锐的反应，也预示了中国城市发展道路的理性转型。据统计，2008 年年底中国拥有 656 个城市，城镇人口超过 6 亿。每年还将有 1600 万人进入城市，每年城镇化率提高 1%，2025 年城市人口将超过 10 亿。中国城市排放的 $CO_2$ 占全国的近 90%，消耗能源占全国的 80%。所以，仇保兴博士提出了低碳城市发展之路——C 模式（Chinese model），建立高效、和谐、健康、可持续发展的人类聚居环境，建设低污染、低排放、低能耗、高效能、高效率、高效益的低碳生态城市。

在实践中，中国已经产生了多个不同的行动概念，包括：环境保护模范城市（1996—2006 年，国家环境保护总局）、全国生态示范市试点（国家环保局、部，1995 年至今）、循环经济试点城市（国家环保局、部，2002. 5、2007. 11）、国家生态园林城市试点城市（国家建设部，2002. 5、2007. 6）、"低碳发展示范城市"（国家建设部与世界自然基金会 WWF）等。列入这些行动的包括上海、广州、伊春、保定、深圳、佛山、武汉、重庆等 100 多个城市。最新的进展是以天津中新生态新城、深圳光明新区为代表的各类生态新城，在实践目标和体系上则表现出更前瞻性的追求和更广泛的探索性。

对比这些行动计划的纲要、标准和实施重点，可以看出，中国城市发展的转型过程日渐深入、目标日渐具体、导向日渐清晰。从国家环保部门倡导的生态示范市试点指标体系来看，生态城市实际是对一个城市总体发展模式提出了系统性的要求，体现了"社会——经济——自然复合生态系统"的理论模式（马世骏和王如松，1984）。从生态系统的构成角度分析，这一指标体系可以分解为生态景观格局、生态治理体系和生态协调系统等三大方面（见图 2）。其中，生态景观格局包括森林覆盖率、受保护地区占国土面积比例、城镇人均公共绿地面积 3 项指标。这说明，中国生态城市建设的基本模式是生态格局为基础、生态治理为核心，社会经济协调为保障。国家环保部门倡导的循环经济试点城市则涵盖了资源产出与

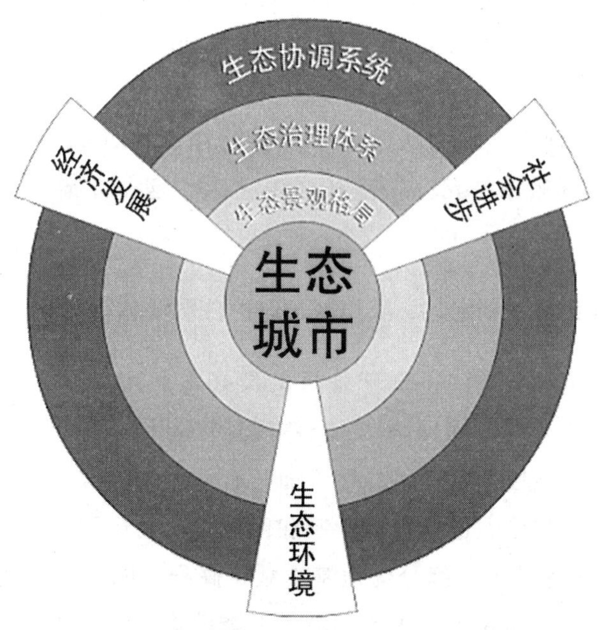


图 2　生态城市建设的基本模式

消耗、资源综合利用和废物排放等4大类、22项指标，反映了以“减量化，再利用，再循环”为原则的新经济发展要求，可以看做对生态城市建设的重要补充性标准。而“低碳城市”更侧重和聚焦在生态城市发展的碳减排方面，是生态城市建设的一个更具有操作性和指针性的目标。“低碳城市”实质上是中国探索城市发展新途径的一个最新最明确也最具体的目标导向，是在生态城市基础上的深化，“低碳城市”和生态城市无论是理论还是实践都是一脉相承的。

## 二、以生态格局为重心——武汉“低碳发展”的核心理念

武汉市是湖北省省会，位于中国中部，长江中游。全市面积达到8494平方公里，2009年市域常住人口达到910万人，城镇化超过了70%。武汉也是一个自然资源十分丰富、自然环境十分独特的城市，其水资源更是得天独厚，水域面积约2200平方公里，占全市面积接近四分之一；有长江、汉江两条大河，市区内现存湖泊27个，山体58座，形成了“一城江水半城山”的空间格局。武汉具备建设生态城市和“低碳城市”的优越条件。

2008年，国家批准武汉城市圈为全国建设“资源节约型和环境友好型”社会的试验区。作为武汉城市圈的核心城市，本轮《武汉市城市总体规划》将建设“低碳城市”作为重要导向，将构建符合“低碳城市”和生态城市要求的城市空间结构作为关键。

### 1. 运用“生态足迹”研究方法，确定和控制低碳城市发展规模

从建设低碳城市的角度确定人口规模，目前较适用的方法是运用“生态足迹”分析法。本轮武汉《总体规划》运用生态足迹分析法，对全市化石能源用地、耕地、牧草地、林地、建筑用地、水域6大类进行核算。2003年全市人均生态足迹为2.3980$hm^2$/人，引入消费调整系数后，武汉市的消费型生态足迹为人均0.9311$hm^2$，可利用的人均生态承载力为0.3076，生态赤字为人均0.6235$hm^2$。

《总体规划》按照目前生态压力缓解25%测算，建议到2020年武汉市总人口应控制在1200万人以内，规划实际采用的人口规模为1180万人。这一方案是所有5个人口专项研究中控制得最为严格的。

### 2. 基于生态敏感性评价，划定禁、限建区，保护自然资源

按照要求，生态城镇绿化空间不低于总面积的40%，且其中至少有50%是公共的、管理良好的、高质量的绿色开放空间网络。《总体规划》运用了地理信息系统（GIS）技术在定量评价、精确性、时效性以及管理信息化方面具有强大的优势，对全市生态要素的敏感性进行分析，以划定禁、限建区，进行分区管制和保护，从而达到尽量减少碳排量的目的。

《总体规划》将生态评价因子细分为地基承载、高程、园地、林地、水资源分布、湿地分布、水体敏感性、地震地质灾害、土壤环境、土壤敏感性、水土流失和耕地、矿产资源及坡度、距离和可达性等17个因子，根据权重，将各生态评价因子进行叠加，分析生态敏

感性。

根据评价结论，武汉市生态不敏感区占 8.5%、较敏感区占 27.4%、中敏感区占 44.9%、重敏感区占 19.2%。其中，北部地区、中部东西方向以及南部湖泊水网及滩涂湿地等地区生物多样性极为丰富，是生态功能极强的重度敏感区。《总体规划》依据上述结果，将武汉市域划分为禁止建设区、限制建设区、适宜建设区、已建区等四类用地。

其中，禁止建设区、限制建设区等生态控制用地总量占市域面积达到83%，有效地保护了市域生态资源，从而对减少碳排量发挥了重要作用。

**3. 快速交通走廊引导城镇轴向拓展，构建低碳交通生活方式**

据统计，过去10年间，地球二氧化碳排放量增长了13%，其中交通工具的碳排放量增长高达25%。所以，降低城市碳排放，首先要解决交通带来的排放，而解决交通问题的根本是构建科学合理的城镇空间结构，尽量减少交通出行。

武汉是一个特大中心城市，而且正处于加速拓展阶段。同时城市周边地区湖泊、山体、绿化密布。本轮《总体规划》改变武汉传统的“圈层”式空间发展模式，根据 TOD 模式（Transit-Oriented Development，以公共交通为导向的开发），在武汉都市区内组织了由 18 条高（快）速路、13 条骨架性主干路、7 条轨道交通线组成的“双快一轨”的复合交通走廊，引导城镇空间由主城区向外沿阳逻、豹澥、纸坊、常福、汉江、盘龙等方向轴向拓展，形成东部、东南、南部、西南、西部和北部等 6 个职住相对平衡、具有一定独立性的新城组群。

在“双快一轨”的复合交通走廊中，高（快）速路提供长距离、点到点的快速交通服务，骨架性主干路提供中长距离、面到面的交通服务。这种以 TOD 模式主导的“圈层 + 轴向”的生态化、开放性、集约型城镇空间拓展格局，既减少居民日常的通勤出行和钟摆式的交通生成，又易于在主城与组群、组群之间组织聚合型公共走廊，同时在组群内部也能保证居住组团与产业组团之间通过步行、骑车、公交等便捷联系，有利于整个城市的低碳、高效运营。

**4. 采用 CFD 模拟城市风道，构筑利于自然循环的低碳城市空间框架**

武汉是中国“四大火炉”之一，中心城区人口密度偏高，局部地段超过了 10 万人/平方公里，热岛效应非常突出。2003 年夏曾创下持续 18 天最高气温≥35℃，整个夏季≥35℃日数达 33 天的记录。夏季超常时间的空调降温，也导致了大量的生活碳排放。所以，如何利用自然循环破解热岛效应，将是武汉建设“低碳城市”的重点考虑问题。

《总体规划》运用计算流体力学（CFD）技术构建数字模型，从武汉市的冬、夏主导风向分析发现，在穿越城市的长江和汉水区域，温度明显低于其他区域，而且风速较大，所以长江、汉水可以作为天然的通风道，对其周边热环境进行调节。在城市周边区域，由于受到湖泊的影响，其周围温度相对较低，空气流动顺畅，有利于改善空气质量，能有效地改变周围的热环境。因此，可考虑将长江、汉水、周边湖泊与城市中的公园、绿地、广场等连接起来，形成生态通道，增大城市中的通风，达到降低城市温度的目的。

基于以上分析，《总体规划》组织 6 个大型风景区、5 个国家级和省级湿地自然保护区、

6个城市森林公园、7大郊野公园以及系列湖泊水域、山体绿地、生态农田等生态要素，沿道观河—大东湖、木兰山—武湖、府河、长河—后官湖、鲁湖—青菱湖、梁子湖—汤逊湖方向，构建了大东湖、武湖、府河、后官湖、青菱湖、汤逊湖等6片放射状生态绿楔，形成贯通城市内外、延伸到主城内部的多向生态廊道、城市风道和冷桥。同时，规划还保护和利用府河、倒水、举水、滠水、通顺河、金水、沙河等水系，形成黄陂—新洲片、汉口—东西湖片、汉阳—蔡甸片、武昌—江夏片4大连通水系，并与长江、汉江有机联系，形成覆盖全市的水系网络（见图3、图4）。由此，《总体规划》构筑起符合自然系统需求的低碳城市生态保护框架。

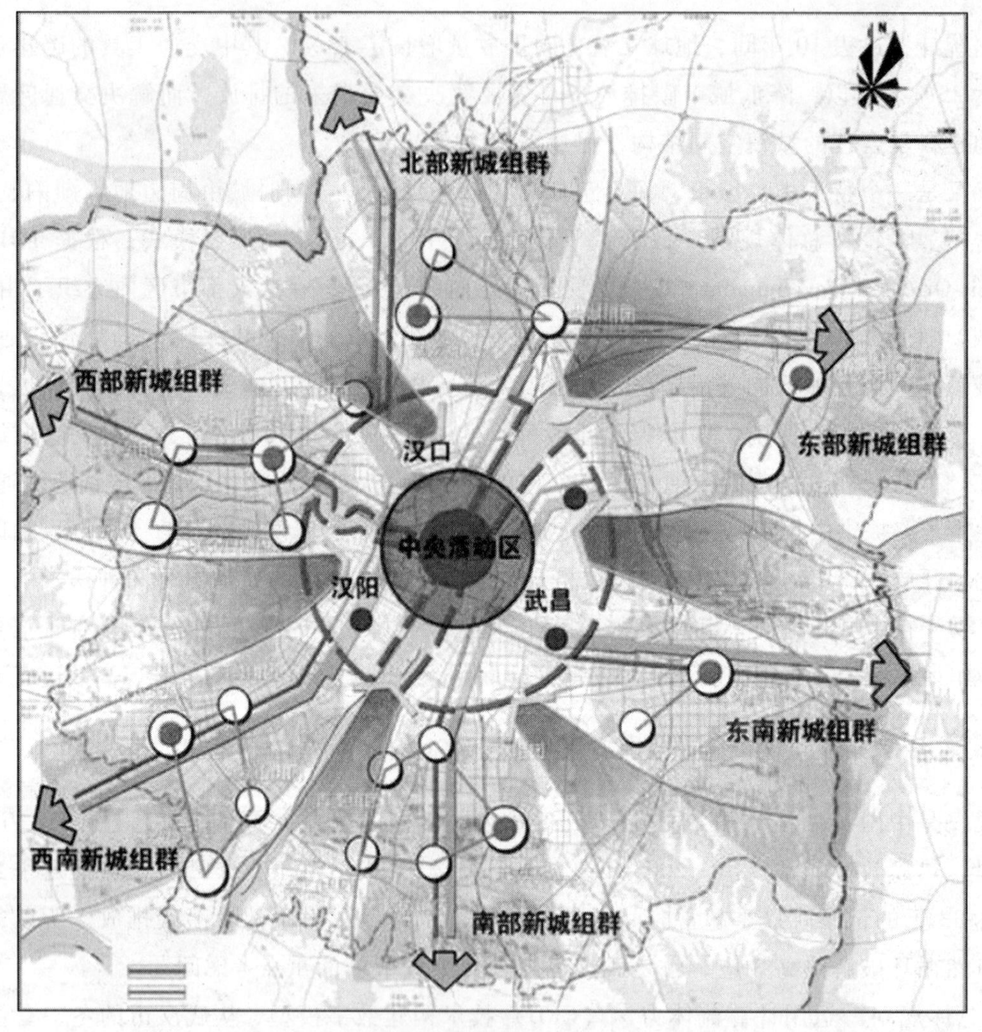


图3　都市发展区规划结构图

国际城市与区域规划师学会给予本轮规划的评价是，从低碳角度对城市规划进行了探索，利用先进的科技手段，通过建立绿色基础设施和交通之间的联系，对微气候学这个既是地方的又是全球的可持续发展问题，从城市规划和设计角度进行解剖，并提出了以可持续发展为目标的战略政策，符合人类聚居形态发展的先进理念。

图 4　都市发展区生态框架规划图

## 三、武汉"低碳城市"建设的最近进展

根据《总体规划》，近年来武汉在低碳城市建设和实践方面取得了一些积极的进展。其重点是围绕生态景观格局的形成和城市发展模式的转变，在城市规划层面落实总体规划的构想。

### 1. 界定了全市生态自然资源，构建了市域生态框架

根据市域生态框架，开展了武汉市生态框架保护规划、武汉市非建设区用地规划、武汉市绿地系统规划、东湖风景区总体规划等规划，保护和促进了武汉各项生态景观要素的彰显和利用。

通过绿楔控制，城市热岛效应得到缓解，武汉城区夏季极端高温天气明显减少，较相同纬度大中城市，夏季平均最高气温排第 6 位，已基本摘掉"火炉"的帽子。

#### 2. 保护和利用滨水环境资源，保障生态空间的开放性

为了保障生态环境资源的公共性、共享性，开展了武汉滨水地区的生态环境改造，扩大了市民亲水、休闲空间，极大地缓解了主城绿化开敞空间缺乏的矛盾，提升了城市宜居环境。武汉滨江公园长度已达26.2公里，面积超过300万平方米，成为我国最大的江滩公园群。

#### 3. 连通全市江河湖泊，构建市域四大水系网络

武汉市水资源丰富，拥有全国人均40倍的水资源量，水域占全市面积的25%。规划串连市域主要湖泊，形成黄陂—新洲片、汉口—东西湖片、汉阳—蔡甸片、武昌—江夏片等4大连通水系，并与长江、汉江有机联系，形成覆盖全市的水系网络。

#### 4. 实施系列水体连通工程，全面开展水功能优化

围绕武汉“水网城市”建设，优化水功能区划，保护武汉的生态环境，保障水系安全，开展了东湖风景区保护规划、汉阳“六湖连通”工程、武昌“大东湖”生态水网构建等水环境工程，开展污染控制、生态修复、水网建设。

#### 5. 严格控制主城建设强度，大力发展外围新城

适当控制主城建设密度，大力推动外围新城建设，改善新城生态环境、增加新城就业、建立快捷的内外交通，引导中心区人口和产业向外围新城疏解，降低中心区热岛效应，整体改善城市的人居环境。

#### 6. 加强轨道交通建设，倡导低碳交通生活模式

在武汉城市圈，建设武汉至黄冈、黄石、仙桃、咸宁、孝感5条高效的城际铁路，总长430公里，率先建立区域铁路公交网络。

实施公交优先，建成轨道交通3条线路，开工建设5条轨道线路，建设引导城市向新城疏散的快速交通走廊，倡导低碳交通模式。

## 四、小结

从武汉的经验来看，建设低碳城市需要在多个方面和各个层次上的突破，包括低碳城市技术的运用、城市生活方式的转变、清洁生产和低碳经济发展、高效的城市管理等等。但从城市规划视角来看，需要将形成合理的城市空间布局作为首要的基础。“规划低碳是最大的低碳”，但这既是一个长期坚持的过程，也需要很长时期的实施才能看到效果。

（作者：张文彤，武汉市国土资源和规划局局长；胡忆东，武汉市规划编制研究和展示中心主任）

# “中国近代第一城”南通的保护与发展

## 一、引言

历史文化名城是指“保存文物特别丰富并且具有重大历史价值或者革命纪念意义的城市”。我国历史文化名城数量丰富，现有国家历史文化名城110座，此外，还有各省省级历史文化名城。历史文化名城的评定和管理是我国保护历史文化的重要举措，国家通过评定历史文化名城肯定城市的历史文化价值，并通过历史文化名城保护的相关法律和规范对历史文化的保护进行严格管理。历史文化名城也日益成为城市的重要名片，成为城市保护和利用历史遗存、彰显城市个性和特色的重要手段。

南通地处美丽富饶的长江三角洲，滨江临海，江湾沃野，民丰物阜，素有崇川福地之美誉。一百多年前，清末状元张謇在南通兴实业、办教育，创造性地开展城市建设，领时代潮流，开风气之先，影响及于全国、绵延至今。南通从20世纪90年代初开始历史文化特色的挖掘和历史文化名城的申报工作，2007年6月江苏省人民政府公布南通为江苏省历史文化名城，2009年1月国务院批复同意将江苏省南通市列为国家历史文化名城。南通旋即全面开展历史文化名城的保护和利用工作。本文以南通为例，对历史文化名城的保护和发展工作进行探讨。

## 二、南通历史文化特色的挖掘

研究历史文化名城的个性特点是保护历史文化名城的基本要求。南通历史文化名城的保护工作从挖掘城市历史文化特色开始。2002年，吴良镛先生经深入调研，反复比较，小心求证，提出南通是“中国近代第一城”的论断。清华大学进行《中国近代第一城》研究，全面系统地阐述了南通“中国近代第一城”的历史渊源、理论基础和史学价值。中国历史文化保护研究中心研究编制《南通市历史文化名城保护规划》，系统研究南通的历史文化价值。通过国内顶尖专家的寻访、研究和论证，南通市挖掘和梳理了历史文化遗存，提炼和界定了历史文化特色。随着国家级历史文化名城的批复，南通的历史文化特色得到了最为权威的认定。

### 1. 南通的历史文化特色和历史文化遗存

南通历史文化特色的确定和历史文化遗存的界定成为南通历史文化保护工作得以开展的基础。

(1) 南通的历史文化特色

《南通历史文化名城保护规划》对南通的历史文化特色进行了明确的界定:

近代“模范”之城——南通在近代的城市建设和发展堪称“中国近代民族第一城”。

古代“典型”之城——南通的形制是中国古代府州县城市的典型。

江海门户之城——南通在中国的航运交通和对外交流史上具有重要地位。

灵山秀水之城——南通“山水相依”、“城河相拥”的格局形成独特山水城市景观。

人文淳厚之城——南通的文人气质、士绅情节构成城市独特的历史人文内涵。

(2) 南通的历史文化遗存

南通的历史文化遗存分为历史文化中物质和非物质两个部分。

物质性的历史文化遗存包括三个层次:一是历史城区,南通历史城区的主要遗存为“一城三镇”格局和主城区“一城两貌”特征;二是历史文化街区,南通遗存濠南、西南营、寺街和唐闸四个历史文化街区;三是文物保护单位,南通遗存各级文物保护单位51处(其中全国重点文物保护单位4处,省级重点文物保护单位12处)。

非物质历史文化遗存方面,南通板鹞风筝制作技艺、蓝印花布印染技艺、沈绣、梅庵古琴、南通童子戏、陆家锣鼓等独特非物质文化遗产全国鲜见。其中板鹞风筝制作技艺和蓝印花布印染技艺还被列入第一批国家级非物质文化保护名录。

### 2. 南通“中国近代第一城”地位的确立

南通的历史文化特色中,尤以“中国近代第一城”最具个性。纵观我国现有的110座国家历史文化名城,除南通以外,基本都是具有突出历史传统、革命纪念意义的城市,尚无以近代历史文化为特色的城市。

2002年,吴良镛先生指出:“南通是中国早期现代化的产物,它不同于租界、商埠或列强占领下发展起来的城市,是中国人基于中国理念,比较自觉的、有一定创造性的、通过较为全面地规划、建设、经营的第一个有代表性的城市。”近代南通的独特地位为南通留下了丰富的近代文化遗存。

(1)“一城三镇”的近代城市格局

清末民初,著名爱国实业家张謇在南通兴办实业的同时,开辟了新工业区和港区,在城内辟商场,办学校,建博物馆,修道路,使城市形态和布局发生了很大的变化,形成了以老城区为政治、金融、商业、文化中心,唐闸工业区、天生港港口区和狼山风景区环绕的“一城三镇”新格局。

(2) 近代工业遗存完整的唐闸历史文化街区

近代唐闸是南通工业的主要承载地区和近代南通的主要发祥地,形成了一条以纱厂为中心的产业链条，包括原料运输、仓储、产品综合利用、设备支持、教育培训和社会支撑等。现存的唐闸工业历史街区包括河东和河西两部分，占地面积为28.1公顷。街区内分布有全国重点文物保护单位1处，市级文物保护单位3处，优秀历史建筑9处（见图1）。其中有用于工业生产的大生纱厂、广生榨油股份有限公司、大生纱厂仓库等，用于生产配套的大储堆栈、大达内河轮船公司旧址、泽生外港水利公司等，以及服务于工业生产生活配套的唐闸红楼、南通纺织专门学校旧址、老公房、西公房、北公房、牙科诊所、三新浴池等。唐闸不仅包括工业生产的历史文化风貌特征，还包括生产配套和社会生活配套的历史文化风貌特征，是保存有较为完整的工业历史文化风貌特征的具有典型意义的工业历史街区。

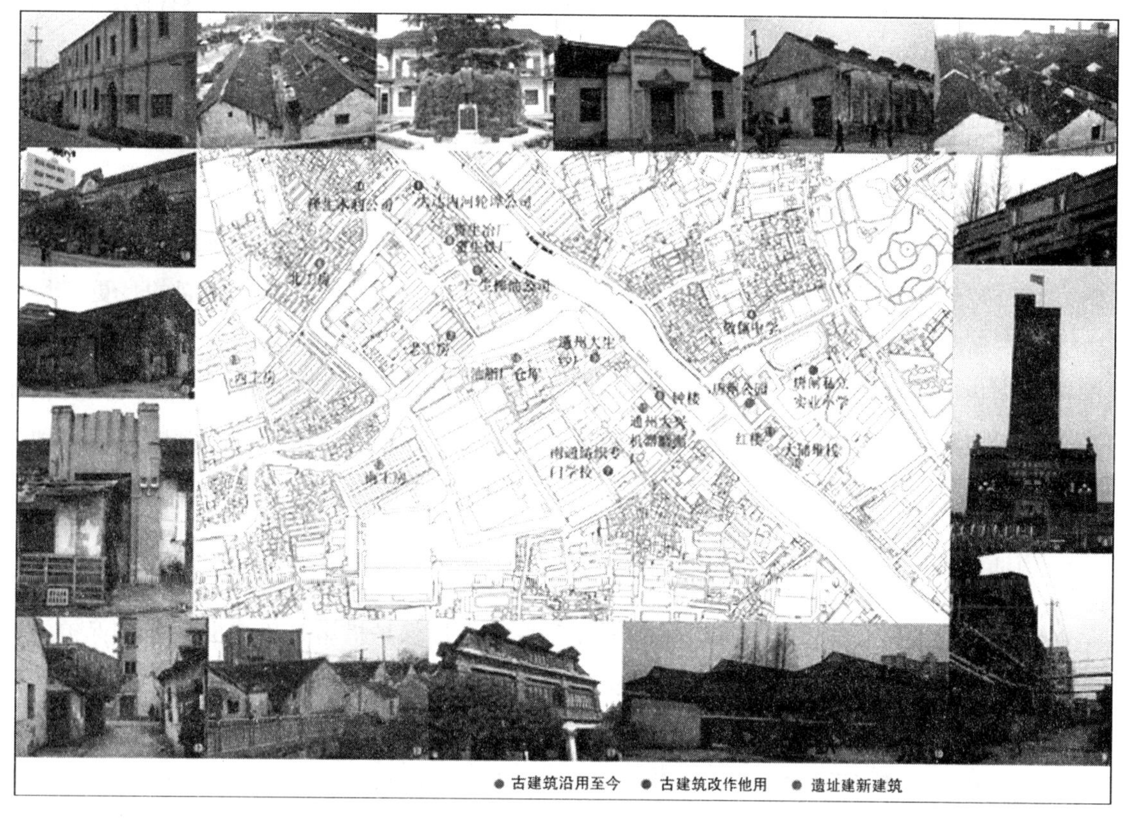


图1 唐闸历史文化街区主要历史建筑、历史遗迹分布图

（3）具有南通特色的近代建筑

张謇在拓展近代南通城市框架的同时，对城市旧城进行了合理扩建，在主城区南门外与桃坞路建设公共行政设施和商业金融、娱乐休闲、餐饮旅馆等服务业，在濠河畔兴建学校、博物苑、图书馆等文教事业。在城市建设中，南通培养出自己的建筑师，以孙之厦为突出代表，创造了中西合璧、洋为中用的具有南通特色的近代建筑风格，在各类建筑特别是公共建筑中进行了具体的实践，为南通留下了宝贵的近代建筑遗存（见图2、图3）。

图2　南通近代建筑——钟楼

图3　南通近代建筑——南通博物苑

## 三、南通历史文化名城的保护利用

温家宝总理讲过："在城市现代化建设中，必须高度重视和切实保护好自然遗产和文化遗产。城市现代化建设与城市历史文化传统的继承和保护之间，不是相互割裂的，更不是相互对立的，而是有机关联、相得益彰的。继承和保护城市的自然遗产和文化遗产，本身就是城市现代化建设的重要内容，也是城市现代文明进步的重要标志。"南通的历史文化名城保护，立足于当地的历史文化特色，致力于整体的历史格局保护，着眼于可持续的积极主动保护，进行了积极的探索。

### 1. 南通历史文化名城的整体性保护

在保护历史文化名城中，从城市整体角度采取综合性保护措施是历史文化名城保护的特点和要旨。只有从全局角度寻求正确处理保护与发展关系的途径，才可以既满足城市发展建设的要求，又为保护文物古迹、历史文化街区创造条件。

(1) 合理的城市发展战略

从城市整体角度采取综合性保护措施，首先要确定合理的城市发展战略。南通已完成新一轮城市总体规划的修编工作。在新一轮城市总体规划中，南通紧扣历史文化名城的城市特色，制定了一系列的城市发展战略，为南通历史文化名城的整体保护提供了基础。

城市总体规划提出"国际港口城市、区域经济中心、历史文化名城、宜居创业城市"的城市发展目标，确定"我国东部沿海江海交汇的现代化国际港口城市，上海北翼的经济中心和门户城市，国内一流的宜居创业城市，历史与现代交相辉映的文化名城"的城市性质，从城市发展战略的角度确定了历史文化名城保护工作的地位。提出历史文化名城保护要"继承和发展以南通市'中国近代第一城'为代表的地方文化遗产，努力提高科技创新和文化创新能力，成为历史与现代交相辉映的历史文化名城"，明确了历史文化名城保护工作的重点。同时，城市总体规划明确南通的城市形态为带状加组团城市，城市发展方向为"南通主城区和通州城区相向发展，主城区主要发展东、南方向，整合西、北方向，通州城区主要发展南、西方向，整合东、北方向"，将引导城市向新城区有效疏导功能，为历史文化名城的保护从空间上提供了有效保障。

（2）"一城三镇"格局的整体性保护

在近代南通独具特色的"一城三镇"城市格局中，工业区建设在城市西郊唐闸、港口区定在长江边的天生港、城市南郊狼山作为花园私宅及风景区，三者以老城为核心，与老城相距各约6公里，并建有道路相通，各城镇相对独立，减少污染，各自可以合理发展，又分工明确，功能互补。这种一城多镇、分片布局的模式极有创意，可以和英国著名的规划师霍华德于1898年创立的、曾对西方现代城市规划产生革命影响的花园城市理论相媲美，甚至早于这一理论的提出。在城市规划和建设史上留下了浓墨重彩的一笔，甚至在今天对于城市发展结构仍具有借鉴意义。"一城三镇"的近代城市格局构成了南通"中国近代第一城"最具特色和最具代表性的城市空间，应从整体上予以保护。

基于这一认识，南通的历史文化名城保护首先确定了"一城三镇"格局整体保护的基本思路，构建了一城（主城区）、三片（唐闸片区、天生港片区、狼山片区）的保护框架。主城区划定了寺街历史文化街区、西南营历史文化街区和濠南历史文化街区作为核心保护区域，重点保护南通主城区"中轴对称"、"城河相拥"的格局，切实有效地保护主城区中的寺街、西南营、濠南三个历史文化街区，以及大量的文物保护单位、历史建筑和历史环境要素；加强对主城区内其他区域的城市建设控制，调整城市功能，提升城市环境品质，体现城市的文化内涵。唐闸片区划定以南通近代产业遗产为主要特色的唐闸历史文化街区，规划重点保护唐闸近代产业城镇的格局，切实有效地保护唐闸历史文化街区，加强对文物保护单位和历史建（构）筑物的保护和合理再利用，加强对其他区域的城市建设控制。天生港片区划定天生港历史地段，规划重点保护历史街道、历史建筑等元素，加强对历史建（构）筑物的保护和合理再利用。狼山片区保护狼山片区的历史文化遗产和山水格局，并划定新港镇历史地段，规划重点保护历史街道、历史建筑等元素，加强对历史建（构）筑物的保护和合理再利用。一城和三片之间通过历史文化轴线和自然景观轴线联系，并塑造若干视线通廊（见图4）。

**2. 南通历史文化名城的可持续保护**

历史文化名城保护的关键是有机更新，增加城市活力。保护与发展二者的关系，保护不是目的，发展才是目的，保护是为了更好的发展。基于这一认识，南通的历史文化名城保护从保护规划编制伊始，就确定了可持续保护的思路。在保护工作具体开展后，提出将历史文化保护和历史文化产业发展相结合的工作方向。立足于南通历史文化特色，经过多轮踏访，以及多方咨询和研讨，对历史文化遗存的保护和利用进行主题策划，根据保护历史文化遗存、彰显历史文化特色和适应市场发展需求的要素，在"一城三镇"的基本框架下，确定各历史文化街区的保护利用主题，为南通历史文化名城的可持续保护明确方向。

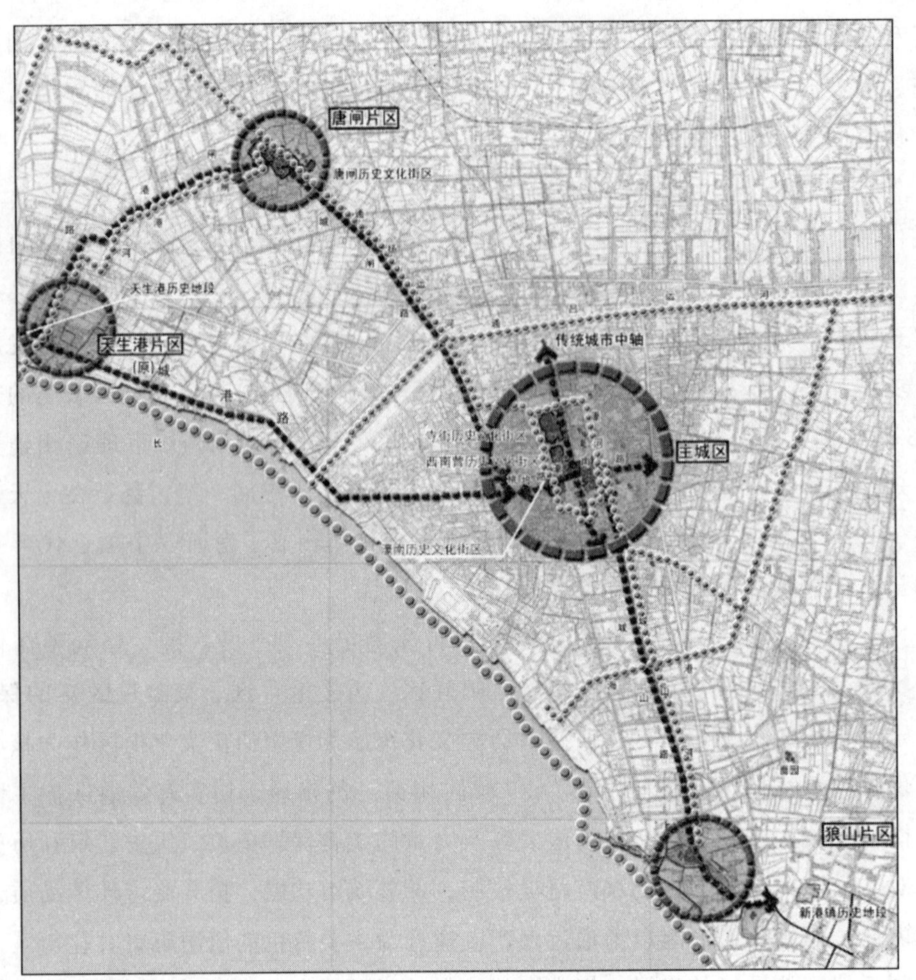


图4　南通历史文化名城保护框架图

(1) 围绕老城文化特色，依托寺街、西南营历史文化街区，发展“寺街·名人文化区”

依托“一城三镇”框架中的“一城”，策划“寺街·名人文化区”。该区包括寺街、西南营历史文化街区及周边用地，总面积约29公顷。区内保存着以国家重点文保单位天宁寺为中心的建筑群，以及从宋元明清直至21世纪的民居建筑，承载了南通古城千年的历史积淀。其中，被列为全国重点文保单位的有1处，江苏省文保单位的有2处，南通市文保单位的有5处，被列为优秀历史建筑的有16处。同时该区域人杰地灵，拥有许多历史文化名人和革命先烈，蕴含深厚的人文底蕴。

策划“寺街·名人文化区”以“名寺、民俗，名人、民居”为主题，以增强生命力，创造生产力为出发点，通过发挥寺街、西南营历史文化街区的历史文化资源优势，挖掘南通历史文脉，开展寺院文化、民俗文化、名人名宅调研、挖掘、梳理的工作。以建筑为载体，采用积极保护、有机更新的方法，保护历史遗存，优化环境品质，改善空间品质，保留城市街巷格局及建筑肌理，强化古城特色。依托名人名宅、千年古刹，打造民俗博览与寺院文化相互交融的文化产业聚集区和旅游休闲生活街区，做到放大优点、突出重点、形成卖点，以吸引游客，使寺街、西南营历史文化街区焕发新的生机，成为南通的城市名片。

(2) 围绕近代工业特色，依托唐闸历史文化街区，发展"南通·1895"

依托"一城三镇"框架中的唐闸镇，策划"南通·1895"。该区位于唐闸老镇，以唐闸河西、河东历史文化街区为主体，同时向东扩展包含唐闸公园及周边用地，向西扩展包含造纸厂、油脂厂、大生纱厂及周边用地，总面积约73公顷。区内现存全国重点文物保护单位1处，南通市文物保护单位2处，优秀历史建筑10处。该区域为南通近代工业的发祥地，也是近代工业遗存最为集中和完整的区域。

策划"南通·1895"以唐闸工业遗迹遗址为载体，新型第三产业发展为主导，将申报世界工业遗产与保护改造利用结合起来，形成集近代工商业发展展示、生态工业展示、非物质文化遗产传承、创意产业、休闲娱乐为一体的综合性片区。彰显南通作为中国近代第一城文化底蕴与近代工业重镇的辉煌历史，同时通过保护、改造和建设，改变唐闸老镇风貌，改善民生，促进社会协调发展。

(3) 围绕近代港口特色，依托天生港历史风貌区，发展"天生·古港风情"

依托"一城三镇"框架中的天生港镇，策划"天生·古港风情"。该区包括"城市绿谷"、天生港泽生街及长江堤岸一线。该区域保留有大量反映南通近代港口码头繁荣景象和近代通埠、水利方面成就的历史遗存。

策划"天生·古港风情"，重现古港当年的繁荣景象，全面反映天生港作为南通第一港的历史文化与风貌，充分展示南通滨江生态城市的风采和近代第一城的风姿及其历史文化内涵，打造以滨江古港、古镇历史文化及生态为主题的国家级4A景区，成为南通旅游新亮点。

此外，"一城三镇"中的狼山镇位于狼山省级风景名胜区，其景观和休闲功能一直以风景名胜区的形式得到保护和发展。通过主题策划，南通在保证"一城三镇"框架完整性的基础上，将凸显历史特色、保留文化要素与适应市场需求二者较为协调地结合起来，为可持续的保护和利用创造了必要的条件。

### 3. 南通历史文化名城的有序性保护

历史文化保护的有序实施和高效管理是历史文化保护规划得以实现的重要保障，也是历史文化名城工作面临的重要课题。众多历史文化名城结合自身实际情况，都进行了积极的探索。南通的历史文化保护，按照政府主导，整体推进，统一规划，分期实施的思路推进，致力于实现有序性的保护。

(1) 政府主导，整体推进

2009年4月，南通成立了历史文化保护项目建设工程指挥部。由分管市长任指挥部总指挥，分管秘书长以及区政府与相关部门的主要负责人任副总指挥。指挥部下设指挥部办公室、工程管理办公室、动迁安置办公室和督察办公室。指挥部办公室主要负责历史文化保护项目的综合协调、方案策划、政策研究、宣传推介、行政事务和日常管理工作。工程管理办公室具体负责历史文化保护项目工程的建设管理，根据项目建设需要，工程管理办公室内设"寺街·名人文化区"、"南通·1895"、"天生·古港风情"等若干个项目组，对各项目进行全面推进。动迁安置办公室具体负责项目用地范围内动迁调查摸底、产权认定工作，研究制定动迁安置办法，指导推进资产清理、产权置换、拆迁安置等工作。

历史文化保护项目由政府主导，在指挥部的统一领导下，由市国有公司与相关单位组建的机构作为历史文化保护建设项目的实施主体，进行保护性开发利用，并承担项目运营。

（2）统一规划，分期实施

前期对历史文化名城保护、各历史文化街区保护以及“一城三镇”保护框架和各历史文化保护项目进行整体规划和策划。在具体实施中，按照分期实施的工作方法，首先确定各区的启动片区和启动项目。通过近期项目的实施，有利于降低实施的难度，集中力量完成局部地区的保护和更新，初步形成“一城三镇”的历史文化保护完整框架，发挥历史文化保护的示范效应。同时，在分期实施过程中可根据具体情况及时进行有效的反馈，有利于历史文化保护的整体工作的顺利推进。

## 四、小结

历史是城市的根，文化是城市的魂。历史文化名城的保护和发展需要以科学发展观为指导，根据科学原理，结合具体情况，科学规划，科学实施。南通对历史文化名城的保护和发展进行了积极的探索，挖掘以“中国近代第一城”为核心的城市历史文化特色，构建“一城三镇”的城市历史文化整体保护和发展框架，以科学策划启动城市历史文化可持续保护和发展，并通过政府主导、整体推进、统一规划、分期实施保障历史文化保护和发展的推进，对历史文化名城保护的基本原理进行了具体的实践和应用。虽然，南通的历史文化名城保护和发展的探索还要通过实践的结果来进行检验，但是，可以预期，立足对城市历史文化的科学认识，把握城市历史文化的个性特色，确立城市历史文化保护和发展的科学思路，城市历史文化的保护和发展必将成为历史文化名城经济和社会发展的战略动力。

（作者：吴骏莲，南通市规划局总师室副主任）

### 参考文献

［1］王景慧．城市历史文化遗产保护的政策与规划［J］．城市规划，2004，（10）

［2］王景慧，阮仪三，王林．历史文化名城保护理论与规划［M］．同济大学出版社，1999

［3］吴良镛．张謇与“中国近代第一城”［M］．北京：中国建筑工业出版社

［4］汪光焘．历史文化名城的保护与发展［J］．建筑学报，2005，（2）

［5］清华大学城市规划设计研究院．中国近代第一城研究［Z］．2004

［6］上海同济城市规划设计研究院．南通历史文化名城保护规划［Z］．2008

［7］江苏省城市规划设计研究院．南通市城市总体规划［Z］．2010

# 北川县石椅村低碳生态村落示范案例

在汶川大地震发生一年多之际，2009 年 9 月，清华大学建筑节能研究中心在中国国际经济技术交流中心和中国城市规划设计研究院的领导和组织下，开始负责实施可持续民生下的灾区低碳生态村落示范项目。

该项目针对当时灾后恢复重建工作已经全面开展、灾区的工作重点已从应急处置阶段进入重建和生计恢复阶段的基本情况，在世界范围内高度重视气候变化的大背景下，确立了建设低碳生态示范村的思路。基本原则是从可持续民生的思路出发，按照与北川县总体规划相结合的原则，在尊重群众意愿的基础上，体现生态性和可持续发展的理念。针对村落所处的特殊地理位置、环境特征和功能定位，正确处理经济发展同人口、资源、环境的关系，合理确定石椅村产业结构和发展规模，坚持污染防治与生态环境保护并重、生态环境保护与经济发展并举的方法，实现整个村落的协调可持续发展，为政府大规模的重建和后续开发工作发挥示范作用。

本项目在进行前期充分调研，并认真考虑当地的自然资源特点和现有工作条件的基础上，最终选取北川羌族自治县曲山镇石椅村作为示范地。该村位于曲山镇南部，位于县城东大门，紧临安北公路。石椅村距北川老县城 3.5 公里，距新县城址约 10 余公里，距绵阳市 60 公里，距省会成都市 150 公里，因其有一块形状像一把巨型石椅的石头而得名。该村现有 91 户，总人口 328 人，95% 以上都是羌族。全村总辖区面积 0.61 万亩，现有耕地面积 215 亩，人均耕地 0.56 亩。从 1988 年开始，该村实施了水果优化工程。石椅村以盛产早、中、晚熟的绿色无公害李子、枇杷、梨等水果而闻名，枇杷、李子等水果的种植面积达到 1000 亩，成为“中国的李子之乡”，并通过了省无公害水果生产示范基地的认证。

## 一、主要示范内容

一是在曲山镇石椅村开展沼气、生物质燃料等能源综合利用技术与民居重建相结合的示范建设，改变当地生活方式，改善当地人居室内外环境，探索创建节能低碳示范村，主要活动包括：

（1）开展沼气、生物质燃料利用技术与民居重建相结合措施的国内外调研分析；

（2）通过分析研究所掌握的沼气、生物质燃料利用技术与民居重建相结合的信息，结

图1 示范点地理位置

合示范点建设经验，提出创建和推广节能低碳示范村的政策和建议；

(3) 提出改善农村居民室内外居住环境的技术方案；

(4) 指导当地居民进行实际工程建设。

二是组织开展节能低碳技术等培训，提升石椅村的整体旅游接待服务水平，提高当地居民的收入，推广节能低碳示范村建设经验，主要活动包括：

(1) 进一步提升石椅村的整体旅游接待水平，通过全村的环境改善吸引更多的游客前来观光旅游，把发展旅游业、拓展旅游产业链条作为切入点，以此带动整个村的经济发展；

(2) 对示范地群众进行低碳节能示范与技术专题培训，推广节能低碳示范村建设经验。

三是总结本项目的成果和经验，为制定地震灾区节能低碳与民居建设相结合方案提供建议，主要活动包括：

(1) 评估总结地震灾区节能低碳与民居建设相结合的技术措施；

(2) 通过公众参与、媒体、研讨会对试点项目进行宣传，以便宣传、推广成功经验。

## 二、示范项目实施情况

### 1. 对示范对象开展深入调研

(1) 村庄整体情况

本项目在实施之前，对全村农户进行了普查，结果发现全村的经济发展水平参差不齐，全年户平均收入为 24441 元，人年均收入为 6781 元。收入最多的村民年收入 10 万元，收入最少的村民年收入 2000 元，相差达 50 倍，有 22% 的村民年收入低于 1 万元。由于在教育、医疗、住宅维护等方面花费比较大，所以，扣除花费后的实际剩余收入很少，23% 的农户家庭入不敷出。

从建筑形式来说，该村二层楼房最多，这也是当地政府灾后重建的房屋主要形式。平顶平房和坡顶平房也占了比较大的比例，由于北川地区气候比较温和，对于保温隔热并无特别要求，所以各种建筑形式的分布也没有很明显的倾向性。其中住宅房间和卧室数量较多，5 间以上占了 70%，住宅面积 80% 都在 90 平方米以上，50% 在 150 平方米以上，可以用来做住宿旅店等。图 2 给出了石椅村几种典型的建筑外观图。

图 2　石椅村不同形式的建筑外观图

该村的墙体材料以实心砖为主，同时有 30% 左右使用木头材料，厚度约为 24cm，其中绝大多数的房子是正面朝西，而且东西向的窗墙相对较大，这样容易造成夏季时室内下午过热。

窗框材料以木头为主，铝合金和塑钢也占据近两成。一般单层木窗传热系数 5.7W/($m^2 \cdot K$)，单层铝合金窗传热系数 4.5W/($m^2 \cdot K$)，还是比较大，保温性能不好。除了窗户本身的热阻之外，密封性也是影响窗户热工特性的主要因素。窗户的密封性与窗户本身的材质有密切关系，通常来说木窗和钢窗的密封性最差，铝合金窗居中，塑钢窗的密封性最好。

在屋顶中层材料中，青瓦的使用率最高（52%），其次是木头（34%），这说明农民会适当地选择当地材料作为屋顶的一部分。屋顶外层主要采用砖瓦，其使用率可达42%，其次是灰泥、水泥和其他材料，其使用率基本都在27%左右。住宅的吊顶使用情况不明显，使用者与没使用者各占50%。

（2）能源消费总量及结构

对调研数据进行整理所得到的石椅村每户每年生活用能量情况，包括炊事、采暖、降温和照明的能耗。统计的能源种类主要包括：木柴、秸秆、液化石油气、电能。经过统计后，得到该村全年能源消耗总量为267.9吨标准煤，其中商品能总量为10.3吨标准煤，比例很低，仅占3.8%，这为在当地实现低碳的目标提供了得天独厚的优势条件。分析其原因是：由于当地煤炭资源匮乏，加上地处山区运输不便，所以使用较少。

另外，根据调研所得到的每户建筑面积进行进一步计算，可以得出该村生活用能单位面积消耗量，计算结果为14公斤标准煤/平方米。

从能源利用种类来说，秸秆主要用作生活燃料（60%），其他主要用作冬季取暖（12%）和就地废弃（22%），制作沼气所用秸秆量很少（2%）。另外，石椅村现有太阳能19户，占20.7%，相对较少，设备还处于开始推广阶段。

（3）其他方面的情况

通过上述对农民室内的冷热感觉的调研数据及分析发现，大部分农民感觉冬季室内偏冷，也就是农宅室内热舒适性比较差。由于石椅村地处山区，所以夏季感觉舒适和凉爽，降温需求不是很迫切。在调研中还了解到，有40%的人认为做饭的时候呛人，当地农民长期在这种环境下生活，适应了做饭时炉灶产生的烟气，因此，即使他们感觉不呛人的情况下，室内的烟气也可能很重。

同时，该村95%以上的农户冬季都有烤腊肉的习惯，熏制过程中产生的烟气成为当地室内环境中的主要污染物之一。

目前，石椅村的生活垃圾处理方式还比较原始，主要是自由倾倒的形式，这样会带来比较严重的环境污染问题。

**2. 完成低碳节能技术和环境健康知识专项培训**

本项目第一阶段工作临近结束前，清华大学建筑节能研究中心、北川县政府和曲山镇政府，按照“可持续民生下的灾区民居建设与安置示范”项目办的总体部署，结合项目自身特点，在曲山镇石椅村开展了对村民的专项培训。

具体内容包括：在石椅村开展生物质半气化炊事炉使用方法现场培训。其一是介绍生物质半气化炊事炉的使用方法，其二是让村民现场体验生物质气化炉的使用过程及其难易程度。通过专家为村民的现场演示，农户充分认识到了生物质气化炉的实用性和经济性。

图3 生物质半气化炊事炉使用现场演示培训

现场演示活动结束后，来自国内五家知名单位的专家分别作了题为“生物质成型燃料技术及设备”、“生物质炊事炉介绍”、“我国农村户用沼气的基本池型介绍”、“农村环境与健康”和“农村利用生物质成型燃料的技术和前景”的专题讲座。农户对于讲座中与他们日常生活密切相关的内容，表现出浓厚的兴趣。同时，村民也对培训内容提出了一些很好的建议，例如增强讲座的通俗性，扩充讲座内容覆盖面（果树种植和家禽养殖），并期望增加示范工程中所涉及的具体实物和设备的现场使用培训。

图4 石椅村现场培训情况

总体来说，此次培训按照先期制定的培训计划顺利开展，达到了预期目标，所取得的成果包括三个方面：一是通过多种节能技术、环境卫生及健康知识的现场演示和专题讲座，起到了很好的宣传作用，提升了当地村民的节能环保意识和改造意愿，使村民更好地理解和掌握节能低碳和环保技术；二是相关专家对工程现场实施条件有了更加清楚的了解，可以确保后续工程方案的顺利实施；三是加强了与农户的沟通，为后续工作的顺利开展奠定了良好的基础。

### 3. 完成生物质颗粒燃料厂房设计与设备加工

石椅村具有丰富的生物质资源。据初步统计，全村秸秆产量约为 50 吨/年（主要为玉米），果树枝产量约为 200 吨/年，平均每户有相当于 1.5 吨标准煤的生物质资源量，完全可以满足生活用能需求。基于此，本示范项目将在石椅村安装一套生物质固体燃料成型设备，首先利用削片机将果树枝切成较小的木屑，然后利用粉碎机将木屑进行进一步粉碎，再利用压缩成型设备将粉碎后的粉末挤压成形状规则的颗粒，供炊事炉燃烧使用。

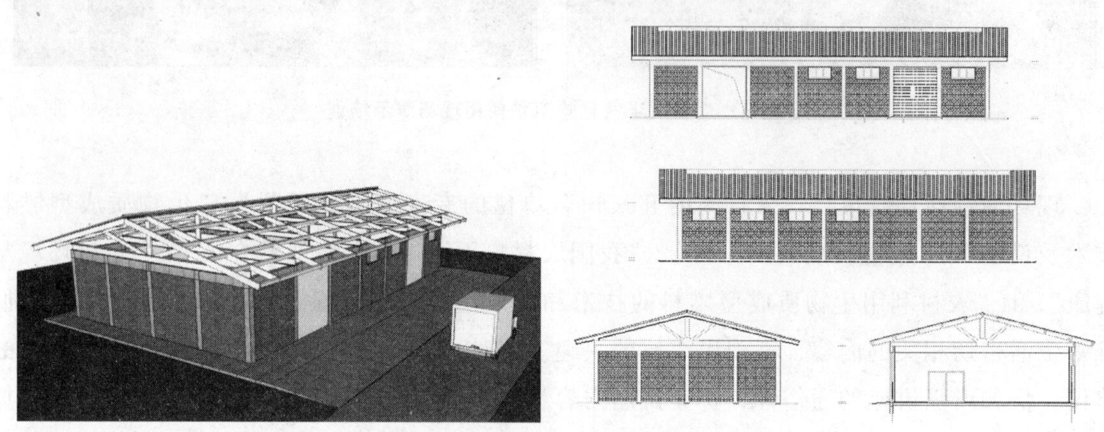

图 5　生物质颗粒燃料加工厂房效果图及立面图

目前该部分工作已经完成了生物质颗粒燃料生产厂房的设计工作，如图 5 所示，加工设备也已经制造完成。另外，利用石椅村当地的果树枝生物质原料进行了加工试验，得到的产品性能良好，说明技术上可靠，如图 6 所示。该项目后续将为每个农户安装一台生物质半气化高效炊事炉。

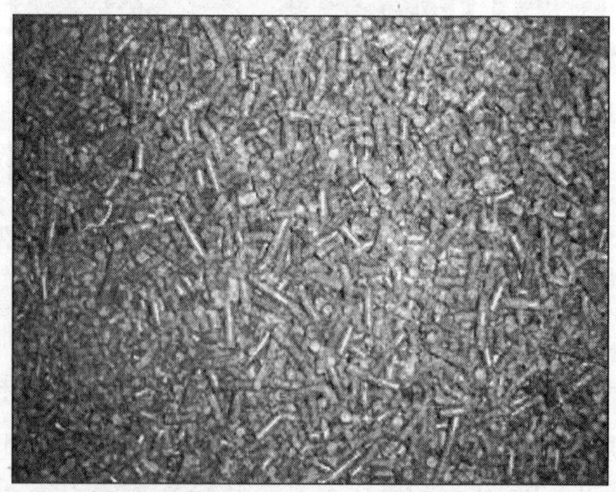

图 6　石椅村生物质原料生产加工试验

### 4. 完成太阳能与沼气节能技术推广

太阳能和沼气在当地均是重要的可再生能源，值得大力推广。截至 2010 年 5 月 30 日，石椅村有 64 户具备条件的农户完成了沼气池建设工作，普及面达到全村的 69.6%。截至 2010 年 7 月 30 日，石椅村完成了 84 台太阳能热水器的安装工作，普及面达到全村的 91.3%。

图 7　石椅村农户所安装的太阳能和沼气灶

## 三、示范效果与展望

目前，针对石椅村的低碳节能规划和示范工作已经基本结束，从已经完成的工作来看，全村的农户都从该项目中直接受益，在当地取得了良好的环境效益、社会效益和示范效果。

石椅村已经具备了良好的优势条件和工作基础，目前该村在建筑用能方面已经完全摒弃了对煤炭、天然气、液化石油气等传统不可再生能源的依赖，转向全部以生物质、沼气、太阳能、水电为消耗对象的可再生能源消费结构，实现了真正意义上的节能低碳目标。据初步估算，该项目所采用的各种节能技术方案，最终可以为该村实现节能 80% 以上的目标，而且实现了建筑用能的“零碳排放”。如果继续以可持续发展为理念，以节能低碳为根本目标，从节约能源、环境改善与经济发展三个方面入手，依靠政府和外界必要的资金支持，群策群力，共同合作，不仅能够将石椅村建设成为一个“村风文明、生活富裕、环境优美、安居乐业、低碳节能”的特色村庄，而且能使其研究成果在该地区得到普遍推广，为当地的新农村建设工作树立典范。

（作者：杨旭东，清华大学建筑节能研究中心教授）

# 实施城镇化主导战略，临沂推动革命老区跨越式发展

临沂市委、市政府按照中央、山东省的部署要求，以科学发展观为指导，坚持把城镇化作为经济社会发展的主导战略，着力做大做强中心城市，提升县城和中心镇承载力，加快推进城乡一体化发展，取得了良好成效。截至2010年年底，全市城镇化率达到48%，高于2000年18个百分点，连续8年年均增长近2个百分点；城镇人口、城镇建成区面积分别达到458.8万人、643平方公里。临沂市城镇面貌的变化、城镇化工作的做法得到了上级领导和各界人士的好评。临沂先后获得全国双拥模范城市、中国优秀旅游城市、全国创建文明城市工作先进市、全国社会治安综合治理优秀市、国家园林城市、中国城乡建设范例城市，通过了国家环保模范城的考核验收，被授予中国书法名城、中国地热城、中国市场名城等称号，全市经济社会发展进入历史上最快最好的时期。

回顾几年来临沂市城镇化工作，主要抓了以下四个方面：

## 一、从实际出发，科学确定临沂城镇化发展思路

临沂市把加快城镇化作为经济社会发展的主导战略，主要是基于对临沂实际情况和城镇化对临沂发展极端重要性的考虑。

一是保持经济平稳较快发展的需要。目前，拉动中国经济发展的两大基本动力，一个是工业化，一个是城镇化。临沂作为革命老区，经济发展处于相对欠发达状态，工业基础相对薄弱，城镇化水平相对较低。在这样的情况下，要与全省、全国同步达到全面小康，进而实现科学发展、和谐发展、率先发展，潜力和出路在于加快城镇化、工业化。而工业化与城镇化是相辅相成、相互促进的关系。加快城镇化，既可以增加城市人口，扩大消费，又可以创造新的市场需求，拉动投资，推动工业和服务业发展。临沂市近几年的实践也证明了这一点。2003年至2010年，临沂市城镇化水平年均增长2个百分点，年均拉动生产总值约4个百分点，对全市经济发展产生了巨大促进作用。

二是统筹城乡发展的需要。临沂市是农业大市，农业人口占比高。加快推进城镇化，是支持“三农”、解决“三农”问题的最现实选择。一方面，可以使大量的农村剩余劳动力转移进入城市，由农民变为市民，有利于扩大城市规模，提升城市现代化水平；另一方面，能

够增强城镇综合承载力和辐射力，促进科技、资金和信息向农村流动，带动农民大力发展优质高效农业和农村二、三产业，推动农业增效、农民增收。近五年，临沂市农民人均纯收入年均增长15%左右，城镇化在其中发挥了很重要作用。

三是改善民生的需要。加快推进城镇化，能够创造大量就业机会，增加居民收入；能够促进城市基础设施向农村延伸、城市公共服务向农村覆盖、城市现代文明向农村辐射，为城乡居民创造良好的生活环境。城镇化进程越快、水平越高，全市人民享受改革发展成果就越多，生活质量就越好。在中央、省对民生社会建设空前重视、要求越来越高的新形势下，实施城镇化战略已成为改善人民群众生产生活条件的有效途径。

四是临沂市推进城镇化具有许多有利条件。临沂是鲁南苏北面积最大、人口最多的地级市，地处长三角经济区与环渤海经济圈交汇地带，文化底蕴深厚，商贸物流业发达，生态环境良好，正处在工业化快速推进时期，城镇化发展空间广阔、潜力巨大，临沂城具备建设区域性特大中心城市的独特优势条件。

基于以上认识，临沂市于2002年把加快城镇化列入经济社会发展的五大战略来抓，市十一次党代会又进一步将其和工业化一并确立为经济社会发展的两大主导战略，全力进行了推进。推进工作中，坚持从实际出发，不断明晰了具有临沂特色的城镇化发展思路。

一是坚持城乡结合。注重城市发展与村镇建设统筹规划，以城带乡，以工促农，重点做大做强中心城市、加速提升各县城城市功能、优化布局重点镇和中心村，以大水城建设带动中心城市和中心镇村建设，推动产业、人口和基础设施向城镇聚集。目前，全市基本形成了中心城市—县城—建制镇—中心村（农村社区）有机结合、合理布局、协调发展的城镇村体系。依托中心城市，郯城、费县等5个县形成了“半小时生活圈”，沂水、苍山等4个县形成了“一小时生活圈”。同时，坚持硬环境与软环境两个一起抓，努力为农民进城镇兴业、居住创造良好条件。2003年临沂在山东省率先实行了一元化户口登记制度，近年来又进一步降低门槛，加快保障性住房建设，着力解决农民进城就业、教育、医疗等难题，有效促进了农民向城镇转移。目前，全市有133万农村人口转化为城镇人口。

二是坚持政府推动和市场化运作结合。城镇化是一项复杂的系统工程，加快推进城镇化关键在于调动各方面积极性。近几年，在搞好规划编制、完善政策法规、维护市场秩序的同时，注重发挥市场机制作用，积极经营城市，鼓励引导各类市场主体参与城镇化建设，全市形成了多元化投资推进城镇化的良好格局。例如，在北城新区开发改造中，坚持“政府主导、财政支持、市场化运作”的经营思路，通过政府投入启动资金吸引运营商直接投资、积极探索政府融资机制等方式，有效拓展了融资渠道，形成了融资—投入—收益—再融资—再投入—再收益的良性循环机制。在财政没有增加投入的情况下，北城新区通过市场化运作、招商引资、政府融资，短短4年多的时间，投入开发建设资金300多亿元，使昔日环境脏乱差的城乡结合部旧貌换新颜，初步建起了设施配套、功能齐全的现代化标志区。

三是坚持城镇建设与经济社会发展结合。加快城镇化的根本目的在于推动发展、改善民生。临沂注重把城镇化置于经济社会发展全局之中，与工业化、市场化、国际化、信息化统筹谋划推进，着力为经济社会发展提供载体、营造环境、增加动力。比如，近几年依托优势明显的商贸物流业和具有地方特色的八大工业支柱产业，规划建设了13个省级开发区和一批新型工业化园区、现代物流园区，取得了经济发展与城镇建设相互促进的良好效果。

## 二、着力增强中心城市的龙头带动作用

城市是一个地方综合竞争力的集中体现，只有大城市才能带动大发展。实施城镇化主导战略，首先要做大做强中心城市。近年来，临沂市坚持中心城市的龙头地位不动摇，制定实施了“以河为轴、两岸开发”、“一河六片、组团发展”的空间发展规划，相继建设了北城新区、涑河片区、滨河景区、临沂大学城、临沂商城等一批重点工程，中心城市的承载力和带动力大幅提升。目前，中心城市建成区面积达到165平方公里、城区人口173万人，比2002年分别增长了1.5倍。

一是抓新区带老城，做到城市规模扩张与质量提升并举。按照“北文、中商、南工”的功能布局，大力实施办公文化区北迁和跨河东进战略，加快建设北城新区和河东新区。目前，北城一期工程23平方公里的现代化新区初步形成，面积29平方公里的二期工程已经动工。河东建成区面积扩展到51平方公里，与河西相对应的“半壁江山”格局初步确立。大力实施以城中村、棚户区改造为重点的老城改造，加快推进现代居民小区建设和公用设施配套，加快完善城市功能，改善居民生活条件，城市道路、路灯等基本功能和排水、排污、疏散交通等减灾功能都有了较大程度的提高。目前，中心城区已完成和正在实施改造的村居200个，累计拆除房屋建筑面积1778万平方米，新建安置房面积1126万平方米；人均道路面积由2002年的10.9平方米提高到24.53平方米，路灯由2002年的8907盏增加到11万余盏。

二是抓水城建商城，做到城市宜居环境与创业平台俱佳。临沂水资源丰富，水资源总量约占全省的六分之一，其中沂河、沭河流域面积占全市总面积的77%，在中心城区形成了近50平方公里的水面；商贸发达，其中临沂商城年市场交易额居全国同类市场前两位，形成了“南有义乌、北有临沂”的格局。可以说，水和商是临沂城市的两大特色。抓住了水城建设，城市就会更有灵气；抓住了商城建设，就会有力促进人流、物流、信息流。为此，近年来，临沂着力建设大水城和物流天下的商贸强市。一方面，立足打造“以水为魂”的城市品牌，积极做活做好水的文章，加快建设水系相连、道路相通、清水绕城的水环境。目前，在城区沿沂河建成了192公里堤坝道路、660万平方米绿地，营造出“一河清水、两岸秀色、人水亲和、城水相依”的城市亲水特色。沂河综合治理工程和临沂城区铁路沿线环境整治工程先后荣获中国人居环境范例奖，沂河湿地被批准为国家城市湿地公园；投资8.6亿元对涑河片区进行了综合治理，对其两岸20平方公里范围进行了以商业为主的开发改造，初步形成了又一道靓丽景观带、商业带；投资4.9亿元，对陷泥河进行清淤、护坡、截污，强化绿化美化亮化硬化，将陷泥河由“臭水沟”改造为“景观河”；实施了梯级拦水和“七河”贯通工程，构成了“七河相通、八水绕城”的环城水系。另一方面，充分发挥商贸物流优势，加快临沂商城批发市场改造，全面提升服务质量和水平，加快建设全国一流的商贸

物流中心。目前，累计投入80多亿元，迁建归并60余处专业批发市场，商城年成交额超过620亿元，从业人员30万人，围绕市场从事地产品加工的业户达100万人。2008年临沂市被授予中国市场名城称号。

三是抓美化活文化，做到城市外部形象与内在品质互映。文化是一个城市的灵魂，优美的环境是城市竞争力的重要体现。近几年，临沂市坚持把美化融入城镇建设之中，把文化不断注入城市内涵之中。在美化方面，以“天蓝、地绿、水清、街净、路畅、灯明、墙洁、楼美”为目标，新建改建城区主次干道103条、公园30余处，总面积1650多万平方米。目前中心城市绿化覆盖率由2002年的17.65%提高到41.02%，人均公园绿地面积由6.97平方米提高到17.04平方米。累计取缔污染性企业7900多家。目前所有出境河流断面水质达到国标要求，空气质量全部达到国家二级标准，在国家对淮河流域水污染防治考核验收中获得了第一名的好成绩。在增加城市文化内涵方面，以建设文化名城为目标，充分挖掘历史文化资源，在核心城区最好地块扩建了王羲之故居、兵学博物馆，新建了书法广场、文化广场等公共文化设施，着力打造书法和兵学文化品牌。依托革命老区的政治优势，建设了沂蒙精神展馆、红嫂广场、沂蒙广场等一批教育基地，积极打造红色文化品牌。这些举措，不仅完善了城市功能，提升了城市形象，而且丰富提升了沂蒙精神内涵，提高了全民文明程度。2009年，在全国城市公共文明指数测评中，临沂在114个城市中位列地级市第7名、山东省第1名。

## 三、着力推进城乡一体化发展

统筹城乡发展是科学发展的内在要求。临沂作为农业大市，推进城乡一体化更具有现实的重要性、紧迫性。近几年，我们在做大做强中心城市的同时，把镇村建设作为城镇化的突出重点，不断加大工作力度，促进城乡一体化发展。

一是以特色镇为重点，着力实现小城镇向小城市的转变。临沂市小城镇数量多、布局分散，发展相对缓慢。为加快小城镇建设，发挥其节点作用，通过积极争取，2000年省政府确定了临沂市29个省级中心镇，2005年临沂又选定了23个市级重点镇，进行重点倾斜、集中建设。工作中，按照“扶优扶强、设施配套、突出特色、统筹兼顾”的原则，进一步确定了12个特色镇优先发展，发挥示范作用，推动小城镇上台阶、上水平。市委、市政府制定了全面规划、资金扶持、产业发展、扩权强镇等一系列政策措施，并从2010年开始，市财政每年设立6000万元专项资金给予扶持，每个镇由两名市级领导同志和一个市直部门对口帮扶，特色镇建设情况纳入对县（区）委、县（区）政府的年度考核评价体系。要求特色镇按照“产业中心、居住中心、基础设施中心、社会服务中心”的定位和小城市的标准进行建设，按省级经济开发区的标准扩大产业园区规模，力争3年左右建设成为产业优势强、人口集聚度高、人居环境优的小城市和县域次中心，城镇化水平达到50%以上。

二是以中心村为引领，着力实现农民居住条件的历史性改观。按照“改造城中村、建设中心村、撤并弱小村、发展重点村、培植特色村、搬迁不宜居住村”的思路，结合新农村建设，以县（区）为单位，科学确定中心村数量及布局，实施合村并点，引导人口向中心村聚集。目前，全市7167个行政村已规划为1130个中心村。2009年以来，按照山东省的决策部署，临沂采取财政扶持、税收减免、建材下乡等措施，加大了农村住房建设和危房改造力度，全市新建农村住房12.7万户，危房改造2万户，直接和间接拉动社会消费280亿元，整体工作走在了山东省前列。2010年，全市在建和竣工农村住房12.7万户，改造危房2.7万户，集中建设改造村庄503个，农村逐步向人口村庄聚集化、建设管理社区化、基础设施配套化、公共服务保障化的“四化”方向发展，较好地改善了农民居住条件、交通状况和生活方式。

三是以城乡环境综合整治为抓手，着力实现现代文明由城市向农村的延伸。在全市范围利用三年时间，以点带面，梯次推进，集中开展了省际边界以及市、县、乡、村之间五个结合部的高速公路、国省道干线公路与铁路沿线等环境整治；大力实施城区“整治工程”和乡村道路硬化、植树绿化、环境卫生净化、广告标语美化、灯光亮化等“五化工程”；全市村镇面貌得到明显改观，农业文明向工业文明逐步过渡，城市文明向农村文明持续延伸，城乡融合步伐不断加快。

## 四、着力打造优美宜居城镇

优美宜居环境，是城镇发展质量和外在形象的重要标志。临沂顺应绿色、环保、节能、可持续成为城镇化发展主潮流的新形势，坚持以环境保护为手段，以基础设施建设为重点，以管理水平提升为保障，将绿色城镇化的理念贯穿于规划、建设、管理的各个层面，加大了打造优美宜居城镇的工作力度。

一是大力改善生态环境。将经济发展、城镇建设、生态环境与节能减排有机结合起来，在全国率先提出了“生态城镇”的概念，并研究制定了《临沂市生态城镇指标评价体系》、《临沂市生态城镇申报与评审办法》，在全市大力开展了“生态城镇”创建活动。为改善能源结构，从根本上降低大气污染，大力推广应用天然气，抢占清洁能源制高点，提出了建设“气化临沂”的目标，争取到2020年，全市所有乡镇、中心村都通上管道天然气。目前，已编制了《临沂市天然气高压管网发展规划》，建设完成了城区次高压环线工程，市政府与中国石油天然气股份有限公司签署了天然气发展利用合作协议。目前，正在建设通往县城的高压管网。

二是不断完善基础设施。基础设施是城镇化发展的基础。临沂坚持基础设施先行，加大集中供热、供水和燃气等基础设施建设力度，7年间全市完成基础设施投资251.1亿元。同时，坚持建管并重，加快建设“数字化”管理城市，理顺“大城管”体制，成立了城市管理局，统一对全市城建公益设施和环境秩序进行管理；创建了“集中受理、分级指挥、分类处置、统一考评”的管理新模式，城市执法和管理效能明显提高。2010年3月31日，临沂市顺利通过国家住房和城乡建设部的验收，成为鲁南经济带、淮海经济区和全国革命老区中第一个、山东省第三个实现数字化管理的城市。

三是高度重视抓好节能减排工作。把节能减排作为城镇化发展的硬约束，严格执行工作目标责任制，强力推进各项节能减排措施的落实。2009 年，69 户省级以上重点用能企业完成节能量 92.95 万吨标煤，提前一年完成“十一五”期间节能任务。列入省、市淘汰计划的企业已关停 52 家，拆除黏土砖厂 138 家。同时，积极推进既有建筑节能改造、供热分户计量、可再生能源建筑应用、新型墙材研发与应用、绿色建筑等工作。沂水县被确定为全国首批可再生能源建筑应用示范县。深入开展省级节水型城市创建活动，强化水污染治理。到 2009 年底，全市建设城镇污水处理厂 25 座，污水集中处理规模达 83.32 万吨/日，城市污水集中处理率达 89%。

（作者：张少军，山东省临沂市委书记）

# 北京市打造"林水融合"生态环境的理论与实践

良好的生态环境是宜居城市的重要支撑，是经济社会可持续发展的重要条件，也是实现"人文北京、科技北京、绿色北京"战略的生态基础。加强生态环境建设，既是转变经济发展方式的必然要求，也是转变经济发展方式的重要着力点。林和水是城市生态环境的两大重要支撑要素，如何统筹好林、水两大要素，打造"林水融合"的生态环境，对实现城市健康发展至关重要。

近年来，首都北京在保持经济社会快速发展的同时，城市人口规模快速膨胀，资源消耗持续增加，整个城市面临着水资源紧缺，生态环境品质不高，服务水平较低等人口、资源、环境等方面的矛盾。如何实现城市生态环境承载力和资源可持续利用和发展，加快创建"环境友好型、资源节约型"社会，成为摆在北京城市建设与管理者面前的一道急需解决的难题。

以奥运会筹办为契机，紧紧围绕"人文北京、科技北京、绿色北京"战略目标，北京市积极研究和探索，努力实践，不断积累，着力加强水资源循环利用水平和城市森林建设步伐，不断提高城市生态环境承载力，构建"以水为魂、以林为体、林水相依"的宜居环境，为建设有中国特色的世界城市奠定了坚实的环境基础。

## 一、实现污水变资源，为生态环境提供稳定可靠水源

1999年以来，北京地区遭遇持续多年干旱，年均降雨量仅472毫米，比多年平均减少20%，水资源量衰减44%，成为建国以来时间最长、旱情最重的连续干旱期。水库蓄水不足，地下水持续超采，城市水源持续紧缺。

针对水资源紧缺不断加剧的形势，北京市采取了厉行节约用水、推进循环利用、建设应急水源等一系列措施，基本实现水资源供需紧平衡，以占全国不足0.2%的水资源供应了全国1.3%的人口，支撑了4.2%的GDP，保障了近年来3.8%的人口增长和11%的经济增长的水资源需求。其中，再生水利用是实现北京水资源供需平衡的关键措施之一。2003年北京市开始规模利用再生水，实现了零的突破，到2010年，全市利用再生水6.8亿立方米，再生水利用量超过地表水供水量，成为缓解水资源紧缺和改善水环境污染的重要水源。

同时，再生水利用还实现提高污水处理率和污水处理水平两大目标。通过再生水厂的建设，北京中心城区污水处理率已达到95%，COD（化学耗氧量）排放指标也由普通污水处理厂的45毫克/升降低到再生水厂的30毫克/升。再生水利用措施的实施，既完成了COD减排任务，减轻了污染排放，也为生态环境提供了满足水体功能的生态水源。

为加强再生水的利用，北京市主要采取了三大措施。

**1. 创新思路，坚持减排与利用结合，大规模开发高品质再生水，实现污水变资源**

转变污水处理模式，从目标单一的削减污染向资源利用和污染减排结合转变，从追求污水处理量提高处理率向提高出水水质转变，升级改造现有污水处理厂为高品质再生水厂，变污水为资源，采取措施充分利用。

目前，北京市已全面启动中心城区污水处理厂升级改造工程，实现了每座新城建设一座高品质再生水厂的目标。加快中心城区清河、高碑店、小红门、卢沟桥、北小河、吴家村、酒仙桥等再生水厂的建设，建成了密云、怀柔、延庆、平谷、昌平、门头沟、亦庄等新城再生水厂，建成了引温入潮水质净化工程，新增再生水生产能力超过400万立方米/日，主要水质指标达到地表水Ⅳ类标准要求。

预计至2015年，全市再生水生产能力将超过10亿立方米/年，供水量将占到全市用水量的1/4，成为城市供水的重要水源。

**2. 依靠科技，积极采用国际领先的膜处理技术，提高再生水水质，满足环境用水的水质要求**

膜技术是目前国际上最先进的水处理技术，利用膜的固液分离作用替代传统的砂过滤等设施，可大幅节约用地，提升出水水质。尤其是膜生物反应器工艺可将传统工艺的串联模式转变为生化反应和过滤为一体的集成模式，成倍提高生化降解作用，大幅提高污水处理效率，并减少工艺环节，是近年来发展迅猛的再生水生产技术。

2006年，北京市密云县采用膜生物反应器工艺建成了京郊首座高品质再生水厂，随后陆续建成了中心城区北小河再生水厂一期工程，怀柔、平谷、门头沟、延庆等新城再生水厂和顺义引温入潮水质净化工程，采取超滤膜工艺建成了清河再生水厂一期等工程。采用膜技术，再生水厂出水的主要指标均能达到地表水Ⅳ类标准，与城市河湖水系的水体功能要求基本一致，同时实现了污染减排和环境改善双重目标。

2008年，中心城区现有污水处理厂升级改造工程全面启动，清河再生水厂二期、高碑店再生水厂、酒仙桥再生水厂二期和小红门再生水厂等工程均采用了先进的膜处理工艺，水质标准均能达到Ⅳ类标准。

**3. 合理利用，通过补充城市河湖水系生态用水，恢复河湖健康生命，同步满足沿线用水需求**

近年来，受水资源紧缺影响，城市河湖水系的生态环境用水被严重挤占，有河多干，有水多污，水环境状况堪忧。为改善河湖水系的生态环境水源，北京市将再生水作为改善河湖水系生态环境的最佳水源，积极推动环境领域的再生水利用工程。

一方面，优化再生水调度和配置体系，灵活高效配置再生水资源。与再生水厂同时规划建设再生水调水工程，进行再生水调水工程建设，将再生水输送到西部永定河、北部清河、南部凉水河等城市河湖上游，补充河湖水系环境用水，基本解决城市生态环境用水问题。

另一方面，利用现状河湖水系的输送、存储和分配功能，实现再生水循环利用。在满足城市河湖水系环境用水的同时，与现有再生水管网实现联合调度，保障沿线工业用户、园林绿化、市政杂用需求，河湖水系退水供下游农业灌溉使用；实现“高水高用，低水低用，一水多用，循环利用”，替代清洁水源，缓解水资源紧缺压力。

图1　北小河再生水保障奥运水系环境用水

## 二、推进园林绿化功能升级，让森林走进城市

随着经济社会的发展，城市化进程、产业发展等对土地开发利用需求大幅增加，城市中有限的绿地空间显得更加珍贵，如何利用好有限的绿地，使其发挥更大的效益，满足经济社会快速发展对生态环境承载力更高的需求，成为城市发展过程中面临的一道难题。向有限的空间要效益，不断扩展绿地功能，实现让森林走进城市，是北京市在探索之路上的基本经验：一是合理利用河滩地、荒滩地、代征绿地、屋顶等未利用空间进行绿化建设，“变废为宝”，增加绿地面积。二是在扩大绿地总量的同时，调整种植结构，以乔木种植为主，提高单位面积绿地的生态效益。三是通过对绿化隔离地区绿地等原有绿地的改造，增加必要的基础设施和服务设施，在形成优美生态景观的同时，满足人们的生态休闲需求，增加绿地

功能。

近年来，北京市在新城建设新城滨河森林公园，在城郊建设郊野公园，在中心城因地制宜建设城市休闲公园，逐步构建起从郊区到中心城区的三级城市森林公园体系，为市民提供多层次、多选择的绿色活动空间，促进城市绿化由景观功能向休闲功能转变。

**1. 林水融合，全面启动11座新城滨河森林公园建设**

新城滨河森林公园是以各新城穿城或环城水系为主线、以水系两侧大规模林木为主体，具有休闲服务功能的带状城市森林公园。11座新城滨河森林公园总面积约10.2万亩。

滨河森林公园建设转变了城市环境建设理念，改变了单一项目单一功能的传统模式，以区域为对象，部门联动、专业融合，在充分利用全市再生水设施建设成果，满足生态用水需求的基础上，有效利用新城滨水空间，充分挖掘环境价值。

新城滨河森林公园建设按照“以水为魂、以林为体、林水相依”的建设理念，充分利用沿河河滩地和荒滩地，以种树为主，注重河流水系与其两侧林木的融合，追求自然生态，同时布设必要的基础设施，突出公园的休闲服务功能，使之成为人们走得进去的森林。

“先栽梧桐树，后引金凤凰”，在新城开发建设之初，建设新城滨河森林公园，先建环境，后建新城，有利于树立新城环境意识，构建新城环境框架，引导新城有序开发；也有利于提高新城品质，增强新城对高新人才、产业的聚集能力，促进高标准高起点高水平新城建设。力争到2012年，为北京市每座新城建设一处有水有林的滨河森林公园，提升新城环境和品质，完善全市城市森林格局，为建设首善之区奠定环境基础。

图2　通州新城滨河森林公园效果图

**2. 提升功能，建设第一道绿化隔离带郊野公园**

按照城市总体规划，自20世纪80年代开始，北京市开始建设第一道绿化隔离带。第一道绿化隔离带位于北京市四环路附近，是市中心区与边缘集团之间以及各边缘集团之间的绿带，规划总面积约297平方公里。其中，规划绿地面积约156平方公里。目前，已实现绿化面积约126平方公里，占规划绿地总面积的八成以上。郊野公园建设是对第一道绿化隔离地区绿地进行近自然化、公园化的改造，可以拓展城市绿化隔离带功能，提供更多休闲游憩空间，让市民更直接、更具体地享受经济社会发展成果，是政府关注民生的重要体现。

郊野公园遵循“以野为魂、以林为体、因地制宜、自然朴野、健康生态”的建设理念，以满足散步休闲为主，推动园林绿化功能由生态景观向休闲服务升级。第一道绿化隔离地区郊野公园从2007年开始建设，截至目前，共建设郊野公园48处，约3.9万亩。郊野公园与第一道绿化隔离地区内现状颐和园、奥林匹克森林公园、朝阳公园等，共形成近8万亩公园，基本形成沿东北五环和西南四环的郊野公园环。

图3　旺兴湖郊野公园

**3. 见缝插绿，建设市民身边的绿色生态休闲空间**

从2008年起，北京市在中心城区，选择空间相对集中、规模较大的代征绿地建设休闲公园。既能够增加中心城区的绿地总量，丰富绿化体系层级，又能满足市民就近健身、享受生态休闲的生活需求。2010年，建成城市休闲森林公园6处，约33公顷。

图 4　东南二环护城河城市休闲森林公园

## 三、未来发展思路

“十二五”时期，北京市将继续全面实施“绿色北京”战略，把资源节约型和环境友好型社会建设作为转变经济发展方式的重要着力点；进一步统筹山区与平原的生态环境建设和功能挖掘，加强绿化建设和水系生态修复，全面改善城市河湖水环境，提升水景观和生态休闲功能，促进水资源与生态建设协调发展，大幅提高首都生态文明水平和可持续发展能力，把北京建设成为既服务于当代市民，又服务于子孙后代的宜居家园。

主要措施包括：

（1）提高污水处理水平，大力推进污水资源化，为生态环境提供充足用水保障，实现首都城市生态环境的可持续发展。按照世界城市的标准，提高污水处理率，在全国率先全面完成城中心区污水处理厂升级改造。新城新建污水处理厂按再生水厂标准一步建成。2015年再生水生产能力超过10亿立方米，全市再生水利用率达到75%。

（2）继续加强城市绿色生态环境建设，建设大尺度森林绿地，进一步夯实“两轴、三环、十放射、多中心”的城市森林体系。加快建设南中轴森林公园、三海子郊野公园等大规模集中成片绿地；积极推动中心城立体绿化建设，在中心城河湖水系沿岸建设滨水林带，千方百计增加中心城绿化面积，继续推动园林绿化功能从生态景观向休闲服务升级。

（3）继续加快河湖水系治理，升级改造河道水系两侧绿地，通过水与绿的融合，挖掘河流的生态价值和经济价值。建设西部永定河绿色生态走廊，实现湖泊溪流相连的自然景观；实施跨流域调水，再现潮白河湖泊水面和芦苇丛生的优美环境；完成北运河流域水系治理，重现古老漕运河道水景。按照“宜弯则弯、宜宽则宽、宜岛则岛、宜滩则滩”的原则，生态治理城市河湖水系，合理规划河岸土地空间，解放滨水资源，建设观水、亲水、近水的休闲滨水空间，打造十大滨水绿线，形成“水秀而可近，岸绿且可亲”的绿色滨水景观。

（作者：刘印春，北京市发展和改革委员会副主任）

**参考文献**

[1] 北京市人民政府《北京市国民经济和社会发展第十二个五年规划纲要》

[2] 北京市人民政府《北京城市总体规划》

[3] 苏德荣，韩烈保，尹淑霞，史小丽．解决城市生态绿地灌溉用水的途径［J］．节水灌溉，2005（04）

[4] 杨小波，等．城市生态学［M］．北京：科学出版社

[5] 王玮琳．生态措施在节约型园林工程中的应用——以昌平新城滨河森林公园为例［J］．北京园林古建设计院

[6] 李宝娟，吕鑑，吴珊，张羽．完善中水利用管理政策的探讨［J］．北京水务，2007（03）

# 珠江三角洲宜居村镇建设实践

## ——以广州番禺大岗镇和增城新塘镇西南村为例

## 一、引言

为切实贯彻《中共广东省委、广东省人民政府关于争当实践科学发展观排头兵的决定》，全面落实《珠江三角洲地区改革发展规划纲要（2008—2020年）》，广东省委、省政府于2009年7月出台了《中共广东省委办公厅、广东省人民政府办公厅关于建设宜居城乡的实施意见》，提出到2020年建设一批生产发展、生活富裕、生态良好、文化繁荣、社会和谐、人民群众具有幸福感的宜居城市、城镇和村庄，成为全国宜居城乡建设的先进省份。从此，广东省拉开全面开展宜居城乡创建活动的帷幕。

2009年10月，广东省政府在中山市召开全省建设宜居城乡工作现场会，会议确定了31个村镇作为全省宜居城乡创建行动的试点。通过开展试点工作，发挥“标杆”示范作用，总结经验，以点带面推动宜居城乡创建活动的广泛深入开展。随后，广东省住房和城乡建设厅2010年1月出台了《广东省宜居城镇、宜居村庄、宜居社区考核指导指标（2010—2012年）（试行）》（以下简称《考核指标》），作为宜居城镇、村庄、社区建设的标准，以指导具体宜居创建行动的开展。

广州番禺大岗镇和增城新塘镇西南村被确定为宜居创建试点中的典型而先行启动。它们不仅之前已开展过宜居建设工作，具备较好的创建基础，而且又结合《考核指标》及时编制了较完善的宜居创建行动计划，在珠江三角洲地区具有较强的代表性。

## 二、大岗镇宜居城镇建设实践与行动计划

### 1. 大岗镇概况

大岗镇位于广州市番禺区南部，与佛山市顺德区一衣带水。镇域面积90平方公里，城区面积14平方公里，辖区内有25个行政村和6个居委会，总人口约13万人。大岗镇发展历史悠久，社会经济发展水平较高，2008年国内生产总值达42.3亿元，财政收入2.76亿

元，税收收入3.19亿元，是番禺南部的经济、文化中心，综合发展指数居全国小城镇前1000名，先后被评为广东省中心镇、“全国发展改革试点城镇”和“联合国开发计划署试点小城镇”，宜居城镇建设基础得天独厚。

**2. 建设实践**

近年，大岗镇通过经济发展、城乡规划、环境建设、民心工程、制度建设等五个方面着力，加强镇、村的规划、建设、管理和整治，改变以前规划混乱、污染严重、城镇面貌脏乱差的局面，打造出富有岭南水乡特色的宜业宜居生态文明新城镇的雏形。

（1）抓经济发展，促产业结构优化

农业方面，大岗镇近几年共投入2亿多元，重点落实农田基础设施建设。同时，以省级农业企业东升农场为龙头，采取“企业+基地+农户”的生产模式，带动2000多户农民奔康致富。

工业方面，大岗镇逐步实现产业向园区集聚，有效地解决了“厂居混合、村村冒烟”的问题。未来，投资额达270亿元的中船柴油机项目将落户大岗新联地区，重点发展船舶配套等大型装备先进制造业。这将大大改变大岗的发展路径，积极促进现有工业企业转型，目前大岗镇已着手发展相关装备制造配套产业，借此机会逐步淘汰低附加值、高污染、高资源消耗产业。

第三产业方面，大岗镇发挥区位优势，促进商业发展。从2002年到2009年，全镇商业网点增长了99.9%，从业人员增长了117%，社会消费品零售总额增长了2.5倍。

（2）抓城乡规划，促持续协调发展

2008年，大岗镇积极面向珠三角大型装备产业基地落户的机遇，按照《珠江三角洲地区改革发展规划纲要》中“在珠三角建设一个世界先进制造业基地”的要求，对《广州市番禺区大岗镇总体规划》的总体空间格局进行了调整，规划以十八罗汉山森林公园为中心、以旧镇中心与装备产业基地综合服务中心为两翼、以南北中三条放射发展轴为基本骨架，建设3条高快速路、5条区域性主干道和3条快速轨道线的交通体系，形成组团发展，大岗镇区与装备基地既联系便捷，又互不干扰，和谐融合为一个整体。

（3）抓环境建设，促城乡面貌改善

近年来，大岗镇大力推进人居生态环境的建设改造：一是大力推动文明村建设，目前全镇25个行政村全部达到广州市文明村的标准。二是加快道路桥梁建设。目前大岗镇人均道路面积达15平方米以上，全镇25个行政村全部实现村村通公路。三是投入5000多万元建设十八罗汉山森林公园，全镇人均公园绿地面积超过30平方米，城区绿化覆盖率达49.5%。四是在2007年年底兴建番禺区首个镇级污水处理厂，污水处理厂总投资2.7亿元，日处理污水12万吨。五是大力整治镇域环境卫生，每年投入400多万元处理垃圾，做到日产日清、统一转运、集中处理，同时成立水上环卫队伍，及时对城区内的河涌垃圾进行清理。

(4) 抓民生工程，促公共服务完善

大岗镇坚持以民为本，破除"见物不见人"的观念，积极抓好各项公共配套设施建设。一是2002年以来全镇累计投入教育资金4.7亿元，在已规划城区范围内的学生都可以享受到市一级学校以上的普教教育，做到幼教、职教、成教协调发展，城镇、农村教育均衡发展，2005年被授予"广东省教育强镇"。二是镇村藏书约30万册，镇文化站顺利通过省特级文化站评审。三是位于镇内的番禺区第二人民医院发展水平较高，已获得国家专利13项，还有17项正在申报中，其中"内镜微创保胆取石"技术已达到国际领先水平，农民参加新型城乡合作医疗覆盖率达到98%。四是逐步建立城镇住房保障体系，投入733.6万元为困难家庭建房228间，建筑面积10260平方米。

(5) 抓制度建设，促城乡管理规范

大岗镇坚持实行城镇管理联席会议制度，每月镇政府定期召开联席会议，通报建设、管理工作，形成了党政一把手亲自抓、分管领导具体抓、部门城乡联动抓的局面，在社会宣传、队伍建设、设施建设、制度建设方面逐步建立城镇管理长效机制。如积极利用电视专栏、墙报标语、宣传单张等形式，开展丰富多彩的城镇管理宣传教育活动；开展"创建平安社区（村）"工作，投入400多万元在15个行政村新增加220个视频监控点，利用高科技手段防控各类犯罪；每季召开一次情况通报会，及时研究和解决城乡管理遇到的新情况、新问题；城管部门采用正面宣传、严格执法、媒体曝光等办法加强管理，有效地遏制了"两违"和"六乱"现象的发生。

**3. 宜居城镇创建行动计划**

(1) 大岗镇宜居建设的完善方向

从上述大岗镇建设实践可以看出，大岗镇已经是一个发展基础很好、发展水平较高的小城市。将大岗镇现状宜居建设情况与广东省建设厅《宜居城镇考核指标》的18项指标进行比照，达标14项，未达标4项，达标率77.8%。从考核指标来看，大岗镇已基本达到了省宜居城镇的标准。

大岗的宜居城镇建设仍有较大的提升空间。

首先，从未达标项来看，包括收入房价比、基本社会保险覆盖率、生活污水处理率、人均公共体育设施场地面积等4项。大岗基本社会保险覆盖率刚刚开展，覆盖率未达标情有可原。另外，在大岗污水处理厂建成以后，城镇生活污水处理率即可达到100%，因此，大岗该两项未达标项短期达标的可能性很大。收入房价比较低说明大岗居民总体收入水平还不高，改善现有住房条件能力还不足。这一方面固然需要继续提高大岗居民的收入水平；另一方面也说明政府应进一步考虑加大保障性住房的供应，保证中低收入居民拥有改善现有居住条件的需要。人均体育用地面积低于标准，则说明提高体育用地面积是大岗下一阶段宜居建设的重点内容。

表1　大岗镇宜居建设现状与考核指标对照情况

| 考核内容 | 序号 | 考核指标 | 建设目标 | 现状情况 | 是否达标 |
|---|---|---|---|---|---|
| 舒适性 | 1 | 城镇低保、住房困难家庭住房保障率 | 100% | 100% | 是 |
| | 2 | 宜居社区比例 | 80% | 91% | 是 |
| | 3 | 收入房价比 | >10 平方米/年 | 5.3 平方米/年 | 否 |
| | 4 | 人均公园绿地面积 | >10 平方米 | 14.9 平方米 | 是 |
| | 5 | 基本社会保险覆盖率 | >90% | 39.6% | 否 |
| 健康性 | 6 | 集中式饮用水源地水质达标率 | 100% | 区水厂 100% | 是 |
| | 7 | 生活污水处理率 | >80% | 未启用(已有污水处理厂,现已投入 1.7 亿元,规模为 4 万吨/日,终极规模为 12 万吨/日。2010 年 6 月启用主管网,支管网正在设计) | 否 |
| | 8 | 生活垃圾无害化处理率 | >80% | 100% | 是 |
| | 9 | 工业废水、废气达标率 | 90% | 100% | 是 |
| | 10 | 社区卫生服务机构覆盖率 | >80% | 100% | 是 |
| 方便性 | 11 | 人均道路面积 | >15 平方米 | 15.3 | 是 |
| | 12 | 公共交通出行率 | >30% | 45%(搭乘公交 4005507 人/全年) | 是 |
| | 13 | 每万人公交车辆数量 | >10 标台 | 11.6(151 台公交车/全镇) | 是 |
| | 14 | 人均公共体育设施场地面积 | >1.2 平方米 | 0.7 平方米 | 否 |
| | 15 | 综合文化站建设 | 有一个省一级以上文化站 | 省特级文化站 1 处 | 是 |
| | 16 | 义务教育学校达到规范化学校标准 | 100% | 2006 年省教育强镇(由 31 所学校合并成 17 所学校,合并后全部达到区要求标准) | 是 |
| 安全性 | 17 | 每年万人刑事案件立案数 | ≤30 起 | 28.38 起 | 是 |
| | 18 | 综治信访维稳中心建设 | 有 | 有 | 是 |

其次，在对大岗镇居民和政府部门访谈的结果来看，绝大部分居民对大岗的宜居建设，对自身的居住条件基本满意，尤其是教育、医疗、购物、公共交通等方面。而对居住环境不满意的方面同样比较集中，主要是水环境、文体设施、公园绿地的质量等方面。另外，对社区的治安环境的评价也并不高。可见，有些项目尽管已经达到了相关的标准（如绿地、治安等），但却不能满足居民的需求，意味着需要进一步对现有的宜居标准进行深化和完善，如绿地需要增加绿地质量指标、服务半径指标。安全性指标宜更为具体，如提出治安设施布局要求，立案率改为出警率等。

最后，从未来发展趋势来看，大岗在中船装备基地建设带动下，尚有巨大的发展潜力。基地建设除带来相关产业的布局外，也带来规模庞大、学历层次较高的外来人口。因此，大岗镇区不仅要担当起提供配套服务的场所，更应成为一个新型产业与传统产业融合、外来人口与本地人口融合的平台，这就对大岗镇宜居建设提出了更高的要求。

（2）大岗镇宜居的重点建设目标

按照马斯洛需求层次理论，人的需求是具有层次的，低层次的需求得到满足，就会产生高层次需求。大岗镇居民目前在生理需求、安全需求方面已基本得到满足，具备向更高的需求层次转化的条件。

如前所述，大岗镇近期宜居的重点建设需求为：需要更多的绿地、广场等公共空间满足居民社交的需求；需要完善体育设施、文化设施，营造优美的居住环境，满足居民“自我实现”的需求、巩固对安全（健康）的需求；需要营造自身的特色，加强原居民、新移民对大岗的认同感、归属感，满足“被他人承认的需要”。据此提出大岗镇2010—2015年的城镇建设目标：宜居城镇考核指标全部达标，进一步改善居住条件，重点增加公共空间、文体设施的设置，整治重点城市节点，建设成为设施完备、富有特色、环境优美的广东省宜居城镇。为达到建设目标，提出下一步的宜居建设计划。

（3）大岗镇宜居建设行动计划

① 显山露水，营造公共空间。密集的河网、逐水而居形成的聚落空间机理是番禺地区独特的居住文化，而十八罗汉山则是大岗镇得天独厚的生态资源，成为大岗区别于番禺南部其他地区的主要自然标志。继续加大对十八罗汉山景观整治、功能升级。对镇区河涌加强治污，美化滨水空间，打造山水相融的城镇空间格局是创造大岗独特形象，推进宜居建设的重要主题。结合显山露水工程，在镇区营造生动、多样化的公共空间，如对大岗沥两侧岸线的整治，十八罗汉山周边工业区、旧村居地改造等，发挥生态、景观、休闲、文化功能、商业、旅游等功能，为加强居民间交往提供空间，从而提升城镇居民生活的品质以及加强居民对大岗的认同感。

② 活跃文体，完善服务设施。根据《广州市居住区公共服务设施配套标准》逐渐完善镇区公共服务设施，保证设施的种类、质量、便利性满足要求。在已编的控制性详细规划基础上，结合调研，明确大部分设施的适宜布局位置，重点增加居民需求最为迫切的文化娱乐、体育类公共服务设施，如文化活动中心、文化站、居民健身场所等，丰富居民的日常生活。此外根据镇发展需要，落实水厂扩建、供电设施、环卫设施等市政配套。

③ 因地制宜，解决用地瓶颈。大岗宜居建设中面临的一个重要问题是可用的土地资源不多，这使大岗镇在配套公共服务设施、拓展公共空间时更需要考虑对现有存量土地的挖潜。建设计划提出了利用存量土地资源解决用地瓶颈的思路。例如，结合十八罗汉山、镇区河涌的整治，在不影响生态环境的基础上，布局体育文化设施、广场绿地等，使市民可以在充满生态特色的环境中进行文体活动；将镇区内效益较低的部分“三旧”用地改造成保障性住房、公服设施，改善居民居住条件。

④ 扩大辐射，延伸服务半径。从区域发展前景来看，除大岗自身强烈的工业发展潜力外，大岗周边地区如顺德五沙地区、榄核墩塘—顺河地区，东涌南部地区都将是工业发展的重要区域，仅有大岗镇区具有发展基础的公共服务中心。因此，大岗的宜居建设不仅仅要服务于自身，还应面向整个番禺南部地区。通过改善交通、提供高品质居住区、服务设施布局考虑镇域以外地区等手段，延伸大岗宜居的服务范围，不断提升大岗的区域地位。在设施布

局、道路建设方面，充分体现了这一思路。

## 三、西南村宜居村庄建设实践与行动计划

**1. 西南村概况**

西南村位于广州增城市（县级市）新塘镇东北部，南临广园快速路，荔新公路和广深铁路从村中部穿过。村域面积2.06平方公里，现状户籍人口1214人，村民集中居住区基本无外来人口。村集体经济发展较好，年土地租金、厂房租金等收入约800万元，村民人均分红5000多元，人均年收入约12000元。

西南村是广州市社会主义新农村建设示范村，曾获得增城市首批“文明示范村”、广州市“文明村”、广东省“卫生村”、全国“绿色小康村”等称号。

**2. 建设实践**

得益于社会主义新农村的建设，西南村的宜居村庄建设工作可以说自2004年即开始了。虽然这些工作主要是在本次宜居城乡创建活动之前开展的，但却有不少值得总结的实践经验，而且已取得了显著的成效，为进一步创建宜居示范村庄奠定了良好的基础。

(1) 科学规划建设

规划先行是宜居村庄建设的前提。西南村首先组织编制了村庄规划和旧村整治规划，规划不仅明确将全村分为居住区、工业区和农业种养区三大功能区，而且制订了详细的土地利用和建设实施方案，提出了操作性强的建设和整治指引，从而有效地发挥了规划对各项建设活动的龙头指导作用。

(2) 推进住有所居

西南村把改善村民居住条件作为宜居建设的重中之重，按照村庄整治规划开展了三次大规模的整治行动。尤其是旧村整治，共拆除了200余幢弃置、不符合规划和没有保留价值的破旧房屋和全部的违章建筑（如猪舍、牛棚、柴房、旱厕、塘厕等），使旧村的居住条件得到了根本性的改善。同时回收整合了一批宅基地，并把符合规划的宅基地重新划给村民新建房屋使用，其余的作为疏通路网和绿化用地使用。经过整治，西南村基本实现了居住条件社区化，部分原来在村外城市小区居住的村民甚至搬回村里居住。

由于村庄整治涉及大量的拆迁工作，西南村把村民的意愿放在首位，通过村民代表会议、拆迁户动员会议、整治效果现场展示宣传、入户沟通等方式获得了广大村民的支持和积极参与，并组成了专门的拆迁补偿评估小组，保证拆迁补偿的公平公正，从而实现了村庄整治的快速有序推进。

(3) 完善公共设施

经过扎实的宜居村庄建设，西南村的公共设施得到了极大的完善，种类齐全，使用便利，基本达到了城市社区的配置标准。村内的道路、街、巷全部实现了水泥硬底化，各种市

政管线进行了重新架设，美观整齐。全村不仅实现了清洁用水，而且沿主要道路铺设了地下排污管线，建设了污水集中处理设施。尤其值得指出的是，行政办公、文体娱乐、医疗卫生、社会福利等各种服务设施主要利用旧祠堂修复改造而来，不仅大大提高了祠堂的利用率，有效保护了传统风貌，而且具有突出的岭南特色。

（4）改善人居环境

为了使村民更舒适地居住生活，西南村在人居环境改善方面也做了大量工作，包括：①绿化环境的营造，充分利用村内空间进行植树绿化，并结合旧村改造拆出的空地建设了 8 个绿化公园。②建筑立面整饰，对村内主要道路两旁建筑立面进行装修改造，既完好保留自然村的生态特点和传统风貌，又充分体现了岭南农村朴实、自然的特点。③彻底拆除旱厕、塘厕，住户卫生厕所普及率达到 100%，并建设有水冲式公厕 3 处。西南村对新建卫生厕所的住户每户补贴 1000 元，极大提高了村民建设卫生厕所的积极性。④按照规划将生活区与养殖区进行分离，家禽牲畜统一迁移到农业种养区圈放和养殖，既方便了卫生管理，又提高了居住质量。此外，西南村聘请了 5 位环卫工人和 4 位绿化工人，实现了人居环境维护的制度化和常态化。

人居环境的逐步改善，使村民对宜居村庄建设的工作更加理解和支持，部分不支持的村民的态度也发生了根本的转变，建设工作逐步进入良性循环的轨道。

### 3. 宜居村庄创建行动计划

与大岗镇一样，按照宜居城乡创建活动的要求，西南村作为先行试点在之前建设的基础上编制了宜居村庄创建行动计划。行动计划主要包括宜居建设现状评价、村委及村民意愿调查、建设目标及行动计划三部分。本文重点介绍基于考核指标的现状评价和行动计划两部分内容。

（1）基于考核指标的现状评价

广东省宜居村庄的《考核指标》分农业型和城郊型村庄两类，两类考核指标的结构相同，均包括舒适性、健康性、方便性、安全性四方面的内容，在具体考核指标和建设目标上有细微差异。西南村是典型的农业型村庄。

与《考核指标》对照，西南村已基本达到宜居村庄的建设标准，12 项考核指标中有 9 项完全达标，3 项尚需进一步改善。未达标的 3 项分别是“社会救助和保障覆盖率”指标的“符合农村社会养老保险参保条件的村民参保比例达到 100%”、“交通条件”指标的“已通客车行政村建有车亭或客运站点”和“自然灾害问题”指标的“配置完善的防灾设施”。可以看出，3 个未达标项均属于非刚性的指标，且其中“已通客车行政村建有车亭或客运站点”对人口较少的西南村而言并非必须设置的。

**表2　西南村宜居建设现状与考核指标对照情况**

| 考核内容 | 序号 | 考核指标 | 建设目标 | 是否达标 |
|---|---|---|---|---|
| 舒适性 | 1 | 居住条件 | ①危房、泥砖房和茅草房改造率达到80%以上<br>②生活区与养殖区分离<br>③住房建设符合村庄规划的要求 | 是 |
| | 2 | 村道建设 | ①村道硬底化80%以上,主要道路机动车可通达<br>②村庄主要道路两侧和重要路口进行简单绿化,增设照明设施,设置排水沟渠 | 是 |
| | 3 | 绿化环境 | ①有1个以上供村民(及外来人口)乘凉、休憩的绿化小公园、小绿荫地等<br>②村域河涌、池塘水面无垃圾,无异味、臭味 | 是 |
| | 4 | 社会救助和保障覆盖率 | ①新型农村合作医疗参保率或参合率达到90%以上<br>②家庭人均纯收入低于当地最低生活保障标准的家庭享受最低生活保障的比例达到100%以上<br>③符合农村社会养老保险参保条件的村民参保比例达到100%以上 | 否 |
| 健康性 | 5 | 生活垃圾收集、处理情况 | ①建设垃圾收集点,定点收集、定时清运,保持环境整洁<br>②大力推行改厕工程,80%农户建有卫生厕所,村庄建有一个以上水冲式公共厕所<br>③人畜粪便要进行无害化处理<br>④生活垃圾运往附近垃圾场处理 | 是 |
| | 6 | 污水处理 | 有简易污水处理设施 | 是 |
| | 7 | 安全用水 | 通过集中供水、分户设置水箱等方法,实现全部村民用水清洁卫生 | 是 |
| 方便性 | 8 | 综合服务设施 | ①有小商铺<br>②有医疗卫生服务场所,并常备医疗设备和药品<br>③有文体活动场所 | 是 |
| | 9 | 交通条件 | ①符合客车安全通行条件的行政村通达客车<br>②已通客车行政村建有车亭或客运站点 | 否 |
| | 10 | 柴草灶的农户比例 | 低于10% | 是 |
| 安全性 | 11 | 社会治安状况 | ①近两年未发生过刑事案件<br>②基本无私彩、无吸毒<br>③无集体上访事件 | 是 |
| | 12 | 自然灾害问题 | ①配置完善的防灾设施,已制定防治自然灾害的长效机制<br>②考核期间没有出现群死、群伤的自然灾害事件 | 否 |

(2) 创建行动计划

通过现状评价可知，西南村具备较好的宜居村庄建设基础。因此，结合发挥典型示范作用的要求，提出西南村宜居村庄建设的目标是：在完成查缺补漏的前提下高标准推进宜居村庄建设，并积极推进民主政治和社会文化建设，将西南村建成安居、康居、乐居、具有岭南特色的全省宜居示范村庄。

在建设目标指引下，行动计划结合西南村的实际特点提出了相应的建设项目，包括建筑整改、旧街区风貌塑造、环境美化、安全宁静社区、公共设施、宜居体验旅游共6类16个项目。可以看出，这些项目除满足《考核指标》的要求外，更多的是宜居提升型的项目。这正是我们对宜居深入理解的体现，人的宜居需求是动态变化的，宜居建设并没有终点。因此，基础条件较好的村庄，应结合发展实际追求更高层次的宜居建设，不仅包括物质建设，也包括精神文化和民生政治的综合发展。

表3 西南村宜居村庄建设项目一览表

<table>
<tr><th>序号</th><th colspan="2">项目名称</th><th>项目规模</th><th>实施时间</th><th>资金来源</th><th>投资估算（万元）</th></tr>
<tr><td>1</td><td colspan="2">建筑整改项目</td><td>全村范围</td><td>2010—2012 年</td><td>公共财政、村集体收入</td><td>798</td></tr>
<tr><td>2</td><td colspan="2">旧街区风貌塑造项目</td><td>南方九街</td><td>2011—2012 年</td><td>村集体收入、市场资金</td><td>—</td></tr>
<tr><td>3</td><td rowspan="4">环境美化项目</td><td>立面绿化工程</td><td>全村范围</td><td>2010—2011 年</td><td>公共财政、村集体收入、村民参与</td><td>30</td></tr>
<tr><td>4</td><td>花木添彩</td><td>主要公共设施周围、主要道路路灯</td><td>2010—2011 年</td><td>公共财政、村集体收入</td><td>5</td></tr>
<tr><td>5</td><td>设置绿化节点</td><td>旧村范围</td><td>2010—2012 年</td><td>公共财政、村集体收入</td><td>14</td></tr>
<tr><td>6</td><td>建设绿色步行道</td><td>旧村范围</td><td>2010—2012 年</td><td>公共财政、村集体收入</td><td>38</td></tr>
<tr><td>7</td><td rowspan="4">安全宁静社区项目</td><td>光亮工程</td><td rowspan="2">村巷出入口、交叉口、公共活动空间等易发生治安事件的地区</td><td>2010—2011 年</td><td>公共财政、村集体收入</td><td>17</td></tr>
<tr><td>8</td><td>电子监控系统</td><td>2010—2011 年</td><td>公共财政、村集体收入</td><td>10</td></tr>
<tr><td>9</td><td>应急避难设施</td><td>中央公园、停车场</td><td>2010—2011 年</td><td>公共财政、村集体收入</td><td>2</td></tr>
<tr><td>10</td><td>广深铁路隔离带</td><td>约 350 米</td><td>2010—2011 年</td><td>公共财政、村集体收入</td><td>7</td></tr>
<tr><td>11</td><td rowspan="4">公共设施项目</td><td>新建幼儿园</td><td>180 平方米</td><td>2011—2012 年</td><td>公共财政、村集体收入</td><td>81</td></tr>
<tr><td>12</td><td>新建垃圾池</td><td>10 平方米</td><td>2010—2011 年</td><td>公共财政、村集体收入</td><td>2.5</td></tr>
<tr><td>13</td><td>新建通往沙头小学道路</td><td>约 200 米</td><td>2010—2011 年</td><td>公共财政</td><td>63</td></tr>
<tr><td>14</td><td>拓宽通往工业园区道路</td><td>约 1000 米</td><td>2011—2012 年</td><td>公共财政</td><td>315</td></tr>
<tr><td>15</td><td rowspan="2">宜居体验旅游项目</td><td>旅游产品开发</td><td>全村范围</td><td>2011 年开始，持续开发</td><td>村集体收入、市场资金、村民参股</td><td>—</td></tr>
<tr><td>16</td><td>配套建设项目（标志性门楼、综合服务区、标识物等）</td><td>全村范围</td><td>2011—2012 年</td><td>村集体收入、市场资金、村民参股</td><td>—</td></tr>
<tr><td>合计</td><td>—</td><td>—</td><td>—</td><td>—</td><td>—</td><td>1382.5</td></tr>
</table>

注：部分项目属市场经营型项目，且包含较多不确定因素，故暂不进行投资估算。

## 四、小结

宜居村镇的建设，是一个长期持续的动态过程。珠江三角洲地区前几年各种形式的建设活动已经积累了不少实践经验，奠定了良好的建设基础。这次全省宜居城乡创建活动的开展，为宜居村镇的建设进一步明确了目标和标准。大岗镇和西南村是珠江三角洲地区宜居村镇建设的典型代表。本文不仅总结了它们积累的建设经验，也介绍了正在实施的宜居村镇创建行动计划，以期为其他地区的宜居村镇创建工作提供借鉴和参考。

（作者：闫永涛，广州市城市规划勘测设计研究院规划研究中心工程师；刘松龄，广州市城市规划勘测设计研究院规划研究中心工程师）

# 高速铁路对沿线城市的影响

## ——以武广高铁为例

### 一、国内高速铁路建设对城市发展的影响

从国际上第一条高铁开通到现在，高速铁路的发展为世界上多个地区的发展带来新的机遇和强劲动力。1964 年日本新干线、1983 年法国 TGV、1988 年德国 ICE、1990 年意大利 FS 的实践证明，高速铁路为这些地区发展带来了巨大机遇。

2010 年，中国在沪杭高速与京沪高速的试运行中，两次刷新了世界铁路运营试验的最高速度。从高铁最高时速的不断刷新到京津高铁、武广高铁等的相继开通，一切都在昭示着中国高铁进入一个快速发展期。在硬件条件提升、高铁网络逐步成形的今天，需要充分把握高速铁路对于城市发展的影响，积极利用这一发展机遇，带动沿线城市实现质的飞跃。

**1. 高铁对城市发展的影响**

（1）高速铁路带动了沿线城市的城市化进程

纵观多数发达国家的发展史，不难看出，高速铁路与沿线地区城市化进程有着密切的关系。1964 年的日本在国力尚弱的情况下，建设并开通了当时世界上第一条高速铁路——时速 210 公里的东海道新干线。此后的 30 年间，沿线城市格局发生重大变化并趋于成熟，形成了今日亚洲最大的都市圈——大东京都市圈。20 世纪 70 年代，法国、德国、西班牙等发达国家陆续开始建设高速铁路，也拉开了诸如大巴黎这样现代意义上的大都市圈形成的序幕。

（2）高铁车站在城市规划布局中获得枢纽地位

随着工业国家 20 世纪 60 年代以后私人汽车化及航空业的发展，火车站在城市经济发展的中心地位被动摇。但是，在全球环境污染日趋严重和环保意识普及后，高速铁路作为污染少、高速、舒适和经济的公共交通工具而得到新的评估，高铁车站的建设也在城市规划的布局调整中获得交通枢纽地位。

（3）高铁车站引发了城市高端服务功能的集聚

由于高速铁路具有准点、安全、舒适、高速等多重优点，使得中远距离出行的中高端旅

客选择高速铁路的人越来越多。这为高铁车站地区的功能发展提供了宝贵资源，车站地区逐步成为会展、餐饮娱乐、酒店办公等城市高端服务功能的集聚地。

## 2. 中国高速铁路的规划与发展

（1）中国高速铁路的建设历程

中国的高速铁路建设始于1999年开始兴建的秦沈客运专线。经过10多年的高速铁路建设和对既有铁路的高速化改造，中国目前已经拥有全世界最大规模以及最高运营速度的高速铁路网。截至2010年10月底，运营时速200公里以上的高速铁路运营里程已经达到7431公里。

**表1　中国部分已运营高速铁路一览表**

| 序号 | 线路名称 | 开通运营时间 | 沿线车站 | 备　注 |
|---|---|---|---|---|
| 1 | 京津城际铁路 | 2008年8月1日 | 北京南、亦庄、武清、天津4个车站。 | 第一条具有完全自主知识产权、世界一流水平的高速铁路。 |
| 2 | 武广高速铁路 | 2009年12月26日 | 湖北段：武汉、咸宁北、赤壁北3个车站。<br>湖南段：岳阳东、汨罗东、长沙南、株洲西、衡山西、衡阳东、耒阳西、郴州西8个车站。<br>广东段：韶关、清远、广州北、广州南4个车站。 | 世界上一次建成里程最长、工程类型最复杂的高速铁路。 |
| 3 | 郑西高速铁路 | 2010年2月6日 | 河南段：郑州东、新荥阳、新巩义、洛阳龙门站、新渑池、新三门峡、新灵宝7个车站。<br>陕西段：新华山、新渭南、新临潼、西安北、咸阳西、（新）杨凌、五丈原、（新）宝鸡8个车站。 | 世界首条修建在湿陷性黄土地区的高速铁路。 |
| 4 | 昌九城际高铁 | 2010年8月28日 | 九江、庐山、德安、共青城、永修、乐化、南昌北等7个车站。 | |
| 5 | 沪杭高速铁路 | 2010年10月26日 | 上海虹桥站、松江南、金山北、嘉善南、嘉兴南、桐乡、海宁西、余杭南、杭州东站等9个车站。 | 最高时速达到416.6公里。 |
| 6 | 京沪高速铁路 | 2010年12月3日（试运行） | 北京南、天津西、济南西、南京南、上海虹桥站5个始发终到站。 | 最高时速达到486.1公里。 |

资料来源：笔者据有关资料整理

（2）中国高速铁路网的规划设想

中国高速铁路网规划，主要依据2004年1月国务院常务会议讨论并原则通过的《中长期铁路网规划》，并于2008年11月正式发布的《中长期铁路网规划（2008年调整）》。根据《中长期铁路网规划（2008年调整）》，为满足快速增长的旅客运输需求，建立省会城市及大中城市间的快速客运通道，规划“四纵四横”等客运专线以及经济发达和人口稠密地区城际客运系统。

①“四纵”客运专线

北京—上海客运专线，包括蚌埠—合肥、南京—杭州客运专线，贯通京津至长江三角洲东部沿海经济发达地区；

北京—武汉—广州—深圳客运专线，连接华北和华南地区；

北京—沈阳—哈尔滨（大连）客运专线，包括锦州—营口客运专线，连接东北和关内地区；

上海—杭州—宁波—福州—深圳客运专线，连接长江、珠江三角洲和东南沿海地区。

②“四横”客运专线

徐州—郑州—兰州客运专线，连接西北和华东地区；

杭州—南昌—长沙—贵阳—昆明客运专线，连接西南、华中和华东地区；

青岛—石家庄—太原客运专线，连接华北和华东地区；

南京—武汉—重庆—成都客运专线，连接西南和华东地区。

同时，建设南昌—九江、柳州—南宁、绵阳—成都—乐山、哈尔滨—齐齐哈尔、哈尔滨—牡丹江、长春—吉林、沈阳—丹东等客运专线，扩大客运专线的覆盖面。

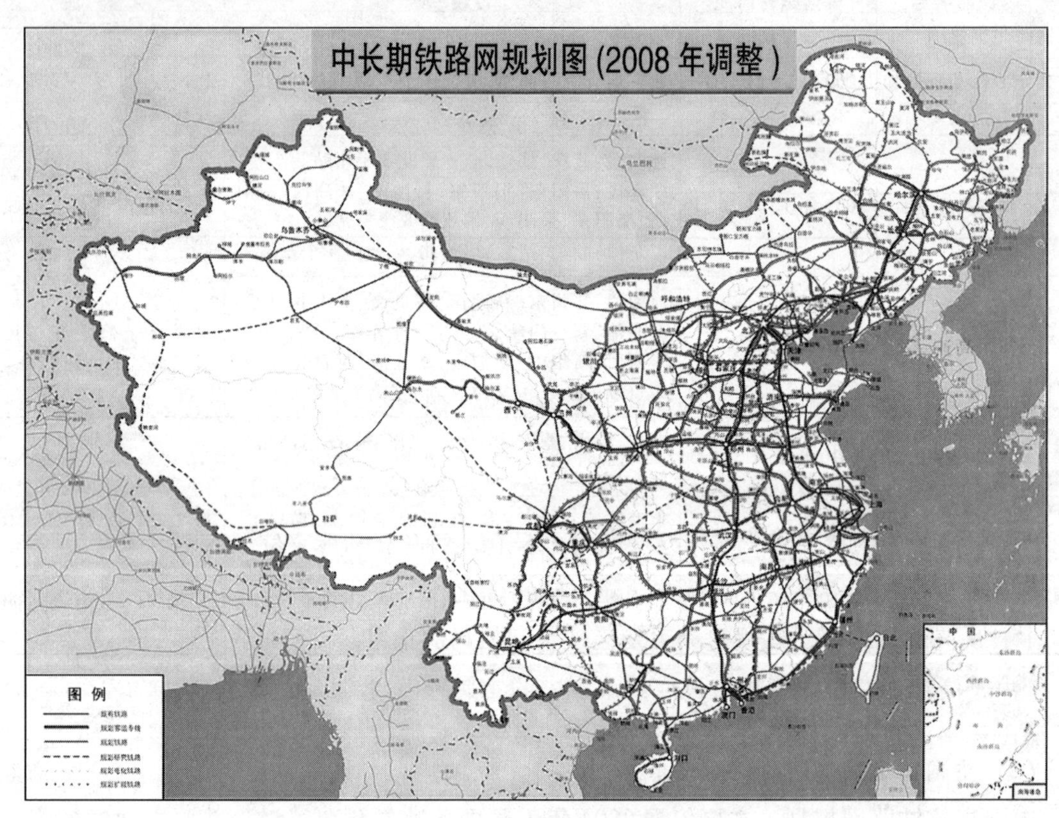


图1　高速铁路网规划图

资料来源：《中长期铁路网规划（2008年调整）》

### 3. 中国高速铁路对城市发展的作用

（1）“十一五”期间中国高速铁路对社会经济的拉动效应

①对国民经济的直接拉动

铁道部在“十一五”期间的5年建设时间内，安排全国建设7000公里的高速铁路新线，总投资额为12500亿元，平均每年投入2500亿元，每年建设1400公里。

高速铁路建设对国民经济拉动的直接效益，主要体现在高速铁路建设投资对GDP的直接拉动作用上，即“十一五”期间高速铁路建设投资对国民生产总值的净贡献。根据《铁路规划战略研究》，每1亿元建设铁路投资对社会总产出的影响为3.014亿元，“十一五”期间高速铁路建设可拉动社会总产出7535亿元①。

②对相关产业的影响分析

高速铁路建设投资对国民经济其他产业或部门产出的影响比较大的主要是第二产业。因此，“十一五”期间，我国投资12500亿元用于7000公里高速铁路新线的建设，在一定程度上拉动了国内第二产业一些部门或行业的发展。

**表2　每1亿元高速铁路建设投资对国民经济各部门产出的影响**

| 主要行业 | 总产出(亿元) | 主要行业 | 总产出(亿元) |
|---|---|---|---|
| 铁路建筑业 | 0.693 | 机械工业 | 0.172 |
| 金属冶炼及压延加工业 | 0.322 | 金属制品业 | 0.099 |
| 交通运输设备制造业 | 0.319 | 建筑材料以及其他非金属矿制品业 | 0.098 |
| 商业 | 0.197 | 货运邮电业 | 0.089 |
| 化学工业 | 0.184 | 电子及通信设备制造业 | 0.070 |

资料来源：《铁路“十五”规划战略研究》

③对就业的拉动分析

高速铁路建设投资可以为社会带来更多的就业岗位。“十一五”期间，我国高速铁路建设投资每年可为社会提供1337.25万个就业岗位。

(2)中国高速铁路对沿线城市空间结构的影响

在区域发展的格局下，城市之间通过差异化、特色化功能定位形成竞合关系，城市内部通过高铁站点客流发展，促进城市功能空间的优化。

①从区域范围看，高铁建设引发区域空间格局的重组。

由于高速铁路串联了城市群或城市圈中的主要城市，加快城市之间的联系，有利于实现区域内要素的再分配，形成串联经济效应，最终形成城市群、城市带的发展格局。

以京津城市铁路为例，在京津城际开始建设后，线路通过的11个城区中有5个城区陆续出台和调整了沿线地区的城市发展规划②。这些城区在新的发展规划中均瞄准了区域的差异化或补充化功能，如丰台区丽泽金融商务区被明确为首都金融业发展新空间，而天津市武清区则将城区定位在“京津之间的高新技术产业基地、现代服务业基地和生态宜居城市”。

②从单一城市的范围看，高铁建设带动车站周边的空间发展。

由于高铁吸引大量的高端商务群体、旅游群体，所以，高铁车站往往可以引发商务、商

① 数据来源：骆玲，曹洪著．高速铁路的区域经济效应研究．2010

② 资料来源：尹冰，吕成文，赵晨．高速铁路对城市发展的影响研究．铁道经济研究，2010（4）

业、休闲、居住等城市功能的聚集，刺激城市新城的开发建设。

以武广高铁沿线城市发展为例，几乎每个城市都认识到高速铁路带来的开发价值，把新火车站作为依托，加快城市化步伐，完善城市功能，打造城市的副中心，借此带动一片新区域的发展。其中，广州南站作为中国六大铁路客运枢纽之一，更成为广州与佛山之间的“都市结”，促进了广州与佛山交接地区的空间发展。以广州新客站为中心，整合番禺区长隆—万博、南海区三山港、顺德区陈村商贸区等周边各类功能区，大力发展现代商贸、物流、休闲娱乐等现代服务业，合力打造区域性物流中心、商贸中心，建成广佛乃至全省对外的展示窗口和商业交流大平台。

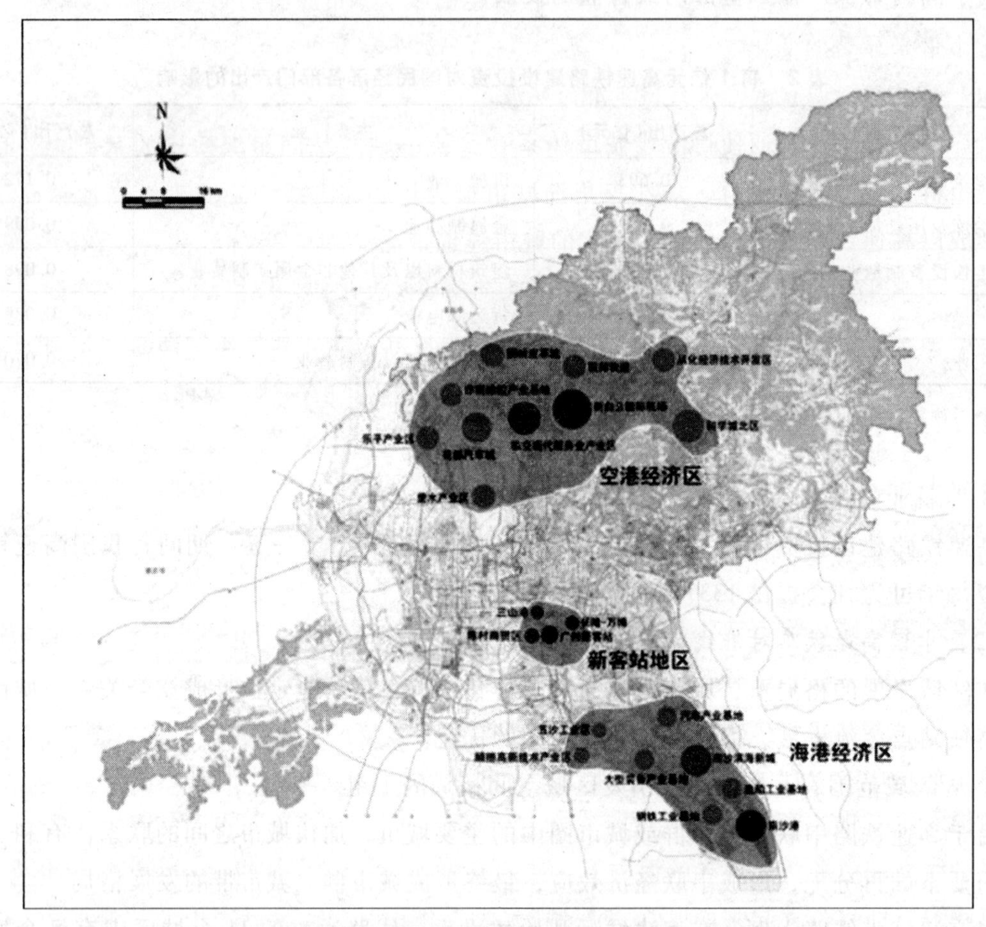


图2　广佛重大设施共享区布局示意图

资料来源：《广佛同城化发展规划（2009—2020年）》

在2010年公布的《广州南站地区城市设计》中，36.1平方公里的南站地区将成为广州继老城区、珠江新城之后的第三增长极，建成以商务、商贸为主导功能的现代服务业集聚区。南站地区主要功能是交通服务，其次是商务、商贸功能，并包括部分城市服务功能（如商业、酒店、旅游购物等）和文化、体育、教育、医疗、住宅、公寓、办公、研发等。居住功能为辅助功能。在广佛同城化战略中，该地区的发展更快，规模更大。

## 二、武广高铁沿线“武广新城”的规划建设

### 1. 武广高铁沿线城市的发展变化

2009年年底，武广高铁开通，广州至武汉出行时间缩短至3小时零8分。高铁拉近了城市距离，节约了旅行时间，改变了人们的生活方式，同时对资源配置和产业布局产生了积极的影响，进而对沿线城市和区域经济产生了深远的影响。

武广高铁开通一年多以来，城际间、区域经济以及城市原有的交通枢纽等方面，为沿线发展城市带来显著的变化。

（1）城市群效应：武广沿线城市群的发展

武广高速铁路的开通使得沿线城市体系在“点—轴”空间组织模式的基础上，促进以武汉城市群、长株潭城市群、珠江三角洲城市群为核心，沿线中心城市沿高速铁路两侧集聚，形成以高速铁路为走廊的葡萄串式的城市连绵带。

（2）同城化效应：交往活动的多样化以及范围的扩大化

武广高铁3小时通达三个省——武广高铁的城际化运输，使广东、湖北、湖南三省同城化的观念深入人心。从10小时到3小时，使三省的同城化渐渐成为可能。

统计显示，平均每天有5万余人选择搭乘武广高铁这条世界运营速度最快的高速铁路。开通短短1年，日开行列车最高达160列，始发站最小发车间隔仅5分钟，加快了三地人员交流和资源配置，大大拉动了三地的旅游、休闲等城市消费，形成了独具特色的“3小时经济圈”。

与传统的铁路运输方式不同，武广高铁的客流成分更多地集中在高中端客流，包括商务、旅游等高端客流，也有学生和往返于大城市之间的城际客流。

（3）新城效应：沿线城市借势打造武广新城区

高速铁路作为一种全新的交通运输方式，它的引入将会使城市的可达性重新组合，促使城市结构发生变化。

在沿线高端商务活动需求的促进下，武广高铁引发了新一轮的站点引导开发热潮。如，韶关新站附近即将矗立起来的“芙蓉新城”，湖南衡山县因高铁站而生的“开云新城”，长沙东部雨花区黎托乡即将建成的“武广新城”。武广高铁途经了15座城市，其中有3大省会城市、7大地级市，连同5座县级市。以高铁枢纽地区为触媒的“新城”群起与武广一同应运而生。

### 2. 武广新城区的规划建设

武广高铁为中国新建的高速铁路工程之一，连接鄂、湘、粤三省，北起武汉新火车站，南到广州的广州南站，全长1068公里，共设车站25座，途经3大省会城市，7大地级市以及5座县级市。武汉、咸宁、岳阳、长沙、广州等15座城市火车站周边崛起的新城，将成

为城市的新门户和新增长极。"武广新城"的开发掀起了新一轮"造城运动"。

(1) 特大城市作为城市副中心开发的"武广新城"

①广州南站新城

广州南站新城规划面积约36.1平方公里，总建筑规模将达到2200万平方米。建成后，该地区将容纳35万人，其中居住人口约14.4万，就业人口约26.8万。

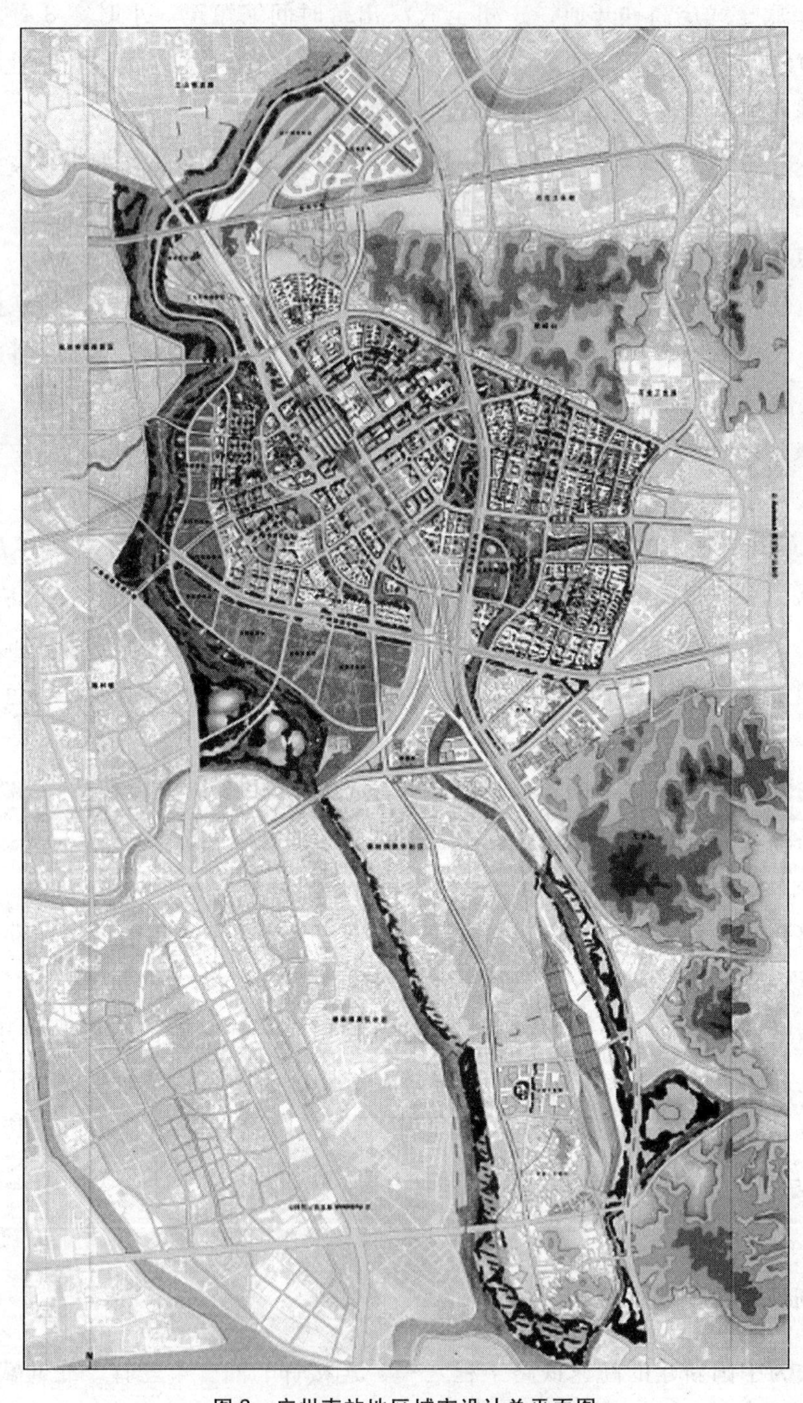

图3　广州南站地区城市设计总平面图

资料来源：《广州南站地区城市设计》

②新武汉站杨春湖地区

杨春湖城市副中心依托于京广客运专线武汉站的交通枢纽型城市综合服务中心，将成为武汉未来新门户。目前，武汉站杨春湖地区规划已获得省政府通过。

杨春湖城市副中心作为武汉市主城区的二级中心，其商业、商务、酒店、办公等核心功能集聚区的面积将小于1平方公里。结合武汉市主城中心结构体系布局，核心功能集聚区的用地面积将在0.8平方公里左右。

图4　武汉杨春湖城市副中心城市设计效果图

③长沙南站武广新城

位于长沙东南部的黎托小镇，因为武广高铁长沙南站的落户，正聚集成千上万的工人和大批现代化机械，掀起兴建武广新城的热潮。在长沙市的规划中，这个以长沙南站为中心的周边8平方公里区域，被定位为“中南地区区域性的铁路客运中心和具有商务功能的交通枢纽型城市副中心”。

(2) 地级城市依托武广高铁打造的“特色新城”

地级城市依托各自城市的特点，力图通过武广高铁的牵引作用，打造城市未来的副中心。各城市“武广新城”的规划情况如表3所示：

表3　地级城市的武广新城规划

| 序号 | 武广新城 | 规　模 | 功能定位 |
|---|---|---|---|
| 1 | 清远市武广客运专线新清远站周边地区 | 总用地面积约为4.96平方公里 | 综合交通枢纽、现代商业、旅游服务以及休闲娱乐 |
| 2 | 武广高铁韶关站“芙蓉新城” | 规划建设用地面积17.8平方公里，承载人口约25万人 | 成为韶关未来的行政、交通、旅游休闲和金融中心 |

续表 3

| 序号 | 武广新城 | 规　模 | 功能定位 |
|---|---|---|---|
| 3 | 郴州“武广新城” | 新城核心区占地面积 0.23 平方公里，总建筑面积 70 万平方米 | 郴州市未来的中央商务区 |
| 4 | 衡阳市武广客运站站前片地区 | 规划总用地面积 2.18 平方公里 | 集贸易、商业办公、文化娱乐、旅游观光为一体的，体现衡阳本土风貌的生态复合型的现代化城市新区 |
| 5 | 株洲“武广新城” | 总用地面积约 10 平方公里 | 建设一个集商务、旅游、生态居住的“武广新城” |
| 6 | 岳阳岳东新城 | 总用地面积 8.7 平方公里 | 岳阳交通、体育、居住、商贸、工农业于一体城市副中心的角色 |
| 7 | 咸宁北站城市新城区 | 总用地面积 3 平方公里 | 包括商务中心、游客接待中心、土特产展销中心、新型住宅区等，以吸引商务人士来安居投资兴业 |

(3) 小城市以承接产业转移为目标的“发展新城”

①赤壁市武广新城

赤壁市依托高铁新设立经济开发区，已有来自广州、深圳等地的数控、光电和旅游企业落户，首批引资近 100 亿元。

②衡山开云新城

衡山开云新城囊括了衡山站所在区域的 6.8 平方公里。开云新城定位为富有个性的旅游服务基地、自然和谐的生态城区、贡献突出的经济实体。要着力将新衡山站区打造成衡山风景名胜区游客集散和旅游服务基地，彰显城市形象及地域文化的名片和生态城区，成为未来区域经济发展的重要增长极。

③武广耒阳新城

武广耒阳新城未来将是耒阳市新的增长极。在高标准建设好武广耒阳新城的规划下，耒阳市将新城规划面积由 11.8 平方公里调整至 30 平方公里。

### 3. 武广高铁的影响作用分析

武广高铁自 2009 年 12 月开通以来，共运送旅客 2058 万余人，日均运送旅客 5.6 万人，高峰日输送量达到 13.5 万人。总运送人数相当于整体搬运了广州、长沙和武汉三座城市的户籍人口，相当于欧洲之星高速列车一年客运量的两倍左右①。

在高铁“大运量、高密度、公交化”的运输组织模式下，武广高铁对沿线城市的影响可以从城市群、区域以及城市三个角度进行分析。

(1) 城市群的角度：武广高铁牵起“武广大都市带”

武广高铁将贯通“两湖”与珠三角三大城市群，形成“武广大都市带”，并成为带动区域城市发展的新引擎。武广高速铁路通车后，对武汉、长沙和广州这 3 个城市所在的武汉城市圈和长株潭城市群以及珠三角城市群，会带来三个方面的改变：

① 数据来源：武广高铁通车 1 周年：速度改变南中国，袁钢，http://www.gzrailway.com.cn/print.aspx? id=644

首先是空间范围的变化。目前三大城市群的范围，是相对于当今的中心城市规模和交通运输状况形成的。当城市群形成的条件变化之后，城市群的范围当然会变化。区域经济联系空前紧密，未来的“武广大都市带”的骨架就跃然图上了。

其次是产业结构的变化。目前，珠三角、长株潭和大武汉三大城市群的产业结构有一定的专业化分工，但不是很明显。高速铁路通车后形成的交通条件的大变化，会使区域的产业结构向两个方向变化：一方面是综合性的方向，即取长补短，相互融通；另一方面是专业化的方向，“武广大都市带”内的制造业部门向最佳区位集中。

最后是发展理念的变化。武广高铁的建成，将大幅度拉近湖南、湖北与珠三角的经济距离，珠三角地区的市场经济理念北上对长株潭城市群和武汉城市圈扩散，湖南、湖北的人才优势、资源优势也可以得到充分发挥。

(2) 区域的角度：“武广经济带”的集聚与扩散

武广高铁开通半年，人流、物流、资金流沿武广线开始“动起来”，沿线大中小城市悄然形成崭新的经济格局——“武广经济带”。比亚迪就是一个很好的例子。目前，比亚迪在深圳、西安、长沙建立三大生产基地，而这些城市都是“高铁城市”。

武广沿线的大部分资金、人才在珠三角沿海地区集中到一定程度后，开始向成本相对低的湘鄂两省腹地推进，走廊产业经济带逐渐形成。而形成走廊产业经济带的重要催化剂就是武广高铁。它的开通运营，使得粤港澳、珠三角“腾笼换鸟”式产业转移变得更快，沿线城镇加速融入珠三角经济圈。

而对于武广高铁经过的中部地区而言，武广沿线房地产、旅游及其他一般服务业的集聚效应更明显，资本的流动将为中部地区创造崛起的契机。

武广沿线城市旅游景点众多，丹霞山、衡山、岳阳等，高铁开通一年以来，游客人数均大为增加。衡山接待游客人数同比增长 30% 以上①。

2010 年 1—8 月，韶关全市旅行社共接待境外游客同比增长 1056.5%，其中接待香港游客同比增长 1111.58%。以前韶关也在香港进行过旅游推广，但推行了 10 多年都不成功，武广高铁一开通，原来冷清的格局马上改变，现在很多香港游客专门来体验高铁的“贴地飞行”。②

2010 年 1 至 3 季度，长沙市接待游客数量比上年同期增长了 20% 以上，增幅为近 10 年来的最高水平③。

(3) 城市的角度：推动城市自身的建设发展

以高铁新客站及新城区域建设为起点，引发新城功能与形象的重构，进而影响城市发展重心的调整，为整个城市的发展注入了新的源泉。这在武广高铁沿线城市中达成了共识。

武广高铁的开通推动城市化进程的加速，为进一步推动城镇化进程提供了新的机遇。

---

① 数据来源：解读高铁“武广现象”，大公报，2010 年 10 月 29 日

② 数据来源：解读高铁“武广现象”，大公报，2010 年 10 月 29 日

③ 数据来源：武广高铁通车 1 周年：速度改变南中国，袁钢，http://www.gzrailway.com.cn/print.aspx? id = 644

基础设施建设方面，武广高铁推进内陆城市的交通基础设施建设，实现了城市交通建设的大跨越。

长沙则先期启动了地铁中心。根据长沙近期轨道交通规划，到2015年，从武汉或广州方向乘高速列车沿武广客运专线进入长沙的乘客，就能乘地铁快速进入长沙市区。同时，国家发改委还正式批复《长株潭城市群城际轨道交通网规划（2009—2020年）》，这一规划标志着长株潭城市群城际轨道已经进入实质性阶段。

在武汉，地铁轻轨连通全城。乘客走出武广专线，可乘地铁迅速到达武汉新区、后湖、常青花园、东湖开发区、关山等地观光。

此外，中国人口众多、土地资源有限，特别需要铁路这种节能环保的交通工具。武广高铁对于发挥高速铁路相对节约土地、能源消耗以及污染较小、安全性好等优势，集约利用土地，减少交通运输的环境污染，降低全社会的运输成本，也具有极为重要的示范意义。

（作者：蔡云楠，广州市城市规划勘测设计研究院副院长，教授级高级规划师；李洪斌，广州市城市规划勘测设计研究院规划一所所长，高级规划师）

# 我国资源型城市转型与发展

资源型城市是我国一个重要的城市类型。为了防止因资源枯竭导致资源型城市产业衰退，党的十六大提出“支持东北地区等老工业基地加快调整和改造，支持以资源开采为主的城市和地区发展接续产业”，正式拉开了中国资源型城市转型的序幕。2007 年 12 月，国务院又出台了《促进资源型城市可持续发展的若干意见》，对我国资源型城市转型攻坚战进行深入的指导。资源型城市经过这些年来的转型发展，已发生深刻变化。

## 一、资源型城市数量与空间演化新特征

改革开放以来，我国社会经济飞速发展，从而带动了对各种能源、原材料需求的迅猛增长。通过新一轮国土资源大调查，目前全国已初步形成藏中铜矿基地、滇西北有色金属资源基地、新疆东天山有色金属资源基地、新疆罗布泊钾盐资源基地、北方可地浸砂岩型铀矿基地、新疆阿吾拉勒铁资源基地、新疆乌拉根铅锌资源基地、西藏念青唐古拉山有色金属基地、祁漫塔格有色金属基地、青海大场金资源基地等十大新的资源接替基地。“十一五”期间，全国集中建设了晋北、晋中、晋东、神东、陕北、黄陇、鲁西、两淮、冀中、河南、云贵、蒙东、宁东十三个大型煤炭基地，产量 26 亿吨。2010 年新疆又正式被国家规划为全国第 14 个大型煤炭基地。这些资源与能源富集区的开发为当地经济插上了腾飞的翅膀，采掘业、能源化工业发展对资源型城市数量与空间演化产生了新的影响。

### 1. 资源型城市数量不断增长，增幅与经济社会对资源的需求相关

我国经济发展与城市建设对能源、原材料保持旺盛的需求，使得不少资源开采和加工基地跃入资源型城市的行列。特别是西部大开发战略的实施，具有得天独厚的资源优势的西部，使一批原本落后的城市的资源产业发展成为其支柱性产业，经济连续多年快速提升。例如，内蒙古的鄂尔多斯、呼伦贝尔，陕西的渭南、榆林、延安，甘肃平凉，另外还有山西晋中、四川广安、云南曲靖等。其中，陕西榆林为全国提供了 5% 以上煤炭和 5% 以上油气，是全国第一产能大市，经济增速连续七年全省最快，昔日极度贫困的边塞之地一举成为能源新都。内蒙古鄂尔多斯，能源开发造就不少“一夜暴富”神话。“十二五”期间，中国面临加快转变经济发展方式的突出任务，发展环境面临资源环境约束增强的重大变化，大西北能

源基地在“十二五”期间将肩负更重的任务，面临全新的挑战。

**2. 资源型城市类别更加丰富，再生资源将得到重视**

随着不可再生资源的枯竭和环境问题日益突出，资源供需矛盾越来越突出。为了满足与日俱增的资源需求，新能源、新材料等可再生资源和生态资源将得到充分重视。过去五年间，新能源和可再生能源异军突起，在加强油气资源勘探开发同时，加快西南地区和黄河上游水电开发，大力发展风能和太阳能。“十二五”期间，新能源产业都被寄予了厚望。将有序推进大型风电基地建设，重点发展内蒙古、甘肃、新疆、河北、江苏、山东、吉林及东北地区等千万千瓦级风电基地。在内蒙古、甘肃、青海、新疆、西藏的适宜地区，开展太阳能热发电试点。资源型城市的类别也会更加丰富。

**3. 资源型城市空间格局逐渐向西部转移**

“十一五”时期，已经逐渐形成长距离、大规模的北煤南运、西电东送、北油南运、西气东输的能源运输基本格局。“十二五”原则是“加快西部、稳定中部、优化东部”。随着中东部能源资源的衰竭，我国能源发展战略西移的特征越来越明显。

资源具有不可再生性，随着大规模的资源开采。城市转型成为历史的必然。伴随着“西部大开发”和“中部崛起”战略的实施，到2007年，东、中、西部资源型城市所占比重分别为36%、33.7%和30.7%。中部六省有资源型城市59个。同时，我国森林资源主要分布在东北和西南地区，煤炭、石油、盐类矿产资源主要分布在中西部的大型沉积盆地，而黑色和有色金属则位于中西部的褶皱山系，随着“西部大开发的深入”、中国经济重心的转移和基于资源地的指向性，决定了资源型城市空间格局的西移。

## 二、资源型城市产业结构发展与变化

**1. 资源型城市产业结构变动率**

一个地区的产业结构是否合理，在很大程度上决定经济发展的速度与效益。笔者从我国92个地级资源型城市中①选取其中45个城市进行了研究，其中把煤炭城市28个、石油城市5个、有色城市6个、冶金城市3个和森工城市3个作为研究对象，应用产业结构变动率、产业结构偏离度分析了资源型城市产业结构变化情况。

(1) 产业结构变动度高于全国水平

以1998年为基期，以1999—2008年为报告期，我国45个地级资源型城市产业结构变动系数见表1，并选择大庆、铜陵等4个资源型城市与资源型城市平均水平和全国产业结构变化进行了比较（见图1）。结果显示：①资源型城市产业结构变动态势和全国相同，但变

① 余际从，刘粤湘等．矿业城市界定及可持续发展能力研究．北京：地质出版社，2009

动幅度却大于全国平均水平。②资源型城市总体产业结构变动平稳，但各城市却变化不同。如大庆市变化呈倒 U 形；大同变动态势呈波浪形；有色城市铜陵在 2004 年前，产业结构变动不明显，变动值维持在 5 左右，2004 年后逐渐上升，2008 年产业结构变动值高达 23.92；白山市各年产业结构变动不大，变动值大多数年均小于 5，而近些年份产业结构变动明显。

**表 1　资源型城市产业结构变动率（1999—2008 年）**

（单位：%）

| 城市＼年份 | 1999 | 2000 | 2001 | 2002 | 2003 | 2004 | 2005 | 2006 | 2007 | 2008 |
|---|---|---|---|---|---|---|---|---|---|---|
| 唐山 | 1.6 | 3.3 | 6.7 | 8.8 | 10.6 | 14.6 | 18.3 | 21.2 | 22.8 | 25.4 |
| 邯郸 | 2.9 | 7.4 | 9.3 | 10.4 | 11.7 | 14.7 | 17.0 | 16.4 | 18.3 | 20.6 |
| 邢台 | 2.3 | 7.6 | 11.8 | 13.9 | 15.7 | 17.2 | 18.7 | 17.7 | 20.3 | 23.7 |
| 大同 | 7.6 | 17.5 | 15.7 | 17.6 | 11.8 | 5.1 | 5.5 | 13.1 | 16.3 | 16.1 |
| 阳泉 | 8.2 | 15.5 | 16.0 | 16.2 | 14.0 | 12.6 | 8.7 | 18.7 | 15.4 | 15.8 |
| 长治 | 2.9 | 5.9 | 6.7 | 8.4 | 10.0 | 6.4 | 10.3 | 14.0 | 15.3 | 18.4 |
| 晋城 | 5.9 | 11.5 | 12.1 | 11.2 | 9.2 | 4.3 | 8.5 | 9.8 | 10.7 | 8.5 |
| 朔州 | 2.3 | 10.2 | 10.3 | 15.3 | 9.1 | 7.0 | 14.1 | 16.8 | 23.7 | 23.6 |
| 乌海 | 5.9 | 6.5 | 6.3 | 5.3 | 2.8 | 7.8 | 12.2 | 12.0 | 11.4 | 6.6 |
| 赤峰 | 3.9 | 7.8 | 15.3 | 16.6 | 14.9 | 19.1 | 17.0 | 18.5 | 25.3 | 33.4 |
| 抚顺 | 9.0 | 11.5 | 8.6 | 8.1 | 9.7 | 11.2 | 7.7 | 19.6 | 17.9 | 16.0 |
| 本溪 | 0.9 | 5.8 | 8.2 | 9.5 | 10.6 | 3.4 | 7.1 | 6.8 | 9.0 | 15.2 |
| 阜新 | 19.9 | 12.2 | 15.6 | 14.2 | 7.9 | 4.7 | 7.8 | 6.6 | 1.8 | 6.6 |
| 盘锦 | 6.3 | 5.1 | 12.8 | 6.1 | 5.3 | 5.2 | 6.2 | 6.3 | 7.7 | 7.1 |
| 葫芦岛 | 1.9 | 8.8 | 11.2 | 8.5 | 10.1 | 11.5 | 11.0 | 10.3 | 12.4 | 11.4 |
| 辽源 | 14.0 | 18.7 | 10.6 | 10.1 | 7.7 | 1.6 | 10.0 | 24.1 | 32.7 | 41.8 |
| 白山 | 1.0 | 2.0 | 3.8 | 4.6 | 4.3 | 2.5 | 5.9 | 10.6 | 14.0 | 19.4 |
| 松原 | 13.8 | 9.4 | 12.6 | 9.3 | 9.4 | 11.7 | 19.3 | 26.1 | 34.9 | 42.4 |
| 鸡西 | 7.3 | 16.5 | 13.2 | 11.8 | 17.9 | 13.8 | 12.8 | 18.0 | 16.7 | 19.7 |
| 鹤岗 | 4.1 | 9.3 | 9.9 | 10.2 | 15.3 | 11.7 | 14.2 | 16.3 | 18.1 | 16.9 |
| 双鸭山 | 2.3 | 5.1 | 4.2 | 4.3 | 6.1 | 7.9 | 12.8 | 6.6 | 8.6 | 11.7 |
| 大庆 | 4.1 | 3.5 | 13.4 | 11.4 | 6.2 | 5.1 | 4.7 | 5.9 | 5.3 | 4.9 |
| 伊春 | 6.8 | 6.1 | 8.3 | 3.2 | 3.2 | 12.8 | 11.2 | 23.6 | 23.8 | 25.7 |
| 七台河 | 4.4 | 12.3 | 11.9 | 14.8 | 13.6 | 10.0 | 9.2 | 9.6 | 9.7 | 17.2 |
| 淮南 | 9.8 | 12.9 | 17.4 | 18.2 | 16.3 | 15.2 | 9.2 | 9.5 | 7.9 | 11.6 |
| 马鞍山 | 5.0 | 6.1 | 13.6 | 14.3 | 14.1 | 7.5 | 7.2 | 12.4 | 14.3 | 12.3 |
| 淮北 | 5.4 | 7.9 | 15.5 | 16.6 | 14.0 | 11.5 | 5.1 | 9.3 | 13.8 | 10.2 |
| 铜陵 | 4.5 | 5.4 | 4.8 | 5.8 | 6.7 | 8.5 | 16.7 | 13.0 | 23.6 | 23.9 |
| 萍乡 | 16.2 | 5.0 | 6.1 | 7.8 | 9.7 | 12.5 | 13.7 | 12.5 | 15.2 | 20.4 |
| 枣庄 | 2.0 | 9.4 | 8.1 | 9.1 | 8.1 | 10.4 | 16.9 | 20.8 | 21.2 | 19.7 |
| 东营 | 3.2 | 5.6 | 8.2 | 8.4 | 9.5 | 10.4 | 11.6 | 12.9 | 13.8 | 16.3 |
| 平顶山 | 3.8 | 5.0 | 5.2 | 5.5 | 5.3 | 6.4 | 8.1 | 12.1 | 15.2 | 22.2 |

续表 1

| 城市＼年份 | 1999 | 2000 | 2001 | 2002 | 2003 | 2004 | 2005 | 2006 | 2007 | 2008 |
|---|---|---|---|---|---|---|---|---|---|---|
| 鹤壁 | 4.6 | 5.8 | 5.0 | 6.4 | 7.8 | 7.7 | 6.9 | 18.2 | 20.6 | 31.2 |
| 焦作 | 3.9 | 23.7 | 22.7 | 21.0 | 20.1 | 20.8 | 12.2 | 11.0 | 13.2 | 14.8 |
| 濮阳 | 2.5 | 8.7 | 4.4 | 3.8 | 5.5 | 14.6 | 13.1 | 19.5 | 22.9 | 27.0 |
| 郴州 | 3.9 | 7.0 | 11.5 | 15.2 | 14.9 | 18.4 | 18.8 | 22.8 | 26.4 | 25.2 |
| 韶关 | 5.1 | 6.9 | 7.9 | 11.6 | 14.0 | 17.5 | 19.8 | 23.2 | 24.5 | 27.6 |
| 攀枝花 | 6.2 | 5.5 | 3.3 | 1.9 | 3.5 | 6.8 | 11.1 | 6.0 | 7.2 | 12.8 |
| 广元 | 13.6 | 8.6 | 7.6 | 1.6 | 3.8 | 2.0 | 3.8 | 7.7 | 13.7 | 13.5 |
| 六盘水 | 0.5 | 0.5 | 2.4 | 5.1 | 7.4 | 9.9 | 16.7 | 17.5 | 19.4 | 23.2 |
| 铜川 | 5.6 | 7.3 | 7.9 | 23.0 | 21.7 | 19.9 | 13.4 | 12.0 | 6.4 | 8.7 |
| 金昌 | 2.1 | 5.1 | 4.3 | 9.3 | 10.5 | 14.0 | 24.3 | 21.5 | 24.9 | 25.7 |
| 白银 | 5.0 | 10.6 | 12.4 | 14.6 | 14.6 | 14.6 | 8.5 | 18.1 | 14.4 | 13.5 |
| 石嘴山 | 0.9 | 2.7 | 4.9 | 7.1 | 14.0 | 11.0 | 13.2 | 15.3 | 16.9 | 30.1 |
| 克拉玛依 | 3.5 | 2.5 | 8.5 | 10.2 | 7.5 | 11.1 | 15.3 | 17.2 | 19.7 | 22.2 |
| 以上平均 | 5.4 | 8.1 | 9.5 | 10.1 | 10.1 | 10.3 | 11.6 | 14.4 | 16.3 | 19.1 |
| 全国平均 | 2.98 | 5.58 | 8.55 | 10.47 | 10.00 | 8.33 | 10.71 | 12.51 | 12.86 | 14.4 |

注：以1998年为基期。

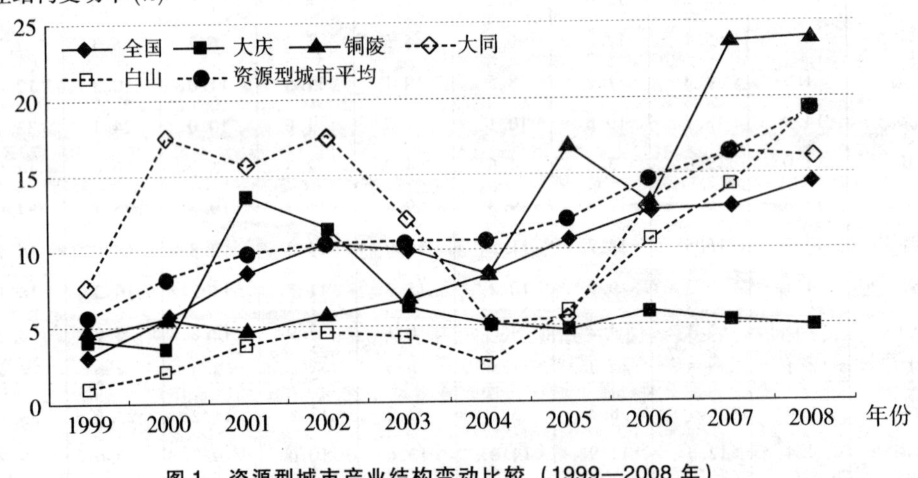


图 1　资源型城市产业结构变动比较（1999—2008 年）

（2）市场状况决定了不同资源型城市转型力度

由表 2 可知，在 2004 年前煤炭市场不景气的情况下，煤炭城市成为转型的主要动力，产业结构变动情况整体高于资源型城市平均水平。之后，随着有色等行业延长产业链条，增加产品附加值情况下，有色和森工城市逐渐取代了煤炭城市成为资源型城市产业结构变动的主要动力。石油、冶金城市变动情况则相对平稳，一直在资源型城市平均水平下变动。

表 2　资源城市按资源类型产业结构变动均值（1999—2008 年）

| 城市类型＼年份 | 1999 | 2000 | 2001 | 2002 | 2003 | 2004 | 2005 | 2006 | 2007 | 2008 |
|---|---|---|---|---|---|---|---|---|---|---|
| 森工城市 | 7.18 | 5.81 | 8.24 | 5.73 | 5.62 | 8.98 | 12.13 | 20.10 | 24.21 | 29.16 |
| 石油城市 | 3.92 | 5.08 | 9.46 | 7.98 | 6.80 | 9.28 | 10.15 | 12.36 | 13.90 | 15.52 |
| 冶金城市 | 4.01 | 6.10 | 9.16 | 10.24 | 10.78 | 9.04 | 11.04 | 12.02 | 14.47 | 16.57 |
| 有色城市 | 3.38 | 7.48 | 8.18 | 9.53 | 10.46 | 12.15 | 15.11 | 15.71 | 18.83 | 18.63 |
| 煤炭城市 | 6.11 | 9.57 | 10.26 | 11.37 | 11.28 | 10.60 | 11.56 | 14.46 | 16.03 | 18.31 |

（3）第一、二产业成为变动情况较大的部门

从三次产业分别变动情况来看，由图 2 可知，第一、二产业变动情况不断地提高。在 2004 年以前，第三产业成为产业结构变动的主要推动力，产业结构变动幅度高于第二产业。而 2004 年以后，第三产业结构变动幅度减低，第一、二产业成为变动较大的产业部门，第一产业比重不断减低，第二产业比重不断加强。说明在经济发展过程中，第一产业产值增加，但比重不断减低；通过发展接替产业、延伸产业链条等使得第二产业产值不断增加；第三产业在这些类型城市中缓慢发展。

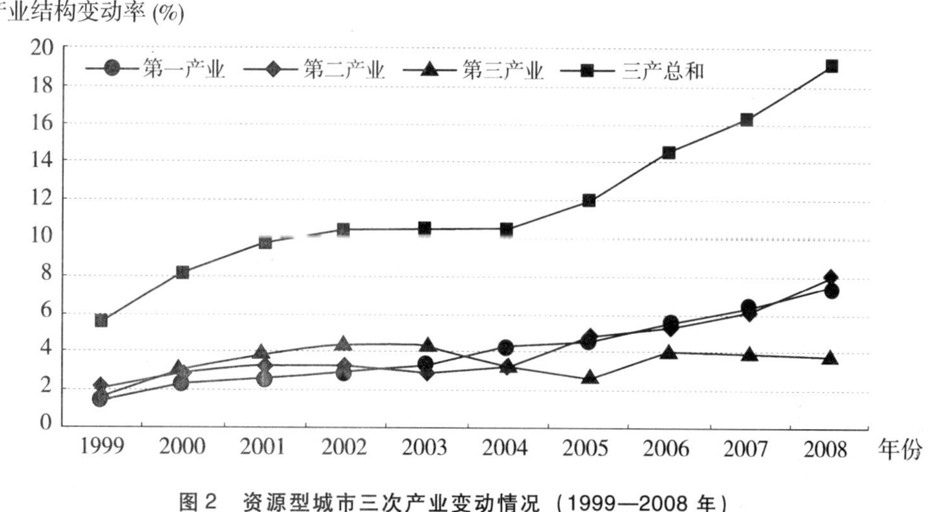


图 2　资源型城市三次产业变动情况（1999—2008 年）

## 2. 资源型城市产业结构协调性

产业结构偏离度是一种直接反映产业结构效益的重要量化指标。当产业结构偏离度为零时，该产业的产业结构与就业结构达到均衡状态；结构偏离度越接近零，该产业的产业结构与就业结构就越合理。

（1）产业结构和就业结构逐渐向协调的方向发展，且优于全国水平

在这 10 年中，我国资源型城市的产业结构偏离度逐渐减小（表 3），表明我国资源型城市的产业结构和就业结构逐渐向协调的方向发展，结构较全国合理。而 10 年间我国产业结

构偏离度下降缓慢，由1999年的67.16，下降为2008年的56.6。资源型城市与全国产业结构偏离度来看，资源型城市的协调性较好：2008年资源型城市第一产业结构偏离度仅为8.14，显著地好于全国水平28.3；第二产业偏离度为10.73，也好于全国水平21.4；第三产业全国优于资源型城市，分别为6.9和14.93。因此，资源型城市要处理好第二、三产业的协调性问题，而我国要重点处理好第一、二产业就业比重和产值比重差距过大的问题。

表3 资源型城市与全国产业结构协调性比较（1999—2008年）

| 年份 | 1999 | 2000 | 2001 | 2002 | 2003 | 2004 | 2005 | 2006 | 2007 | 2008 |
|---|---|---|---|---|---|---|---|---|---|---|
| 第一产业 | 17.23 | 16.36 | 13.31 | 12.97 | 12.01 | 10.6 | 10.54 | 9.91 | 8.91 | 8.14 |
| 第二产业 | 13.82 | 12.43 | 10.12 | 10.23 | 8.34 | 7.34 | 8.46 | 9.37 | 9.24 | 10.73 |
| 第三产业 | 9.19 | 10.14 | 10.73 | 11.08 | 11.05 | 11.48 | 12.95 | 13.34 | 13.6 | 14.93 |
| 资源城市 | 39.36 | 39.72 | 34.97 | 35.06 | 32.15 | 30.10 | 32.61 | 33.24 | 32.37 | 33.80 |
| 全国 | 67.16 | 69.87 | 71.12 | 72.51 | 72.61 | 67.01 | 65.20 | 62.60 | 59.35 | 56.60 |

(2) 各类型资源型城市产业结构偏离情况不同

这10年资源型城市产业结构逐渐向合理的方向转变，但各类型城市结构偏离情况并不相同。由图3可知，冶金、有色城市产业结构偏离度均小于资源型城市平均水平，且偏离度基本稳定；煤炭城市与资源型城市平均水平基本相同，10年变化轨迹与资源型城市变动基本重合；而森工城市多数年份均高于资源城市平均水平；石油城市结构偏离度呈U形，1999年偏离度为50.18，2002年下降到10年中的最低值37.74，而后又升高，2008年偏离度为54.83。这两种类型城市是我国资源型城市产业结构偏离度下降较慢的主要原因。但从各种资源型城市内部各城市表现来看，形态又各不相同。

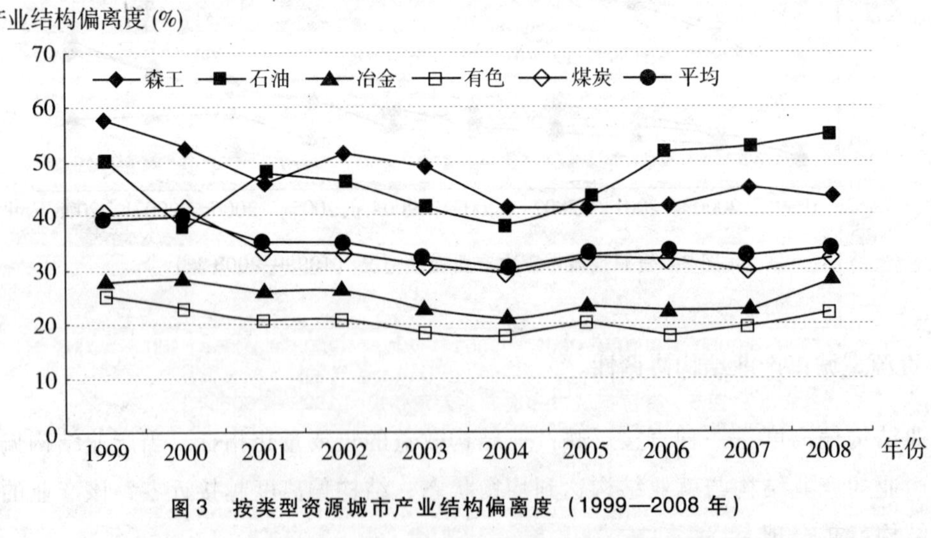


图3 按类型资源城市产业结构偏离度（1999—2008年）

由图4得，冶金城市攀枝花除1998年外，其余各年偏离度均在15以下波动，波动平稳，也表现了冶金城市的总体态势。煤炭城市总体基本稳定，10年中大同和阜新产业偏离度波动较大年份也相同，都发生在2001年。大同当年偏离度为57.6，阜新为66.1（图4）。

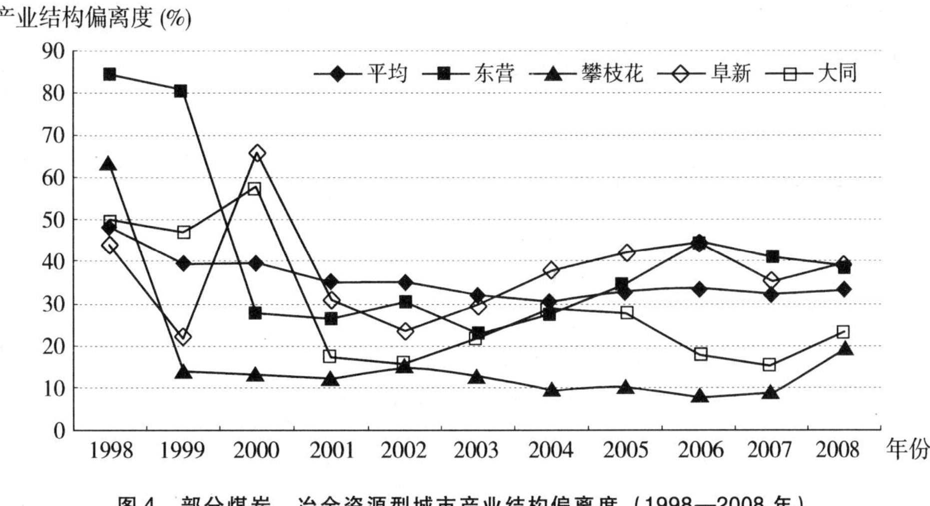


图 4　部分煤炭、冶金资源型城市产业结构偏离度（1998—2008 年）

然而，石油类各城市表现却不尽相同，东营表现了石油城市的总体呈 U 形态。

（3）第三产业成为资源型城市产业结构偏离的主要原因

从资源型城市三次产业各自偏离度动态轨迹（图 5）来看，一、二产业由不协调向协调的方向转变。一、二产业偏离度由 1998 年的 22.44、19.94 减低为 2008 年的 8.14 和 10.73。在 2002 年以前，一、二产业为我国资源型城市产业结构偏离的主要力量，而此后，第三产业成为产业结构偏离的主要原因。1998 年，第三产业结构偏离度为 6.99，2008 年上升为 14.93，占 2008 产业结构偏离度的 44.17%。

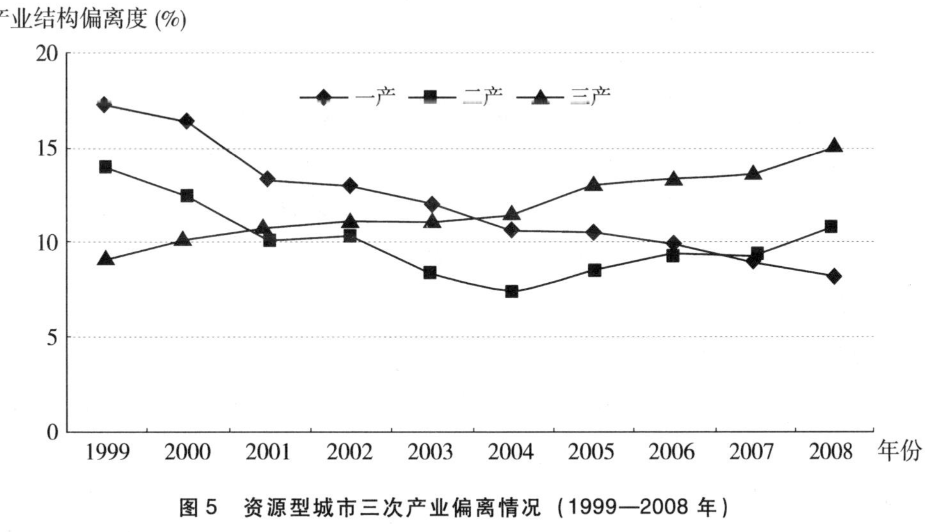


图 5　资源型城市三次产业偏离情况（1999—2008 年）

## 三、资源型城市转型案例与发展模式

资源型城市转型是指改变城市发展过度依赖自然资源开发的状况，并解决由此引起的经济、社会、环境问题，实现可持续发展。具体说就是，通过培育接续产业，发展替代产业，改变资源型城市主要依赖自然资源的开发和利用为其主导产业的现状，形成合理的产业结构，以发展、稳定、生态为目标带动城市经济形态、经济体制、生产方式、发展战略和发展模式等方面的系列变化，最终实现城市的可持续发展。

**1. 资源型城市转型的典型案例**

(1) 以现代农业为特色的阜新转型

阜新市彻底打破过去单一的煤电经济结构，推动农业和农产品加工产业发展，形成了食品及农产品加工业、新型能源产业及精细化工、装备制造业配套等优势特色产业为主的多元化工业经济结构，国民生产总值逐年攀高，城市居民人均可支配收入不断增加，城市转型取得了阶段性成效。同时，还实现多种产业并举；加强周边矿区勘探力度；参与开发内蒙古东部煤田，适度转移富余生产能力；推进矿区生态建设。

(2) 以非油气采掘业重点培育为特色的盘锦转型

自1996年以后，辽河油田的油气生产进入递减阶段。为了实现可持续发展，盘锦选择了重点培育壮大石油化工业、装备制造业、塑料及新型建材业、绿色有机食品业、现代服务业等五大接续产业发展战略。到2007年，盘锦市非油气采掘业增加值占地区生产总值的比重已经达到63.7%。按照盘锦市的“十二五”战略部署，将建设石化及精细化工、石油天然气装备、船舶及海洋工程装备、新材料、农产品生产加工“五大产业基地”。石化及精细化工产业集群产值力争达到3000亿元；石油天然气装备产业集群产值力争达到1000亿元；海洋工程装备产业集群产值力争达到600亿元；新材料产业集群产值力争达到1000亿元；农产品生产加工产业集群产值力争达到300亿元，农产品综合加工率达到60%以上。

(3) 以旅游业为特色的焦作转型

以旅游业为龙头，带动全市第三产业快速发展，是焦作推进城市经济转型的重要一环。目前，全市旅游业的综合收入占GDP比例高达10%，云台山、青龙峡、青天河、神农山、峰林峡五大景区，通过整体包装、资源整合，被联合国教科文组织正式命名为世界地质公园。焦作市已成为“中国优秀旅游城市”，“焦作山水”和“云台山”被评为“中国旅游知名品牌”，云台山入选首批世界地质公园。

(4) 以高科技产业为特色的白银转型

在长期的转型过程中，白银市形成了以中科院白银高技术产业园和白银西区经济开发区为载体，高新技术产业为主导的城市转型特色。2002年成立了中科院白银高技术产业园。一大批新材料、微电子、生物制药等高技术项目入驻园区。其中，碳酸锂加工、特大功率电子加速器、在恩制药等项目均为国家高新技术产业化项目。与此同时，科技园也诞生了新能源和洁净能源产业。利用产业园现有的碳酸锂、氧化钴等上游材料，建设锂离子动力电池和锌空气动力电池产业化基地，形成一个以锂产业为主导的多元化、多层次发展的产业群体。

(5) 以生态立市为特色的白山转型

依托长白山、鸭绿江、松花江“一山两江”，以“生态立市”为理念，拓宽资源开发领域，延长资源转换链条。目前白山市已经发展成为以能源、矿产冶金、林木深加工为支柱产业，以绿色食品、医药、旅游为希望产业的门类比较齐全的新兴工业城市。到2010年，实现工业增加值185亿元，年均增长21.6%。

**2. 资源型城市转型的发展模式**

资源型城市转型是个复杂巨大的系统工程。根据我国不同资源型城市的转型实践等方面情况，从资源产业处置方式、接续产业选择、转型运行机制等方面可归纳出资源型城市转型中选择的发展模式（表4）。

表4　资源型城市转型中的发展模式

| 划分依据 | 类型 | 特点 | 适用城市 |
|---|---|---|---|
| 矿业处置方式 | 整体退出型 | 矿产资源已经枯竭，资源型城市按原有的产业链条继续发展的空间很小，或资源开采条件恶化，开采成本过高，产品市场竞争乏力，企业不堪负重。或城市在原有优势资源基础上建立起来的产业体系，受资源供应的影响表现出缺乏活力甚至衰退的迹象；或由于保城限采、环境保护等方面的原因，尤其在国家政策发生重大变化的特殊情况下，资源型产业全线退出 | 适用于一些矿产资源开发成本很高或处于衰竭期的资源型城市 |
| | 局部退出型 | 对单一资源型城市的原有主导产业通过向纵向发展和技术改造，扩展原有产业链，增加产品的加工深度，从而带动区域产业的转型和区域的可持续发展，属于内、外界共同参与式转型模式 | 适用于资源储量及开发成本虽然具有一定优势，但由于产业附加值低，辐射影响力不大，从而影响城市产业可持续发展的单一资源型城市 |
| | 重新进入型 | 寻到了资源新储量或发现了非传统资源，以及市场利好因素影响，地位和作用明显下降资源性产业的获得新生 | 适用于具有勘查工作突破潜力的资源型城市 |
| 接续产业选择 | 产业链扩展模式 | 通过对原有主导资源开发产业进行产业纵向发展和技术进步及产业改造，扩展原有产业链，增加产品的加工深度，提高资源的附加价值，从而带动区域产业的转型和区域的可持续发展。如发展矿产品加工业、矿业装备制造业、现代服务业（矿业咨询等）、矿山旅游业等 | 适用于矿产资源储量及开发成本尚具有一定优势，但由于产业附加值低，辐射影响力不大，从而影响城市产业可持续发展的单一资源型城市 |
| | 新型产业替代模式 | 选择合适的新型产业，直接在资源型城市植入，从而较为彻底地改变对原有资源优势的依赖，带动建立新的城市产业体系。需要雄厚的资金、丰富的科技人才、畅通的信息、便捷的交通以及成熟的转化中介机构等 | 适用于资源开发成本很高和资源已经枯竭的资源型城市 |
| | 多元模式 | 以上两种模式的复合。主要依靠资源型城市区域内部产业结构调整优化，达到产业转型的目的 | 适用于虽然对资源开发依赖性很强，但也具有一定的其他产业优势的单一资源型城市 |
| 转型运行机制 | 政府主导型 | 根据国家对某个资源型城市的试点与分类指导进行的一种转型。政府成立专门委员会和其他组织，制定详细目标、计划和政策，各部门与各界通力合作促进转型 | 适用于工业历史悠久、城市具有一定规模、人口密度大、矿业在城市经济中的比重较大、转型难度较大的资源型城市 |
| | 市场主导型 | 政府很少控制资源型城市兴盛衰败，企业投资流向对资源型城市发展起决定性作用。区位好的资源型城市渐渐发展为综合性城市，区位较差的资源型城市则走向衰落或被遗弃 | 适用于从业人员少、城市规模小、转型较容易的矿业城镇 |
| | 政府与市场联动型 | 政府根据国内外市场的变化情况和资源战略的实施状况，制定和修改产业政策，设定目标和措施，各矿区的地方政府和企业依照中央政府的规划实施 | 普遍适用 |

总之，在资源型城市的发展过程中，要进行科学转型，避免城市发展对资源的过度依赖。对我国典型资源型城市发展与转型进行分析与总结，旨在为资源型城市制定中长期发展战略提供决策参考。

（作者：刘粤湘，中国矿业联合会矿业城市工作委员会副秘书长，教授）

# 附录篇

# 附录1　2010年中国城市规划发展大事记

**2010年1月4日**　国务院发布《关于推进海南国际旅游岛建设发展的若干意见》，将海南建设国际旅游岛上升为国家战略。海南国际旅游岛的战略定位是我国旅游业改革创新的试验区、世界一流的海岛休闲度假旅游目的地、全国生态文明建设示范区、国际经济合作和文化交流的重要平台、南海资源开发和服务基地、国家热带现代农业基地。到2020年，海南将初步建成世界一流的海岛休闲度假旅游胜地，旅游业增加值占地区生产总值比重达到12%以上，第三产业增加值占地区生产总值比重达到60%，第三产业从业人数比重达到60%，力争全省人均生产总值、城乡居民收入和生活质量达到国内先进水平，生态环境质量保持全国领先水平。

**2010年1月7日**　国务院办公厅发布《关于促进房地产市场平稳健康发展的通知》（以下简称《通知》）。《通知》强调，要加快中低价位、中小套型普通商品住房建设；增加住房建设用地有效供应，提高土地供应和开发利用效率。各地要根据房地产市场运行情况，把握好土地供应的总量、结构和时序。城市人民政府要在城市总体规划和土地利用总体规划确定的城市建设用地规模内，抓紧编制2010—2012年住房建设规划，重点明确中低价位、中小套型普通商品住房和限价商品住房、公共租赁住房、经济适用住房、廉租住房的建设规模，并分解到住房用地年度供应计划，落实到地块，明确各地块住房套型结构比例等控制性指标要求。

**2010年1月9—10日**　"第二届（2010）中国创新大会"在北京举行。住房和城乡建设部副部长仇保兴在会上提出，目前我国城市化发展有三个不平衡，即沿海与内地发展不平衡，大城市与小城市发展不平衡，城市发展与能源的保障不平衡。这三个不平衡，是当前我国城市化进程中的三大症结。

**2010年1月11日**　天津滨海新区政府揭牌成立，此举标志着天津滨海新区不仅是一个经济区，还是一个享有宪法赋予各种权力的行政区，天津滨海新区开发开放也由此翻开新的一页。

**2010年1月12日**　国务院正式批准实施《皖江城市带承接产业转移示范区规划》（以下简称《规划》），这标志着皖江城市带承接产业转移示范区建设正式纳入国家发展战略。《规划》从国家战略层面，明确了皖江城市带承接产业转移示范区发展的总体思路、重点任务和政策措施，为当前和今后一个时期皖江城市带加快发展指明了方向。

**2010年1月12日** 国家发展和改革委员会继不久前批准深圳市创建国家创新型城市试点之后，扩大试点范围，"原则同意" 大连、青岛等16个城市申报创建国家创新型城市总体方案，支持这些城市开展创建国家创新型城市试点。发展改革委还要求相关城市不断优化区域创新环境，形成创新友好型政策法律制度环境；围绕创新型城市建设总目标，弘扬科学思想，尊重首创精神，激发创造热情，营造鼓励创新、宽容失败的创新文化氛围，促进创新创业发展。

**2010年1月13日** 国务院新闻办举行新闻发布会，住房和城乡建设部副部长齐骥和国家发展改革委等部门相关领导介绍了《国务院办公厅关于促进房地产市场平稳健康发展的通知》的有关内容。齐骥说，鉴于当前房地产市场交易较为活跃，一些地方投资投机性购房比重较大，为合理调节住房需求，在继续支持居民首次贷款购买普通自住房需求的同时，有必要进一步严格二套房信贷政策，加强住房信贷管理。因此，《通知》明确规定："对已利用贷款购买住房、又申请购买第二套（含）以上住房的家庭（包括借款人、配偶及未成年子女），贷款首付款比例不得低于40%，贷款利率严格按照风险定价。"

**2010年1月16日** 国家住房和城乡建设部与深圳市人民政府共同签署了我国首个低碳生态示范市框架协议。作为住建部首个批准的国家低碳生态示范市，深圳将以"部市共建"的模式，以全新的面貌向低碳生态城市启航。

**2010年1月20日** 上海市政府公布了最新制定完成的《崇明生态岛建设纲要（2010—2020）》，明确力争到2020年形成崇明现代化生态岛建设的初步框架。据上海市发展和改革委副主任王建平介绍，为实现2020年的长远发展目标，崇明岛的建设聚焦在"六大行动领域"，包括自然资源的保护利用、循环经济和废弃物的综合利用、能源利用和节能减排、环境污染治理和生态环境建设、发展生态型产业、完善基础设施和公共服务。按照建设世界级生态岛的总体目标，《纲要》紧紧围绕生态环境建设，在上海市科委组织有关专家筛选的核心指标和上海市环保局确定的重点控制性指标的基础上，聚焦形成了2020年崇明生态岛建设的评价指标体系。该指标体系吸收了国际组织和发达国家对可持续发展、生态建设等方面的理论和应用成果，具有国际先进性和通用性。

**2010年1月25日** 环境保护部部长周生贤在2010年全国环境保护工作会议上公布2010年减排目标，"据初步测算，2009年全国化学需氧量和二氧化硫排放量继续保持双下降态势，二氧化硫'十一五'减排目标提前一年实现。2010年的减排目标是，二氧化硫排放量力争比2009年再削减40万吨，化学需氧量减排在完成'十一五'目标的基础上，力争再削减20万吨以上。"

**2010年1月25日** 北京市市长郭金龙代表市政府向人民代表大会报告政府工作，报告提出"着眼建设世界城市"，这也成为2010年政府工作报告的一个新亮点。北京市市委书记刘淇在审议报告时表示，北京市已经组织专家在研究世界城市的目标体系等框架。北京市规划委主任黄艳表示，按照北京城市总体规划确定的北京城市发展目标定位，第一步要构建现代国际城市的基本构架，第二步到2020年全面建成现代化国际城市，第三步到2050年成为世界城市。

**2010年1月29日** 国务院法制办公布《国有土地上房屋征收与补偿条例（草案)》，并向社会公开征求意见。

**2010年1月30日** “世界现代化400年暨《中国现代化报告（2010)》专家座谈会”在中科院举行。《中国现代化报告（2010)》是全球第一部世界现代化概览，是中国现代化报告的第十本报告，它是课题组十年潜心研究成果的一个集中体现。课题组负责人何传启先生汇报了《中国现代化报告（2010)》的主要结果。

**2010年1月31日** 新华社受权播发了《中共中央、国务院关于加大统筹城乡发展力度，进一步夯实农业农村发展基础的若干意见》。中央一号文件再度锁定“三农”，推出了一系列含金量高的强农惠农新政策，强力推动资源要素向农村配置是其最大亮点。从健全强农惠农政策体系、提高现代农业装备水平、加快改善农村民生、协调推进城乡改革、加强农村基层组织建设5个方面，着力推动资源要素向农村配置，促进农业发展方式转变，努力缩小城乡公共事业发展差距，增强农业农村发展活力，巩固党在农村的执政基础。文件强调两大方面：一是修改土地法推动土地改革，城乡建设用地增减挂钩要严格限定在试点范围内，农村宅基地和村庄整理后节约的土地仍属农民集体所有，确保城乡建设用地总规模不突破，确保复垦耕地质量，确保维护农民利益。二是新生代农民工将市民化，鼓励有条件的城市将有稳定职业并在城市居住一定年限的农民工逐步纳入城镇住房保障体系。着力解决新生代农民工问题。统筹研究农业转移人口进城落户后城乡出现的新情况、新问题。

**2010年2月2日** 国土资源部强调，经济适用住房、廉租住房以及城市、国有工矿棚户区改造中符合经济适用住房、廉租住房条件的安置用地，应当以划拨方式供地。土地供应后，不得改变保障性住房用地的性质。城乡规划调整后需要改变用地性质的，应由政府收回土地。国土资源部土地利用司司长廖永林展示了“土地动态监测系统”，通过这个在线监测系统，全国105个主要城市的每宗土地的出让、开发进度等均能被国土资源部实时掌握。廖永林表示，新土地出让合同全面推行以后，以合同管地将成为土地利用管理的主要思路。

**2010年2月5日** 国务院批复《湘潭市城市总体规划（2010—2020年)》。

**2010年2月28日** 《中国省域经济竞争力发展报告（2008—2009)》蓝皮书由社会科学文献出版社出版发行，报告根据中国省域经济综合竞争力指标评价体系和数学模型，向社会公布了中国内地31个省级行政区以及港澳台地区经济综合竞争力的评价结果。蓝皮书显示，上海和北京的省域经济综合竞争力分列全国一、二位，这是自我国首部中国省域竞争力蓝皮书出版以来的稳定序位。蓝皮书还报告，截至2009年年底，中国内地已有14个省市的GDP总量突破万亿元大关，几乎占到全部省区市的一半。

**2010年3月5日** 国务院总理温家宝在十一届全国人大三次会议上所作的政府工作报告中，提出了2010年中国经济的10个关键数据：GDP（国内生产总值）增长8%左右；城镇新增就业900万人以上；城镇登记失业率控制在4.6%以内；CPI（居民消费价格）涨幅3%左右；今年拟安排财政赤字10500亿元人民币，其中中央财政赤字8500亿元，继续代发地方债2000亿元并纳入地方财政预算；新增人民币贷款7.5万亿元左右；新增8000万吨标准煤的节能能力；中央财政拟安排“三农”投入8183亿元，比上年增加930亿元；各级政府要进一步增加社会保障投入，中央财政拟安排3185亿元；中央财政拟安排保障性住房专项补助资金632亿元，比上年增加81亿元。

**2010年3月8日** 国务院批复《武汉市城市总体规划（2010—2020年）》。

**2010年3月10日** 国土资源部公布了《关于加强房地产用地供应和监管有关问题的通知》，明确保障性住房用地供应、商品房用地出让、打击囤地等方面的具体要求，全方位加强土地市场监管。同时通过土地竞买人资格审查、严格规范土地出让底价等手段，进一步提高土地出让门槛。要求各地确保保障性住房用地供应，保障性住房、棚户改造和自住性中小套型商品房建房用地，不低于住房建设用地供应总量的70%。保障性住房用地不得从事商业性房地产开发，因城市规划调整需要改变的，应由政府收回，另选地块供应。

**2010年3月12日** 《2010第十届中国房地产发展年会暨2009—2010中国房地产政策评估成果发布会》在北京召开，会上首发了研究成果《2009年度中国房地产政策评估报告》(以下简称《报告》)。《报告》认为，2009年的房地产政策在总体上实现了既定的保增长、惠民生的政策目标，预计2010年房地产市场将呈现“价涨量缩，前低后高”的态势，其中，商品房销售面积将比2009年下降4.4%到6.5%，而商品房均价将上涨3.3%到6.0%。

**2010年3月15日** 国务院批复《青海省柴达木循环经济试验区总体规划》。根据《规划》，试验区将遵循循环经济“减量化、再利用、资源化”的原则，重点规划建设格尔木工业园等四个循环经济工业园，构建以盐湖化工为核心的六大循环经济主导产业体系，形成资源、产业和产品多层面联动发展的循环型产业格局。

**2010年3月18日** 博鳌国际旅游论坛新闻发布会举行。海南省副省长谭力宣布成立中国5A级旅游景区城市联盟。目前，我国共有67家5A级旅游景区，分布在55个城市。成立中国5A级旅游景区城市联盟，旨在加强中国5A级景区及所在城市之间的合作，协调互动，提升中国精品旅游景区及优秀旅游城市品牌，推动各旅游城市的长足发展，共同打造国际化旅游目的地，并充分发挥示范带头作用，开创中国旅游产业发展新局面。

**2010年3月22日** 广东珠三角绿道网建设启动仪式在广州亚运城举行。广东省委书记汪洋在仪式上宣布，珠三角绿道网建设正式启动。1月7日广东省委十届六次全会公布的最新的《珠三角绿道网总体规划纲要》提出，广东将在3年内建设6条长度不一的“绿色道路”，连接广佛肇、深莞惠、珠中江三大都市区，全长1690公里，服务人口超过2500万人。此前，广州、中山等城市已率先启动绿道网建设。

**2010年3月26日** 在浙江嘉兴召开的长三角城市经济协调会第十次市长联席会议宣布，协调会成员由此前16个增至22个，即长三角核心城市群扩容，不仅吸收盐城、淮安、金华、衢州等4个苏浙城市为新会员，而且让泛长三角区域内的合肥、马鞍山两个安徽省的城市也正式“加盟”。

**2010年3月28日** 历时近3年时间综合改造的百年上海外滩宣告竣工。上海市市长韩正致辞说，“外滩是上海的象征。它承载着上海开埠近170年的历史，浓缩了百年中国政治、经济和文化的变迁”。他指出，新外滩不仅保护和延续了外滩历史文脉，还将对“促进浦江两岸功能转换”发挥重大作用。所谓浦江两岸功能转换，意味着改造之后的外滩，不仅有中国最璀璨夺目的华丽江景，还将出现一个占地2.6平方公里、建筑面积超过460万平方米的“外滩金融聚集带”，重点集聚以金融为主的现代服务业。此次上海外滩综合改造的核心工程是外滩地下通道工程，需要在滨江核心区从地下穿越33幢著名历史建筑，其难度堪比“心脏搭桥”。与此同时，和外滩地下通道形成配套的新建路隧道和人民路隧道也宣布建成，一举将外滩金融聚集带、已初露峥嵘的北外滩航运服务聚集区与浦东小陆家嘴金融核心区紧密相连。

**2010年3月29日**　国土资源部公布《中国城市地价状况（2009）》，首次提到了与“租售比”相似的“租价比”概念，并明确表示从这一概念角度分析，国内热点城市的住宅市场已经出现了比较严重的泡沫。

**2010年3月29日**　国务院新闻办公室举行新闻发布会，国家发展改革委、人力资源社会保障部、国土资源部、住房和城乡建设部、农业部有关负责人介绍中国城镇化发展的有关情况。国家发展改革委发展规划司司长李守信介绍了中国城镇化发展的成就：一是城镇化率明显提高。到2009年，我国的城镇人口按统计口径算，已经达到了6.22亿人，城镇化率提高到46.6%；二是我国城镇体系在逐步完善，以大城市为中心，中小城市为骨干，小城镇为基础的多层次的城镇体系已经形成；三是我国城镇经济实力不断增强。城市经济蓬勃发展，到2008年，地级以上的地区生产总值达到18.6万亿，占全国的62%。服务业增加值达到8.6万亿元，占全国的71.4%；四是相关的体制机制改革取得了积极进展。

**2010年3月29—31日**　第六届国际绿色建筑与建筑节能大会在北京召开。大会的主题是“加快可再生能源应用，推动绿色建筑发展”。住房和城乡建设部副部长仇保兴在第六届国际绿色建筑与建筑节能大会上指出，我国是世界上每年新建建筑量最大的国家，每年20亿平方米新建面积，相当于消耗了全世界40%的水泥和钢材，而只能持续25~30年。

**2010年4月6日**　辽宁省政府新闻办举行新闻发布会，宣布经国务院同意，国家发展改革委正式批复沈阳经济区为国家新型工业化综合配套改革试验区，这标志着沈阳经济区成为继上海浦东、天津滨海新区、成都、重庆、武汉城市圈、长株潭城市群和深圳等七个地区后，国务院批准设立的第八个国家综合配套改革试验区。沈阳经济区综合配套改革的主要任务是：以区域发展、企业重组、科技研发、金融创新四个方面体制机制创新为重点，紧扣走新型工业化道路主题率先突破；配套推进资源节约、环境保护、城乡统筹、对外开放、行政管理等体制机制创新，为走新型工业化道路提供支撑平台和配套措施。

**2010年4月13日**　国土资源部发出信号，土地招拍挂制度有其合理性，仍要坚持，但同时又要在民生用地方面加以完善，今后涉及民生普通住宅用地或采用“一次报价”方式。

**2010年4月14日**　由中国社科院编纂的首部《宏观经济蓝皮书》发布。蓝皮书称，中国将在2013年左右（在2011年至2016年之间）结束高速城市化过程。蓝皮书预测，到2015年，中国的城市化率为52.28%，2020年为57.67%，2030年为67.81%。而68%左右可能是中国未来20年城市化发展的顶部，此后城市化水平将在较长一个时期维持在这一水平。

**2010年4月15日**　国土资源部发布2010年各省、自治区、直辖市住房供地计划公告。

全国2010年度住房用地计划拟供应量约18万公顷，比2009年及前5年平均年度实际供地量大幅度增加，其中保障性住房用地比去年增加1倍多，廉租房用地比去年实际供地增加达4.7倍。

**2010年4月20日** 指导深圳未来城市发展的纲领性文件《深圳2040城市发展策略》的编制工作启动。在2005年年底，该市发布《深圳2030城市发展策略》，其中关于深圳未来将是“可持续发展的先锋城市”的定位将作为深圳未来发展的长期战略目标。其后不久，该市人大常委会行使重大事项决定权，将《深圳2030城市发展策略》法定化。

**2010年4月22日** 中国社会科学院公布了评估低碳城市的新标准体系。这是迄今我国首个最为完善的标准。该标准具体分为低碳生产力、低碳消费、低碳资源和低碳政策等四大类共12个相对指标。如果一个城市的低碳生产力指标超过全国平均水平的20%，即可被认定为“低碳”。社科院报告说，把低碳发展的理念和标准整合到“十二五”发展规划中是至关重要的。

**2010年4月26日** 中国社会科学院在京举办2010年《城市竞争力蓝皮书》发布暨中国城市竞争力研讨会，会上发布了《城市竞争力蓝皮书：中国城市竞争力报告NO.8》。蓝皮书对全国294个地级以上城市综合竞争力进行比较发现，中国最具竞争力的前10名城市依次是：香港、深圳、上海、北京、台北、广州、天津、高雄、大连、青岛。

**2010年4月27日** 住房和城乡建设部印发了《关于加强经济适用住房管理有关问题的通知》（建保［2010］59号，以下简称《通知》）。《通知》针对部分地方经济适用住房存在的准入退出管理机制不完善、日常监管和服务不到位等问题，做出了有关规定。《通知》提出，经济适用住房的建设规模由各地结合当地居民收入、住房状况等实际情况确定。商品住房价格过高、上涨过快的城市，要大幅度增加经济适用住房供应，并适当扩大供应范围。《通知》要求，经济适用住房申请人应当如实申报家庭收入、财产和住房状况，并对申报信息的真实性负责。

**2010年5月1日至10月31日期间** 在上海市举行了2010年上海世界博览会。上海世博会以“城市，让生活更美好”（Better City，Better Life）为主题，总投资达450亿元人民币，创造了世界博览会史上最大规模纪录。被视为上海世博会思想成果的《上海宣言》，提出“和谐城市”的理念，蕴含着宝贵的价值。《上海宣言》这样表述：“和谐城市，应该是建立在可持续发展基础之上的合理有序、自我更新、充满活力的城市生命体；和谐城市，应该是生态环境友好、经济集约高效、社会公平和睦的城市综合体。”《上海宣言》同时指出：“我们一致认为，通过创新来建设和谐城市，是城市可持续发展的解决之道。”

**2010年5月4日** 国土资源部在京召开挂牌督办违法案件及2009年土地例行督察公告新闻发布会。会议通报了2010年一季度国土资源违法形势；通报了2009年国家土地督察工作情况；公布了9起国土资源违法案件查处情况和4起挂牌督办案件，通报中央治理工程建设领域突出问题工作领导小组办公室、国土资源部、监察部联合挂牌督办的5起国土资源违法案件处理结果。

**2010年5月5日** 《横琴新区控制性详细规划》编制完成，获得通过。106平方公里的横琴岛，54%的面积为绿色山体，横琴绿色生态系统将最大限度得到保护，半个岛都是“禁建区”；全岛将实行管道直供，长达32公里的共同管沟，将是上海世博园6.6公里地下管沟系统的5倍。按照该《控规》，禁建区、限建区加上建设用地规划中的绿地面积，2020年横琴新区绿地面积将达到82.45平方公里，而届时横琴人口规划为28万人，人均绿地面积将达到294平方米。

**2010年5月5日** 国务院召开全国节能减排工作电视电话会议，动员和部署加强节能减排工作。国务院总理温家宝出席并作重要讲话。温家宝强调，要坚持节能与发展相促进，开发与节约相协调，政府调控和市场机制相结合，综合运用经济、法律、技术和必要的行政手段，抓好节能减排工作，确保实现“十一五”节能减排目标。

**2010年5月11日** 由中国市长协会主办、国际欧亚科学院中国科学中心承办的《中国城市发展报告（2009）》卷，在京举行首发式。《中国城市发展报告（2009）》卷以“构建和谐城市，应对金融危机，扩大社会保障”为主题，特邀数十位院士、专家和学者撰稿，全面记叙了我国城市发展的进程、热点、焦点和典型案例。《报告》分为六大篇章：论坛篇、综论篇、观察篇、专题篇、案例篇、附录篇，全书共60万字，插图51幅。

**2010年5月17—19日** 中央新疆工作座谈会在北京举行。中共中央总书记、国家主席、中央军委主席胡锦涛在会上发表重要讲话。强调做好新形势下的新疆工作，是提高新疆各族群众生活水平、实现全面建设小康社会目标的必然要求，是深入实施西部大开发战略、培育新的经济增长点、拓展我国经济发展空间的战略选择，是我国实施互利共赢开放战略、发展全方位对外开放格局的重要部署，是加强民族团结、维护祖国统一、确保边疆长治久安的迫切要求。加快建设繁荣富裕和谐稳定的社会主义新疆，是全党全国各族人民的共同意志，是全体中华儿女的共同责任。全党全国必须充分认识做好新疆工作对党和国家工作全局的重大意义，深刻理解邓小平同志“两个大局”战略思想和中央西部大开发战略决策的重大意义，切实做好新形势下新疆工作，把新疆经济社会发展搞上去，把新疆长治久安工作搞扎实，推进新疆跨越式发展和长治久安，不断开创新疆工作新局面。会上同时公布，新疆区域振兴规划即将由国务院审核发布。

**2010年5月24日** 国务院正式批准实施《长江三角洲地区区域规划》（以下简称《规划》），这是贯彻落实《国务院关于进一步推进长江三角洲地区改革开放和经济社会发展的指导意见》（国发［2008］30号）、进一步提升长江三角洲地区整体实力和国际竞争力的重大决策部署，是深入实施区域发展总体战略、促进全国经济平稳较快发展的又一重要举措。

**2010年5月24日** 山东省政府公布，国务院已同意选择山东半岛蓝色经济区作为全国海洋经济科学发展实现路径的试点区域。据介绍，山东省目前已编制完成蓝色经济区的规划纲要和24个专项规划，规划纲要也正式报送国家发改委。尽管距离正式获批国家级海洋经济科学发展示范区规划尚有时日，山东省已然开始敲定322个重点建设项目，启动了蓝色经济区的发展引擎。

**2010年5月24日** 国土资源部、监察部通报了清查出来的逾61万亩的“未报即用”违法用地，16个地级市被点名。据国土资源部部长徐绍史介绍，31个省区市不同程度存在

“未报即用”违法用地现象，其中国家和省级重点项目超过三成。

**2010年5月27日** 国务院转发了国家发改委《关于2010年深化经济体制改革重点工作的意见》，这是首次在国务院文件中提出在全国范围内实行居住证制度。该意见在“推进城乡改革”部分提到，深化户籍制度改革将加快落实放宽中小城市、小城镇特别是县城和中心镇落户条件的政策。进一步完善暂住人口登记制度，逐步在全国范围内实行居住证制度。

**2010年6月2日** 深圳市第五届人大一次会议举行。会上披露，国务院就广东省《关于延伸深圳经济特区范围的请示》作出批复，同意将深圳经济特区范围扩大到深圳全市，包括宝安、龙岗以及光明和坪山两个新区纳入到经济特区里面，特区总面积由395平方公里扩容为1948平方公里，扩容5倍。7月1日深圳正式步入大特区时代。特区一体化的内涵是“六个一体化”，即：法规政策一体化，规划布局一体化，基础设施一体化，城市管理一体化，环境保护一体化，以及基本公共服务一体化。“一市两法”问题成为特区外扩后需解决的首要问题。深圳市五届人大常委会第一次会议6月29日决定，7月1日前制定的101项经济特区法规今起适用于扩大后的经济特区。与此同时，深圳市政府常务会议6月30日审议并原则通过了《关于深圳经济特区规章在宝安、龙岗两区实施有关事项的决定》，41项特区规章的实施范围今日起扩大至全市。

**2010年6月2日** 中国社科院2010年《休闲绿皮书》新闻发布会在北京举行。这是国内第一本有关休闲发展的绿皮书，是社科院财贸所受国家旅游局综合协调司委托所做的一项关于《2009—2010年中国休闲发展报告》专项研究。该书指出，2009年我国休闲相关产业在应对金融危机中，以较高的增长速度实现了逆势上涨。2009年我国休闲核心消费大约达到1.7万亿元，相当于社会消费品零售总额的13.56%，相当于GDP的5.07%。

**2010年6月2日** 国务院新闻办举行新闻发布会，文化部副部长王文章在会上介绍中国非物质文化遗产保护与传承取得的进展和成果等方面情况时表示，目前全国非物质文化遗产资源共有近87万项，中央和省级财政已累计投入17.89亿元用于非物质文化遗产保护。2007年6月至2010年5月，文化部先后设立了闽南文化、徽州文化、热贡文化、羌族文化、客家文化（梅州）和武陵山区（湘西）土家族苗族文化等6个文化生态保护实验区。

**2010年6月5日** 《2010中国新型城市化报告》在成都发布。该报告是由中科院可持续发展战略研究组组长、首席科学家牛文元教授牵头，组织多名专家历时1年完成的研究成果。牛文元说，报告从全球的视野和战略的高度，深入探讨了中国新型城市化战略的低碳发展之路。在对“2010年新型城市化水平的总体评价”中，上海、北京、深圳分列前三名，重庆排名第八。

**2010年6月8日** 国家发改委正式批复了《海南国际旅游岛建设发展规划纲要（2010—2020)》，这是进一步贯彻落实《国务院关于推进海南国际旅游岛建设发展的若干意见》的重大举措。该规划纲要阐述了未来十年海南国际旅游岛建设发展的指导原则、发展目标、空间布局、主要任务和政策措施，具有较强的指导性和可操作性，是今后一个时期海南国际旅游岛建设发展的基本蓝图和行动纲领。

**2010年6月8日**　住房和城乡建设部等七部门联合发布加快发展公共租赁住房的指导意见，意见强调了六大方面：一、加快发展公共租赁住房的重要意义；二、基本原则；三、租赁管理；四、房源筹集；五、政策支持；六、监督管理。

**2010年6月9—27日**　由中组部、住房和城乡建设部主办，由中国市长协会具体组织实施的经济结构转型与城市建设管理专题研讨班（暨第30期中德城市管理研讨会）在北京和德国柏林、法兰克福、卡尔斯鲁厄、慕尼黑市举办。

**2010年6月10日**　世界银行在对《2010年全球经济展望》报告进行的夏季更新中，调高了对今年全球经济增长的预期，并指出，发展中国家正引领全球经济复苏，特别是得益于中国的经济增长。但报告同时认为，欧洲主权债务危机将给世界经济可持续增长蒙上阴影，全球经济复苏的过程仍然缓慢且脆弱。

**2010年6月11日**　住房和城乡建设部、发展改革委、财政部、国土资源部、农业部、国家林业局联合发出《关于做好住房保障规划编制的通知》，部署2010—2012年保障性住房建设规划和“十二五”住房保障规划编制工作。

**2010年6月12日**　由住房和城乡建设部等七部门联合制定的《关于加快发展公共租赁住房的指导意见》（以下简称《意见》）正式对外发布，旨在解决城市中等偏低收入家庭住房困难。《意见》指出，近年来，一些中等偏下收入住房困难家庭无力通过市场租赁或购买住房的问题比较突出。同时，随着城镇化快速推进，新职工的阶段性住房支付能力不足矛盾日益显现，外来务工人员居住条件也亟须改善。

**2010年6月12日**　国务院总理温家宝主持召开国务院常务会议，审议并原则通过《全国主体功能区规划》，决定取消和下放184项行政审批项目。会议指出，根据不同区域的资源环境承载能力、现有开发强度和发展潜力，统筹谋划未来人口分布、经济布局、国土利用和城镇化格局，确定不同区域主体功能，并据此明确开发方向和政策，推进形成主体功能区，是党中央、国务院作出的重要战略部署，是深入贯彻落实科学发展观的重大战略举措。

**2010年6月12日**　是我国第五个文化遗产日。文化遗产日的设立，充分体现了我们党和国家对保护、发展文化遗产的高度重视，对于弘扬中华民族优秀传统文化、激发人民群众参与保护、发展文化遗产的热情，发挥了积极的推动作用。

**2010年6月13日**　中国政府网公布了国务院下发的《关于加强地方政府融资平台公司管理有关问题的通知》，要求地方各级政府要对融资平台公司债务进行一次全面清理，并按照分类管理、区别对待的原则，妥善处理债务偿还和在建项目后续融资问题。

**2010年7月17—18日**　由中国市长协会和哈尔滨市人民政府共同主办的“2010中国市长论坛暨中国市长协会四届四次常务理事扩大会”在哈尔滨市隆重召开。

**2010年6月18日**　重庆“两江”新区挂牌成立。黄奇帆市长在新闻发布会上说，国务院文件里专门明确了五条重庆两江新区的功能定位。一是统筹城乡综合配套改革实验区的先行区；二是内陆重要的先进制造业和现代服务业的基地；三是长江上游地区金融中心和创新中心；四是内陆地区对外开放的重要门户；五是科学发展的示范窗口。

**2010年6月20日**　在陕西安康举办第七届陕川甘旅游区域协作年会，会上宣布，地处秦巴地区的陕西、甘肃和四川三省18个市将共建秦巴国际生态旅游圈。18个协作城市签署发布了《携手共建秦巴国际生态旅游圈安康宣言》，旨在突破行政区域界限，建立无障碍旅游区，围绕三省共有的生态旅游资源，整体开发区域内旅游资源。

**2010年6月25日** 是第20个全国“土地日”，主题确定为“土地与转变发展方式——依法管地集约用地”，其含义是以土地利用方式的转变，促进经济发展方式的转变，主旨是集约用地。它进一步唤醒我们节约土地的意识，提醒我们把握好形势要求，倍加珍惜土地，集约利用土地。集约用地是我国当前乃至今后相当长一个时期必须坚持的土地利用方式。

**2010年6月26日** 国土资源部总规划师胡存智在“中国房地产2010年夏季峰会”上透露，国土资源部将大力推进城乡建设用地增减挂钩工作。经过测算，预计将置换出10%的农村建设用地指标。这意味着，约2700万亩农村集体建设用地转变为城镇建设用地。

**2010年6月26日** 国土资源部下发《关于进一步做好征地管理工作的通知》，对提高征地补偿标准，补偿直接给农民等作出明确规定。通知强调对农民利益的切实保护。首先，征地之前，有关征地的重要信息必须由政府告知农民，农民的知情权、参与权和申述权将会得到充分的尊重。在征地之前有一个告知的、确认的和听证的程序。按照规定，征地补偿款应在征地实施方案批复后三个月之内支付给农民，还有3项措施来确保补偿安置费准时到达农民的手中。

**2010年7月1日** 国务院正式批复了北京市政府关于调整首都功能核心区行政区划的请示，同意撤销北京市东城区、崇文区，设立新的北京市东城区，以原东城区、崇文区的行政区域为东城区的行政区域；撤销北京市西城区、宣武区，设立新的北京市西城区，以原西城区、宣武区的行政区域为西城区的行政区域。

**2010年7月6日** 2010年大运河保护和申遗工作会议在运河名城江苏省扬州市召开。国家文物局局长单霁翔出席会议并讲话。讲话在回顾过去一年大运河保护和申报世界文化遗产工作进展情况的基础上，分析总结了各项保护和申报准备工作中存在的问题，并对下一阶段的工作进行了全面部署。

**2010年7月12日** 文化部、国家文物局发出《文化部办公厅 国家文物局办公室关于把握正确导向做好文化遗产保护开发工作的通知》。通知要求，各地在对名人故里、故居或文化遗址等进行合理适度的开发利用时，要加强监管，防止过度的商业开发和对文化遗产内涵的肆意歪曲和滥用。对历史文化遗产要进行科学甄别，对历史文化名人的故里、故居、重要文物所在地的认定，要本着积极有益、少而精的原则，由权威的学术机构和专家参与进行认定。对于有争议的、未经认定的，不宜命名或宣传。严禁利用历史或文学作品中反面或负面的人物形象建设主题文化公园、举办主题文化活动等。为保证命名的严肃性，各地不宜对文艺作品中虚构的人物进行命名故里等活动。

**2010年7月14日** 中国社会科学院在京发布《全球城市竞争力报告（2009—2010）》。通过比较竞争力指数及其具体构成指标数据，报告全面解析了全球500个城市的发展和竞争格局，其中，纽约、伦敦、东京位列全球城市综合竞争力排名前三甲。中国唯有香港挤进了前十，但排名最末。综合竞争力50强城市中，欧美继续遥遥领先，其中，美国有20个入围，欧盟则占16个，两者占到50强的72%。在经济增长率排名上，除了排名第5的巴库来自阿塞拜疆外，其余9个经济增长最快的城市均来自中国，依次是：鄂尔多斯、包头、烟台、呼和浩特、东莞、中山、日照、惠州和威海。

**2010年7月15日** 北京世界城市研究基地成立大会暨揭牌仪式在北京社科院举行。北京世界城市研究基地是市委宣传部领导下，专门研究世界城市建设的机构。它以北京社科院为依托，汇聚学术界和实际工作部门的各类相关资源，为研究世界城市构建跨学科、跨单位、跨地区的联合攻关平台，将为北京建设世界城市提供决策、咨询等方面的服务，也是市委、市政府的重要“智库”。

**2010年7月17日** 北京市政协通过《关于促进首都人口与资源环境协调发展的建议案》。该建议案涉及的调研显示，截至2009年年底，北京市实际常住人口已达1972万人，其中居住半年以上的流动人口726万人。2006年起的4年内，北京人口年均增长54.3万人，70%是流动人口。北京市政协建议尽快成立首都人口委员会，并建议北京市府向国务院申请对首都人口规模调控的特殊管理政策。同时，还建议多部门联动形成“全员人口信息管理系统”，逐步实现对全市人口的实时动态监测及预测预警机制。

**2010年7月18日** 北京唐家岭村正式启动宅基地腾退搬迁工作。随着腾退协议书的签订，首批8个村民宅院开始拆迁。按照该村的拆迁政策，从即日起在30日内搬迁的村民，最高可获得50多万元的奖励。

**2010年7月25日** 第三十四届世界遗产大会在巴西利亚开幕。这次大会审议和批准了20余处新的世界遗产。中国登封的“天地之中”历史建筑群和中国丹霞地貌分别被列入文化和自然遗产。中国“三江并流”也被批准扩大遗产保护区域。同时，马达加斯加阿钦安阿纳雨林、美国大沼泽地国家公园、格鲁吉亚巴格拉特大教堂及格拉特修道院、乌干达卡苏比王陵被列入《濒危世界遗产名录》。

**2010年7月28日** 厦门市十三届人大常委会举行第23次会议，决定从8月1日起，50部涉及厦门民生的经济特区法规，将适用于岛外。这50部特区法规，涵盖经济建设、市政管理、科教卫生、环境保护等各个方面，将其正式适用于岛外，打破了“一市两法”的尴尬局面，使岛内外一体化有法可依。

**2010年7月28日** 中国科学院发布《中国科学发展报告（2010）》（以下称《报告》），该报告是国内第一部以自然科学与人文科学的交叉研究为特征，探讨科学发展理论、总结科学发展实践、评估科学发展水平的综合研究报告。《报告》指出，中国要实现绿色发展，必须有序地通过三大基本台阶，实现三大基本目标，即理论上所称的三大“非对称零增长时间节点”。一是到2030年，实现人口数量和规模的“零增长”，同时在对应方向上实现人口质量的极大提高；二是到2040年，实现资源和能量消耗速率的“零增长”，同时在对应方向上实现社会财富的极大提高；三是到2050年，实现生态环境退化速率的“零增长”，同时在对应方向上实现环境质量和生态安全的极大提高。

**2010年7月28日** 重庆官方公布了中国首个大规模户籍制度改革计划，按计划，到2020年，重庆市1000万农村人群将转户为城镇人口。为稳妥推进改革，当地转为城镇居民的农民最长将在3年内保留其农村土地的收益权。此间公布的《重庆市人民政府关于统筹城乡户籍制度改革的意见》提出，要充分兼顾政府的承受力和城镇资源的承载力，防止农民流离失所，防止出现城市贫民窟现象。前述“缓冲”政策意味着，即使“进城”，农民3年内在城镇中经济状况不佳，其保留的农村土地权益仍可为其生活提供一定保障。

**2010年7月29日** “《2010年城市蓝皮书》发布暨中国城市发展战略转型高层论坛”在中国社会科学院举办，《中国城市发展报告（2010）》正式发布。本书以中国城市发展的“十一五”回顾与“十二五”展望为主题，对中国城市发展状况及趋势进行了全面的分析。本书认为，“十二五”期间，中国城市将展开更大规模的城市建设，在建设中将更加关注改善外来劳动力的生活条件，将更加关注绿色城市环境的营造。统筹大中小城市协调发展，形成东部地区和中西部地区城市群并立的格局，将成为推动城乡和区域结构优化调整、协调经济长期平稳较快发展的重要任务，“十二五”期间的中国城市建设将在城镇化的进程中肩负更加重要的使命。

**2010年8月12日** 珠三角五个一体化规划正式公布，即基础设施、产业布局、基本公共服务、城乡规划和环境保护五个一体化规划。规划分近期、远期两个目标，近期规划目标到2012年，远期规划到2020年。项目设施一体化重拳出击，150个重大项目总投资近2万亿元；构建珠三角地区“530”产业体系；公共教育、公共卫生、生活保障、住房保障、就业保障等十项公共服务将无障碍对接流转；依托省、市、县三级绿道建成1小时区域休闲生活圈；2020年珠三角环境质量接近或达到世界先进水平……作为推进珠三角一体化的重要行动指引，五个一体化规划从目标任务、实施机制、保障措施等方面科学谋划布局，大胆先行先试，突破行政界限，统筹规划布局，整合各类资源，助力推进珠三角一体化进程。

**2010年8月12日** 为加强“中国丹霞”世界自然遗产地的保护管理，住房和城乡建设部下发了《关于加强“中国丹霞”世界自然遗产地保护管理工作的通知》，要求严格执行国家有关景区门票价格管理的规定，不得擅自随意提高遗产地的门票价格；涉及门票价格调整的，要提前半年向社会公布，并按规定程序履行相关手续后方可实施。

**2010年8月16日** 国务院批复《深圳市城市总体规划（2010—2020年）》。

**2010年8月19日** 国务院批复《郑州市城市总体规划（2010—2020年）》。

**2010年8月26日** 在珠海迎来建立经济特区30周年纪念日的当日，经国务院批准，从2010年10月1日起，珠海经济特区范围正式扩大到全市。国务院在《关于扩大珠海经济特区范围的批复》中要求，广东省和珠海市要做好特区范围扩大后的统筹规划工作，要按照走集约化、内涵式发展道路的要求，切实做好特区城市管理、产业布局、土地利用和城市规划等工作，进一步发挥特区在改革开放中“窗口”和“试验田”作用，着力转变经济发展方式，逐步建立以创新为内在驱动力的发展模式，更加注重改善民生和加强社会建设，为全面建设社会主义和谐社会探索经验，为推动珠三角经济区又好又快发展、促进珠港澳地区共同繁荣作出新的贡献。

**2010年9月1日** 国务院正式批准杭州、南昌、郑州、武汉、南宁、平顶山、安阳、荆州、湘潭、柳州10个城市土地利用总体规划，标志着市级土地利用总体规划正式进入批准阶段。

**2010年9月2日** 全国国土规划纲要编制工作领导小组第一次会议在京召开，会议通过了《全国国土规划纲要编制工作方案》，《全国国土规划纲要（2011—2030年）》前期研究和编制工作正式启动。国土资源部部长徐绍史在会上强调，随着国土空间开发的广度和深度不断加大、资源环境保护问题更加凸显，加强国土规划工作日益重要和紧迫，要扎实做好《纲要》前期研究和编制工作，提高国土规划的科学性、针对性和可操作性。

**2010年9月7日** 住房和城乡建设部下发通知，要求各地深刻认识保护世界遗产的重要意义，科学推进申报工作，依法开展保护工作，加大宣传力度，加强能力建设，全面改进世界遗产保护管理工作，推进我国世界遗产保护事业健康发展。通知要求，各地要认真贯彻落实《城乡规划法》、《风景名胜区条例》、《城市绿化条例》等法律法规以及国家关于风景名胜区、历史文化名城（名镇、名村）和城市园林的有关保护管理规定，通过法制、行政和技术等多种手段，加大对世界遗产保护监管的力度，增强履约意识，提高履约能力，切实维护世界遗产的真实性和完整性。

**2010年9月16日** 国家主席胡锦涛在出席第五届亚太经合组织人力资源开发部长级会议开幕式致辞中再次用较大篇幅论“包容性增长”。胡锦涛指出，中国是包容性增长的积极倡导者，更是包容性增长的积极实践者。中国既强调加快转变经济发展方式、保持经济平稳较快发展，又强调坚持把发展经济与改善民生紧密结合起来，以解决人民最关心最直接最现实的利益问题为着力点，大力推进以改善民生为重点的社会建设。在应对国际金融危机冲击的过程中，中国提出保增长、保民生、保稳定的方针，实施积极的财政政策和适度宽松的货币政策，既积极推动经济发展、提高经济发展质量，又加大社会领域投入，加强社会保障体系建设，着力解决民生问题。

**2010年9月17日** 加快保障性安居工程建设工作座谈会在北京召开。中共中央政治局常委、国务院副总理李克强出席会议并讲话。他强调，要坚持以人为本、执政为民，着力推进保障性安居工程，加快发展公共租赁住房，促进人民群众安居乐业。

**2010年9月20—23日** 在肯尼亚内罗毕举行的第四十六届国际规划大会上，广州市战略规划项目获“国际杰出范例奖”，成为我国首个获得全球规划最高级别奖项的城市。大会奖项评审团一致认为：2000年开始的广州战略规划实践，充分学习和吸收了20世纪60年代以来世界各国在编制城市发展战略规划方面的有益经验，结合中国的社会经济现实进行了深入的制度创新，其战略规划的编制与实施模式，值得全世界的发展中城市广泛借鉴。

**2010年9月21日** 最新一期全球金融中心指数（GFCI）揭晓，在本期评价的75个全球金融中心城市中，深圳的金融中心竞争力排名第14位，同期上榜的中国内地城市上海和北京分列第6位和第16位。

**2010年9月21—23日** 在联合国成立65周年之际，国务院总理温家宝出席联合国“千年发展目标”高级别会议和第六十五届联大一般性辩论，就进入“倒计时”阶段的“千年发展目标”进展与“后金融危机时代”的世界和平发展，向世界阐述中国主张。此次高级别首脑会议以“我们能够在2015年前消除贫困”为口号，充分表明了国际社会的广泛共识与“集体决心”。

**2010年9月25日** 国家发展和改革委员会公布《促进中部地区崛起规划实施意见》(以下简称《意见》),要求中部地区的山西、安徽、江西、河南、湖北、湖南六省人民政府和有关部门积极落实这份文件提出的各项任务要求,努力推动中部地区经济社会又好又快发展。《意见》指出,2015年,中部地区要实现《规划》确定的主要目标,即人均地区生产总值达到36000元,城镇化率达到48%,城镇居民人均可支配收入和农村居民人均纯收入分别达到24000元和8200元,耕地保有量不低于《全国土地利用总体规划纲要(2006—2020)》下达的指标。

**2010年9月26日** 国土资源部、住房和城乡建设部联合发布《关于进一步加强房地产用地和建设管理调控的通知》,通知明确,进一步加强房地产用地和建设的管理调控,积极促进房地产市场继续向好发展,将严格住房建设用地出让管理,强化住房用地和住房建设的年度计划管理,在房价高的地区,应增加中小套型限价住房建设供地数量。

**2010年10月4日** “2010年世界人居日”庆典活动在上海发布了《中国城市状况报告2010—2011》。《报告》指出,由于现行住房政策还不完善,一些政策措施推进和落实力度不够,中国住房领域还存在一些深层次矛盾问题。报告还指出,2008年全国城镇居民人均住房使用面积达23平方米(人均住房建筑面积接近30平方米),住房的质量和居住环境有较大提高和改善,城镇居民的自有住房拥有率大幅提高,至2008年已达87.8%。

**2010年10月11日** 国家文物局公布了第一批国家考古遗址公园名单和立项名单。圆明园国家考古遗址公园等12个项目入选第一批国家考古遗址公园名单。

**2010年10月13日** 全球商业杂志《福布斯》中文版推出“2010中国大陆经营成本最高城市”子榜单,揭晓中国大陆经营成本最高的25个城市。上海超越北京成为经营成本最高城市,上海、北京、杭州位列前三甲。《福布斯》中文版对2009年全市GDP在360亿元以上的132个大陆城市进行了调查,并参考劳动力成本、税收成本、能源价格、办公用地租金和企业四险负担等5个指标,加权计算出商业城市的经营成本,并进行综合排名。

**2010年10月15—18日** 中国共产党十七届五中全会在北京举行,全会的主要议程之一是审议并通过《中共中央关于制定国民经济和社会发展的第十二个五年规划(2011—2015年)的建议》。全会将“城乡居民收入普遍较快增加”作为今后五年经济社会发展主要目标之一,将“民富”目标摆在更加突出的位置。这一追求至少包含两方面:一是要进一步改善人民收入的整体水平,将“蛋糕”继续做大;二是要缩小贫富差距,将蛋糕切得更加合理,促进社会公平。而后者较于前者,更具有现实性和紧迫性。全会提出,将合理调整收入分配关系,努力提高居民收入在国民收入分配中的比重、劳动报酬在初次分配中的比重等,作为未来五年着力保障和改善民生的核心举措。这将理性发展与保障民生提到空前重要的地位,诠释了此前国家主席胡锦涛提出的“包容性增长”的内涵。

**2010年10月18日** 国务院下发《关于加快培育和发展战略性新兴产业的决定》,《决定》称,战略性新兴产业是引导未来经济社会发展的重要力量,发展战略性新兴产业已成为世界主要国家抢占新一轮经济和科技发展制高点的重大战略,我国必须按照科学发展观的要求，加快培育和发展战略性新兴产业。

**2010年10月21日**　北京成立了历史文化名城保护委员会，这意味着今后关于旧城保护的问题均要通过该委员会来决定，也标志着政府将北京历史文化名城保护提到了前所未有的高度。其中最引人注目的是，重新设立的专家顾问组将在制订规划、科学决策和挖掘文化内涵方面建言献策。

**2010年10月24日**　全球商业杂志《福布斯》中文版推出了“2010年中国最佳商业城市排行榜”，广州击败上海在排行榜上位居第一。排在前十名的城市分别是：上海（第二）、深圳（第三）、杭州（第四）、苏州（第五）、北京（第六）、无锡（第七）、宁波（第八）、南京（第九）、天津（第十）。

**2010年10月25日**　中国社会科学院发布《国家竞争力蓝皮书——中国国家竞争力报告》，指出中国的国家竞争力已由1990年的第73位上升至2008年的第17位，力争在2020年进入G20五强，2050年成为仅次于美国的世界第二强国，而实现目标应采取的战略是“梯次追赶”。蓝皮书认为，从规模竞争力来看，中国经济总量巨大，位居全球前列，目前已直逼前三。在增长竞争力方面，中国也保持了长期领先的优势，10来年间始终未跌出世界前五名，保持着强劲的增长态势。同时蓝皮书也指出，20世纪90年代到21世纪初的10年间，中国的规模竞争力提升速度趋缓，这主要是由于找不到新的经济增长点和粗放型的增长模式缺乏可持续性引起的。中国如果继续提升自身的规模竞争力，不仅要扩大数量，还要从结构和效率上下工夫，加快经济转型。

**2010年10月26日**　财政部、国家发展改革委、住房和城乡建设部下发《关于保障性安居工程资金使用管理有关问题的通知》（以下简称《通知》）。《通知》明确提出，从2010年起，各地在确保完成当年廉租住房保障任务的前提下，可从现行土地出让净收益中安排不低于10%的廉租住房保障资金，统筹用于发展公租房，包括购买、新建、改建、租赁公共租赁住房，贷款贴息，向承租公租房的廉租住房保障家庭发放租赁补贴。从2010年起，各地在完成当年廉租住房保障任务的前提下，可以将住房公积金增值收益中计提的廉租住房保障资金，统筹用于发展公共租赁住房。

**2010年10月29日**　北京国际城市发展研究院在国际城市论坛2010年年会上发布了其最新研究成果——《2006—2010中国城市价值报告》。报告对“十一五”期间中国城市价值进行了系统研究，对“十一五”中国城市价值新变化和“十二五”城市发展新方向进行了分析和展望。通过对全国286个地级以上城市的调查研究发现，中国城市化进入加速发展期，城市价值不断提升。与此同时，中国城市发展也面临着人口、资源、环境制约、区域发展不平衡不协调、“大城市病”日益蔓延等诸多挑战。“十二五”时期，我国城镇化率将突破50%，加快城镇化进程是转变经济发展方式的主要动力。城市将向着增长方式集约化、公共服务均等化、城乡发展一体化方向发展。报告还阐述了我国城市的十大变化与十大发展新趋势。

**2010年10月30—31日**　国际欧亚科学院中国院士第十四次全体会议在北京国家会议中心隆重召开。会议开幕式由国际欧亚科学院秘书长、中国科学中心常务副主席汪光焘主持，国际欧亚科学院院长邦杜尔及北京市副市长陈刚先后致辞，国际欧亚科学院执行院长、中国科学中心主席蒋正华做了题为“团结进取，开拓创新，为强化中心建设继续努力奋斗”的工作报告。10月30日下午，在毗邻奥林匹克森林公园的国际欧亚科学院中国科学中心的新址，国际欧亚科学院秘书处（北京）举行了挂牌仪式。随后，中共中央政治局委员、北京市市委书记刘淇同志接见了以邦杜尔院长为首的国际欧亚科学院有关领导，蒋正华执行院长、汪光焘秘书长等陪同接见。刘淇同志表达了北京市加强与国际性科技组织联系的意愿，以及对国际欧亚科学院秘书处（北京）成立的支持。10月30日晚上，国际欧亚科学院中国科学中心名誉主席成思危在人民大会堂宴请了总院代表团一行，中俄双方进行了友好的交流。

**2010年11月4日** 联合国开发计划署发表了《2010年人类发展报告》，对1970年至2010年间的人类发展趋势进行了系统评价。报告中对全球169个国家和地区的人类发展指数进行了排名，中国在这份榜单上排第89位，与去年的排名相比前进了三位，在人类发展指数进步最快国家中排名第二。

**2010年11月9日** 国务院批复广西壮族自治区人民政府，同意将广西北海市列为“国家历史文化名城”。

**2010年11月10日** 国务院总理温家宝主持召开国务院常务会议，研究部署规范农村土地整治和城乡建设用地增减挂钩试点工作。会议称，近年来，一些地方开展城乡建设用地增减挂钩试点，对统筹城乡发展发挥了积极作用，但也出现违背农民意愿强拆强建，侵害农民利益等问题。会议提出明确要求：要充分尊重农民意愿，涉及村庄撤并等方面的土地整治，必须由农村集体经济组织和农户自主决定，不得强拆强建。严禁违法调整、收回和强迫流转农民承包地。坚决防止违背农民意愿搞大拆大建、盲目建高楼等现象。会议强调，要严格控制城乡建设用地增减挂钩试点规模和范围。经批准开展城乡建设用地增减挂钩试点的地方要严格按照有关规定，坚持局部试点、封闭运行、规范管理，不得扩大试点范围。

**2010年11月12—27日** 2010年广州第16届亚运会暨第10届亚残运会在中国广州进行。

**2010年11月16日** 中国工程院召集曾参与《新疆可持续发展中有关水资源的战略研究》项目组的主要成员召开发布会，公布研究成果。会上，10多位院士、专家认为近期广受关注的引渤海水入新疆工程“不可行”、“没法想象”。

**2010年11月16日** 联合国教科文组织保护非物质文化遗产政府间委员会在肯尼亚首都内罗毕举行第五次会议，讨论保护非物质文化遗产。经审议决定将把中国的京剧和中医针灸、法国大餐、比利时的阿尔斯特狂欢节、墨西哥传统烹饪、地中海餐、秘鲁传统剪刀舞仪式、土耳其油脂摔角节、西班牙佛朗明哥舞、哥伦比亚的瓦尤人社区规范体系、伊朗的卡山地毯编织传统技艺、韩国歌谣及大木匠等46项申报项目列入人类非物质文化遗产名录。中国申报项目《中国水密隔舱福船制造技艺》、《中国活字印刷术》以及《麦西热甫》被列入2010年“急需保护的非物质文化遗产名录”。

**2010年11月16日** 成都正式出台《关于全域成都城乡统一户籍实现居民自由迁徙的

意见》。按照这一《意见》，成都市将彻底破除城乡“二元”结构，消除隐藏在户籍背后的身份差异和基本权利不平等，计划到2012年，将实现全域成都统一户籍，城乡居民可以自由迁徙，并实现统一户籍背景下的享有平等的基本公共服务和社会福利。《意见》具有三大特点：一是破除了长期以来束缚城乡居民自由迁徙的制度障碍，全面建立了户籍、居住一元化管理的体制机制；二是农民进城不以牺牲承包地、宅基地等财产权为代价，充分保障了农民的基本权益；三是破除了长期附着在户籍上的城乡权利不平等，实现统一户籍背景下享有平等的教育、住房、社保等基本公共服务和社会福利。

**2010年11月17日**　审计署发布了19个省市2007年至2009年政府投资保障性住房审计调查结果。重点包括：廉租住房保障工作快速开展——3年间，保障资金增长6.25倍，保障总户数增长2.58倍；22个城市提取廉租住房保障资金比例不达标——北京、上海、重庆、成都等城市共计少提取146.23亿元；政策在执行中出现偏差——2132户不符合条件家庭获补助，1.32万户将租赁补贴变成“生活补贴”；一些地方配套设施不完善——南京等13城市出现廉租住房配租困难、房源闲置等问题；出现租金、物业费收取难等问题——天津等12个城市欠收租金和物业费238.05万元；一些地方存在套取、挪用保障资金等问题——1.5亿元廉租房保障资金被挪用，34个项目套取补助资金6129万元。

**2010年11月23日**　住房和城乡建设部向各地发出《关于报送城镇保障性安居工程任务的通知》（以下简称《通知》）。《通知》明确提出，2011年计划建设保障性安居工程任务上调至1000万套。较之2010年中央政府确定的580万套保障性住房的建设规划，2011年版的规划总量，已近翻番。

**2010年11月26日**　住房和城乡建设部副部长仇保兴在北京举行的中国城市科学研究会住房政策和市场调控研究专业委员会成立大会上，指出房地产市场调控的六大难点。一是中国城镇化发展带来的刚性需求；二是民间资本投资领域过窄；三是全球化的热钱涌动与人民币升值预期相结合；四是房产持有环节税收制度缺失；五是地方政府对土地财政的依赖，使得房价越高，土地价格越高。而土地价格越高，地方政府用于城市基础设施的钱就更多；六是中国各地区之间经济发展差距十分巨大。

**2010年11月29日**　坎昆联合国气候变化大会召开。来自190多个国家和地区的官员、专家学者以及非政府组织成员就气候变化问题展开磋商。会场上的博弈主要围绕两个问题展开，一个是对《京都议定书》的地位认定问题；另一个是资金和技术问题。

**2010年12月1日**　经国务院同意，国家发改委以发改经体［2010］2836号《国家发展改革委关于设立山西省国家资源型经济转型综合配套改革试验区的批复》，正式批复设立“山西省国家资源型经济转型综合配套改革试验区”，成为我国设立的第九个综合配套改革试验区，也是我国第一个全省域、全方位、系统性的国家级综合配套改革试验区。山西将把“转型试验区”作为全省“十二五”规划的重要内容，细化金融、土地、财税、投资等多方面的支撑措施。根据中央要求，山西省国家资源型经济转型综合配套改革试验区将通过大胆探索，先行先试，率先突破，破解长期制约全省经济社会发展的瓶颈，实现资源型地区的全面协调可持续发展。

**2010 年 12 月 1 日** 住房和城乡建设部出台《商品房屋租赁管理办法》，住房和城乡建设部房地产市场监管司副司长姜万荣表示，实践中，出租人将房屋分割出租的情况比较突出，已经成为一个各方面反映比较强烈集中的问题，因此考虑多方因素，在《办法》中作出了规范分割出租行为的规定。规范分割出租行为有其现实意义，合理的合租行为仍然受到保护，中低收入人群租房问题可通过保障性租赁住房解决。

**2010 年 12 月 6 日** 北京市委通过的《关于制定北京市国民经济和社会发展第十二个五年规划的建议》（以下简称建议）对外公布。建议分析，首都城市建设管理中面临着人口膨胀、交通拥堵等问题；城乡一体化建设任务仍然十分繁重，基本公共服务均等化水平需要进一步提高；社会管理工作亟待加强。与五年前北京市委对“十一五”规划的建议稿相比，此次建议更多强调北京未来的“科学发展”与“可持续发展”，对发展主要目标的建议不再强调量化指标，而更多着墨于交通、人口管理、改善住房条件等方面，更加注重“主要保障和改善民生”。

**2010 年 12 月 7 日** 由中国社会科学院等单位主办的“2011 年《经济蓝皮书》发布暨中国经济形势分析与预测研讨会”在北京举行，正式发布了由社会科学文献出版社出版的《2011 年中国经济形势分析与预测》。蓝皮书指出，从季度经济运行情况看，2010 年我国经济运行将呈现“前高后低”的局面，预计全年 GDP 增长速度将达到 9.9% 的较高水平。2011 年，影响我国经济运行的基本因素没有发生明显变化，在保持宏观调控政策力度相对稳定的条件下，2011 年我国经济仍将保持高位平稳较快增长态势，与 2010 年增长速度基本持平，GDP 增长率预计可达 10% 左右。该书总结出了 2010 年中国社会建设面临的 5 个主要矛盾和挑战。一是经济运行进入新成长阶段，发展模式亟待转变；二是部分地区劳动关系冲突显化，新生代农民工备受关注；三是收入分配改革举步维艰，警惕进入“中等收入国家陷阱”；四是“土地城市化”再现热潮，警惕损害农民利益；五是半城市化问题突出，部分地区乡村凋敝。

**2010 年 12 月 8 日** 由中国社会科学院财政与贸易经济研究所、社会科学文献出版社联合主办的“2011 年《住房绿皮书》发布暨 2010—2011 年住房形势与政策研讨会”在北京举行。会议研讨了中国住房发展面临的现实问题和重大挑战，分析了 2009—2010 年中国住房及相关市场走势，预测了 2010—2011 年我国住房发展趋势，会议正式对外发布由中国社会科学院财政与贸易经济研究所、中国社会科学院城市与竞争力研究中心完成的国家重大社科基金阶段性成果：住房绿皮书《中国住房发展报告（2010—2011）》。

**2010 年 12 月 10—12 日** 中央经济工作会议在北京举行。胡锦涛总书记在会上发表重要讲话，深刻总结今年及“十一五”时期我国经济社会发展取得的成就，全面分析当前国际国内经济形势，明确提出明年经济工作的总体要求、重要原则、主要任务。温家宝总理在讲话中全面总结今年经济工作，阐述明年经济社会发展主要预期目标和宏观经济政策，对明年经济工作作出具体部署。

**2010 年 12 月 11 日** 重庆公布了《关于进一步加强房地产市场调控的通知》（下称《通知》），其中，原计划在 2020 年前建设 4000 万平方米公租房的目标被提前到 2012 年完成。《通知》中列出了当地遏制房价快速上涨的6条调控措施，包括努力增加保障性住房和普通商品住房供应，进一步加强土地供应及监管，严格执行差别化住房信贷政策，强化房地产行业税收管理，以及严厉查处违法违规行为、积极发挥舆论引导作用等。

**2010年12月15日** 《国有土地上房屋征收与补偿条例（第二次征求意见稿）》（以下简称“二次征求意见稿”）公布，全文共31条，再次向社会公开征求意见。

**2010年12月16日** 国土资源部以国家土地督察机构的名义约谈土地违法情况严重的12名地方政府行政“一把手”，就土地违法问题进行通报，同时要求被约谈地方政府积极整改。相关县级以上地方政府主要领导人员可能被处以警告、记过、记大过、降级直至撤职处分。这标志着由国土资源部、监察部、人力资源和社会保障部联合进行的2009年度土地违法约谈和问责行动正式启动。

**2010年12月19日** 国土资源部发出通知，要求各省、自治区、直辖市国土资源行政主管部门及派驻地方的国家土地督察局采取有力措施，严格落实房地产监管和调控政策措施，打击囤地炒地闲置土地等违法违规行为，坚决抑制少数城市地价过快上涨趋势。

**2010年12月21日** 中国环境保护部部长周生贤在2010年度及“十一五”主要污染物总量减排核查核算视频会议上表示，“十一五”期间，中国排污总量大幅下降，减排目标可超额实现，预计“十一五”全国二氧化硫减排14%、化学需氧量（COD）减排12%左右。

**2010年12月22日** 中央农村工作会议闭幕。会议对2011年及“十二五”时期“三农”工作进行了部署，提出了保三农的六大举措。1. 首要任务是“稳粮”；2. 重要信号：加快水利发展；3. 加大投入，夯实农业基础；4. 征地力保农民权益；5. “菜篮子”“菜摊子”都要抓；6. 加大气象服务，提高防灾能力。

**2010年12月29日** 全国住房和城乡建设工作会议在北京召开。会议指出，今年保障性安居工程建设规模创历年之最，全国各类保障性住房和棚户区改造住房开工590万套，基本建成370万套；农村危房改造开工136万户，基本竣工108万户；均超额完成年初国务院部署的任务。今年，国家加大了对房地产市场的调控力度，房地产市场投机性需求得到一定抑制，调控取得一定效果。

（编辑整理：金晓春，中国城市规划设计研究院学术信息中心主任工程师；郭磊，中国城市规划设计研究院学术信息中心城市规划师）

# 附录2　2010年中国城市政策法规文件索引

| 名称 | 批号(文号) | 发布机构 | 发布日期 | 实施日期 |
|---|---|---|---|---|
| 国务院办公厅关于促进房地产市场平稳健康发展的通知 |  | 中华人民共和国国务院办公厅 | 2010-01-07 |  |
| 建设领域违法违规行为稽查工作管理办法 | 建稽[2010]4号 | 中华人民共和国住房和城乡建设部 | 2010-01-07 | 2010-01-07 |
| 城市轨道交通工程安全质量管理暂行办法 | 建质[2010]5号 | 中华人民共和国住房和城乡建设部 | 2010-01-08 | 2010-01-08 |
| 关于发布《地面交通噪声污染防治技术政策》的通知 | 环发[2010]7号 | 中华人民共和国环境保护部 | 2010-01-11 |  |
| 促进中部地区崛起规划 |  | 中华人民共和国国家发展和改革委员会 | 2010-01-12 |  |
| 城市综合交通体系规划编制办法 | 建城[2010]13号 | 中华人民共和国住房和城乡建设部 | 2010-02-02 | 2010-02-02 |
| 国务院办公厅关于批准湘潭市城市总体规划的通知 | 国办函[2010]33号 | 中华人民共和国国务院办公厅 | 2010-02-05 |  |
| 国务院关于武汉市城市总体规划的批复 | 国函[2010]24号 | 中华人民共和国国务院 | 2010-03-08 |  |
| 国土资源部关于加强房地产用地供应和监管有关问题的通知 | 国土资发[2010]34号 | 中华人民共和国国土资源部 | 2010-03-08 |  |
| 国家发展和改革委员会关于批准设立沈阳经济区国家新型工业化综合配套改革试验区的通知 | 发改经体[2010]660号 | 中华人民共和国国家发展和改革委员会 | 2010-04-06 |  |
| 国务院关于坚决遏制部分城市房价过快上涨的通知 | 国发[2010]10号 | 中华人民共和国国务院 | 2010-04-17 |  |
| 生活垃圾处理技术指南 | 建城[2010]61号 | 中华人民共和国住房和城乡建设部、中华人民共和国国家发展和改革委员会、中华人民共和国环境保护部 | 2010-04-22 | 2010-04-22 |
| 关于加强经济适用住房管理有关问题的通知 | 建保[2010]59号 | 中华人民共和国住房和城乡建设部 | 2010-04-22 |  |
| 关于加强廉租住房管理有关问题的通知 | 建保[2010]62号 | 中华人民共和国住房和城乡建设部 | 2010-04-23 |  |
| 省域城镇体系规划编制审批办法 | 中华人民共和国住房和城乡建设部令第3号 | 中华人民共和国住房和城乡建设部 | 2010-04-25 | 2010-07-01 |

续表

| 名称 | 批号(文号) | 发布机构 | 发布日期 | 实施日期 |
|---|---|---|---|---|
| 关于城市和国有工矿棚户区改造项目有关税收优惠政策的通知 | 财税[2010]42号 | 中华人民共和国财政部、中华人民共和国税务总局 | 2010-05-04 | |
| 关于促进中部地区城市群发展的指导意见 | 发改地区[2010]967号 | 中华人民共和国国家发展和改革委员会 | 2010-05-09 | |
| 关于城市停车设施规划建设及管理的指导意见 | 建城[2010]74号 | 中华人民共和国住房和城乡建设部、中华人民共和国公安部、中华人民共和国国家发展和改革委员会 | 2010-05-19 | |
| 国务院关于做好玉树地震灾后恢复重建工作的指导意见 | 国发[2010]14号 | 中华人民共和国国务院 | 2010-05-24 | |
| 城市综合交通体系规划编制导则 | 建城[2010]80号 | 中华人民共和国住房和城乡建设部 | 2010-05-26 | 2010-05-26 |
| 关于规范商业性个人住房贷款中第二套住房认定标准的通知 | 建房[2010]83号 | 中华人民共和国住房和城乡建设部、中国人民银行、中国银行业监督管理委员会 | 2010-05-26 | |
| 国务院关于支持玉树地震灾后恢复重建政策措施的意见 | 国发[2010]16号 | 中华人民共和国国务院 | 2010-05-27 | |
| 城市照明管理规定 | 中华人民共和国住房和城乡建设部令第4号 | 中华人民共和国住房和城乡建设部 | 2010-05-27 | 2010-07-01 |
| 关于进一步加强汶川地震灾后恢复重建工程质量管理的通知 | 建质[2010]85号 | 中华人民共和国住房和城乡建设部 | 2010-06-03 | |
| 国家发展和改革委员会关于印发长江三角洲地区区域规划的通知 | 发改地区[2010]1243号 | 中华人民共和国国家发展和改革委员会 | 2010-06-07 | |
| 关于加快发展公共租赁住房的指导意见 | 建保[2010]87号 | 中华人民共和国住房和城乡建设部、中华人民共和国国家发展和改革委员会、中华人民共和国财政部、中华人民共和国国土资源部、中国人民银行、国家税务总局、中国银行业监督管理委员会 | 2010-06-08 | |
| 国务院关于印发玉树地震灾后恢复重建总体规划的通知 | 国发[2010]17号 | 中华人民共和国国务院 | 2010-06-09 | |
| 国务院关于进一步加强防震减灾工作的意见 | 国发[2010]18号 | 中华人民共和国国务院 | 2010-06-09 | |
| 关于切实加强政府办公和大型公共建筑节能管理工作的通知 | 建科[2010]90号 | 中华人民共和国住房和城乡建设部 | 2010-06-10 | |
| 关于做好住房保障规划编制工作的通知 | 建保[2010]91号 | 中华人民共和国住房和城乡建设部、中华人民共和国国家发展和改革委员会、中华人民共和国财政部、中华人民共和国国土资源部、中华人民共和国农业部、国家林业局 | 2010-06-11 | |
| 国土资源部关于发布《国家地质公园规划编制技术要求》的通知 | 国土资发[2010]89号 | 中华人民共和国国土资源部 | 2010-06-12 | 2010-06-12 |

续表

| 名称 | 批号(文号) | 发布机构 | 发布日期 | 实施日期 |
|---|---|---|---|---|
| 关于切实加强城市照明节能管理严格控制景观照明的通知 | 建城[2010]92号 | 中华人民共和国住房和城乡建设部、中华人民共和国国家发展和改革委员会 | 2010-06-17 | |
| 中央补助城市棚户区改造专项资金管理办法 | 财综[2010]46号 | 中华人民共和国财政部、中华人民共和国住房和城乡建设部 | 2010-06-25 | 2010-06-25 |
| 关于加强城市轨道交通安防设施建设工作的指导意见 | 建城[2010]94号 | 中华人民共和国住房和城乡建设部 | 2010-06-28 | |
| 国务院办公厅关于进一步加强地质灾害防治工作的通知 | 国办发明电[2010]21号 | 中华人民共和国国务院办公厅 | 2010-07-16 | |
| 国务院办公厅印发贯彻落实国务院关于加快发展旅游业意见重点工作分工方案的通知 | 国办函[2010]121号 | 中华人民共和国国务院办公厅 | 2010-07-23 | |
| 房屋建筑和市政基础设施工程质量监督管理规定 | 中华人民共和国住房和城乡建设部令第5号 | 中华人民共和国住房和城乡建设部 | 2010-08-01 | 2010-09-01 |
| 国务院办公厅关于有序做好支援甘肃舟曲灾区有关工作的通知 | 国办发明电[2010]22号 | 中华人民共和国国务院办公厅 | 2010-08-10 | |
| 国家发展和改革委员会关于印发促进中部地区崛起规划实施意见的通知 | 发改地区[2010]1827号 | 中华人民共和国国家发展和改革委员会 | 2010-08-12 | |
| 关于加强建筑市场资质资格动态监管完善企业和人员准入清出制度的指导意见 | 建市[2010]128号 | 中华人民共和国住房和城乡建设部 | 2010-08-13 | |
| 国务院关于深圳市城市总体规划的批复 | 国函[2010]78号 | 中华人民共和国国务院 | 2010-08-16 | |
| 国务院关于郑州市城市总体规划的批复 | 国函[2010]80号 | 中华人民共和国国务院 | 2010-08-19 | |
| 关于国家级风景名胜区数字化景区建设工作的指导意见 | 建城函[2010]226号 | 中华人民共和国住房和城乡建设部 | 2010-08-25 | |
| 关于试行住房公积金督察员制度的意见 | 建稽[2010]102号 | 中华人民共和国住房和城乡建设部、中华人民共和国财政部、中华人民共和国国家发展和改革委员会、中国人民银行、中华人民共和国审计署、中国银行业监督管理委员会 | 2010-08-27 | |
| 文化馆建设标准 | 建标[2010]136号 | 中华人民共和国住房和城乡建设部 | 2010-08-30 | |
| 地方残疾人综合服务设施建设标准 | 建标[2010]135号 | 中华人民共和国住房和城乡建设部 | 2010-08-30 | |
| 国务院关于中西部地区承接产业转移的指导意见 | 国发[2010]28号 | 中华人民共和国国务院 | 2010-08-31 | |
| 住房公积金督察员管理暂行办法 | 建稽[2010]139号 | 中华人民共和国住房和城乡建设部 | 2010-09-07 | 2010-09-07 |
| 关于进一步加强世界遗产保护管理工作的通知 | 建城函[2010]240号 | 中华人民共和国住房和城乡建设部 | 2010-09-07 | |

续表

| 名称 | 批号(文号) | 发布机构 | 发布日期 | 实施日期 |
|---|---|---|---|---|
| 生活垃圾堆肥处理工程项目建设标准 | 建标[2010]147 号 | 中华人民共和国住房和城乡建设部 | 2010-09-07 | 2011-01-01 |
| 生活垃圾填埋场封场工程项目建设标准 | 建标[2010]146 号 | 中华人民共和国住房和城乡建设部 | 2010-09-14 | 2011-01-01 |
| 固定资产投资项目节能评估和审查暂行办法 | 中华人民共和国国家发展和改革委员会令第 6 号 | 中华人民共和国国家发展和改革委员会 | 2010-09-17 | 2010-09-17 |
| 国土资源部、住房和城乡建设部关于进一步加强房地产用地和建设管理调控的通知 | 国土资发[2010]151 号 | 中华人民共和国国土资源部、中华人民共和国住房和城乡建设部 | 2010-09-21 | |
| 关于支持公共租赁住房建设和运营有关税收优惠政策的通知 | 财税[2010]88 号 | 中华人民共和国财政部、中华人民共和国税务总局 | 2010-09-27 | |
| 关于调整房地产交易环节契税个人所得税优惠政策的通知 | 财税[2010]94 号 | 中华人民共和国财政部、中华人民共和国税务总局、中华人民共和国住房和城乡建设部 | 2010-09-29 | |
| 国务院关于加快培育和发展战略性新兴产业的决定 | 国发[2010]32 号 | 中华人民共和国国务院 | 2010-10-10 | |
| 国务院办公厅关于批准柳州市城市总体规划的通知 | 国办函[2010]150 号 | 中华人民共和国国务院办公厅 | 2010-10-11 | |
| 国家发展和改革委员会关于印发加强区域产业创新基础能力建设工作指导意见的通知 | 发改高技[2010]2455 号 | 中华人民共和国国家发展和改革委员会 | 2010-10-13 | |
| 国务院关于支持舟曲灾后恢复重建政策措施的意见 | 国发[2010]34 号 | 中华人民共和国国务院 | 2010-10-18 | |
| 国务院办公厅关于批准淮南市城市总体规划的通知 | 国办函[2010]145 号 | 中华人民共和国国务院办公厅 | 2010-10-21 | |
| 关于保障性安居工程资金使用管理有关问题的通知 | 财综[2010]95 号 | 中华人民共和国财政部、中华人民共和国国家发展和改革委员会、中华人民共和国住房和城乡建设部 | 2010-10-26 | |
| 国务院关于印发舟曲灾后恢复重建总体规划的通知 | 国发[2010]38 号 | 中华人民共和国国务院 | 2010-11-04 | |
| 关于中央企业工程建设领域突出问题专项治理整改工作的指导意见 | 国资发纪检[2010]171 号 | 国务院国有资产监督管理委员会 | 2010-11-05 | |
| 国务院关于同意将广西壮族自治区北海市列为国家历史文化名城的批复 | 国函[2010]121 号 | 中华人民共和国国务院 | 2010-11-09 | |
| 国务院关于确定三亚市城市总体规划由国务院审批的通知 | 国函[2010]123 号 | 中华人民共和国国务院 | 2010-11-16 | |
| 社区老年人日间照料中心建设标准 | 建标[2010]193 号 | 中华人民共和国住房和城乡建设部、中华人民共和国国家发展和改革委员会 | 2010-11-17 | 2011-03-01 |
| 老年养护院建设标准 | 建标[2010]194 号 | 中华人民共和国住房和城乡建设部、中华人民共和国国家发展和改革委员会 | 2010-11-17 | 2011-03-01 |

续表

| 名称 | 批号(文号) | 发布机构 | 发布日期 | 实施日期 |
|---|---|---|---|---|
| 儿童福利院建设标准 | 建标[2010]195号 | 中华人民共和国住房和城乡建设部、中华人民共和国国家发展和改革委员会 | 2010-11-17 | 2011-03-01 |
| 城镇燃气管理条例 | 中华人民共和国国务院令第583号 | 中华人民共和国国务院 | 2010-11-19 | 2011-03-01 |
| 商品房屋租赁管理办法 | 中华人民共和国住房和城乡建设部令第6号 | 中华人民共和国住房和城乡建设部 | 2010-12-01 | 2011-02-01 |
| 城市、镇控制性详细规划编制审批办法 | 中华人民共和国住房和城乡建设部令第7号 | 中华人民共和国住房和城乡建设部 | 2010-12-01 | 2011-01-01 |
| 中央补助廉租住房保障专项资金管理办法 | 财综[2010]110号 | 中华人民共和国财政部 | 2010-12-01 | 2011-01-01 |
| 关于印发《全国绿色建筑创新奖实施细则》和《全国绿色建筑创新奖评审标准》的通知 | 建科[2010]216号 | 中华人民共和国住房和城乡建设部 | 2010-12-23 | |
| 国家发展和改革委员会关于实行政府重大投资项目公示工作的指导意见 | 发改投资[2010]3131号 | 中华人民共和国国家发展和改革委员会 | 2010-12-28 | |
| 国土资源部关于房地产闲置土地情况的公告 | 2010年第27号 | 中华人民共和国国土资源部 | 2010-12-29 | |
| 关于印发《黄土高原地区综合治理规划大纲(2010—2030年)》的通知 | 发改农经[2010]3152号 | 中华人民共和国国家发展和改革委员会 | 2010-12-30 | |
| 关于加强重点流域水污染防治规划编制工作的通知 | 环办[2010]177号 | 中华人民共和国环境保护部 | 2010-12-30 | |

(编辑整理:金晓春,中国城市规划设计研究院学术信息中心主任工程师;郭磊,中国城市规划设计研究院学术信息中心城市规划师)

# 附录 3　中国城市基本数据（2008 年）

| 城市名称 Name of Cities | | 行政级别 Admini－strative Rank | 行政区土地面积（平方公里）Area of City's Administrative（sq. km） | 年末总人口（万人）Total Population（year-end）（10 thousand） | 非农业人口（万人）Non-agricultural Population（10 thousand） | 建成区面积（平方公里）Area of Built-up District（sq. km） | 地区生产总值（万元）Gross Regional Product（10 000 yuan） | 人均地区生产总值（元）Per Capita Gross Regional Product（yuan） | 市政公用设施固定资产投资总额（万元）Total Fixed Assets Investment in Municipal Service Facilities（10 000 RMB） | 污水处理率（%）Wastewater Treatment Rate（%） | 生活垃圾处理率（%）Domestic Garbage Treatment Rate（%） | 用水普及率（%）Water Coverage Rate（%） | 人均公园绿地面积（平方米）Per Capita Public Green Space（sq. m） |
|---|---|---|---|---|---|---|---|---|---|---|---|---|---|
| 北京市 | Beijing | 直辖市 | 16 411 | 1 299. 85 | 950. 71 | 1 310. 94 | 104 880 500 | 63 029 | 5 189 156 | 78. 92 | 97. 71 | 100. 00 | 8. 56 |
| 天津市 | Tianjin | 直辖市 | 11 760 | 968. 87 | 538. 27 | 640. 85 | 63 543 800 | 55 473 | 1 661 826 | 72. 40 | 93. 52 | 100. 00 | 7. 53 |
| 河北省 | Hebei | | | | | | | | | | | | |
| 石家庄市 | Shijiazhuang | 地级市 | 15 848 | 966. 48 | 398. 31 | 190. 86 | 28 383 712 | 28 923 | 598 526 | 77. 21 | 100. 00 | 100. 00 | 9. 30 |
| 唐山市 | Tangshan | 地级市 | 13 472 | 729. 41 | 244. 39 | 213. 00 | 35 611 900 | 48 054 | 586 650 | 90. 61 | 100. 00 | 100. 00 | 10. 53 |
| 秦皇岛市 | Qinhuangdao | 地级市 | 7 523 | 285. 85 | 120. 10 | 87. 48 | 8 089 526 | 27 481 | 254 536 | 89. 01 | 96. 86 | 100. 00 | 12. 12 |
| 邯郸市 | Handan | 地级市 | 12 062 | 928. 08 | 299. 70 | 104. 06 | 19 903 633 | 22 651 | 217 422 | 76. 86 | 100. 00 | 100. 00 | 12. 01 |
| 邢台市 | Xingtai | 地级市 | 12 434 | 706. 36 | 164. 92 | 70. 00 | 9 890 039 | 14 315 | 202 929 | 81. 01 | 100. 00 | 100. 00 | 9. 34 |
| 保定市 | Baoding | 地级市 | 20 584 | 1 141. 73 | 301. 40 | 129. 00 | 15 808 884 | 14 518 | 99 450 | 93. 81 | 100. 00 | 100. 00 | 8. 03 |
| 张家口市 | Zhangjiakou | 地级市 | 36 873 | 459. 67 | 147. 18 | 80. 00 | 7 203 705 | 17 134 | 450 321 | 75. 86 | 61. 62 | 100. 00 | 7. 55 |
| 承德市 | Chengde | 地级市 | 39 548 | 369. 38 | 98. 05 | 83. 70 | 7 149 413 | 21 048 | 124 975 | 56. 04 | 72. 18 | 100. 00 | 24. 14 |
| 沧州市 | Cangzhou | 地级市 | 14 053 | 710. 10 | 214. 87 | 44. 25 | 17 161 616 | 24 665 | 129 757 | 76. 98 | 90. 89 | 100. 00 | 4. 71 |
| 廊坊市 | Langfang | 地级市 | 6 429 | 408. 28 | 122. 40 | 55. 98 | 10 514 939 | 25 757 | 254 751 | 83. 01 | 95. 05 | 100. 00 | 12. 11 |
| 衡水市 | Hengshui | 地级市 | 8 815 | 432. 51 | 98. 07 | 43. 56 | 6 338 142 | 14 843 | 49 505 | 86. 97 | 88. 59 | 100. 00 | 6. 50 |
| 辛集市 | Xinji | 县级市 | 951 | 61. 40 | 23. 85 | 23. 89 | | | 11 228 | 100. 00 | 100. 00 | 100. 00 | 6. 69 |
| 藁城市 | Gaocheng | 县级市 | 836 | 76. 40 | 21. 45 | 17. 60 | | | 8 399 | 97. 66 | 97. 50 | 96. 37 | 6. 38 |
| 晋州市 | Jinzhou | 县级市 | 619 | 52. 80 | 9. 11 | 16. 00 | | | 10 842 | 91. 03 | 100. 00 | 100. 00 | 6. 29 |
| 新乐市 | Xinle | 县级市 | 525 | 47. 70 | 12. 28 | 13. 00 | | | 5 033 | 79. 86 | | 100. 00 | 6. 75 |

续表

| 城市名称 Name of Cities | | 行政级别 Admini－strative Rank | 行政区土地面积(平方公里) Area of City's Administrative (sq. km) | 年末总人口(万人) Total Population (year-end) (10 thousand) | 非农业人口(万人) Non-agricultural Population (10 thousand) | 建成区面积(平方公里) Area of Built-up District (sq. km) | 地区生产总值(万元) Gross Regional Product (10 000 yuan) | 人均地区生产总值(元) Per Capita Gross Regional Product (yuan) | 市政公用设施固定资产投资总额(万元) Total Fixed Assets Investment in Municipal Service Facilities (10 000 RMB) | 污水处理率(%) Wastewater Treatment Rate(%) | 生活垃圾处理率(%) Domestic Garbage Treatment Rate(%) | 用水普及率(%) Water Coverage Rate(%) | 人均公园绿地面积(平方米) Per Capita Public Green Space (sq. m) |
|---|---|---|---|---|---|---|---|---|---|---|---|---|---|
| 鹿泉市 | Luquan | 县级市 | 603 | 37.60 | 9.05 | 18.04 | | | 9 308 | 83.15 | 100.00 | 100.00 | 6.64 |
| 遵化市 | Zunhua | 县级市 | 1 513 | 71.50 | 10.71 | 19.12 | | | 71 747 | | 100.00 | 100.00 | 6.78 |
| 迁安市 | Qianan | 县级市 | 1 208 | 71.00 | 13.33 | 26.00 | | | 54 810 | 93.35 | 100.00 | 100.00 | 13.80 |
| 武安市 | Wuan | 县级市 | 1 806 | 75.60 | 24.58 | 25.00 | | | 36 363 | 80.52 | 100.00 | 100.00 | 10.51 |
| 南宫市 | Nangong | 县级市 | 854 | 46.80 | 8.33 | 12.00 | | | 12 547 | 29.33 | 58.82 | 100.00 | 8.82 |
| 沙河市 | Shahe | 县级市 | 999 | 48.80 | 11.68 | 14.00 | | | 27 421 | 81.94 | 100.00 | 100.00 | 9.17 |
| 涿州市 | Zhuozhou | 县级市 | 742 | 62.80 | 19.02 | 25.40 | | | 16 917 | 84.17 | 82.02 | 100.00 | 6.76 |
| 定州市 | Dingzhou | 县级市 | 1 274 | 119.30 | 27.79 | 25.21 | | | 17 193 | 11.02 | 100.00 | 100.00 | 5.28 |
| 安国市 | Anguo | 县级市 | 486 | 40.70 | 9.82 | 12.60 | | | 14 758 | 17.54 | 100.00 | 100.00 | 6.63 |
| 高碑店市 | Gaobeidian | 县级市 | 672 | 59.80 | 12.22 | 16.65 | | | 6 705 | 4.16 | 100.00 | 100.00 | 3.49 |
| 泊头市 | Botou | 县级市 | 1 007 | 57.50 | 18.61 | 19.72 | | | 15 000 | 29.72 | 47.22 | 100.00 | 3.45 |
| 任丘市 | Renqiu | 县级市 | 1 012 | 81.90 | 36.53 | 41.43 | | | 16 056 | 46.55 | 100.00 | 100.00 | 6.30 |
| 黄骅市 | Huanghua | 县级市 | 1 545 | 43.30 | 16.30 | 20.08 | | | 32 690 | 74.78 | 100.00 | 100.00 | 7.61 |
| 河间市 | Hejian | 县级市 | 1 333 | 79.80 | 17.29 | 15.06 | | | 11 829 | | | 100.00 | 1.84 |
| 霸州市 | Bazhou | 县级市 | 784 | 58.90 | 24.30 | 17.60 | | | 34 735 | | 100.00 | 100.00 | 5.54 |
| 三河市 | Sanhe | 县级市 | 643 | 52.00 | 17.95 | 18.60 | | | 42 348 | 72.10 | 100.00 | 100.00 | 6.68 |
| 冀州市 | Jizhou | 县级市 | 922 | 36.70 | 7.03 | 15.50 | | | 8 500 | | 57.25 | 100.00 | 9.65 |
| 深州市 | Shenzhou | 县级市 | 1 253 | 57.00 | 9.78 | 16.44 | | | 15 007 | 53.65 | 99.40 | 100.00 | 6.75 |
| 山西省 | Shanxi | | | | | | | | | | | | |
| 太原市 | Taiyuan | 地级市 | 6 989 | 360.23 | 260.65 | 238.00 | 14 680 851 | 42 378 | 363 822 | 68.40 | 90.01 | 100.00 | 7.58 |
| 大同市 | Datong | 地级市 | 14 127 | 312.00 | 146.45 | 91.20 | 5 696 268 | 17 974 | 210 830 | 69.99 | | 100.00 | 5.16 |
| 阳泉市 | Yangquan | 地级市 | 4 570 | 129.34 | 77.17 | 51.23 | 3 106 529 | 23 593 | 48 434 | 64.99 | 81.00 | 100.00 | 8.80 |
| 长治市 | Changzhi | 地级市 | 13 896 | 327.40 | 97.30 | 45.30 | 6 821 316 | 20 821 | 46 984 | 82.72 | 100.00 | 77.58 | 5.67 |
| 晋城市 | Jincheng | 地级市 | 9 421 | 221.59 | 53.36 | 31.00 | 5 275 490 | 23 680 | 8 172 | 94.97 | 92.08 | 100.00 | 11.61 |
| 朔州市 | Shuozhou | 地级市 | 11 066 | 155.17 | 39.78 | 29.00 | 4 204 038 | 27 458 | 34 189 | 94.24 | 47.77 | 91.53 | 9.00 |

续表

| 城市名称 Name of Cities | | 行政级别 Admini－strative Rank | 行政区土地面积（平方公里）Area of City's Administrative (sq. km) | 年末总人口（万人）Total Population (year-end) (10 thousand) | 非农业人口（万人）Non-agricultural Population (10 thousand) | 建成区面积（平方公里）Area of Built-up District (sq. km) | 地区生产总值（万元）Gross Regional Product (10 000 yuan) | 人均地区生产总值（元）Per Capita Gross Regional Product (yuan) | 市政公用设施固定资产投资总额（万元）Total Fixed Assets Investment in Municipal Service Facilities (10 000 RMB) | 污水处理率（%）Wastewater Treatment Rate (%) | 生活垃圾处理率（%）Domestic Garbage Treatment Rate (%) | 用水普及率（%）Water Coverage Rate (%) | 人均公园绿地面积（平方米）Per Capita Public Green Space (sq. m) |
|---|---|---|---|---|---|---|---|---|---|---|---|---|---|
| 晋中市 | Jinzhong | 地级市 | 16 404 | 317. 90 | 89. 20 | 38. 28 | 5 678 066 | 18 219 | 69 964 | 65. 64 | 0. 39 | 96. 24 | 9. 37 |
| 运城市 | Yuncheng | 地级市 | 14 181 | 499. 40 | 89. 61 | 30. 00 | 6 914 452 | 12 313 | 36 950 | 75. 00 | 56. 00 | 90. 66 | 7. 55 |
| 忻州市 | Xinzhou | 地级市 | 25 117 | 303. 26 | 67. 55 | 21. 40 | 3 112 485 | 10 101 | 25 227 | 88. 02 | | 87. 49 | 1. 13 |
| 临汾市 | Linfen | 地级市 | 20 275 | 431. 92 | 108. 58 | 37. 40 | 7 546 316 | 18 031 | 64 279 | 82. 86 | 11. 00 | 93. 24 | 11. 26 |
| 吕梁市 | Lvliang | 地级市 | 21 241 | 376. 63 | 81. 21 | 15. 00 | 6 296 438 | 17 553 | 96 192 | 45. 07 | 100. 00 | 93. 47 | 10. 36 |
| 古交市 | Gujiao | 县级市 | 1 527 | 21. 70 | 14. 14 | 15. 80 | | | 12 518 | 86. 43 | | 89. 35 | 5. 93 |
| 潞城市 | Lucheng | 县级市 | 630 | 22. 10 | 4. 53 | 7. 30 | | | 7 902 | 92. 21 | 92. 39 | 97. 41 | 7. 77 |
| 高平市 | Gaoping | 县级市 | 946 | 47. 60 | 7. 30 | 8. 30 | | | 8 533 | 75. 79 | | 100. 00 | 10. 43 |
| 介休市 | Jiexiu | 县级市 | 757 | 39. 70 | 11. 54 | 17. 55 | | | 25 570 | 33. 60 | | 98. 72 | 7. 31 |
| 永济市 | Yongji | 县级市 | 1 221 | 43. 10 | 8. 87 | 20. 60 | | | 1 263 | 68. 00 | 18. 00 | 47. 52 | 2. 85 |
| 河津市 | Hejin | 县级市 | 593 | 38. 90 | 10. 14 | 18. 00 | | | 9 900 | 59. 33 | | 66. 81 | 10. 78 |
| 原平市 | Yuanping | 县级市 | 2 571 | 49. 30 | 12. 76 | 9. 57 | | | 4 996 | 93. 35 | | 96. 80 | 1. 69 |
| 侯马市 | Houma | 县级市 | 221 | 24. 30 | 13. 02 | 18. 47 | | | 33 621 | 69. 04 | 50. 00 | 85. 96 | 9. 30 |
| 霍州市 | Huozhou | 县级市 | 764 | 30. 30 | 11. 62 | 14. 00 | | | 29 750 | | | 93. 64 | 6. 18 |
| 孝义市 | Xiaoyi | 县级市 | 946 | 46. 20 | 21. 29 | 12. 00 | | | 43 716 | 68. 02 | | 85. 44 | 13. 92 |
| 汾阳市 | Fenyang | 县级市 | 1 180 | 41. 50 | 8. 60 | 12. 00 | | | | | | 86. 72 | 14. 27 |
| 内蒙古自治区 | Inner Mongolia | | | | | | | | | | | | |
| 呼和浩特市 | Huhehaote | 地级市 | 17 224 | 224. 30 | 105. 50 | 154. 00 | 13 163 700 | 49 606 | 209 213 | 44. 11 | 95. 18 | 95. 34 | 15. 74 |
| 包头市 | Baotou | 地级市 | 27 768 | 217. 76 | 135. 58 | 180. 00 | 17 600 038 | 70 004 | 438 795 | 67. 32 | 97. 25 | 78. 00 | 11. 21 |
| 乌海市 | Wuhai | 地级市 | 1 754 | 48. 27 | 44. 53 | 37. 51 | 2 401 000 | 50 036 | 35 873 | 64. 10 | 82. 68 | 100. 00 | 10. 66 |
| 赤峰市 | Chifeng | 地级市 | 90 659 | 456. 49 | 107. 19 | 77. 00 | 7 523 927 | 17 242 | 140 354 | 90. 65 | 82. 99 | 58. 74 | 5. 54 |
| 通辽市 | Tongliao | 地级市 | 59 535 | 316. 92 | 119. 47 | 50. 50 | 7 419 620 | 25 402 | 49 066 | 100. 00 | 100. 00 | 88. 53 | 11. 00 |
| 鄂尔多斯市 | Eerduosi | 地级市 | 86 752 | 149. 69 | 46. 89 | 71. 68 | 16 030 184 | 10 218 | 607 733 | 76. 31 | 100. 00 | 93. 03 | 8. 01 |
| 呼伦贝尔市 | Hulunbeier | 地级市 | 253 356 | 272. 48 | 180. 28 | 28. 00 | 6 326 600 | 23 413 | 146 568 | 97. 25 | | 74. 36 | 20. 00 |
| 巴彦淖尔市 | Bayannaoer | 地级市 | 64 413 | 185. 00 | 62. 79 | 32. 47 | 4 390 600 | 25 237 | 4 411 | 85. 05 | 94. 86 | 92. 23 | 4. 64 |

续表

| 城市名称 Name of Cities | | 行政级别 Admini-strative Rank | 行政区土地面积(平方公里) Area of City's Administrative (sq. km) | 年末总人口(万人) Total Population (year-end) (10 thousand) | 非农业人口(万人) Non-agricultural Population (10 thousand) | 建成区面积(平方公里) Area of Built-up District (sq. km) | 地区生产总值(万元) Gross Regional Product (10 000 yuan) | 人均地区生产总值(元) Per Capita Gross Regional Product (yuan) | 市政公用设施固定资产投资总额(万元) Total Fixed Assets Investment in Municipal Service Facilities (10 000 RMB) | 污水处理率(%) Wastewater Treatment Rate(%) | 生活垃圾处理率(%) Domestic Garbage Treatment Rate(%) | 用水普及率(%) Water Coverage Rate(%) | 人均公园绿地面积(平方米) Per Capita Public Green Space (sq. m) |
|---|---|---|---|---|---|---|---|---|---|---|---|---|---|
| 乌兰察布市 | Wulanchabu | 地级市 | 54 492 | 287.11 | 71.82 | 35.00 | 4 346 864 | 20 358 | 22 300 | 87.50 | | 85.29 | 26.12 |
| 霍林郭勒市 | Huolinguole | 县级市 | 585 | 8.20 | 7.89 | 18.00 | | | 10 045 | 100.00 | | 77.25 | 2.49 |
| 满洲里市 | Manzhouli | 县级市 | 732 | 30.00 | 16.52 | 27.06 | | | 84 968 | 17.36 | 29.12 | 97.82 | 9.30 |
| 牙克石市 | Yakeshi | 县级市 | 27 830 | 37.90 | 36.44 | 15.70 | | | 4 010 | 80.00 | | 40.37 | 5.18 |
| 扎兰屯市 | Zhalantun | 县级市 | 16 800 | 43.20 | 16.86 | 19.20 | | | 3 540 | 76.67 | | 40.27 | 8.19 |
| 额尔古纳市 | Erguna | 县级市 | 28 400 | 8.50 | 7.76 | 10.38 | | | 2 751 | | | 36.44 | 8.89 |
| 根河市 | Genhe | 县级市 | 20 012 | 16.30 | 16.31 | 17.50 | | | 7 951 | | | 76.31 | 4.69 |
| 丰镇市 | Fengzhen | 县级市 | 2 704 | 34.10 | 9.56 | 25.00 | | | 5 480 | 27.29 | 98.87 | 57.14 | 7.93 |
| 乌兰浩特市 | Wulanhaote | 县级市 | 2 332 | 31.50 | 23.64 | 25.38 | | | 29 935 | 92.86 | 100.00 | 80.41 | 13.70 |
| 阿尔山市 | Aershan | 县级市 | 7 409 | 4.70 | 4.79 | 10.44 | | | 4 279 | | | 41.25 | 1.25 |
| 二连浩特市 | Erlianhaote | 县级市 | 4 015 | 9.40 | 2.40 | 20.20 | | | 11 908 | | | 100.00 | 2.72 |
| 锡林浩特市 | Xilinhaote | 县级市 | 14 592 | 16.60 | 14.40 | 30.40 | | | 126 403 | 57.01 | 91.11 | 85.82 | 2.51 |
| 辽宁省 | Liaoning | | | | | | | | | | | | |
| 沈阳市 | Shenyang | 地级市 | 12 980 | 713.51 | 460.49 | 370.00 | 38 604 745 | 54 248 | 2 571 800 | 77.26 | 100.00 | 100.00 | 12.12 |
| 大连市 | Dalian | 地级市 | 12 574 | 583.37 | 347.83 | 258.00 | 38 582 471 | 63 198 | 634 382 | 90.00 | 100.00 | 100.00 | 10.46 |
| 鞍山市 | Anshan | 地级市 | 9 252 | 351.42 | 177.17 | 148.04 | 16 078 635 | 45 830 | 98 106 | 34.56 | 100.00 | 96.21 | 8.69 |
| 抚顺市 | Fushun | 地级市 | 11 272 | 223.19 | 147.30 | 123.90 | 6 624 377 | 29 645 | 102 500 | 56.89 | 100.00 | 98.16 | 7.85 |
| 本溪市 | Benxi | 地级市 | 8 411 | 155.66 | 104.27 | 106.50 | 6 108 589 | 39 199 | 56 627 | 42.80 | 97.25 | 99.70 | 8.27 |
| 丹东市 | Dandong | 地级市 | 15 030 | 242.70 | 101.74 | 53.40 | 5 638 618 | 23 223 | 48 775 | | 100.00 | 94.11 | 6.15 |
| 锦州市 | Jinzhou | 地级市 | 10 111 | 310.19 | 123.37 | 68.82 | 6 904 436 | 22 287 | 57 019 | 51.50 | 100.00 | 100.00 | 8.35 |
| 营口市 | Yingkou | 地级市 | 5 402 | 233.80 | 108.31 | 97.12 | 7 035 683 | 30 177 | 149 473 | 63.20 | 89.87 | 95.86 | 10.36 |
| 阜新市 | Fuxin | 地级市 | 10 355 | 192.46 | 86.17 | 66.00 | 2 339 120 | 12 134 | 19 427 | | 90.89 | 93.46 | 7.79 |
| 辽阳市 | Liaoyang | 地级市 | 4 743 | 183.39 | 80.07 | 92.02 | 5 666 088 | 30 897 | 34 367 | 98.38 | 100.00 | 100.00 | 8.12 |
| 盘锦市 | Panjin | 地级市 | 4 071 | 129.20 | 104.70 | 57.85 | 6 750 045 | 51 214 | 61 371 | 53.58 | 91.25 | 100.00 | 7.16 |
| 铁岭市 | Tieling | 地级市 | 12 980 | 305.93 | 97.98 | 43.96 | 5 363 280 | 17 543 | 159 725 | 83.51 | 86.04 | 97.40 | 9.31 |

续表

| 城市名称 Name of Cities | | 行政级别 Admini－strative Rank | 行政区土地面积（平方公里）Area of City's Administrative（sq. km） | 年末总人口（万人）Total Population（year-end）（10 thousand） | 非农业人口（万人）Non-agricultural Population（10 thousand） | 建成区面积（平方公里）Area of Built-up District（sq. km） | 地区生产总值（万元）Gross Regional Product（10 000 yuan） | 人均地区生产总值（元）Per Capita Gross Regional Product（yuan） | 市政公用设施固定资产投资总额（万元）Total Fixed Assets Investment in Municipal Service Facilities（10 000 RMB） | 污水处理率（%）Wastewater Treatment Rate（%） | 生活垃圾处理率（%）Domestic Garbage Treatment Rate（%） | 用水普及率（%）Water Coverage Rate（%） | 人均公园绿地面积（平方米）Per Capita Public Green Space（sq. m） |
|---|---|---|---|---|---|---|---|---|---|---|---|---|---|
| 朝阳市 | Chaoyang | 地级市 | 19 699 | 340. 92 | 93. 70 | 35. 00 | 4 466 114 | 13 114 | 18 522 | 32. 31 | 100. 00 | 76. 97 | 8. 15 |
| 葫芦岛市 | Huludao | 地级市 | 10 415 | 280. 40 | 86. 73 | 67. 50 | 4 578 221 | 16 351 | 12 182 | 87. 20 | 100. 00 | 100. 00 | 11. 43 |
| 新民市 | Xinmin | 县级市 | 3 315 | 69. 90 | 14. 12 | 18. 00 | | | 22 562 | | | 92. 15 | 10. 65 |
| 瓦房店市 | Wafangdian | 县级市 | 3 794 | 102. 50 | 35. 56 | 32. 50 | | | 12 564 | 88. 80 | 100. 00 | 100. 00 | 10. 51 |
| 普兰店市 | Pulandian | 县级市 | 2 913 | 82. 80 | 25. 64 | 30. 00 | | | 9 436 | 47. 56 | 100. 00 | 94. 75 | 15. 35 |
| 庄河市 | Zhuanghe | 县级市 | 4 086 | 92. 30 | 18. 80 | 25. 00 | | | 20 872 | | | 92. 37 | 9. 56 |
| 海城市 | Haicheng | 县级市 | 2 732 | 114. 00 | 29. 30 | 32. 85 | | | 11 509 | 61. 15 | 100. 00 | 96. 21 | 5. 83 |
| 东港市 | Donggang | 县级市 | 2 414 | 61. 20 | 13. 27 | 31. 72 | | | 10 790 | | 100. 00 | 90. 37 | 7. 51 |
| 凤城市 | Fengcheng | 县级市 | 5 513 | 58. 70 | 17. 91 | 16. 99 | | | 3 074 | | 100. 00 | 96. 75 | 5. 22 |
| 凌海市 | Linghai | 县级市 | 2 586 | 53. 50 | 12. 25 | 17. 59 | | | 10 081 | | 100. 00 | 100. 00 | 9. 58 |
| 北镇市 | Beizhen | 县级市 | 1 694 | 52. 90 | 11. 15 | 8. 00 | | | 5 028 | | 100. 00 | 72. 21 | 2. 15 |
| 盖州市 | Gaizhou | 县级市 | 2 925 | 73. 20 | 18. 08 | 24. 00 | | | 2 242 | | 100. 00 | 91. 32 | 4. 89 |
| 大石桥市 | Dashiqiao | 县级市 | 1 598 | 71. 80 | 20. 87 | 29. 75 | | | 4 270 | | 100. 00 | 94. 74 | 6. 24 |
| 灯塔市 | Dengta | 县级市 | 1 331 | 51. 00 | 9. 68 | 10. 00 | | | 6 721 | | 100. 00 | 67. 56 | 2. 60 |
| 调兵山市 | Diaobingshan | 县级市 | 262 | 24. 20 | 17. 89 | 13. 50 | | | 6 730 | 92. 29 | 100. 00 | 92. 10 | 9. 07 |
| 开原市 | Kaiyuan | 县级市 | 2 828 | 59. 20 | 14. 15 | 13. 60 | | | 42 800 | 17. 85 | 100. 00 | 99. 89 | 9. 08 |
| 北票市 | Beipiao | 县级市 | 4 469 | 59. 70 | 20. 72 | 18. 40 | | | 8 827 | | 100. 00 | 87. 49 | 4. 22 |
| 凌源市 | Lingyuan | 县级市 | 3 278 | 64. 50 | 13. 72 | 21. 40 | | | 4 255 | | | 80. 00 | 5. 48 |
| 兴城市 | Xingcheng | 县级市 | 2 118 | 55. 40 | 13. 39 | 24. 12 | | | 1 404 | | | 72. 82 | 5. 49 |
| 吉林省 | Jilin | | | | | | | | | | | | |
| 长春市 | Changchun | 地级市 | 20 604 | 752. 53 | 331. 85 | 327. 71 | 25 618 985 | 34 193 | 545 193 | 74. 01 | 90. 19 | 97. 14 | 12. 11 |
| 吉林市 | Jilin | 地级市 | 27 120 | 438. 29 | 211. 97 | 165. 63 | 13 000 948 | 30 016 | 79 492 | 80. 07 | 100. 00 | 98. 40 | 10. 48 |
| 四平市 | Siping | 地级市 | 14 080 | 337. 56 | 127. 36 | 39. 00 | 5 965 476 | 17 739 | 16 000 | 44. 98 | 100. 00 | 69. 79 | 7. 28 |
| 辽源市 | Liaoyuan | 地级市 | 5 139 | 123. 33 | 55. 60 | 42. 00 | 2 711 856 | 21 989 | 46 930 | 20. 11 | 100. 00 | 78. 92 | 4. 69 |
| 通化市 | Tonghua | 地级市 | 15 195 | 227. 70 | 104. 82 | 47. 34 | 4 473 262 | 19 703 | 46 242 | | 100. 00 | 89. 73 | 9. 21 |

续表

| 城市名称 Name of Cities | | 行政级别 Admini－strative Rank | 行政区土地面积（平方公里）Area of City's Administrative (sq. km) | 年末总人口（万人）Total Population (year-end) (10 thousand) | 非农业人口（万人）Non-agricultural Population (10 thousand) | 建成区面积（平方公里）Area of Built-up District (sq. km) | 地区生产总值（万元）Gross Regional Product (10 000 yuan) | 人均地区生产总值（元）Per Capita Gross Regional Product (yuan) | 市政公用设施固定资产投资总额（万元）Total Fixed Assets Investment in Municipal Service Facilities (10 000 RMB) | 污水处理率（%）Wastewater Treatment Rate(%) | 生活垃圾处理率（%）Domestic Garbage Treatment Rate(%) | 用水普及率(%) Water Coverage Rate(%) | 人均公园绿地面积（平方米）Per Capita Public Green Space (sq. m) |
|---|---|---|---|---|---|---|---|---|---|---|---|---|---|
| 白山市 | Baishan | 地级市 | 17 485 | 129.68 | 88.57 | 65.00 | 3 003 488 | 23 159 | 33 621 | | 100.00 | 95.70 | 6.70 |
| 松原市 | Songyuan | 地级市 | 21 090 | 285.09 | 79.14 | 36.93 | 8 067 183 | 28 486 | 34 609 | 61.43 | 60.00 | 90.40 | 11.02 |
| 白城市 | Baicheng | 地级市 | 25 745 | 202.90 | 80.74 | 38.11 | 2 907 212 | 14 327 | 16 340 | | 88.69 | 89.80 | 7.62 |
| 九台市 | Jiutai | 县级市 | 3 375 | 70.90 | 18.12 | 25.00 | | | 1 112 | | 90.91 | 95.63 | 5.52 |
| 榆树市 | Yushu | 县级市 | 4 723 | 128.90 | 19.94 | 35.50 | | | 2 088 | | 100.00 | 46.96 | 4.78 |
| 德惠市 | Dehui | 县级市 | 3 435 | 82.70 | 14.69 | 30.50 | | | 1 462 | | 88.44 | 59.02 | 3.32 |
| 蛟河市 | Jiaohe | 县级市 | 6 364 | 45.40 | 17.28 | 12.50 | | | 9 261 | 91.18 | 88.61 | 94.38 | 20.79 |
| 桦甸市 | Huadian | 县级市 | 6 625 | 45.60 | 19.45 | 17.20 | | | 796 | | | 51.88 | 15.09 |
| 舒兰市 | Shulan | 县级市 | 4 557 | 66.10 | 19.81 | 25.00 | | | 4 603 | | 100.00 | 89.55 | 7.21 |
| 磐石市 | Panshi | 县级市 | 3 867 | 54.20 | 17.56 | 13.27 | | | 5 763 | | 73.47 | 72.08 | 6.00 |
| 公主岭市 | Gongzhuling | 县级市 | 4 028 | 107.80 | 32.58 | 25.07 | | | 13 753 | 42.00 | 80.12 | 94.40 | 1.58 |
| 双辽市 | Shuangliao | 县级市 | 3 121 | 41.60 | 14.21 | 19.26 | | | 5 480 | 100.00 | 100.00 | 63.36 | 4.71 |
| 梅河口市 | Meihekou | 县级市 | 2 174 | 61.90 | 26.01 | 21.64 | | | 19 283 | | 89.29 | 95.32 | 6.17 |
| 集安市 | Jian | 县级市 | 3 217 | 22.60 | 8.09 | 13.80 | | | 13 930 | | 93.10 | 94.24 | 10.20 |
| 临江市 | Linjiang | 县级市 | 3 008 | 17.40 | 10.88 | 6.00 | | | 16 500 | | 85.88 | 96.00 | 8.67 |
| 洮南市 | Taonan | 县级市 | 5 031 | 43.70 | 15.38 | 17.40 | | | 4 360 | | 46.60 | 44.12 | 6.67 |
| 大安市 | Daan | 县级市 | 4 879 | 42.10 | 14.77 | 13.90 | | | 5 190 | | 100.00 | 91.42 | 7.54 |
| 延吉市 | Yanji | 县级市 | 1 748 | 44.30 | 39.93 | 34.68 | | | 50 434 | 99.09 | 97.14 | 98.41 | 8.41 |
| 图们市 | Tumen | 县级市 | 1 142 | 13.10 | 10.58 | 8.67 | | | 4 995 | | | 91.73 | 6.75 |
| 敦化市 | Dunhua | 县级市 | 11 545 | 48.40 | 26.72 | 17.20 | | | 29 592 | 78.07 | 100.00 | 93.74 | 20.64 |
| 珲春市 | Huichun | 县级市 | 5 145 | 22.10 | 15.81 | 17.89 | | | 6 331 | | 81.84 | 80.80 | 5.36 |
| 龙井市 | Longjing | 县级市 | 2 208 | 23.80 | 13.92 | 9.93 | | | 8 061 | | 100.00 | 92.82 | 7.66 |
| 和龙市 | Helong | 县级市 | 5 069 | 20.40 | 12.74 | 9.23 | | | 2 949 | | 100.00 | 83.14 | 4.27 |
| 黑龙江省 | Heilongjiang | | | | | | | | | | | | |
| 哈尔滨市 | Haerbin | 地级市 | 53 068 | 989.86 | 476.95 | 340.33 | 28 681 851 | 29 012 | 843 415 | 74.75 | 91.75 | 80.94 | 8.37 |

续表

| 城市名称 Name of Cities | | 行政级别 Admini－strative Rank | 行政区土地面积（平方公里）Area of City's Administrative (sq. km) | 年末总人口（万人）Total Population (year-end) (10 thousand) | 非农业人口（万人）Non-agricultural Population (10 thousand) | 建成区面积（平方公里）Area of Built-up District (sq. km) | 地区生产总值（万元）Gross Regional Product (10 000 yuan) | 人均地区生产总值（元）Per Capita Gross Regional Product (yuan) | 市政公用设施固定资产投资总额（万元）Total Fixed Assets Investment in Municipal Service Facilities (10 000 RMB) | 污水处理率（%）Wastewater Treatment Rate (%) | 生活垃圾处理率（%）Domestic Garbage Treatment Rate (%) | 用水普及率（%）Water Coverage Rate (%) | 人均公园绿地面积（平方米）Per Capita Public Green Space (sq. m) |
|---|---|---|---|---|---|---|---|---|---|---|---|---|---|
| 齐齐哈尔市 | Qiqihaer | 地级市 | 42 469 | 569. 20 | 204. 70 | 115. 27 | 6 658 807 | 12 272 | 33 454 | 57. 98 | 45. 67 | 93. 61 | 7. 01 |
| 鸡西市 | Jixi | 地级市 | 22 531 | 190. 84 | 120. 01 | 79. 23 | 3 158 814 | 16 541 | 2 160 | | 92. 86 | 98. 15 | 9. 13 |
| 鹤岗市 | Hegang | 地级市 | 14 648 | 109. 41 | 88. 21 | 43. 00 | 1 846 919 | 16 887 | 12 265 | | | 69. 30 | 12. 75 |
| 双鸭山市 | Shuangyashan | 地级市 | 23 202 | 150. 46 | 93. 69 | 58. 80 | 2 600 512 | 17 285 | 7 435 | | | 97. 40 | 12. 89 |
| 大庆市 | Daqing | 地级市 | 21 219 | 277. 23 | 136. 80 | 175. 77 | 22 203 734 | 80 655 | 286 198 | 98. 35 | 100. 00 | 96. 03 | 15. 22 |
| 伊春市 | Yichun | 地级市 | 32 759 | 127. 63 | 109. 38 | 160. 90 | 1 790 114 | 14 029 | 33 351 | | | 65. 69 | 17. 83 |
| 佳木斯市 | Jiamusi | 地级市 | 32 704 | 251. 64 | 124. 04 | 62. 39 | 3 985 000 | 15 871 | 28 466 | 60. 13 | 77. 36 | 85. 92 | 9. 71 |
| 七台河市 | Qitaihe | 地级市 | 6 221 | 90. 22 | 50. 91 | 62. 37 | 1 871 613 | 20 826 | 20 122 | | 74. 24 | 81. 04 | 9. 13 |
| 牡丹江市 | Mudanjiang | 地级市 | 40 583 | 269. 90 | 148. 40 | 65. 30 | 5 060 872 | 17 983 | 34 857 | 37. 19 | 100. 00 | 94. 07 | 8. 08 |
| 黑河市 | Heihe | 地级市 | 68 726 | 173. 90 | 97. 58 | 19. 00 | 2 056 219 | 11 800 | 8 182 | | | 76. 43 | 8. 07 |
| 绥化市 | Suihua | 地级市 | 34 964 | 577. 20 | 151. 60 | 30. 50 | 5 417 896 | 9 397 | 25 400 | | | 77. 14 | 3. 81 |
| 双城市 | Shuangcheng | 县级市 | 3 112 | 81. 80 | 16. 96 | 27. 70 | | | 17 870 | | | 95. 35 | 12. 16 |
| 尚志市 | Shangzhi | 县级市 | 8 825 | 61. 60 | 24. 18 | 18. 30 | | | 21 026 | | | 96. 26 | 11. 46 |
| 五常市 | Wuchang | 县级市 | 7 512 | 98. 00 | 22. 33 | 21. 51 | | | 1 607 | | | 90. 06 | 7. 20 |
| 讷河市 | Nehe | 县级市 | 6 648 | 73. 60 | 13. 74 | 10. 69 | | | 14 152 | 38. 46 | | 73. 53 | 5. 96 |
| 虎林市 | Hulin | 县级市 | 9 334 | 20. 50 | 18. 69 | 10. 76 | | | 8 530 | | | 98. 44 | 6. 79 |
| 密山市 | Mishan | 县级市 | 7 843 | 36. 20 | 18. 25 | 22. 00 | | | 1 881 | | | 98. 83 | 17. 80 |
| 铁力市 | Tieli | 县级市 | 6 730 | 38. 90 | 28. 04 | 16. 50 | | | 7 375 | | | 79. 55 | 7. 48 |
| 同江市 | Tongjiang | 县级市 | 6 300 | 13. 10 | 10. 00 | 10. 00 | | | 2 451 | | | 61. 70 | 12. 50 |
| 富锦市 | Fujin | 县级市 | 8 227 | 38. 80 | 18. 28 | 14. 80 | | | 2 321 | | | 71. 43 | 7. 14 |
| 绥芬河市 | Suifenhe | 县级市 | 422 | 6. 30 | 5. 30 | 14. 23 | | | 27 056 | | | 61. 59 | 4. 51 |
| 海林市 | Hailin | 县级市 | 8 814 | 42. 90 | 24. 99 | 12. 45 | | | 32 343 | 0. 17 | 100. 00 | 94. 81 | 11. 38 |
| 宁安市 | Ningan | 县级市 | 7 924 | 42. 10 | 15. 26 | 8. 40 | | | 9 759 | | 100. 00 | 71. 36 | 1. 64 |
| 穆棱市 | Muling | 县级市 | 6 673 | 32. 60 | 13. 56 | 10. 83 | | | 7 230 | | | 99. 46 | 8. 91 |
| 北安市 | Beian | 县级市 | 7 194 | 39. 90 | 27. 50 | 19. 81 | | | 4 765 | | | 64. 73 | 5. 96 |

续表

| 城市名称 Name of Cities | | 行政级别 Admini－strative Rank | 行政区土地面积(平方公里) Area of City's Administrative (sq. km) | 年末总人口(万人) Total Population (year-end) (10 thousand) | 非农业人口(万人) Non-agricultural Population (10 thousand) | 建成区面积(平方公里) Area of Built-up District (sq. km) | 地区生产总值(万元) Gross Regional Product (10 000 yuan) | 人均地区生产总值(元) Per Capita Gross Regional Product (yuan) | 市政公用设施固定资产投资总额(万元) Total Fixed Assets Investment in Municipal Service Facilities (10 000 RMB) | 污水处理率(%) Wastewater Treatment Rate(%) | 生活垃圾处理率(%) Domestic Garbage Treatment Rate(%) | 用水普及率(%) Water Coverage Rate(%) | 人均公园绿地面积(平方米) Per Capita Public Green Space (sq. m) |
|---|---|---|---|---|---|---|---|---|---|---|---|---|---|
| 五大连池市 | Wudalianchi | 县级市 | 9 874 | 36.70 | 20.30 | 5.62 | | | 1319 | | | 51.89 | 10.61 |
| 安达市 | Anda | 县级市 | 3 586 | 51.80 | 19.34 | 18.42 | | | 4 512 | | | 84.47 | 3.27 |
| 肇东市 | Zhaodong | 县级市 | 3 905 | 93.30 | 27.05 | 48.77 | | | 5 200 | | 27.27 | 75.00 | 2.50 |
| 海伦市 | Hailun | 县级市 | 4 667 | 84.20 | 17.16 | 20.56 | | | 3 824 | | | 90.91 | 5.34 |
| 上海市 | Shanghai | 直辖市 | 6 340 | 1 391.04 | 1 216.56 | | 136 981 500 | 73 124 | 6 900 678 | 79.82 | 79.01 | 100.00 | 7.82 |
| 江苏省 | Jiangsu | | | | | | | | | | | | |
| 南京市 | Nanjing | 地级市 | 6 582 | 624.46 | 517.22 | 592.07 | 37 750 000 | 60 808 | 1 316 438 | 85.96 | 96.93 | 100.00 | 13.20 |
| 无锡市 | Wuxi | 地级市 | 4 788 | 464.20 | 325.15 | 208.00 | 44 195 000 | 95 460 | 1 164 119 | 90.07 | 100.00 | 99.80 | 12.59 |
| 徐州市 | Xuzhou | 地级市 | 11 258 | 946.86 | 336.65 | 186.60 | 20 073 600 | 21 367 | 284 702 | 80.75 | 89.29 | 99.85 | 13.00 |
| 常州市 | Changzhou | 地级市 | 4 385 | 358.74 | 177.73 | 120.51 | 22 022 300 | 61 503 | 910 537 | 86.21 | 100.00 | 100.00 | 12.12 |
| 苏州市 | Suzhou | 地级市 | 8 488 | 629.75 | 368.43 | 317.72 | 67 012 900 | 106 863 | 778 674 | 88.86 | 100.00 | 100.00 | 17.06 |
| 南通市 | Nantong | 地级市 | 8 001 | 763.72 | 321.60 | 68.66 | 25 101 300 | 32 815 | 530 000 | 85.85 | 100.00 | 100.00 | 11.35 |
| 连云港市 | Lianyungang | 地级市 | 7 500 | 488.25 | 233.75 | 95.00 | 7 501 000 | 15 458 | 321 823 | 79.30 | 100.00 | 100.00 | 10.98 |
| 淮安市 | Huaian | 地级市 | 10 072 | 536.91 | 152.84 | 100.00 | 9 158 300 | 17 104 | 22 550 | 81.00 | 100.00 | 99.20 | 9.81 |
| 盐城市 | Yancheng | 地级市 | 16 972 | 811.71 | 303.82 | 79.20 | 16 032 600 | 19 775 | 242 464 | 80.79 | 100.00 | 100.00 | 11.40 |
| 扬州市 | Yangzhou | 地级市 | 6 634 | 459.79 | 217.03 | 75.00 | 15 732 900 | 34 238 | 279 168 | 86.03 | 100.00 | 100.00 | 18.71 |
| 镇江市 | Zhenjiang | 地级市 | 3 847 | 268.77 | 120.50 | 98.18 | 14 081 351 | 52 391 | 283 055 | 77.70 | 100.00 | 100.00 | 14.97 |
| 泰州市 | Taizhou | 地级市 | 5 797 | 500.89 | 178.69 | 58.50 | 13 943 800 | 27 843 | 161 098 | 81.38 | 100.00 | 100.00 | 8.29 |
| 宿迁市 | Suqian | 地级市 | 8 555 | 534.58 | 238.29 | 58.40 | 6 550 600 | 12 289 | 50 617 | 78.74 | 99.94 | 97.20 | 11.33 |
| 江阴市 | Jiangyin | 县级市 | 988 | 120.00 | 48.40 | 52.03 | | | 36 898 | 85.27 | 100.00 | 100.00 | 15.50 |
| 宜兴市 | Yixing | 县级市 | 2 177 | 106.80 | 52.93 | 59.64 | | | 48 963 | 80.35 | 100.00 | 100.00 | 15.50 |
| 新沂市 | Xinyi | 县级市 | 1 611 | 100.30 | 19.42 | 29.30 | | | 16 748 | 82.15 | 91.67 | 100.00 | 12.38 |
| 邳州市 | Pizhou | 县级市 | 2 088 | 169.70 | 43.25 | 38.00 | | | 3 855 | 76.63 | 69.44 | 100.00 | 15.31 |
| 溧阳市 | Liyang | 县级市 | 1 536 | 77.80 | 28.37 | 20.30 | | | 18 825 | 71.35 | 100.00 | 100.00 | 9.33 |
| 金坛市 | Jintan | 县级市 | 976 | 54.60 | 31.08 | 21.72 | | | 42 225 | 84.76 | 100.00 | 100.00 | 10.54 |

续表

| 城市名称 Name of Cities | | 行政级别 Admini－strative Rank | 行政区土地面积（平方公里）Area of City's Administrative (sq. km) | 年末总人口（万人）Total Population (year-end) (10 thousand) | 非农业人口（万人）Non-agricultural Population (10 thousand) | 建成区面积（平方公里）Area of Built-up District (sq. km) | 地区生产总值（万元）Gross Regional Product (10 000 yuan) | 人均地区生产总值（元）Per Capita Gross Regional Product (yuan) | 市政公用设施固定资产投资总额（万元）Total Fixed Assets Investment in Municipal Service Facilities (10 000 RMB) | 污水处理率（%）Wastewater Treatment Rate(%) | 生活垃圾处理率（%）Domestic Garbage Treatment Rate(%) | 用水普及率（%）Water Coverage Rate(%) | 人均公园绿地面积（平方米）Per Capita Public Green Space (sq. m) |
|---|---|---|---|---|---|---|---|---|---|---|---|---|---|
| 常熟市 | Changshu | 县级市 | 1 094 | 106. 50 | 50. 47 | 97. 62 | | | 155 478 | 82. 13 | 100. 00 | 100. 00 | 34. 31 |
| 张家港市 | Zhangjiagang | 县级市 | 772 | 89. 80 | 43. 55 | 62. 63 | | | 114 988 | 84. 56 | 100. 00 | 100. 00 | 17. 76 |
| 昆山市 | Kunshan | 县级市 | 928 | 69. 00 | 69. 04 | 44. 92 | | | 146 856 | 86. 05 | 100. 00 | 100. 00 | 13. 42 |
| 吴江市 | Wujiang | 县级市 | 1 093 | 79. 50 | 27. 00 | 76. 75 | | | 117 496 | 82. 31 | 100. 00 | 100. 00 | 15. 03 |
| 太仓市 | Taicang | 县级市 | 620 | 46. 60 | 20. 31 | 23. 75 | | | 61 522 | 82. 55 | 100. 00 | 100. 00 | 13. 27 |
| 启东市 | Qidong | 县级市 | 1 208 | 111. 40 | 22. 39 | 14. 70 | | | 42 622 | 68. 45 | 100. 00 | 100. 00 | 5. 34 |
| 如皋市 | Rugao | 县级市 | 1 492 | 140. 90 | 49. 00 | 12. 89 | | | | 68. 04 | 100. 00 | 100. 00 | 8. 79 |
| 通州市 | Tongzhou | 县级市 | 1 166 | 124. 30 | 46. 78 | 9. 18 | | | 5 142 | 75. 61 | 100. 00 | 100. 00 | 7. 70 |
| 海门市 | Haimen | 县级市 | 939 | 100. 10 | 47. 61 | 17. 47 | | | 20 296 | 65. 07 | 100. 00 | 100. 00 | 6. 63 |
| 东台市 | Dongtai | 县级市 | 3 221 | 114. 60 | 41. 78 | 27. 73 | | | 30 027 | 76. 33 | 100. 00 | 100. 00 | 10. 01 |
| 大丰市 | Dafeng | 县级市 | 3 059 | 72. 50 | 25. 51 | 15. 00 | | | 15 450 | 75. 24 | 90. 96 | 100. 00 | 4. 96 |
| 仪征市 | Yizheng | 县级市 | 853 | 56. 80 | 22. 99 | 37. 00 | | | 8 378 | 76. 08 | 100. 00 | 100. 00 | 7. 41 |
| 高邮市 | Gaoyou | 县级市 | 1 962 | 82. 40 | 27. 46 | 20. 95 | | | 15 506 | 70. 11 | 100. 00 | 98. 88 | 8. 49 |
| 江都市 | Jiangdu | 县级市 | 1 332 | 106. 80 | 40. 83 | 29. 00 | | | 23 316 | 73. 90 | 100. 00 | 99. 80 | 10. 54 |
| 丹阳市 | Danyang | 县级市 | 1 047 | 80. 70 | 20. 03 | 18. 57 | | | 63 539 | 73. 29 | 100. 00 | 100. 00 | 8. 40 |
| 扬中市 | Yangzhong | 县级市 | 331 | 27. 50 | 7. 43 | 9. 51 | | | 11 238 | 78. 75 | 100. 00 | 100. 00 | 8. 47 |
| 句容市 | Jurong | 县级市 | 1 387 | 57. 80 | 27. 18 | 15. 19 | | | 12 244 | 70. 46 | 100. 00 | 100. 00 | 10. 74 |
| 兴化市 | Xinghua | 县级市 | 2 394 | 154. 40 | 28. 69 | 18. 60 | | | 24 297 | 71. 56 | 100. 00 | 100. 00 | 7. 88 |
| 靖江市 | Jingjiang | 县级市 | 665 | 66. 60 | 30. 16 | 32. 80 | | | 25 389 | 67. 01 | 100. 00 | 100. 00 | 13. 53 |
| 泰兴市 | Taixing | 县级市 | 1 172 | 119. 70 | 46. 24 | 22. 15 | | | 41 466 | 80. 42 | 100. 00 | 100. 00 | 10. 09 |
| 姜堰市 | Jiangyan | 县级市 | 927 | 79. 60 | 30. 64 | 19. 08 | | | 1 6741 | 79. 25 | 100. 00 | 100. 00 | 9. 44 |
| 浙江省 | Zhejiang | | | | | | | | | | | | |
| 杭州市 | Hangzhou | 地级市 | 16 596 | 677. 64 | 340. 76 | 367. 26 | 47 811 649 | 70 832 | 1 547 800 | 84. 47 | 100. 00 | 100. 00 | 13. 90 |
| 宁波市 | Ningbo | 地级市 | 9 817 | 568. 09 | 198. 49 | 241. 57 | 39 640 472 | 69 997 | 635 778 | 81. 29 | 100. 00 | 100. 00 | 10. 31 |
| 温州市 | Wenzhou | 地级市 | 11 784 | 711. 99 | 164. 44 | 164. 00 | 24 242 923 | 31 555 | 246 786 | 58. 07 | 93. 33 | 100. 00 | 6. 81 |

续表

| 城市名称 Name of Cities | | 行政级别 Admini－strative Rank | 行政区土地面积(平方公里) Area of City's Administrative (sq. km) | 年末总人口(万人) Total Population (year-end) (10 thousand) | 非农业人口(万人) Non-agricultural Population (10 thousand) | 建成区面积(平方公里) Area of Built-up District (sq. km) | 地区生产总值(万元) Gross Regional Product (10 000 yuan) | 人均地区生产总值(元) Per Capita Gross Regional Product (yuan) | 市政公用设施固定资产投资总额(万元) Total Fixed Assets Investment in Municipal Service Facilities (10 000 RMB) | 污水处理率(%) Wastewater Treatment Rate(%) | 生活垃圾处理率(%) Domestic Garbage Treatment Rate(%) | 用水普及率(%) Water Coverage Rate(%) | 人均公园绿地面积(平方米) Per Capita Public Green Space (sq. m) |
|---|---|---|---|---|---|---|---|---|---|---|---|---|---|
| 嘉兴市 | Jiaxing | 地级市 | 3 915 | 338.07 | 130.14 | 83.50 | 18 152 979 | 43 129 | 223 115 | 77.48 | 100.00 | 100.00 | 11.36 |
| 湖州市 | Huzhou | 地级市 | 5 818 | 258.50 | 80.75 | 72.20 | 10 348 945 | 40 089 | 171 943 | 82.92 | 100.00 | 100.00 | 9.92 |
| 绍兴市 | Shaoxing | 地级市 | 8 256 | 437.06 | 139.97 | 90.40 | 22 229 451 | 50 909 | 85 600 | 83.76 | 100.00 | 100.00 | 15.55 |
| 金华市 | Jinhua | 地级市 | 10 941 | 461.41 | 105.31 | 69.67 | 16 818 457 | 36 538 | 22 658 | 71.01 | 100.00 | 99.79 | 12.00 |
| 衢州市 | Quzhou | 地级市 | 8 841 | 248.85 | 51.95 | 48.40 | 5 800 500 | 23 362 | 74 683 | 63.80 | 100.00 | 96.96 | 11.82 |
| 舟山市 | Zhoushan | 地级市 | 1 440 | 96.77 | 35.79 | 50.19 | 4 902 500 | 50 683 | 71 369 | 62.02 | 100.00 | 99.61 | 14.18 |
| 台州市 | Taizhou | 地级市 | 9 411 | 574.06 | 103.35 | 114.66 | 19 652 660 | 34 374 | 88 124 | 70.15 | 96.25 | 97.85 | 8.71 |
| 丽水市 | Lishui | 地级市 | 17 298 | 255.43 | 44.54 | 26.50 | 5 056 756 | 22 053 | 115 579 | 62.89 | 97.04 | 100.00 | 6.71 |
| 建德市 | Jiande | 县级市 | 2 364 | 51.30 | 12.73 | 8.01 | | | 14 039 | 70.99 | 100.00 | 100.00 | 9.42 |
| 富阳市 | Fuyang | 县级市 | 1 808 | 64.30 | 12.81 | 24.85 | | | 28 721 | 72.18 | 100.00 | 100.00 | 7.17 |
| 临安市 | Linan | 县级市 | 3 124 | 52.70 | 11.09 | 11.86 | | | 37 931 | 83.00 | 100.00 | 98.52 | 4.37 |
| 余姚市 | Yuyao | 县级市 | 1 501 | 83.10 | 17.91 | 36.58 | | | 104 261 | 80.80 | 100.00 | 100.00 | 9.20 |
| 慈溪市 | Cixi | 县级市 | 1 361 | 103.10 | 17.79 | 35.00 | | | 113 238 | 72.19 | 100.00 | 100.00 | 3.55 |
| 奉化市 | Fenghua | 县级市 | 1 268 | 48.20 | 10.53 | 12.58 | | | 23 021 | 75.77 | 100.00 | 100.00 | 8.02 |
| 瑞安市 | Ruian | 县级市 | 1 271 | 117.50 | 21.01 | 22.30 | | | 18 675 | 45.14 | 91.84 | 100.00 | 4.80 |
| 乐清市 | Leqing | 县级市 | 1 174 | 120.90 | 12.49 | 25.03 | | | 15 601 | 5.60 | 77.37 | 100.00 | 3.06 |
| 海宁市 | Haining | 县级市 | 668 | 65.10 | 22.56 | 28.70 | | | 47 417 | 81.76 | 100.00 | 100.00 | 10.90 |
| 平湖市 | Pinghu | 县级市 | 537 | 48.40 | 23.09 | 14.80 | | | 34 948 | 80.07 | 100.00 | 100.00 | 11.88 |
| 桐乡市 | Tongxiang | 县级市 | 727 | 66.90 | 26.13 | 31.50 | | | 60 132 | 83.50 | 100.00 | 100.00 | 12.32 |
| 诸暨市 | Zhuji | 县级市 | 2 311 | 106.40 | 15.75 | 37.70 | | | 19 747 | 80.39 | 100.00 | 100.00 | 10.82 |
| 上虞市 | Shangyu | 县级市 | 1 403 | 77.30 | 24.18 | 20.60 | | | 81 622 | 65.75 | 100.00 | 100.00 | 11.36 |
| 嵊州市 | Shengzhou | 县级市 | 1 790 | 73.40 | 15.61 | 32.50 | | | 4 074 | 44.32 | 100.00 | 99.96 | 6.66 |
| 兰溪市 | Lanxi | 县级市 | 1 313 | 65.70 | 12.61 | 27.80 | | | 10 330 | 25.10 | 100.00 | 97.30 | 8.40 |
| 义乌市 | Yiwu | 县级市 | 1 105 | 72.40 | 22.23 | 78.00 | | | 42 098 | 80.28 | 100.00 | 100.00 | 4.66 |
| 东阳市 | Dongyang | 县级市 | 1 739 | 81.30 | 14.33 | 34.20 | | | 25 733 | 60.11 | 100.00 | 100.00 | 7.04 |

续表

| 城市名称 Name of Cities | | 行政级别 Admini－strative Rank | 行政区土地面积（平方公里）Area of City's Administrative（sq. km） | 年末总人口（万人）Total Population（year-end）（10 thousand） | 非农业人口（万人）Non-agricultural Population（10 thousand） | 建成区面积（平方公里）Area of Built-up District（sq. km） | 地区生产总值（万元）Gross Regional Product（10 000 yuan） | 人均地区生产总值（元）Per Capita Gross Regional Product（yuan） | 市政公用设施固定资产投资总额（万元）Total Fixed Assets Investment in Municipal Service Facilities（10 000 RMB） | 污水处理率（%）Wastewater Treatment Rate（%） | 生活垃圾处理率（%）Domestic Garbage Treatment Rate（%） | 用水普及率（%）Water Coverage Rate（%） | 人均公园绿地面积（平方米）Per Capita Public Green Space（sq. m） |
|---|---|---|---|---|---|---|---|---|---|---|---|---|---|
| 永康市 | Yongkang | 县级市 | 1 049 | 56. 50 | 9. 65 | 36. 53 | | | 13 861 | 50. 99 | 100. 00 | 100. 00 | 6. 18 |
| 江山市 | Jiangshan | 县级市 | 2 019 | 59. 00 | 9. 87 | 14. 23 | | | 27 450 | 72. 26 | 100. 00 | 97. 50 | 9. 62 |
| 温岭市 | Wenling | 县级市 | 836 | 117. 60 | 19. 34 | 30. 50 | | | 65 920 | 82. 37 | 98. 57 | 98. 97 | 9. 11 |
| 临海市 | Linhai | 县级市 | 2 171 | 114. 70 | 15. 06 | 36. 21 | | | 16 019 | 66. 75 | 100. 00 | 99. 77 | 7. 93 |
| 龙泉市 | Longquan | 县级市 | 3 059 | 28. 50 | 4. 33 | 11. 26 | | | 26 610 | 25. 12 | 100. 00 | 100. 00 | 15. 43 |
| 安徽省 | Anhui | | | | | | | | | | | | |
| 合肥市 | Hefei | 地级市 | 7 047 | 486. 73 | 209. 99 | 268. 00 | 16 648 400 | 34 482 | 768 530 | 99. 16 | 100. 00 | 96. 67 | 10. 30 |
| 芜湖市 | Wuhu | 地级市 | 3 317 | 230. 79 | 113. 72 | 126. 31 | 7 496 460 | 32 500 | 666 690 | 70. 17 | 100. 00 | 98. 72 | 9. 08 |
| 蚌埠市 | Bengbu | 地级市 | 5 952 | 358. 31 | 100. 26 | 99. 75 | 4 863 852 | 13 632 | 104 293 | 72. 08 | 100. 00 | 90. 83 | 8. 88 |
| 淮南市 | Huainan | 地级市 | 2 585 | 240. 88 | 112. 98 | 95. 77 | 4 536 200 | 19 809 | 122 653 | 99. 41 | 100. 00 | 99. 04 | 11. 65 |
| 马鞍山市 | Maanshan | 地级市 | 1 686 | 128. 10 | 63. 06 | 72. 00 | 6 363 000 | 49 824 | 116 606 | 81. 40 | 100. 00 | 100. 00 | 13. 25 |
| 淮北市 | Huaibei | 地级市 | 2 741 | 215. 78 | 93. 23 | 62. 83 | 3 490 900 | 17 029 | 28 893 | 73. 87 | 86. 00 | 91. 96 | 12. 42 |
| 铜陵市 | Tongling | 地级市 | 1 113 | 73. 89 | 43. 47 | 47. 00 | 3 253 100 | 44 100 | 55 025 | 48. 11 | 54. 22 | 100. 00 | 10. 86 |
| 安庆市 | Anqing | 地级市 | 15 318 | 613. 89 | 108. 93 | 65. 50 | 7 047 175 | 12 595 | 130 251 | 71. 67 | 100. 00 | 93. 94 | 9. 18 |
| 黄山市 | Huangshan | 地级市 | 9 807 | 148. 35 | 35. 69 | 39. 71 | 2 499 000 | 16 867 | 37 168 | 95. 46 | 94. 09 | 99. 30 | 14. 51 |
| 滁州市 | Chuzhou | 地级市 | 13 523 | 447. 37 | 97. 60 | 43. 89 | 5 201 110 | 11 626 | 31 058 | 54. 64 | 100. 00 | 99. 63 | 7. 30 |
| 阜阳市 | Fuyang | 地级市 | 9 775 | 987. 79 | 121. 81 | 68. 60 | 5 412 700 | 6 475 | 105 512 | 86. 86 | 100. 00 | 91. 23 | 4. 39 |
| 宿州市 | Suzhou | 地级市 | 9 787 | 626. 06 | 82. 27 | 45. 70 | 5 111 031 | 8 982 | 42 739 | 59. 19 | 94. 01 | 98. 97 | 7. 35 |
| 巢湖市 | Chaohu | 地级市 | 9 394 | 456. 80 | 75. 21 | 36. 50 | 4 793 300 | 11 600 | 21 257 | 71. 82 | 100. 00 | 93. 78 | 8. 07 |
| 六安市 | Liuan | 地级市 | 17 976 | 701. 64 | 98. 71 | 51. 29 | 5 339 470 | 7 473 | 50 284 | 67. 85 | 98. 52 | 98. 94 | 7. 92 |
| 亳州市 | Bozhou | 地级市 | 8 374 | 588. 77 | 65. 06 | 32. 00 | 4 042 200 | 7 918 | 56 937 | 84. 85 | 100. 00 | 98. 41 | 7. 59 |
| 池州市 | Chizhou | 地级市 | 8 271 | 158. 93 | 27. 79 | 26. 33 | 1 924 000 | 14 147 | 146 233 | 60. 74 | 100. 00 | 96. 20 | 14. 82 |
| 宣城市 | Xuancheng | 地级市 | 12 323 | 276. 75 | 49. 55 | 33. 51 | 4 116 100 | 15 953 | 153 412 | 34. 30 | 100. 00 | 98. 55 | 7. 63 |
| 桐城市 | Tongcheng | 县级市 | 1 546 | 75. 10 | 11. 24 | 20. 81 | | | 24 044 | 5. 83 | 100. 00 | 75. 84 | 4. 40 |
| 天长市 | Tianchang | 县级市 | 1 751 | 62. 90 | 16. 51 | 23. 00 | | | 13 052 | 69. 64 | 42. 18 | 95. 63 | 0. 49 |

续表

| 城市名称 Name of Cities | | 行政级别 Admini－strative Rank | 行政区土地面积(平方公里) Area of City's Administrative (sq. km) | 年末总人口(万人) Total Population (year-end) (10 thousand) | 非农业人口(万人) Non-agricultural Population (10 thousand) | 建成区面积(平方公里) Area of Built-up District (sq. km) | 地区生产总值(万元) Gross Regional Product (10 000 yuan) | 人均地区生产总值(元) Per Capita Gross Regional Product (yuan) | 市政公用设施固定资产投资总额(万元) Total Fixed Assets Investment in Municipal Service Facilities (10 000 RMB) | 污水处理率(%) Wastewater Treatment Rate(%) | 生活垃圾处理率(%) Domestic Garbage Treatment Rate(%) | 用水普及率(%) Water Coverage Rate(%) | 人均公园绿地面积(平方米) Per Capita Public Green Space (sq. m) |
|---|---|---|---|---|---|---|---|---|---|---|---|---|---|
| 明光市 | Mingguang | 县级市 | 2 359 | 65.20 | 12.26 | 17.90 | | | 6 623 | 100.00 | 100.00 | 90.01 | 3.57 |
| 界首市 | Jieshou | 县级市 | 666 | 77.20 | 14.60 | 16.40 | | | 7 469 | 74.28 | 64.76 | 70.99 | 2.88 |
| 宁国市 | Ningguo | 县级市 | 2 487 | 38.40 | 7.76 | 18.08 | | | 34 220 | 12.55 | 100.00 | 65.87 | 8.97 |
| 福建省 | Fujian | | | | | | | | | | | | |
| 福州市 | Fuzhou | 地级市 | 13 047 | 635.95 | 262.91 | 176.59 | 22 841 602 | 33 615 | 854 092 | 75.12 | 100.00 | 96.16 | 10.21 |
| 厦门市 | Xiamen | 地级市 | 1 573 | 173.67 | 118.58 | 197.00 | 15 600 218 | 62 651 | 902 036 | 96.45 | 100.00 | 97.93 | 11.04 |
| 莆田市 | Putian | 地级市 | 4 119 | 316.64 | 60.82 | 52.21 | 6 099 627 | 21 515 | 115 300 | 73.18 | 100.00 | 97.75 | 11.26 |
| 三明市 | Sanming | 地级市 | 23 061 | 270.15 | 93.12 | 24.52 | 6 669 222 | 25 407 | 15 504 | 70.12 | 93.96 | 99.08 | 9.10 |
| 泉州市 | Quanzhou | 地级市 | 11 015 | 677.73 | 194.80 | 81.00 | 27 052 915 | 34 840 | 445 000 | 85.01 | 100.00 | 99.31 | 9.84 |
| 漳州市 | Zhangzhou | 地级市 | 12 873 | 468.50 | 135.12 | 47.52 | 10 020 167 | 21 073 | 112 468 | 73.56 | 98.56 | 99.24 | 9.51 |
| 南平市 | Nanping | 地级市 | 26 315 | 308.13 | 106.98 | 26.10 | 5 591 439 | 19 348 | 55 052 | 62.45 | 98.12 | 94.99 | 10.22 |
| 龙岩市 | Longyan | 地级市 | 19 063 | 291.30 | 86.50 | 35.00 | 6 728 476 | 24 334 | 47 366 | 82.98 | 95.45 | 99.17 | 10.59 |
| 宁德市 | Ningde | 地级市 | 13 248 | 335.03 | 100.94 | 17.18 | 5 426 716 | 17 851 | 22 605 | 8.95 | 99.46 | 98.74 | 12.93 |
| 福清市 | Fuqing | 县级市 | 1 917 | 124.80 | 35.72 | 28.00 | | | 26 407 | 64.81 | 100.00 | 95.17 | 9.76 |
| 长乐市 | Changle | 县级市 | 724 | 67.00 | 23.83 | 19.09 | | | 14 497 | 19.82 | 100.00 | 97.54 | 12.90 |
| 永安市 | Yongan | 县级市 | 2 932 | 32.10 | 16.93 | 18.01 | | | 11 241 | 60.39 | 100.00 | 94.63 | 10.47 |
| 石狮市 | Shishi | 县级市 | 160 | 31.30 | 9.70 | 17.26 | | | 3 524 | 61.01 | 100.00 | 99.70 | 6.54 |
| 晋江市 | Jinjiang | 县级市 | 649 | 105.00 | 37.16 | 32.00 | | | 66 773 | 78.91 | 99.59 | 99.67 | 9.13 |
| 南安市 | Nanan | 县级市 | 2 036 | 149.70 | 37.34 | 20.50 | | | 61 029 | 61.82 | 100.00 | 98.89 | 8.47 |
| 龙海市 | Longhai | 县级市 | 1 128 | 80.40 | 15.94 | 15.35 | | | 27 947 | 27.04 | 99.11 | 95.82 | 13.71 |
| 邵武市 | Shaowu | 县级市 | 2 951 | 30.10 | 13.26 | 13.47 | | | 11 988 | 52.64 | 98.64 | 96.71 | 16.73 |
| 武夷山市 | Wuyishan | 县级市 | 2 814 | 22.70 | 10.39 | 7.39 | | | 7 839 | 56.06 | 90.00 | 91.50 | 9.03 |
| 建瓯市 | Jianou | 县级市 | 4 233 | 52.70 | 16.35 | 8.98 | | | 11 324 | | 100.00 | 99.50 | 10.35 |
| 建阳市 | Jianyang | 县级市 | 3 378 | 33.90 | 12.38 | 9.30 | | | 3 663 | | 80.00 | 95.64 | 10.59 |
| 漳平市 | Zhangping | 县级市 | 2 975 | 27.50 | 8.75 | 8.00 | | | 11 520 | 45.52 | 95.73 | 96.85 | 13.42 |

续表

| 城市名称 Name of Cities | | 行政级别 Admini－strative Rank | 行政区土地面积（平方公里）Area of City's Administrative (sq. km) | 年末总人口（万人）Total Population (year-end) (10 thousand) | 非农业人口（万人）Non-agricultural Population (10 thousand) | 建成区面积（平方公里）Area of Built-up District (sq. km) | 地区生产总值（万元）Gross Regional Product (10 000 yuan) | 人均地区生产总值（元）Per Capita Gross Regional Product (yuan) | 市政公用设施固定资产投资总额（万元）Total Fixed Assets Investment in Municipal Service Facilities (10 000 RMB) | 污水处理率（%）Wastewater Treatment Rate (%) | 生活垃圾处理率（%）Domestic Garbage Treatment Rate (%) | 用水普及率（%）Water Coverage Rate (%) | 人均公园绿地面积（平方米）Per Capita Public Green Space (sq. m) |
|---|---|---|---|---|---|---|---|---|---|---|---|---|---|
| 福安市 | Fuan | 县级市 | 1 880 | 64.40 | 18.12 | 8.80 | | | 8 271 | | 100.00 | 98.55 | 5.22 |
| 福鼎市 | Fuding | 县级市 | 1 526 | 57.30 | 19.79 | 14.08 | | | 16 849 | 29.17 | 100.00 | 90.54 | 9.68 |
| 江西省 | Jiangxi | | | | | | | | | | | | |
| 南昌市 | Nanchang | 地级市 | 7 402 | 494.73 | 233.16 | 185.00 | 16 600 847 | 36 105 | 414 553 | 68.95 | 100.00 | 100.00 | 8.36 |
| 景德镇市 | Jingdezhen | 地级市 | 5 256 | 158.23 | 62.64 | 72.84 | 3 219 756 | 20 646 | 18 585 | 54.52 | 100.00 | 99.62 | 13.61 |
| 萍乡市 | Pingxiang | 地级市 | 3 824 | 185.77 | 57.71 | 41.48 | 3 876 366 | 21 002 | 51 850 | 59.97 | 100.00 | 99.26 | 9.18 |
| 九江市 | Jiujiang | 地级市 | 18 823 | 484.67 | 133.10 | 89.47 | 7 005 984 | 14 785 | 79 818 | 86.65 | 100.00 | 99.98 | 11.45 |
| 新余市 | Xinyu | 地级市 | 3 181 | 123.20 | 41.10 | 46.00 | 4 023 218 | 35 629 | 165 335 | 89.22 | 100.00 | 99.52 | 13.53 |
| 鹰潭市 | Yingtan | 地级市 | 3 554 | 116.11 | 33.89 | 23.68 | 2 566 218 | 23 222 | 22 415 | 85.04 | 91.77 | 98.52 | 14.55 |
| 赣州市 | Ganzhou | 地级市 | 39 380 | 888.95 | 185.30 | 55.00 | 8 348 486 | 10 016 | 108 036 | | 100.00 | 100.00 | 8.14 |
| 吉安市 | Jian | 地级市 | 24 922 | 485.25 | 110.38 | 29.12 | 5 050 046 | 10 571 | 56 623 | 74.57 | 100.00 | 95.11 | 9.64 |
| 宜春市 | Yichun | 地级市 | 18 669 | 543.97 | 144.36 | 32.20 | 6 150 000 | 11 336 | 44 902 | 71.01 | 100.00 | 98.89 | 13.52 |
| 抚州市 | Fuzhou | 地级市 | 18 820 | 387.74 | 95.00 | 44.98 | 4 340 496 | 11 233 | 78 441 | 61.16 | 98.47 | 87.05 | 10.96 |
| 上饶市 | Shangrao | 地级市 | 22 791 | 716.35 | 133.83 | 27.08 | 6 283 382 | 9 718 | 48 641 | 81.02 | 100.00 | 99.66 | 10.06 |
| 乐平市 | Leping | 县级市 | 1 975 | 84.60 | 19.18 | 16.10 | | | 21 057 | | 100.00 | 95.98 | 11.91 |
| 瑞昌市 | Ruichang | 县级市 | 1 423 | 43.90 | 11.45 | 11.02 | | | 1 955 | | 100.00 | 96.48 | 9.96 |
| 贵溪市 | Guixi | 县级市 | 2 480 | 58.50 | 11.79 | 19.50 | | | 30 055 | | 100.00 | 99.08 | 25.50 |
| 瑞金市 | Ruijin | 县级市 | 2 448 | 64.40 | 12.37 | 18.30 | | | 11 050 | | 100.00 | 96.69 | 19.02 |
| 南康市 | Nankang | 县级市 | 1 845 | 80.00 | 13.19 | 20.50 | | | 16 528 | | 100.00 | 90.00 | 7.95 |
| 井冈山市 | Jinggangshan | 县级市 | 1 276 | 15.70 | 4.24 | 7.29 | | | 7 514 | 94.61 | 100.00 | 56.81 | 35.36 |
| 丰城市 | Fengcheng | 县级市 | 2 845 | 134.50 | 51.79 | 29.80 | | | 49 088 | | 100.00 | 73.23 | 6.89 |
| 樟树市 | Zhangshu | 县级市 | 1 287 | 54.00 | 16.03 | 19.30 | | | 15 331 | | 100.00 | 87.14 | 8.86 |
| 高安市 | Gaoan | 县级市 | 2 439 | 80.90 | 19.82 | 20.43 | | | 24 157 | | 100.00 | 98.46 | 11.12 |
| 德兴市 | Dexing | 县级市 | 2 082 | 31.50 | 12.49 | 10.00 | | | 7 569 | | 100.00 | 92.28 | 9.38 |
| 山东省 | Shandong | | | | | | | | | | | | |

续表

| 城市名称 Name of Cities | | 行政级别 Admini－strative Rank | 行政区土地面积(平方公里) Area of City's Administrative (sq. km) | 年末总人口(万人) Total Population (year-end) (10 thousand) | 非农业人口(万人) Non-agricultural Population (10 thousand) | 建成区面积(平方公里) Area of Built-up District (sq. km) | 地区生产总值(万元) Gross Regional Product (10 000 yuan) | 人均地区生产总值(元) Per Capita Gross Regional Product (yuan) | 市政公用设施固定资产投资总额(万元) Total Fixed Assets Investment in Municipal Service Facilities (10 000 RMB) | 污水处理率(%) Wastewater Treatment Rate(%) | 生活垃圾处理率(%) Domestic Garbage Treatment Rate(%) | 用水普及率(%) Water Coverage Rate(%) | 人均公园绿地面积(平方米) Per Capita Public Green Space (sq. m) |
|---|---|---|---|---|---|---|---|---|---|---|---|---|---|
| 济南市 | Jinan | 地级市 | 8 177 | 603. 99 | 350. 23 | 326. 20 | 30 174 243 | 45 724 | 643 575 | 82. 55 | 79. 21 | 99. 57 | 9. 81 |
| 青岛市 | Qingdao | 地级市 | 10 978 | 761. 56 | 276. 25 | 267. 12 | 44 361 800 | 52 677 | 582 109 | 81. 93 | 92. 00 | 100. 00 | 14. 53 |
| 淄博市 | Zibo | 地级市 | 5 965 | 420. 62 | 157. 05 | 213. 06 | 23 167 800 | 51 547 | 153 590 | 93. 80 | 96. 45 | 100. 00 | 14. 75 |
| 枣庄市 | Zaozhuang | 地级市 | 4 563 | 383. 24 | 82. 74 | 106. 39 | 10 928 300 | 29 978 | 164 833 | 87. 16 | 96. 49 | 98. 75 | 9. 82 |
| 东营市 | Dongying | 地级市 | 7 923 | 183. 97 | 63. 29 | 96. 72 | 2 0526 200 | 102 741 | 124 649 | 83. 89 | 91. 99 | 100. 00 | 16. 84 |
| 烟台市 | Yantai | 地级市 | 13 746 | 651. 69 | 128. 14 | 211. 18 | 34 341 900 | 49 012 | 337 631 | 92. 54 | 95. 40 | 99. 86 | 16. 38 |
| 潍坊市 | Weifang | 地级市 | 16 005 | 862. 48 | 124. 91 | 132. 00 | 24 918 100 | 28 106 | 198 204 | 69. 72 | 73. 58 | 99. 66 | 8. 00 |
| 济宁市 | Jining | 地级市 | 11 194 | 822. 75 | 56. 94 | 88. 00 | 21 221 600 | 26 721 | 98 860 | 91. 65 | 73. 02 | 99. 20 | 10. 61 |
| 泰安市 | Taian | 地级市 | 7 762 | 554. 72 | 66. 28 | 97. 40 | 15 133 000 | 27 794 | 139 649 | 83. 05 | 92. 34 | 99. 80 | 15. 70 |
| 威海市 | Weihai | 地级市 | 5 698 | 252. 23 | 47. 86 | 120. 00 | 17 803 493 | 63 519 | 194 631 | 83. 92 | 92. 02 | 100. 00 | 23. 92 |
| 日照市 | Rizhao | 地级市 | 5 363 | 284. 54 | 60. 53 | 69. 65 | 7 731 401 | 28 300 | 334 098 | 87. 10 | 100. 00 | 100. 00 | 19. 22 |
| 莱芜市 | Laiwu | 地级市 | 2 247 | 125. 96 | 49. 52 | 56. 50 | 4 557 900 | 35 845 | 132 756 | 86. 02 | 100. 00 | 100. 00 | 18. 27 |
| 临沂市 | Linyi | 地级市 | 17 182 | 1 034. 47 | 140. 67 | 142. 56 | 19 582 000 | 19 949 | 301 749 | 98. 64 | 99. 64 | 100. 00 | 18. 87 |
| 德州市 | Dezhou | 地级市 | 10 356 | 564. 19 | 41. 81 | 46. 50 | 14 009 100 | 25 606 | 70 368 | 61. 93 | 88. 13 | 99. 95 | 18. 97 |
| 聊城市 | Liaocheng | 地级市 | 8 703 | 584. 91 | 97. 02 | 63. 31 | 12 526 700 | 22 556 | 37 724 | 95. 20 | 92. 00 | 97. 81 | 16. 12 |
| 滨州市 | Binzhou | 地级市 | 9 454 | 375. 68 | 49. 43 | 78. 00 | 12 368 300 | 33 610 | 80 704 | 77. 25 | 79. 12 | 100. 00 | 18. 17 |
| 菏泽市 | Heze | 地级市 | 12 239 | 919. 94 | 68. 61 | 60. 40 | 8 217 900 | 10 050 | 109 706 | 74. 08 | 87. 46 | 94. 00 | 9. 70 |
| 章丘市 | Zhangqiu | 县级市 | 1 855 | 100. 80 | 40. 86 | 35. 00 | | | 150 426 | 79. 52 | 92. 02 | 100. 00 | 13. 62 |
| 胶州市 | Jiaozhou | 县级市 | 1 313 | 79. 60 | 29. 41 | 37. 74 | | | 31 655 | 85. 12 | 91. 98 | 100. 00 | 14. 42 |
| 即墨市 | Jimo | 县级市 | 1 780 | 111. 10 | 49. 00 | 50. 00 | | | 28 858 | 81. 01 | 91. 99 | 100. 00 | 14. 44 |
| 平度市 | Pingdu | 县级市 | 3 167 | 137. 00 | 43. 07 | 40. 90 | | | 17 565 | 84. 82 | 91. 98 | 100. 00 | 11. 07 |
| 胶南市 | Jiaonan | 县级市 | 1 802 | 83. 40 | 38. 79 | 53. 20 | | | 34 857 | 91. 13 | 100. 00 | 100. 00 | 16. 29 |
| 莱西市 | Laixi | 县级市 | 1 522 | 73. 20 | 31. 72 | 30. 34 | | | 25 000 | 89. 97 | 91. 97 | 100. 00 | 15. 37 |
| 滕州市 | Tengzhou | 县级市 | 1 496 | 165. 80 | 41. 59 | 43. 63 | | | 50 186 | 81. 58 | 85. 85 | 100. 00 | 9. 03 |
| 龙口市 | Longkou | 县级市 | 893 | 63. 00 | 29. 46 | 40. 13 | | | 54 250 | 82. 03 | 92. 03 | 99. 90 | 8. 70 |

续表

| 城市名称 Name of Cities | | 行政级别 Admini－strative Rank | 行政区土地面积（平方公里）Area of City's Administrative (sq. km) | 年末总人口（万人）Total Population (year-end) (10 thousand) | 非农业人口（万人）Non-agricultural Population (10 thousand) | 建成区面积（平方公里）Area of Built-up District (sq. km) | 地区生产总值（万元）Gross Regional Product (10 000 yuan) | 人均地区生产总值（元）Per Capita Gross Regional Product (yuan) | 市政公用设施固定资产投资总额（万元）Total Fixed Assets Investment in Municipal Service Facilities (10 000 RMB) | 污水处理率（%）Wastewater Treatment Rate (%) | 生活垃圾处理率（%）Domestic Garbage Treatment Rate (%) | 用水普及率（%）Water Coverage Rate (%) | 人均公园绿地面积（平方米）Per Capita Public Green Space (sq. m) |
|---|---|---|---|---|---|---|---|---|---|---|---|---|---|
| 莱阳市 | Laiyang | 县级市 | 1 732 | 87. 50 | 29. 36 | 31. 99 | | | 13 080 | 84. 20 | 92. 02 | 98. 53 | 8. 01 |
| 莱州市 | Laizhou | 县级市 | 1 878 | 85. 90 | 35. 89 | 35. 00 | | | 10 549 | 89. 54 | 92. 04 | 98. 71 | 9. 13 |
| 蓬莱市 | Penglai | 县级市 | 1 129 | 44. 80 | 17. 59 | 25. 53 | | | 21 324 | 70. 90 | 91. 94 | 92. 55 | 13. 23 |
| 招远市 | Zhaoyuan | 县级市 | 1 433 | 56. 90 | 19. 14 | 26. 46 | | | 22 504 | 86. 83 | 91. 95 | 99. 76 | 16. 91 |
| 栖霞市 | Qixia | 县级市 | 2 016 | 63. 00 | 15. 22 | 13. 00 | | | 3 100 | 83. 05 | 100. 00 | 99. 17 | 10. 89 |
| 海阳市 | Haiyang | 县级市 | 1 887 | 68. 00 | 20. 60 | 30. 00 | | | 23 010 | 80. 11 | 92. 00 | 97. 29 | 14. 57 |
| 青州市 | Qingzhou | 县级市 | 1 569 | 90. 30 | 30. 15 | 37. 50 | | | 58 514 | 91. 99 | 91. 94 | 100. 00 | 12. 89 |
| 诸城市 | Zhucheng | 县级市 | 2 183 | 106. 80 | 47. 67 | 39. 31 | | | 45 079 | 94. 25 | 78. 22 | 100. 00 | 10. 85 |
| 寿光市 | Shouguang | 县级市 | 2 057 | 102. 50 | 47. 82 | 46. 89 | | | 40 095 | 92. 46 | 92. 02 | 100. 00 | 10. 95 |
| 安丘市 | Anqiu | 县级市 | 1 710 | 93. 00 | 39. 14 | 33. 43 | | | 8 235 | 85. 86 | 100. 00 | 98. 82 | 26. 24 |
| 高密市 | Gaomi | 县级市 | 1 527 | 84. 90 | 27. 85 | 42. 20 | | | 33 397 | 81. 34 | 91. 92 | 96. 68 | 28. 92 |
| 昌邑市 | Changyi | 县级市 | 1 582 | 58. 00 | 25. 95 | 24. 95 | | | 11 171 | 92. 39 | 92. 00 | 100. 00 | 16. 92 |
| 曲阜市 | Qufu | 县级市 | 896 | 63. 70 | 17. 97 | 20. 00 | | | 22 990 | 85. 61 | 100. 00 | 100. 00 | 22. 73 |
| 兖州市 | Yanzhou | 县级市 | 648 | 62. 30 | 17. 09 | 30. 80 | | | 86 148 | 71. 37 | 73. 72 | 100. 00 | 10. 70 |
| 邹城市 | Zoucheng | 县级市 | 1 616 | 114. 00 | 40. 01 | 32. 50 | | | 11 485 | 66. 06 | 91. 99 | 95. 06 | 15. 09 |
| 新泰市 | Xintai | 县级市 | 1 933 | 137. 80 | 39. 71 | 60. 00 | | | 42 253 | 80. 02 | 92. 13 | 99. 88 | 16. 11 |
| 肥城市 | Feicheng | 县级市 | 1 277 | 97. 10 | 27. 07 | 26. 56 | | | 23 100 | 83. 28 | 92. 00 | 99. 57 | 15. 51 |
| 文登市 | Wendeng | 县级市 | 1 780 | 64. 20 | 25. 08 | 41. 00 | | | 61 774 | 87. 57 | 91. 98 | 100. 00 | 18. 76 |
| 荣成市 | Rongcheng | 县级市 | 1 392 | 66. 70 | 32. 15 | 43. 10 | | | 65 290 | 87. 06 | 92. 02 | 100. 00 | 22. 31 |
| 乳山市 | Rushan | 县级市 | 1 654 | 57. 40 | 15. 69 | 24. 58 | | | 50 527 | 76. 74 | 91. 93 | 100. 00 | 15. 06 |
| 乐陵市 | Leling | 县级市 | 1 172 | 68. 30 | 17. 95 | 48. 00 | | | 19 400 | 94. 31 | 41. 07 | 94. 60 | 3. 91 |
| 禹城市 | Yucheng | 县级市 | 990 | 51. 80 | 16. 46 | 20. 80 | | | 6 820 | 80. 21 | 84. 31 | 97. 77 | 8. 70 |
| 临清市 | Linqing | 县级市 | 950 | 73. 80 | 30. 31 | 21. 50 | | | 40 771 | 76. 07 | 98. 38 | 98. 71 | 13. 66 |
| 河南省 | Henan | | | | | | | | | | | | |
| 郑州市 | Zhengzhou | 地级市 | 7 446 | 719. 61 | 301. 77 | 328. 66 | 30 039 925 | 40 616 | 457 778 | 92. 80 | 87. 62 | 89. 22 | 5. 34 |

续表

| 城市名称 Name of Cities | | 行政级别 Admini－strative Rank | 行政区土地面积(平方公里) Area of City's Administrative (sq. km) | 年末总人口(万人) Total Population (year-end) (10 thousand) | 非农业人口(万人) Non-agricultural Population (10 thousand) | 建成区面积(平方公里) Area of Built-up District (sq. km) | 地区生产总值(万元) Gross Regional Product (10 000 yuan) | 人均地区生产总值(元) Per Capita Gross Regional Product (yuan) | 市政公用设施固定资产投资总额(万元) Total Fixed Assets Investment in Municipal Service Facilities (10 000 RMB) | 污水处理率(%) Wastewater Treatment Rate(%) | 生活垃圾处理率(%) Domestic Garbage Treatment Rate(%) | 用水普及率(%) Water Coverage Rate(%) | 人均公园绿地面积(平方米) Per Capita Public Green Space (sq. m) |
|---|---|---|---|---|---|---|---|---|---|---|---|---|---|
| 开封市 | Kaifeng | 地级市 | 6 444 | 518. 48 | 98. 36 | 89. 49 | 6 893 747 | 14 713 | 42 918 | 56. 20 | 72. 00 | 98. 84 | 5. 09 |
| 洛阳市 | Luoyang | 地级市 | 15 200 | 686. 50 | 188. 02 | 163. 95 | 19 196 384 | 30 084 | 45 156 | 94. 27 | 81. 97 | 66. 36 | 7. 65 |
| 平顶山市 | Pingdingshan | 地级市 | 7 882 | 523. 94 | 129. 70 | 61. 71 | 10 677 008 | 21 998 | 47 665 | 87. 01 | 85. 56 | 90. 11 | 8. 35 |
| 安阳市 | Anyang | 地级市 | 7 413 | 567. 37 | 124. 90 | 73. 00 | 10 360 548 | 19 924 | 66 700 | 90. 46 | 94. 02 | 100. 00 | 8. 36 |
| 鹤壁市 | Hebi | 地级市 | 2 182 | 157. 74 | 50. 76 | 48. 00 | 3 423 523 | 24 070 | 18 685 | 75. 87 | 70. 00 | 97. 10 | 10. 10 |
| 新乡市 | Xinxiang | 地级市 | 8 169 | 589. 57 | 163. 71 | 94. 59 | 9 494 928 | 17 217 | 46 474 | 86. 04 | 100. 00 | 97. 09 | 8. 51 |
| 焦作市 | Jiaozuo | 地级市 | 4 071 | 361. 25 | 106. 03 | 89. 96 | 10 315 860 | 30 356 | 42 988 | 61. 40 | 83. 59 | 100. 00 | 9. 40 |
| 濮阳市 | Puyang | 地级市 | 4 266 | 396. 24 | 74. 17 | 36. 00 | 6 572 798 | 18 803 | 6 383 | 39. 21 | 95. 45 | 92. 11 | 12. 52 |
| 许昌市 | Xuchang | 地级市 | 4 996 | 478. 95 | 121. 24 | 65. 30 | 10 620 503 | 24 706 | 21 076 | 80. 16 | 93. 27 | 97. 99 | 11. 18 |
| 漯河市 | Luohe | 地级市 | 2 617 | 272. 87 | 65. 48 | 51. 30 | 5 502 627 | 22 237 | 23 250 | 33. 41 | 100. 00 | 94. 83 | 16. 78 |
| 三门峡市 | Sanmenxia | 地级市 | 10 496 | 227. 69 | 67. 65 | 28. 50 | 6 542 124 | 29 515 | 19 662 | 92. 98 | 99. 01 | 94. 33 | 16. 07 |
| 南阳市 | Nanyang | 地级市 | 26 400 | 1 147. 61 | 179. 11 | 87. 39 | 16 364 296 | 16 367 | 63 399 | 56. 00 | 78. 91 | 70. 99 | 10. 96 |
| 商丘市 | Shangqiu | 地级市 | 10 704 | 901. 11 | 166. 53 | 58. 50 | 9 313 905 | 12 092 | 17 102 | 83. 07 | 85. 71 | 62. 69 | 4. 93 |
| 信阳市 | Xinyang | 地级市 | 19 541 | 845. 21 | 150. 47 | 58. 20 | 8 667 899 | 13 015 | 20 899 | 80. 28 | 93. 94 | 95. 53 | 11. 34 |
| 周口市 | Zhoukou | 地级市 | 11 959 | 1 188. 08 | 147. 97 | 42. 00 | 9 841 251 | 9 905 | 52 904 | 76. 39 | | 91. 51 | 9. 88 |
| 驻马店市 | Zhumadian | 地级市 | 15 083 | 865. 18 | 130. 37 | 49. 24 | 8 129 755 | 10 610 | 25 846 | 91. 89 | 84. 39 | 57. 70 | 7. 14 |
| 巩义市 | Gongyi | 县级市 | 1 041 | 80. 90 | 15. 89 | 22. 00 | | | 32 079 | 56. 54 | 50. 51 | 99. 09 | 15. 36 |
| 荥阳市 | Xingyang | 县级市 | 908 | 60. 00 | 11. 13 | 21. 00 | | | 11 380 | 96. 00 | 93. 86 | 90. 47 | 10. 46 |
| 新密市 | Xinmi | 县级市 | 978 | 76. 70 | 18. 80 | 22. 60 | | | 9 660 | 73. 45 | 87. 50 | 97. 66 | 9. 64 |
| 新郑市 | Xinzheng | 县级市 | 887 | 62. 30 | 16. 06 | 21. 00 | | | 6 882 | 85. 77 | 100. 00 | 70. 38 | 5. 97 |
| 登封市 | Dengfeng | 县级市 | 1 219 | 65. 20 | 20. 16 | 18. 50 | | | 9 891 | 66. 67 | 87. 12 | 86. 45 | 10. 62 |
| 偃师市 | Yanshi | 县级市 | 948 | 85. 20 | 10. 70 | 14. 60 | | | 7 658 | 90. 06 | 98. 85 | 99. 31 | 10. 76 |
| 舞钢市 | Wugang | 县级市 | 641 | 32. 70 | 10. 13 | 13. 92 | | | 14 275 | 53. 86 | | 82. 96 | 9. 71 |
| 汝州市 | Ruzhou | 县级市 | 957 | 95. 20 | 11. 18 | 25. 00 | | | 3 031 | 78. 06 | 99. 14 | 47. 56 | 6. 81 |
| 林州市 | Linzhou | 县级市 | 2 046 | 100. 10 | 17. 40 | 18. 00 | | | 12 658 | 64. 86 | 54. 92 | 90. 85 | 11. 49 |

续表

| 城市名称 Name of Cities | | 行政级别 Admini－strative Rank | 行政区土地面积（平方公里）Area of City's Administrative（sq. km） | 年末总人口（万人）Total Population（year-end）（10 thousand） | 非农业人口（万人）Non-agricultural Population（10 thousand） | 建成区面积（平方公里）Area of Built-up District（sq. km） | 地区生产总值（万元）Gross Regional Product（10 000 yuan） | 人均地区生产总值（元）Per Capita Gross Regional Product（yuan） | 市政公用设施固定资产投资总额（万元）Total Fixed Assets Investment in Municipal Service Facilities（10 000 RMB） | 污水处理率（%）Wastewater Treatment Rate（%） | 生活垃圾处理率（%）Domestic Garbage Treatment Rate（%） | 用水普及率（%）Water Coverage Rate（%） | 人均公园绿地面积（平方米）Per Capita Public Green Space（sq. m） |
|---|---|---|---|---|---|---|---|---|---|---|---|---|---|
| 卫辉市 | Weihui | 县级市 | 862 | 49.00 | 12.06 | 18.90 | | | 5 143 | 44.75 | | 84.51 | 7.78 |
| 辉县市 | Huixian | 县级市 | 2 007 | 81.00 | 37.73 | 21.31 | | | 5 937 | 53.08 | | 100.00 | 7.30 |
| 济源市 | Jiyuan | 县级市 | 1 894 | 68.00 | 25.57 | 28.30 | | | 22 530 | 80.33 | 100.00 | 99.73 | 9.04 |
| 沁阳市 | Qinyang | 县级市 | 624 | 48.90 | 9.41 | 17.50 | | | 16 418 | 82.58 | 28.02 | 95.07 | 9.01 |
| 孟州市 | Mengzhou | 县级市 | 542 | 37.70 | 5.83 | 14.18 | | | 10 959 | 87.74 | 92.65 | 97.65 | 10.33 |
| 禹州市 | Yuzhou | 县级市 | 1 461 | 123.90 | 19.86 | 31.30 | | | 13 433 | 80.00 | 74.16 | 97.54 | 11.02 |
| 长葛市 | Changge | 县级市 | 650 | 70.60 | 16.16 | 18.10 | | | 8 017 | 91.66 | 96.05 | 77.94 | 10.80 |
| 义马市 | Yima | 县级市 | 112 | 16.70 | 13.27 | 15.14 | | | 13 040 | 35.56 | | 72.24 | 9.01 |
| 灵宝市 | Lingbao | 县级市 | 3 011 | 74.30 | 12.22 | 19.00 | | | 25 760 | 72.33 | 92.46 | 87.22 | 7.95 |
| 邓州市 | Dengzhou | 县级市 | 2 370 | 156.00 | 16.71 | 21.00 | | | 5 933 | 67.07 | 81.76 | 80.00 | 5.95 |
| 永城市 | Yongcheng | 县级市 | 1 994 | 147.40 | 19.71 | 23.00 | | | 16 151 | 71.20 | 85.00 | 66.81 | 8.08 |
| 项城市 | Xiangcheng | 县级市 | 1 083 | 128.80 | 22.29 | 27.10 | | | 4 851 | 81.64 | 90.33 | 94.22 | 10.16 |
| 湖北省 | Hubei | | | | | | | | | | | | |
| 武汉市 | Wuhan | 地级市 | 8 494 | 833.24 | 537.24 | 460.00 | 39 600 819 | 44 290 | 2 459 180 | 87.08 | 99.99 | 99.83 | 9.25 |
| 黄石市 | Huangshi | 地级市 | 4 583 | 257.31 | 93.68 | 62.00 | 5 565 700 | 22 980 | 71180 | 71.09 | 100.00 | 100.00 | 11.66 |
| 十堰市 | Shiyan | 地级市 | 23 680 | 351.03 | 101.92 | 59.50 | 4 876 426 | 13 892 | 49 232 | 20.00 | 95.84 | 90.72 | 9.09 |
| 宜昌市 | Yichang | 地级市 | 21 048 | 400.83 | 133.70 | 81.56 | 10 265 600 | 25 445 | 85 648 | 84.33 | 91.00 | 100.00 | 10.73 |
| 襄樊市 | Xiangfan | 地级市 | 19 724 | 584.38 | 194.71 | 79.26 | 10 024 600 | 18 458 | 83 896 | 79.94 | 100.00 | 100.00 | 10.09 |
| 鄂州市 | Ezhou | 地级市 | 1 504 | 106.82 | 40.99 | 47.30 | 2 697 900 | 26 142 | 53 621 | 61.35 | 99.80 | 100.00 | 11.37 |
| 荆门市 | Jingmen | 地级市 | 12 404 | 300.11 | 79.99 | 48.53 | 5 203 600 | 18 309 | 13 613 | 79.83 | 99.35 | 100.00 | 10.29 |
| 孝感市 | Xiaogan | 地级市 | 8 910 | 525.06 | 152.31 | 32.50 | 5 930 600 | 12 698 | 32 861 | 80.37 | 98.85 | 97.39 | 9.15 |
| 荆州市 | Jingzhou | 地级市 | 14 205 | 658.50 | 163.53 | 64.88 | 6 239 800 | 9 554 | 27 262 | 52.75 | 99.97 | 100.00 | 6.03 |
| 黄冈市 | Huanggang | 地级市 | 17 446 | 735.14 | 167.26 | 28.52 | 6 007 500 | 6 520 | 33 210 | 70.19 | 91.55 | 100.00 | 10.47 |
| 咸宁市 | Xianning | 地级市 | 9 861 | 288.21 | 78.23 | 30.80 | 3 591 900 | 14 299 | 30 923 | 30.95 | 92.59 | 96.55 | 13.59 |
| 随州市 | Suizhou | 地级市 | 9 636 | 256.11 | 50.63 | 43.00 | 3 102 000 | 14 074 | 6 570 | 47.38 | 100.00 | 97.42 | 8.67 |

续表

| 城市名称 Name of Cities | | 行政级别 Admini－strative Rank | 行政区土地面积(平方公里) Area of City's Administrative (sq. km) | 年末总人口(万人)Total Population (year-end) (10 thousand) | 非农业人口(万人) Non-agricultural Population (10 thousand) | 建成区面积(平方公里) Area of Built-up District (sq. km) | 地区生产总值(万元) Gross Regional Product (10 000 yuan) | 人均地区生产总值(元) Per Capita Gross Regional Product (yuan) | 市政公用设施固定资产投资总额(万元) Total Fixed Assets Investment in Municipal Service Facilities (10 000 RMB) | 污水处理率(%) Wastewater Treatment Rate(%) | 生活垃圾处理率(%) Domestic Garbage Treatment Rate(%) | 用水普及率(%) Water Coverage Rate(%) | 人均公园绿地面积(平方米) Per Capita Public Green Space (sq. m) |
|---|---|---|---|---|---|---|---|---|---|---|---|---|---|
| 大冶市 | Daye | 县级市 | 1 566 | 93.40 | 93.11 | 20.00 | | | 7 599 | 50.00 | 65.18 | 96.99 | 5.50 |
| 丹江口市 | Danjiangkou | 县级市 | 3 121 | 49.70 | 20.77 | 27.60 | | | 14 890 | | 96.67 | 83.70 | 9.09 |
| 宜都市 | Yidu | 县级市 | 1 357 | 39.50 | 11.62 | 12.00 | | | 10 514 | 85.38 | 82.67 | 100.00 | 11.94 |
| 当阳市 | Dangyang | 县级市 | 2 159 | 48.60 | 12.42 | 20.50 | | | 4 587 | 55.03 | 87.50 | 100.00 | 6.58 |
| 枝江市 | Zhijiang | 县级市 | 1 310 | 50.10 | 13.72 | 12.80 | | | 8 400 | 73.03 | 94.21 | 100.00 | 12.74 |
| 老河口市 | Laohekou | 县级市 | 1 032 | 52.90 | 29.73 | 27.00 | | | 14 120 | 88.66 | 100.00 | 97.98 | 7.94 |
| 枣阳市 | Zaoyang | 县级市 | 3 277 | 110.60 | 18.55 | 20.10 | | | 4 683 | 67.89 | 99.39 | 93.93 | 9.39 |
| 宜城市 | Yicheng | 县级市 | 2 115 | 56.50 | 23.15 | 14.20 | | | 10 340 | | 100.00 | 100.00 | 3.97 |
| 钟祥市 | Zhongxiang | 县级市 | 4 488 | 104.00 | 21.94 | 18.00 | | | 18 194 | 60.00 | 100.00 | 100.00 | 11.73 |
| 应城市 | Yingcheng | 县级市 | 1 103 | 68.00 | 16.02 | 19.55 | | | 10 862 | 72.81 | 97.45 | 92.70 | 8.47 |
| 安陆市 | Anlu | 县级市 | 1 355 | 62.90 | 11.23 | 16.16 | | | 8 585 | 21.15 | 91.68 | 81.11 | 7.61 |
| 汉川市 | Hanchuan | 县级市 | 1 663 | 110.60 | 25.03 | 15.68 | | | 15 381 | 37.32 | 94.40 | 97.09 | 4.22 |
| 石首市 | Shishou | 县级市 | 1 427 | 63.20 | 15.74 | 22.51 | | | 6 180 | 67.50 | 99.23 | 99.93 | 11.57 |
| 洪湖市 | Honghu | 县级市 | 2 519 | 92.10 | 17.65 | 39.52 | | | 11 494 | 19.34 | 100.00 | 93.94 | 11.30 |
| 松滋市 | Songzi | 县级市 | 2 235 | 84.50 | 15.72 | 15.00 | | | 16 312 | | 100.00 | 97.46 | 24.15 |
| 麻城市 | Macheng | 县级市 | 3 747 | 116.90 | 29.52 | 23.95 | | | 7 245 | 49.93 | 94.39 | 98.16 | 8.62 |
| 武穴市 | Wuxue | 县级市 | 1 246 | 75.60 | 26.13 | 25.36 | | | 4 830 | 54.12 | 88.60 | 99.95 | 12.36 |
| 赤壁市 | Chibi | 县级市 | 1 723 | 51.20 | 16.23 | 22.23 | | | 10 313 | 15.27 | 100.00 | 97.03 | 7.97 |
| 广水市 | Guangshui | 县级市 | 2 641 | 93.50 | 17.72 | 19.80 | | | 9 885 | 38.97 | 86.76 | 80.16 | 11.21 |
| 恩施市 | Enshi | 县级市 | 3 972 | 79.70 | 20.34 | 20.00 | | | 23 130 | 82.53 | 99.57 | 86.50 | 8.36 |
| 利川市 | Lichuan | 县级市 | 4 610 | 88.50 | 13.63 | 12.35 | | | 13 272 | 20.00 | 100.00 | 68.97 | 0.34 |
| 仙桃市 | Xiantao | 县级市 | 2 538 | 148.70 | 40.92 | 38.30 | | | 29 450 | 68.75 | 100.00 | 100.00 | 11.57 |
| 潜江市 | Qianjiang | 县级市 | 2 004 | 100.70 | 30.64 | 38.60 | | | 18 957 | 68.50 | 100.00 | 100.00 | 10.06 |
| 天门市 | Tianmen | 县级市 | 2 622 | 162.20 | 26.00 | 25.50 | | | 15 200 | | 100.00 | 99.22 | 7.78 |
| 湖南省 | Hunan | | | | | | | | | | | | |

续表

| 城市名称 Name of Cities | | 行政级别 Admini－strative Rank | 行政区土地面积（平方公里）Area of City's Administrative（sq. km） | 年末总人口（万人）Total Population（year-end）（10 thousand） | 非农业人口（万人）Non-agricultural Population（10 thousand） | 建成区面积（平方公里）Area of Built-up District（sq. km） | 地区生产总值（万元）Gross Regional Product（10 000 yuan） | 人均地区生产总值（元）Per Capita Gross Regional Product（yuan） | 市政公用设施固定资产投资总额（万元）Total Fixed Assets Investment in Municipal Service Facilities（10 000 RMB） | 污水处理率（%）Wastewater Treatment Rate（%） | 生活垃圾处理率（%）Domestic Garbage Treatment Rate（%） | 用水普及率（%）Water Coverage Rate（%） | 人均公园绿地面积（平方米）Per Capita Public Green Space（sq. m） |
|---|---|---|---|---|---|---|---|---|---|---|---|---|---|
| 长沙市 | Changsha | 地级市 | 11 819 | 645. 14 | 234. 45 | 242. 78 | 30 009 795 | 45 765 | 1 433 136 | 60. 28 | 100. 00 | 100. 00 | 8. 66 |
| 株洲市 | Zhuzhou | 地级市 | 11 276 | 383. 04 | 102. 41 | 89. 58 | 9 095 676 | 24 563 | 235 430 | 63. 89 | 100. 00 | 92. 01 | 8. 21 |
| 湘潭市 | Xiangtan | 地级市 | 5 015 | 293. 99 | 82. 50 | 72. 65 | 6 547 824 | 23 673 | 154 762 | 60. 01 | 100. 00 | 97. 11 | 8. 34 |
| 衡阳市 | Hengyang | 地级市 | 15 303 | 731. 14 | 311. 25 | 93. 00 | 10 000 859 | 14 858 | 84 734 | 39. 93 | 100. 00 | 100. 00 | 8. 85 |
| 邵阳市 | Shaoyang | 地级市 | 20 830 | 754. 09 | 112. 26 | 47. 00 | 5 615 709 | 8 332 | 82 753 | 38. 00 | 100. 00 | 95. 11 | 7. 71 |
| 岳阳市 | Yueyang | 地级市 | 15 087 | 551. 51 | 248. 15 | 78. 60 | 11 057 360 | 21 410 | 277 744 | 68. 00 | 100. 00 | 95. 58 | 8. 75 |
| 常德市 | Changde | 地级市 | 18 190 | 614. 16 | 143. 25 | 72. 54 | 10 496 975 | 19 201 | 30 345 | 66. 65 | 100. 00 | 97. 77 | 9. 33 |
| 张家界市 | Zhangjiajie | 地级市 | 9 516 | 164. 56 | 29. 71 | 21. 75 | 1 839 774 | 12 338 | 55 198 | 55. 65 | 100. 00 | 92. 23 | 7. 09 |
| 益阳市 | Yiyang | 地级市 | 12 144 | 467. 66 | 94. 74 | 50. 50 | 5 112 770 | 12 223 | 72 094 | 62. 31 | 100. 00 | 78. 37 | 6. 06 |
| 郴州市 | Chenzhou | 地级市 | 19 557 | 471. 00 | 194. 50 | 41. 70 | 7 340 633 | 16 668 | 88 423 | 62. 00 | 100. 00 | 91. 58 | 7. 35 |
| 永州市 | Yongzhou | 地级市 | 22 441 | 580. 16 | 93. 12 | 54. 10 | 5 926 853 | 11 551 | 59 505 | 34. 13 | 100. 00 | 99. 05 | 5. 33 |
| 怀化市 | Huaihua | 地级市 | 27 624 | 508. 94 | 95. 14 | 40. 00 | 5 037 856 | 10 950 | 117 089 | 42. 16 | 100. 00 | 93. 09 | 7. 98 |
| 娄底市 | Loudi | 地级市 | 8 117 | 423. 79 | 89. 63 | 41. 00 | 5 284 038 | 13 509 | 56 570 | 52. 18 | 100. 00 | 95. 05 | 8. 31 |
| 浏阳市 | Liuyang | 县级市 | 4 999 | 138. 80 | 15. 25 | 22. 00 | | | 18 648 | 67. 46 | 100. 00 | 83. 04 | 4. 83 |
| 醴陵市 | Liling | 县级市 | 2 157 | 98. 60 | 15. 16 | 26. 00 | | | 32 486 | 25. 58 | 100. 00 | 88. 50 | 9. 67 |
| 湘乡市 | Xiangxiang | 县级市 | 2 011 | 88. 70 | 12. 91 | 13. 82 | | | 6 640 | 33. 08 | 100. 00 | 91. 58 | 7. 38 |
| 韶山市 | Shaoshan | 县级市 | 210 | 10. 10 | 1. 63 | 4. 70 | | | 24 288 | 36. 54 | 100. 00 | 99. 61 | 9. 96 |
| 耒阳市 | Leiyang | 县级市 | 2 656 | 126. 00 | 21. 18 | 31. 50 | | | 4 113 | 23. 73 | 100. 00 | 100. 00 | 7. 01 |
| 常宁市 | Changning | 县级市 | 2 064 | 86. 30 | 16. 79 | 9. 53 | | | 6 413 | 28. 09 | 100. 00 | 98. 88 | 7. 95 |
| 武冈市 | Wugang | 县级市 | 1 532 | 75. 30 | 9. 87 | 14. 21 | | | 11 165 | 12. 14 | 100. 00 | 90. 12 | 10. 86 |
| 汨罗市 | Miluo | 县级市 | 1 562 | 73. 00 | 18. 38 | 13. 80 | | | 6 793 | 26. 15 | 100. 00 | 88. 02 | 9. 50 |
| 临湘市 | Linxiang | 县级市 | 1 744 | 49. 30 | 13. 12 | 15. 00 | | | 29 300 | 58. 90 | 100. 00 | 80. 07 | 6. 00 |
| 津市市 | Jinshi | 县级市 | 558 | 26. 50 | 11. 42 | 10. 66 | | | 5 665 | 30. 11 | 100. 00 | 97. 24 | 9. 16 |
| 沅江市 | Yuanjiang | 县级市 | 1 797 | 74. 60 | 19. 17 | 13. 10 | | | 6 208 | 19. 44 | 100. 00 | 86. 59 | 2. 74 |
| 资兴市 | Zixing | 县级市 | 2 747 | 36. 80 | 13. 00 | 19. 83 | | | 9 995 | 57. 18 | 100. 00 | 85. 24 | 7. 44 |

续表

| 城市名称 Name of Cities | | 行政级别 Admini - strative Rank | 行政区土地面积（平方公里）Area of City's Administrative (sq. km) | 年末总人口（万人）Total Population (year-end) (10 thousand) | 非农业人口（万人）Non-agricultural Population (10 thousand) | 建成区面积（平方公里）Area of Built-up District (sq. km) | 地区生产总值（万元）Gross Regional Product (10 000 yuan) | 人均地区生产总值（元）Per Capita Gross Regional Product (yuan) | 市政公用设施固定资产投资总额（万元）Total Fixed Assets Investment in Municipal Service Facilities (10 000 RMB) | 污水处理率（%）Wastewater Treatment Rate(%) | 生活垃圾处理率（%）Domestic Garbage Treatment Rate(%) | 用水普及率（%）Water Coverage Rate(%) | 人均公园绿地面积（平方米）Per Capita Public Green Space (sq. m) |
|---|---|---|---|---|---|---|---|---|---|---|---|---|---|
| 洪江市 | Hongjiang | 县级市 | 2 174 | 52.40 | 12.21 | 4.50 | | | 7 137 | 15.94 | 100.00 | 73.39 | 6.88 |
| 冷水江市 | Lengshuijiang | 县级市 | 439 | 37.40 | 18.78 | 19.90 | | | 7 520 | 35.26 | 100.00 | 85.71 | 7.34 |
| 涟源市 | Lianyuan | 县级市 | 1 895 | 112.40 | 16.38 | 12.00 | | | 6 627 | 26.91 | 100.00 | 80.33 | 4.15 |
| 吉首市 | Jishou | 县级市 | 1 059 | 29.10 | 12.82 | 19.50 | | | 44 804 | 28.54 | 100.00 | 84.58 | 7.61 |
| 广东省 | Guangdong | | | | | | | | | | | | |
| 广州市 | Guangzhou | 地级市 | 7 434 | 784.14 | 704.17 | 895.00 | 82 158 151 | 81 233 | 2 039 003 | 75.09 | 100.00 | 99.71 | 9.72 |
| 韶关市 | Shaoguan | 地级市 | 18 463 | 323.09 | 124.80 | 78.30 | 5 458 677 | 18 503 | 11 703 | 67.74 | 100.00 | 97.87 | 11.58 |
| 深圳市 | Shenzhen | 地级市 | 1 953 | 228.07 | 228.07 | 787.90 | 78 065 387 | 89 814 | 263 053 | 62.67 | 94.17 | 80.79 | 16.20 |
| 珠海市 | Zhuhai | 地级市 | 1 701 | 99.48 | 99.48 | 118.34 | 9 920 616 | 67 591 | 138 547 | 66.85 | 72.16 | 98.84 | 12.92 |
| 汕头市 | Shantou | 地级市 | 2 064 | 506.57 | 502.01 | 170.39 | 9 747 835 | 19 384 | 65 829 | 31.10 | 64.01 | 98.75 | 11.75 |
| 佛山市 | Foshan | 地级市 | 3 848 | 364.34 | 364.34 | 149.98 | 43 333 044 | 72 975 | 341 706 | 79.15 | 94.53 | 100.00 | 8.10 |
| 江门市 | Jiangmen | 地级市 | 9 541 | 389.93 | 219.77 | 113.75 | 12 805 877 | 30 973 | 87 123 | 33.34 | 100.00 | 96.91 | 7.50 |
| 湛江市 | Zhanjiang | 地级市 | 13 225 | 753.88 | 278.88 | 77.23 | 10 486 608 | 15 297 | 21 689 | 62.88 | 97.33 | 99.12 | 12.50 |
| 茂名市 | Maoming | 地级市 | 11 458 | 725.67 | 270.91 | 67.40 | 12 178 395 | 16 889 | 990 | 64.82 | 95.32 | 100.00 | 9.16 |
| 肇庆市 | Zhaoqing | 地级市 | 15 134 | 410.28 | 117.88 | 70.96 | 7 158 542 | 18 951 | 67 925 | 71.01 | 96.65 | 99.90 | 21.14 |
| 惠州市 | Huizhou | 地级市 | 11 158 | 318.84 | 186.20 | 132.03 | 12 903 608 | 33 077 | 151 331 | 59.64 | 86.48 | 92.94 | 8.15 |
| 梅州市 | Meizhou | 地级市 | 15 870 | 505.28 | 124.71 | 33.37 | 4 778 840 | 11 604 | 3 940 | 83.11 | 100.00 | 95.45 | 11.69 |
| 汕尾市 | Shanwei | 地级市 | 5 271 | 335.99 | 167.35 | 13.40 | 3 502 293 | 12 130 | 11 600 | | 101.22 | 91.55 | 3.60 |
| 河源市 | Heyuan | 地级市 | 15 826 | 346.64 | 83.02 | 26.90 | 3 941 331 | 13 860 | 2 567 | 64.61 | | 91.31 | 8.41 |
| 阳江市 | Yangjiang | 地级市 | 7 946 | 273.29 | 114.34 | 40.10 | 4 838 439 | 20 479 | 8 835 | 97.16 | 77.60 | 95.49 | 9.19 |
| 清远市 | Qingyuan | 地级市 | 19 153 | 405.80 | 111.57 | 41.84 | 7 466 166 | 20 205 | 23 948 | 38.18 | 100.00 | 99.01 | 6.46 |
| 东莞市 | Dongguan | 地级市 | 2 465 | 174.87 | 76.80 | 681.86 | 37 025 344 | 53 285 | 386 466 | 84.95 | 97.34 | 99.93 | 12.12 |
| 中山市 | Zhongshan | 地级市 | 1 800 | 146.43 | 77.26 | 86.10 | 14 085 194 | 56 106 | 63 009 | 93.08 | 100.00 | 100.00 | 8.70 |
| 潮州市 | Chaozhou | 地级市 | 3 100 | 256.13 | 74.20 | 41.68 | 4 427 597 | 17 336 | 19 188 | 76.95 | 100.00 | 100.00 | 10.28 |
| 揭阳市 | Jieyang | 地级市 | 5 240 | 641.24 | 219.60 | 47.00 | 7 250 296 | 12 679 | 41 186 | | 81.99 | 97.00 | 12.22 |

续表

| 城市名称 Name of Cities | | 行政级别 Admini－strative Rank | 行政区土地面积（平方公里）Area of City's Administrative (sq. km) | 年末总人口（万人）Total Population (year-end) (10 thousand) | 非农业人口（万人）Non-agricultural Population (10 thousand) | 建成区面积（平方公里）Area of Built-up District (sq. km) | 地区生产总值（万元）Gross Regional Product (10 000 yuan) | 人均地区生产总值（元）Per Capita Gross Regional Product (yuan) | 市政公用设施固定资产投资总额（万元）Total Fixed Assets Investment in Municipal Service Facilities (10 000 RMB) | 污水处理率（%）Wastewater Treatment Rate(%) | 生活垃圾处理率（%）Domestic Garbage Treatment Rate(%) | 用水普及率（%）Water Coverage Rate(%) | 人均公园绿地面积（平方米）Per Capita Public Green Space (sq. m) |
|---|---|---|---|---|---|---|---|---|---|---|---|---|---|
| 云浮市 | Yunfu | 地级市 | 7 779 | 272. 68 | 100. 59 | 18. 60 | 3 198 566 | 13 439 | 556 | 91. 43 | 100. 00 | 98. 45 | 10. 28 |
| 增城市 | Zengcheng | 县级市 | 1 616 | 82. 70 | 34. 03 | 24. 00 | | | 23 775 | 45. 34 | 50. 53 | 73. 47 | 13. 93 |
| 从化市 | Conghua | 县级市 | 1 975 | 55. 70 | 24. 31 | | | | 19 146 | 53. 88 | 100. 00 | 65. 82 | 15. 75 |
| 乐昌市 | Lechang | 县级市 | 2 421 | 52. 40 | 24. 77 | 12. 30 | | | 600 | 86. 96 | 100. 00 | 84. 85 | 4. 09 |
| 南雄市 | Nanxiong | 县级市 | 2 361 | 46. 40 | 11. 63 | 10. 67 | | | 997 | 38. 81 | 99. 68 | 95. 76 | 12. 82 |
| 台山市 | Taishan | 县级市 | 3 296 | 98. 40 | 26. 81 | 23. 40 | | | 3 926 | 57. 63 | 100. 00 | 100. 00 | 14. 48 |
| 开平市 | Kaiping | 县级市 | 1 659 | 68. 50 | 24. 49 | 27. 40 | | | 716 | 68. 75 | 99. 07 | 99. 17 | 6. 49 |
| 鹤山市 | Heshan | 县级市 | 1 083 | 36. 30 | 14. 44 | 19. 91 | | | 12 983 | 28. 48 | 100. 00 | 100. 00 | 9. 53 |
| 恩平市 | Enping | 县级市 | 1 698 | 50. 00 | 17. 45 | 21. 55 | | | 2 085 | | 100. 00 | 90. 50 | 8. 42 |
| 廉江市 | Lianjiang | 县级市 | 2 840 | 161. 80 | 35. 20 | 18. 50 | | | 1 462 | | 94. 65 | 87. 65 | 34. 26 |
| 雷州市 | Leizhou | 县级市 | 3 662 | 161. 50 | 30. 29 | 20. 88 | | | 88 | | 95. 29 | 62. 21 | 8. 31 |
| 吴川市 | Wuchuan | 县级市 | 849 | 106. 90 | 30. 43 | 17. 00 | | | 1 435 | | 94. 07 | 73. 05 | 11. 09 |
| 高州市 | Gaozhou | 县级市 | 3 276 | 167. 80 | 48. 06 | 15. 16 | | | 1 995 | | 98. 57 | 97. 81 | 4. 38 |
| 化州市 | Huazhou | 县级市 | 2 354 | 155. 80 | 24. 95 | 24. 80 | | | 755 | | 100. 00 | 100. 00 | 4. 91 |
| 信宜市 | Xinyi | 县级市 | 3 081 | 135. 00 | 34. 97 | 22. 00 | | | 4 017 | | 99. 60 | 96. 65 | 6. 99 |
| 高要市 | Gaoyao | 县级市 | 2 200 | 74. 50 | 11. 84 | 18. 34 | | | 1 580 | 87. 73 | 73. 21 | 96. 34 | 17. 86 |
| 四会市 | Sihui | 县级市 | 1 259 | 51. 20 | 21. 30 | 24. 68 | | | 18 332 | 55. 23 | 83. 83 | 94. 21 | 9. 06 |
| 兴宁市 | Xingning | 县级市 | 2 104 | 114. 00 | 32. 11 | 16. 50 | | | 692 | | 98. 89 | 80. 43 | 7. 86 |
| 陆丰市 | Lufeng | 县级市 | 1 681 | 171. 20 | 65. 82 | 19. 93 | | | 245 | | 100. 00 | 96. 02 | 1. 15 |
| 阳春市 | Yangchun | 县级市 | 4 054 | 109. 90 | 29. 84 | 20. 00 | | | 4 343 | 87. 05 | | 98. 93 | 8. 60 |
| 英德市 | Yingde | 县级市 | 5 671 | 109. 40 | 20. 10 | 21. 37 | | | | 48. 86 | | 62. 86 | 7. 14 |
| 连州市 | Lianzhou | 县级市 | 2 663 | 52. 20 | 8. 99 | 12. 95 | | | | | | 49. 11 | 4. 79 |
| 普宁市 | Puning | 县级市 | 1 635 | 223. 90 | 66. 27 | 26. 16 | | | 5 640 | | | 98. 61 | 0. 38 |
| 罗定市 | Luoding | 县级市 | 2 327 | 116. 10 | 38. 73 | 23. 00 | | | 310 | 40. 17 | | 91. 49 | 10. 39 |
| 广西壮族自治区 | Guangxi | | | | | | | | | | | | |

续表

| 城市名称 Name of Cities | | 行政级别 Admini－strative Rank | 行政区土地面积（平方公里）Area of City's Administrative (sq. km) | 年末总人口（万人）Total Population (year-end) (10 thousand) | 非农业人口（万人）Non-agricultural Population (10 thousand) | 建成区面积（平方公里）Area of Built-up District (sq. km) | 地区生产总值（万元）Gross Regional Product (10 000 yuan) | 人均地区生产总值（元）Per Capita Gross Regional Product (yuan) | 市政公用设施固定资产投资总额（万元）Total Fixed Assets Investment in Municipal Service Facilities (10 000 RMB) | 污水处理率（%）Wastewater Treatment Rate(%) | 生活垃圾处理率（%）Domestic Garbage Treatment Rate(%) | 用水普及率（%）Water Coverage Rate(%) | 人均公园绿地面积（平方米）Per Capita Public Green Space (sq. m) |
|---|---|---|---|---|---|---|---|---|---|---|---|---|---|
| 南宁市 | Nanning | 地级市 | 22 112 | 691.69 | 188.94 | 179.06 | 13 162 137 | 19 142 | 501 683 | 97.06 | 100.00 | 100.00 | 10.29 |
| 柳州市 | Liuzhou | 地级市 | 18 617 | 364.90 | 128.45 | 126.88 | 9 098 522 | 21 181 | 458 741 | 73.10 | 100.00 | 99.80 | 10.70 |
| 桂林市 | Guilin | 地级市 | 27 809 | 508.32 | 122.64 | 59.54 | 8 830 250 | 17 435 | 109 941 | 84.60 | 100.00 | 76.74 | 6.44 |
| 梧州市 | Wuzhou | 地级市 | 12 611 | 313.20 | 62.65 | 36.10 | 4 001 238 | 13 115 | 14 556 | 4.30 | 90.60 | 98.96 | 7.13 |
| 北海市 | Beihai | 地级市 | 3 337 | 157.71 | 46.68 | 68.80 | 3 138 785 | 20 093 | 32 436 | 58.29 | 100.00 | 54.29 | 3.23 |
| 防城港市 | Fangchenggang | 地级市 | 6 181 | 84.76 | 28.58 | 18.96 | 2 121 817 | 25 375 | 34 400 | | 30.09 | 98.22 | 4.86 |
| 钦州市 | Qinzhou | 地级市 | 10 843 | 364.51 | 41.40 | 53.78 | 3 774 232 | 11 740 | 122 942 | 84.40 | 81.67 | 91.79 | 5.47 |
| 贵港市 | Guigang | 地级市 | 10 606 | 501.86 | 56.49 | 52.91 | 3 985 273 | 9 386 | 55 544 | 65.81 | 89.71 | 100.00 | 11.69 |
| 玉林市 | Yulin | 地级市 | 12 838 | 641.73 | 72.44 | 52.00 | 6 059 167 | 9 267 | 89 137 | 0.57 | 100.00 | 100.00 | 10.85 |
| 百色市 | Baise | 地级市 | 36 201 | 392.37 | 49.02 | 31.74 | 4 162 366 | 10 037 | 39 983 | | 83.61 | 99.88 | 9.19 |
| 贺州市 | Hezhou | 地级市 | 11 855 | 221.79 | 31.03 | 28.85 | 2 528 364 | 12 103 | 13 632 | | 87.16 | 65.45 | 4.38 |
| 河池市 | Hechi | 地级市 | 33 508 | 404.57 | 57.29 | 17.20 | 3 673 139 | 9 667 | 20 224 | 97.59 | 54.13 | 100.00 | 3.75 |
| 来宾市 | Laibin | 地级市 | 13 411 | 252.74 | 38.03 | 22.67 | 2 715 837 | 11 903 | 52 717 | 0.12 | 220.13 | 100.00 | 6.12 |
| 崇左市 | Chongzuo | 地级市 | 17 351 | 240.00 | 40.66 | 14.50 | 2 648 005 | 12 226 | 14 240 | | | 95.90 | 7.54 |
| 岑溪市 | Cenxi | 县级市 | 2 783 | 86.20 | 13.73 | 16.05 | | | 1 963 | | | 94.98 | 16.63 |
| 东兴市 | Dongxing | 县级市 | 549 | 12.00 | 4.54 | 7.72 | | | 13 577 | | | 84.29 | 7.78 |
| 桂平市 | Guiping | 县级市 | 4 074 | 179.00 | 16.74 | 13.68 | | | 2 990 | 21.14 | | 100.00 | 6.33 |
| 北流市 | Beiliu | 县级市 | 2 457 | 131.00 | 13.72 | 17.22 | | | 35 764 | | 100.00 | 100.00 | 9.19 |
| 宜州市 | Yizhou | 县级市 | 3 869 | 64.30 | 10.40 | 11.91 | | | 11 572 | 60.37 | | 100.00 | 9.98 |
| 合山市 | Heshan | 县级市 | 360 | 13.90 | 5.92 | 5.90 | | | 4 220 | | | 100.00 | 4.66 |
| 凭祥市 | Pingxiang | 县级市 | 650 | 10.90 | 3.24 | 5.10 | | | 5 191 | | | 98.25 | 9.05 |
| 海南省 | Hainan | | | | | | | | | | | | |
| 海口市 | Haikou | 地级市 | 2 304 | 155.82 | 94.13 | 91.42 | 4 431 808 | 24 420 | 183 621 | 82.97 | 100.00 | 96.50 | 9.25 |
| 三亚市 | Sanya | 地级市 | 1 915 | 54.58 | 27.50 | 20.00 | 1 443 178 | 30 572 | 37 486 | 67.14 | 100.00 | 69.38 | 9.19 |
| 五指山市 | Wuzhishan | 县级市 | 1 128 | 11.50 | 5.61 | 6.55 | | | 2 967 | | 100.00 | 98.90 | 10.62 |

续表

| 城市名称 Name of Cities | | 行政级别 Admini－strative Rank | 行政区土地面积（平方公里）Area of City's Administrative（sq. km） | 年末总人口（万人）Total Population（year-end）（10 thousand） | 非农业人口（万人）Non-agricultural Population（10 thousand） | 建成区面积（平方公里）Area of Built-up District（sq. km） | 地区生产总值（万元）Gross Regional Product（10 000 yuan） | 人均地区生产总值（元）Per Capita Gross Regional Product（yuan） | 市政公用设施固定资产投资总额（万元）Total Fixed Assets Investment in Municipal Service Facilities（10 000 RMB） | 污水处理率（%）Wastewater Treatment Rate（%） | 生活垃圾处理率（%）Domestic Garbage Treatment Rate（%） | 用水普及率（%）Water Coverage Rate（%） | 人均公园绿地面积（平方米）Per Capita Public Green Space（sq. m） |
|---|---|---|---|---|---|---|---|---|---|---|---|---|---|
| 琼海市 | Qionghai | 县级市 | 1 710 | 48. 30 | 14. 81 | 22. 20 | | | 33 070 | | 100. 00 | 88. 69 | 17. 36 |
| 儋州市 | Danzhou | 县级市 | 3 265 | 114. 60 | 41. 33 | 25. 13 | | | 1 676 | | 100. 00 | 67. 39 | 8. 57 |
| 文昌市 | Wenchang | 县级市 | 2 484 | 59. 90 | 12. 37 | 14. 00 | | | 14 980 | | 100. 00 | 64. 86 | 6. 41 |
| 万宁市 | Wanning | 县级市 | 1 884 | 67. 40 | 17. 77 | 9. 60 | | | 11 368 | | 100. 00 | 79. 10 | 6. 39 |
| 东方市 | Dongfang | 县级市 | 2 256 | 44. 80 | 11. 20 | 15. 90 | | | 6 574 | | 100. 00 | 73. 10 | 4. 68 |
| 重庆市 | Chongqing | 直辖市 | 82 826 | 3 257. 05 | 907. 38 | 708. 37 | 50 966 600 | 18 025 | 2 889 371 | 84. 20 | 92. 82 | 93. 20 | 9. 62 |
| 四川省 | Sichuan | | | | | | | | | | | | |
| 成都市 | Chengdu | 地级市 | 12 390 | 1 124. 96 | 612. 08 | 427. 65 | 39 009 857 | 30 855 | 1 783 619 | 85. 19 | 100. 00 | 94. 12 | 11. 43 |
| 自贡市 | Zigong | 地级市 | 4 373 | 325. 58 | 103. 11 | 53. 20 | 4 868 510 | 17 348 | 98 412 | 72. 81 | 74. 48 | 83. 26 | 5. 24 |
| 攀枝花市 | Panzhihua | 地级市 | 7 440 | 111. 18 | 59. 58 | 54. 60 | 4 276 138 | 37 278 | 33 610 | 28. 80 | 93. 56 | 91. 92 | 8. 26 |
| 泸州市 | Luzhou | 地级市 | 12 247 | 493. 38 | 86. 56 | 53. 13 | 5 084 223 | 11 831 | 36 305 | 65. 31 | 100. 00 | 77. 40 | 8. 02 |
| 德阳市 | Deyang | 地级市 | 5 954 | 387. 37 | 90. 77 | 44. 09 | 6 950 411 | 19 084 | 27 016 | 74. 01 | 100. 00 | 98. 41 | 7. 86 |
| 绵阳市 | Mianyang | 地级市 | 20 249 | 540. 71 | 135. 69 | 80. 48 | 7 431 645 | 15 012 | 50 045 | 83. 57 | 99. 48 | 93. 62 | 7. 99 |
| 广元市 | Guangyuan | 地级市 | 16 314 | 310. 37 | 64. 45 | 32. 62 | 2 335 589 | 8 550 | 14 879 | 70. 61 | 73. 31 | 90. 42 | 8. 08 |
| 遂宁市 | Suining | 地级市 | 5 325 | 384. 94 | 79. 93 | 43. 65 | 3 726 708 | 10 454 | 35 373 | 77. 94 | 81. 87 | 83. 31 | 7. 71 |
| 内江市 | Neijiang | 地级市 | 5 386 | 425. 05 | 84. 00 | 37. 00 | 4 882 791 | 12 309 | 11 895 | 33. 90 | 12. 06 | 65. 52 | 2. 91 |
| 乐山市 | Leshan | 地级市 | 12 826 | 353. 50 | 95. 70 | 49. 82 | 5 623 939 | 16 737 | 13 029 | 49. 80 | 83. 72 | 86. 83 | 7. 23 |
| 南充市 | Nanchong | 地级市 | 12 479 | 749. 49 | 150. 10 | 64. 05 | 6 019 472 | 9 687 | 36 620 | 42. 51 | 81. 69 | 97. 11 | 8. 63 |
| 眉山市 | Meishan | 地级市 | 7 186 | 346. 58 | 86. 55 | 40. 40 | 4 127 098 | 13 716 | 9 648 | 64. 16 | 100. 00 | 87. 46 | 11. 47 |
| 宜宾市 | Yibin | 地级市 | 13 283 | 530. 81 | 96. 53 | 49. 04 | 6 458 619 | 14 489 | 70 204 | 11. 88 | 78. 79 | 78. 59 | 14. 64 |
| 广安市 | Guangan | 地级市 | 6 344 | 466. 45 | 74. 68 | 21. 00 | 4 049 030 | 10 862 | 27 928 | 87. 46 | 88. 28 | 85. 00 | 14. 68 |
| 达州市 | Dazhou | 地级市 | 16 591 | 655. 97 | 121. 69 | 23. 20 | 6 039 863 | 10 580 | 23 638 | 51. 98 | 84. 23 | 97. 58 | 11. 89 |
| 雅安市 | Yaan | 地级市 | 15 302 | 154. 54 | 34. 60 | 20. 40 | 2 132 237 | 14 051 | 7 562 | 52. 29 | 92. 78 | 99. 43 | 7. 88 |
| 巴中市 | Bazhong | 地级市 | 12 301 | 398. 57 | 69. 65 | 16. 32 | 2 137 624 | 6 806 | 8 919 | 61. 94 | 71. 91 | 83. 67 | 8. 23 |
| 资阳市 | Ziyang | 地级市 | 7 962 | 497. 15 | 72. 00 | 28. 30 | 4 676 250 | 11 068 | 28 829 | 80. 00 | 95. 15 | 88. 96 | 6. 26 |

续表

| 城市名称 Name of Cities | | 行政级别 Admini－strative Rank | 行政区土地面积（平方公里）Area of City's Administrative (sq. km) | 年末总人口（万人）Total Population (year-end) (10 thousand) | 非农业人口（万人）Non-agricultural Population (10 thousand) | 建成区面积（平方公里）Area of Built-up District (sq. km) | 地区生产总值（万元）Gross Regional Product (10 000 yuan) | 人均地区生产总值（元）Per Capita Gross Regional Product (yuan) | 市政公用设施固定资产投资总额（万元）Total Fixed Assets Investment in Municipal Service Facilities (10 000 RMB) | 污水处理率（%）Wastewater Treatment Rate(%) | 生活垃圾处理率（%）Domestic Garbage Treatment Rate(%) | 用水普及率(%) Water Coverage Rate(%) | 人均公园绿地面积（平方米）Per Capita Public Green Space (sq. m) |
|---|---|---|---|---|---|---|---|---|---|---|---|---|---|
| 都江堰市 | Dujiangyan | 县级市 | 1 208 | 61. 20 | 16. 84 | 26. 34 | | | 30 824 | 46. 58 | 97. 21 | 71. 17 | 8. 00 |
| 彭州市 | Pengzhou | 县级市 | 1 420 | 80. 00 | 25. 64 | 18. 11 | | | 17 622 | 83. 81 | 81. 67 | 64. 59 | 4. 56 |
| 邛崃市 | Qionglai | 县级市 | 1 384 | 65. 60 | 18. 65 | 16. 80 | | | 16 375 | 60. 10 | 89. 80 | 82. 41 | 8. 28 |
| 崇州市 | Chongzhou | 县级市 | 1 090 | 67. 00 | 17. 41 | 19. 93 | | | 16 334 | 57. 61 | 98. 61 | 94. 38 | 11. 84 |
| 广汉市 | Guanghan | 县级市 | 551 | 59. 80 | 15. 66 | 31. 07 | | | 10 939 | 44. 55 | 47. 97 | 74. 81 | 5. 23 |
| 什邡市 | Shifang | 县级市 | 863 | 43. 30 | 9. 51 | 11. 00 | | | 203 | | 99. 52 | 77. 20 | 7. 14 |
| 绵竹市 | Mianzhu | 县级市 | 1 245 | 51. 30 | 11. 50 | 11. 66 | | | 4 436 | | 99. 06 | 82. 59 | 8. 97 |
| 江油市 | Jiangyou | 县级市 | 2 720 | 88. 30 | 24. 72 | 24. 08 | | | 22 078 | 55. 76 | 100. 00 | 83. 63 | 4. 21 |
| 峨眉山市 | Emeishan | 县级市 | 1 168 | 43. 60 | 16. 44 | 13. 80 | | | 12 410 | 89. 98 | 98. 04 | 82. 54 | 8. 36 |
| 阆中市 | Langzhong | 县级市 | 1 877 | 87. 70 | 19. 63 | 17. 20 | | | 25 340 | 57. 89 | 82. 16 | 96. 52 | 8. 12 |
| 华蓥市 | Huaying | 县级市 | 466 | 35. 70 | 9. 86 | 6. 65 | | | 4 790 | | | 74. 15 | 8. 05 |
| 万源市 | Wanyuan | 县级市 | 4 065 | 60. 00 | 9. 72 | 8. 43 | | | 300 | | | 92. 48 | 4. 79 |
| 简阳市 | Jianyang | 县级市 | 2 215 | 145. 10 | 22. 04 | 18. 60 | | | 16 800 | | 100. 00 | 97. 41 | 4. 41 |
| 西昌市 | Xichang | 县级市 | 2 654 | 60. 80 | 19. 84 | 29. 06 | | | 12 131 | 71. 08 | 100. 00 | 80. 00 | 4. 43 |
| 贵州省 | Guizhou | | | | | | | | | | | | |
| 贵阳市 | Guiyang | 地级市 | 8 034 | 363. 93 | 181. 42 | 132. 00 | 8 110 521 | 20 638 | 254 872 | 41. 74 | 93. 36 | 93. 43 | 9. 58 |
| 六盘水市 | Liupanshui | 地级市 | 9 974 | 312. 97 | 69. 08 | 38. 00 | 3 842 663 | 12 944 | 12 402 | 64. 11 | 100. 00 | 95. 77 | 2. 54 |
| 遵义市 | Zunyi | 地级市 | 30 762 | 744. 02 | 115. 45 | 51. 00 | 6 557 276 | 9 570 | 23 255 | 41. 00 | 85. 60 | 96. 37 | 4. 92 |
| 安顺市 | Anshun | 地级市 | 9 267 | 270. 30 | 41. 34 | 31. 50 | 1 676 482 | 6 617 | 25 563 | | 100. 00 | 73. 17 | 1. 27 |
| 清镇市 | Qingzhen | 县级市 | 1 492 | 50. 10 | 10. 67 | 15. 52 | | | 16 080 | | 100. 00 | 51. 93 | 0. 37 |
| 赤水市 | Chishui | 县级市 | 1 883 | 30. 00 | 7. 22 | 8. 00 | | | 385 | 91. 29 | 93. 75 | 84. 93 | 8. 77 |
| 仁怀市 | Renhuai | 县级市 | 1 788 | 63. 80 | 8. 41 | 10. 00 | | | | 77. 78 | 69. 52 | 72. 88 | 1. 78 |
| 铜仁市 | Tongren | 县级市 | 1 514 | 37. 40 | 13. 12 | 21. 00 | | | 11 305 | 20. 80 | 64. 00 | 82. 05 | 3. 85 |
| 兴义市 | Xingyi | 县级市 | 2 911 | 77. 30 | 14. 34 | 26. 70 | | | 14 592 | 50. 17 | 100. 00 | 92. 81 | 5. 18 |
| 毕节市 | Bijie | 县级市 | 3 412 | 138. 70 | 17. 30 | 20. 00 | | | 11 007 | 94. 68 | 95. 00 | 69. 06 | 0. 45 |

续表

| 城市名称 Name of Cities | | 行政级别 Admini－strative Rank | 行政区土地面积（平方公里）Area of City's Administrative (sq. km) | 年末总人口（万人）Total Population (year-end) (10 thousand) | 非农业人口（万人）Non-agricultural Population (10 thousand) | 建成区面积（平方公里）Area of Built-up District (sq. km) | 地区生产总值（万元）Gross Regional Product (10 000 yuan) | 人均地区生产总值（元）Per Capita Gross Regional Product (yuan) | 市政公用设施固定资产投资总额（万元）Total Fixed Assets Investment in Municipal Service Facilities (10 000 RMB) | 污水处理率（%）Wastewater Treatment Rate(%) | 生活垃圾处理率（%）Domestic Garbage Treatment Rate(%) | 用水普及率（%）Water Coverage Rate(%) | 人均公园绿地面积（平方米）Per Capita Public Green Space (sq. m) |
|---|---|---|---|---|---|---|---|---|---|---|---|---|---|
| 凯里市 | Kaili | 县级市 | 1 306 | 48.20 | 17.90 | 29.41 | | | 9 802 | 64.40 | 98.79 | 85.94 | 4.01 |
| 都匀市 | Duyun | 县级市 | 2 274 | 48.20 | 17.28 | 14.69 | | | 3 443 | | 100.00 | 99.44 | 8.49 |
| 福泉市 | Fuquan | 县级市 | 1 688 | 31.70 | 6.20 | 9.60 | | | 350 | | 98.04 | 97.07 | 10.85 |
| 云南省 | Yunnan | | | | | | | | | | | | |
| 昆明市 | Kunming | 地级市 | 20 832 | 528.52 | 222.37 | 280.20 | 15 116 795 | 25 826 | 255 116 | 72.98 | 97.13 | 99.88 | 7.06 |
| 曲靖市 | Qujing | 地级市 | 28 904 | 608.09 | 75.36 | 37.00 | 7 875 678 | 13 684 | 160 350 | 90.01 | 100.00 | 88.68 | 7.61 |
| 玉溪市 | Yuxi | 地级市 | 15 285 | 212.98 | 33.00 | 22.60 | 5 960 973 | 26 260 | 26 790 | 79.31 | 88.00 | 99.48 | 10.68 |
| 保山市 | Baoshan | 地级市 | 19 637 | 248.22 | 27.09 | 18.60 | 1 940 496 | 7 898 | | 35.71 | 61.28 | 86.42 | 4.32 |
| 昭通市 | Zhaotong | 地级市 | 22 666 | 549.52 | 45.56 | 22.50 | 2 722 801 | 5 162 | 51 978 | 55.18 | 55.00 | 89.67 | 3.27 |
| 丽江市 | Lijiang | 地级市 | 21 219 | 119.49 | 17.55 | 22.00 | 1 011 490 | 8 301 | 9 880 | 66.64 | 100.00 | 87.61 | 27.61 |
| 普洱市 | Puer | 地级市 | 45 385 | 258.10 | 32.27 | 20.00 | 1 798 569 | 6 975 | 1 347 | 37.67 | 100.00 | 82.26 | 2.17 |
| 临沧市 | Lincang | 地级市 | 24 469 | 224.66 | 24.52 | 12.18 | 1 568 740 | 6 605 | 7 326 | | 50.00 | 81.53 | 1.95 |
| 安宁市 | Anning | 县级市 | 1 302 | 26.60 | 14.05 | 19.20 | | | 22 457 | 77.17 | 100.00 | 100.00 | 13.66 |
| 宣威市 | Xuanwei | 县级市 | 6 053 | 144.20 | 14.31 | 24.50 | | | 35 857 | 89.42 | 98.77 | 87.84 | 4.57 |
| 楚雄市 | Chuxiong | 县级市 | 4 482 | 50.60 | 15.31 | 23.00 | | | 10 634 | 91.72 | 100.00 | 93.60 | 10.23 |
| 个旧市 | Gejiu | 县级市 | 1 587 | 39.00 | 21.54 | 12.15 | | | 2 400 | 82.10 | 100.00 | 100.00 | 13.28 |
| 开远市 | Kaiyuan | 县级市 | 1 950 | 26.80 | 10.77 | 19.50 | | | 7 891 | 96.72 | 100.00 | 94.95 | 7.09 |
| 景洪市 | Jinghong | 县级市 | 6 959 | 39.00 | 15.70 | 18.80 | | | 37 661 | 72.17 | 100.00 | 100.00 | 15.18 |
| 大理市 | Dali | 县级市 | 1 815 | 61.40 | 21.63 | 37.53 | | | 33 382 | 95.13 | 100.00 | 94.01 | 6.86 |
| 瑞丽市 | Ruili | 县级市 | 1 020 | 12.20 | 4.72 | 19.00 | | | 8 733 | 56.00 | | 100.00 | 9.01 |
| 潞西市 | Luxi | 县级市 | 2 987 | 35.90 | 7.97 | 15.00 | | | 5 091 | 59.85 | 94.75 | 55.43 | 5.03 |
| 西藏自治区 | Tibet | | | | | | | | | | | | |
| 拉萨市 | Lasa | 地级市 | | 47.72 | 19.41 | 59.00 | 1 420 500 | 20 404 | 24 968 | | 94.81 | 96.39 | 3.32 |
| 日喀则市 | Rikaze | 县级市 | 3 654 | 10.60 | 3.82 | 20.00 | | | | | | 41.61 | 16.30 |
| 陕西省 | Shanxi | | | | | | | | | | | | |

续表

| 城市名称 Name of Cities | | 行政级别 Admini－strative Rank | 行政区土地面积(平方公里) Area of City's Administrative (sq. km) | 年末总人口(万人) Total Population (year-end) (10 thousand) | 非农业人口(万人) Non-agricultural Population (10 thousand) | 建成区面积(平方公里) Area of Built-up District (sq. km) | 地区生产总值(万元) Gross Regional Product (10 000 yuan) | 人均地区生产总值(元) Per Capita Gross Regional Product (yuan) | 市政公用设施固定资产投资总额(万元) Total Fixed Assets Investment in Municipal Service Facilities (10 000 RMB) | 污水处理率(%) Wastewater Treatment Rate(%) | 生活垃圾处理率(%) Domestic Garbage Treatment Rate(%) | 用水普及率(%) Water Coverage Rate(%) | 人均公园绿地面积(平方米) Per Capita Public Green Space (sq. m) |
|---|---|---|---|---|---|---|---|---|---|---|---|---|---|
| 西安市 | Xian | 地级市 | 10 108 | 772.30 | 363.87 | 272.71 | 21 900 400 | 26 259 | 1 681 700 | 65.12 | 90.35 | 100.00 | 7.80 |
| 铜川市 | Tongchuan | 地级市 | 3 882 | 85.06 | 40.26 | 37.36 | 1 286 500 | 15 362 | 30 800 | 59.02 | 98.65 | 92.12 | 7.61 |
| 宝鸡市 | Baoji | 地级市 | 18 172 | 377.95 | 95.25 | 71.35 | 7 140 700 | 18 992 | 61 300 | 89.66 | 100.00 | 99.83 | 12.45 |
| 咸阳市 | Xianyang | 地级市 | 10 196 | 510.45 | 110.63 | 54.55 | 7 645 560 | 15 286 | 37 098 | 70.29 | 100.00 | 98.95 | 9.49 |
| 渭南市 | Weinan | 地级市 | 13 046 | 551.88 | 162.65 | 38.20 | 4 897 150 | 9 535 | 10 283 | 99.88 | 99.50 | 99.17 | 7.61 |
| 延安市 | Yanan | 地级市 | 37 037 | 223.31 | 61.09 | 25.95 | 7 132 720 | 33 332 | 9 372 | 70.74 | 81.67 | 84.99 | 8.53 |
| 汉中市 | Hanzhong | 地级市 | 27 215 | 380.14 | 75.56 | 31.00 | 3 526 120 | 10 049 | 3 317 | 96.00 | 38.46 | 81.97 | 14.29 |
| 榆林市 | Yulin | 地级市 | 43 578 | 353.12 | 64.68 | 36.00 | 10 082 610 | 30 243 | 106 031 | 58.66 | 96.48 | 94.69 | 5.44 |
| 安康市 | Ankang | 地级市 | 23 529 | 301.87 | 47.66 | 29.00 | 2 336 744 | 8 802 | 33 810 | | | 86.38 | 11.20 |
| 商洛市 | Shangluo | 地级市 | 19 292 | 242.48 | 39.85 | 13.10 | 1 740 360 | 7 291 | 38 790 | | 100.00 | 85.71 | 8.93 |
| 兴平市 | Xingping | 县级市 | 509 | 58.40 | 12.04 | 14.80 | | | 21 956 | | | 96.65 | 5.44 |
| 韩城市 | Hancheng | 县级市 | 1 621 | 39.30 | 19.91 | 17.72 | | | 6 450 | | | 99.64 | 7.74 |
| 华阴市 | Huayin | 县级市 | 817 | 26.10 | 14.37 | 18.00 | | | 10 100 | | 100.00 | 95.05 | 4.95 |
| 甘肃省 | Gansu | | | | | | | | | | | | |
| 兰州市 | Lanzhou | 地级市 | 13 085 | 322.28 | 201.63 | 182.88 | 8 462 811 | 25 628 | 333 251 | 61.04 | 100.00 | 92.14 | 9.33 |
| 嘉峪关市 | Jiayuguan | 地级市 | 2 935 | 18.59 | 16.52 | 42.30 | 1 441 043 | 69 415 | 12 605 | 66.57 | 100.00 | 100.00 | 14.29 |
| 金昌市 | Jinchang | 地级市 | 8 896 | 47.29 | 22.68 | 31.58 | 1 944 259 | 41 231 | 15 027 | 64.95 | 100.00 | 90.40 | 15.41 |
| 白银市 | Baiyin | 地级市 | 21 158 | 178.06 | 45.27 | 51.00 | 2 442 835 | 13 954 | 8 494 | 49.08 | 51.52 | 96.69 | 6.27 |
| 天水市 | Tianshui | 地级市 | 14 359 | 357.21 | 96.79 | 42.24 | 2 265 698 | 6 626 | 10 181 | 61.32 | 100.00 | 75.87 | 5.46 |
| 武威市 | Wuwei | 地级市 | 33 238 | 197.60 | 35.74 | 24.64 | 2 101 088 | 11 021 | 1 067 | 83.33 | 94.00 | 88.71 | 3.94 |
| 张掖市 | Zhangye | 地级市 | 41 924 | 129.56 | 35.33 | 27.83 | 1 698 559 | 13 285 | 3 346 | 77.00 | 89.88 | 92.31 | 12.31 |
| 平凉市 | Pingliang | 地级市 | 11 170 | 228.23 | 35.40 | 36.00 | 1 750 618 | 7 982 | 28 806 | 65.18 | 96.07 | 96.67 | 7.95 |
| 酒泉市 | Jiuquan | 地级市 | 193 974 | 95.80 | 33.10 | 36.00 | 2 480 173 | 24 759 | 16 435 | 66.00 | 82.87 | 72.73 | 8.34 |
| 庆阳市 | Qingyang | 地级市 | 27 119 | 258.23 | 31.21 | 16.34 | 2 484 991 | 9 872 | 13 040 | 32.39 | 88.39 | 96.22 | 2.97 |
| 定西市 | Dingxi | 地级市 | 20 330 | 297.81 | 31.75 | 22.83 | 1 056 400 | 3 602 | 21 119 | 71.15 | 62.79 | 89.39 | 9.17 |

续表

| 城市名称 Name of Cities | | 行政级别 Admini－strative Rank | 行政区土地面积（平方公里）Area of City's Administrative（sq. km） | 年末总人口（万人）Total Population（year-end）（10 thousand） | 非农业人口（万人）Non-agricultural Population（10 thousand） | 建成区面积（平方公里）Area of Built-up District（sq. km） | 地区生产总值（万元）Gross Regional Product（10 000 yuan） | 人均地区生产总值（元）Per Capita Gross Regional Product（yuan） | 市政公用设施固定资产投资总额（万元）Total Fixed Assets Investment in Municipal Service Facilities（10 000 RMB） | 污水处理率（%）Wastewater Treatment Rate（%） | 生活垃圾处理率（%）Domestic Garbage Treatment Rate（%） | 用水普及率（%）Water Coverage Rate（%） | 人均公园绿地面积（平方米）Per Capita Public Green Space（sq. m） |
|---|---|---|---|---|---|---|---|---|---|---|---|---|---|
| 陇南市 | Longnan | 地级市 | 27 915 | 277.44 | 42.27 | 6.59 | 1 216 011 | 4 396 | 12 232 | | 100.00 | 48.73 | 1.30 |
| 玉门市 | Yumen | 县级市 | 13 496 | 18.20 | 8.41 | 23.18 | | | 3 988 | 11.11 | 96.77 | 95.60 | 10.32 |
| 敦煌市 | Dunhuang | 县级市 | 31 200 | 18.30 | 4.04 | 14.89 | | | 11 390 | 27.84 | 96.00 | 95.96 | 8.46 |
| 临夏市 | Linxia | 县级市 | 88 | 22.20 | 12.16 | 14.00 | | | 22 734 | 70.00 | 91.67 | 76.59 | 1.04 |
| 合作市 | Hezuo | 县级市 | 2 291 | 9.10 | 5.32 | 8.98 | | | 2 813 | 70.32 | | 81.37 | 3.07 |
| 青海省 | Qinghai | | | | | | | | | | | | |
| 西宁市 | Xining | 地级市 | 7 649 | 217.79 | 115.05 | 64.92 | 4 221 885 | 19 494 | 101 232 | 53.78 | 92.70 | 100.00 | 9.25 |
| 格尔木市 | Geermu | 县级市 | 118 954 | 21.20 | 9.53 | 30.51 | | | 17 128 | 30.27 | 95.83 | 100.00 | 4.51 |
| 德令哈市 | Delingha | 县级市 | 27 358 | 7.00 | 4.18 | 15.22 | | | 26 887 | | 96.08 | 100.00 | 5.50 |
| 宁夏回族自治区 | Ningxia | | | | | | | | | | | | |
| 银川市 | Yinchuan | 地级市 | 9 555 | 152.27 | 98.13 | 110.77 | 5 141 138 | 31 436 | 101 733 | 87.61 | 100.00 | 89.03 | 8.40 |
| 石嘴山市 | Shizuishan | 地级市 | 5 310 | 74.04 | 44.20 | 94.20 | 2 287 270 | 32 102 | 68 283 | 31.11 | | 100.00 | 21.50 |
| 吴忠市 | Wuzhong | 地级市 | 20 394 | 135.68 | 41.23 | 24.49 | 1 729 879 | 12 982 | 30 512 | 89.91 | 98.78 | 85.64 | 14.31 |
| 固原市 | Guyuan | 地级市 | 12 849 | 148.36 | 20.59 | 31.95 | 757 929 | 5 108 | 8 775 | 74.03 | 43.96 | 73.29 | 3.00 |
| 中卫市 | Zhongwei | 地级市 | 17 391 | 114.17 | 27.30 | 25.78 | 1 191 009 | 10 498 | 9 467 | 89.94 | 82.72 | 67.40 | 11.07 |
| 灵武市 | Lingwu | 县级市 | 4 529 | 23.40 | 10.93 | 6.89 | | | 10 184 | 90.06 | 100.00 | 73.85 | 8.15 |
| 青铜峡市 | Qingtongxia | 县级市 | 2 445 | 26.80 | 7.98 | 16.81 | | | 25 696 | 96.17 | 83.33 | 99.20 | 12.31 |
| 新疆维吾尔自治区 | Xinjiang | | | | | | | | | | | | |
| 乌鲁木齐市 | Urumuchi | 地级市 | 14 216 | 236.05 | 174.48 | 302.80 | 10 203 488 | 37 343 | 211 596 | 58.98 | 91.75 | 86.27 | 6.00 |
| 克拉玛依市 | Kelamayi | 地级市 | 9 548 | 38.62 | 26.83 | 53.29 | 6 612 062 | 100 216 | 107 064 | 91.15 | 100.00 | 100.00 | 8.72 |
| 吐鲁番市 | Tulufan | 县级市 | 13 589 | 27.00 | 8.62 | 9.03 | | | 1 791 | 60.65 | 100.00 | 98.02 | 2.38 |
| 哈密市 | Hami | 县级市 | 85 035 | 44.00 | 29.26 | 34.00 | | | 52 525 | 41.74 | 100.00 | 100.00 | 7.74 |
| 昌吉市 | Changji | 县级市 | 8 385 | 36.10 | 22.77 | 30.09 | | | 40 222 | 100.00 | 100.00 | 100.00 | 9.38 |
| 阜康市 | Fukang | 县级市 | 11 726 | 16.90 | 9.64 | 6.29 | | | 15 724 | 90.91 | 100.00 | 90.23 | 7.03 |
| 博乐市 | Bole | 县级市 | 7 956 | 26.30 | 15.76 | 14.01 | | | 8 499 | 100.00 | 90.13 | 99.29 | 17.43 |

续表

| 城市名称 Name of Cities | | 行政级别 Admini－strative Rank | 行政区土地面积(平方公里) Area of City's Administrative (sq. km) | 年末总人口(万人) Total Population (year-end) (10 thousand) | 非农业人口(万人) Non-agricultural Population (10 thousand) | 建成区面积(平方公里) Area of Built-up District (sq. km) | 地区生产总值(万元) Gross Regional Product (10 000 yuan) | 人均地区生产总值(元) Per Capita Gross Regional Product (yuan) | 市政公用设施固定资产投资总额(万元) Total Fixed Assets Investment in Municipal Service Facilities (10 000 RMB) | 污水处理率(%) Wastewater Treatment Rate(%) | 生活垃圾处理率(%) Domestic Garbage Treatment Rate(%) | 用水普及率(%) Water Coverage Rate(%) | 人均公园绿地面积(平方米) Per Capita Public Green Space (sq. m) |
|---|---|---|---|---|---|---|---|---|---|---|---|---|---|
| 库尔勒市 | Kuerle | 县级市 | 7 219 | 48. 50 | 31. 00 | 45. 53 | | | 38 552 | 99. 15 | 100. 00 | 100. 00 | 9. 02 |
| 阿克苏市 | Akesu | 县级市 | 18 000 | 46. 50 | 25. 05 | 28. 10 | | | 54 830 | 100. 00 | 100. 00 | 100. 00 | 9. 70 |
| 阿图什市 | Atushi | 县级市 | 16 151 | 23. 40 | 7. 65 | 8. 30 | | | 3 399 | 75. 66 | 93. 33 | 94. 10 | 2. 13 |
| 喀什市 | Kashi | 县级市 | 555 | 45. 10 | 26. 44 | 41. 55 | | | 15 139 | 100. 00 | 100. 00 | 100. 00 | 8. 89 |
| 和田市 | Hetian | 县级市 | 496 | 28. 50 | 12. 44 | 17. 32 | | | 1 160 | 80. 05 | 82. 50 | 96. 35 | 9. 98 |
| 伊宁市 | Yining | 县级市 | 525 | 45. 20 | 30. 56 | 35. 61 | | | 30 043 | 67. 04 | 95. 26 | 100. 00 | 8. 01 |
| 奎屯市 | Kuitun | 县级市 | 1 110 | 15. 20 | 27. 83 | 24. 56 | | | 24 037 | 67. 34 | 100. 00 | 100. 00 | 9. 19 |
| 塔城市 | Tacheng | 县级市 | 4 353 | 14. 90 | 10. 51 | 13. 80 | | | 8 759 | 86. 67 | 90. 59 | 90. 18 | 14. 66 |
| 乌苏市 | Wusu | 县级市 | 13 729 | 21. 90 | 7. 84 | 15. 99 | | | 5 105 | 81. 72 | 86. 67 | 89. 94 | 6. 15 |
| 阿勒泰市 | Aletai | 县级市 | 10 829 | 19. 50 | 15. 01 | 10. 62 | | | 2 806 | 100. 00 | 97. 11 | 97. 49 | 18. 46 |
| 石河子市 | Shihezi | 县级市 | 7 762 | 63. 20 | 54. 53 | 27. 05 | | | 6 371 | 75. 53 | 100. 00 | 100. 00 | 10. 70 |
| 阿拉尔市 | Alaer | 县级市 | 4 196 | 17. 50 | 11. 95 | 11. 98 | | | 3 040 | | 92. 86 | 94. 69 | 11. 88 |
| 图木舒克市 | Tumushuke | 县级市 | 1 901 | 15. 00 | 13. 72 | 6. 88 | | | 2 135 | 92. 17 | | 53. 18 | 30. 34 |
| 五家渠市 | Wujiaqu | 县级市 | 711 | 9. 30 | 8. 70 | 14. 16 | | | 10 876 | | | 97. 24 | 7. 76 |

(本统计数据和资料均未包括香港特别行政区、澳门特别行政区和台湾省)

## 一、数据来源（Data Resources）

1. 行政区土地面积（Area of city's administrative）

2. 年末总人口（Total population（year-end））

3. 地级及以上城市地区生产总值（Gross regional product）

来源：国家统计局城市社会经济调查司编，《中国城市统计年鉴—2009》，北京：中国统计出版社，2010.2。（注：该统计年鉴未发表2008年全国386个县级市的地区生产总值。）

4. 建成区面积（Area of built-up district）

5. 市政公用设施固定资产投资总额（Total fixed assets investment in municipal service facilities）

6. 污水处理率（Wastewater treatment rate）

7. 生活垃圾处理率（Domestic garbage treatment rate）

8. 用水普及率（Water coverage rate）

9. 人均公园绿地面积（Per capita public green space）

来源：住房和城乡建设部计划财务与外事司编，《中国城市建设统计年鉴（2008年）》，北京：中国建筑工业出版社，2009.9

10. 人均地区生产总值（Per capita gross regional product）

地级及以上城市人均地区生产总值来源于《中国城市统计年鉴—2009》。

（注：2008年全国386个县级市的人均地区生产总值空缺。）

11. 非农业人口（Non-agricultural population）

地级及以上城市（不包括山东地级及以上城市）非农业人口来源于《中国城市统计年鉴—2009》。

山东地级及以上城市、全国县级市非农业人口来源：住房和城乡建设部城乡规划司，住房和城乡建设部城乡规划管理中心编，《2008年全国设市城市及其人口统计资料（内部资料）》，2009.10

## 二、指标解释

1. 行政区域土地面积：是指在该行政区划内的全部土地面积（包括水面面积）。计算土地面积是以行政区划为准。

——《中国城市统计年鉴—2009》. p481

2. 年末总人口：是指本市本年12月31日24时的人口总数。

——《中国城市统计年鉴—2009》. p481

3. 非农业人口：

其中，地级及以上城市（不包括山东地级及以上城市）的非农业人口所采用的定义是“指从事农业以外的职业维持生活的人口以及由他们抚养的人口，采用按农业、非农业分类的户籍统计口径。”

——《中国城市统计年鉴—2009》. p481

山东地级及以上城市、全国县级市非农业人口则主要摘自公安部编2008年《全国分县市人口统计资料》。

——《2008年全国设市城市及其人口统计资料（内部资料）》. p1

4. 建成区面积：城市建成区内实际已成片开发建设、市政公用设施和公共设施基本具备的区域。对核心城市，它包括集中连片的部分以及分散的若干个已经成片建设起来，市政公用设施和公共设施基本具备的地区；对一城多镇来说，它包括由几个连片开发建设起来的，市政公用设施和公共设施基本具备的地区组成。因此建成区范围，一般是指建成区外轮廓线所能包括的地区，也就是这个城市实际建设用地所达到的范围。

——《中国城市建设统计年鉴（2008年）》. p787

5. 地区生产总值：指按市场价格计算的一个国家（地区）所有常住单位在一定时期内生产活动的最终

成果。

——《中国城市统计年鉴—2009》. p481

6. 污水处理率：指报告期内污水处理总量与污水排放总量的比率。计算公式：

污水处理率 = 污水处理总量/污水排放总量 ×100%

——《中国城市建设统计年鉴（2008 年）》. p786

7. 生活垃圾处理率：指报告期内生活垃圾处理量与生活垃圾产出量的比率。计算公式：

生活垃圾处理率 = 生活垃圾处理量/生活垃圾产生量 ×100%

在统计时，由于生活垃圾产生量不易取得，用清运量代替。

——《中国城市建设统计年鉴（2008 年）》. p787

8. 用水普及率：指报告期末城区内用水人口与总人口的比率。计算公式为：

用水普及率 = 城区用水人口/（城区人口 + 城区暂住人口）×100%

——《中国城市建设统计年鉴（2008 年）》. p786

9. 人均公园绿地面积：指报告期末城区内平均每人拥有的公园绿地面积。计算公式：

人均公园绿地面积 = 城区公园绿地面积/（城区人口 + 城区暂住人口）

——《中国城市建设统计年鉴（2008 年）》. p787

**注：**

1. 2007 年 1 月 21 日，国务院发布《国务院关于同意云南省思茅市及相关县区更名的批复》，在《中国城市建设统计年鉴（2008 年）》和《2008 年全国设市城市及其人口统计资料》中已更名为普洱市；但《中国城市统计年鉴—2009》仍沿用思茅市的称谓。在本次“2008 年中国城市基本数据”的统计工作中，统一采用“普洱市”这一称谓。

2. 目前，由于各城市户籍改革步伐进展不一，一些地区已经把暂住人口完全纳入当地人口管理范畴，而另一些地区则仍维持原来的户籍人口管理办法，把暂住人口排除在外，导致各城市总人口概念差异较大。因此，本统计中的总人口及在此基础上计算出的各项人均指标均采用所引资料中的定义，可能与其他渠道统计数据存在出入，仅供参考。

（数据收集整理：毛其智，清华大学教授，国际欧亚科学院院士；厉基巍，清华大学建筑学院博士研究生）

# 附录4　中国最具幸福感城市调查推选活动简介

## 一、2010 年活动情况简述

### 1. 活动概述

2010 年 10 月 8 日“创造幸福，享受尊严”，为全面彰显党的十七大以来科学发展与和谐社会建设成果，展现民众的幸福生活，由《瞭望东方周刊》与中国市长协会《中国城市发展报告》工作委员会联合主办的“2010 年中国最具幸福感城市调查推选活动”启动。

### 2. 评价体系与新增项目

为了进一步保障调查和推选活动的科学性、公正性、严谨性，提高调查结果的公信力。2010 年，组委会再次邀请美国芝加哥大学幸福学课题组对调查体系及内容进行了调整和完善，增加了有关民生建设与保障方面的内容，将 12 项指标扩展到 20 项，以期更加全面地了解影响市民幸福度的因素。同时，为了使调查活动科学、完整，采用了入户调查和公共调查两种不同的调研方式，了解居民对于自住城市的幸福感知，并特别增设了候选城市材料申报的环节。

### 3. 调查范围

调查范围为大陆地区的 60 个地级城市和 60 个县级城市。组委会根据全国综合实力前 100 名的地级以上城市和综合竞争力百强县，以及排名以外的地级和县级城市的自荐和推荐情况，划定了候选城市范围。

地级以上候选城市 60 座：上海、北京、天津、重庆、深圳、广州、南京、大连、杭州、沈阳、哈尔滨、成都、东莞、济南、佛山、无锡、长沙、武汉、宁波、长春、苏州、青岛、珠海、大庆、福州、厦门、石家庄、常州、郑州、秦皇岛、烟台、乌鲁木齐、西安、合肥、南宁、呼和浩特、东营、昆明、威海、中山、南昌、绍兴、太原、惠州、温州、徐州、扬州、淄博、镇江、鞍山、保定、银川、南通、鄂尔多斯、洛阳、嘉兴、大同、海口、包头、通化。

县级候选城市60座：江阴市、昆山市、张家港市、常熟市、晋江市、吴江市、慈溪市、绍兴县、宜兴市、荣成市、余姚市、义乌市、太仓市、诸暨市、温岭市、文登市、福清市、乐清市、增城市、瑞安市、海宁市、邹城市、龙口市、桐乡市、胶南市、丹阳市、即墨市、富阳市、寿光市、胶州市、滕州市、南安市、章丘市、平度市、惠安县、海门市、海城市、莱州市、通州市、新泰市、库尔勒市、上虞市、迁安市、双流县、巩义市、瓦房店市、平湖市、石狮市、兖州市、诸城市、泰兴市、启东市、长沙县、溧阳市、遵化市、江都市、招远市、东阳市、临海市、扬中市。

组委会采用随机抽样入户访问和公共调查（网络、报纸）两种方式对居民进行调查。入户调查中每个城市收集200个有效问卷，总计样本数量为24000个。公共调查中，网络调查收集有效样本数1789645份，报纸调查收集有效样本数1673225份。网络投票数5853821份。总样本数创历史新高。

**4. 活动影响**

为了扩大活动的影响，提升当选城市的品牌形象。结果产生以后，组委会在长沙举行了隆重的颁奖典礼，并通过20个当选城市的电视台向全国现场直播典礼盛况，超过1亿电视观众收看节目。颁奖典礼中一个重要的环节是当选城市的杰出市民为城市市长颁奖，这是此项活动的一个亮点，体现了活动的宗旨是由人民大众评价自己的城市。

本次调查是四年来规模最大、参与人数最多、影响力最大的一次城市调查推选活动。评选进程及调查结果吸引了大量媒体的关注，并引发了一系列关于城市民生建设与保障内容人情味、交通状况、医疗条件、教育质量、自然环境、房屋价格、物价水平以及幸福与尊严话题等各方面的问题讨论，社会反响强烈。共有超过300家网络媒体、15家中央媒体、100家地方媒体对本次活动及相关事件进行了报道，新闻传播覆盖范围广，基本覆盖了全国与地方的重要媒体。

**5. 获奖城市**

本次调查的最终结果根据入户调查、公共调查（报纸网络调查）的数据，并参考城市材料申报的内容产生。活动历时两个月，推选结果于2010年12月26日在长沙揭晓。杭州、成都、长沙、昆明、南京、长春、重庆、广州、无锡、通化获得地级及以上“2010年中国最具幸福感城市”，江阴、宜兴、长沙县、余姚、滕州、铜梁县、海城、太仓、莱州、胶州获得县级“2010年中国最具幸福感城市”。其中，杭州市、成都市同时获得中国最具幸福感城市最高荣誉奖——民生贡献特别大奖，昆明市、长春市、长沙市获得中国最具幸福感城市金奖，长沙市还获得民生满意大奖。县级市中，宜兴市、余姚市获得民生贡献大奖。

## 二、中国最具幸福感城市评价体系解读

务实与发展是当今世界发展的主旋律，经济的发展程度经常决定一个国家或地区在世界

上的话语权。国家追求经济发展，企业追求经济回报，个人追求经济地位，但是经济就真的是一切终极目的吗？大多数人思考一下，应该都会予以否定。经济只是一个手段或过程，我们追求的终极目标应该是人生的幸福。幸福是一种对生活的满足，是感到生活有巨大乐趣并自然地希望持续的愉快心情。就如马斯洛需求理论一样，对于一些发展比较落后的国家或者个人，经济的提高当然能够提高幸福度。但是，当经济发展到一定阶段的时候，经济与幸福之间的关系会大大减弱。比如，在美国过去的50年中，人均GDP翻了3倍，但主观幸福感却没有提高多少。

经过几代人的努力，中国的经济飞速发展，GDP年均增长近10%，即使在经济危机的大环境下仍然能够保持8%的增长率。但与此同时，对于幸福感的质疑却越来越明显，流行的词汇也都是像“房奴”、“杯具”（“悲剧”的谐音）这样的负面词汇。人们对于幸福感的质疑越来越明显。

我们不禁反思到，经济增长与否、经济增长快慢，并不能代表社会和谐、健康发展的程度，我们应该更加关注社会总体幸福感的增长程度。而人们主观幸福感的高低在很大程度上取决于很多和经济无直接关系的因素，例如情感状况、社交关系、生活环境。为了探求我国全民的主观幸福度现状及改进方向，我们对全国各地的幸福感进行客观的调研及分析，把研究重点放在调研对象的主观感受上，即了解他们想到城市某个方面时的主观感受如何。研究采用直接调研和侧面了解两种方式，一方面了解居民对自己所在城市的感知，另一方面了解居民对其他城市的感知，并结合两个方面进行对比分析。具体调研方式采用网络调研、实地调研、传统媒介调研等多种方式进行。

研究采用的是美国芝加哥大学奚恺元教授提出的城市幸福学评估体系。奚恺云教授是最早系统地将幸福学和幸福指数引入中国，并在中国倡导研究城市幸福感的学者。

**1. 研究目的**

（1）采用入户调查、网络调查和报纸调查三种方式探索地级市和县级市不同城市市民的生活总体幸福度和城市具体幸福度；

（2）探索市民对其他城市的幸福度的预期；

（3）探索市民对其他城市的幸福度预期与该城市的实际幸福度的异同点。

针对上述研究目标，本次研究主要分为三个部分，即地级市和县级市市民对自住城市幸福度的评估、市民对其他城市的幸福度的预期、对于其他城市幸福度的投票结果与自住城市幸福度的调查结果比较。考虑到地级市和县级市在经济、人口等因素上的差别，本次研究中，所有的比较研究都对两者分别研究。

**2. 生活总体幸福度**

一个城市的市民是否觉得自己幸福是多方面的，它涉及诸如交际、职业发展、生活等多个方面。为了相对准确地衡量出他的生活总体幸福度，需要考虑到多个方面的影响。本次研究测量了市民在人情味、交通状况、医疗的便利程度和质量、教育质量、文体设施、餐饮及娱乐设施、购物便利性、治安状况、气候、污染程度、自然环境、城区建设、赚钱机会、房价、房价以外的物价、经济发展、生活节奏、工作压力、市民文明程度和文化底蕴具体方面的幸福度。最后采取将各个指标的分数加总从而得到总分的方式获得总体幸福度，虽然简单但是客观，同时回避了一些问卷设计的偏差和受调研者对问卷感知的偏差。

具体幸福度指标体系包括20项评价指标，详见下表：

表1 幸福度指标体系

| 评价指标 | 指标解释 |
| --- | --- |
| 人情味 | 受调研者对当地人情味浓厚感到的幸福程度 |
| 交通状况 | 受调研者对当地整体交通状况感到的幸福程度 |
| 医疗的便利程度和质量 | 受调研者对当地医疗的便利程度和质量感到的幸福程度 |
| 教育质量 | 受调研者对当地学校质量、教学质量等感到的幸福程度 |
| 文体设施 | 受调研者对当地文化体育设施等感到的幸福程度 |
| 餐饮及娱乐设施 | 受调查者对当地的餐饮设计，以及娱乐设施的便利感到的幸福程度 |
| 购物便利 | 受调研者对购买各种生活相关产品的便利程度感到的幸福程度 |
| 治安状况 | 受调研者对当地整体的治安状况感到的幸福程度 |
| 气候 | 受调研者对当地的气温及天气舒适度感到的幸福程度 |
| 污染程度 | 受调研者对当地的空气、水质及道路干净程度等感到的幸福程度 |
| 自然环境 | 受调研者对当地的绿化、山水等感到的幸福程度 |
| 城区建设 | 受调研者对当地的建筑、街道设计建设等感到的幸福程度 |
| 赚钱机会 | 受调研者对当地就业机会与赚钱机会感到的幸福程度 |
| 房屋价格 | 受调研者对当地房屋价格感到的幸福程度 |
| 房价以外的物价 | 受调研者对当地除房价以外的其他物价感到的幸福程度 |
| 经济发展 | 受调研者对当地近年来经济方面发展感到的幸福程度 |
| 生活节奏 | 受调研者对当地的生活节奏感到的幸福程度 |
| 工作压力 | 受调研者对当地工作的压力感到的幸福程度 |
| 市民文明程度 | 受调研者对当地居民整体文明程度感到的幸福程度 |
| 文化底蕴 | 受调研者对当地的历史、传统等感到的幸福程度 |

**3. 历届中国最具幸福感城市调查推选活动获奖名单为**

2007年

杭州、沈阳、中山、宁波、青岛、台州、珠海、上海、北京、成都。

2008年

杭州、宁波、昆明、天津、唐山、佛山、绍兴、长春、无锡、长沙。

2009年

地级市：西安、南京、昆明、宁波、杭州、成都、银川、长沙、南昌、长春。

县级市：山东邹平县、江苏宜兴市、江苏吴江市、湖南长沙县、江苏江都市、浙江余姚市、云南安宁市、四川都江堰市、辽宁海城市、广东增城市。

2010年

地级市：杭州、成都、长沙、昆明、南京、长春、重庆、广州、通化、无锡。

县级市：浙江江阴市、浙江宜兴市、湖南长沙县、浙江余姚市、山东滕州市、重庆铜梁县、辽宁海城市、江苏太仓市、山东莱州市、山东胶州市。

（作者：新华社《瞭望东方周刊》，中国市长协会《中国城市发展报告》工作委员会）

# 附录5　中国历史文化名街名单

为进一步推进城市文化建设和文化遗产保护，全面落实科学发展观，经中华人民共和国文化部、国家文物局批准，由中国文化报社、中国文物报社等联合举办“中国历史文化名街”推介活动。该活动已于2009年、2010年连续举办两届，共评选出20条中国历史文化名街。

**第一批中国历史文化名街（共10条）**

北京市国子监街
山西省平遥县南大街
黑龙江省哈尔滨市中央大街
江苏省苏州市平江路
安徽省黄山市屯溪老街
福建省福州市三坊七巷
山东省青岛市八大关
山东省青州市昭德古街
海南省海口市骑楼街（区）（海口骑楼老街）
西藏自治区拉萨市八廓街

**第二批中国历史文化名街（共10条）**

江苏省无锡市清名桥历史文化街区
重庆市沙坪坝区磁器口古镇传统历史文化街区
上海市虹口区多伦路文化名人街
江苏省扬州市东关街
天津市和平区五大道
江苏省苏州市山塘街
黑龙江省齐齐哈尔市昂昂溪罗西亚大街
北京市烟袋斜街
福建省漳州市历史文化街区（漳州古街）
福建省泉州市中山路

（资料整理：廖远涛，陶琳，广州市城市规划勘测设计研究院）

# 附录6　国家城市湿地公园名录

为更好地保护和利用湿地公园，对城市湿地公园进行有效的跟踪监督管理，住房和城乡建设部于2008年（建城［2008］117号），2009年（建城［2009］277号），2010年（建城［2010］214号）分别公布第五批、第六批、第七批国家城市湿地公园，共14处。

**第五批国家城市湿地公园（共4处）**

吉林省镇赉县南湖

江苏省昆山市城市生态公园

江西省新余市孔目江

广东省湛江市绿塘河

**第六批国家城市湿地公园（共7处）**

浙江省台州市鉴洋湖城市湿地公园

河南省平顶山市平西湖城市湿地公园

河南省平顶山市白鹭洲城市湿地公园

贵州省贵阳市花溪城市湿地公园

甘肃省张掖市城北城市湿地公园

辽宁省铁岭市莲花湖城市湿地公园

黑龙江省哈尔滨市群力城市湿地公园

**第七批国家城市湿地公园（共3处）**

江苏省南京市高淳县固城湖城市湿地公园

山东省昌邑市潍水风情湿地公园

福建省厦门市杏林湾湿地公园

（资料整理：廖远涛，陶琳，广州市城市规划勘测设计研究院）

# 附录7　第七批国家级风景名胜区名单

风景名胜区是中华民族珍贵的、不可再生的自然文化遗产。为强调开发利用与资源保护的关系，科学规划、统一管理地做好风景名胜资源的保护和管理工作，国务院于2009年12月28日（国函［2009］152号）公布了第七批国家级风景名胜区名单，共计21处。

**黑龙江省**

太阳岛风景名胜区

**浙江省**

天姥山风景名胜区

**福建省**

佛子山风景名胜区

宝山风景名胜区

福安白云山风景名胜区

**江西省**

灵山风景名胜区

**河南省**

桐柏山—淮源风景名胜区

郑州黄河风景名胜区

**湖南省**

苏仙岭—万华岩风景名胜区

南山风景名胜区

万佛山—侗寨风景名胜区

虎形山—花瑶风景名胜区

东江湖风景名胜区

**广东省**

梧桐山风景名胜区

**贵州省**

平塘风景名胜区

榕江苗山侗水风景名胜区

石阡温泉群风景名胜区

沿河乌江山峡风景名胜区

瓮安江界河风景名胜区

**西藏自治区**

纳木错—念青唐古拉山风景名胜区

唐古拉山—怒江源风景名胜区

（资料整理：廖远涛，陶琳，广州市城市规划勘测设计研究院）

# 附录8　第五批中国历史文化名镇（村）

为进一步加强对历史文化名镇名村的保护，更好地保护、继承和发展我国优秀建筑历史文化遗产，弘扬民族传统和地方特色，让文物保护真正实现可持续发展，根据《中国历史文化名镇（村）评选办法》（建村［2003］199号）等规定，在各地初步考核和推荐的基础上，经专家评审并按《中国历史文化名镇（村）评价指标体系》审核，住房和城乡建设部、国家文物局于2010年7月22日（建规［2010］150号）公布了第五批中国历史文化名镇（村）名单，共99个。其中，历史文化名镇38个，历史文化名村61个。

## 第五批中国历史文化名镇名村名单

**山西省（共12个）**

天镇县新平堡镇
阳城县润城镇
太原市晋源区晋源镇店头村
阳泉市义井镇大阳泉村
泽州县北义城镇西黄石村
高平市河西镇苏庄村
沁水县郑村镇湘峪村
宁武县涔山乡王化沟村
太谷县北洸镇北洸村
灵石县两渡镇冷泉村
万荣县高村乡阎景村
新绛县泽掌镇光村

**福建省（共11个）**

宁德市蕉城区霍童镇
平和县九峰镇
武夷山市五夫镇
顺昌县元坑镇
长汀县三洲乡三洲村
龙岩市新罗区适中镇中心村
屏南县棠口乡漈头村
连城县庙前镇芷溪村
长乐市航城街道琴江村
泰宁县新桥乡大源村
福州市马尾区亭江镇闽安村

**浙江省（共11个）**

景宁畲族自治县鹤溪镇
海宁市盐官镇
建德市大慈岩镇新叶村
永嘉县岩坦镇屿北村
金华市金东区傅村镇山头下村
仙居市白塔镇高迁村
庆元县松源镇大济村
乐清市仙溪镇南阁村

宁海县茶院乡许家山村

金华市婺城区汤溪镇寺平村

绍兴县稽东镇冢斜村

**江苏省（共6个）**

苏州市吴中区东山镇

无锡市锡山区荡口镇

兴化市沙沟镇

江阴市长泾镇

张家港市凤凰镇

无锡市惠山区玉祁镇礼社村

**江西省（共6个）**

吉安市青原区富田镇

吉安市吉州区兴桥镇钓源村

金溪县双塘镇竹桥村

龙南县关西镇关西村

婺源县浙源乡虹关村

浮梁县勒功乡沧溪村

**广东省（共6个）**

中山市黄圃镇

大埔县百侯镇

仁化县石塘镇石塘村

梅县水车镇茶山村

佛冈县龙山镇上岳古围村

佛山市南海区西樵镇松塘村

**湖南省（共6个）**

绥宁县寨市镇

泸溪县浦市镇

双牌县理家坪乡坦田村

祁阳县潘市镇龙溪村

永兴县高亭乡板梁村

辰溪县上蒲溪瑶族乡五宝田村

**上海市（共4个）**

嘉定区南翔镇

浦东新区高桥镇

青浦区练塘镇

金山区张堰镇

**四川省（共4个）**

屏山县龙华镇

富顺县赵化镇

犍为县清溪镇

阆中市天宫乡天宫院村

**云南省（共4个）**

宾川县州城镇

洱源县凤羽镇

蒙自县新安所镇

祥云县云南驿镇云南驿村

**贵州省（共4个）**

三都县都江镇怎雷村

安顺市西秀区大西桥镇鲍屯村

雷山县郎德镇上郎德村

务川县大坪镇龙潭村

**重庆市（共3个）**

荣昌县路孔镇

江津区白沙镇

巫溪县宁厂镇

**海南省（共3个）**

三亚市崖城镇保平村

定安县龙湖镇高林村

文昌市会文镇十八行村

**湖北省（共3个）**

潜江市熊口镇

赤壁市赵李桥镇羊楼洞村
宣恩县椒园镇庆阳坝村

**河北省（共3个）**
武安市冶陶镇
邯郸市涉县固新镇
井陉县南障城镇大梁江村

**安徽省（共2个）**
休宁县商山乡黄村
黟县碧阳镇关麓村

**陕西省（共2个）**
商洛市柞水县凤凰镇
宁强县青木川镇

**新疆维吾尔自治区（共2个）**
哈密市五堡乡博斯坦村
特克斯县喀拉达拉乡琼库什台村

**北京市（共1个）**
顺义区龙湾屯镇焦庄户村

**天津市（共1个）**
蓟县渔阳镇西井峪村

**山东省（共1个）**
淄博市周村区王村镇李家疃村

**甘肃省（共1个）**
榆中县金崖镇

**河南省（共1个）**
郏县冢头镇

**广西壮族自治区（共1个）**
南宁市江南区江西镇扬美村

**青海省（共1个）**
玉树县仲达乡电达村

（资料整理：廖远涛，陶琳，广州市城市规划勘测设计研究院）

# 附录9　国家园林城市、县城、城镇名单

## 一、园林城市名单（180个）

第一批3个（1992年）：北京市、合肥市、珠海市。

第二批2个（1994年）：杭州市、深圳市。

第三批3个（1996年）：马鞍山市、威海市、中山市。

第四批4个（1997年）：大连市、南京市、厦门市、南宁市。

第五批7个（1999年）：青岛市、濮阳市、十堰市、佛山市、三明市、秦皇岛市、烟台市。

第六批16个（2002年）：江门市、惠州市、茂名市、肇庆市、海口市、三亚市、襄樊市、石河子市、常熟市、长春市、济南市、常德市、葫芦岛市、洛阳市、漯河市、峨眉山市。

第七批17个（2003年）：上海市、宁波市、福州市、唐山市、吉林市、无锡市、扬州市、苏州市、绍兴市、桂林市、绵阳市、荣成市、张家港市、昆山市、富阳市、开平市、都江堰市。

第八批31个（2005年）：武汉市、郑州市、邯郸市、廊坊市、长治市、晋城市、包头市、伊春市、日照市、淄博市、寿光市、新泰市、胶南市、徐州市、镇江市、吴江市、宜兴市、安庆市、嘉兴市、泉州市、漳州市、许昌市、南阳市、宜昌市、岳阳市、湛江市、安宁市、遵义市、乐山市、宝鸡市、库尔勒市。

第九批14个（2005年申报，2006年整改通过）：成都市、焦作市、黄山市、淮北市、湖州市、广安市、青州市、偃师市、太仓市、诸暨市、临海市、桐乡市、宜春市、景德镇市。

第十批34个（2007年）：石家庄市、迁安市、沈阳市、调兵山市、四平市、松原市、常州市、南通市、江阴市、衢州市、义乌市、淮南市、铜陵市、永安市、南昌市、新余市、莱芜市、胶州市、乳山市、文登市、新乡市、济源市、舞钢市、登封市、黄石市、株洲市、广州市、东莞市、潮州市、贵阳市、银川市、克拉玛依市、昌吉市、奎屯市。

第十一批8个（2007年申报，2008年整改通过）：敦化市、淮安市、上虞市、赣州市、

长沙市、宜都市、南充市、西宁市。

第十二批41个（2009年申报，2010年命名）：重庆市、承德市、武安市、太原市、潞城市、侯马市、铁岭市、开原市、宿迁市、泰州市、金坛市、台州市、平湖市、海宁市、池州市、萍乡市、吉安市、潍坊市、临沂市、泰安市、章丘市、肥城市、三门峡市、安阳市、商丘市、平顶山市、巩义市、鄂州市、湘潭市、韶关市、梅州市、汕头市、柳州市、遂宁市、昆明市、玉溪市、景洪市、西安市、青铜峡市、哈密市、伊宁市。

## 二、园林城区名单（7个）

1999年　上海浦东区（国家园林城区）
2002年　上海市闵行区（国家园林城区）
　　　　上海市金山区（国家园林城区）
　　　　重庆市北碚区（国家园林城区）
2007年　天津市塘沽区（国家园林城区）
　　　　重庆市南岸区（国家园林城区）
　　　　重庆市渝北区（国家园林城区）

## 三、园林县城名单（61个）

### 第一批10个（2006年）

北京市延庆县
重庆市铜梁县
河北省滦县
山东省长岛县
浙江省安吉县
湖北省秭归县
湖南省长沙县
甘肃省阿克塞哈萨克族自治县
宁夏回族自治区贺兰县
新疆维吾尔自治区布尔津县

### 第二批20个（2007年）

北京市密云县
天津市蓟县
重庆市大足县
山西省壶关县
吉林省通化县
黑龙江省嘉荫县
江苏省射阳县
江苏省沛县
江苏省宝应县
浙江省绍兴县
浙江省长兴县
浙江省嘉善县
安徽省凤台县
福建省惠安县
江西省武宁县
山东省邹平县
河南省新县
湖北省兴山县

海南省保亭县
新疆维吾尔自治区且末县

**第三批 31 个（2009 年）**

重庆市荣昌县、重庆市云阳县、河北省乐亭县、山西省怀仁县、山西省武乡县、辽宁省桓仁满族自治县、吉林省抚松县、江苏省溧水县、江苏省高淳县、江苏省金湖县、浙江省海盐县、安徽省歙县、福建省沙县、江西省吉安县、山东省广饶县、山东省沂源县、山东省平邑县、河南省修武县、河南省夏邑县、河南省桐柏县、四川省金堂县、云南省石林彝族自治县、云南省弥勒县、甘肃省华亭县、陕西省凤翔县、陕西省千阳县、陕西省麟游县、宁夏回族自治区彭阳县、新疆维吾尔自治区新源县、新疆维吾尔自治区沙湾县、新疆维吾尔自治区哈巴河县

## 四、国家园林城镇名单（15 个）

**第一批 10 个（2007 年）**

上海市青浦区朱家角镇
安徽省颍上县迪沟镇
重庆市九龙坡区西彭镇
江西省萍乡市安源区安源镇
河北省唐山市黄各庄镇
山东省文登市茼山镇
山西省阳城县北留镇
广东省中山市小榄镇
浙江省嘉兴市南湖区余新镇
云南省玉溪市红塔区大营街镇

**第二批 5 个（2009 年）**

江苏省江阴市新桥镇
四川省成都市大邑县安仁镇
山东省肥城市石横镇
云南省安宁市青龙镇
广东省东莞市塘厦镇

（资料整理：李如生，严胜虎，住房和城乡建设部城市建设司）

# 编后记

2010年，对于中国人民来说是很不平常的一年。面对国际国内环境的复杂变化，中国人民团结一心、开拓前进，成功举办了上海世博会、广州亚运会，战胜了青海玉树强烈地震、甘肃舟曲特大山洪泥石流等重大自然灾害，保持经济平稳较快发展，着力提高人民群众生活水平和质量，胜利实现“十一五”规划确定的目标任务，经济实力和综合国力进一步增强。特别是上海世博会，成为中国走向世界、让世界了解中国的重要历史机遇。“一切始于世博”——这句广为传诵的名言道出了一个多世纪以来世博会对创新的不懈追求。“城市，让生活更美好”的主题表明了上海世博会是一次探讨人类城市生活的盛会，这同时也是2010年《中国城市发展报告》的主题。本年度《报告》专题篇对上海世博会“城市创新与可持续发展”高峰论坛，以及“信息化与城市发展”、“城市更新与文化传承”、“科技创新与城市未来”、“环境变化与城市责任”、“经济转型与城乡互动”、“和谐城市与宜居生活”等六个主题论坛做了全面的介绍。上海世博会围绕人与自然和谐相处和可持续发展的主线，彰显了人类追求永续发展的长期目标。低碳将成为未来城市发展之路，经济转型是未来城市发展关键，创新引领现代化城市发展，《上海宣言》汇聚了本届世博会的思想成果。

继1990年北京举办第十一届亚洲运动会后，亚运盛会时隔20年再次回到中国。这也是中国继2008年北京奥运会后举办的又一次大型国际综合性运动会。第十六届亚运会和第十届亚残运会在广州精彩召开，获得了巨大的成功。在本年度《报告》论坛篇中，广州市委张广宁书记为举办亚运做了专题论述。在论坛篇中，我们还特别邀请了曾培炎、吴良镛、宋春华、张广宁、孔德涌、林珲、陈勇、葛仁等领导和院士们就城市发展中的重要课题发表了专题论文或研究成果。

综论篇中，除了对2010年中国城市发展做了中英文综述、对中国城市发展十大事件做了回顾外，我们还对中国城市经济发展、中国住房发展、中国城市土地利用、中国城市交通进展、城市市政公用设施建设、中国城市信息化进展等问题做了综论。

观察篇中，针对广大人民关注的焦点、热点问题，如“2010年全国‘两会’城乡规划建设与管理热点问题”、“城市保障性住房”、“城市休闲经济与休闲产业”、“四川地震灾后城镇恢复重建状况观察”、“中国城市热岛问题”、“近年来我国区域发展规划”等问题，我们分别邀请专家、教授做了论述。

案例篇中，本报告选了十多个城市发展的不同案例作为典型或示范，期望对国内各类城市发展交流有所参考。

附录篇中，本年度新增加了“2010 年度最具幸福感城市评选”，由中国市长协会与《瞭望东方周刊》杂志负责整理有关资料。

2011 年是我国进入“十二五”规划的开局之年，又是“后世博”、“后亚运”的第一年。在国际金融危机阴霾未散、国内宏观经济平稳运行但也面临复杂形势的背景下，在这个非同寻常的“开局之年”，中国城市发展如何抓住新机遇、应对新挑战备受关注。“城市，让生活更美好”这一主题在中国城市发展可持续旋律中，在共建和谐城市的进程中，必将谱写美好生活的新篇章。

最后，我们恳切希望城市决策者、管理者和研究人员以及广大读者对《报告》多提宝贵意见，帮助我们提高编写质量，把《中国城市发展报告》编写得更好。

国际欧亚科学院中国科学中心
城市科学学部副主任，国际欧亚科学院院士
戴逢院士　执笔
2011 年 3 月 31 日